MW01202074

Lewis Cass

and the Politics

of Moderation

Lewis Cass
by Francis Bicknell Carpenter, mid-1850s
(Courtesy of the Chicago Historical Society, P & S—1960.0439)

Lewis Cass and the Politics of Moderation

Willard Carl Klunder

The Kent State University Press

KENT, OHIO, & LONDON, ENGLAND

Library of Congress Catalog Card Number 95-37385
ISBN 0-87338-536-5
Manufactured in the United States of America

04 03 02 01 00 99 98 97 96 5 4 3 2 1

Library of Congress Cataloging-in-Publication Data
Klunder, Willard Carl, 1947–
Lewis Cass and the politics of moderation / Willard Carl Klunder.
p. cm.
Includes bibliographical references and index.
ISBN 0-87338-536-5 (hc : alk. paper) ∞
1. Cass, Lewis, 1782–1866. 2. Statesmen—United States—Biography.
3. United States—Politics and government—1783–1865.
4. Governors—Michigan—Biography. 5. Michigan—Politics and government—To 1837. I. Title.
E340.C3K57 1996
977.4'03'092—dc20
[B] 95-37385

British Library Cataloging-in-Publication data are available.

For Kathy and for Kristin, Catherine, & Erica,

who taught me the art

of compromise.

CONTENTS

PREFACE

LEWIS CASS is a curiously neglected historical figure. Born in 1782, he survived the Civil War and, during a career that spanned more than half a century, variously served as a prosecuting attorney, state legislator, federal marshal, army officer, territorial governor, secretary of war, minister to France, United States senator, and secretary of state.

Two comprehensive biographies of Cass written by William T. Young and William L. G. Smith were designed to drum up support for the Democratic presidential nomination in the 1850s. Young, for instance, fawningly portrays Cass as "the first statesman of his country, scarcely less known and celebrated among the Great Powers of Europe, than in his own country, and wherever known commanding attention, esteem and respect." Despite limitations of analysis and scope, these works contain important source materials not conveniently assembled elsewhere.

Andrew C. McLaughlin was the other nineteenth-century biographer of Lewis Cass. His work was published in 1891 and revised eight years later as part of the American Statesman Series. Although McLaughlin provides a more judicious characterization of his subject than either Young or Smith, he confesses to being "somewhat hampered" by the lack of Cass's private papers.[1]

More recent studies of Cass have drawn upon the expanding collections of his correspondence, notably those of the William L. Clements Library at the University of Michigan and the Burton Historical Collection of the Detroit Public Library. Nevertheless, it is a tedious and sometimes virtually impossible task to decipher the available documents. The problem, as Cass personally acknowledged, was the "miserable scrawl" in which he wrote. In a confidential note penned by a secretary, Cass explained to the addressee that he avoided "inflict[ing] my hieroglyphics upon you . . . because I hate the mechanical labor of writing, and because when I do write nobody can read it." Andrew Stevenson, U.S. minister to Great Britain, echoed this theme in his reply to a letter from Cass: "The names of the individuals for whom you ask information; I am totally unable to make out. . . . You should moreover remember, my good friend, that I have never been to the Holy Land, and although pretty good at *common*, I am not at all up to such pure Egyptian Hieroglyphics, as yours."[2]

In light of the delay in gathering his papers and the difficulties encountered in "translating" them, it is not surprising modern scholars have been reluctant to undertake studies of Lewis Cass. It is, moreover, a bit daunting to tackle the sheer scope of his extensive public life; Cass played a role in major historical events from the Burr conspiracy through the *Trent* affair. In 1950, Frank B. Woodford of the *Detroit Free Press* presented a popular and highly laudatory biography. Twenty years later, Willis F. Dunbar provided a reasoned sketch of Cass's political career. Several dissertations likewise shed considerable light on various aspects of Cass's public life, but no comprehensive, scholarly biography exists.[3] It is hoped that this book will contribute to a better understanding of the significance of Lewis Cass to the course of American history.

I incurred numerous obligations in the course of writing this biography. Robert W. Johannsen, my graduate adviser at the University of Illinois, suggested the topic and guided my initial study. His authoritative work on Stephen A. Douglas both inspired and deflated me with its sweeping scope, erudition, and seemingly effortless style. Fredrick J. Blue and Eugene H. Berwanger conscientiously read earlier versions of the manuscript and provided thoughtful suggestions. Fran Majors typed several drafts and aided me in meeting deadlines. My colleagues, notably Ralph Gray at Indiana University, Indianapolis, and Jim Duram at Wichita State University, repeatedly bolstered my spirits. The generally gentle proddings of John Dreifort, chairman of the WSU history department, also encouraged me to complete this project.

The editorial staff of The Kent State University Press, under the leadership of John T. Hubbell, has been extrememly supportive. Senior Editor Julia Morton and Assistant Editor Linda Cuckovich have been unflaggingly cordial and receptive to my proposals; unsung copyeditors have deftly improved the quality of the text. It has been a pleasant experience working with everyone connected with this publication.

I am, of course, indebted to more people than can possibly be acknowledged individually. The personnel of the libraries and depositories listed in the bibliography were uniformly courteous and helpful. I owe a special word of appreciation to those who facilitated my research at the University of Illinois, the Burton Historical Collection, the William L. Clements Library, the Michigan State Archives, and the Library of Congress. Wichita State University provided a reduced teaching load one semester and a summer research grant. The J. K. Sowards professional development fund partially underwrote my search for potential illustrations.

Others contributed to this book as well. Craig Torbenson, who makes up the geography department at Wichita State, prepared the maps. Henry Ledyard of Grosse Pointe Farms, Michigan, the namesake of Cass's son-in-law, graciously shared with me his family recollections. Members of my own family responded to my prolonged labors in various ways, depending on their predilections and level of maturity, ranging from insensibility to enthusiasm. And, ultimately, I am profoundly grateful to my mother, Dorothy Ross Pollack, who instilled in me the love of learning she inherited from Jack and Irene. Thank you all.

INTRODUCTION

Lewis Cass scribbled an affectionate letter to his young grandson during the summer of 1858. "My dear Child," wrote the seventy-five-year-old secretary of state, "I send you five dollars for piscatory purposes. Every one to his taste. Fishing is not to mine. Dr. Johnson defined a fishing rod to be a pole, with a hook and line at one end, and a fool at the other."[1] Political opponents at times thought Lewis Cass the fool, but all would agree that for more than half a century he lacked the leisure time to spend fishing, even had he so wished. Cass's life spanned the period of American history from the Revolution through the Civil War. From the time of his election as a prosecuting attorney in 1804, he almost continuously held some public office. Cass received his first federal appointment from President Thomas Jefferson, and he remained in the political arena past Abraham Lincoln's election.

Lewis Cass was educated at Phillips Exeter Academy and trained as a lawyer. He served as a general officer during the War of 1812 and was included in General William Hull's ignominious surrender of Detroit. Appointed governor of Michigan Territory in 1813, Cass held that post for eighteen years as Michigan grew to the brink of statehood. In 1831, he was selected as Andrew Jackson's secretary of war, an office he resigned five years later to become United States minister to France. He returned to America in 1842, after quarreling with the secretary of state over the Webster-Ashburton Treaty. Cass was a disappointed aspirant for the Democratic presidential nomination of 1844, but the following year the Michigan legislature sent him to the United States Senate. He remained a member of that body until 1857, resigning briefly after his nomination for the presidency in 1848. Following his defeat by Zachary Taylor, Senator Cass again sought the presidential nomination and nearly succeeded in capturing it at the Democratic convention—only the two-thirds rule blocked his selection during the early balloting. The election of 1852 foreshadowed the end of Cass's national political influence. His fellow Democrat, Franklin Pierce, did not consult him regarding cabinet appointments, and the aged Michigan senator took himself out of consideration for the presidential nomination four years later. James Buchanan selected Cass as his secretary of state in 1857, but Buchanan was motivated by political considerations and expected to take firm personal command of American foreign affairs. Cass spent the Civil War years in quiet support of the Union cause.

Lewis Cass subscribed to the Jeffersonian political philosophy. He embraced the principles of individual liberty, the sovereignty of the people, equality of rights and opportunities for all citizens, and a strictly construed and balanced constitutional government of limited powers. Cass was also a champion of spread-eagle expansionism and an ardent nationalist who steadfastly sought compromise on the explosive issues that threatened the stability of the republic. His letter to Alfred O. P. Nicholson, in December 1847, was a nationally recognized effort to use the ideal of self-government to repudiate the Wilmot Proviso.[2] As the "Father of Popular Sovereignty," he denied that Congress possessed the power to regulate slavery in the territories. He believed that slavery was evil but supported the right of citizens of each state or territory to decide the question for themselves. He denounced both abolitionists and disunionists and, in turn, was vilified by those who did not agree with his moderate position. To antislavery forces, he was a "doughface": a northern man with southern principles. He was similarly castigated as a man whom southerners could not trust, since planters came to view popular sovereignty as a smoke screen behind which slavery would be prohibited from the western territories. At the time of his death, Lewis Cass was a repudiated symbol of antebellum political moderation.

Lewis Cass

and the Politics

of Moderation

Lake Superior
Sault Ste. Marie
Drummond Is.
Mackinac
Lake Huron
Lake Michigan
Ft. Howard (Green Bay)
Butte des Mortes
Lake Winnebago
Fox
Fond du Lac
Mississippi
Wisconsin
Ft. Crawford (Prairie du Chien)
Fever (Galena)
Dubuque
Rock
Des Plaines
Illinois
St. Louis
Ft. Dearborn (Chicago)
Grand
Ft. Saginaw
Ft. Gratiot
Battle of Thames
Thames
R. Rouge
Detroit
Ft. Malden
Lake Erie
R. Raisin
Ft. Meigs
Toledo Strip
Maumee
Black Swamp
Sandusky
Upper Sandusky
Tippecanoe Cr.
Ft. Wayne
St. Mary's
Prophet's Town
Greenville
Urbana
Dayton
Scioto
Salt Cr.
Zanesville
Muskingum
Marietta
Vienna
Wabash
Ft. Hamilton
Miami
Chillicothe
Ohio

Chapter One

Youth and Soldier (1782–1813): "I Saw the Constitution Born"

Lewis Cass was nearly eighty years old in 1861, retired from politics and living quietly in Detroit, when he was visited by James Garfield, a young man destined to attain the presidential prize that so long eluded Cass. The Union was sundered, and the old Democrat looked back upon a happier time. Cass noted that his native New Hampshire had been the ninth state to ratify the Constitution, thereby giving the nation a new government. "It was a day of great rejoicing," he recounted. "My mother held me, a little boy of six years, in her arms at a window, and pointed me to the bonfires that were blazing in the streets of Exeter, and told me that the people were celebrating the adoption of the Constitution. So, . . . I saw the Constitution born, and I fear I may see it die." Cass earnestly concluded he had "loved the Union ever since the light of that bonfire greeted my eyes. I have given fifty-five years of my life, and my best efforts, to its preservation."[1]

The constitutional Union to which Lewis Cass devoted his life did not exist when he was born in Exeter on October 9, 1782, the first of six children of Jonathan and Mary Gilman Cass. Both parents traced their New England ancestry back more than a century. John Cass arrived in America around 1640 and married Martha Philbrick; together they raised nine children on a two-hundred-acre New Hampshire farm formerly owned by the Reverend John Wheelwright. John served frequently as a selectman, initiating a family tradition of political service. Another such tradition was answering the call to arms. "Captain" Joseph Cass responded during King Philip's War, and Jonathan joined the successful campaign against Fort Louisbourg in 1745. Jonathan's grandson and namesake—Lewis's father—was born in Salisbury, Massachusetts, in 1753.

When Jonathan Cass was about four years old, his parents moved to Epping, New Hampshire. Following the death of his mother, Jonathan got a taste of military life by serving for a year at Fort William and Mary, situated across the Piscataqua River from Portsmouth. Upon his return home the restless young man found civilian life too tame, and when news arrived of the clashes at Lexington and Concord, he enlisted as a private in the patriot ranks.

Jonathan Cass saw action in several major engagements during the early years of the Revolution, fighting bravely at Bunker Hill, Brandywine Creek, Germantown, and Saratoga. He endured the encampment at Valley Forge in the winter of 1777 and marched up the Susquehanna River valley with General John Sullivan's expedition against the Iroquois. As the fighting diminished in the northern states, Captain Cass was stationed at Exeter, where he wed Mary Gilman in late 1781. Mary was the daughter of Theophilus, a prosperous merchant engaged in the West Indies trade, and Deborah Webster Gilman. The Gilmans were more affluent and influential than the Casses; several served in the Continental Congress, and one was a signer of the Constitution. Captain Cass's contributions to the Revolutionary cause were warmly appreciated by his in-laws, and his patriotism was evident in the names selected for his sons: Lewis, in honor of America's royal ally; George Washington; Charles Lee; and John Jay, who died in early childhood. Lewis's two sisters, Mary and Deborah, were named for their immediate maternal relatives.[2]

Lewis Cass's political moderation and social conservatism were shaped by his father, a fervent Federalist who later supported the National Republicans. Jonathan Cass was appointed federal marshal for the New Hampshire district following the Revolution and took a strong stand in maintaining public order during Shays's Rebellion. The elder Cass was also personally concerned with passage of Alexander Hamilton's funding scheme. Lewis retained his father's economic leanings, never feeling truly comfortable with antimonopolistic attacks on the national bank, for example. Jonathan Cass was less successful in imbuing his eldest child with other Federalist principles, but he kindled a fierce sense of nationalism—fueled by the bonfires that greeted the adoption of the Constitution—in the soul of Lewis Cass. Unmistakably, the father's influence was strong, and political opponents later charged that young Lewis's hat was adorned with a black cockade, a symbol of the Federalist party.[3]

In March 1791, Jonathan Cass rejoined the army, and within two years he was promoted to major. He served in the Northwest Territory under General Anthony Wayne but was not present at the decisive Battle of Fallen Timbers because of a broken leg. Major Cass soon recovered, and with the exception of Lewis his family joined him at Fort Hamilton, Ohio, where he commanded for two years. When Congress set aside a portion of the territory as military bounty lands, Jonathan applied for forty warrants totaling four thousand acres. In due course his request was fully granted, and the family settled at Wakatomaka, a few miles above Zanesville, Ohio. There Jonathan spent his remaining years, living comfortably and dabbling in real estate.[4] Many years before his death in 1830, Jonathan Cass divided the bulk of his estate among his children. It was this patrimony that established the foundation for the personal fortune amassed by Lewis Cass.

Lewis did not accompany his family on their initial journey to the western frontier. Instead, he moved into the home of an uncle, Simeon Ladd, and continued attending Phillips Exeter Academy. He studied for seven years under the able tutelage of Benjamin Abbot, who instilled in the young man a lifelong devotion to literature and scholarship. Years later, while on various errands through the northwestern wilderness, Cass carried books to be read around the evening's campfire. Jonathan Cass was so taken with Lewis's academic progress that he sent his other sons to join their brother back in New Hampshire.

Lewis applied himself to his studies but took time to enjoy the pleasant fields and woods near Exeter. He was a headstrong, robust lad who organized fellow students into a military company—the Washington Whites—which he commanded and drilled. The youthful Cass was apparently deficient only in the field of romance. Decades later, Leverett Saltonstall wistfully acknowledged that the two of them were "no great gallants" at the academy. Daniel Webster, another schoolmate, remembered Cass as "a clever fellow, good-natured, kind-hearted, amiable, and obliging."[5]

Jonathan Cass was not concerned with his absent son's late-blooming social graces, but he joined the rest of the family in lamenting Lewis's failure to write regularly. Debby Cass informed her brother in December 1794 that no word had been received from him since February, and she was "extremely anxious" to learn whether he was ill. Eventually, Lewis was stirred into action, and the arrival of a letter in the spring of 1796 triggered responses from each family member. George expressed happiness at hearing of his brother's good health and extolled the bucolic virtues of the Ohio country: "I believe nature never form'd a place more calculated for a person fond of rural life." (George would contentedly spend his adult life as a farmer, looking after his parents in their declining years.) Charles, who pursued a military career, was not yet eight years old in 1796 and pressed his tutor into service to answer Lewis's letter. Major Cass commanded his son "to continue writing us once a month without fail" and added that Lewis should also pay more attention to improving his handwriting. The elder Cass was bound to be disappointed: Lewis corresponded sporadically, and his handwriting actually deteriorated with maturity, forcing him to employ an amanuensis when possible.[6]

Jonathan Cass was delighted with the education Lewis received at Phillips Exeter, and with the self-discipline and quiet assurance the seventeen-year-old demonstrated. Upon leaving the academy, Lewis was issued a certificate that confirmed his proficiency in "the English, French, Latin, & Greek languages, Geography, Arithmetic, & practical Geometry." Furthermore, he had made "very valuable progress in the study of Rhetoric, History, Natural & Moral Philosophy, Logic, Astronomy, & Natural Law," all the while sustaining a "good moral character."[7]

His formal education completed, Lewis moved with his family to Wilmington, Delaware, where his father served as a recruitment officer. Lewis tutored his younger siblings and joined the local academy as a Latin instructor. Debby boasted that her brother's prospects were "very flattering, he teaches a school at 6 dollars a quarter & will probably have 30 or 40 scholars." The sojourn at Wilmington proved to be a learning experience for the young teacher as well, who was exposed there to the institution of slavery. Delaware was a border state where slaves were relatively well treated in comparison to the Deep South. In fact, Cass blindly discerned little difference between bondsmen and free blacks; certainly, he developed no moral abhorrence toward slavery. Lewis Cass's teaching career ended after only a few months, when his father was transferred to Harpers Ferry in western Virginia. That assignment proved to be equally brief, and the Cass family slowly made its way to Pittsburgh, Pennsylvania. Lewis hiked with some of his father's recruits over the Allegheny Mountains during this odyssey, making the acquaintance of William Henry Harrison, soon to become governor of Indiana Territory.[8]

When the bounty lands near Zanesville were granted, Jonathan Cass resigned from the army and transported his family down the Ohio River to Marietta. They arrived in October 1800, and Lewis began to study law under Return Jonathan Meigs. The following spring the Cass men traveled the final seventy miles up the Muskingum River, built a two-story cabin, and began clearing the land. By the end of the year the family was settled at Wakatomaka. Lewis returned to Marietta and continued reading law in the office of Matthew Backus, where he formed a friendship with the lawyer's nephew, William Woodbridge. (Their professional and personal relationship would carry them both to Michigan Territory and stretch over decades, running the gamut from intimacy to estrangement.) During this period, Lewis's sister Debby married Wyllys Silliman, a lawyer. The Sillimans resided briefly at Marietta, where sister Mary joined their household before marrying John Munro, a Zanesville merchant.[9]

Lewis Cass's studies proceeded apace, and in late 1802 he was licensed to practice law. The following year he was admitted to the state bar. Cass additionally did some work for the surveyor general's office, and his father reported he was earning a thousand dollars annually. Lewis Cass soon turned his undivided attention to his expanding law practice, as Backus and Silliman steered business his way. Ohio, a new state recently carved out of the northwestern frontier, was undergoing major and rapid changes in its population and commerce. Lawsuits abounded over land titles and contracts, and within a few years Cass was asking William Woodbridge to undertake several cases for him.

Dividing most of his time between Zanesville and Chillicothe, the state capital, Lewis Cass formed lasting professional relationships. He fondly recalled the camaraderie engendered among the lawyers and judges who rode circuit together through woods and across swollen streams, taking shelter for the night in a rude cabin or around a campfire. On one such occasion Cass was thrown from his horse into the Salt Creek, and his saddlebags continued a journey that conceivably ended at New Orleans. It was a life perfectly suited for a vigorous young man embarked on a promising career, and Cass reveled in it. Debby bragged that her brother was "doing extremely well, is called one of the best lawyers in the state, and is quite an honor to the family."[10]

With his law practice prospering, Cass sought admittance "to the Sacred Mysteries of Free Masonry." In the spring of 1804, he became a master mason in American Union Lodge No. 1 of Marietta. This secret organization was composed of the region's leading citizens, and membership amplified the young lawyer's social and professional standing. Cass later joined the Zion Lodge of Detroit and served as the first grand master of the Masonic Order of Michigan. Characteristically, when a political backlash against Masonry swept the country in the 1820s, Cass recommended that the Detroit members disband in order to defuse the potentially explosive situation. His lodge brothers, naturally, claimed Cass took the path of least resistance rather than jeopardize his political aspirations.[11]

Jonathan Cass was proud of his successful son but regretted his changing political ideology. The young lawyer was interested in entering politics and realized that the future lay with Thomas Jefferson's Democratic-Republican party. Although Federalists were well represented in the ranks of the Ohio judiciary, the legislature and congressional delegations were firmly controlled by the Jeffersonians.[12] Lewis therefore embraced the principles espoused by Return J. Meigs and Thomas Worthington, one of the state's original federal senators and political mentor to Cass until his death in 1827. This conversion was not simply a cynical abandonment of principle for political preferment. The young Lewis had been strongly influenced by his father's New England Federalism, but his early manhood was spent on the Ohio frontier, a territory imbued with the western spirit of rough-hewn democracy. While Cass understood the political expediency involved in joining the Democratic-Republicans, he believed sincerely in such Jeffersonian principles as popular rule and a federal government of limited powers. Cass was easily elected prosecuting attorney of Muskingum County in 1804. Zanesville was the seat of justice for the newly created county, and brother-in-law Wyllys Silliman was the only other resident lawyer. In October 1806, Cass won a seat in the Ohio legislature, although at twenty-four he failed to fulfill the minimum age requirement for state representatives. This turned out to be the last time in his extensive career that Lewis Cass was elected by popular vote to a public office.

Shortly before his election to the legislature, Cass married nineteen-year-old Elizabeth Spencer. Lewis was no longer an awkward youth, more comfortable drilling his Washington Whites than in a drawing room. With long black hair and distinctly homely features, he was a strapping, sturdily built man of medium height. His face was round and full and marked with prominent warts and moles; it would soon turn jowly. He was, in short, an unprepossessing physical specimen. And yet, he was a self-assured, quick-witted lawyer and politician who was clearly "going places." One observer noted that "Cass has become much of a Gallant, . . . his rough eloquence & noisy bluster seem to please the Ladies amazingly." He certainly impressed Elizabeth, daughter of Dr. Joseph Spencer and the former Deborah Selden. Elizabeth's maternal grandfather died while a prisoner of the British during the Revolutionary War; her other grandfather, General Joseph Spencer, was a veteran of the French and Indian War and the Revolution. Her father served the American cause as a surgeon before moving his family across the Ohio River from Marietta to the small town of Vienna, Virginia. Lewis Cass and Elizabeth were married there in the spring of 1806, and their enduring union proved to be happy and fruitful. Before being hindered by chronic ill health, Elizabeth bore seven children, five of whom survived infancy. One daughter, the namesake of her mother, died in 1832 during a cholera epidemic. Mary, Matilda, Isabella, and Lewis, Jr., outlived their mother, who died in 1853.[13]

Lewis and Elizabeth Cass honeymooned at the Ohio River island estate of Harman Blennerhassett. Their host regaled the young couple with tales of Aaron Burr, another recent guest, who had totally captivated Blennerhassett with grandiose schemes of western conquest. When rumors of Burr's machinations reached Washington, President Jefferson dispatched John Graham of the State Department to investigate. After conferring with Graham, Governor Edward Tiffin sent the legislature a confidential message outlining Burr's alleged illegal activities and recommending prompt action.

Lewis Cass was a member of the Ohio House committee selected to investigate the Burr conspiracy. The freshman legislator had no desire even to be at Chillicothe in the winter of 1806; it was his first separation from Elizabeth. In what turned out to be ironic speculation, Cass pleaded with his wife to "write me as often as possible. Tell me your whole thoughts, and how you do. Do you think of me as often as I do of you? I don't think that anything will induce me to leave you again." Momentarily putting aside thoughts of Elizabeth and the gracious hospitality Blennerhassett had provided the newlyweds, Cass drafted a bill passed by the legislature empowering the governor to "seize all persons" connected to the Burr plot. Governor Tiffin acted swiftly, and militiamen confiscated the flotilla gathered at Blennerhasset Island. Insofar as it concerned Ohio, the Burr conspiracy was ended.[14]

Cass was not content merely with foiling Burr's schemes. He composed an address to President Jefferson, unanimously adopted by the legislature, that emphasized Ohio's firm attachment to the federal government: "No acts of intriguing men—no real or visionary prospects of advantage—will ever induce us to sever that bond of union, which is our only security against domestic violence and foreign invasion." Demonstrating a sycophancy worthy of an aspiring politician, Cass hoped President Jefferson would "live long to enjoy the confidence and attachment of the American people." Cass also dashed off a letter to Senator Worthington, relating "that a great proportion" of the legislative proceedings against Burr "were originated by myself."

Cass took a firm stand against domestic disorder that threatened the federal union, much as his father did at the time of Shays's Rebellion, and he made certain his actions were brought to the attention of party leaders. Their response was gratifying. Governor Tiffin recommended him for the office of U.S. marshal, and Cass "hesitated not to tell him, that the appointment would be very acceptable." Cass sought Worthington's aid in securing the post, and in return pledged he would "ever be proud of an occasion to testify my gratitude." President Jefferson endorsed Tiffin's nomination and named Cass federal marshal for Ohio. Thus ended a brief yet propitious legislative career. The office of marshal allowed Cass to extend his circle of political acquaintances, as did his thriving law practice.[15]

In January 1809, Cass was selected as one of the defense counselors in the trial of Ohio Supreme Court Justice George Tod, who was impeached after declaring an act of the legislature unconstitutional. The stature Cass enjoyed as an attorney was demonstrated when he was chosen to present the closing arguments, and a Chillicothe newspaper reported that his summation "was, beyond description, beautiful and sublime." The correspondent praised Cass as "a friend to his country—and a firm and able advocate of her unalienable rights and privileges." By a narrow margin, Tod was not removed from the bench; with a two-thirds majority necessary for conviction, nine legislators voted for the judge, fifteen against. In this partisan case, Cass did not support the Democratic-Republican position regarding popular democracy and judicial review. Clearly, he feared an omnipotent legislature as much as despotic judges (or, for that matter, governors). Early in his public career, Lewis Cass served notice he had the courage to differ from his party when constitutional issues were at stake.[16]

Cass continued to practice law and serve as federal marshal until shortly before war was declared against Britain in June 1812. He was not yet thirty years old, an ambitious and unflappable young man with complete confidence in himself. Although he lacked formal military training and experience, professional and political influence led to his appointment as a brigadier general in the Ohio militia. His military duties were primarily of an administrative nature, aptly suited to a lawyer whose father was a professional soldier. Jonathan Cass, indeed, had many reasons to be proud of his firstborn. Lewis was a successful attorney and advancing politician who had not strayed completely from the political path his father trod, despite a public adherence to Jeffersonian principles. At least, that was the way Jonathan chose to view it.[17] It was typical of the younger Cass to mute his political sentiments in the company of his father. Throughout his life, Lewis Cass attempted to accommodate people and compromise political issues; he avoided personal confrontations whenever it was possible to do so without a sacrifice of principle.

As the conflict with Britain approached, Congress authorized the president to federalize one hundred thousand militiamen and recruit half that number of volunteers. Governor Meigs, Cass's former law tutor, ordered the Ohio soldiers to assemble at Dayton. Twelve hundred men responded, and three regiments were formed under Duncan McArthur, James Findlay, and Lewis Cass. The men and officers brought their own weapons. Most wore civilian clothes, but Colonel Cass was arrayed in full uniform and sported "the highest plume of any officer in the Army." The sword his father carried so bravely during the Revolution banged against his thigh as he reviewed the raw troops. On March 27, 1812, Governor Meigs urged the men to do their duty, and Cass called for three cheers in honor of their commander, Brigadier General William Hull, "the revolutionary veteran . . . who fought and bled in achieving our independence." As the shouts echoed, an American flag was unfurled, and Colonel Cass addressed the assembled volunteers. In the fervid style of the day, the young colonel expressed sentiments that governed his public life: "Fellow Soldiers: The standard of your Country is displayed. You have rallied around it to defend her rights, and avenge her injuries. . . . And should we ever meet in the hostile field, I doubt not but the Eagle of liberty, which it bears, will be found more than a match for the Lion of England." Cass firmly believed that the United States was superior to Great Britain, and this conviction broadened over the years into a confirmed case of Anglophobia.[18]

William Hull, a decorated fifty-eight-year-old veteran of the Revolution, realized his days as an energetic military commander of frontier recruits were long past. Moreover, a recent stroke had exacerbated his innate stubborness and vacillation. But Hull had served as governor of

Michigan Territory since 1805, and members of his family resided in Detroit. He therefore had grudgingly accepted command of the army raised to defend the Northwest and invade Canada.

Colonel Cass lacked confidence in his military commander. Before Hull joined the Ohio forces, Cass predicted, "He is not our man. I saw him at Cin[cinnati] and was prepossessed in his favour. But I am now told by men capable of appreciating his talents that he is indecisive and irresolute, leaning for support upon persons around him." Swayed himself by the opinions of fellow officers, Colonel Cass would take every available opportunity to counsel the general.[19]

The Ohio soldiers arrived at Fort Detroit on July 6, four days after receiving official notification of the declaration of war. Hull's command totaled about twenty-five hundred men, including a detachment of regulars under Lieutenant Colonel James Miller.[20] The Americans outnumbered the enemy garrison at Fort Malden, near Amherstburg, and as Cass later pointed out, the British position was extremely vulnerable. General Hull, however, waited until the early hours of July 12 to cross the Detroit River, and then suspended offensive operations pending the arrival of siege cannon. This was the first invasion of Canadian territory during the War of 1812, and Colonel Cass led the landing party. Much would be made of this incident in future political campaigns, when Democratic literature referred to Lewis Cass as "the first man in arms who leapt ashore from the boats" onto enemy soil.[21]

Upon crossing into Canada, General Hull issued a blustering manifesto warning that if the enemy turned "the savages . . . loose to murder our citizens, and butcher our women and children, this . . . will be a war of extermination. The first stroke of a tomahawk, the first attempt with the scalping-knife, will be the signal for one indiscriminate scene of desolation. *No white man found fighting by the side of an Indian will be taken prisoner.*" After Hull's death, Lewis Cass publicly claimed to be the author of this proclamation, and although the general's kinsmen disputed his assertion, the florid style was typical of Cass's earlier literary efforts. Invariably praised by the American press, the proclamation was denounced as insidious by the British commander at Fort Malden.[22]

Mere words would not conquer Canada. While their comrades waited impatiently for the delivery of artillery, Cass and Miller led a three-hundred-man reconnaissance mission against British emplacements four miles north of Fort Malden. At a bridge spanning the Aux Canards River (which the natives called the Tarontee), the Americans attacked a detachment of Canadian militia and their Indian allies under Tecumseh. Cass reported that the bridge was seized without the loss of a single man, although two wounded soldiers were captured; the British suffered about ten casualties. Colonel Cass exceeded his orders in attacking the enemy position but sent word to Hull the crossing would be held if he elected to advance the main body of troops against Fort Malden. Ever cautious, the general ordered a retreat unless Cass or Miller would take complete responsibility for the military outcome. Upon receiving this startling reply, the officers at the bridge held a council, and only Captain Josiah Snelling agreed with Cass to stand firm. Overruled, a chagrined Colonel Cass marched his men back to the main camp. Newspaper accounts exaggerated the importance of this initial skirmish of the war, and Cass was dubbed the intrepid "Hero of the Tarontee."

General Hull did not take advantage of Cass's initiative in capturing the Aux Canards crossing because he was not prepared to attack Fort Malden without cannon and believed it would be foolhardy to leave a small contingent of troops only four miles from the main enemy force. In fact, the bridge was within range of the long guns aboard the brigantine *Queen Charlotte,* which lay in the Detroit River off the mouth of the Canard. Hull's course was prudent, especially in light of the fact that only a few days earlier Cass acknowledged the "high spirits" of the American troops but doubted they were "adequate to the reduction of Malden." Regardless of Cass's personal misgivings, Hull's failure to take decisive action exacerbated the mistrust between the Ohio colonels and their commander.[23]

Subsequent events further alienated Hull from his senior officers. Colonels Cass and McArthur disregarded the general's instructions and fired three rounds from a six-pound gun at the *Queen Charlotte,* exposing their troops to a much heavier bombardment. If General Hull wished to reassert control over his eroding command, he should have immediately disciplined his subordinate officers. Instead, he did nothing. While Cass privately doubted Hull's fitness, the old general rightly questioned the ability of his senior officers to follow orders.

The problems faced by the American troops in the Northwest were soon compounded. On July 28, word was received that Mackinac Island had fallen to a combined force of British regulars, Canadian voyageurs, and Indians. Fearing the imminent arrival at Fort Malden of some four thousand Indian reinforcements, General Hull ordered a retreat from Canadian soil on August 8. Democratic campaign literature in 1848 emphasized that

"Colonel Cass remonstrated bitterly," but vainly, against the withdrawal. When Hull suggested pulling back to the Maumee River to protect his eastern lines of communication, Cass warned of mutiny among the Ohio volunteers.[24]

With the American troops on the verge of rebelling, Hull's officers plotted against him. Shortly after the retreat from Canada, a letter passed between the Ohio colonels "requesting the arrest or displacement" of their ineffectual commander. On August 12, Colonel Cass underscored the urgency of the situation when he beseeched Senator Worthington to send reinforcements and provisions to Detroit, adding that the Indians in the region had flocked to the British standard after the loss of Mackinac. An ominous postscript signed by Cass and the other Ohio officers implored Worthington to "believe all the bearer will tell you! Believe it! . . . Even a c[apitulation] is talked of" by General Hull.[25]

In an effort to prevent the abandonment of Detroit, a round-robin letter was circulated among the soldiers and civilian residents. Cass and seventy-nine others pledged to depose General Hull and "defend the fort at all hazards." Hull eventually became aware of these widespread conspiracies and effectively removed Cass and McArthur from the plotting. He ordered them to lead a four-hundred-man force to the River Raisin and escort to Detroit an anticipated relief expedition.[26]

While the Americans were preoccupied with internal intrigue, General Isaac Brock arrived at Fort Malden with ninety British regulars and three hundred militiamen. After assuming command, Brock resolutely demanded the surrender of Detroit. Hull refused, and the opposing batteries exchanged fire for six hours. Brock then led his troops across the river and advanced against the American fort. Faced with what he perceived as an overwhelming enemy force, General Hull ordered a white flag of surrender hoisted on August 16. Hull feared an Indian massacre if the resistance continued, and the presence of his daughter and grandchildren inflated his natural timidity into full-blown panic.

Hull had no illusions about how the surrender of Detroit would be received. He confessed that he dreaded meeting Cass, "as I expect he will censure me very much. My country will also censure me, but . . . I have done what my conscience directed." Hull's forecast was certainly correct. The *National Intelligencer* screamed "DETROIT IS TAKEN!!" and placed complete responsibility on the commanding general. "A tale remains to be told, which will make the blood of every American boil with indignation." Other accounts of the capitulation were equally blunt in excoriating the general, who was frequently and pointedly compared to Benedict Arnold.[27]

Colonel Cass joined in the condemnation of General Hull, but his own conduct deserves scrutiny. Cass and McArthur failed to contact the relief expedition at the River Raisin, and so they returned to within three miles of Detroit by the early morning hours of August 16, before camping for the night. They inexplicably neglected to notify General Hull of their whereabouts, even though they heard cannonading during the day and had received orders for their immediate return. No explanation was ever given by Cass to account for this, although political supporters later postulated he and McArthur hoped to avoid being included in the surrender terms. This is an insufficient defense; Cass had no way of knowing Hull was about to capitulate. Subsequently informed by a French resident that Detroit was in British hands, Cass and McArthur retreated a few miles before being notified that their detachment was included in the surrender.

The capitulation of Detroit was a mortifying experience for Colonel Cass, who had marched off to war in the glorious military tradition of his father. Lewis Cass devoted the remainder of his public life to defending his country's honor from British pretensions, but he never fully expunged the personal humiliation suffered on August 16, 1812. In the heat of subsequent political campaigns, Democratic apologists emphasized that Cass broke his father's sword rather than surrender it to the British. One campaign tract further embellished Cass's reaction: "'Traitor,' he exclaimed to General Hull's messenger bringing the news and telling him his command was included in the surrender, 'he has verified our worst fears, he has eluded our grasp, and disgraced the country. But the enemy shall never receive the hilt of *my* sword.' So saying, he snapped his sword in two, and cast it on the ground." One officer present during these events claimed it was McArthur who refused to surrender his sword, while Cass, concerned with the safety of those already held prisoner, reasoned that further resistance jeopardized American lives. If Cass did break his sword (and it is doubtful such an event took place), it was one of the few times in the entire campaign that he drew his weapon in anger. Cass's rage was directed at Hull, but his own actions directly contributed to the ignominious surrender of Detroit. And in a broader perspective, the loss of Detroit was due more to the manner in which the Madison administration conducted the war than to the faults of any individual.[28]

Colonel Cass did not take a larger view of the debacle at Detroit; it was perfectly clear to him that General Hull was solely to blame. After his release on parole, Cass hastened to Washington to argue the case against Hull, who remained in British custody. He suffered a fever on this journey that resulted in baldness and led him to wear reddish-black wigs for the remainder of his life. While prostrated for several days, Cass composed a letter to Secretary of War William Eustis that borrowed heavily from the journal of Robert Lucas, an eyewitness to the surrender of Detroit. Cass insisted the subordinate officers would have deposed Hull, had he and McArthur not been ordered to escort the relief party to Detroit. Colonel Cass drew a melancholy picture of "at least 500" soldiers "shedding tears because they were not allowed to meet their Country's foe, and to fight their Country's battles." The capitulation "excited sensations, which no American has ever before had to feel."[29]

Attorney General Richard Rush recognized the value of Cass's report to the administration and urged Eustis to publish it. He added that the fate of General Hull "is and must be sealed. The issue is made up between him and the nation, and this letter will promulgate the true and righteous decision." Eustis hesitated, but Cass's report reached the public the day after the president returned to Washington and personally took charge of the situation.[30]

The Madison administration had its scapegoat, and William Hull's court-martial convened at Albany, New York, in January 1814. Martin Van Buren served as a special judge advocate and Major General Henry Dearborn presided. Dearborn was scarcely a disinterested judge; his vacillation on the Niagara front gave General Brock time to march reinforcements to Fort Malden, effect the surrender of Detroit, and return to the eastern theater. Additionally, in a transparent attempt to single out Hull for blame, all the prosecution witnesses were promoted before the trial. Not surprisingly, Hull was found guilty of cowardice and neglect of duty, although he was acquitted on the charge of treason. President Madison approved the verdict but remitted the death sentence in recognition of the general's Revolutionary War record. William Hull was dishonorably discharged and spent the remainder of his years living quietly with his family in Newton, Massachusetts.

Lewis Cass was one of the court-martial witnesses promoted after the loss of Detroit. Elected a major general in the Ohio militia following his release from parole, Cass actively sought an appointment to the regular army. The humiliation of the capitulation hung over him like a dark cloud, and he wrote to Senator Worthington seeking yet another political favor. "Perhaps I have no right to expect it, but I must confess if a

Brigadier General is to be appointed in this State, I should be most happy to receive the appointment." Cass then busied himself with raising a regiment of volunteers. In March 1813, he received a regular army commission as brigadier general and resigned as federal marshal, confessing his "military mania must be gratified, . . . I must once more see the American standard wave over Canada." Cass subsequently served as an unofficial aide-de-camp to General William Henry Harrison at the Battle of the Thames, drawing praise as "an officer of the highest merit." A campaign biography described how Cass "threw himself on the left of the battalion of the mounted regiment, under the command of Lieutenant-Colonel Johnson, and shared with them in the decisive charge." That was patently false; General Cass took no part in the actual fighting. After the victory at the Thames secured the Northwest for the United States, General Harrison appointed Cass military governor of Michigan and the occupied Canadian territory. Harrison knew Cass was politically acceptable to the administration, since his report on the surrender of Detroit focused exclusively on Hull's shortcomings, and the two generals agreed that peaceful Indians should be treated fairly and with respect. On October 29, 1813, President Madison seconded Harrison's action by appointing Cass civil governor of Michigan Territory.[31]

General Hull experienced understandable bitterness when Cass testified for the prosecution at his trial. Cass was a brigadier general in the regular army and Hull's successor as governor of Michigan Territory. In an effort to place the onus of Detroit's surrender squarely on the shoulders of William Hull, the administration unstintingly rewarded his subordinates, and Cass was among the chief beneficiaries. It is certain that Hull's blunders greatly contributed to the loss of the Northwest; yet this was but the first episode in Cass's public life when his actions appeared motivated by the pursuit of personal or political gain. Although Cass had hoped to avoid being called as a witness, his testimony tacitly defended the administration's military policy by placing sole responsibility for the capitulation on Hull. That was too much for one political observer, who chastised Cass for the sycophancy he demonstrated "to old Hull, succeeded by his wiley abuse of him to subserve his own elevation." Such truckling placed Cass "below the grade of Honorable Political Scoundrels." This was an intemperate characterization, but not unfounded. Above all else in his public career, Lewis Cass was a politician, and as governor of Michigan Territory he would employ his political skills well.[32]

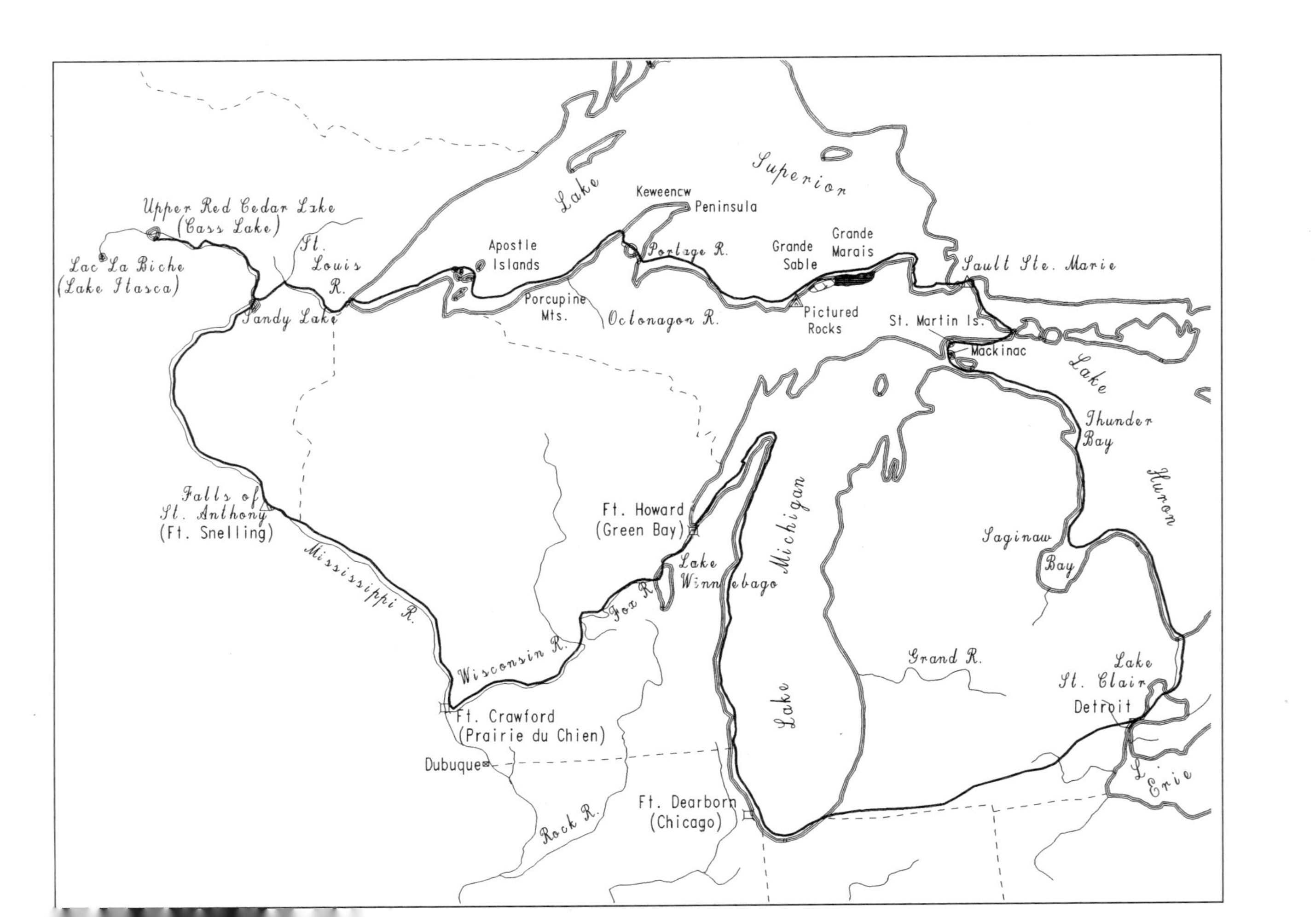
Upper Red Cedar Lake
(Cass Lake)
Lac La Biche
(Lake Itasca)
St. Louis R.
Sandy Lake
Lake Superior
Apostle Islands
Porcupine Mts.
Keweencw Peninsula
Portage R.
Octonagon R.
Grande Sable
Grande Marais
Pictured Rocks
Sault Ste. Marie
St. Martin Is.
Mackinac
Lake Huron
Thunder Bay
Saginaw Bay
Falls of St. Anthony
(Ft. Snelling)
Mississippi R.
Ft. Howard
(Green Bay)
Lake Winnebago
Fox R.
Lake Michigan
Wisconsin R.
Grand R.
Lake St. Clair
Detroit
Ft. Crawford
(Prairie du Chien)
Dubuque
Ft. Dearborn
(Chicago)
Rock R.
L. Erie

Chapter Two

Governor of Michigan Territory (1813–1831): "A More Consummate Politician . . . Will Rarely Be Found"

It is difficult to picture Lewis Cass as a robust young man; the more common image is of aged, phlegmatic "Senator Gass." But Cass was an enterprising man of only thirty-one years when appointed governor and ex officio superintendent of Indian affairs for Michigan Territory. He leaped at the opportunity. It was clear by now that he was not cut out to follow in the martial footsteps of his father, and the governorship of Michigan Territory was a political plum for the former Ohio legislator and federal marshal. Cass modestly remarked he neither sought nor expected the appointment, convinced as he was that it resulted from "my peculiar situation"; nonetheless, he moved swiftly to secure Senate approval of his nomination. On the journey to Albany to testify at the court-martial of William Hull, General Cass paused at Fort Meigs to write Charles Larned, a political confidant in Detroit. Cass acknowledged the Senate might look with disfavor upon his holding both a military commission and a civil office, and he asked Larned to circulate a petition among Michigan residents supporting his appointment. Cass also called upon his longtime mentor, Ohio senator Thomas Worthington. Such persistence paid off. The nomination was confirmed, and shortly after Hull's trial, Cass resigned his military commission, thereby removing that barrier to civil office. The ambitious young man enthusiastically hitched his political future to that of Michigan Territory. It proved to be an astute move, as the reputation and public career of Lewis Cass grew with the Old Northwest.[1]

When Cass became the governor of Michigan, he embarked on a remarkably successful phase of a long and varied public life, during which he was reappointed six times by three different presidents. Michigan had been formally detached from Indiana Territory just eight years previously, and Cass succeeded the disgraced William Hull as the territory's second governor. He retained the post for eighteen years, until Michigan reached the threshold of statehood. Governor Cass enjoyed the longest tenure in American territorial history by keeping his political fences well mended, through traveling frequently to Washington; negotiating a score of Indian treaties; and aggressively promoting settlement of the Northwest. During his governorship, too, Cass developed a reputation as a moderate politician and an astute businessman. In brief, this period laid the foundation for his personal wealth and national political career.

It was especially advantageous that Cass enjoyed a vigorous mind and constitution at the time he became governor, because he faced a staggering challenge. The United States was still engaged in the conflict with Great Britain and her Indian allies, and Michigan was a war zone populated primarily by French-speaking residents with little interest in the military outcome. The brunt of the fighting soon shifted to the east, and Cass's immediate tasks were the survival of Michigan's inhabitants and the establishment of American sovereignty and government over the region. Although circumstances kept him away from Detroit for much of the year following his appointment, Cass accomplished these goals. Until the Treaty of Ghent brought a formal end to hostilities, Cass's jurisdiction extended to the occupied regions of Upper Canada. After Illinois was admitted as a state in 1818, Michigan Territory encompassed its present boundaries and Wisconsin, eastern Minnesota, and the "Toledo Strip" of Ohio.

General Cass returned to Fort Detroit with British prisoners in late October 1813 and took command of some two thousand troops, three-quarters of them regulars led by Lieutenant Colonel George Croghan. After the mounted militiamen under Richard Mentor Johnson returned to Kentucky, Cass organized a troop of cavalry to deal with the Indians and any remaining enemy soldiers lingering in the vicinity. The British had burned the barracks before evacuating, and the American troops spent an unusually harsh winter in log huts with leaky roofs that turned the dirt floors to mud. The officers took shelter in taverns and private homes, leaving the enlisted men to drown their troubles in cheap whiskey. Fortunately, the British were incapable of launching an assault on Detroit, and most of the troops were withdrawn in the spring. It was not until the war was nearly concluded that adequate barracks and officer quarters were built within the fort, and the remaining soldiers settled into the boredom of garrison duty.[2]

Michigan's civilian population suffered a similar ordeal. Prior to the outbreak of hostilities, the non-Indian population of Michigan numbered fewer than five thousand. Almost one-third of the residents were clustered in Detroit, an outpost only recently recovered from the devastating fire of 1805. After General Hull surrendered the fort, fear of British and Indian retaliation led many residents to flee, and the eight hundred who remained struggled to survive, since it was difficult to raise crops in a war zone.

Governor Cass responded to the plight of Michigan's inhabitants by describing the pitiful conditions to Secretary of War John Armstrong. He warned that unless the people "are assisted from the public stores, they must, literally perish." Indeed, "hunger stalked the land." One newly arrived resident complained "misery—& ruin—& famine—& desolation" were rampant. Federal aid was slow in coming, however, and Cass took it upon himself to issue government rations to destitute civilians. Although instructed to terminate this practice soon after the war ended, he continued to plead for federal assistance since the "moral character" of French habitants differed markedly from resourceful Americans'. Those engaged in the fur trade "spend one half of the year in labour, want, and exposure, and the other in indolence and amusements." Even the French farmers were content merely to eke out an existence. "The spinning wheel and the loom are unknown" to them, and only a dozen years before, "the making of soap for family purposes was a curiosity." Cass saw little hope for the advancement of civilization in Michigan Territory until a migration of Americans could strengthen the moral fiber of its population, but the governor's repeated entreaties for support fell upon deaf ears. The secretary of war made it clear that territorial residents had to provide their own sustenance. Michiganites already had learned to rely primarily upon themselves for protection from their enemies.[3]

The victory at the Thames proved to be the decisive action in the northwestern theater during the War of 1812, but it did not completely dissipate British influence over the Indian tribes of the region. There were some thirty thousand Indians under the superintendency of Governor

Cass, many of whom sought to continue the fight against the white Americans encroaching on tribal lands. Shortly before leaving Detroit to testify at Hull's court-martial, Cass warned that with the spring thaw "they will again take up the tomahawk." In the face of this persistent threat, Cass and William Henry Harrison were commissioned to negotiate a treaty of alliance with the major northwestern tribes. Representatives of the Wyandot, Delaware, Shawnee, Seneca, Miami, Ottawa, and Potawatomi tribes were called together in the summer of 1814, at the site of General Anthony Wayne's famous treaty. No land was ceded, but Cass and Harrison fulfilled their primary goal. By the second Treaty of Greenville, the Indians pledged to join forces against the British if the United States government so requested. In his report to the secretary of war, Governor Cass declared he was "no enthusiastic believer in Indian friendship" but recommended that those who abided by the treaty be rewarded. He subsequently took a party of warriors with him to defend Detroit but discharged them because they lacked discipline. Such incidents made a great impression upon the governor. Forty years later, Cass rose in the United States Senate to oppose the employment of Indian scouts on the western frontier: "You can keep them within no such peaceable limits. . . . They would scent the blood upon the gale, and redden their hands with it." From his earliest contact with Native Americans, Cass prided himself on having no illusions regarding "the noble savage." He was a nineteenth-century frontiersman who viewed Indians as an uncivilized and barbarous people: improvident, cruel, and bloodthirsty. Nonetheless, he argued that "however we may dispise them," they must be taught to live in peace with their white neighbors. Indians responded only to self-interest or superior strength, Cass asserted, and "the only question is, by which of these methods, by presents and gentle treatment or by force and fear we may expect with the most economy to attain the objective."[4]

The Greenville treaty did not end the military threat to Michigan Territory. After an American invasion of Mackinac Island failed in August, Cass warned that Detroit was indefensible against British bombardment. He regretted resigning his army commission: "I find myself a perfect Cypher. In the event of an enemy approaching the Territory I shall retire from it." This was the very action proposed two years before by General Hull which Cass had so vehemently resisted. The governor added he would do his utmost should the president place him in charge of the territorial defenses, and in due course Cass was granted the authority to take command of the regular troops in case of an attack.[5]

Cass did not wait for the Canadians or their erstwhile Indian allies to mount an offensive. Rather, he continued to employ negotiations or military force to maintain peace in the Northwest. In September, he wrote the secretary of war urging that thirty or forty thousand dollars be spent on presents to the Indians, claiming such an expenditure would be the equivalent of one million dollars in troops and arms. Cass was authorized to spend forty thousand dollars for gifts, but at the same time he led a foray against Indian raiders who killed one Detroit resident and carried off his eleven-year-old son. Cass informed the acting secretary of war, James Monroe, that a band of Chippewas had "been for some days hanging upon the settlements, murdering the people and plundering their property—We have fortunately succeeded in killing some of them." Cass and his militia brought back the scalps of the slain Indians (a fact the governor neglected to transmit to the War Department), and three Chippewas were exchanged for the captured boy. The northwestern tribes were especially difficult to pacify because they looked upon the British and Canadians as their natural allies against the white Americans. The British kept prominent chiefs in their pay at the rate of between ten and twenty dollars per month, Cass bitterly reported. In fact, the end of the War of 1812 brought at best an uneasy truce with the Indians, who remained under British influence.[6]

The Treaty of Ghent signaled a major turning point in Cass's tenure as governor. It shifted his attention from the mere survival of Michigan to its growth as an American territory. No longer was Cass absorbed almost exclusively with military matters; he now more fully pursued the civil duties associated with his office and enhanced his political ambitions and personal fortune. Governor Cass, in short, began to shape a commonwealth in Michigan, eventually bringing social order to the frontier territory.

The close of the war found Lewis Cass in Ohio, reunited with his growing family. He had been able to visit his wife and daughter, also named Elizabeth, on only two brief occasions since marching off to war in April 1812. A second child, Mary Sophia, was born in Cass's absence; a son, named for his father, followed two years later. The family spent the winter at the homestead near Zanesville, and in the late spring of 1815, the governor returned to Detroit with Elizabeth and their three youngsters.

The Casses were soon ensconced in an ancient weatherboarded house on a five-hundred-acre farm that stretched, in the French fashion, far back from the river along a narrow front. Local tradition maintained that the one-story oak house had been commissioned by the founder of Detroit, Antoine de la Mothe Cadillac, for the chief of the Huron Indians. It stood on a high bank with a magnificent view. Gardens and meadows were laid out to the rear. Decades later, the house was moved back from the riverbank to the north of Larned Street; it was demolished in 1882. Cass purchased the property from the William Macomb family for twelve thousand dollars, using proceeds from Ohio land he received from his father. One Detroit resident noted in 1817 that the Cass farm provided "a handsome income," and the governor "is accumulating property rapidly." Indeed, in the years immediately following the War of 1812, Cass negotiated a number of real estate contracts with John R. Williams, Gabriel Godfroy, Francis Cicotte, Conrad Ten Eyck, and other territorial businessmen. In 1816, for instance, Cass and Williams entered into an equal partnership for half a dozen Detroit lots. The governor also extended his personal speculations to Brownstown and along the River Rouge. Cass later made extensive land purchases in Macomb and Monroe counties, and his acquisitions continued throughout the region in the decades after his tenure as governor.[7]

His real estate holdings and other commercial investments—in bank and railroad stocks particularly—made Cass one of the wealthier men in the Old Northwest. Nonetheless, he was never quite satisfied with the return from his myriad investments. Although he claimed to be "constitutionally disposed to look on the bright side of things," the governor was a ruthless businessman. This trait would come to the fore most plainly during the Panic of 1837, when Cass was far removed from Detroit.[8]

Cass accumulated his wealth during years of economic fluctuation. When he became governor of Michigan, the territory was in dire financial straits. The small amount of specie in circulation was primarily Spanish and Portuguese gold and French silver pieces. The inhabitants frequently divided these coins into eighths, and this "cut money" stretched the supply of hard cash. So did paper bills from a variety of western banks. Known as "shinplasters," the paper money traded at a steep discount. In an effort to alleviate this situation, the Bank of Michigan was chartered in December 1817, with an authorized capital of one hundred thousand dollars. For more than a decade this was the only financial institution in the territory, and Cass was the largest local shareholder. One of his political supporters, Charles C. Trowbridge, was an officer of the Bank of Michigan; after Cass joined President Jackson's cabinet, the bank became a federal depository. The Bank of Monroe was chartered in 1827, and two years later the Farmers' and Mechanics' Bank was founded to accommodate the burgeoning territorial economy. Although the Panic of 1837 spread ruin throughout the financial community, the local banking industry was thus established during Cass's tenure as governor.[9]

Michigan's precarious economic condition following the War of 1812 did not diminish the enthusiastic welcome extended the governor and his family by the people of Detroit. The social life of the territory resumed with all the flair its French-American denizens could muster, and the Casses fell into a pleasant routine. Each season ushered in different holidays and customs. On New Year's Eve prosperous residents were serenaded by the young dandies of Detroit, who wore masks and accepted donations of old clothes and money for the poorer families. New Year's Day was traditionally spent calling upon the homes of friends and exchanging small gifts. Mardi Gras was a time of celebration and the ceremonial tossing of pancakes. The summer social scene revolved around the Detroit River; picnics on Belle Isle were popular with all ages, and in the evening canoes and sailboats plied the waterway. Cass's enormous birch canoe sported a crimson canopy and turned the heads of those on shore as it meandered along the river.

Public dinners and dances were held whenever a suitable opportunity arose; the governor's return from one of his frequent business trips was reason enough for a gathering of the town's leading citizens. The inauguration of Ann Arbor's Masonic Lodge was attended by Governor Cass, who danced with all the ladies as the festivities continued through the night. Even the opening of a flour mill at Pontiac was commemorated with a public ceremony that included an abundance of food and liquor. The governor headed the Detroit delegation, which was an especially boisterous group. Warmed by alcohol, the men spent much of the afternoon jumping into the hopper and running each other through the mill: "Gen. Cass being properly ground out, was declared to be superfine." A teetotaler from early adulthood, Cass did not participate in the drinking on such occasions, but he joined wholeheartedly in the frivolity. It was truly a satisfying and rewarding life for the governor of Michigan Territory. Two more daughters, Matilda and Isabella (Belle), joined the family during these years, which were seriously marred only by the deaths of two infant children.[10]

As the Casses settled into their roles at the forefront of Detroit society, the governor continued his quest to foster an American commonwealth in Michigan Territory. He observed immediately after the war that "we are sadly deficient in the means necessary to form the morals of a Country. We have neither schools nor preachers, . . . so essential to every well organized community."[11] Nor, he might have added, did the territory have newspapers or courthouses or other symbols of social order. But they would soon come—along with roads, commercial development, and a more democratic form of government—and Governor Lewis Cass was at the center of all this change.

Michigan Territory was still in the first stage of government set forth by the Northwest Ordinance. The governor was appointed for a term of three years as chief executive, commander of the militia, and superintendent of Indian affairs. He was assisted in his duties by a territorial secretary, who served as acting governor when the need arose. The governor was authorized to delineate counties and townships and to appoint local civil officials and militia officers beneath the rank of general. The governor and three territorial judges were appointed by the president; in addition to their executive and judicial roles, they served collectively as the legislative branch of government. In the years that followed, they adopted, executed, and enforced the laws of Michigan Territory, commonly known as the "Cass Code." When the population of the territory reached five thousand adult males, the second stage of government might be implemented. This entailed the election of a nonvoting delegate to Congress and the selection of a legislative council, with the governor assuming an absolute veto over legislation.[12]

Cass wasted little time in asserting his personal control over Michigan Territory. He wrote Senator Worthington in November 1813, unsuccessfully urging that Justice Augustus B. Woodward not be reappointed to the bench. A few months later, Cass petitioned the president for the removal of Reuben Atwater as territorial secretary. Although unacquainted with Atwater, Cass described him as "a weak man, perfectly unqualified for his office," and recommended the appointment of William Woodbridge. President Madison complied, and the longtime friends were reunited at Detroit. Nearly a decade after working closely with Cass in Michigan, Woodbridge revealed, "Tho' we have long ceased to be very intimate, yet we have never quarrelled." Not intimate but never quarreling aptly characterized Lewis Cass. Possibly owing to a disagreement between their wives that led to an estrangement of the two men, Woodbridge exaggerated when he claimed Cass "has no one warm and disinterested friend," but he correctly noted the governor "certainly has no one enemy." From the commencement of his public career, Cass made a conscious effort to placate political foes and work harmoniously with them whenever possible. "I cannot carry political feelings into private life," he wrote. "I cannot denounce as dishonest or unworthy all who differ from me in opinion upon political topics." He likewise was unwaveringly loyal to his friends. "No man ever aided me in life," he proudly proclaimed, "whom I forgot." Cass was genuinely perturbed when political issues threatened personal relationships: "This is the key to my whole conduct publick & private. It is painful for me to be upon bad terms with any body, & perhaps I have rated human nature too high. If so, I am willing to die in the error." This was more than a self-serving declaration. Lewis Cass inveterately eschewed personal confrontations and sought compromise solutions to political problems.[13]

The chief problem Cass faced following the War of 1812 was the lagging settlement of Michigan Territory. The governor therefore did everything in his power to encourage immigration and stimulate public land sales. He devoted considerable energy to additional Indian cessions; the improvement of transportation throughout the region; and the fostering of political, economic, and cultural opportunities—all of which aided immigration. While the War of 1812 was still being contested, Cass urged President Madison to grant lands in the Northwest "to actual settlers, free of expense." The governor was heartened when Congress set aside six million acres in the West as military bounty lands, including one-third of the allotment in Michigan, and he proceeded to harangue Surveyor General Edward Tiffin to get his men in the field. However, he was disappointed with the report Tiffin subsequently submitted to Josiah Meigs, commissioner of the General Land Office. Tiffin's surveyors suffered immense hardships in Michigan and complained of interminable swamps, thick underbrush, and barren sand hills. The surveyor general pessimistically estimated that fewer than one acre in a hundred was suitable for cultivation, and suggested the two million acres of bounty lands slated for Michigan be located elsewhere. This advice was accepted, and Cass was informed by Secretary of War William Crawford that Congress had transferred the military bounties further west.[14]

Cass did not allow the loss of bounty lands to retard the settlement of Michigan. He acknowledged the temporary setback but commenced a steady stream of letters to Washington in an effort to change the false perceptions. To the secretary of war, Cass emphasized the need for increased immigration to defend the territory. He pointed out to Meigs that Tiffin's men ran their surveys during an unusually rainy season, so they were ignorant of the true quality of the land. Since that time other surveyors had been highly impressed, one declaring the region to be "the finest Country he ever saw." The governor repeatedly implored Meigs to authorize additional surveys. And to those politicians who would listen, Cass noted that land sales would provide revenue to the government and open up the heart of Michigan's fine agriculture regions.[15]

Cass's persistent appeals were effective. The surveying of Michigan Territory continued. The loss of the bounty lands ultimately proved a blessing in disguise, since it lessened the influence of speculators and promoted actual settlement. Although Cass complained to Tiffin that the survey lines being run by his men added tracts of Michigan to Ohio and Indiana, overall he was pleased. In 1818, quarter-sections were offered for sale, and even the surveyor general was sanguine about the prospects. "There will be a good deal of excellent land," Tiffin asserted, "that I expect will readily sell." Within a few years, several million acres were purchased. The surveyor general and the governor were by then pulling in tandem, and Cass requested sketches of surveys so he could lay out townships prior to public land sales. By 1825, about one-third of lower Michigan was surveyed, a project completed some fifteen years later.[16]

With the advent of land surveys, Governor Cass began the process of organizing counties. In late 1815, he laid out the present boundaries of Wayne County, which originally comprised nearly the entire region ceded by the Indians. The visit of James Monroe to Detroit two years later provided a dramatic opportunity for the establishment of a second county, named in honor of the newly inaugurated president. Cass arranged for the commander-in-chief to review the troops, and the president received visitors at the Cass home. Over the course of several days, President Monroe was entertained with public dinners and balls, and during the evenings Detroit was illuminated for the celebrations. The president was suitably impressed with both Michigan and its governor and, upon his return to Washington, recommended seeking continued Indian cessions to facilitate settlement of the territory. Macomb County was soon thereafter created by Cass's proclamation. Later in 1818, Michilimackinac, Brown, and Crawford counties were laid out, the latter two in the region west of Lake Michigan. In the decade that followed, as surveyors finished their work in southern Michigan, county governments and townships were established. The legislative council by then had assumed responsibility for delineating county boundaries, but Cass continued to appoint most of the local officials.[17]

Prospective emigrants, taking notice of public lands being offered for sale, were encouraged by improved accessibility to the territory. Throughout his tenure as governor, Lewis Cass pushed for improvements in transportation. The first step was to assist in the military defense of Michigan by connecting the territory to Ohio. Cass, who retained vivid memories of Hull's troops painstakingly carving out a rude trail through the Black Swamp, repeatedly urged the federal government to build a decent road along the route. He secured the Indian title for such a road in September 1817, by the Treaty of Fort Meigs, and army troops soon completed construction through the swamp between Sandusky and Detroit. Meanwhile, Cass appointed district road commissioners and called for the building of highways to carry the mail and the immigrants, many of whom were arriving aboard Lake Erie ships. In 1820, post roads were opened between Detroit and Pontiac and Mount Clemens, and Cass proposed linking Detroit to Chicago. The following year, he acquired permission from the Indians at Chicago to build the road, but more than a decade passed before the entire route was surveyed. It was not until after Cass left the governorship that the Chicago road was completed. Still, during the years of its construction immigrants used it to move westward, settling the lower tiers of Michigan counties. Additional territorial roads and regularly scheduled stagecoaches fostered settlement in southern Michigan. (Road construction in the territory west of Lake Michigan naturally lagged, although after he became Andrew Jackson's secretary of war, Cass authorized the surveying of a military road linking the principal Wisconsin forts.)[18]

Governor Cass likewise supported improved transportation on the Great Lakes. The first steamboat docked at Detroit in August 1818. The *Walk-in-the-Water,* named in honor of a Wyandot chief, ran aground and was lost on only her second voyage, but larger and faster steamships soon were plying the waters of Lake Erie between Buffalo and Detroit. Commerce on the Great Lakes grew enormously during these years. In 1823, Cass requested Michigan's congressional delegate to seek authorization for the erection of a lighthouse near Fort Gratiot at the foot of Lake Huron. With the completion of the Erie Canal, packets such as the *Henry Clay, Pioneer,* and *Superior* landed several hundred passengers a week at Detroit. In 1824, Cass established six new counties to provide local government for the territory's burgeoning population, and the *Detroit Gazette* printed an encouraging letter from an immigrant, which reported that deck passage cost him only about three dollars and the trip from Buffalo had been "exceedingly pleasant."[19]

The advent of inexpensive steamboat passage and the construction of roads between principal Michigan settlements aided in the defense of the territory and its commercial development. In the period after the War of 1812, Lewis Cass recognized that growth of the Northwest was directly tied to its defense. He was painfully aware that relations with both the Indians and British would have to be stabilized before the United States could secure sovereignty over Michigan Territory. He described the region as the "weakest and most exposed frontier of the whole Union," warning that without military protection the residents "could not for one hour resist the efforts of the Indians." While arguing with the Washington authorities to maintain military posts in the territory, he sought to pacify the Indians by lessening their ties with the British and providing for their establishment on reservations or removal to the west. This led Cass to refuse The Prophet, brother of Tecumseh, and two hundred Shawnee followers permission to settle near the River Raisin, a decision swiftly ratified by the War Department. He was not successful, however, in preventing Indians residing in Michigan from crossing into Canada to receive gifts and encouragement from British military authorities. Thousands of tribesmen continued their annual trek to Malden and upon their return assaulted settlers and stole livestock, thereby keeping "this frontier in a continued state of alarm." The governor was compelled to have soldiers assigned to his house at Detroit to regulate the traffic of drunken—or merely curious—Indians. Federal officials eventually responded to the situation, and Cass was authorized to prohibit Michigan Indians from visiting British posts. He proposed several "effectual measures" to put an end to the problem, but they proved to be fruitless. The following year Cass estimated that twice as many Indians crossed the Detroit River to visit Malden. It may be noted that Cass did not wish the Indians to suffer as a result of any interdiction; in fact, he called upon the administration to compensate them for the loss of British goods. Cass was fundamentally concerned that American sovereignty in the region was being undermined by the British.[20]

Foreign influence over the Indians caused anxiety in Michigan settlements. As the governor pointedly asserted, it was "perfectly farcical to assign any philanthropick motive" to the conduct of the British. Still smarting over the humiliating surrender of Detroit, Cass chafed under the imperious attitude displayed by the military commanders at Malden, and he urged the federal government to provide an adequate military force to deal with Indian depredations. Cass applauded the decisions made in 1816 to erect Fort Crawford at Prairie du Chien and Fort Howard at Green Bay and to rebuild Fort Dearborn at Chicago; after negotiating a treaty with the Chippewas several years later, he was instrumental in establishing a garrison in the Saginaw River valley. In addition, he continued to pressure Washington to maintain "a respectable display of military force" at Detroit.[21]

It was difficult, especially during economic hard times, to convince the nation's political leaders to support a large military presence in Michigan. More than eight years after the end of the war, Cass pleaded that the garrisons not be withdrawn from Detroit, Saginaw, Chicago, and Prairie du Chien. In response, Secretary of War John C. Calhoun stated that troops stationed in the interior of the territory must be withdrawn to strengthen garrisons on the frontier, including the post at Michilimackinac. Good soldier and politician that he was, Cass knew when the battle was lost, and he thanked Calhoun for his "judicious distribution" of northwestern troops. As it turned out, owing to road construction and periodic outbreaks of violence between whites and Indians, most of the military posts in Michigan Territory remained garrisoned during Cass's governorship.[22]

In a very real sense, Governor Cass served as America's ambassador to Upper Canada. A series of incidents that took place soon after the War of 1812 gave him the opportunity to oppose British pretensions and champion the supremacy of the United States in the Old Northwest. Lewis Cass, who once marched off to war to defend the American eagle from the British lion, now engaged in truculent diplomacy to uphold national honor and establish a workable relationship with Canadian authorities. In July 1815, the commander at Fort Malden, Lieutenant Colonel Reginald William James, complained that an accidental discharge of ordnance aboard the American brig *Niagara* had seriously damaged the property of a British citizen. James called for an investigation, especially in view of the "great lightness" with which the Americans treated the incident. The governor responded the following day, apologizing for the mishap and expressing "regret that any occurrence should happen tending in the slightest degree to interrupt that harmony which I trust will exist between the American and British Officers upon the frontier." But the northwestern neighbors would not enjoy tranquil borders for a number of years.[23]

A few months following the *Niagara* incident, a more serious altercation was triggered by the desertion of five sailors from the HMS

Confiance. Lieutenant Alexander T. E. Vidal led an armed party into Michigan that captured one of the deserters, Thomas Rymer, and hustled him back to the British schooner. In the meantime, the territorial militia was called out to deal with the incursion. Vidal was arrested for breach of the peace, prompting the British naval commander on Lake Erie, Commodore Sir Edward W. C. R. Owen, to demand his immediate release. Lewis Cass instead used the situation to full advantage. The sight of a British officer standing trial in an American court was certain to impress the Indians as well as Canadian authorities. The governor crisply replied that Lieutenant Vidal "violated the Laws of this Country & subjected himself to the Penalty described for such conduct." Furthermore, Cass requested the return of Rymer, since there were no treaty provisions with Britain calling for the extradition of deserters. A rather perplexed Commodore Owen disingenuously responded that Rymer was not actually a deserter—he simply had been in a drunken stupor aboard the boat stolen by the deserters to make their escape. With national honor at stake, Governor Cass shrewdly offered what appeared to be a compromise. He suggested Rymer be sent back to Michigan and given the opportunity to decide whether to return to British jurisdiction. Owen, realizing that the legal and diplomatic roadblocks Cass had erected left no room to maneuver, refused to return Rymer and ended the debate by turning the entire matter over to the British minister at Washington. Soon thereafter, a Detroit jury found Lieutenant Vidal guilty of incitement to riot; his fine and court costs, totaling nearly seven hundred dollars, were paid from British naval funds. When a presidential pardon for Vidal subsequently arrived, Cass returned it to Washington. The governor informed Secretary of State James Monroe that the fine had been paid, Vidal released, and justice served.[24]

Shortly before Vidal's trial, Governor Cass and Lieutenant Colonel James became involved in another international dispute that threatened the wary truce prevailing along the northwestern border. James protested the "murder" of an Indian on Grosse Ile by an American thought to be a soldier. After investigating the incident, Cass explained an American had killed the Indian in self-defense, and—driving home the point he made earlier to Commodore Owen—he firmly stated the shooting occurred "within the Territorial jurisdiction of the United States, and a British officer has consequently no right to require nor ought an American officer to give any explanation upon the subject." Case closed, in other words. But Colonel James was not about to let the matter rest. He posted a reward of five hundred dollars for the capture of "the perpetrator." Cass responded like a bull to the cape, spurred by the fact the reward was made payable in dollars as an apparent incentive to Americans. In a bellicose proclamation he exhorted all Michigan residents "to repel by force" attempts to apprehend anyone on United States territory. Cass's resolute stand was successful; the reward went unclaimed.[25]

As 1815 drew to a close, Governor Cass wrote that his "British neighbors are rather uncivil. We are daily in contact, and they evince little disposition to forget the past. I hope in a short time this spirit will subside." Of course, Cass himself could not forget the past, and it was quite some time before tensions lessened along the Michigan border. While the United States and Britain withdrew their troops from captured territory shortly after the war ended, the British continued to occupy Drummond Island in northern Lake Huron, despite Cass's claim this violated the Treaty of Ghent. It was not until more than a dozen years later that an international commission ajudicated the question and the British garrison was pulled off the island.[26]

Meanwhile, the issue of maritime search captured the attention of Lewis Cass and his counterparts in Canada. On several occasions after the end of the war, British naval parties boarded American ships on the Great Lakes and inspected crews and cargoes. In June 1816, for example, the schooner *Tecumseh* drew alongside four American merchant vessels lying off Fort Malden and searched them for British deserters. Cass vigorously protested these actions, "for which the laws of nations afford no pretence," and ominously warned Secretary of State James Monroe that repeated offenses were likely to trigger bloodshed. The administration pursued Cass's protests through John Quincy Adams. The British minister to Washington, Charles Bagot, subsequently informed the State Department that his government wished to settle the issue amicably with the United States. Cass thus provided some impetus to the discussions that culminated in the Rush-Bagot Agreement of 1817. Animated by a developing case of Anglophobia, Lewis Cass served his nation well in forcefully defending American sovereignty in the Old Northwest.[27]

Governor Cass believed a strict regulation of Indian trade was needed to prevent British trappers from gaining an unfair economic advantage. His motivation was clear: to support national interests in the struggle for control of Indian markets, thereby augmenting the economic and commercial base needed to sustain the growth of Michigan as an American commonwealth. In his efforts to thwart British traders, Cass proved willing to compromise on the sale of liquor to the Indians. Shortly after taking office, he had issued a proclamation that ordered "all persons to refrain from selling or disposing of any spirituous liquor to any Indians" and warned that violators would be punished. But when it appeared American traders were placed at a disadvantage by their British counterparts, Cass exercised his discretionary powers to permit the use of alcohol in the Michigan fur trade. While he remained true to the ideal of total prohibition in Indian lands under his superintendency, Cass was prepared to grant exceptions in order to support American interests in the face of foreign competition.[28]

Another aspect of Indian affairs colored by Lewis Cass's aversion to British imperialism was the issue of federally subsidized trading posts. Cass believed such "factories" hindered American fur trading companies and individual trappers and diminished Indian respect for the national government. The trading houses had been established at President Washington's suggestion, and although Cass's political lodestar, Thomas Jefferson, was an equally strong advocate of the factory system, the governor contended that engaging in trade made the federal government appear "contemptible" to the Indians. In September 1818, he recommended to Secretary of War Calhoun that the factories be abolished. Cass argued, "A great abundance of American capital has been diverted into this channel, and it would be a reflection upon our national character to suppose, that enterprize could not be found to distribute this capital, or skill to employ it." The governor doubtless had John Jacob Astor's American Fur Company in mind while making these claims. Two years later, he wrote to Michigan's congressional delegate in support of opening the Indian country to private traders. The factory system was abolished in 1822, although the suggestion made by Cass to distribute the remaining goods gratuitously to the Indians was not accepted in Washington. Thomas McKenney, the superintendent of Indian trade, bitterly blamed Astor for the demise of the trading posts.[29]

Lewis Cass and John Jacob Astor agreed that the federal government did not belong in the fur trade. Cass, in fact, was a consistent supporter of Astor and his business organizations. This was a prudent position to take, considering the political influence enjoyed by Astor, a personal acquaintance and financial benefactor of President Monroe. During these years the American Fur Company achieved a virtual monopoly in the region, and Governor Cass responded by appointing several of Astor's associates to minor territorial offices. When grumblings regarding the dominance of the company reached the War Department, Cass replied that the so-called "monopoly is merely the influence of capital, skill & enterprize." The governor, following a directive from the War Department, likewise urged his subordinates to grant Astor's men all possible considerations. William Puthuff, the Indian agent at Mackinac, was ordered to issue licenses to traders recommended by Ramsay Crooks, a field representative of Astor's company. Instead, Puthuff became involved in a lengthy feud with Crooks, and his subsequent dismissal was widely perceived as a political triumph for Astor. Governor Cass underscored the influence of Astor when he authorized Crooks—a British citizen—to investigate the mistreatment of American Fur Company traders at Fort Crawford, Prairie du Chien.[30]

Governor Cass's unshakable support of the American Fur Company led to charges that he accepted a bribe from Astor. Apparently, the bribery accusation originated in 1892, with a New York newspaper article announcing the sale of six American Fur Company account books. One ledger reportedly included an entry that "Lewis Cass took certain money from Montreal to Mackinac on May 3, 1817, amounting to £7,238." Although several of Astor's early biographers embellished this brief story, subsequent examinations of the account books revealed no such entry. It simply would have been out of character for either Cass or Astor to engage in outright bribery. Cass's long public career provides no evidence of venality. He once advised an Indian agent to avoid even the appearance of impropriety: "It is a safe rule for a public officer, never to do an act, which he would not be willing should be disclosed to the whole world." In an era of relaxed professional ethics for politicians, Governor Cass went so far as to keep separate stocks of pens and writing paper in his home, so his children would not use materials provided from government funds. It also is hardly credible that Lewis Cass would have traveled to Montreal to accept a bribe when a more discreet meeting in Washington or New York could easily have been arranged. Plainly, there are less devious explanations for his support of Astor. Throughout his public life Cass gravitated toward the political center, customarily following the more expedient course, and Astor's influence in business and political circles was palpable. Furthermore, Cass had the satisfaction of aiding the premier American fur company in its economic struggle with British competitors. Supporting Astor was simply another manifestation of his broadening Anglophobia.[31]

In the fall of 1819, Lewis Cass proposed to the War Department an expedition under his leadership to the far reaches of Michigan Territory. Six years had passed since General Cass was thrust into the office of governor during the War of 1812. The Michigan frontier was pacific, the underpinnings of a stable society were laid, and the time was ripe to carry the American flag "into those remote regions where it has never been borne by any person in a public station." Such an ambitious venture would tie the Indian tribes of the far Northwest to the federal government and lessen British influence on the fur trade. Furthermore, Cass informed Calhoun, an examination of mineral resources would prove useful, and land cessions might be negotiated at Sault Ste. Marie. To convince the secretary of war, Cass promised that no additional appropriation was needed; the estimated fifteen-hundred-dollar expenditure could come from funds already slated for the Michigan superintendency.[32]

Calhoun granted approval for the expedition in January 1820, authorizing a military escort and an additional one thousand dollars to defray expenses. Captain David B. Douglass, a topographical engineer, and Henry Rowe Schoolcraft were sent to Detroit to join the Cass party. The governor, in the meantime, made preparations for the tour. Supplies were requisitioned, and three large birch canoes were ordered from the Chippewas of Saginaw Bay. Thirty-five feet in length and six feet wide in the middle, the canoes were capable of hauling cargoes totaling four tons, yet could easily be carried across portages by four men. In addition to Captain Douglass and Schoolcraft, who served as mineralogist, the "gentlemen" of the party included Dr. Alexander Wolcott, a physician at the Chicago Indian agency; James M. Doty, official secretary of the expedition; Charles C. Trowbridge, topographical assistant to Douglass; and Robert Forsyth, Cass's private secretary. A small military contingent was under the command of Lieutenant Aeneas Mackay. Ten voyageurs and an equal number of Ottawa, Chippewa, and Shawnee braves provided the crews and hunters for the excursion; the interpreters were James Riley, a mixed-blood Saginaw, and Joseph Parks, a former Shawnee captive.

Late in the afternoon of May 24, the Cass expedition departed to the cheers of Detroit residents lining the river bank. The *Gazette* reported the canoes made rapid progress despite unfavorable winds and currents, "the *voyageurs* regulating the strokes of their paddles by one of their animated row-songs, and the Indians encouraging each other by shouts of exultation." The Indian paddlers soon left the other two canoes behind, but the entire party was driven ashore near Grosse Point by a storm. The expedition was to be frequently delayed by inclement weather, and Cass made the best of the unscheduled pauses by drawing upon the small library he carried on his travels. The voyageurs were entertained around the evening campfires as the governor or one of the other gentlemen read aloud from a well-thumbed volume.[33]

The first portion of the journey was uneventful as the canoes traversed Lake St. Clair and coasted along the western shore of Lake Huron. After a "tedious" voyage, as Schoolcraft characterized it, the expedition arrived at Michilimackinac on June 6. Governor Cass made arrangements to refit the canoes, while Schoolcraft examined the gypsum deposits on nearby St. Martin's Island. On June 13, the refreshed party embarked for the Sault de Ste. Marie, a half-mile stretch of rapids on the St. Mary's River that impeded navigation between Lakes Superior and Huron. The expedition was accompanied by a detachment of twenty-two soldiers from the Mackinac garrison under Lieutenant John Pierce, brother of a future president. Cass thought it prudent to strengthen the military escort, because the Chippewas opposed ceding land for a United States fort. The party, now numbering sixty-four, reached the Sault before sunset on the fourteenth, and the governor sent out a call to meet with the Chippewas.[34]

The personal courage of Lewis Cass was tested many times in his dealings with Indians but never more dramatically than on June 16, 1820. The governor explained to the Chippewa negotiators that the Treaty of Greenville in 1795 granted the United States title to the old French fort at the Sault. Although Chief Shinabawsin was in favor of accommodating the Americans, most of the Chippewas were not. They were especially reluctant to cede tribal burial grounds, but Cass was convinced the British were surreptitiously encouraging the recalcitrants. The North West Company's buildings on the Canadian side of the border were clearly visible, and many of the Indians wore British medals and carried English guns. The spokesman for those opposing any cession, Sassaba, was clothed in a scarlet military coat with the gold epaulettes of a British general; his brother had died with Tecumseh at the Battle of the Thames. Sassaba kicked aside the presents brought by Cass and heatedly asked those braves preparing peace pipes: "How dare you accept of tobacco thrown on the ground as bones thrown to dogs?"[35] The young chief thrust a war lance into the ground at Cass's feet before stalking back to his lodge and defiantly hoisting the British flag. The council was a shambles; as Indian women and children fled to safety, warriors put on their paint and the American soldiers braced for an attack.

Governor Cass did not hesitate in the face of the dangerously deteriorating situation. Shouting to an interpreter to accompany him, he marched into the Indian village and stopped before Sassaba's lodge. Cass resolutely tore down the British ensign and trampled it underfoot to demonstrate the Chippewas were under the jurisdiction of the United States. He then carried the British colors back to the American camp and prepared his outnumbered party to fight.

Cass's intrepid action stunned the Chippewas, and several of the older chiefs counseled peace. So did George Johnston, son of the Indian agent at the Sault, and his Chippewa mother, "Susan" (Ozha-Gus-coday). Sassaba and a few disgruntled braves sullenly withdrew. The remaining Chippewas negotiated a treaty that granted the federal government a tract of land four miles square. All present then joined in a celebration fueled by bottles of Madeira and the smoking of calumets. Cass made several important concessions to Chippewa sensibilities in order to secure this treaty. The amount of land ceded was considerably less than the ten miles square Cass was authorized to seek, the governor guaranteed fishing and camping rights to the Indians at the rapids, and he advised the War Department not to include the tribal burying ground in the cession. All in all, both sides were pleased with the bargain made, and a United States fort was constructed at the Sault, better enabling army troops to regulate Indian trade and protect the increasing number of settlers.[36]

At six o'clock the morning after the signing of the Sault treaty, the Cass expedition portaged the rapids and entered Lake Superior. They camped that night on Canadian soil before coasting along the southern shore of the largest Great Lake. Each day brought new natural wonders into sight as the canoes passed the extensive marshland of the Grande Marais; the Grande Sable sand dunes; and the twelve-mile stretch of eroded bluffs, waterfalls, and colorful mineral veins known as the Pictured Rocks. Cass met with a number of Chippewa bands and learned they were again at war with their Sioux enemies. Ten days after leaving the Sault, the expedition completed the portage across the Keweenaw Peninsula and entered the mouth of the Ontonagon River. The governor divided his party to search for the famed boulder which, according to Indians, was of pure copper. Schoolcraft and seven others set out overland, while Cass led a group up the river by canoe before proceeding on foot. It was an exceedingly hot and humid afternoon, and an exhausted Cass turned back six miles short of the objective. Schoolcraft's party managed to find the boulder, only to be disappointed that its size and purity did not live up to reports. In the meantime, Cass and his guide lost their way in the woods and wandered aimlessly until signal guns led them to the campsite.

The governor was happy to return to his canoe the following day as the tour continued past the Porcupine Mountains and through the Apostle Islands. The Fourth of July was observed as the expedition completed its passage across Lake Superior. Cass led his party some twenty miles up the St. Louis River, where they took shelter at an American Fur Company post. He was impressed with the industry displayed by Astor's men in the interior of the Northwest and gained additional insight into the keen British competition American traders faced in their struggle for Indian markets.

Once the expedition traversed Lake Superior, Cass exchanged the canoes for seven smaller ones. The immediate goal was to discover the source of the Mississippi River. After several days of difficult progress against the current and over muddy portages of the St. Louis, the expedition arrived at Sandy Lake and took refuge in another American Fur Company trading house. Cass held a council with the local Chippewas and learned they were willing to seek peace with the Sioux. The governor offered to mediate, and the Chippewas agreed to send a delegation with the expedition when it returned from the source of the Mississippi.

On July 17, Cass, Doctor Wolcott, Captain Douglass, Schoolcraft, Forsyth, and Lieutenant Mackay embarked in three canoes manned by nineteen voyageurs and Indians. They carried provisions for twelve days and were confident the source of the mighty river was within reach. Once again, however, the elements conspired to thwart their plans. On the afternoon of the twenty-first, the party arrived at Upper Red Cedar Lake, which Schoolcraft renamed Cassina Lake in honor of the governor. Schoolcraft erroneously labeled Cassina "the source of the Mississippi," perhaps induced to make this claim because the expedition was forced to turn back at this juncture due to falling water levels.[37] Governor Cass knew better; he had planned to proceed to Lac La Biche (Elk Lake), which the Chippewas and white traders agreed was the true source of the Father of Waters.

The Cass party returned to the Sandy Lake trading post and, accompanied by a Chippewa peace delegation, began the voyage down the Mississippi. Despite the daily—and nightly—battles with mosquitoes that continued unabated, on July 30 the expedition reached the falls of St. Anthony, the site of downtown Minneapolis. They received a warm welcome from Colonel Henry Leavenworth, commander of the post later named Fort Snelling. Cass called together representatives of the Sioux nation and the Chippewas from Sandy Lake, and a peace treaty was negotiated. Neither Cass nor Leavenworth was sanguine that the traditional enmity between the two tribes would be so easily ended. In fact, within a half dozen years, Governor Cass would preside at another council seeking a boundary agreement between the Sioux, Chippewa, and other major tribes of the region west of Lake Michigan, but for a time the truce held.

The next stop was Prairie du Chien. Governor Cass was pleased to see that the seat of justice for Crawford County was a thriving village. Some eighty buildings housed the five hundred residents, and a company of infantry garrisoned at Fort Crawford provided protection. While the other members of the expedition enjoyed a brief respite, Schoolcraft explored the Dubuque lead mines worked by the Fox Indians. At Cass's urging, the federal government later gained permission to exploit a portion of the lead district. The governor, meanwhile, acquired a great deal of information about the Indians of the Wisconsin country. Clearly, boundary disputes stemming from hereditary hostilities needed to be settled before peace would prevail among the Sioux, Chippewa, Fox, Potawatomi, Winnebago, and Menominee tribes.

After a few days at the Prairie, Cass gave orders for the expedition to begin the ascent of the Wisconsin River. On August 20, they reached Green Bay, seat of Brown County. This marked the conclusion of the most dangerous portion of the excursion, the passage through ill-explored territory. The governor dispatched the military escort and Indian guides to their respective posts and villages and split the remaining company into two parties for the next leg of the journey. Eight men under Trowbridge and Doty traveled by canoe along the western shore of Lake Michigan to Mackinac, while sixteen men accompanied Cass in two canoes to Chicago, a village of little more than a dozen houses and a population of sixty. Doctor Wolcott, home at last, resumed his duties as resident Indian agent at Fort Dearborn. Cass further divided his company, sending a group under Douglass and Schoolcraft to study the topography of the eastern shore of Lake Michigan between Chicago and Mackinac while his own party proceeded by horseback to Detroit. Following an old Indian trail that became part of the Michigan road linking the two great northwestern cities, Governor Cass arrived home on September 10.[38]

Cass reported to the secretary of war that he had completed "a very fortunate journey of four thousand miles, and an accomplishment without any adverse accident, of every object entrusted to me." Indeed he had. Lewis Cass carried the United States flag to the far reaches of Michigan

Territory, thereby demonstrating to various Indian tribes they were under the protection and jurisdiction of the federal government. He gained first-hand knowledge of the intense competition between American and British trading companies, and was appreciative of the assistance provided by the American Fur Company and its representatives, including Ramsay Crooks. The Cass expedition also accumulated a wealth of scientific data from the upper Northwest; the governor urged the War Department to expand topographical and geological surveys and negotiate with the Indians for permission to develop the mineral resources of the country. Cass sent Schoolcraft to Washington with samples of the copper boulder and other curiosities collected during the journey. In a reference antedating the "moon rocks" by well over a century, Cass remarked to Secretary Calhoun that "it will probably be agreeable to you to have these specimens of the mineralogical products of our country" distributed among influential public figures.[39]

Governor Cass was lavish in his praise of those who participated in the expedition, focusing attention on the contributions of Captain Douglass and Schoolcraft. After Cass recommended Douglass for a position on the West Point faculty, Secretary Calhoun appointed the captain to the mathematics chair. Schoolcraft served as Cass's secretary the following year during treaty negotiations at Chicago, and he became Indian agent at the Sault in 1822. In his official report to the secretary of war, Schoolcraft complimented Cass's "fertility of resource, personal energy, and a suavity of deportment peculiar to himself under the most untoward circumstances." Years later, Schoolcraft wrote a private letter to his wife in which he extolled Cass as a "truly great and excellent man. I believe, were his casual, everyday observations written down, they would afford a richer report to the literary, the philosophical, & the political world, than those which have been so studiously recorded of Napoleon, & other great men who have set the world agape." James Doty, partly thanks to Cass's recommendation, was appointed in 1823 to a territorial judgeship for the western counties and later elected governor of Wisconsin. And George Johnston's efforts to maintain the peace during treaty negotiations at the Sault were not forgotten: he was appointed to an Indian subagency by Cass following the Fond du Lac treaty council of 1826. So ended the Cass expedition of 1820. It was an extraordinarily successful venture that paid scientific and geopolitical dividends for years to come.[40]

Lewis Cass spent a pleasant winter reunited with his family, and in the spring of 1821, he and Solomon Sibley were appointed joint commissioners for a treaty council at Chicago. The objective was the cession of all remaining Indian lands in southern Michigan. Accompanied by Schoolcraft and a crew of voyageurs, the commissioners left Detroit on July 3 and began a circuitous journey to the council site. They traveled by canoe up the Maumee River and switched to horseback for the ride to Fort Wayne, where Cass visited the missionary school run by Isaac McCoy. Pushing on to the Wabash, Cass and his party rejoined the voyageurs and descended the Ohio River to Shawneetown, where they boarded a stagecoach for St. Louis. From that old river town, they again took to the water, ascending the Mississippi and Illinois Rivers before reaching Chicago. The council convened on August 17, within sight of the guns at Fort Dearborn. An estimated three thousand Potawatomis, Chippewas, and Ottawas were on hand to hear Cass's familiar refrain. The governor argued that the fur-bearing animals and game were seriously depleted, and their Great Father in Washington was offering presents and annuities worth far more than their lands. In an attempt to seal the bargain, Cass assured the Indians they would not be asked to give up their country for a number of years, while government payments would commence immediately.

It became clear during the negotiations that the Chippewas and Ottawas, with only nebulous claims to the lands, favored a treaty; the Potawatomis did not, but faced with the defection of the other tribes they reluctantly agreed to sell. The Chicago treaty ceded some five million acres, areas south of the Grand River in Michigan and northern stretches of Indiana and Illinois, and granted permission for roads to be constructed linking Detroit with Fort Wayne and Chicago. In return, the Indians received about $10,000 worth of goods and $6,500 in specie at the conclusion of the council, as well as annuities (including agricultural supports) to total about $150,000 over the next twenty years. After Cass and his retinue departed for Detroit, the Indians were lured some ten miles into the woods with the promise of whiskey. The casks were opened, and after consuming all the liquor, the Indians returned to their respective villages—leaving behind the bodies of several braves killed in drunken brawls. It was a sordid end to the Chicago council. Cass adhered to his policy of withholding alcohol until the treaty was signed, but the promise of whiskey must have preyed on many Indian minds during the negotiations.[41]

The Chicago treaty spurred settlement in the southwestern portion of Michigan, and Governor Cass continued to nurture societal and governmental development throughout the region. Demonstrating considerable political skills, he nudged the territory toward a more democratic government than that provided by the first stage of the Northwest Ordinance. Cass had discarded the Federalism learned at his father's knee, and one of the Jeffersonian principles he embraced was the ideal of local self-government. Cass believed that "in proportion as all governments recede from the people, they become liable to abuse." He complained to federal officials shortly after assuming the governorship that Michigan citizens had no voice in their government, but Cass made little headway against the intransigence of the habitants. The vast majority of longtime residents were satisfied with the rule of the governor and judges. In fact, they evinced no desire for self-government, spurning the establishment of a legislature and the higher taxes that would ensue. Contemptuous Yankees, who wanted a more democratic system, castigated these "Muskrat Frenchmen." As early as 1817, more than a hundred citizens mainly of New York or New England background petitioned Cass in support of a territorial assembly. The *Detroit Gazette* published a series of letters promoting this idea; the most vociferous, signed "Rousseau," claimed that "the government of the territory, in its formation, is despotic—as it exists at present, it is an anarchy." In sympathetic response to demands for a more representative territorial government, Cass called a referendum for February 1818, at which time the voters soundly rejected any change in the structure of government. Parsimony, coupled with complacency, carried the day. Nevertheless, William Woodbridge was elected territorial delegate to Congress the following year, and in 1823 Michigan entered the second stage of government under the Northwest Ordinance. A nine-member legislative council was chosen by the president from a list of eighteen candidates who had been selected by the voters. The legislative function of the governor and judges was thereby abolished, an action which displeased many of the habitants but reflected the demographic changes taking place in Michigan. In 1827, the legislative council was elected directly by the people.[42]

The first meeting of the territorial assembly, in June 1824, gave Governor Cass the opportunity to emphasize that the popular election of the legislature was "not only correct in principle, but will be found most salutary in its operation." He called for the establishment of township government throughout the settled regions of Michigan, and Congress responded affirmatively the following year. In filling township posts, Cass continued the practice he originated for county appointments, frequently sending blank commissions with instructions for the local voters to select their officers. To some extent, of course, this form of popular rule elevated Cass above the fray of petty political squabbles—entanglements which the master politician scrupulously sought to evade. He confided to William Woodbridge that it was better to withdraw from those political "excitements, to which all communities are liable. Silence gives no offence, but active interference will long be remembered." Such was his motivation in writing the sheriff of Washtenaw County: "The papers I have received . . . for and against the re-appointment of Dr. Pomeroy have rendered it impossible for me to decide what ought to be done. I have therefore determined to request the people of the district to elect a person for that office." Allowing the voters to make the decisions enabled Cass to avoid offending the losing candidates, but such a practice was feasible only because there were no organized political parties in the territory to force him to make a choice. Nonetheless, Cass supported self-government in theory as well as practice, and with his later adherence to the doctrine of popular sovereignty, he remained true to the democratic principles espoused while governor of Michigan Territory.[43]

Although there were no formal political party organizations in Michigan during the years Cass served as territorial governor, two factions appeared during the 1820s. The Junto, led by William Woodbridge, supported the principles embraced by the emerging National Republican party; their opposition, headed by the editor and publisher of the *Detroit Gazette,* John P. Sheldon, championed the aspirations of Andrew Jackson. It is revealing that both factions claimed the support of Governor Cass, who worked smoothly with all concerned. Indeed, a member of the Junto privately complained he could not understand why the *Gazette* received Cass's patronage, and Woodbridge fumed that one of the governor's appointees was a "malignant, . . . contemptible fellow."[44]

It is reflective of Cass's genius as a politician that he was able to attract personal supporters of varied political stripe. The mercurial Woodbridge, in fact, was the most prominent officeholder to benefit from a connection with the governor. While decrying a friendship "based only upon political convenience—which is . . . heartless—soulless!," Woodbridge acknowledged he would not "despise, or fly from it." He served simultaneously as territorial secretary, collector of customs at Detroit, and Michigan's first delegate to Congress. Austin E. Wing, a decade younger than Cass, was appointed sheriff of the territory and served three terms as congressional delegate. Robert Forsyth was Cass's personal secretary for a number of years, a member of the territorial council, and an officer in the Michigan militia. John R. Williams was appointed adjutant general of the militia, and several other business and political cohorts of the governor were rewarded with commissions. Henry Rowe Schoolcraft, although long since removed to New York, wrote a laudatory campaign biography of Cass for the presidential contest of 1848. The youngest of Cass's intimate political circle, Charles Trowbridge, was a teenager when he arrived at Detroit in 1819. He served briefly as an Indian agent and interpreter, and several years after accompanying Cass on his northwestern expedition, he began a thirty-year career with the Bank of Michigan. Trowbridge eventually joined Woodbridge in the Whig party but remained a close business associate of Cass. Woodbridge could not mask his personal admiration for the governor's ability to attract men who loyally supported his public aspirations. "He has originated & kept in operation here a system of political machinery—which few perhaps or none would have devised—or could have maintained." In short, "a more consummate politician, upon the machiavel[l]ian model (softened perhaps & *americanized*)—will rarely be found."[45]

Michigan Territory made great strides toward a more democratic government under Cass's political tutelage, and a corollary to the principle of self-government was public education. The Northwest Ordinance proclaimed, "Schools and other means of education shall forever be encouraged," and the former schoolmaster certainly agreed with that sentiment. Cass fervently believed in the Jeffersonian precept of an enlightened citizenry. He credited the institution of public schools to the Pilgrims, who thereby instilled in the American consciousness a love of republican government. An address to the New England Society of Michigan provided the occasion for a reaffirmation of the principles that guided his tenure as governor of Michigan Territory. Cass told his listeners that in the entire "compass of human legislation, there is no object more worthy the attention of the law-giver, than the diffusion of the means of education, freely and equally, among the whole community." Speaking at the Hamilton College commencement exercises in 1830, Cass declared that Americans "must look forward to an enlarged and vigorous system of education, as the sheet-anchor of our institutions."[46]

An ambitious attempt to establish a system of higher education was made while Cass was governor of Michigan Territory. The Catholepistemiad, or University of Michigania, was created in 1817. Cass served as one of the trustees for this grandiose institution, the brainchild of Judge Woodward. The Reverend John Montieth, a Princeton graduate whom

Cass helped bring to Detroit in 1816, served as president and held half of the professorships; his faculty colleague was Father Gabriel Richard. Four years later the Catholepistemiad was replaced by a University of Michigan, which proved to be equally short-lived; Cass again sat on the board of trustees. These institutions were established while Governor Cass was absent from the territory on official business, but they reflected his belief in the efficacy of education.

The emergence of public grammar and secondary schools likewise proceeded haltingly. In 1820, Cass encouraged the superintendent of the Detroit Academy "to establish a female school connected with your own." A decade later, Cass served as president of a society for the promotion of female education that donated a Detroit lot to the city. The property and a three-story school building subsequently were transferred to the University of Michigan. Clearly, attempts by individual citizens to promote education in the territory fell far short of what was needed.[47]

Cass made an eloquent plea to the territorial council in 1826 for a publicly supported school system. An enlightened electorate was the cornerstone upon which the American republic was founded, because "whenever education is diffused among the people generally, they will appreciate the value of free institutions." The governor drew upon personal experience when he asserted, "The wealthy will provide for their own children, but those who have been less fortunate in life must look to their country for assistance." The assembly responded to the governor's request and passed a bill the following year that required every township with fifty or more families to employ a schoolmaster to teach reading and writing (English or French), arithmetic, spelling, and "decent behaviour." Townships with at least two hundred families were directed to build grammar schools. Unfortunately, a tax system to support public schools was not enacted until 1843. Shortly before he retired, Cass made another contribution to his lifelong support of education: he donated a block of Detroit real estate with the proviso that a public school be built on the site.[48]

Lewis Cass fostered adult educational and cultural associations, and took pains that his own family members be properly educated. The governor served as the first president of the Michigan Historical Society, the Lyceum, and the Athenaeum, short-lived institutions that pointed the way for more enduring historical societies and public libraries. His eldest daughter, Elizabeth, attended Emma Willard's school in the mid-1820s, and Lewis, Jr., was sent off to college in New York. George Washington Cass, Jr., a nephew, lived in the governor's home while attending the Detroit Academy; he later graduated from West Point. C. C. Gilbert, at Uncle Lewis's urging, returned to the Point after his father died.[49]

In an effort to cultivate an informed electorate, Cass promoted newspapers as "the safeguards of freedom." While Father Richard published at least one number of the *Michigan Essay; or, the Impartial Observer* in 1809, at the end of the War of 1812 the territory did not have a single newspaper in circulation. Cass encouraged two enterprising eastern journalists, John Sheldon and Ebenezer Reed, to establish the *Detroit Gazette* in 1817. Newspapers, Cass noted, functioned as "the nerves which convey sensation through the political body," and Michigan Territory was the scene of a thriving, stridently partisan press. The editors of the *Michigan Herald,* established in 1825 by leaders of the Junto, were frequently at odds with the pro-Jackson stance of the *Gazette.* The *North-Western Journal* was founded in 1829 (the year the *Herald* ceased publication) by disappointed supporters of John Quincy Adams. In the 1830s, the *Journal* became the leading Whig organ in Michigan, changing its name to the *Advertiser.* Its chief rival was the *Democratic Free Press,* which began publishing in 1831 and became the region's first daily four years later. Weekly newspapers were founded in a number of counties. Cass understood the power of the press, and he openly championed organs that supported democratic ideals. In 1822, for example, he urged Schoolcraft to "make every man, woman and child" at the Sault subscribe to Thomas McKenney's *Washington Republican.*[50]

Lewis Cass was a product of the age of deism and the American Enlightenment. He believed in tolerance and public education and the efficacy of religion in maintaining social order. The French residents of Michigan had long been ministered to by Father Richard and other clerics, but following the war there was no permanent Protestant congregation in the territory. Although he lacked personal religious convictions, Cass was instrumental in securing the services of John Monteith, Detroit's first resident Protestant minister (and university president). A nondenominational church was erected in 1819 under his leadership that eventually affiliated with the Presbyterians. Episcopalians formed the second Protestant congregation in the territory. Elizabeth Cass was a devout Presbyterian. Every Sunday that the governor was in Detroit, he drove his wife and children in a high-wheeled "French cart" to church, and returned to pick them up after the sermon. On those rare occasions when he attended services, Cass was generous with his praise and purse. Cass's wife fruitlessly exhorted him over the years to join the church, and daughter

Elizabeth urged his friends to raise the question of eternal salvation. The governor conceded his lack of religious belief to one of those individuals concerned with his spiritual welfare: "As I advance in life, its realities become more and more important, but not with that conviction, which will alone justify a person in making a publick profession" of faith. Ever the politician, Cass concluded by stating he "rejoiced that your own mind is clear upon this awful topic, and I trust it will prove a blessing to you."[51]

Cass plainly was not voicing his personal religious beliefs in supporting missionary work among the Indians or advocating temperance. Characteristically, he aided Isaac McCoy and his Baptist mission school solely in an effort to "civilize" the Indians, not to save their immortal souls. And although Cass became a national spokesman for the temperance movement, his sincere opposition to the evils of drink stemmed from neither religious nor moral impulses. Temperance did not serve as a secular religion to Cass; he took pains not to annoy his friends on this issue. Neighbors and political acquaintances were frequently invited to call at his house and "take a glass of wine," and he did not stint on ardent spirits while entertaining dinner guests. (Elizabeth Cass, on one occasion, requisitioned ten gallons of whiskey from the Detroit commissary.) Cass's religious skepticism helped mold his moderate political philosophy. He failed to comprehend the zealotry of those who based their principles on theological underpinnings. Cass preferred the middle ground of mainstream religions that strengthened the American social fabric and did not threaten to rend it.[52]

During Cass's administration, the foundations for social order were laid with the expansion of popular government and educational opportunities. Yet one segment of Michigan's inhabitants—Negro slaves—did not participate in the democratization of politics and schooling. The Northwest Ordinance prohibited slavery in the territory, of course, although slaves were owned by British and French settlers under treaty agreements, and those held by Americans prior to the extension of United States sovereignty over the region remained in bondage. Some slaves were also owned in violation of the laws, but their number was never great. The census of 1810 recorded twenty-four slaves; twenty years later, thirty-two were tallied, out of a total black population of fewer than three hundred. Most of the slaves were owned by fur traders or merchants, and one Detroit resident recalled that "most every prominent man in those days had a slave or two." Governor Cass, the territory's most prominent citizen, owned a household servant during this period, despite his later claim he was never a slaveholder. A note written to Cass by General Alexander Macomb reveals that the governor was negotiating with the general's cousin, David Betton Macomb, to sell a slave. The entire communication, dated October 10, 1818, is as follows: "My dear Sir, David states that he is about purchasing your servant Sally and wishes me to become his security. I whereby engage to see that he faithfully performs his contract for Sally at the price of three hundred dollars."[53]

It is not surprising that Cass briefly owned at least one slave. The governor's household employed several servants, and since his sojourn in Wilmington, Delaware, Cass viewed the "peculiar institution" as constitutionally and socially acceptable. So did his wife, who lived before their marriage in Virginia. Cass simply did not consider slavery a moral issue, and he deplored its potential for sectional divisiveness. As early as 1826, he declared that discussion of the slavery question "excited too much sensation. I doubt whether it is right, morally or politically, for those portions of our Country, exempt from the evil, to interfere in its operation. The political effect is nothing, literally nothing." Correspondingly, he sympathized with the owners of escaped slaves. In a commiserating letter to Jefferson Scott, a Kentuckian seeking the return of a female slave, Cass wrote that the fugitive had been discovered in Canada but refused to return to her master. He acknowledged, "Where this evil, which threatens so much injury to the holders of this species of property in Kentucky, is to end, I cannot see—it has increased to an alarming extent." It was little comfort to Scott that Cass suggested "some conventional arrangement between ours and the British Govt. by which their apprehension and restoration may be enforced by legal authority." Cass's later positions on the expansion of slavery into the western territories and the Fugitive Slave Act of 1850 were conditioned by his acceptance of the institution of slavery. Throughout his life, Lewis Cass considered the black race to be "inferior" to the white, and he repudiated "all political equality and social connection with its descendants."[54]

Understandably concerned with building a commonwealth in Michigan Territory, Lewis Cass did not neglect his duties as superintendent of Indian affairs. His responsibilities extended beyond the borders of Michigan to include agencies in the states of Ohio, Indiana, and Illinois. The number of Indians living in this region was probably close to thirty thousand, although Cass placed the figure at forty thousand. Only William Clark's superintendency west of the Mississippi compared similarly in geographic size and Indian population. During these years, the administration of Indian affairs was centered in the Department of War, and in March 1824, Secretary Calhoun appointed Thomas McKenney, former superintendent of the Office of Indian Trade, chief clerk for all Indian matters. Thus was born the Office (or Bureau) of Indian Affairs, known also as the Indian Department. Nevertheless, a succession of secretaries of war continued to grant Cass wide-ranging discretionary powers in negotiating treaties and administering Indian affairs under his superintendency. Shortly after the end of the war, Cass recommended the establishment of agencies at Michilimackinac and "Chikago" under Major William H. Puthuff and John Kinzie, and later he proposed building an agency at Prairie du Chien to supplement the post at Green Bay. These suggestions were accepted; the Mackinac agency, in fact, was established solely at Cass's request. The governor even found a minor sinecure for his brother, Charles Lee Cass, after he left the army. Captain Cass accompanied his older brother to the treaty negotiations at Saginaw in 1819, and was appointed subagent at Upper Sandusky, Ohio.[55]

In addition to selecting many of the Indian agents, Cass allocated and dispersed the annual appropriations from Washington and authorized all major expenditures and construction projects for each agency. When George Boyd, the agent at Mackinac, complained to the War Department in 1820 that he was not receiving enough of the $45,000 appropriated for Cass's superintendency, Secretary Calhoun curtly told Boyd to take up his problem with Cass. The governor's greatest challenge in administering Indian affairs during this period came not from disgruntled agents, however, but from Congress, which was forced by an economic panic to halve the annual appropriation for the Indian Department. Calhoun, in turn, reduced the allocation for the northwestern superintendency to $24,000 in 1821 but allowed Cass to draw an additional $19,000 from contingency funds. Secretary Calhoun showed "great confidence" in the governor's "judgement and experience in the management of Indian affairs." He demonstrated this trust by not permitting Indians to circumvent the superintendent in their dealings with the federal government: by order of the War Department, no chief was allowed to travel to Washington without first gaining permission from Governor Cass, whose jurisdiction over the Indians and agencies of the Northwest was paramount.[56]

Lewis Cass and John C. Calhoun formed a close professional relationship during these years. It was a mark of the governor's stature as a western politician that Calhoun discussed his presidential prospects in a number of personal letters. The secretary of war counted on Cass to bolster his chances in Ohio; by the spring of 1823, the governor assured Calhoun he was the choice of the West. After thc Calhoun forces lost the Pennsylvania elections early the next year, however, Cass advised him not to seek the vice presidency. Calhoun naturally had his own political agenda, but he gave "great weight" to the governor's opinions and appreciated his "disinterested friendship."[57]

Cass's involvement in the political future of John C. Calhoun was hardly disinterested, nor was it exclusive. He supported Calhoun's aspirations in the campaign of 1824 because of the South Carolinian's nationalistic stance and their warm professional relationship. Governor Cass also enjoyed the luxury—since Michigan Territory had no electoral votes—of privately supporting Calhoun while having to make no public pronouncements antagonizing other national figures. In fact, he kept open his lines of communication with a number of influential politicians during this period. He occasionally sent New York governor De Witt Clinton barrels of wild rice, only partly in appreciation for the boost to Michigan's economy brought by the Erie Canal. And just a month after President John Quincy Adams unleashed a storm of protest from Jackson's men by appointing Henry Clay secretary of state, Cass penned a sycophantic missive to the Kentuckian. This was typical behavior for Cass, who was constitutionally incapable of allowing political issues to color his relations with those he respected.[58]

As Governor Cass solidified his ties with key national politicians, he labored assiduously with the Indians entrusted to his superintendency. He informed Secretary Calhoun that the survival of the Indians was too important a matter to be ignored "by a sound politician, or by a humane man." Cass, who fit both categories, actively encouraged tribesmen to assimilate the white American way of life. The governor embodied many of the convictions and prejudices of his era, including ethnocentrism; he viewed Indians as barbarous and impetuous children who needed to be treated with paternal care. Cass characterized his charges as "so capricious in their tempers, so irresolute in their decisions, and withal so jealous, that their opinions might vary many times between now and then." Indians were "habitually improvident" and would even give up their blankets or guns to procure passage across a toll bridge. "Like the bear, and deer, and buffalo," Cass wrote in an article that received national attention, "an Indian lives as his father lived, . . . in a succession of listless indolence and vigorous exertion to provide for his animal wants or to gratify his baleful passions." Cass stressed to Calhoun, "We must think for them." After all, "there are but two serious occupations, connected with the ordinary business of life, to which an Indian willingly devotes himself. These are *war* and *hunting*. Labor is performed exclusively by the women, and this distribution of duties is a marked characteristic of all barbarous nations." Before Indians could enter the mainstream of American civilization, he wrote, they had to embrace farming.[59]

Cass called upon the federal government to assist Indians in making the switch from a hunting society. He urged that seed corn, agricultural implements, and livestock be distributed "gratuitously to such of them as wish it" and petitioned the War Department to employ at Detroit a saddler, carpenter, cooper, wheelwright, tailor, and armorer, "to make such articles of various kinds as the necessity and comfort of the Indians may require." The governor also repeatedly requested rations to feed temporarily distressed Indians, although he took pains not to impose "a pauper system" of welfare assistance "which would be as expensive to us, as injurious to the Indians." Material aid from the American government, coupled with the educational and spiritual guidance provided by Christian missionaries, would enable the tribes to live at peace with their white neighbors. So Cass believed. He inserted in the Chicago treaty a provision authorizing him to appoint a teacher for the Potawatomis, and he also supported the building of schools at Indian agencies. Those tribes that sought assimilation should be afforded every opportunity, secular and religious; Indians opposed to assimilation should be removed from the path of encroaching white civilization.[60]

The position Cass took on the issue of Indian "removal" evolved from qualified to wholehearted support. In September 1818, he and Duncan McArthur negotiated a treaty at St. Mary's in western Ohio. This pact did not stipulate removal for the Wyandot, Shawnee, Seneca, and Ottawa signatories because, as Cass explained to the secretary of war, white settlement would have to surround the Indians before they felt compelled to move westward. In an article published in 1826, Cass emphasized the problems of providing suitable new lands for the Indians in light of traditional tribal enmities. He concluded that in some circumstances, "it is better to do nothing, than to hazard the risk of increasing their misery" by relocating them.[61]

When the Indians themselves were amenable to selling their lands, Cass encouraged them to do so, and over the years he earned a reputation as a humane proponent of removal. He urged the War Department, for example, to pay the Delawares all their improvement claims "without scrutiny," since they were impoverished and needed funds to ease the pain of moving. Secretary of War Calhoun frequently called upon Cass to arbitrate the value of improvements and the exchange of lands before tribes relocated in the West. As Calhoun explained to a Shawnee spokesman, Cass was known "as a just & upright man & as a friend of the Red Men." This was stretching the point, considering the governor's ethnocentrism, but Cass declared he would not push for "the lowest possible sum," nor distribute whiskey during land cession negotiations, since inebriated Indians were all too willing to make ill-conceived bargains. In summary, Governor Cass gave qualified support to the policy of Indian removal prior to the election of President Andrew Jackson.[62]

When Old Hickory entered the White House, debate ended among Democratic politicians over Indian removal. Cass accepted relocation as administration policy, encouraged partly by a growing conviction that assimilation into white society was not a viable option for the vast majority of Indians. The governor feared the Native Americans were "destined to disappear" with the forests, as game diminished and exposure to alcohol increased. "We have extinguished their council fires, and ploughed up the bones of their fathers. Their population has diminished with lamentable rapidity. . . . We have taught them neither how to live, nor how to die." Cass supported a general removal policy as the only acceptable means of ensuring the survival of the Indians, because "a barbarous people . . . cannot live in contact with a civilized community." He insisted that "no force should be used" and that the Indians be "liberally remunerated" for their cessions. Nonetheless, the actual process of relocation was invariably a brutal experience.[63]

Owing to his paternalistic concern for their welfare and his straightforwardness in treaty negotiations, Cass gained the trust of northwestern Indians. He took pains to explain to Indian agents that the laws of the United States "recognize no difference between a white man and an Indian." Elizabeth Cass Goddard recalled that her grandfather "often said to me with great impressiveness, 'My child, remember that I tell you I never broke my word to an Indian, and no Indian ever broke his word to me.'" The governor was designated "the Great Father at Detroit," and taking note of his ever-increasing girth, Indians dubbed him the considerably less distinguished "Os-Kotchee," which translates as "Big Belly."[64]

Regardless of the personal trust Indians placed in Lewis Cass, most tribes were understandably reluctant to cede their hereditary lands. The negotiations conducted with the Chippewas at Saginaw, in September

1819, were typical in this respect. One of the younger chiefs woefully recounted to Cass:

> We are here to smoke the pipe of peace, but not to sell our lands. Our American Father wants them. Our English Father treats us better; he has never asked for them. Your people trespass upon our hunting grounds. . . . Our land melts like a cake of ice; our possessions grow smaller and smaller; the warm wave of the white man rolls in upon us and melts us away. Our women reproach us. Our children want homes: shall we sell from under them the spot where they spread their blankets?

Eventually, of course, almost all the Indians residing in the Old Northwest were forced to do just that. But Cass recognized the futility of pushing for removal in this particular situation and instead persuaded the Chippewas to part with some six million acres of land. In return, they received annuity payments and, at the governor's suggestion, cattle and "farming utensils." Several years after the Saginaw treaty was signed, Cass wrote to the secretary of war complaining the stipulations regarding agricultural support were not being fulfilled. True to his nature, Cass stated that "every principle of policy and humanity" dictated compliance.[65]

Cass's attitude toward the Indians was formulated during years of intense study of their cultures and influenced by his many journeys throughout the Northwest. He also relied upon the investigations of fur trappers and Indian agents under his supervision. In 1821, the governor distributed a detailed questionnaire seeking information on various topics including tribal traditions, religion, government, and "peculiar societies." From the data he received, Cass wrote two pamphlets. The governor also commissioned portraits of Indian chiefs visiting Detroit, poignantly noting that from "a national point of view, it cannot be unimportant to form a gallery . . . of our most distinguished aborigines, who [are] rapidly passing away, & will ere long disappear." He even came to hold a grudging admiration for Tecumseh, whom he called "an uncommon man." Lewis Cass wrote several articles concerning Indians which appeared in the *North American Review*, and he provided notes for Schoolcraft's *Narrative* and Henry Whiting's *Ontwa* and *Sannilac* and research material for several of Francis Parkman's works. Coupled with his treaty negotiations and duties as Indian superintendent, these scholarly endeavors gained for Cass the reputation as an authority on the American natives.

Daniel Webster was moved to remark after a visit with the governor that "he is probably not overlearned in Indian languages—perhaps [his knowledge] is superficial—but I confess I was astonished to find he knew so much."[66]

In light of their experience, Secretary of War Peter B. Porter called upon Lewis Cass and William Clark to draft a system of regulations and principles for the Indian Department. The two superintendents submitted proposals sent to Congress in 1829 that were incorporated into legislation five years later, during Cass's tenure as secretary of war. Although the Cass-Clark proposals dealt with many issues, Cass focused on alcohol as the major stumbling block for Indians on the road to civilization. He was pleased that Congress moved in 1832 to ban ardent spirits from Indian lands, thereby fulfilling one of his longtime goals.[67]

During the latter years of his administration as Indian superintendent, Cass's attention frequently turned to the western counties. In 1825, he joined Clark at Prairie du Chien for talks with Sioux, Chippewa, Winnebago, Potawatomi, Menominee, Iowa, and Sac and Fox representatives, seeking agreement on common boundaries and an end to tribal warfare. A general peace treaty was signed on August 19, but the delineation of specific boundaries was postponed. The following summer, Cass traveled with Thomas McKenney to Fond du Lac, where they met with Chippewas from the Lake Superior region and secured their assent to the Prairie treaty. The commissioners exceeded their instructions by inserting provisions establishing a school near the Sault for Chippewa children and setting aside tracts of farmland for forty-five mixed-bloods, including relatives of Indian agent Schoolcraft and prominent white traders. The "civilizing" of the Native American and political patronage sometimes went hand in hand. At the conclusion of the Fond du Lac negotiations, Cass confiscated the British medals worn by several of the chiefs, reminding them they were under the protection and jurisdiction of their Great Father in Washington.[68]

Governor Cass returned to Detroit and in October journeyed to the Wabash to negotiate with the local Miami and Potawatomi bands. After gaining their assent to the Prairie du Chien pact, Cass urged these Indians to remove westward. White settlers were destroying their hunting grounds and, "above all, your young men are ruining themselves with whiskey." The governor ominously concluded the Miami and Potawatomi "must remove or perish." Cass promised they would receive "a country abounding with game" that "will be yours as long as the sun shines and the rains fall." The Indians of the Wabash were swayed by Cass's words, and the two bands signed separate treaties. The stage was thus set for the concluding series of negotiations based on the Prairie accord.[69]

Cass and McKenney were selected as commissioners by Secretary of War Barbour for a treaty council held in the summer of 1827, at Butte des Morts, near Lake Winnebago on the Fox River. They were charged with setting the boundaries between the Chippewa, Menominee, and Winnebago tribes. It was not a propitious time for such negotiations. Recent clashes had broken the peace between whites and Indians, and the lead district (near the present Illinois-Wisconsin border) was especially volatile. Unrest among Red Bird's Winnebagos culminated in late June, with the murder of two whites at Prairie du Chien. Days later, another Winnebago band near Prairie la Crosse opened fire on keelboats from Fort Snelling; both sides sustained casualties. These attacks came as Cass and McKenney, accompanied by Schoolcraft and a delegation of northern Chippewas, were on their way to Butte des Morts.

Upon reaching the council site, Cass was informed of the outbreak of hostilities and hurriedly left for Prairie du Chien to investigate. He stopped en route at the main Winnebago camp and attempted to pacify the sullen Indians, but one of the young warriors threatened him with a gun before an older tribesman intervened. Arriving at the Prairie on the Fourth of July, Cass promptly mobilized the terrified white residents cowering in the abandoned military post. He ordered the militia into service, sent riders north to seek reinforcements from Colonel Josiah Snelling, and issued warnings to the local Sioux, Menominee, and Sac and Fox bands to remain peaceful. Cass informed Secretary Barbour of his plans "to overawe the hostile party," trenchantly adding that the old fort should be garrisoned.

After bolstering defenses at Prairie du Chien, Cass began a descent of the Mississippi, urging peaceful Fox and Menominee chiefs to send braves to the abandoned post. Arriving at the Fever (Galena) River in the heart of the lead district, Cass rallied the panicked miners and sent a hundred volunteers marching off to protect the more exposed settlers at the Prairie. He then continued his trek downriver to St. Louis, where he conferred with William Clark and General Henry Atkinson. With military preparations underway, Cass paused to discuss the causes of this "Winnebago War" in a letter to Secretary Barbour. Recognizing that the Indians had a legitimate quarrel with white miners despoiling tribal lands near the ceded lead district, the governor recommended to the War Department that the federal government seek additional cessions once peace was restored.

Cass returned to Butte des Morts, via the Illinois and Des Plaines rivers and Lake Michigan. In less than a month, he traveled more than a thousand miles, stiffening the resolve of settlers and miners, bolstering defenses, and isolating hostile Winnebagos from potential allies. In the meantime, military forces led by Snelling and Atkinson converged on Prairie du Chien and took several Winnebago chiefs hostage. Red Bird and half a dozen of his braves ultimately surrendered, and the northwestern frontier was again pacific.[70]

On August 11, 1827, a treaty was signed at Butte des Morts delineating the boundaries between the Chippewa, Menominee, and Winnebago tribes. Once back in Detroit, Cass suggested the Winnebago chiefs be sent on a tour of American cities to acquaint them with the strength of their white neighbors. McKenney agreed, and in November 1830 several of the chiefs passed through Detroit on their way to visit President Jackson. The federal government, meanwhile, pursued the governor's proposal that additional lands be purchased in the lead district. Cass and Colonel Pierre Menard concluded such a treaty on August 25, 1828, although it did not deter whites from trespassing on the remaining Indian territory. The Winnebago uprising underscored Cass's call for a continued strong military posture in the region. Shortly after he was appointed commanding general of the army, Alexander Macomb decided the posts in Michigan Territory (including Prairie du Chien) would remain garrisoned and a new fort would be constructed at the portage of the Wisconsin and Fox rivers. General Macomb, not so incidentally, was a member of the family that had sold Cass his farm, and the governor had supported his rise through the military. The commanding general, in turn, recognized Cass's "extensive knowledge of the affairs and dispositions of the Indians and our [British] neighbors" and frequently sought his advice.[71]

The network of political contacts that Cass so devotedly fostered stretched far beyond the borders of Michigan Territory; indeed, it reached into the White House. President Jackson, politically weakened by "Eaton malaria" and determined that Vice President Calhoun should not succeed him, reorganized his cabinet in the spring of 1831. Secretary of State Martin Van Buren and Secretary of War John Eaton resigned, and the Calhoun faction was purged. Lewis Cass was a leading candidate for a cabinet post. He was considered for the war office during the Monroe administration, and it had been rumored that President John Quincy

Adams would appoint Cass postmaster general. Andrew Jackson realized that Cass was the most prominent northwestern Democrat, and the two shared the same basic political philosophy. Van Buren assured the president that Governor Cass was "a most able administrator" who maintained close contact with national party leaders. Cass was also a recognized authority on the American Indian and supported the president's removal policy. Furthermore, Jackson and Cass shared a bond as brothers in arms. Both answered their country's call in 1812: Cass marched off to defend Detroit and the Northwest, while Jackson emerged as "the Hero of New Orleans." It could be assumed by the president that Cass would willingly follow the orders of his commander-in-chief. Finally, Jackson was blissfully unaware of the governor's earlier support of Calhoun. So while Jackson may not have embraced Cass as a personal friend or intimate political supporter, he recognized him as a sound administrator whose experiences were well suited for the War Department.

Despite his qualifications, Cass was not President Jackson's first choice to succeed Eaton. Old Hickory informed Van Buren that Hugh Lawson White and William Drayton rejected the nomination before it was offered to Cass, "who I suppose, will accept." Cass did accept, and formally became secretary of war on August 1, 1831, the same day his resignation as governor of Michigan Territory took effect. Secretary of War Cass, while not completely fulfilling the president's expectations of a good soldier blindly following orders, was destined to play a major role in the important political issues that dominated the latter years of the Jackson administration. Thus closed a long chapter in the public life of Lewis Cass, who served as the territorial governor of Michigan for nearly eighteen years.[72]

Before he left for Washington, Cass was honored at a public dinner tendered by the people of Detroit. John Biddle, territorial delegate to Congress and brother of the head of the Bank of the United States, presided. He assured Cass Michiganites would long remember his "zealous and successful exertions to promote their welfare." A contemporary chronicler concluded that Cass found the territory "weak from the devastations of war, and left it strong. . . . It can be affirmed safely, that the present prosperity of Michigan is now more indebted to Governor Cass than to any other man, living or dead." This did not overstate the case. Under the tutelage of Lewis Cass, Michigan became a truly American commonwealth.[73]

Responding to the laudatory speeches at the public dinner held in his honor, Cass noted that "all the elements of social order and prosperity have been called into action."[74] Michigan Territory was poised to enter the Union; the population, enumerated at 31,639 in the census of 1830, swelled to 175,000 in the next seven years. During Governor Cass's administration, the foundations of social and political order were laid. Settlement was boosted by public land sales, improved transportation, and the augmentation of educational and political opportunity. Cass made strenuous efforts to bring democracy to all levels of territorial government, calling upon the legislative council and local residents to join in the selection of county and township officials formally appointed by the governor. He cultivated the desire for self-government among Yankee emigrants to the region and steered reluctant habitants along the road to increased political participation. In the process, Cass came to appreciate the fact this insulated him from local partisan quarrels and volatile political issues. This proved to be a valuable lesson. Indeed, the seeds of the popular sovereignty doctrine were sown during this period of increased democratic participation in government. Michigan certainly had come a long way from the war-ravaged border territory of 1813; and so, too, had Lewis Cass.

When Cass joined the cabinet of Andrew Jackson, he brought to Washington a distinguished reputation as a moderate politician and staunch defender of national sovereignty. He was a man who bristled at British pretensions, favored local self-government and public education, dealt firmly but fairly with Indians, and readily accepted the institution of slavery where it existed. This reputation as a conservative Democrat and steadfast supporter of American honor was molded by the provisions of the Constitution and the Northwest Ordinance and the precepts of Jefferson; it remained constant for his entire career. The forty-eight-year-old Cass was also an accomplished politician. William Woodbridge observed, "This world to him, is but a play-house & that drama, with him, is best—which is best performed. . . . The men & women who move, or strut, upon this theatre are, with him, mere automata—without heart or soul." With his appointment to the War Department, Cass's political instincts would be further developed. If the world to him was indeed but a play-house, Lewis Cass was now a player in the theater of national politics.[75]

Chapter Three

Secretary of War (1831–1836): "An Amiable Talented Man"

Lewis Cass took up the reins of the War Department in August 1831 and was unanimously confirmed by the Senate when it convened in December. President Jackson's revamped cabinet was a disparate group that included Secretary of State Edward Livingston, Louis McLane at the Treasury Department, Attorney General Roger Brooke Taney, and Secretary of the Navy Levi Woodbury. Postmaster General William Barry, the sole survivor from the original cabinet, was a staunch supporter of the president but an incompetent administrator. Taney demonstrated both loyalty and talents that made him indispensable to Jackson. Livingston was an intelligent, cogent writer but lacked basic political instincts. Woodbury, in contrast, was a consummate politician who frequently allied himself with McLane, Livingston, and Cass on major issues faced by the administration. It was McLane, a man of boundless political ambition, who was the driving force in this cabinet coalition. A former Federalist, chairman of the Ways and Means Committee, and minister to Great Britain, McLane was an ardent supporter of the national bank and a close friend of its president, Nicholas Biddle. He quickly formed a personal and ideological bond with Lewis Cass, who shared his conservative sentiments.[1]

Cass's appointment was praised by military commanders and politicians from both sides of the political fence. His talents and experience were a good fit for the war office, and since he had not publicly participated in national party politics while governor of Michigan Territory, even Jackson's opponents hoped for the best. Democrats Richard M. Johnson and Thomas Hart Benton sent their good wishes. Nicholas Biddle congratulated the new secretary of war, hopeful of gaining an ally in the cabinet; no Locofoco, Cass was a successful real estate and stock investor and a fiscal conservative. Benjamin Abbot likewise sent his congratulations, proud that another student from Phillips Exeter was making a mark in national affairs. General Winfield Scott flattered Cass by writing that "all, without a single exception, regard your appointment as your personal friends regard it—as the best which could have been made." General William Henry Harrison, Cass's commander at the Battle of the Thames, did not equal Scott in effusiveness: "You possess all the qualities necessary for the discharge of the duties of y[ou]r appointment in a greater degree than any other incumbent *at least* since the days of Calhoun. This is paying you no great compliment you will say & in truth I think so myself but I do not aim to be complimentary."[2]

General Harrison's estimation of Cass's ability to cope with the varied tasks of the War Department was well founded. In addition to its military responsibilities, the department during these years had jurisdiction over Indian affairs, public lands, river and harbor improvements, and military pensions. A chief clerk and several subordinates aided the secretary of war in his administrative duties. There was no assistant secretary, simply a few civilian clerks under the army staff officers who headed the various military bureaus. Major General Alexander Macomb was the commanding general of the army. Keeping a keen eye on America's military affairs was Commander in Chief Andrew Jackson.

The Age of Jackson was a period of momentous change. The nation was expanding and the population exploding, in large measure because of a surge in immigration. Business activity quickened. The accumulation of wealth became the benchmark of success. Capital investment, implementation of the factory system, and technological innovations—coupled with abundant natural resources—fostered industrial growth. New cities and markets were created, and the economy was further fueled by a transportation network linking roads, canals, and railroads.

The American political process also underwent a transformation during these years of expansion. A new generation was enfranchised as the drive for universal white manhood suffrage gathered momentum. Mass political parties, molded by professional politicians, led to the invention of national nominating conventions and to active campaigning for public offices. The forces of democratization carried the day; equality of opportunity became the watchword, as the ideology of "republicanism" flourished. Third parties emerged—such as the Workingmen's and the Antimasonic—organized in opposition to aristocratic and privileged elites. The Antimasons, in particular, profoundly affected Cass's political career.

The Democratic party likewise proclaimed its opposition to privilege, monopoly, and aristocracy and encouraged economic opportunity. But when Democratic politicians such as Jackson and Cass called for equality in the marketplace, they were not including women, Negroes, or Indians. Politicians and private citizens with a more egalitarian outlook than mainstream Democrats, and those with a philosophically or religiously based antipathy toward crass materialism, tended to support humanitarian and societal reform movements that embraced a greater portion of the population. Transcendentalists and evangelical Protestants (in distinctly different ways) glorified the human soul and provided impetus for reform. Advocates of abolitionism and women's rights, educational reformers, promoters of humane treatment for the physically and mentally afflicted, and temperance crusaders organized to promote their goals. Utopian communities sprang up from New England to the western territories as Americans sought to perfect society. The Jacksonian era was characterized by ferment and change, and in many ways Lewis Cass was a product of the age.

The Cass family members soon acclimated themselves to Washington society during the Jackson administration, especially the four daughters, Elizabeth, Mary, Matilda, and Belle. They briefly resided several blocks west of the White House, in a house on F Street, before moving to a more capacious dwelling with a carriage house on G Street, between Nineteenth and Twentieth. The capital city was gaining a sophistication that Detroit could not match, and a staff of servants enabled the secretary of war to assume his place in society. The Casses entertained on a grand scale. Austin Wing, Michigan's congressional delegate, proclaimed his old friend to be the most popular man in the capital. Lewis Cass, Jr., was still an awkward teenager unappreciative of all the excitement, but his sisters reveled in the swirl of soirées and balls and dinner parties. Indeed, although Lewis and Elizabeth enjoyed the quiet evenings they were able to spend together, their daughters blossomed in the glow of Washington society. Emily Mason, a Detroit acquaintance, was clearly impressed, calling the young Cass women some of "the most intelligent, interesting & amiable girls I have ever known." As a member of President Jackson's cabinet, Lewis Cass attained a national stature that delighted his family members.[3]

The major challenge confronting Secretary of War Cass was that faced by his immediate predecessors: maintaining the efficiency of the armed forces as economically as possible. Following the War of 1812, Congress authorized an army of some twelve thousand men and officers, but full strength was never attained. In a spirit of retrenchment, the actual number of troops was cut in half during the early 1820s, as were appropriations for the War Department. Additionally, the U.S. Military Academy was assailed as being too costly and elitist; many Jacksonians wished to abolish West Point. Secretary Cass joined the president in looking to the militia as the bulwark of national defense, but he had been impressed with regular army forces during the War of 1812 and later Indian clashes. Cass also appreciated the sense of nationalism engendered in the cadets at West Point, "where young men are brought into friendly contact and emulation, from every part of the Union, and are sent out to defend their country, with their sectional prejudices diminished." Any republican institution that fostered nationalism—especially during a period rife with sectional disputes over slavery and tariffs—deserved the support of the federal government. And on a more mundane level, Cass was cognizant of the political value of appointments to the Military Academy. He therefore deflected all attempts to abolish West Point and force the country to rely solely on a civilian officer corps.[4]

Cass discovered that in addition to the daily routine of the War Department, he was besieged with entreaties and unsolicited suggestions. Mrs. Stephen Decatur, the widow of America's naval hero, sought financial relief after selling off the captain's plate and medals. General John E. Wool complained his $3,300 annual salary was not enough to cover the costs of a personal servant. Thomas Ritchie wrote from Richmond, urging Cass to prevent a duel scheduled to take place in Washington between two young army engineers. General William Henry Harrison resigned from the Board of Visitors at West Point when General Macomb was chosen to preside; perhaps the secretary could soothe the Harrison's injured feelings. As secretary of war, Cass had some influence over the selection of cadets and faculty at the military academy, and President Jackson forwarded several applications for his perusal. The list of politicians who sent cadet recommendations included James Buchanan, Louis McLane, Richard M. Johnson, and Roger Brooke Taney. (Cass's nephew, George Washington Cass, Jr., passed the entrance examination on his own merits.) When the drawing instructor at the Point resigned, William Cullen Bryant and Washington Irving suggested a replacement. After speaking to General Macomb, Cass assured John A. Dix his brother would receive a commission in the Topographical Corps. Ever the politician, Cass did his best to accommodate the numerous requests he received, doubtless wishing he could exercise the same patronage clout within the War Department itself. One of Henry Clay's correspondents reported that Cass hired a clerk but when the new worker arrived the next day to begin, the chagrined secretary announced the position had instead been filled by chief clerk John Robb, a member of Jackson's inner circle.[5]

Lewis Cass exerted even less control over patronage and political affairs in Michigan Territory while a member of Jackson's cabinet. His relationship with William Woodbridge was indicative of his waning influence. Woodbridge requested the secretary's aid in collecting six thousand dollars in expenses, but Cass regretfully responded he could not act officially on the claim. Furthermore, Cass was unsuccessful in persuading Andrew Jackson to allow Woodbridge to remain on the territorial supreme court; since President John Quincy Adams had made the original appointment, Justice Woodbridge was doomed. Several months later, Cass assured Woodbridge he was doing everything possible to facilitate payment of the original compensation claims, despite suffering from dyspepsia. As late as January 1835, Cass continued to work on Woodbridge's case, although by then the two longtime friends were politically estranged. Woodbridge eventually served as a Whig governor of Michigan and a United States senator.[6]

There were more gratifying aspects to serving as Andrew Jackson's secretary of war. Cass was in the happy position of authorizing the construction of military roads he had proposed while governor of Michigan Territory. He ordered the surveying of a route between Forts Howard and Crawford to link Green Bay with Prairie du Chien; Colonel Zachary Taylor was given responsibility for its western section. In February 1836, Cass recommended the building of a major military road running north and south, paralleling the western frontier. Its chief purpose was "to form a line of communication . . . along which troops may be moved with facility, and which may become a barrier against the incursions of the Indians." Forces concentrated along a cordon of posts would protect not only white settlements from hostile tribes but also the thousands of Indians recently removed from the East. Congress appropriated one hundred thousand dollars in July to begin construction, and Cass directed that the road run between Fort Snelling and Fort Towson (near the Red River, in what is now Oklahoma). Cass appointed a three-member survey commission, headed by Colonel Stephen Watts Kearny after Zachary Taylor declined the assignment, still smarting from Cass's lack of support following the colonel's expulsion of white trespassers from Indian lands in the lead district. Work continued on the military road after Cass left the War Department despite opposition to the project from Joel R. Poinsett, Van Buren's secretary of war. It was completed in 1845, although within a few years increased emigration to the Oregon country and the acquisition of the vast Mexican cession made the original purpose of the road obsolete. Instead, cavalry units that were organized while Cass was secretary of war became indispensable to the defense of the expanding American West.[7]

To protect Americans along the frontier, a troop of mounted riflemen was organized at Secretary Cass's suggestion. The War Department had received entreaties from western traders and politicians; Thomas Hart Benton, for example, reported from St. Louis that a caravan setting out for Santa Fe carried field artillery for protection against bandits and marauding Indians. The Mounted Ranger Battalion was raised in 1832 and, at Cass's direction, was converted into a dragoon unit the following year. Eventually this troop became the First Cavalry Regiment. The recruitment of a cavalry force was a sound military move; in 1835, Cass reported that the dragoons under Colonel Henry Dodge were "usefully employed in . . . exhibiting to the Indians a force well calculated to check or to punish any hostilities they may commit."[8]

Cass also devoted considerable energies to promoting the welfare of the American soldier. In the first annual report of the War Department prepared under his leadership, he called for additional army surgeons and urged Congress to increase the salary of medical corps personnel. The individual soldier, Cass contended, was adequately fed and clothed, but his "moral culture" was totally neglected. The secretary noted that since most garrisons were beyond the bounds of civilized society, troops were in particular need of religious instruction, and so he recommended the appointment of chaplains at military posts: "Where moral and religious principles are practically acknowledged," the enlisted man will perform his duties "with more fidelity and alacrity. As he becomes a better man, he will become a better soldier." Cass's religious skepticism was unaltered—as was his firm conviction that religion fostered a stable social environment, even among veteran army troops.[9]

Lack of religious instruction was only one obstacle to elevating the character of the American soldier; the chief problem was alcohol abuse.

Cass's personal committment to the cause of temperance was revealed in the War Department report of 1831, which stated that "a very large proportion of all the crimes committed in the army may be traced to habits of intemperance. This vice is, in fact, the prevalent one of our soldiery." He called for an end to the daily liquor ration. In place of the 72,537 gallons of whiskey issued in 1830, the secretary advocated the dispensation of tea, coffee, and sugar. Congress accepted the suggestion, and the following year Cass was pleased to report that four pounds of coffee and eight pounds of sugar were being issued with every hundred rations. The sale of ardent spirits by army sutlers was also prohibited.[10]

Cass took an active role in the temperance crusade during the early 1830s. His opposition to alcohol abuse was heartfelt, and the reforms instituted at his behest aided the cause of temperance in the army. And yet, there was naturally a political aspect to this campaign against drink. The temperance movement was led by industrious middle-class Americans who melded patriotic appeals with a moral fervor that attracted members of the lower classes, especially evangelical Protestants. Temperance ideology promised economic and moral progress, and Cass wholeheartedly supported these goals—although he ultimately disassociated himself from the more zealous crusaders. He was too good a judge of human nature and too much the politician to be unbending on this issue.

A lifelong advocate of abstinence, Cass was warmly welcomed into Washington's inner circle of moral reformers. Responding to an inquiry from the secretary of the American Temperance Society, he asserted he had "never tasted ardent spirits, nor have I, at any time . . . been in the habit of drinking wine." The secretary of war acknowledged that in spite of military service during wartime and arduous travels throughout the northwestern reaches of the United States, all he knew about the effects of stimulating liquors was what he observed in others. "I can only say that I have done well enough without them," he superciliously concluded. Such sentiments placed Cass in the forefront of the capital's reform movement, and he was elected first president of the Congressional Temperance Society. Secretary Cass presided at the inaugural meeting of the society, held in the Hall of the House of Representatives during the evening of February 24, 1833, and delivered an impassioned address. As an inveterate Anglophobe, Cass estimated that the amount of gin consumed annually in England "would form a river three feet deep, fifty feet wide and five miles long. Well may such a stream be called the river of death!" Bringing the argument back home, Cass painted a dismal picture of the American family destroyed by the ravages of alcohol. The true victims of drink were "the heart-broken wife" and "the children, whose father is a stranger to their love and affection, and who barters their happiness and his own for scenes of dissipation." The sole solution to the evils of alcohol was teetotalism. "Abstinence, and abstinence only, from ardent spirits, will shield us from their injurious consequences." He thus broadened his earlier condemnation of demon rum; he now lamented the debilitating effects on all elements of American society, not simply the Indians.[11]

Cass tempered his public opposition to alcohol in an effort to avoid offending those with differing views. Partly, of course, he did so to minimize adverse political reactions. Lewis Cass did not foist his morals on other American citizens; rather, he supported their right to decide such questions for themselves. Not everyone appreciated his subtlety. Congressman John Fairfield described a dinner party hosted by the secretary of war at which "we had everything and a little more to eat and drink." Cass "drinks nothing himself, but keeps his glass of wine before him, and is every few minutes inviting some one to take a glass with him, when he puts his to his lips and goes through the form without drinking any. This is one way to cheat the 'Old Fellow,' which I don't like." Ever the politician, Cass played down his personal adherence to teetotalism in social situations. In a similar vein, he withdrew from the Congressional Temperance Society when it came under the dominance of anti-Jackson politicians. The entire temperance movement lost much of its mass appeal during these years. More of its leaders advocated the total prohibition of alcohol and prohibition was anathema to most immigrants, the vast majority of whom joined the Democratic party. Throughout his career, Lewis Cass avoided public commitments on potentially divisive subjects when principle was not directly at stake—and the temperance crusade was such an issue during the 1830s.[12]

In addition to instituting temperance reforms that benefited the health of the individual soldier, Secretary Cass implemented changes in the structure of the army. He called for augmenting the engineering and topographical corps and turned his attention to the military bureaucracy. Purchasing procedures were so muddled, he directed the War Department to hold original contractors responsible for any problems caused by their subcontractors. As for the administration of military affairs, General Wool expressed concern that the bureau chiefs "may give you unnecessary trouble." There was no such worry regarding the highest-ranking officer of the United States Army. Cass and Commanding General Alexander

Macomb continued the smoothly functioning professional relationship established while Cass served as governor of Michigan Territory. This was especially fortunate, since Macomb's official duties were not clearly defined; the inevitable bureaucratic friction between the military command and the executive branch of government was kept to a minimum. The general served as the active commander of the army, and the civilian heads of the War Department's administrative bureaus formed the "General Staff," which reported directly to Cass. A "Military Board" was established in 1832, composed of the bureau chiefs and key staff officers and chaired by the commanding general, but this embryonic version of a modern general staff was dissolved shortly before Cass left the War Department. The administration of the nation's armed forces thus remained bifurcated, with the commanding general and bureau chiefs often acting autonomously. The lack of a coordinated administrative structure plagued the U.S. military throughout the nineteenth century.[13]

In a similar vein, Cass made an effort to reorganize the Indian service. He urged Congress to create the post of commissioner of Indian affairs, and he worked closely with congressional leaders to overhaul the inefficient field staff and implement many of the Cass-Clark proposals submitted in 1829. Congress established the office of Indian commissioner in 1832, to which post President Jackson appointed the head of the Indian Bureau, Elbert Herring. Two years later, when Congress created the Office of Indian Affairs, Commissioner Herring was placed in charge. This administrative structure (which remained in operation well into the twentieth century) provided the Jackson administration with the machinery to formulate and execute an Indian policy that focused on pacifying hostile bands and removing eastern tribes to the West. Jackson, in fact, became almost obsessed with the idea of relocating all Indians beyond the Mississippi River.[14]

Andrew Jackson was a willful man who occasionally became petulant and irascible, especially when the constant pain he suffered from various ailments and injuries intensified. He was also an opinionated man who personally determined administration policy. Although he met regularly with the cabinet, the president sought merely the advice of his department heads and expected them to execute his decisions. Lewis Cass certainly understood this and during his first months as secretary of war demonstrated a deference toward the president that bordered on irresolution.

A visitor to Washington in late 1831 wrote: "Nothing of any interest is going on here, except that they say Mr. Cass & Gen. Jackson are pouting at each other." Decades later, James Buchanan claimed President Jackson became exasperated with his secretary of war because he "comes to me constantly with great bundles of papers, to decide questions for him which he ought to decide for himself." This critical assessment of Cass came after his abrupt resignation as Buchanan's secretary of state, but it contains more than a kernel of truth. Lewis Cass habitually eschewed personal confrontations over political questions. He consequently appeared indecisive and even timorous or vacillating. Several months after Cass took over at the War Department, Jackson confided to Van Buren that the new secretary was "an amiable talented man, a fine writer, but unfortunately it is hard for him to say no, and he thinks all men honest, this is a virtue in private, but unsafe in public life." Nonetheless, President Jackson made the most of Cass's writing talents, notably during the nullification crisis and the debate over Cherokee removal, and appreciated his decisiveness in dealing with the Black Hawk hostilities in 1832.[15]

Secretary Cass had scarcely settled into the daily routine of the War Department when he was confronted with a crisis on the western frontier. Under increasing pressure from aggressive white settlers, Black Hawk and his chiefs in the summer of 1831 pledged that the Sac and Fox Indians of northwestern Illinois would relocate across the Mississippi. A month later, Black Hawk led a retaliatory raid against an unarmed camp of Menominees at Prairie du Chien, and about thirty Indians under the protection of the United States flag were killed. Cass, drawing upon past experience in the Old Northwest, realized decisive action was needed to prevent an outbreak of intertribal warfare. This became increasingly clear when Black Hawk reneged on his treaty promises and, in the spring of 1832, moved back to the Rock River country with some two thousand warriors, women, and children. The Sac and Fox people had come under attack in the West from their traditional Sioux enemies and fled to Illinois in peace, although this violated the removal agreement. To further complicate the situation, other disgruntled Indians, chiefly Winnebagos, joined Black Hawk's camp.

Cass responded with alacrity to the apparent threat posed by Black Hawk. The War Department ordered General Henry Atkinson to demand the surrender of those Sacs and Foxes responsible for the attack on the Menominees, and Cass requested Governor John Reynolds of Illinois to provide the general with "such a militia force, as he may call for."[16] One of the 1,700 men who responded to Reynolds's call was Abraham Lincoln. The volunteers joined 340 regulars under the command of Colonel Zachary Taylor. On May 14, an advance party of militia panicked and opened fire on three Indians carrying a flag of truce; one was killed, and the others escaped to warn their tribesmen. Black Hawk rallied his warriors and ambushed the advancing militia, killing a dozen whites.

When word of the outbreak of the Black Hawk War reached Washington, Cass ordered General Atkinson to take "the most prompt and efficient measures to chastise these Indians and to ensure the peace of the frontiers." Acting in concert with the president, Cass called upon the governors of Illinois, Indiana, Missouri, and Michigan Territory for additional militia. At the same time, he sent Major General Winfield Scott to assume command, informing him that it was "very desirable, that the whole country between Lake Michigan and the Mississippi, and south of the Ouisconsin should be freed from the Indians." In an effort to improve lines of communication with his principal field commanders—who reported directly to him—Cass hastened to Detroit.[17]

General Scott and his troops arrived in Chicago with unprecedented celerity. One company, utilizing railroads for part of the journey, covered the eighteen hundred miles from Old Point Comfort in just eighteen days. But Scott's command was unfit for military action. Asiatic cholera broke out aboard troop transports docked at Detroit, killing more than two hundred soldiers. The epidemic proved to be a personal tragedy as well for Secretary Cass: his eldest child, Elizabeth, was among the hundred civilians at Detroit who succumbed to the disease. Although the Casses had sustained the deaths of two infant children years before, the loss of Elizabeth was more deeply felt. Writing from the Hermitage, President Jackson extended his condolences, adding his "hope that the war will be brought to a speedy termination."[18]

Indeed, General Atkinson soon ended the sordid conflict. A detachment of mounted troops attacked the retreating Indians as they attempted to cross the Wisconsin River. This Battle of Wisconsin Heights was followed in early August by the final action of the war. As the remnants of Black Hawk's band crossed the Mississippi, they were annihilated by Atkinson's forces; fewer than one hundred Indians survived. Following Cass's suggestion, General Scott ordered Black Hawk and a number of other influential braves held as hostages. Peace treaties were subsequently negotiated, ceding Sac and Fox lands east of the Mississippi and Winnebago territory southeast of the Wisconsin River. The Black Hawk War was another sad episode in relations between the two races, and Secretary Cass must be held ultimately accountable for the shameful behavior of certain militia units.[19]

The Black Hawk War had an unforeseen impact on the political future of Lewis Cass, in that Zachary Taylor emerged from the conflict with a very unfavorable opinion of him. Colonel Taylor was instructed by the War Department, in September 1832, to evict white trespassers from Indian territory in the lead district. He executed the orders so zealously, a civil suit was brought by the displaced squatters and miners. After fruitlessly appealing to the secretary of war for a deposition stating he was merely following orders, Taylor complained that "Cass has acted a mean, & contemptable part, and I am now induced to believe he is blessed with a most convenient memory." Zachary Taylor was convinced the secretary of war acted from "timidity, or perhaps from worse motives," in failing to support him, and he would exact sweet revenge in the presidential election of 1848.[20]

The Black Hawk conflict was the only instance in which northwestern Indians were forcibly removed by the military while Cass was secretary of war, but other tribes were also relocated by the Jackson administration. The Chicago treaty of 1833, with the Potawatomis, Chippewas, and Ottawas, called for their removal and the cession of tribal lands in Michigan, Illinois, Wisconsin, and Iowa. Similar treaties were signed with other Indians of the Old Northwest and the region west of the Mississippi—including the Miami, Wyandot, Menominee, Kickapoo, Delaware, Shawnee, Wea, Pinkeshaw, Peoria, and Pawnee. By the time Cass left the War Department, the Indian population north of the Ohio was estimated to number no more than a few thousand. Removal opened up vast tracts to settlement and enabled the surviving Indians to establish themselves—at least temporarily—beyond the reach of avaricious whites.[21]

Jackson had appointed Cass secretary of war in large measure because he backed the administration's position on Indian removal. Governor Cass, in fact, supported the principle of the Removal bill in an article published in the *North American Review* of January 1830. Drawing upon personal experiences, he contended that removal from the path of white settlement was the only humane way to ensure the survival of barbarous tribes. This blatantly racist position was naturally castigated by those who opposed removal. Joseph Blunt wrote a pamphlet to refute his arguments, and Samuel Worcester agreed that the governor of Michigan Territory knew little about the Indians of the Southwest. Jeremiah Evarts in the *American Monthly Magazine* denounced the "slanderous insinuation, . . . and the reckless nature" of Cass's assertions, concluding that his ulterior motive was "to trim his sails, in such a manner as to catch the breeze of government favor and patronage." While Cass was not motivated simply by political sycophancy, he wholeheartedly embraced Jackson's policy before joining his cabinet.[22]

In his first annual report, Secretary Cass warned that Indians living near white settlement who refused to relocate were under state jurisdiction and could not turn to the federal government for a redress of grievances. He enumerated seven "fundamental principles" by which the administration would implement removal, including a guarantee of perpetual Indian ownership of their new lands, federal protection from hostile tribes, the prohibition of liquor, and educational and agricultural assistance. Cass remained convinced that only through relocation beyond white civilization could the Indians hope to survive.[23]

Lewis Cass promoted removal as a humane alternative to the depravity and destitution that inevitably afflicted Indians who lived in close contact with whites and alcohol, but moving westward was at best a wrenching experience. The Choctaws of Mississippi, for instance, signed a treaty at Dancing Rabbit Creek in 1830, agreeing to emigrate during the next three years. Under the guidance of Lewis Cass, the War Department made extensive plans for their relocation; after all, this operation was expected to serve as a model for later removals. Cass placed General George Gibson in charge of operations and appointed George S. Gaines to oversee the removal east of the Mississippi. Gaines had gained the trust of the Choctaws through years of trading with them. Captain John B. Clark was given the responsibility for escorting the Indians to their new lands in present-day Oklahoma. But despite all the planning, the removal of the Choctaws did not go smoothly. It was difficult to coordinate operations from Washington, and adequate supplies were late in reaching the West. Captain Clark asked to be relieved rather than be held accountable for the defalcations of civilian agents, many of whom viewed the operation as a golden opportunity to line their pockets. To add to the difficulties, the first band of Choctaws left Mississippi late in the year and suffered through a harsh winter. Secretary Cass glossed over these problems when he reported to Congress in November 1832 that the relocated Indians were "highly gratified with the climate and country, and satisfied with the exchange they have made." The second group of Choctaw emigrants arrived that same year, after enduring a bout of cholera. By the time the remaining members of the tribe reached their new home, some fifteen thousand Choctaws had been removed from Mississippi under conditions that contradicted Cass's sanguine assessment of their fate.[24]

Cass was vividly aware of the problems encountered during the Choctaw removal operations. The first group cost the government "two to three times the original estimate," and Cass responded by discharging all civilian officials and replacing them with military personnel. To further economize, rations were decreased and transportation was "provided only for the very young and the sickly." This policy reduced federal expenditures, certainly, but the cost in human suffering was great. It is not surprising that hundreds of the Choctaws who survived chose to continue their trek until they reached Mexico.[25]

Sensitive to the hardships endured by the Choctaws during removal, Cass took steps to alleviate the suffering of those to follow. He convinced Congress to establish the position of Indian commissioner and appointed a three-man board "to visit and examine the country set apart for the emigrating Indians west of the Mississippi." Montford Stokes, the father-in-law of "Major" William B. Lewis and a Democrat from North Carolina, chaired the commission. He was joined by Henry I. Ellsworth of Connecticut and the Reverend John F. Schermerhorn of New York. Cass hoped the northeastern flavor of the delegation would deflect criticism of the administration's removal policy, and he charged the commissioners with locating suitable tracts in the West for emigrating tribes. "There is country enough for all, and more than all; and the President is anxious that full justice should be done." The Stokes commission filed a lengthy report with Cass in early 1834, in which they expressed confidence that the Indians already removed had received fertile lands and recommended the creation of a territorial government to guarantee that whites would not interfere with them. Cass forwarded this suggestion to Congress, but no substantive action was taken. In the meantime, the removal of the eastern tribes continued.[26]

The Creeks residing in Alabama fared no better than the Choctaws, despite their resistance to removal. Cass warned the Creeks they were under the jurisdiction of the state and could not rely upon the federal government to intercede on their behalf. The people of Alabama "claim the right of governing you, as they govern your white brethren. . . . I trust you will yield cheerful obedience." The Creeks, however, remained reluctant to depart from their homeland and, in early 1832, Cass urged them to relocate "where no bad white men will trouble you, where no ardent spirits will tempt or debauch you, and where the land will be yours, as long as the grass grows or the rivers run." He assured the Creeks that removal was "not a question of money with your great father, but one of peace, comfort and security for his red children. He will deal with you in a spirit of the utmost liberality." These repeated appeals had an impact, as did the increasing number of white squatters on Indian lands. The Creeks still opposed wholesale removal, but their leaders signed a treaty with Secretary Cass which ceded to the federal government approximately five million acres of land. In return, the Indians received cash annuities and 320 acres for each family, although Cass encouraged them to sell their allotments and emigrate to the West. Most of the tribe ignored his advice and chose to remain in Alabama, believing they could reside peacefully among their white neighbors. In this, they were tragically mistaken.[27]

As white intrusions continued, the Creeks turned to the federal government for the protection promised in the treaty of 1832. Secretary Cass directed federal marshal Robert Crawford to expel the squatters, and orders were issued for the commander at Fort Mitchell, Major Philip Wager, to enforce the evictions, but this had little impact. To make matters worse, speculators and traders blatantly defrauded the Creeks of their allotments. In a further effort to pressure the Creeks to leave Alabama, Cass transferred the Indian agency at Fort Mitchell to the West.

The situation in Alabama continued to deteriorate. Wholesale fraud was the norm, and after a period of inaction, Cass gave orders in 1833 to remove all squatters after they harvested their crops. The white trespassers refused to comply, and Francis Scott Key, district attorney for the District of Columbia, was sent to mediate. A compromise settlement suspended the evictions until the Indian holdings were surveyed, and then only those squatting on Creek allotments were to be expelled. This agreement, naturally, did not stop some whites from defrauding the Indians of their homesteads, livestock, and crops; and incessant charges of corruption finally forced the administration to take further action. Cass appointed John B. Hogan as a special investigator in the fall of 1835, but it was too late. The sporadic violence between the exploited Indians and white trespassers erupted into the "Creek War" the following spring. Cass immediately suspended the fraud investigations and sent General Thomas S. Jesup to effect the unconditional surrender of the Creeks and remove the entire tribe—even those who had not joined in the war. Jesup's forces easily subdued the embattled Indians and sent sixteen hundred Creeks in chains to Mobile, where they embarked for the West. The remaining fifteen thousand were removed by the end of the year. Negotiation had failed; it took the army to transport the Creek nation to their new home.[28]

The Chickasaws of northern Mississippi and Alabama, not as numerous as the Creeks or Choctaws, held lands also coveted by whites. Unlike their Indian neighbors, however, the Chickasaws recognized the inevitability of removal and struck a better bargain with the federal government. In the fall of 1832, the Chickasaws ceded most of their holdings in return for generous allotments that ultimately brought the tribe more than three million dollars. It was not until after Lewis Cass left the War Department that five thousand Chickasaws and their twelve hundred slaves emigrated to western lands purchased from the Choctaws. The Chickasaws fared better than neighboring tribes, but the process of removal was typically marred by corruption and fraud, and forsaking hereditary lands was in itself a melancholy experience.

The trappings of white civilization did not save the Cherokees from the fate of less assimilated tribes. Several thousand Cherokees had relocated years before to lands west of the Mississippi River, and Jackson encouraged the remaining tribesmen to join the "Old Settlers." Lewis Cass naturally played a leading role in the administration's efforts; in fact, he helped lay the groundwork for Cherokee removal even before joining the War Department. In an article published in the *North American Review* of January 1830, Cass denigrated the achievements of the Cherokee people: "We are well aware, that the constitution of the Cherokees, their press, and newspaper, and alphabet, their schools and police, have sent through all our borders the glad tidings, that the long night of aboriginal ignorance was ended, and that the day of knowledge had dawned. Would that it were so." Comfortable with his ethnocentric perspective, Cass claimed that opposition to removal arose from an educated, mixed-blood elite who selfishly put their personal interests above the vast majority of full-blooded Cherokees scarcely touched by the advances of white civilization. (This was not a sudden conversion to curry Jackson's favor. As early as 1816, Cass wrote that "an Indian who can read and write is generally the greatest rascal of his tribe." In his first annual report, Cass insisted "the great mass" of Cherokees lived "in ignorance and poverty," dissatisfied with a leadership opposed to removal.) At President Jackson's request, he appointed Benjamin Currey of Tennessee to inform the tribe "they had better remove and soon." The Cherokees remained unconvinced, however, and turned to the federal courts for protection.[29]

The ensuing legal dispute centered on a series of Georgia laws designed to extend state jurisdiction over both the Cherokees and white missionaries who opposed removal. In separate proceedings, Samuel

Worcester and Elizur Butler (missionaries sentenced to four years in prison for defying Georgia law) and the Cherokee nation sued for relief. The Supreme Court ruled that the state laws were unconstitutional, but the Georgia government ignored the decisions and continued to pressure the Indians to remove. Worcester and Butler, meanwhile, languished in the penitentiary, unwilling to pledge obedience to the Georgia legislation if pardoned.[30]

President Jackson supported the state's position and asked Cass to prepare a rebuttal to the Supreme Court rulings. The result was published in the *Washington Globe.* Cass contended the legal debate hinged on one general question: "Has the State of Georgia a right to extend her laws over the Cherokee lands within her boundaries?" The answer was clear. "Civilized communities have a right to take possession of a country inhabited by barbarous tribes, [and] to assume jurisdiction over them." There were only three passages in the Constitution with even "the remotest connexion" to the controversy, and neither the war power nor the authority to regulate commerce with the Indian tribes proved relevant in this case. As for the clause granting Congress the "Power to dispose of and make all needful Rules and Regulations respecting the territory or other Property belonging to the United States," Cass argued it was "inapplicable to the Cherokee country in Georgia" because the federal government had relinquished all claims to the region. He later presented a contradictory interpretation of this provision in support of the popular sovereignty doctrine; in some respects it served as an "elastic clause" in his constitutional ideology. This lengthy apologia represented Cass's definitive statement regarding removal. "The decree has gone forth; it is irreversible, that the white and the red man can not live together." Despite the hardships entailed, Indians had to be relocated for their own survival and the advancement of white civilization. Since that was his irrefragable conclusion, Cass rhetorically inquired: "Had they not better go, and speedily?"[31]

Cass informed the Cherokee people, in January 1832, that there was "no remedy but in a removal beyond the immediate contact of the white people." A few months later, he met with a Cherokee delegation and outlined the terms of a treaty subsequently rejected by the tribe. The Cherokee General Council then convened at Red Clay and notified Cass they would not relocate in the West. But as months passed and the administration's position remained unbending, a faction within the tribe became convinced removal was the only viable option. This "Treaty party" was led by Major Ridge; his son, John Ridge; and two nephews, Stand Watie and Elias Boudinot, editor of the *Cherokee Phoenix*. The majority of the tribe continued to oppose removal and rallied around Principal Chief John Ross (who was primarily of white ancestry, only one-eighth Cherokee) and the "National party." This split within the Cherokee nation was shrewdly exploited by the Jackson administration.[32]

At the same time he pressured the Cherokees to relocate, Lewis Cass privately urged Georgia governor Wilson Lumpkin to release Worcester and Butler. The administration was in the midst of the tariff-related nullification crisis, and Cass informed the governor he might be called upon for militia support. In light of this perilous situation, the secretary of war argued that the Cherokee "matter should be closed, amicably and forever." But Lumpkin was not to be rushed. While he assured Cass that Georgians "abhor nullification," until the missionaries gave up their legal proceedings and requested a pardon, he would stand on principle. Worcester and Butler, recognizing that the battle was lost, acceded to these stipulations and were freed in January 1833.[33]

Following the release of the missionaries and the formation of the Treaty party, a settlement was reached in the Cherokee removal controversy. The Reverend John Schermerhorn, a member of the Stokes commission, in December 1835 negotiated at New Echota a removal agreement acceptable to the Ridge faction. The Treaty party ceded all Cherokee holdings east of the Mississippi, in return for western lands and five million dollars. The U.S. Senate narrowly ratified the removal treaty, over the vehement protests of John Ross and his supporters, and some two thousand Cherokees emigrated within the stipulated two years. More than fifteen thousand, however, stood with John Ross and refused to comply with the duplicitous agreement. Shortly before leaving the War Department, Cass sent General Wool to Georgia to coerce the recalcitrants, but they adamantly refused to leave. In May 1838, when the deadline for removal expired, Lewis Cass was in France. At that time, troops under General Winfield Scott enforced the treaty. The soldiers were ordered to treat their charges with respect, but thousands of Cherokees perished during the eight-hundred-mile journey known as "the Trail of Tears." Thus closed another iniquitous chapter in the removal saga.[34]

While the administration engaged in negotiations to remove the Cherokees and placate the citizens of Georgia, the nullification controversy threatened disunion. This sectional issue grew out of southern resistance to protective tariffs that supported northern manufacturing at the expense of agricultural interests. Political opposition to high tariffs centered in South Carolina, where the legislature issued an exposition written by John C. Calhoun to protest the "Tariff of Abominations" of 1828. Calhoun based the theory of nullification upon state sovereignty and minority rights within the republican union. The South Carolina legislature took no further action at the time, but resentment against protection festered as the Jackson administration failed to make any meaningful effort to lower tariff schedules.

Southerners viewed the tariff passed in the summer of 1832 as only slightly less objectionable than the Tariff of Abominations, and Governor James Hamilton, Jr., a disciple of nullification, convened the South Carolina legislature in special session. The nullifiers were in control, and over the spirited objections of the state's unionist minority, led by Joel Roberts Poinsett, a call was issued for a convention that passed an ordinance declaring the tariffs of 1828 and 1832 null and void within South Carolina. The nullifiers threatened secession if the federal government used force to collect the revenues after February 1, 1833.

The nullification crisis imperiled the Union, and President Jackson, ably seconded by his secretary of war, took a staunch nationalistic stance. It was one thing for Georgia to defy the Supreme Court on an issue which found the president supporting the state; it was quite another for Calhoun to put South Carolina on a collision course with the federal government that jeopardized the very foundations of the republic. At the convening of the special legislative session, Jackson sent Cass a confidential memorandum directing that measures be taken to guard the federal posts in Charleston harbor. The same day, Commanding General Macomb issued orders to defend the forts "to the last extremity." While the state convention debated the merits of a nullification ordinance, Cass ordered Major General Winfield Scott to inspect the fortifications at Charleston and reinforce the garrisons, "as you may think prudence and a just precaution require." The secretary of war scarcely needed to add that this duty required "great delicacy." Scott reported personally to Cass upon his return from Charleston and was instructed "to take care that the forts . . . be finished as rapidly as possible, and that every necessary step is taken for their security."[35]

Andrew Jackson's annual message to Congress on December 4, 1832, made no mention of the military preparations to defend the forts at Charleston. Instead, the president predicted the national debt would be completely paid off within a year and recommended the gradual lowering of tariff rates. Jackson hoped a peaceful solution to the tariff controversy could be attained, but he decided to refute the theory of nullification with a public proclamation dated December 10. Old Hickory equated nullification with disunion, and forcible disunion was treasonous. South Carolina governor Robert Y. Hayne, who succeeded Hamilton, accelerated efforts to raise a military force to defend the state.[36]

The president and secretary of war sought a political resolution to the crisis while continuing their preparations to collect the federal revenues. At Jackson's request, Lewis Cass wrote a letter to editor Thomas Ritchie, which appeared, unsigned, in the *Richmond Enquirer* of December 13. Ritchie, who introduced the letter as an appeal from "one of the ablest men in the country," supported Cass's suggestion that Virginia intercede in the tariff controversy to effect a compromise. The Virginia legislature responded by appointing Benjamin Watkins Leigh commissioner to Charleston. The administration's plan was bearing fruit: South Carolina's nullification ordinance was not sustained by the largest southern state, and the question now was whether an acceptable compromise tariff could be fashioned before the confrontation turned violent.[37]

On December 17, Jackson directed Secretary Cass to prepare three divisions of artillery for immediate service and to report on the condition of weapons available to arm the unionists of Charleston. Additionally, two naval vessels were dispatched to assist in collecting the revenues. In the interim, a tariff bill drafted by Treasury Secretary Louis McLane was introduced in Congress by the chairman of the House Ways and Means Committee, Gulian Verplanck. This bill would lower rates precipitously by the end of 1835, and it was vigorously promoted by both Cass and the vice president–elect, Martin Van Buren. Jackson also requested explicit congressional authority to enforce the federal revenue laws, should they be resisted by South Carolinians. When reports of the Verplanck bill reached Charleston, a mass meeting was called, where it was decided to postpone implementation of the nullification ordinance until Congress completed its work. Responding to the lessening tensions, Cass diligently attempted to prevent any mishap that might precipitate a military clash. He informed Major General Scott that if the garrison at Charleston was attacked, the troops necessarily would have to defend themselves, but he admonished the general to "be mindful of the great delicacy of the subject, & of the anxiety of the President to avoid, if possible, a resort to force."[38]

A military collision was averted. Congress ultimately passed a compromise tariff introduced by Henry Clay. The president signed it into law on March 2—along with the Force bill, providing for the collection of customs duties. The South Carolina convention subsequently rescinded the nullification ordinance, but it defiantly declared the Force Act nullified. This was little more than a symbolic statement of principle; nullification was scotched. And yet, although they failed to attract support from other southern states, South Carolinians achieved a reduction in tariff rates through the threat of secession. For his part, while compromising on the tariff as he was willing to do all along, President Jackson rejected the right of secession and upheld the sovereignty of the federal government. He was fully and ably supported in his unwavering stand by Secretary of War Cass. The nullification crisis united the president and his cabinet with a nationalistic fervor. Unfortunately, that concord was broken during the administration's next challenge, the "Bank War."

Following his second inaugural, Andrew Jackson rearranged his cabinet and made plans for a triumphal tour of the northeastern states. Secretary of State Edward Livingston, a Francophile who did not share Jackson's hatred toward the Bank of the United States, was sent to replace William C. Rives as minister to France. Jackson shifted Louis McLane to the State Department, and selected William J. Duane, a Pennsylvanian with an antibank reputation, to head the Treasury. The president then embarked on a tour of major cities, intending to travel as far north as Portland, Maine, before returning to the White House and the fight over the national bank.

The presidential entourage, which included several cabinet members, departed the capital on June 6. A three-day sojourn at Baltimore set the tone for the tour, when Jackson was lustily cheered by enthusiastic crowds as the defender of the Union. The next stop was Philadelphia, where, flanked by Cass and McLane, Jackson stoically sat on horseback for five hours and reviewed a military parade. On the afternoon of June 12, the presidential party landed at New York. As the sounds of the guns saluting his visit reverberated, Jackson was greeted by Governor William Marcy and Vice President Van Buren. Then a minor mishap occurred. After the president led the procession over an old causeway connecting the Castle Garden wharf with the Battery, the timbers collapsed, spilling into the water a startled group including Marcy, Van Buren, and Cass. While most suffered only a momentary loss of dignity at the soaking,

Cass bobbed to the surface without his wig. Seba Smith, a popular humorist who wrote under the pseudonym of "Major Jack Downing," assured his bemused readers the secretary of war would certainly have no difficulty in finding "a scalp to suit him."[39] Cass quickly regained his composure—if not his wig—and joined in the discussions held by Jackson regarding Biddle's bank. The president's physical strength was sagging, even as his resolution was growing to crush the Bank of the United States.

From New York, the tour proceeded through Connecticut and Rhode Island. In Providence, Lewis Cass visited the campus of Brown University and delivered a short speech that "left a favorable impression . . . with whigs as well as Democrats." The secretary of war took his leave of Jackson shortly thereafter and joined his family at Detroit. The president continued his journey to Boston and Cambridge, where he received an honorary degree from Harvard College, and traveled to Concord, New Hampshire, before ill health forced him to return abruptly to Washington, where he arrived on the Fourth of July. The presidential procession through the northeastern states following the nullification crisis proved a stunning success, stirring in the American people a reactive spirit of nationalism and patriotism.[40]

Back in the White House, Jackson determined to destroy the Bank of the United States. The political skirmishing had begun a year earlier when Congress passed a recharter bill, to which Jackson responded with a stinging veto message that attacked the Bank as monopolistic, elitist, and unconstitutional. In his annual message to Congress in December, Jackson called for an investigation into the safety of the federal deposits, but a perfunctory examination by a congressional committee sympathetic to Nicholas Biddle concluded the funds were secure. So the president tried a new tack, reorganizing his cabinet in preparation for an all-out assault against the Bank. Despite the absence of Livingston and the shift of McLane from the Treasury, however, Jackson still faced a serious division within the administration. Vice President Van Buren; Jackson's intimate adviser, Major Lewis; McLane; and Lewis Cass supported the concept of a national bank. In fact, the secretary of war had revoked the directive of his predecessor for the removal of military pension funds from the New York branch. Clearly, the views of Treasury Secretary William Duane were crucial, and Jackson discovered he had blundered in appointing Duane without first securing a promise to halt federal deposits.

On Tuesday, September 17, at the cabinet's regular weekly session, President Jackson appealed for unity on the bank issue. He did not receive it. McLane and Duane spoke against the withdrawal of federal funds. Cass simply stated, "You know, sir, I have always thought, that the matter rests entirely with the secretary of the treasury." This was not an attempt by Cass to dodge the issue, nor was it a timid acquiescence to Jackson's proposal: everyone at the meeting was well aware of Duane's position. Secretary Cass was going on record in opposition to the president's plan. Secretary of the Navy Woodbury announced he had come around to Jackson's way of thinking, while Attorney General Taney continued to advocate the immediate removal of the deposits. Plainly, Jackson did not preside over a harmonious cabinet, and he adjourned the meeting. The next day the cabinet listened as Jackson read a paper that traced the evolution of his opposition to the Bank of the United States. The president bluntly informed his department heads that removal of the deposits would commence no later than October 1. The following Monday, Jackson replaced Duane with Taney. The president managed to force his will upon a reluctant cabinet, but in so doing he pushed Lewis Cass and Secretary of State McLane to the brink of resignation. On the day after Duane's dismissal, Cass notified Major Lewis that he and McLane were determined to leave the administration. Cass intimated that Jackson's decision to publish the paper read to the cabinet implied that the department chiefs conformed to Old Hickory's views. Major Lewis was aghast. The unprecedented dismissal of a cabinet member and the voluntary departure of two other disgruntled department heads would play right into the hands of Nicholas Biddle. Lewis pleaded with Cass to speak directly with President Jackson before he and McLane submitted their resignations, assuring the secretary of war that the president's "confidence in both of them was unimpaired."[41]

Cass readily acceded to Lewis's request. Constitutionally unsuited for personal confrontations, he hoped a satisfactory arrangement could be reached. He and McLane visited the president that very morning, explaining that under the circumstances they could no longer honorably remain in the cabinet. Jackson summoned all of his considerable charm and urged them to stay at their posts, affirming that he took sole responsibility for removal of the federal funds. All he asked of his department chiefs was that they attend to their respective duties; there was no need to sacrifice personal principle. Cass and McLane, satisfied with the president's explication, informed him the next day they would remain. Clearly relieved with their decision, Jackson inserted a sentence in the paper before it was published: "The President again repeats that he begs his

Cabinet to consider the proposed measure as his own, in the support of which he shall require no one of them to make a sacrifice of opinion or principle." To emphasize the point, Francis P. Blair announced in the *Washington Globe*, on September 26, that the removal of the funds "was not to be considered a cabinet measure." Andrew Jackson avoided a major political embarrassment by inducing Cass and McLane to remain in the cabinet, and the secretary of war faithfully removed all military pension funds from the national bank in early 1834. After the popularity of the removal policy was settled, Cass extolled it "as the wisest and most heroic" act of Jackson's presidency.[42]

Cass was grateful to continue in the cabinet while registering private opposition to the removal of the deposits, but some of the president's closest supporters were disappointed he and McLane did not resign. Taney remarked to Blair (who agreed) that the president's claim of sole responsibility "saved Cass and McLane; but for it they would have gone out [of the cabinet] and have been ruined—as it is, they will remain and do us much mischief." In Taney's opinion, Cass lacked decisiveness because he was "unwilling to come in conflict with his associates, upon any measure of policy strongly and perserveringly urged." William Henry Harrison contrastingly saluted his former comrade in arms, delighted that Cass and McLane had extricated themselves from a sticky political controversy. General Harrison noted the national bank was *"the most popular institution we ever had"* in the western states and promised the secretary of war his actions would be remembered. Indeed, the Bank War demonstrated that Cass would remain true to his principles even while seeking solutions to contentious partisan issues; after all, he had been prepared to resign rather than compromise his conservative fiscal views.[43]

Lewis Cass did not neglect his burgeoning business interests after joining President Jackson's cabinet. Charles Trowbridge, a member of the Cass expedition of 1820, was authorized to act as his personal agent in real estate dealings, and a bit later Edmund A. Brush assumed similar responsibilities. Trowbridge and Brush were faithful stewards, and the routine management of Cass's investments proved to be in capable hands. The secretary of war kept a watchful eye on his financial concerns through frequent visits to Detroit, where the Cass family spent part of each summer. He also speculated on town lots in neighboring communities and entered into a number of real estate partnerships with John R. Williams and Austin Wing, among others. Cass additionally invested in the capital stock of corporations, favoring railroads and insurance companies.

In the summer of 1835, Lewis and Elizabeth Cass sold the family farm for $100,000 to a group of investors. The self-styled "Cass Company" agreed to pay 7 percent interest on the unpaid principal, and the Casses were confident their financial security was assured. Vice President Van Buren congratulated Cass on the "good fortune" that would permit him to concentrate on "public service and literary pursuits." That certainly appeared to be a reasonable assumption, as the land boom in Detroit continued unabated through 1836. One speculator caught up in the frenzy offered to bet a new "suit of clothes worth $75" that the Cass Company would realize a profit of at least $500,000. Brush excitedly informed the secretary of war that lots were selling for $1,000 an acre, and in September he forwarded $7,000 in annual interest payments from the Cass Company. The following month, a third of the farm front was sold by the investors for $175,000. Brush was ecstatic. At the time Cass left the War Department, his Detroit agent declared all was proceeding smoothly: "Your business is beyond the reach of any accident, but such a catenation as never yet happened in one man's history." Prophetic words indeed; however, the only current predicament was that the Cass children, now young adults, were fully capable of spending whatever money their parents accumulated. Lewis, Jr., in seeking a loan of $500 from Trowbridge, acknowledged, "Pa . . . is harassed and annoyed almost to death with paying bills and spending money—he is so good . . . that the girls and myself are unworthy to ask for more." The young man promised to repay the loan, "even if I have to forego many pleasures," but as a rule he chose diversions over serious endeavors. As for the daughters, they soon demonstrated an uncanny affinity for extravagance that would peak when the family settled in Paris.[44]

A recurring dispute dating back to his years as governor of Michigan Territory captured the attention of Lewis Cass during the last years of Jackson's presidency. Shortly after Indiana was admitted as a state, in the process pushing its boundary ten miles north into Michigan, two separate surveys were run to delineate the Ohio-Michigan border. Between these competing lines was the "Toledo Strip," encompassing nearly five hundred square miles. Governor Cass denounced these usurpations in an address to the territorial legislature in 1826, recommending the federal government protect the territorial integrity of Michigan.[45] There the matter rested until the question of statehood for Michigan renewed the dispute.

When the Toledo Strip controversy heated up in the mid-1830s, neither the "Boy Governor" of Michigan, Stevens T. Mason, nor Robert Lucas, his Ohio counterpart, was amenable to compromise. Events soon took on overtones of an *opéra bouffe,* as Mason mustered the militia to drive out of the disputed district two commissioners sent to re-mark the survey line favorable to Ohio. Lucas protested to President Jackson and called a special session of the state legislature, which created Lucas County with Toledo as the seat of justice. Secretary Cass, meanwhile, worked behind the scenes to calm the situation. He privately assured Governor Mason, in May 1835, that he supported Michigan's claims, but added that as a member of Jackson's cabinet, "I have felt . . . I ought to interfere as little as possible, either officially or personally." This was not the response the Boy Governor sought from his predecessor; he feared the territory was being sold out to secure Ohio's electoral votes in 1836 and warned the result would be "a sad blow to the democratic party in Michigan."[46]

For a time it appeared the border dispute would erupt in violence, and Cass did his utmost to prevent a military clash while visiting Detroit in the summer of 1835. He hired dispatch riders to carry his personal message of peace to Governor Mason, then in the field with the territorial militia: "The crisis is one for calm deliberation, and not for rash action." Cass feared the worst, going so far as to authorize Mason "to use my name, if you think it would be useful." As it turned out, Cass was publicly drawn into the controversy when Governor Lucas charged that the Michigan militiamen were armed from federal stores at Detroit. The secretary of war vehemently denied the accusation and withdrew as a secret mediator in the Toledo Strip dispute shortly after Mason was removed from office by President Jackson. In late 1835, Cass implored Mason "to make no further reference to me. Let me drop out of the matter, quietly, as is my nature. And I beg you to make not the most distant allusion to any thing I have communicated to you." Thus he turned his back on an extremely muddled situation. The territorial voters had recently ratified a state constitution, elected Mason governor, and selected a congressional delegation, leaving it to the Twenty-fourth Congress to craft a bloodless end to the "Toledo War."[47]

After consultation with Henry Rowe Schoolcraft and Michigan senator-elect Lucius Lyon, political confidants of Lewis Cass, Senator Thomas Hart Benton presented an enabling bill that recognized Ohio's claims to the Toledo Strip. To complete the compromise, Michigan was compensated with territory north of Mackinac. Cass supported this arrangement, since it promised a peaceful end to the controversy and because he was well aware of the Upper Peninsula's rich natural resources.

The immediate reaction in Michigan, however, was generally unfavorable. A convention rejected the offer in the fall of 1836. But when it became clear the territory would not receive any of the federal treasury surplus to be distributed to the states, a second convention approved the compromise on December 14. Michigan was formally admitted into the Union the following month, and Michiganites soon came to appreciate the bargain made with Cass's support to attain the Upper Peninsula.

Whereas the Toledo Strip controversy ended in political compromise, the Jackson administration proved incapable of preventing a military clash with the Seminole nation of Florida. The Seminoles, numbering fewer than five thousand, were the descendants of Creeks and local tribes. They violently resisted removal to the West. The issue was complicated by the presence of hundreds of slaves from Georgia and Alabama who sought refuge in Florida; their new Indian masters were comparatively indulgent, and the blacks frequently intermarried and became allies of the Seminoles. Eventually, the continuing encroachment of whites on tribal lands, and the friction caused by attempts to recover escaped slaves, led to war.

The federal government negotiated a treaty at Payne's Landing, in May 1832, with a particularly destitute remnant of the Seminole tribe. These Indians agreed to remove within three years, and a delegation sent to investigate the suitability of western lands signed the Treaty of Fort Gibson the following March. Although the tribe as a whole repudiated this agreement, the Jackson administration accepted it as ratification of the Payne's Landing treaty and pressured the Seminoles to cede their lands and join the Creeks in the West. The majority of the tribe, however, questioned the validity of the removal treaty because it was not ratified by the Senate until April 1834, too late to fulfill the original terms. Governor John Eaton of Florida Territory, Cass's capable predecessor in the War Department, believed the delay in ratifying the treaty raised serious doubts about its implementation. He warned that if the federal government chose to use the military to remove the Seminoles, "a strong, imposing, *regular force*" was needed. "Send only a handful of men," Eaton concluded, "and difficulties will come upon you." Cass responded by stating the attorney general considered the treaty valid, and the Seminoles were required to relocate in the next three years. Confident that Indian agent Wiley Thompson and General Duncan Clinch would be able to manage removal operations, he informed Thompson that "nothing less than insanity, or an utter ignorance of their own position," could induce the Seminoles to hope they could remain.[48]

Lewis Cass underestimated both the resistance to removal among the Seminoles and the ability of the federal government to compel them to leave their homes. The Indians petitioned Clinch and Thompson to postpone removal for at least another year, and in an effort to avoid needless bloodshed, General Clinch seconded this request and forwarded it to the War Department. Cass commended the general's "equally judicious and humane" views and assured him the administration had no desire to oppress disgruntled Seminoles. Nevertheless, the Indians had agreed to remove, "and the sooner they are satisfied of this fact the better it will be for them. Still, however, I should much prefer a voluntary and peaceful removal to one effected by force." In characteristic fashion, the secretary of war closed by referring the matter "entirely to your discretion, and that of General Thompson." The Seminoles thereby received a temporary reprieve, but they were expected to begin their westward trek the following spring.[49]

Tensions mounted as Osceola, a mixed-blood the whites called "Powell," exerted increasing influence over the growing number of warriors opposed to removal. General Clinch, understandably concerned with the threat of violence, warned the War Department that if a military force sufficient to overcome the Seminoles' objections was not sent to Florida, "the whole frontier may be laid waste by a combination of Indians, Indian negroes, and the negroes on the plantations." Thompson and Lieutenant Joseph Harris, special disbursing agent for removal operations, also chimed in with requests for reinforcements. Cass ordered an additional fourteen companies placed under General Clinch's command, but these proved to be woefully inadequate to avert a military disaster.[50]

In the spring of 1835, Wiley Thompson had Osceola put in irons to cow the Seminole chieftain into giving up the fight. At first Osceola reacted violently to this affront, but eventually he became strangely calm and silent. A short time later he was freed, after acknowledging the validity of the Payne's Landing treaty and promising to encourage his people to migrate west. He subsequently returned with scores of Seminoles who solemnly pledged to accept removal. Thompson, completely won over by these events, reported to Secretary Cass he had no doubt of the Seminole chief's "sincerity, and as little that the greatest difficulty is surmounted." Lieutenant Harris, too, was convinced the danger had passed. He estimated that three thousand Seminoles were resigned to their fate and preparing to leave Florida.[51]

Cass was encouraged by the reports he received, and in November he informed the president the removal operations would soon commence. Cass observed that the Seminoles were expected to relocate peaceably, although "some of them exhibit a refractory spirit." His years of dealing with northwestern Indians made him less trusting of Osceola's intentions than was Wiley Thompson, but he believed that even the recalcitrants "will, probably, when the time for operations arrives, quietly follow their countrymen. Should they not, measures will be adopted to ensure this course."[52]

Osceola, of course, had other plans. The humiliation he suffered from the white man's chains could not be forgotten; the proud chieftain's degradation would be purged with blood. Osceola gained revenge in late December, by leading a raiding party against Fort King. Wiley Thompson was killed in the attack; and a detachment of more than one hundred men under the command of Major Francis Dade was massacred as it marched to the relief of the fort. A short time later, General Clinch skirmished with Osceola at the Withlacoochee River. The southeastern frontier was once again a battleground.

Cass responded with swift resolution to the news of hostilities in Florida. The recently appointed territorial governor, Richard Keith Call, was instructed to raise one thousand volunteers, and General Clinch was authorized to call out twenty-five hundred Tennessee militiamen. The militias of Georgia and Alabama were engaged in subjugating the Creeks, so Brigadier General Abraham Eustis was ordered to reinforce Clinch with the garrisons of Charleston and Savannah. Additionally, five steamboats were sent from Pensacola to interdict Indian communications along the Chattahoochee. And before the end of January 1836, Major General Winfield Scott was given overall command of the Florida forces—partly to defuse the bickering between Clinch and Call over who held higher rank. Scott received carefully worded orders from Cass in which the general was given great latitude:

> It is impracticable here to prescribe the amount of force which ought to be carried into the field. That must depend upon the actual circumstances which you may find existing when you reach the scene of operations. It is of course highly desirable that no unnecessary force should be employed, as the expense may be thereby greatly increased. Still, I would not have you hesitate for a moment

> in calling out such a number of the militia as will enable you, with promptitude and certainty, to put an immediate termination to these difficulties. The horrors of such a warfare are too great to run any risk in its immediate suppression. This subject is, therefore, committed entirely to your own discretion.

But on one point there was to be no compromise by Scott. Cass informed the general he was to "allow no terms to the Indians, until every living slave in their possession, belonging to a white man, is given up." Local civilians enthusiastically aided in the search for escaped slaves by importing bloodhounds from Cuba (during the presidential campaign of 1848, Zachary Taylor was unjustly accused of concocting this plan).[53]

General Scott never got the opportunity to dictate terms to the Seminoles. For seven years, through a procession of eight field commanders, the war dragged on inconclusively. The majority of the Seminoles were eventually rounded up and forced to remove, but a brave remnant remained in the Everglades after the federal government proclaimed an end to the hostilities in August 1842. During the conflict some 10,000 regular troops and about 30,000 volunteers saw action against an enemy that never numbered more than 1,200 warriors. The death toll was 1,466 soldiers, 69 seamen, and 55 militiamen; there are no accurate statistics regarding the Indians, but Osceola was among those who perished. The monetary cost of the conflict is estimated at between thirty and forty million dollars. In short, the Second Seminole War was the bloodiest and costliest chapter in the annals of Indian removal.[54]

Although he resigned as secretary of war shortly after the commencement of hostilities, Lewis Cass's political reputation was damaged by the Second Seminole War. John Eaton warned him, in early 1836, of "ill timed & unfounded" efforts to cast the blame for the military disasters "upon you, & other functionaries at Washington." Eaton sympathized with the secretary of war: "Who could, who did dream, that a few miserable, . . . starved, naked Indians could be induced to such open, bold revolt." General Duncan Clinch, for one, had such dreams, and he publicly blamed Cass for the debacle unfolding in Florida. Testifying before a court of inquiry held at Frederick, Maryland, to examine General Scott's conduct, Clinch charged that Cass had made inadequate military preparations to preserve the peace, in light of the Seminole resistence to removal. Cass replied that at the time, the number of Osceola's warriors was thought to be fewer than five hundred, and he concluded with an appeal clearly directed to the American people: "I have received, during a public life of more than thirty years, many favors I neither expected nor merited. I am encouraged to hope that when I ask only rigid justice, I shall not be found a vain suppliant."[55]

General Clinch resumed his verbal attack in a Washington newspaper. Referring to Cass's disclaimer regarding unwarranted favors, the general dryly remarked that Cass "should be considered a good witness as respects his own merits." Clinch further contended that "nine-tenths" of the army officers believed the secretary of war was negligent in reinforcing the Florida command. This assessment was shared by many. A visitor to Washington, in January 1836, wrote: "As to Mr. Cass, I should suppose from what Capt. Turnbill said yesterday that he is unpopular with the officers of the Army and unskilled in management." According to Amos Adams Lawrence, President Jackson expressed doubts about Cass's resolution, likening the secretary of war to "an old woman." Compared to Jackson and his volatile temperament, Lewis Cass at times appeared to be placidly irresolute—but not, however, regarding the Florida war. Clinch, angry at Cass for sending Scott to take command following the battle at the Withlacoochee, erred in his accusations. Prior to the outbreak of hostilities, Cass actually sent more companies of reinforcements to Florida than Clinch requested, and the general neglected to concentrate his troops (including the garrison at Key West) as he was authorized to do. Once the fighting started, Cass's broad instructions to the field commanders gave them the means to raise adequate forces, although they had to rely heavily on militiamen. The regular army, after all, numbered only 7,000 men when the war started; it was enlarged during the conflict to 12,500.[56]

Lewis Cass did bear some of the responsibility for the confusion that reigned during the first year of the war. The fighting raged in an area that cut through the eastern and western army command zones, and this circumstance led to wrangling between Generals Scott and Gaines that the secretary of war should have mediated. The situation was further complicated when President Jackson authorized Governor Call to conduct military maneuvers against the Indians. Unquestionably, better coordination was needed within the executive branch and also between the War Department and the field commanders. The president and secretary of war were distracted during this period by a diplomatic dispute with France, but this does not absolve them of their responsibilities. Ultimately, it was the courage and desperation of the Seminoles—and their ability to take advantage of the fastnesses of the Everglades—that resulted in a protracted war and foiled the removal of the entire tribe.

Lewis Cass left the War Department in the fall of 1836, shortly before the end of Andrew Jackson's presidency. By that time, about forty-five thousand Indians had been relocated west of the Mississippi. The process was invariably brutal and harsh; confusion and greed combined to cause the deaths of thousands of Indians. Cass conceded as much in an address to the American Historical Society: "I do not mean to say that the white man was always right, and the red man always wrong. I do not mean to deny that the ancient possessor had too often just cause to complain, that his inheritance was violently reft from him, or craftily obtained."[57] And yet Cass joined Jackson in supporting removal as a humanitarian movement—as the only feasible way to guarantee the survival of eastern tribes. The ethnocentrism and paternalism of the age were reflected in his attitude toward Indian removal (and, for that matter, toward slavery). The removal policy of the Jackson era left an ambiguous legacy: some tribes were able to maintain their heritage and culture beyond the reach of white racism and avarice, but the cost in human suffering was staggering.

His service as secretary of war enhanced Cass's national reputation to the extent that he was mentioned as a candidate for the Democratic presidential nomination in 1836. Following Calhoun's fall from grace, and before Vice President Van Buren was clearly designated the heir apparent, Cass and Supreme Court Justice John McLean were discussed as challengers for the White House. Duff Green, editor of the *United States Telegraph* and a Calhoun supporter, fretted during the summer of 1833 that if the South Carolinian did not soon announce his candidacy, he would not overcome the momentum of Van Buren or, perhaps, Cass or McLean. At about the same time, Cass wrote a Michigan admirer denying any presidential aspirations: "You know I am not ambitious and, if I know myself, I am desirous of no further elevation." Such private protestations could not persuade the voting public Cass was not a serious contender. One of Henry Clay's correspondents, in fact, was convinced the Democratic choice was between Van Buren, Cass, and McLean. Justice McLean, more candid than Cass regarding his political ambitions, was "at a loss to account for the movement in behalf of Gen. Cass" and surmised he was a stalking horse for the vice president. Such was not the case, and once Jackson's preference for Van Buren became known, the Democratic nomination was a foregone conclusion. Cass's presidential aspirations would not be gratified in 1836.[58]

Another issue that proved to have a significant impact on Cass's political future surfaced as the election campaign approached. This was the Texas question, which threatened to disrupt the delicate sectional balance of American politics. When the Texas revolution broke out in the spring of 1836, Andrew Jackson declared the United States would remain scrupulously neutral. The president was sensitive to the charge that intrigues in Mexico City by heavy-handed American diplomats had led to deteriorating relations between the neighboring countries and encouraged the Texans to rebel. Moreover, Texas was slave territory, and Jackson did not want the controversy to jeopardize Van Buren's presidential campaign. To add to the diplomatic turmoil in the Southwest, the boundary between Louisiana and Texas—based upon the Transcontinental Treaty—had not been definitively surveyed. Cass issued orders to Major General Edmund Pendleton Gaines to maintain the American neutrality proclaimed by Jackson. Gaines responded from Baton Rouge, suggesting he augment his forces with militia and cross "our supposed or imaginary national boundary" into Texas, ostensibly to prevent "savage marauders" from raiding Louisiana settlements. Cass authorized the general to set up defensive operations, "on either side of the imaginary boundary line," but emphasized it was "not the wish of the President to take . . . possession of any portion of the Mexican territory." In a final communication to Gaines, Cass drove home the message: "Your great objects, as I have before stated to you, are to defend our frontier, and to fulfill the neutral obligations of the government." The Texans proved capable of attaining their freedom without American military intervention, and in March 1837, President Jackson extended formal diplomatic recognition to the Lone Star Republic. It remained, however, for a future administration to deal with the sectionally charged question of Texas annexation.[59]

Another dangerous diplomatic controversy threatened to embroil the United States in a conflict with France during the latter years of Cass's tenure as secretary of war. At issue were the spoliation claims for damages incurred by American shipping interests at the time of the Napoleonic wars. On July 4, 1831, William Rives, the minister to France, signed an indemnity treaty by which the French government agreed to pay twenty-five million francs in six annual installments. Ratifications were exchanged early the next year, and Rives returned home in triumph, but difficulties soon arose in collecting the indemnity payments. The Chamber of Deputies delayed passage of an appropriation bill, and when the Treasury draft presented to the Bank of the United States by the

American government bounced, Nicholas Biddle tacked on a 15 percent service fee. Jackson was furious—at both Biddle and the French. After the Chamber, in April 1834, defeated an appropriation bill to pay the first installment on the spoliation settlement, Old Hickory seethed. He called a cabinet meeting and suggested that letters of marque and reprisal be issued against French vessels. Cass and Secretary of State McLane, who until recently had been at odds with the president over the bank controversy, promptly agreed that a stern show of force was necessary to preserve national honor. But Taney, dismayed at the bellicose nature of the discussion, urged caution, and the president decided to wait until Congress convened in December before taking action. McLane then resigned, upset that his advice had been ignored on major issues.

France made no effort to pay the indemnity before Jackson, in his annual message to Congress on December 1, asked for a bill authorizing reprisals against French property. Gallic pride was at stake, and the Chamber finally passed an indemnity appropriation in April 1835, contingent upon Jackson's apologizing for offending French sensibilities. Fortunately, Great Britain offered to mediate the dispute, and once tempers cooled, an agreement was reached. France quickly paid four installments on the claims indemnity, and Jackson announced in May 1836 that cordial diplomatic relations would be resumed. Two weeks later, Edward Livingston died, and Andrew Jackson turned to Secretary of War Cass as his replacement.

President Jackson nominated Cass to be minister to France in late June. It was an astute choice. As a man who sought compromise rather than confrontation, Cass was temperamentally suited for the diplomatic corps. Jackson also took note of Cass's experiences in dealing with the British in Canada and his deserved reputation as a steadfast defender of American honor. Cass's Anglophobia certainly did not disqualify him for the mission to France. Furthermore, the sole remaining cabinet member from the reshuffling of 1831 had lent the president his support throughout the spoliation crisis. The appointment was plainly meant as a reward for five years of loyal service to the Jackson administration, and it also afforded the president the opportunity to strengthen Martin Van Buren's influence on the cabinet at the height of the presidential campaign. Attorney General Benjamin Franklin Butler, a protégé of the Democratic candidate, was selected as acting secretary of war. Cass accepted the mission to France with the understanding he would be permitted to spend some months touring Europe and the Holy Land before assuming his routine diplomatic duties. He hoped to recoup his health, which had deteriorated during his extended residence in Washington.

One incident marred the cordial resumption of relations with France. Major Lewis wished to have his son-in-law, Alphonse Pageot, reappointed as the French chargé d'affaires to the United States. Pageot, however, incurred the president's displeasure during the spoliation controversy, so Lewis asked Cass to sound out Jackson about the possibility of his return. By then Jackson had been apprised by the British minister at Washington, Henry Stephen Fox, that Pageot simply followed the instructions of his government regarding the claims issue, and the president informed Cass that his "personal feelings towards Mr. Pageot are very kind." Cass was pleased to relate this good news in a letter to Lewis, and he included an oblique reference to the confidential information Jackson obtained from Fox, although he made no mention of either the British minister or his government. Cass closed by stating that "this letter has been read by the President."[60]

Major Lewis proudly forwarded Cass's note to his son-in-law in Paris, who showed it to King Louis Philippe, recently installed as constitutional monarch. As a mark of respect to the American president, the king appointed Pageot chargé to Washington. Jackson was livid when he discovered his confidential discussion with Fox had been indirectly leaked to the French government. The president claimed in a personal memorandum that had he known the Cass letter "was intended to have been shewn to the King, it would never have been authorized to have been made to Major Lewis." Jackson vented most of his anger toward Cass, accusing him of "an act of great impropriety." As the president explained to Lewis: "I have never blamed Mr. Pajoet [*sic*], nor have I you for your attachment to your children but, I never can but blame Govr. Cass for not giving you the real situation between France and us." This censure was misdirected. Cass acted as a friendly intermediary between Lewis and Jackson and received the president's approval of his reference to Pageot. His letter to Lewis, couched in cautious language, was not intended to reach the French monarch. The fault for this diplomatic wrangling rests squarely with Major Lewis, who used a private communication to further the career of his son-in-law. He thereby violated the trust and strained the friendship of Andrew Jackson and Lewis Cass.[61]

Harvard College awarded Lewis Cass an honorary doctorate in recognition of his public service and literary attainments shortly before he left the War Department. Cass by that time had written a number of articles for the *North American Review* and the *American Quarterly Review* and had promised Edgar Allan Poe a manuscript for the *Southern Literary Messenger.* In the years to come, Cass would publish articles in the *Knickerbocker* and the *Democratic Review.* The secretary of war also held honorary memberships in several state historical and literary societies and was chosen the first president of the American Historical Society. In his inaugural address, delivered at Washington on January 30, 1836, Cass called for the preservation of historical documents (especially newspapers) and research into the vanishing traditional lifestyles of Indian tribes. "We have one advantage over every other people," Cass reminded his audience. "Our origin and progress are within the reach of authentic history; we have no fabulous nor doubtful eras to perplex investigation and to provoke discussion." A simplistic view, certainly, but "Dr. Cass" noted that the historian must discriminate between fact and fable. This perspective was tested during his service as U.S. minister to France.[62]

The Cass family spent the summer months in Detroit preparing for their residence in Europe. Lewis, Jr., Mary, Matilda, and Belle were excited about the journey and the prospect of living in France. The elder Casses were more subdued. The minister-designate was particularly concerned about whether the French language skills he had acquired while governor of Michigan Territory would suffice in Paris. Meanwhile, George Washington Cass, Jr., sought Uncle Lewis's help securing a well-paying job as a construction engineer. All in all, it was a hectic summer.

Lewis Cass returned to Washington and submitted his formal resignation as secretary of war on October 4, 1836, the same day he was appointed U.S. envoy extraordinary and minister plenipotentiary to France. Andrew Jackson took "great pleasure in expressing the confidence, inspired by our past relations, that the post which you are about to assume will be filled with the same fidelity and ability that have been displayed in that which you leave." General Wool and the clerks of the Ordnance Office sent their best wishes. So did James Buchanan, who enclosed a letter of introduction and added that, "should it ever become necessary . . . to stand forth in your defense during your absence, I shall be one of the numerous band of your friends." Kind words, certainly, but Buchanan evinced no desire to become embroiled in the fiasco of the Seminole removal controversy; Cass capably presented his own defense from Paris. His appointment as U.S. minister to France provided Cass with the opportunity to hone his diplomatic skills and enhance his stature in international politics. These were important considerations for a politician who, notwithstanding personal disclaimers, harbored presidential ambitions. Thanks in no small measure to actions taken while minister to France, upon his return home six years hence, Lewis Cass would emerge as a candidate to head the Democratic ticket in 1844.[63]

Chapter Four

Minister to France (1836–1842): "I Have Presumed that I Express the Feelings of the American Government and People"

WITH HIS appointment as United States minister to France in the autumn of 1836, Lewis Cass commenced a challenging phase of his multifaceted career. He and his family, accompanied by Henry Ledyard, who served as personal secretary to the minister, embarked for Europe on the *Quebec* in October, anxious to cross the Atlantic before the winter storms. After a brief stay in London to ascertain that a French minister had been selected for Washington, the Casses arrived in Paris and settled in a residence on the Champs Élysées. The backlog of official business that had accumulated during the suspension of relations between the United States and France was soon discharged, and Cass arranged for interest payments on the twenty-five million francs indemnity, thereby bringing the spoliation claims controversy to a satisfactory conclusion.

Cass was instrumental in restoring cordial relations with the French government. He proved to be an accomplished diplomat—at least, when not dealing with his old bugbear, Great Britain—and quickly established a warm and harmonious relationship with the French monarch. Louis Philippe, the "citizen king" who ascended the throne by vote of the Chamber of Deputies after the July Revolution of 1830, had spent several years in the United States and styled himself a republican ruler. The king faced opposition from Bourbon royalists, liberal republicans, and Bonapartist supporters of Louis Napoleon; politically motivated insurrections were commonplace. Cass witnessed one such disturbance during the Days of

May 1839. At the intersection of four narrow streets, a group of working-class Parisians erected a barricade, but they swiftly dispersed upon the approach of a detachment of troops. The commanding officer prepared his men to open fire on the fleeing crowds—most of whom by then were simply bystanders—when Cass stepped forward and told him the guilty had escaped. The French officer, "a discreet man," ordered the troops to shoulder their weapons, and the American minister returned to his residence, satisfied he had experienced an *émeute*.[1]

Cass lauded the intelligence and scrupulous attention to duty of Louis Philippe, the namesake of the French monarch who aided the American Revolutionary cause, and extolled him as the epitome of "all magistrates, monarchical or republican." The American minister turned a blind eye to the king's dynastic designs and his reluctance to broaden the franchise, and the esteem in which Cass held Louis Philippe became a minor campaign issue in 1848. But then, Cass was not in Paris to reform the French government; he was there to promote American interests, and that he did admirably.[2]

The new minister's rapport with King Louis Philippe was the envy of the diplomatic corps. The two men spoke frankly and familiarly about international matters and agreed British pretensions in the Western Hemisphere must be stymied—particularly in Cuba and Texas. Shortly after arriving in Paris, Cass informed the king the interests of their two nations were identical. "I told him I felt sure," the minister reported to President Jackson, "the government of the United States would be very unwilling, that England should acquire the sovereignty of Cuba," emphasizing the "powerful considerations" the island presented to the southern states specifically. In a similar vein, Cass encouraged the French government to extend diplomatic recognition to the fledgling Republic of Texas and arranged for a meeting between Texas representative, General James Pinckney Henderson, and the aged Marshal Soult, who fought with Napoleon and was between terms as minister for war. Cass was gratified when France joined the United States in establishing formal relations with Texas, thus neutralizing British influence over the cotton-producing republic. As a member of the Texas legation later expressed it, Cass's "dispositions were very friendly towards our country." The American minister was doubly pleased that his nationalistic support of the Lone Star Republic dealt a diplomatic blow to Great Britain.[3]

By the spring of 1837, the Paris legation was functioning smoothly, and before the annual throng of American visitors descended upon the French capital, Cass escorted his family on a tour of the Mediterranean and the Middle East. At Marseilles, the Casses boarded the fabled frigate *Constitution* as the guests of Commodore Jesse Duncan Elliott, commander of the Mediterranean squadron. Elliott and Cass served together in the Northwest during the War of 1812, and during the cruise they shared reminiscences of the victories on Lake Erie and at the Thames. The commodore recommended the Cass women be prepared to don male attire, "to check the curiosity of the wild Arab and the Turk," and suggested they pass the time aboard ship learning to play the piano or guitar.[4] It was an enlightening and relaxing excursion for the entire family.

Lewis Cass was fascinated with the history, economy, and geography of the ports of call during this extended tour, although he remained incorrigibly provincial in his attitude toward foreign lands and customs. The crystal waters of Lake Superior compared favorably to the Aegean Sea; the Nile reminded him of nothing so much as the turgid Missouri; and even the Dead Sea was "surpassed" by the dreariness of the Ontonagon River, which he encountered during the Northwest expedition of 1820. His ethnocentrism permeated several articles he wrote for the *Southern Literary Messenger* describing his experiences during the tour. He submitted the manuscripts at the request of the journal's editor, Edgar Allan Poe, who placed Cass among the nation's "most distinguished literati." A typical piece, "A Recent Visit to Lady Hester Stanhope," depicted the lifestyle of a granddaughter of the Earl of Chatham who dwelt in the hills of Lebanon. Cass graphically portrayed the English woman, "dressed like an Arab, clothed in white, with a turban upon her head, and smoking a long pipe." He was appalled at Lady Hester's reduced circumstances, and departed "wishing her more happiness than I am afraid is in store for her." In a condescending reference to the devotions of Muslims on the island of Cyprus, Cass hypocritically proclaimed, "There is something touching in the earnestness and punctuality with which the duties of prayer are peformed; and the more absurd their tenets, the more regret is felt, that a people thus docile to a false faith have not received their inspirations at a purer fountain." The moralizing tone of these articles was leavened occasionally by humor. For example, Cass disclosed that his progress while examining an Egyptian catacomb was checked "by a latitude which prohibited all passage through the narrow entrance, except to those who had been more ascetic than myself." In November, the Casses returned to Paris; the health of the minister was much improved by his seven-month hiatus from official duties, but his perspective remained parochial. Only three works of nature or man "surpassed his most sanguine anticipations": St. Peter's Cathedral in Rome, the ruins of Baalbec (Heliopolis), and the River Nile—despite its similarity to the Missouri.[5]

Additional, more modest travels were in store for Cass. He took every opportunity to roam the French countryside observing the people, society, and government; and in the spring of 1838, he and Elizabeth and their daughters attended Queen Victoria's coronation. Ledyard accompanied the Casses to London, doubtless keeping close to his future bride, Matilda Cass. Lewis, Jr., was in Detroit studying law, although he returned briefly to Paris the next year after being admitted to the Michigan bar.

Lewis Cass wrote a series of articles based upon his various travels that were collected and published as *France, Its King, Court, and Government; and Three Hours at St. Cloud.* The minister emphasized the superiority of the American democratic system to either the French or British brand of monarchy. He pointed out that between thirty and fifty thousand troops were quartered in Paris "to put down any insurrectionary movements, and to give aid to the civil authority." Extremes of poverty and wealth were also prevalent throughout France, and Cass exclaimed: "Thank God! we have in our country *'neither poverty nor riches,'* in the European acceptance of those terms." His sharpest barbs were slung at a familiar target. After dismissing British travelers who published recollections of their journeys through the United States as "mere gossips in pantaloons or petticoats," Cass presented his equally biased impressions of English society: drunkenness, gambling, and a general dissoluteness were endemic among the upper classes, and traditional sinecures stultified the workings of government. Cass cited the new master of her majesty's buck hounds, Lord Kinnaird, "a peer of England, a hereditary judge of the court of the last resort, *a keeper of the Queen's dogs!*" He humorously referred to an even more extreme case. "I find one appointment in the Red Book which I trust, during the reign of a Queen, and for the sake of conjugal happiness, will be a sinecure, that of *'leather breeches maker'* to her Majesty!"

Cass took the British government to task for "those scenes of lawless violence which marked our maritime history for many years." Although the impressment of sailors from American vessels was suspended during periods of peace, the "right of search" remained an issue of contention between the two countries because British warships, in an attempt to eradicate the African slave trade, detained and searched suspected slavers flying the United States flag. Cass vigorously protested such actions and berated hypocritical Englishmen who condemned black slavery while condoning "the slavery of impressment." He viewed impressment as a greater evil than the slave trade, ominously warning that the United States must be prepared to defend its maritime rights with a force of arms. This was an enduring theme in the public life of Lewis Cass.[6]

During his tenure as U.S. minister to France, Cass devoted a great deal of his energy to social obligations. He graciously welcomed visiting Americans to Paris and presented to King Louis Philippe all who requested that honor, on occasion introducing fifty of his compatriots in a single evening. One traveler to the French capital wrote home that there was "no want of amusements & gayety—and the family of Gen. Cass manage to make themselves quite popular." Charles Sumner, who spent several years touring Europe after graduating from Harvard Law School, was invited to dine with the minister and his family. He noted, "The table was splendid, and the attendance perfect; servants in smallclothes constantly supplying you with some new luxury." An obviously captivated Sumner concluded that Cass was "a man of large private fortune, and is said to live in a style superior to that of any minister ever sent by America." Even the Panic of 1837 did not curtail the sumptuous style in which the Casses received visitors to their home, although the seemingly endless procession was especially taxing on Elizabeth, who suffered from ill health during the latter decades of her life. She eventually was forced to limit her Paris social functions to Monday evenings.[7]

John Middleton Clayton, a prominent Delaware politician who later served as Zachary Taylor's secretary of state, called upon the hospitality of the Casses in a different fashion when his sixteen-year-old son was sent to study in France. Clayton asked that Lewis and Elizabeth act as guardians for Charles, whose mother had died shortly after he was born: "The kind and maternal advice of your excel[l]ent lady would be of infinite service to so young a boy." The American minister oversaw Charles's financial affairs, and the young man attended church services with the Cass family. The elder Clayton was deeply appreciative.[8]

The most famous American visitor to the French capital during these years was an old school chum of Lewis Cass. In October 1839, Senator Daniel Webster and his wife, Caroline, and several traveling companions arrived for a two-week stay in Paris. The American minister outdid himself entertaining the distinguished visitor, taking Webster on a personal tour of the city's attractions. Caroline Webster confided in her diary that Cass obligingly offered "to do anything for us, show us anything, or send us anywhere." The Websters and their entourage were honored at "a superb dinner" presided over by the Casses and attended by the British and Spanish ambassadors. The highlight of the Websters' sojourn in France was a soirée at the palace of St. Cloud. Cass last called upon the Websters the morning of their departure, satisfied he had helped make their stay in Paris a memorable one.[9]

Although the Casses entertained lavishly, neither Lewis nor Elizabeth was entranced by Paris society. Cass confided to Andrew Stevenson, the American minister at London, that "Mrs. Cass and myself are so much too old . . . we shall always feel as exotics." He echoed this sentiment several months later, claiming, "There is a continual whirl. A succession of amusements, rather, it seems to me, to keep up an excitement and to get rid of time, than for any thing else." Cass's insufficient grasp of the French language added to his discomfort. In the ensuing months he made "a little progress" in this regard, but it was plainly "uphill work," and had he not acquired "some proficiency in early life, I should abandon the task in despair." Cass did relish delving into French archival depositories in search of materials pertaining to the colonial Old Northwest. His time for historical research was even more limited than his French, however, and he hired the young Pierre Margry to copy relevant documents that Francis Parkman, among others, later perused. Recently graduated from college, Margry was launched on a long and successful career as a historian.[10]

Lewis, Jr., Mary, Matilda, and Isabella, in contrast to their parents, reveled in the social whirl of the French capital. Paris was the center of fashion, and they made the most of it. Young Lewis was soon sporting cuff links with diamonds the size of hazelnuts, while his sisters became "a little bit Frenchified," in the eyes of at least one of their Detroit acquaintances. The Cass siblings cut quite a swath through Parisian society, and flirtations turned into romances for the two younger sisters. In 1839, Matilda and Henry Ledyard were wed, and Belle became a baroness when she married Theodore Marinus Roest von Limburg—Baron von Limburg—who later served as the Netherlands ambassador to the United States and minister of foreign affairs. Mary, the eldest of the surviving children, married Captain Augustus Canfield of the Topographical Corps following her return to the United States. Lewis, Jr., was to take a distinctly rockier road to the altar.[11]

Admirably fulfilling the social and diplomatic responsibilities of the French mission, Cass served as minister for six years under Democratic and Whig administrations. Martin Van Buren had no intention of replacing Cass, who supported him for vice president in 1832 and campaigned for the Democratic national ticket four years later. Cass, after all, was appointed to the Paris post by Old Hickory himself. William Henry Harrison, a Whig who died one month after being inaugurated in March 1841, probably would not have removed Cass if he lived. Cass served under Harrison at the Battle of the Thames, and it was Old Tippecanoe who first appointed him governor of Michigan Territory. The two former generals maintained a close professional relationship during the intervening years that blossomed into a warm friendship by the time Cass joined the Jackson cabinet. Harrison doubtless was aware of Cass's ties to leading Whig businessmen and bankers in Detroit, and Secretary of State Daniel Webster appreciated firsthand the esteem in which the minister was held by the French government. Furthermore, the Whig party eschewed the principle of removal based solely on political grounds. By the time John Tyler, Harrison's successor and a former Democrat from Virginia, began making sweeping changes, Cass had returned to the United States.[12]

Although the possibility of being recalled from Paris for partisan reasons caused Cass few anxious moments, concern over his private financial affairs, and a continuing maritime controversy with Britain, ultimately contributed to his resignation. Shortly after arriving in France, Cass placed his economic portfolio in order. Charles Trowbridge was given power of attorney to handle legal matters regarding the Cass farm, and Edmund Brush continued to oversee the minister's myriad commercial and real estate investments. Writing from Marseilles in April 1837, Cass asked Austin Wing to keep him apprised of their extensive holdings along the River Raisin. Cass was a bit apprehensive about not being able to keep a close watch on his far-flung enterprises, and his troubles increased with the Panic of 1837. He was forced to draw heavily upon personal resources to finance the lavish residency at Paris; his annual nine thousand dollar salary as minister plenipotentiary proved to be inadequate.[13]

Cass never fully grasped the extent of the economic depression that struck in 1837, although Brush attempted to paint a realistic picture of the financial woes paralyzing the country. The Detroit agent acknowledged in late April, "The first word you expect to see is Money—& the subject is awful. . . . We don't ask a man now, how *he* is this morning, but 'how's money'!" The following month, as Michigan banks suspended specie payments, Brush wrote that the business community was operating in "a heavy fog, but we have no fear of foundering," since enough payments on the interest and principal of the Cass farm were still being made to "keep you floating clear." Unmistakably, the five-hundred-acre Cass farm proved to be extremely lucrative. It was by now part of the downtown Detroit waterfront, and the Cass Company had expended $50,000 clearing and grading the portion purchased in 1835, planning to turn it into a mercantile and manufacturing district. The ensuing panic severely depressed land values, of course, and many of the company's investors were unable to fulfill their annual $700 interest payments. Trowbridge, for instance, sold half of his one-tenth share to Henry Schoolcraft and Andrew McReynolds for a total of $16,000, prior to the economic downturn, but since they were unable to make their payments, Trowbridge fell in arrears to Cass. Benjamin Kercheval, who enticed Henry Hubbard and Daniel Webster to join in an investment purchased from a member of the farm company, found himself in similar straits. By the end of the year, Trowbridge notified Cass that "a general gloom will overspread the land" if the business situation was not soon remedied.[14]

The economic depression continued through 1838. Brush did his best to collect rents and interest payments due Cass, but he was the only member of the farm company still able to meet his obligations in full. Trowbridge gloomily revealed that runs on the Bank of Michigan and the Farmers' and Mechanics' Bank so discredited paper currency that Detroit merchants accepted only specie. It was needless to add that bank stocks had paid no dividends since the panic commenced. In short, Trowbridge had "never witnessed such a year as this, . . . in regard to pecuniary distress in this state." Despite such reports, Cass did not wholly comprehend the financial difficulties back home. In the spring, he blithely asked the American minister at London: "Why could not you and I have been born with the silver spoon of £50,000 in our mouths?" With typical perspicacity, Brush chided Cass for believing, "like Astor—that a man worth $500,000 is just as well off as if he was rich, *though a little more would do no harm.*" Cass's repeated demands for security, when the farm company investors had sunk nearly $100,000 into improvements, was not unlike "bleeding a man half to death for fear he will run away from you, & then letting him go about his day's work." Still, Brush collected mortgage payments and interest from loans whenever possible, and occasionally sold some of Cass's lots in Detroit and neighboring communities such as Brownstown. All the while, the Detroit agent implored Cass to accept a "living price" for his property—to renegotiate contracts so investors could keep making payments rather than default. But the American minister remained inflexible, and an exasperated Brush grumbled: "I perceive that you come back again to the idea that nothing must be cancelled & that interest must be continually compounded *until the debtor is stripped. . . .* You do not & have never realized the revulsion & its consequences here, & never will, until, if it lasts so long, you see it." Such was not to be.[15]

Although he suffered some financial setbacks—most notably the loss of $32,000 when the Bank of Michigan failed—Cass weathered the depression in fine shape. By the time of his return to Detroit, most of the farm company holdings had reverted to him by default. Cass subsequently divided the land into lots and over an extended period of time realized a profit of more than $750,000 from their sale. As Brush prophesied, however, Cass came under withering criticism for his rigid stance toward business associates who fell on hard times. A Detroit neighbor scathingly characterized him as "a perfect Shylock" whose "merciless rapacity is making him odious. . . . I had much rather be indebted to *Satan.*" In truth, the former governor conveniently forgot that some years before the organization of the Cass Company he had agreed to sell the property for $34,000 and, when subsequently offered $50,000, used his influence to cancel the original contract. In future political campaigns, Democratic party managers naturally played down his personal wealth and expansive standard of living during this period, insisting his Paris "house was always open to American citizens, and he became proverbial for kindness and hospitality." Those in his debt did not always receive such kindness or understanding, and one of the reasons Cass returned to the United States at the end of 1842 was to reassert personal control over his business affairs. Another motivation was his dispute with Secretary of State Webster regarding Britain and the right-of-search issue.[16]

A number of incidents threatened to erupt in war between the United States and Great Britain during these years of peace in Europe. The most volatile situation was the *Caroline* controversy. Writing from Paris, in March 1841, to Daniel Webster—whom he assumed would be named secretary of state in the new Whig administration—Cass warned that if Alexander McLeod were executed, "it is the *casus belli.*" A usually reliable informant had reported that the British Mediterranean fleet was preparing to sail for Halifax, and Cass urged Webster "to create without delay a steam marine" to guard American ports. A new era of naval warfare was dawning, Cass predicted, and permanent fortifications would soon be obsolete. "Bend all your efforts *to steam,*" he exhorted; establish "powerful steam-batteries in the exposed ports." Such preparations were imperative because "the English are the most *credulous* people upon the face of the earth in all that concerns their own wishes or pretensions. They are always right and everybody else wrong." He grudgingly added that "if we have war, they will fight bitterly." McLeod's subsequent acquittal defused the *Caroline* dispute, but the diplomatic wrangling between the United States and Britain was abated only temporarily.[17]

The right-of-search issue underlay the debate over ratification of the Quintuple Treaty. Once again, Cass and the British government were at loggerheads. In 1841, representatives of Britain, Austria, Russia, Prussia, and France met in London and signed a treaty declaring the slave trade to be piracy and agreeing to a qualified right of mutual search to eradicate the traffic. Since the Mediterranean was specifically exempted from the treaty (and Austria, Russia, and Prussia had never engaged in the African slave trade), the Quintuple Treaty was little more than a formal declaration of principle. The British government, however, viewed this "holy alliance" as an opportunity to bolster its claims to search and visitation, and American ships suspected of being slavers were frequently detained and occasionally seized by the Royal Navy. Andrew Stevenson, on his own initiative, protested in London that such actions were "an insult to the flag of the United States, and an outrage upon the rights of its citizens." Cass agreed, not believing his lifelong nemesis was motivated solely by philanthropy. Instead, he viewed the Quintuple Treaty as a pretext by the British to institute a general policy of searching ships of all nations, and as such it represented a grave menace to the rights and freedom of Americans. Cass therefore took it upon himself to oppose ratification of the treaty by the French government. In so doing, he pushed to the limits the great latitude afforded American ministers by the State Department. Nevertheless, the U.S. government previously rebuffed a British proposal calling for a mutual search policy to suppress the African slave traffic, and Cass was secure in the knowledge that President Tyler's position agreed with his own.[18]

After privately voicing his opposition to the Quintuple Treaty, Cass escalated the ratification fight in early 1842, with the publication in Paris of *An Examination of the Question, Now in Discussion, Between the American and British Governments, Concerning the Right of Search: By an American.* This pamphlet was widely disseminated among political circles in France and England; Edward Everett, Stevenson's successor as American minister to Britain, distributed copies to government officials and leading newspapers. Journals in the United States also reprinted the pamphlet, identifying it as the work of Lewis Cass.[19]

In the pamphlet, Cass sought to divorce the search issue from efforts to suppress the slave trade, dismissing the connection as "incidental." He blindly contended the extent of American involvement was grossly exaggerated: "Not a slave has been imported into the United States for thirty years." The relatively few American ships engaged in the nefarious traffic transported their cargoes to Portuguese and Spanish colonies in South America, "but even this is much rarer than is supposed." Cass maintained it was "not African slavery, the United States wish to encourage. It is . . . the slavery of American sailors, they seek to prevent." Thus, it fell to the United States to defend its flag and enforce its laws on the high seas; this was not and should not be Britain's responsibility. Mutual search was merely a guise for exercising impressment in time of peace, and Cass warned in no uncertain language that the first American seized "from a ship of his country, and detained, with an avowal of the right, by order of the British government, will be the signal of war." After raising the specter of the Royal Navy harassing foreign merchant vessels and impressing sailors, he addressed the charge that slavers could escape justice simply by flying the American flag. He proposed a distinction between a systematic policy of search and "a casual act of trespass" to investigate suspicious ships: "The latter may be pardoned. The former is intolerable." Cass entangled the separate issues of impressment and suppression of the slave trade. "It is strange indeed, but so it is, that one of the modes proposed for the liberation of the negro, from the traffic of his flesh and blood, will, necessarily lead to the bondage of the American seaman."

The American minister discussed at some length his attitudes toward the slave trade—which he strongly condemned—and the institution of slavery. The traffic in human beings was "unjustifiable, and ought every where to be proscribed, and rigorously punished," but, Cass cautioned, care must be taken to protect maritime rights while combatting the illegal trade. "It is not permitted," he reasoned, "in order to attain a great good, to commit a great evil." Cass couched his opposition to the institution of slavery in equally ambivalent language. He disingenuously declared he had never been and never would be a slaveholder, but he lessened the impact of this statement by remarking that American slaves were generally well treated and lived long lives. Indeed, "the patriarchal relation between the Southern planter and slave" meant that the blacks were better off than the lower classes of European society. Cass had "seen far more, and more frightful misery" since landing in Europe—although he had *"not visited Ireland yet"*—than he observed among the American slave population.

On the subject of emancipation, Cass's language was cautious. He believed slavery was morally wrong in the abstract; still, he rejected social or political equality for free blacks. Cass called for abolition, if it could "be effected justly, and peaceably, and safely for both parties. But we would not carry fire, and devastation, and murder, and ruin into a peaceful community, to push on the accomplishment of the object." He viewed slavery as southern whites portrayed it—as a benevolent institution—and agreed with most Americans that the Constitution left the question to the state governments. Cass held these positions for the remainder of his public life.

The pamphlet concluded on a somber note. The minister expressed some hope Britain and the United States would resolve their differences over the right of search, but overall he remained pessimistic. He was convinced compromise was impossible because of the intractable position of the British government. War ultimately would settle the issue.[20]

The arguments Cass put forth were swiftly attacked in England. The London *Times* disparagingly remarked that his protest was "a violation of all the customs of diplomatic intercourse" and was riddled with "bad reasoning and false assertions." The *Examiner* similarly declared: "As a diplomatic agent his occupation is gone. And the sooner he takes himself off, the better for the influence of his Government in Paris!" The most comprehensive denunciation—*Reply to An American's Examination*—came from the pen of Sir William Gore Ouseley, who rejected Cass's contention that the right of search would lead to impressment of American sailors. Ouseley contemptuously dismissed Cass's "quibbling attempts at argument [which] might perhaps be expected in the pettifogging practice of a village attorney, but are novel in the discussion of the law of nations." Americans, Ouseley asserted with a chauvinism worthy of Lewis Cass, were generally "incapacitated from seeing or arguing with their usual clearness and talent on the subject of slavery. The dictation of southern feelings on this matter continually involves them, nationally and individually, in startling contradictions." He emotionally appealed to Americans to refrain from going to war on behalf of the slave trade.[21]

The Cass pamphlet was criticized in the United States as well. Charles Sumner, emerging as a spokesman for the antislavery crusade, noted that the American minister "mixed up questions which are not at all related" in his discussion of search and impressment. Sumner pointed out that under international maritime law, a British cruiser could search any vessel suspected of being a slaver, even if the ship sailed under an American flag. Cass was guilty of muddling the terms "search" and "visitation" in his haste to castigate "a perpetual right to stop, to search, and to seize" American ships by British cruisers in times of peace. The British government emphatically disclaimed any such right. Foreign Secretary Aberdeen had informed Edward Everett, in December 1841, that his government renounced the right "to search American vessels in time of peace. The right of search, except when specially conceded by treaty, is a purely belligerent right." This distinction between the right of visit and the right of search was repeated by British political leaders after the publication of Cass's pamphlet.[22]

Lewis Cass was more successful in his efforts to sway the French government. On February 14, he delivered to François Guizot, minister of foreign affairs, a personal protest against ratification of the Quintuple Treaty. Cass conceded that the treaty itself furnished "no just cause of complaint" but warned that if Britain implemented a general search policy, Americans were prepared "for one of those desperate struggles which have sometimes occurred in the history of the world." The clear implication was that France would be drawn into the military conflict. Cass divulged to Guizot: "I have presumed . . . that I express the feelings of the American government and people. If in this I have deceived myself, the responsibility will be mine." The minister concluded that as soon as instructions arrived from the United States, "I shall . . . declare to you either that my conduct has been approved by the president, or that my mission is terminated."[23]

Although he acted without specific instructions from Washington, Cass remained a man of caution. He knew his views regarding the right of search corresponded with those of the president; both were aware it was politically advantageous to oppose British pretensions. In fact, Cass quoted from President Tyler's first annual message to Congress: "However desirous the United States may be for the suppression of the slave trade, they can not consent to interpolations into the maritime code at the mere will and pleasure of other governments." Tyler understood that Cass's protest to Guizot supported this position, and he remarked to Secretary of State Webster he was "essentially in favor of General Cass's course." Hoping a French rejection of the Quintuple Treaty would give the United States "more sea-room" in its negotiations with Britain, Tyler directed Webster to inform Cass his actions were approved by the administration. The secretary of state complied most reluctantly. Although Webster had recently called Cass a "respectable" ambassador, he described the letter to Guizot, in a conversation with John Quincy Adams, as a ploy "to make great political headway upon a popular gale." Webster elaborated on his criticism in a letter to Edward Everett, claiming the Cass pamphlet lacked logic and contained "passages which yield all that is contended for on the other side." John Quincy Adams's personal opinion was even more acerbic: he characterized the protest as "a compound of Yankee cunning, of Italian perfidy, and of French légèreté, cemented by shameless profligacy, unparalleled in American diplomacy. Tyler's approval of it is at once dishonest, mean, insincere, and hollow-hearted."[24]

Lewis Cass made certain his opposition to the Quintuple Treaty was broadcast across the United States. In late April, he wrote former minister William Rives, then a Whig senator from Virginia, acknowledging he had ventured onto "dangerous ground" in opposing the treaty without a specific directive from Washington. Cass expressed gratitude for Rives's support and urged him to call for publication of the Guizot letter, because "its effect would be decisive upon France." Two weeks later the American minister sent Duff Green copies of his protest to distribute among leading American newspapers, emphasizing that his personal honor and reputation were at stake in the ratification debate. The Guizot letter was reprinted in European and American newspapers, and Rives informed Cass that "the more it is canvassed, the better it will be for you." The British press naturally excoriated the American minister, and Cass crowed: "I am afraid I shall be accused at home of bribing the English Journals to ante me up to be [a] great man. If their object was to do me the greatest possible good, they could not take more certain means of affecting it." Simply put, "The true facts of the insufferable arrogance of the English character were never more strikingly developed." Nor did condemnation of his actions from Americans discourage him. "As to all Mr. Adams has said, it is nothing. It does not weigh as a hair in the solution of the great matters." Cass was correct in this assessment.[25]

By the middle of May, Cass proudly reported that the Quintuple Treaty "has received the coup de grace. . . . It is dead, never to be resuscitated." He officially advised the State Department that "no ministry will venture to recommend ratification." Furthermore, Guizot assured the American minister the French government would never accept an interpretation of international law, without specific treaty provisions, that sanctioned the searching of foreign vessels.[26]

Cass's intervention was a factor in blocking French ratification of the Quintuple Treaty, and the American minister also received credit in the United States for objecting to the British search policy. Attorney General

Hugh S. Legaré informed Cass his actions met "with the perfect & hearty approbation of the President," and added: "I envy you the opportunity of acquiring the reputation which such occasion alone can give." Senator Rives reported that Cass's views were eliciting encomiums from Democratic journals, and the few discordant voices "will but enhance the popular sympathy, & approval of your course."[27]

Lewis Cass clearly understood that his stand against the Quintuple Treaty and British maritime pretensions enhanced his budding presidential ambitions, but he was motivated by more than personal political gain. The American minister believed Great Britain was an imperial power bent on dominating world trade, and the United States therefore could not allow the Royal Navy to implement an unrestricted search policy. Cass was aware, too, of the risks involved in opposing Britain. "All I have is upon the frontier liable to be ruined by war," he confided to Webster, "but let all go, rather than yield an inch to that haughty nation." This was not mere bombastic saber rattling: the fires of nationalism, stoked during the War of 1812, still seared his soul. "I hope we shall have peace," Cass wrote several months later, "but if we cannot have peace without dishonour, then I hope we shall have war." He was not alone in these sentiments. Even such a refined New Englander as Edward Everett wrote from London that he was "for peace, if it can be preserved upon honorable terms; if not, I am ready to take my humble portion of the responsibility of meeting the crisis."[28]

The rest of Cass's family returned to Detroit in the spring of 1842, leaving the minister in Paris to continue the right-of-search debate. Their homecoming turned out to be quite an occasion, as "the whole town ran to see them . . . to stare at their Paris clothes & criticize their appearance." Elizabeth Cass, "in excellent preservation—not a grey hair yet in her head," impressed her neighbors with the same "lady like" presence they remembered. The family members were welcomed with a party that turned out to be ill attended due to the "squally" weather. Elizabeth soon had the Cass household functioning smoothly, an easier task now that the daughters were marrying and setting up households of their own. Lewis, Jr., balancing a law practice and the management of some of his father's business affairs, during this time developed a lasting friendship with Emily Mason, whose brother declined to run for reelection as governor. Lewis could be charming; he frequently called upon Emily bearing volumes of literature and spent the evening reading aloud. And yet, he was developing into something of a self-indulgent wastrel, relying for subsistence on the parental purse. He was characterized as "a sottish-looking fellow" who would come to no good—a prediction that nearly proved all too accurate. In November, with Detroit covered by a deep blanket of snow, Lewis confided to brother-in-law Henry Ledyard that in places which provide so few "temptations to go out as our respectable city, cold weather is quite a blessing." Unfortunately, Lewis soon discovered an illicit attraction that opened an ignominious chapter in his life. For the moment, however, Elizabeth Cass and her children settled back comfortably into Detroit society, while Lewis, Sr., hoped an honorable solution to the search controversy was in the offing.[29]

Secretary of State Webster and Lord Ashburton began negotiations, in the spring of 1842, to settle the major issues of disagreement between the United States and Great Britain. Prior to Ashburton's arrival in Washington, Lewis Cass served notice that "a formal renunciation should be made of the monstrous pretension of England to search our vessels." The minister to France suggested that Ashburton clarify the British position to the satisfaction of the American government before Webster commenced substantive discussions. The issue was clear: "War is a great evil; but there are evils greater than war, and among these is national degradation." Without a straightforward rejection by the British diplomat of the right of search, the honor of the United States would be sullied, and so, too, the public reputation of Lewis Cass.[30]

Webster was aware the British government would not lightly disavow the right of search; nor was he certain it was in the best interests of a rapidly expanding maritime power such as the United States to push for a repudiation. And since Ashburton received no specific instructions on the issues of search or impressment, an exchange of notes was agreed upon to deal with those divisive subjects. President Tyler took the trouble late in the negotiations to inform Cass that the American government "shall yield nothing of the right of search, but may enter into arrangements which will be satisfactory." Indeed, while Webster and Ashburton sidestepped the search issue, article 8 of the treaty pledged both nations to maintain independent naval squadrons off the African coast, "in order that no slave-ship, under whatever flag she may sail, shall be free from visitation and search." In private letters to Cass, the secretary of state vowed not "to surrender any point of national interests or national honor," and gave assurances "that, in the absence of treaty stipulations, the United States will maintain the immunity of merchant vessels on the seas to the fullest extent." Webster made it plain to Cass that the abolition of the slave trade was a more important issue than British renunciation of the right of search. At the same time, Webster declared to Cass, if the treaty did not specifically refer to the search controversy, the position of the United States remained unchanged.[31]

No mention was made of search or visitation in the Treaty of Washington, signed by Webster and Ashburton in August 1842. As Cass warned, this omission led to complications. The British government maintained that the right of visit was unaffected by the treaty. Webster disagreed, claiming British cruisers "have no right at all to detain an American merchant vessel." President Tyler supported this interpretation and declared that the pact removed "all possible pretext . . . to visit and detain our ships upon the African coast." But that patently was not the case. Although the U.S. Senate overwhelmingly ratified the Webster-Ashburton Treaty, the right-of-search dispute was not laid to rest.[32]

A copy of the ratified treaty arrived in Paris on September 17, and the American minister was deeply disturbed by the lack of any provision dealing with the search issue. Cass, a staunch defender of his country's maritime rights, felt betrayed because Webster had not pressed the British envoy to disavow the right to board ships flying the American flag. Cass immediately communicated to the secretary of state his desire "to retire from this mission" (a decision made before the arrival of the Webster-Ashburton Treaty), declaring he could "no longer be useful here." Cass and Webster then entered into an acrimonious exchange of letters.[33]

Before he left Paris, Cass opened the debate with Webster by contending the Treaty of Washington did not "change, in the slightest degree, the pre-existing right claimed by Great Britain to arrest and search our vessels." More disturbing still, Webster's pact was a departure from the fundamental foreign policy principle of "avoiding European combinations upon subjects not American." What the secretary of state should have done, Cass insisted, was to settle the search issue before committing the United States to an entangling naval alliance with Britain. He closed by stating he had been placed "in a false position" by the Webster-Ashburton Treaty, since the president approved of his protest to Guizot. Cass's only recourse was to resign and return home.[34]

As word of his resignation circulated among the American community in Paris, a committee was formed to organize a public dinner in Cass's honor. Enos T. Throop and Nathaniel Niles were prominent among those who planned the affair, held at the Trois Frères Provençaux on the evening of November 11. The dinner "went off with great éclat," and the toast to Cass was enthusiastically greeted "with three times three cheers." The following morning, Cass put the affairs of the mission under the capable supervision of chargé Henry Ledyard and took his leave of King Louis Philippe and France. He had served six years as the U.S. minister and now planned to focus attention on private affairs and presidential politics. First, however, there remained to be settled his differences with Webster over the right-of-search controversy.[35]

Daniel Webster replied, on November 14, that Cass's attack on the Treaty of Washington and subsequent resignation "caused the President considerable concern." Cass appeared to be using the search controversy as a pretext for resigning, and Webster chided him for remonstrating "against a transaction of the government to which you were not a party, in which you had no agency whatever, and for the results of which you were in no way answerable." The secretary of state took Cass to task for writing a "public despatch" by which Britain might bolster its position on the right-of-search issue—although why the British government should accept Cass's construction of a treaty in which he played no role was not explained. Webster dismissed as "a tissue of mistakes" Cass's contention that the British had initiated the joint-squadron proposal.[36]

Following an uneventful passage from Liverpool on the *Columbia,* Lewis Cass arrived at Boston on December 6. A few days later, while pausing at New York, he received a copy of Webster's letter and hastily composed a heated response. It pained Cass to quarrel with his old schoolmate, but his sense of personal honor was stung. Cass seethed at the tone of Webster's letter, which implied American ministers should simply carry out official instructions without regard to their own opinions or principles: "There is no government—certainly none this side of Constantinople—which would not encourage, rather than rebuke, the free expression of the views of their representatives in foreign countries." Moreover, his note of October 3 was not intended as a public protest that strengthened the British stand in this controversy; since the decision to publish the dispatch rested with the government, it could just as easily have been "buried in the archives of the [State] department, and thus forgotten and rendered harmless." Cass then turned to Webster's "tissue of mistakes" remark, and acknowledged his error in assuming Lord Ashburton proposed the joint-naval-squadron provision. That did not, however, change the fundamental shortcomings of the treaty. Webster had missed the chance during negotiations to force Britain to disavow the right of search, thereby placing his government in an unfortunate position, Cass reiterated. The joint-squadron agreement of article 8 enmeshed the United States in the very type of "entangling alliances" the Founding Fathers warned against, and it set an ominous precedent. "Ruinous consequences" lay ahead if the U.S. government engaged in similar humanitarian crusades. American foreign policy should be firmly based on national interests and principles and grounded in the ability of the United States to enforce such a policy. Insofar as Cass was concerned, this ended his debate with the secretary of state.[37]

The administration was nettled by Cass's persistent objections to the Treaty of Washington and his harping on Webster's failure to insist Britain renounce the right of search. President Tyler urged the secretary of state to answer Cass's letter of December 11 and, when Webster dawdled, added, "Every day's delay will injure us." By February, he was imploring Webster to publish the entire correspondence with Cass. "Let the whole blast be at once over," as the president phrased it. Webster's belated reply to Cass was antedated December 20, postmarked February 23, 1843, at Washington, and delivered to Cass in early March. This deceitful attempt to present the final argument prior to the official publication of the correspondence conjures up (in a decidedly different context) John Quincy Adams's reference to Yankee cunning. Regarding Cass's contention the secretary of state should have insisted upon Britain's disavowal of the right to search American ships before concluding his negotiations with Ashburton, Webster argued that since the treaty was silent on the issue, "a declaration against such a right would have been no more suitable . . . than a declaration against the right of sacking our towns in time of peace, or any other outrage." Webster ridiculed the idea of the United States relying on a "skilfully extorted" pledge from Britain to guarantee American maritime rights. Such vague promises "are not likely to be more effectual than the Chinese method of defending their towns, by painting grotesque and hideous figures on the walls, to fright[en] away assailing foes." The secretary of state concluded his part in the correspondence with an admonition from President Tyler: "that it would have been far better on all accounts" if Cass had never precipitated this debate.[38]

The final word belonged to Cass, who penned a lengthy rebuttal dated March 7. He pointedly noted the "unintentional" error Webster made in antedating his final missive and launched into a protracted recapitulation of his arguments. Cass's resignation as minister to France was necessitated by the failure of the Webster-Ashburton Treaty to support his recognized position on the right of search, an issue on which he had staked his reputation as a diplomat. Cass also excoriated the secretary of state for the "uncourteous tone" of his letters, "a kind of official loftiness, which, however it may suit other meridians, does not belong to an American functionary writing to an American citizen." This was not meant as a private reproach; Cass informed Webster he intended to publish this letter. The former minister made the most of his public forum with a passionate appeal to resist future British encroachments: "I think the pretension she advances to search our vessels, and to call this search a 'visitation,' is one of the most injurious and unjustifiable claims of modern days. I would meet the first exercise of it by war. It leads directly to impressment, and . . . is but another step in her march towards universal domination." All he "feared and foretold has come to pass," Cass smugly summarized. The recent British claim to "visit" ships flying the American flag to ascertain their nationality was an egregious assumption of power. "Our flag is to be violated, to see if it has been abused!" The United States stood in the way of Britain's determination to dominate the world, and such a perilous situation threatened war. Nonetheless, Cass was not about to yield on the search issue. "I think it is better to . . . fight for the first inch of territory rather than for the last; to maintain our honor when attacked, rather than wait till we have none to be attacked or maintained." Nor did he accept the idea that the eighty guns pledged to combat the slave trade was a fair exchange for violating "one of the articles of our political faith," the "old principle of avoiding European combinations upon subjects not American." There was no reason the United States could not have continued its unilateral attempts to eradicate the illegal traffic in African slaves. On this issue, Lewis Cass remained squarely in the ranks of the Founding Fathers.[39]

Thus ended the correspondence between Cass and Webster over the Treaty of Washington. While each believed he bested the other, the results of the debate were inconclusive. To Webster's credit, the treaty was easily ratified by the Senate and generally well received by the American people. He made a telling point with his claim that Cass should have approached the issue as a private citizen. And his assertion that—since the British government would not have renounced the right of search—it was better to reach agreements on those matters that could be settled amicably, has some merit. On the other hand, Cass's recommendation that Britain be urged to give up the right of search before treaty negotiations were concluded was never given a chance. Since the administration (or at least President Tyler) supported this position, it was unfortunate Webster made no attempt to press the point. And throughout their correspondence, Webster never squarely addressed the central question posed by Cass of why it was in America's interest to engage in a naval alliance with Britain, rather than continue to combat the slave trade independently. Cass's contention that his resignation was unavoidable, under the circumstances, was valid: he clearly identified himself with the search controversy and viewed the treaty's silence on the issue as a personal rebuke. His assertion that the treaty did not alleviate the possibility of further conflicts with Britain off the African coast (as Webster and Tyler claimed) was also well-founded. In fact, the arguments between the United States and Britain over visitation continued until 1858, at which time Secretary of State Lewis Cass took particular pleasure in the British government's renunciation of the right of search.

Cass consistently stated that his motivation regarding the Quintuple and Webster-Ashburton pacts was to protect American rights on the high seas. Nevertheless, he was inspired not only by a keen sense of national honor but his virulent Anglophobia. The humiliation he had suffered during the surrender of Detroit burned deep within his breast, and he never truly trusted the British or their motives—unlike Webster, who opposed the War of 1812 and was much more willing to compromise with the British on controversial issues. Cass, in summary, denounced the joint-squadron provision of the Webster-Ashburton Treaty for ideological and emotional reasons. He held fast to Thomas Jefferson's dictum to avoid entangling alliances, and resisted any type of military accord with the detested British.[40]

Anglophobia and protection of American maritime rights were important factors in Cass's fight against the British search policy, but political ambition, too, cannot be discounted. Cass was being mentioned as a candidate for the Democratic presidential nomination of 1844, and his actions (especially after his resignation as minister to France) may be viewed as a bid for political support. As early as March 1842, Edward Everett insisted Cass was posturing for the White House. The following month, Lord Ashburton reported from Washington that Cass's intervention in the search controversy was "an attempt to attract attention to himself as one of the numerous candidates in the field for the next Presidency." Articles appeared in American newspapers at this time lauding the minister's staunch stand against British pretensions and hinting he might be suitable presidential timber. This talk was not lost upon his British detractors. Following France's rejection of the Quintuple Treaty, Lord Brougham castigated Cass's "discreditable conduct" in a particularly vituperative speech to the House of Lords. Cass, "the promoter of discord between America and England," had no more conception about international law "than he had of the language spoken on the moon." The "impertinent" letter to Guizot was motivated by a desire to become president, and to attain that goal, Cass "pandered to the mob feeling of the lowest rabble in the United States."[41]

Democrats hoped to regain the White House in 1844, and many welcomed Cass among the leading contenders for the party's nomination upon his return to the United States. By opposing the British position regarding visitation and search, Cass found himself the champion of Americans who supported the institution of slavery. He plainly identified himself with those unconcerned with the morality of slavery, who favored allowing the southern states to decide the future of their peculiar institution. It is not fair to claim, as Horace Greeley later did, that Cass's opposition to a mutual right of search "was really a bid for the favor of the Slave Power." Cass was not a vocal defender of slavery; rather, he condoned the institution where it existed, believing its continuation or abolition rested in the hands of those directly involved. He sought unification over this divisive issue. Nonetheless, Cass's political ambitions henceforth were linked irrevocably with slavery supporters and moderate northerners who favored allowing the South to regulate its own domestic institutions.[42]

Chapter Five

Candidate for the Presidential Nomination (1842–1844): "The Best Man, Undoubtedly, for the Democrats"

AT THE TIME Lewis Cass had left Andrew Jackson's cabinet for France, a two-party political system was developing in the United States that pitted the Democrats and Whigs in fairly even national campaigns for two decades. With a nucleus of National Republicans who followed John Quincy Adams and Henry Clay, the Whig party drew additional support from old-line Federalists, Antimasons, and opponents of "King Andrew." The Democrats rallied behind the banner of Old Hickory and his handpicked successor, Martin Van Buren, the architect of political party organization. Both major parties were in a state of flux during these years, as the nation underwent a tremendous economic and social transformation. Transportation and technological advances, westward expansion, and a revitalized spirit of reform—including abolitionism—swept the country, with the South lagging behind in these movements. The Whigs generally came to grips better than their opponents with the momentous changes and the new political issues that arose, but they were not a unified national organization as the presidential campaign of 1836 approached. The Democrats contrastingly spoke of "principles, not men," although a debate raged within their ranks over economic issues in particular. The radical antibank, hard-money Van Burenites such as Thomas Hart Benton, Silas Wright, and Francis Blair struggled with conservative supporters of paper currency and state banks, who counted among their leadership William Rives and New Yorkers Nathaniel Tallmadge and

William Marcy.[1] The Democrats were able to mute their internal differences and Van Buren succeeded Jackson in the White House, but the New Yorker was destined to be a one-term president. His administration was racked by the Panic of 1837, the seemingly interminable Second Seminole War, and notorious corruption scandals. The Whigs parlayed economic hard times and dissatisfaction with Van Buren into a presidential victory in 1840. Ironically, they did not enjoy the fruits of their success. Following the death of William Henry Harrison, just one month after his inauguration, party unity was fragmented as Henry Clay bitterly fought for leadership with President John Tyler. None of this was lost upon Lewis Cass, who, from Paris, viewed the American political scene with more than passing interest.

The Democrats were deeply divided after their defeat in 1840. Van Buren retained the allegiance of most party officeholders and hard-money men, and his embittered followers vowed to recapture the White House. Many other party members either disagreed with Van Buren's policies or believed he could not be reelected. Democrats were encouraged by bickering within the Whig ranks and the lack of divisive issues; arguments over slavery and the annexation of Texas were temporarily abated, as attention turned to the selection of a presidential candidate for 1844. There was no shortage of contenders for the nomination, especially since Democrats predicted victory. John C. Calhoun was considered Van Buren's chief challenger. The South Carolinian advocated traditional party principles such as retrenchment and a federal government of limited powers, and he demonstrated strength among sectionalist southerners and antitariff men in the free states. Calhoun set his political machinery in motion by late 1842—as did Van Buren—in an attempt to garner the nomination, although nullification and a hardening stance in the defense of slavery weakened his candidacy. Democrats such as James Buchanan of Pennsylvania and Richard M. Johnson, Van Buren's vice president from Kentucky, were "available"; it was assumed their nomination would ensure an electoral triumph. Another candidate for the Democratic nomination touted for his availability was Lewis Cass, whose principles placed him in a position to serve as a compromise selection.[2]

The groundwork for his candidacy was laid long before Cass resigned as minister to France. Midway through the presidency of Martin Van Buren, a visitor to Paris noted Cass was busy corresponding with politicians who were urging him to run for the White House. Van Buren's reelection plans put an end to such speculation, but Cass's opposition to the Quintuple and Webster-Ashburton treaties kept his name before the national electorate. The minister also responded to inquiries from political conventions and public meetings regarding his presidential ambitions and political principles. Cass informed a group of Philadelphians he would accept a nomination only from a national party convention, although he pointedly added, "The first elective office in the world is not a charge to be sought." Such protestations were characteristic of the period—no one was expected to seek the presidency—but Cass prudently complied with requests to express his political views, always avoiding specific issues and couching his principles in grand generalizations. He belonged "to the old Jeffersonian school, and shall die in it." When Duff Green, an intimate of Calhoun, sounded out Cass on his plans for 1844, the minister dissembled. "As to political views, my friend, I have none. It is a subject upon which I can give no explanations, because I have none to give." Should the Democratic party select him as its nominee, Cass claimed it would make him "the most miserable man alive. I therefore sit still, *in fear & trembling.*" And in truth, supporters in Pennsylvania were complaining the minister was *"throwing cold water"* upon their efforts. Cass played well the political game expected of candidates for the presidential nomination; he disclaimed any personal aspirations for the White House while encouraging political friends and self-styled campaign organizers.[3]

Following Van Buren's unsuccessful bid for reelection, a disparate group of Democrats commenced a national movement to win the presidential nomination for Cass. Senator Rives, slowly gravitating toward the Whig ranks, reminded Cass of his "solemn duty" not to discourage the efforts of his supporters. Rives was convinced that if Cass returned to the United States he "would, at once, become the rallying-point for the true Democracy of the country." Nathaniel Niles, a New Englander who spent much of the 1830s on various diplomatic missions to Europe, was motivated by an intense dislike of Martin Van Buren and the belief that Cass could carry the party to victory. Indeed, his principles and extensive public career made Cass an attractive contender for the nomination in the eyes of many Americans. Military service during the War of 1812, a long and successful tenure as governor of Michigan Territory, and his contributions to Jackson's administration added luster to Cass's political appeal. Furthermore, his principles placed him in the Democratic mainstream. He was not associated with either economic or slavery radicals. He was a strident nationalist, belligerently opposed to British pretensions, and a fervid expansionist who promoted the Texas Republic and championed claims to the Oregon country. The Michigan politician garnered support in the North and the South, and his chances were enhanced by the mission to France, which left him personally untainted by the Panic of 1837 or the recent electoral debacle. It remained only for Cass to leave Paris and strike out on the campaign trail back home. At least, that is what his friends insisted.[4]

Cass's return to the United States ostensibly was triggered by the Webster-Ashburton Treaty, but he was largely influenced by growing political support for his nomination. Three days before a copy of the treaty reached Paris, Cass indicated he was "sick of the contests of parties" and feared a national campaign would "kill" him, and yet, he was willing to take the plunge if his friends were convinced a "decided expression of publick feeling" existed on his behalf. Cass clearly was caught up in the maneuvering for the Democratic nomination, and he wrote Major Lewis to find out how Andrew Jackson's supporters placed his name in contention. Although Lewis absentmindedly neglected to respond until after the national convention, Cass pressed forward.[5]

The announcement of Cass's resignation as minister to France cheered his political backers. A brief article in the *Niles Weekly Register* served notice of a Democratic gathering at Shelbyville, Indiana, to select delegates for the state convention, and anyone favoring the nomination of Lewis Cass or fellow westerner Richard Johnson was encouraged to attend. Cass was nominated for president at a rally held at Harrisburg, Pennsylvania, despite Buchanan's control of the state party organization. Governor David Porter, a political opponent of Buchanan with wide-ranging commercial interests, originally backed Johnson for the presidency but turned to Cass when the Kentuckian generated only tepid support. The governor was convinced that delegates pledged to Van Buren and Calhoun would deadlock the national convention. George M. Dallas joined in Porter's appraisal, and Cass was buoyed by the efforts of his Pennsylvania supporters. Levi Reynolds, the self-proclaimed "prime mover in the Cass movement," wrote that two thousand copies of the Harrisburg proceedings were distributed along with a campaign biography, and added some unsolicited advice to the candidate: Cass should ask the voters to rely upon his "disposition to do right if elected" and avoid taking controversial positions. Plainly, Reynolds was not well acquainted with Lewis Cass, who had no intention of committing himself on divisive political issues.[6]

The other Democratic contenders and their advisers were unconcerned with the nascent Cass movement. Enos T. Throop, a staunch Van

Buren man, reported from Paris that Cass returned to the United States prepared to employ "all his means" in a doomed attempt to secure the White House. After Cass spent two days in London en route home, Edward Everett was convinced he vainly expected to receive the presidential nomination. Calhoun believed the demonstrations on Cass's behalf lacked substance: "His hold on the country is slight." Van Buren agreed. The *New York Herald* hopefully argued that the disdain with which his opponents treated Cass "lets the cat out of the bag. . . . They cannot disguise the fact that they are more afraid of General Cass than any rival candidate who has yet appeared in the field." Cass himself was determined to "let things take their course" in the race for the Democratic nomination.[7]

Cass hit full stride on the campaign trail when he disembarked at Boston in early December. He soon found the going rough. Nathaniel Niles attempted to smooth the way in the Northeast by writing to prominent Democrats seeking their support. William Marcy, however, expressed astonishment upon learning of the "high esteem and great regard, Gov. Cass entertained for me and the brilliant prospects which were opening before me if I took a proper course." Niles intimated to Marcy he would be an excellent choice for secretary of state, but the New Yorker was not swayed by such blandishments and made no plans to meet privately with Cass. Niles was no more successful with the Massachusetts Democracy. George Bancroft declined to arrange a public reception for Cass, claiming the minister's stand on the Webster-Ashburton Treaty doomed his chances, "for here *his friends are the Webster Whigs*."[8]

Although Niles failed to convince Bancroft, a nonpartisan committee of business and civic leaders headed by Abbot Lawrence, David Henshaw, and Josiah Quincy, Jr., invited Cass to attend a public gathering at Faneuil Hall honoring his services in France. The former minister responded with gratitude for the invitation but informed the citizens of Boston he could not tarry in their city. Cass was inexperienced on the campaign circuit—he had not run for public office since his brief term in the Ohio legislature—and this inept rejection was characteristic of his stilted public demeanor. Unmistakably, Cass did not galvanize the voters of Boston with a captivating personality or brilliant political philosophy. He was, instead, a colorless extemporaneous speaker and plodding (albeit persuasive) writer who advocated moderate compromise solutions to the divisive issues of the day. George Bancroft summarily dismissed the political impact of Cass's visit. "On the whole, I am confident Gen. Cass can have no party," he assured Van Buren. "The few who were ready to hail his coming, are chilled through."[9]

Cass had a campaign problem extending beyond an unattractive public image. He needed to rally those who agreed with his principles if he expected to elicit unwavering political support, but few voters were familiar with his beliefs, beyond the resentment he harbored toward the British. His protracted residency in France had removed Cass from the American political scene, and he consistently avoided taking stands on controversial domestic issues. One recent visitor to Michigan spoke with residents "who had known Genl. Cass for years and yet could give no opinion as to his political sentiments." Conrad Ten Eyck noted that during the election campaign of 1840, Lewis, Jr., in the absence of his father, declined to contribute to the Democratic cause. Lewis explained he held no political opinions, and while the elder Cass "was *deemed* a Democrat yet—if he subscribed to the Democratic party—he would feel it his duty to subscribe the same am[oun]t to the Harrison Party." Ten Eyck, a Van Buren appointee to federal office, incorrectly proclaimed that Lewis Cass "never was a Democrat," but there was a legitimate question as to which political party he belonged. After all, Cass served as territorial governor of Michigan under Madison, Monroe, and John Quincy Adams; opposed Andrew Jackson's war against the national bank; remained as minister to France following Harrison's victory in 1840; and retained close business and personal associations with leading Whigs. The *New York Herald* suggested, shortly before Cass returned to the United States, "that the only hope of the whigs is in General Scott or General Cass."[10]

In an effort to clarify his political philosophy and invigorate his candidacy, Cass arranged for the publication of an exchange of letters with Mahlon Dickerson, a fellow member of Jackson's cabinet. The aged New Jersey Democrat had assisted in the Van Buren campaign of 1836 and briefly remained secretary of the navy under the New Yorker, but he supported Cass for the nomination in 1844. Concerned about the suspicions held by many voters that Cass favored Whig principles, Dickerson called for a public statement of his political views. Cass answered the same day that he was "a member of the Democratic party, and have been so from my youth." He was a firm believer in the principles espoused by Thomas Jefferson, and "from the faith as taught and received in his day, I have never swerved a single instant." By emphasizing his adherence to Jeffersonianism, Cass subtly distanced himself from the Van Buren branch of the party. He was equally judicious in discussing the only specific issue addressed in the Dickerson letter: "With respect to a National Bank, I think the feelings and experience of the country have decided against it, and that no such institution should be chartered by the General Government." Cass made no reference to state banks, however, and carefully added that "while a due degree of credit is highly useful in the business concerns of a country, a sound specie basis is essential to its permanent prosperity." Cass thus staked out within the Democratic ranks a moderate position on the bank issue.[11]

The letter to Dickerson was written during a brief stay in New York City, where Cass was received by the local Democracy with a warmth distinctly lacking in Boston. Philip Hone, a Whig businessman and civic leader who supported Henry Clay for the presidency, graciously observed that Cass "is all the fashion in New York." Indeed, the common council turned over the Governor's Rooms in the City Hall to the returning minister, who was introduced to notable citizens by the mayor. Hone correctly surmised that his resignation from the French mission and the Dickerson letter, "published with a flourish of trumpets for the benefit of all good Republicans," indicated Cass was in the race for the Democratic nomination. "He will be a thorn in the side of Mr. Van Buren," even more so than Calhoun. The New York Whig had difficulty ascertaining Cass's political principles and admitted if "Clay cannot be elected, I do not know that I shall not be prepared to hurrah for Cass. Any body but Calhoun, even Van Buren." (Sectionalism was clearly playing a role in national politics; four years later, when Cass's conservative views regarding slavery were better known, Hone vehemently opposed his aspirations.) The *Herald,* which previously described Cass as "a liberal, elevated, and most accomplished man" who enjoyed a popularity exceeded only by that of Andrew Jackson, designated him "the best man, undoubtedly, for the democrats." It was clear by now to publisher James Gordon Bennett, at least, that Cass was a member of the Democratic party. John T. Mason, father of the "Boy Governor," never doubted it. Residing in New York at this time, Mason found Cass to be "the same plain, good humoured, unaffected man" he knew in Michigan. Despite published reports the Casses planned to live in Cincinnati for the sake of Elizabeth's delicate health, Mason was pleased the returning minister was "fixed on Detroit as his permanent residence, on which I congratulate its inhabitants, for he has great talent in contributing *a les agréements de la société.*"[12]

Bolstered by the cordial reception he received in New York, Cass resumed his journey toward Washington, pausing en route at Philadelphia. The *Herald* continued its favorable coverage of Cass's candidacy, reporting he was greeted "with great enthusiasm in the city of brotherly love." Richard Rush, George M. Dallas, and Charles J. Biddle, son of the president of the defunct national bank, were among the leading citizens of Philadelphia who commended his services as minister to France. Yet, as in Boston, local Democrats loyal to other contenders for the nomination discerned no groundswell of support for Cass. Rush, for example, had joined forces with Cass years before to limit the political damage that General Hull's surrender of Detroit caused the Madison administration, but he considered Van Buren to be a more desirable candidate regarding the bank issue. Henry D. Gilpin, a Philadelphia attorney and political lieutenant of Van Buren, smugly observed that the "equivocal" nature of Cass's policies rendered "it quite impossible for the Democrats generally to look favourably towards him." Nonetheless, Gilpin was convinced Cass expected to carry the Democratic national convention with the support of "seven states—Vermont, New Jersey, Pennsylvania, Delaware, Ohio, Illinois and Michigan!!"[13]

Ever a cautious man, Cass did not reveal to Gilpin or Rush his sanguine hopes, but he remained optimistic. Elizabeth was in Savannah for the winter, and since there were no pressing family or business concerns to be dealt with, Cass spent the holiday season in Washington seeking support for the Democratic nomination. He met with Thomas Hart Benton, an ardent promoter of Van Buren, who subsequently submitted a Senate resolution calling for publication of his correspondence with Webster concerning the right-of-search controversy. Cass also made arrangements for returning to Detroit, hoping to make the remainder of his journey a triumphal campaign tour. He notified Rives of plans to leave the capital in the middle of January and travel through York, Pennsylvania, where the local Cass committee was arranging a reception. The itinerary called for a two-day visit to Harrisburg, where "things will be *well* managed." Cass was feted at a public dinner hosted by Governor Porter, but the warm tribute he received in Harrisburg belied the fact his candidacy was faltering. His return to the United States did not generate the enthusiasm supporters had predicted, and some Democrats were already shifting their allegiance to more promising candidates. Governor Porter, in fact, was tentatively switching to the Tyler camp. The *New York Tribune* reveled in the divisions displayed among the Democrats and wittily warned that, "if the 'devil' *is* to 'take the hindmost' in this as in some other races," Cass and Van Buren "must take care and back out early or that personage will certainly have one of them."[14]

Undaunted by the lack of widespread interest in his candidacy, Cass resumed his homeward trek through Ohio, the most populous state in the Old Northwest. He took care over the years to maintain a legal residence at his late father's farm, and the *Zanesville Aurora* was an early champion of his presidential aspirations, so it was somewhat as a returning son that Cass was cordially received at Columbus. He took to heart Levi Reynolds's advice to allow "some room for demonstration" once he reached Ohio and was gratified his "friends here are in fine spirits, and consider[ed] the prospects very flattering." In an effort to rally flagging support elsewhere, Cass responded to a request from the Indiana Democratic party with the most detailed statement of his political principles yet written for public scrutiny. He firmly opposed a national bank, conveniently claiming to "have always entertained doubts of the power of Congress to charter such an institution." Cass also disapproved of the distribution to states of proceeds from public land sales, stating it would unduly increase the power of the central government. In the same vein, he called for a frugal federal government that raised needed revenue through land sales, and for the imposition of moderate tariff duties, which afforded "incidental protection" to American industry. Cass concluded by opposing any constitutional change in the veto power of the president. Coupled with the letter to Dickerson, this communication portrayed Cass as a moderate Democrat in the spirit of Jefferson and Jackson, whose nomination for the presidency would be acceptable to most factions of the party and appeal to a majority of the American electorate.[15]

Cass left Columbus and resumed the campaign tour, traveling through various towns and meeting local voters. The welcome he received at Cincinnati was particularly encouraging. He was presented to the citizens of the Queen City at a reception arranged by David T. Disney, a leader of the Democratic wing that favored state banks and paper money. Resolutions passed by the Cincinnati Democracy supporting Cass for the presidency were approved by Governor Wilson Shannon; Rufus Spalding, former speaker of the Ohio legislature; Edson Olds, publisher of the *Chillicothe True Democrat;* and Samuel Lahm, director of a Wooster bank. Other conservative Democrats including George Manypenny, William Sawyer, and Thomas Hamer jumped aboard the Cass bandwagon, and he was endorsed by the *Cleveland Plain Dealer* and the *Cincinnati Daily*

Enquirer, which glowingly described the candidate as "a fine looking man, as all *great men* are supposed to be." The Cincinnati organ conceded he was "a little corpulent," but "if phrenology be true, of the first order of talent." The report tactfully overlooked the reddish wig Cass wore, focusing instead on his robust health and vigorous mind. Naturally, this flattering characterization did not sway Cass's political opponents.[16]

Lewis Cass recognized that his candidacy faced stiff resistence in Ohio from the antibank Van Buren forces. This entrenched faction was led by Senator Benjamin Tappan, an antislavery man; his young law partner, Edwin Stanton; and two influential newspaper editors, Samuel Medary, of the *Ohio Statesman,* and Moses Dawson. Cass met personally with Medary and sought his support by offering confidential assurances he was not a radical foe of the hard-money position. The editor, unimpressed, remained loyal to Van Buren, although Cass was hopeful he would "take a just course" in the *Statesman.* Cass failed to reach an accommodation with any of the other Van Buren men, including Dawson, whose *Cincinnati Advertiser* had endorsed the New Yorker shortly after his failed reelection campaign. Dawson informed Van Buren that Cass had been "perambulating the states of the Union" seeking political support but his efforts were proving ineffectual.[17]

Lewis Cass simply did not understand the mechanics of the second political party system or its impact on presidential races. He failed to appreciate the importance of grass-roots organization in securing delegates to the national nominating convention, and he was naive when it came to campaign funding. The rough-and-tumble of the national political arena was a new experience for Cass, who had governed Michigan Territory before the formation of organized parties in the region and had spent the previous six years in France. To make matters worse, he lacked the innate political instincts of his rivals—especially Van Buren. He would have to learn quickly if he hoped to succeed in 1844.

The inexperience Cass brought to the campaign trail was dramatically demonstrated during his stop in Cincinnati. The three local Masonic lodges, in a show of solidarity for their brother candidate, gathered together in the largest assemblage since Andrew Jackson visited the city. But as the lodge members sat awaiting his arrival, a message was received from Cass that he could not consent to address "free masons clothed in their masonic paraphernalia" without offending other potential supporters. This cursory note insulted the Cincinnati brethren. Most of them bolted the hall, leaving only a few disrobed masons to greet the candidate.

Dawson gleefully reported that Cass and his entourage entered the lodge hall, "remained a few minutes in the room without sitting down and then retired to attend the theatre."[18]

Lewis Cass, past grand master of lodges in Ohio and Michigan, totally miscalculated the impact of his actions on the Cincinnati masons. The mounting hostility during the 1820s to the secret order, which seemed to a growing number of the uninitiated to be an elitist organization bent on controlling American society, had led Governor Cass to suspend lodge activities in Michigan. Antimasonry was a waning force by the early 1840s, but the incident at Cincinnati graphically illustrated the pitfalls that lay ahead as Cass attempted to placate varying points of view. Moderation, he regretfully learned, becomes untenable when morality is infused with politics and partisan ideology brooks no compromise. The immediate lesson learned in Cincinnati, however, was not so inclusive. Rather, as Andrew Jackson subsequently informed Martin Van Buren, "Gov. Cass has destroyed himself" in Ohio.[19]

A subdued Lewis Cass left the Buckeye State, resigned to the notion that Van Buren was building an insurmountable lead in the race for the Democratic nomination. Cass's mood brightened when a "Committee of Escort," consisting of seventy prominent Detroit citizens, joined him at Ypsilanti and accompanied the returning minister on the last leg of his journey home. Douglass Houghton, physician, geologist, and science professor as well as the city's mayor, extended a formal welcome, and the governor made a few appropriate remarks. Cass was then marched in the company of local militia and civic organizations to temporary lodgings at Dibble's Exchange Hotel. At a public dinner held that evening, February 14, Cass graciously responded to the warm reception and pledged that Detroit was his permanent home. A week later, while reflecting upon events since returning to the United States, he insightfully confided: "Nothing could be more satisfactory than the demonstration of publick feeling I met with." Although he had "sense enough to separate those tokens of appreciation, arising out of a peculiar circumstance abroad," from political support, Cass found it impossible to abandon his presidential ambitions.[20]

Nearly a dozen years had passed since Cass accepted a post in Andrew Jackson's cabinet, and the Panic of 1837 combined with prolonged absences to leave his business affairs in disarray. To all outward appearances, he settled into a life of tranquil retirement, husbanding commercial enterprises and overseeing construction of a new house on Fort Street. Some months after his return, Henry Schoolcraft visited Detroit and observed his old mentor directing the digging of drainage ditches and the planting of trees near the family dwelling—"living in a quiet, retired way, in a style of republican simplicity."[21]

While tending to business affairs and slipping into a domestic routine, Cass did not divorce himself from the presidential contest. Despite a feigned disinterest in the outcome, he followed the political fortunes of other contenders for the Democratic nomination, focusing his attention on Van Buren, Calhoun, Johnson, and Buchanan. Buchanan demonstrated little strength outside his native Pennsylvania, but he was a decade younger than the others and could afford to bide his time. Johnson, the reputed slayer of Tecumseh, remained a strong candidate in the western states, although his support was more broadly based than deep. Calhoun held the hearts and minds of southern Democrats, naturally, and did surprisingly well in eastern states, especially among Irish voters with no love for antislavery politicians. Van Buren was the acknowledged front-runner. The most astute politician in the race, the New Yorker was methodically sewing up support among the rank and file in states where Democrats maintained viable organizations following the election of 1840. Cass was plainly aware that "the machinery of party," as he phrased it, would "operate powerfully upon the Presidential question." A Whig newspaper neatly summarized these feelings: "There is nowhere a particle of enthusiasm for Van Buren. . . . Nevertheless he will out general his opponents, and in the face of all his popular coldness, will get the nomination of a National convention."[22]

In the face of these developments, Lewis Cass made no attempt to establish a political organization capable of challenging Van Buren. He did not actively court financial backers or assemble a newspaper network to carry his message to the voters, nor, as Schoolcraft noted, did he surround himself with a "busy committee of correspondence." There was, in fact, "no evidence" that time or money were devoted to the presidential campaign. The forsaken candidate informed Nathaniel Niles he intended "to sit still and take no part personally in what is going on," although he conceded it was "not in human nature" to suppress all thoughts of the contest. Meanwhile, Niles and other supporters, such as Alfred O. P. Nicholson of Tennessee, pursued a political strategy that groomed Cass as a compromise nominee acceptable to both the Van Buren and Calhoun factions. To keep his name before the public and encourage secondary support among followers of rival candidates, Cass wrote several public letters emphasizing basic political principles and policies, ever wary of defining his positions too precisely. In response to a query from a voter from Pontiac, Michigan, Cass reiterated his opposition to a national bank and the distribution of federal treasury surpluses while advocating "a judicious tariff" to provide "incidental protection" to American manufacturers. He also pledged to support "zealously and sincerely" the Democratic nominee. In a note to John Dean of Tennessee, Cass broke new ground in an effort to broaden his appeal in the South. He denounced abolition as "not only unconstitutional, but fraught with dangerous consequences to the peace of our common country." Another campaign letter advocated "taking possession of Oregon at all events" and favored "the most liberal extension of the right of suffrage." Cass hoped these sentiments stimulated Democratic support in all sections of the nation, but he fretted in a private communication that "a man may write too much, and appear too often before the publick. He may display too much eagerness." That, Lewis Cass was determined not to do.[23]

Cass garnered additional campaign capital from an exchange of letters with Andrew Jackson. The former president supported Van Buren and was resolved not to aid any other Democratic contender; thus, when David Disney sought a note of praise for Cass's contributions to his administration, Jackson declined, since "an improper construction might be put upon his motives." This failed attempt by his chief Ohio supporter to smoke out Jackson did not deter Cass from writing a fawning letter in May 1843, in which he claimed that, had Jackson been in the White House when Webster was negotiating with Ashburton, "we should not have been disgraced with a treaty, which will be a black spot upon our national escutcheon forever." When the old general still balked at endorsing Cass's political qualifications, Major Lewis stepped in. Jackson's intimate adviser had wielded little influence during the Van Buren administration, and he owed Cass a personal debt of gratitude for aiding family members Montford Stokes and Alphonse Pageot. Lewis even concocted a story for Jackson's benefit—telling him Cass planned to write a history of his administration—and this had the "intended effect" of softening Old Hickory. Lewis proudly informed Cass a letter from Jackson was in the works and candidly added, "You and your friends will of course know *how* and *when* to get permission to publish it. . . . I have endeavored to help you to some *good cards,* and . . . I am sure you will play them skillfully!"[24]

Jackson's letter, dated July 8, was adroitly exploited by the Cass campaign. While scrupulously avoiding any mention of the Democratic nomination, the former president commended Cass's "discretion and talents," praised his "noble stand" against *"the late disgraceful treaty of Washington,"* and tendered "the thanks of every true republican" for his nationalistic efforts. The Michigan candidate effusively responded that he intended to place Jackson's letter "among my most precious papers, to be preserved by my children, as an enduring testimonial . . . of your friendship." Acting on the advice of John Norvell, whom Jackson had appointed postmaster at Detroit, Cass asked for permission to reprint the letter: "not on my account, tho' I do not dissemble the satisfaction such a measure would give me, but on account of our country, to which your opinion upon all subjects is so acceptable." Norvell did not wait for a reply before sending a copy of Jackson's comments to Francis Blair and John Rives of the *Washington Globe.* This was fortunate, because Jackson still refused to allow his personal opinions to be broadcast for political purposes.[25]

Publication of the Jackson letter was part of a concerted effort by Cass supporters in the year prior to the Democratic national convention. Two campaign biographies of the candidate were circulated: *Sketch of the Life and Services of General Lewis Cass, of Ohio,* published at Harrisburg, and *Biography of General Lewis Cass: Including a Voice from a Friend,* from a New York press. The latter pamphlet appended a series of articles written for the *Richmond Enquirer* by Richard Rush, who rejected Van Buren's candidacy because of his inability "to stir up men's spirits, or excite fervor at the polls." Inconsistent political principles made Calhoun suspect, Rush argued, and Johnson and Buchanan were summarily dismissed as suitable nominees. Lewis Cass, portrayed as an orthodox Democrat and the candidate most capable of winning the national election, was the best choice available.[26]

The numerous invitations that Cass received to address far-flung Democratic meetings demonstrated a renewed national interest in his campaign for the presidential nomination. Since the candidate was unable or unwilling to attend most of these functions, well-worded letters of regret served to convey his political sentiments. At a Philadelphia celebration of Jefferson's birthday, for instance, his note was received enthusiastically, and a toast was offered to General Cass, "the soldier, the diplomatist, and the statesman." To an "Oregon Convention" at Cincinnati, chaired by Richard M. Johnson, Cass sent a forceful message that echoed the sentiments of the delegates, urging the U.S. government to extend its jurisdiction to 54°40'. "I would take and hold possession of the Territory upon the Pacific, come what might," he avowed. America had a rightful claim to the Oregon country, and Cass "would not waste time in fruitless diplomatic discussions" with the British: "Let us keep our own, and keep it with a strong hand, if need be." This bellicose letter propitiously identified Cass with territorial expansion—an issue destined to play a major role in the presidential campaign.[27]

Lewis Cass did not attend the Cincinnati convention because he was at Fort Wayne, Indiana, to deliver a Fourth of July speech. The patriotic celebration marked the completion of the Wabash and Erie Canal, which effectively linked Lake Erie with the Mississippi. With a nationalistic fervor customary to Independence Day orations, Cass extolled the "public virtue and intelligence" of the American people and vowed that "the citadel of freedom" was secure from foreign foes. This visit also permitted Cass to meet with his staunch Hoosier supporters, led by Senator Edward Hannegan.[28]

The candidacy of Lewis Cass for the Democratic nomination was well launched by the summer of 1843, although Martin Van Buren continued to lead in the scramble for convention delegates. Despite disclaimers that he was simply allowing the political process to run its course, Cass was caught up in the excitement of the campaign and indulged in some electioneering. One of his less respectful neighbors disparagingly remarked that "the old cock is making play for the Presidency," receiving at his home on Fort Street "about 20 paddys dressed a la militaire, denominated 'Cass Guards.'" After salutes were exchanged, Cass "invited the posse into his house, to flatter them with a glass of french wine. . . . This is some of the monkeyism a great man plays to attain his objects."[29] Public campaigning in this fashion did not suit Cass, who was ill at ease when soliciting votes, yet the enthusiasm of the "paddys" was undeniable; Irish voters flocked to the Democratic party, and his Anglophobia ensured their loyalty. As it turned out, however, such support was not enough to upset the Van Buren juggernaut as it gathered momentum prior to the Baltimore convention.

Commencing in late 1843, the selection of delegates to the Democratic national convention demonstrated the overwhelming strength of Martin Van Buren among state party organizations. The Massachusetts convention proved to be an accurate barometer of the New England political atmosphere when it convened at Worcester in September. The Van Buren forces succeeded in naming a delegation almost unanimously committed to the former president, and George Bancroft boasted that the single exception "will not dare to avow his secret preference for Calhoun." As expected, Van Buren carried the entire New York slate, headed by his former law associate, Benjamin Butler. James Buchanan, the other contender from the Northeast, responded by gracefully withdrawing from the contest in December. Pennsylvania Democrats subsequently nominated a ticket of Martin Van Buren and Richard M. Johnson, with Lewis Cass receiving the vote of a solitary delegate.[30]

Cass hoped to stem the Van Buren tide when Tennessee Democrats convened at Nashville in November. Jackson continued to favor his former vice president for the nomination, with James Knox Polk as his running mate; the Cass forces were led by Major Lewis and two former federal senators, Alfred O. P. Nicholson and Alexander Anderson. Owing to the influence of Cass supporters, and to the reluctance of delegates pushing Polk for the vice presidency to antagonize any of the contenders, no presidential candidate was specifically endorsed at Nashville. Jackson explained to Van Buren it was thought best not to split the state party into factions, but the delegates "were at least five to one in favour of you & Polk." Indeed, a clear majority of the national delegates chosen by the end of the year were pledged to Van Buren.[31]

In January, attention focused on the Northwest, the region most closely associated with the political career of Lewis Cass. The showdown came in Ohio, where a battle raged for control of the party machinery. The Cass forces won an early skirmish in the Akron area when the Democrats of Summit County nominated their candidate for the presidency, lauding him as a true Jeffersonian, "a man of the people, and most emphatically the "PEOPLE'S MAN." Cass was also the choice at Zanesville, but the regular party members of Muskingum County, where he served as prosecuting attorney before the War of 1812, nominated Van Buren. Local pride fell before superior political organization. The New Yorker was similarly cheered when Buckeye Democrats assembled at Columbus and selected William Medill to chair the meeting. Samuel Medary, Moses Dawson, and Edwin Stanton led the successful fight for Van Buren on the convention floor; the Cass forces, under Governor Shannon and David Disney, were powerless to prevent the nomination of their chief rival. The other northwestern states likewise fell into the Van Buren column.[32]

The outcome of the Michigan Democratic convention sounded an apparent death knell to Cass's presidential ambitions in 1844. The Northwest's favorite son had been nominated for the presidency by a public gathering in Detroit the previous June, but as the state delegates convened at Ann Arbor in January, it was clear a majority either supported or acquiesced in the selection of Van Buren. Nonetheless, the final tabulation was so mortifying—the New Yorker received more than one hundred votes, compared to only five for Cass—it was deleted from the published convention proceedings. With the Democrats of his adopted state failing in their support, Cass could not reasonably expect others to stand by his candidacy. Van Buren ultimately received the backing of party organizations in twenty-four of the twenty-six states; by late spring, three-fourths of the instructed delegates to the Baltimore convention were pledged to vote for him on the first ballot. Although a few stubborn opponents continued to dispute its inevitability, the nomination of Martin Van Buren as the Democratic standard-bearer was generally conceded throughout the country.[33]

From his Detroit home, surrounded by furniture and trappings purchased in France when his prospects for the presidency had appeared so promising, Lewis Cass contemplated the collapse of his candidacy. He ignored the popular following painstakingly cultivated by Van Buren over the years, and complained that his own moderate principles "were not sufficiently extreme to satisfy the violent" Democrats determined to back the New Yorker "at all hazards." In a letter to Lucius Lyon, one of his political supporters and an occasional business associate, Cass foresaw a presidential election pitting Van Buren against Henry Clay. Lyon agreed that Van Buren "must be the nominee of the national convention unless he should die or voluntarily withdraw" and forlornly inquired whether there was "any chance of his withdrawal?" Despite such pessimistic prognostications, Lyon asked Cass to send a list of political friends with whom he and fellow congressman Robert McClelland "might confer confidentially on the subject of your nomination by the Baltimore convention." A dispirited Cass replied that Joseph Wright and Senator Hannegan, aggressive expansionists from Indiana, were his only acknowledged allies in Washington, although several Baltimore delegates privately pledged support. Cass contended his principles were "not ultra enough to satisfy the ultra partisans who in stirring times take the lead"; yet it was just as well, since he suffered "a fit of the blue devils" whenever his chances for the nomination improved. Cass gloomily concluded certain party members would "rather fail with Mr. Van Buren, than succeed with any body else." As the Whig organ in Detroit rightly reported, "Any support which Gov. Cass may give Mr. Van Buren will be cold and reluctant."[34]

Cass was resigned to Van Buren's nomination as late as the middle of April, when an explosive political controversy that had been percolating for years suddenly erupted, destroying the New Yorker's candidacy and severely damaging Henry Clay's chances of winning the White House. The issue was Texas. Although earlier attempts to incorporate the Lone Star Republic into the Union elicited protests from antislavery spokesmen, not until this time did it emerge as a crucial point of contention among Democrats and Whigs. President John Tyler, estranged from both political parties and unable to build a national following through patronage, attempted to spark his reelection hopes with the annexation of Texas. A treaty to that effect was signed on April 12, 1844, and submitted to the Senate for ratification. Accompanying the pact, however, was a letter from Secretary of State Calhoun to the British minister, which linked Texas statehood with the future of American slavery. This turned the question of annexation into a sectional debate, and it doomed ratification.

In an effort to divorce the Texas issue from partisan politics and the spresidential election, Martin Van Buren and Henry Clay presented their thoughts on the subject in Washington newspapers. The *Globe* printed Van Buren's letter to Congressman William H. Hammett, in which he opposed immediate annexation. Clay, too, disappointed expansionists with the "Raleigh letter," published in the *National Intelligencer.* He argued that the acquisition of Texas would result in war with Mexico, would disrupt the sectional equilibrium within the Union, and was "not called for by any general expression of public opinion." The Kentucky Whig greatly misread popular sentiment regarding expansion; the annexation of Texas was not a controversy easily quieted by the efforts of Clay and Van Buren.[35]

Lewis Cass, who had aided the Texas Republic while serving in France and was on record defending America's claim to all of Oregon, realized that the annexation question turned the national political scene topsy-turvy. Democratic ideology was grounded in the inherent wisdom of the people, and Cass upheld this principle during the Texas debate. His passionate expansionism reflected public opinion—especially in the western states—and while his sincerity cannot be doubted, Cass seized upon this argument to derail the Van Buren campaign express as it pulled into Baltimore.

Ardent expansionists clamored for the annexation of Texas, and other Democratic opponents of Van Buren believed they now had an issue capable of blocking his nomination. The efforts of Cass supporters were again charged with hope. An annexation rally held in Washington on April 29, chaired by Senator Robert J. Walker of Mississippi, called for the election of Lewis Cass as president. Major Lewis repeatedly pressed upon Andrew Jackson—who broke with Van Buren over Texas—the virtues of Cass as the Democratic standard-bearer. If the United States encountered "difficulties" with Britain and Mexico over Oregon and Texas, Cass was "the very man, above all others," to be in the White House. Since Van Buren must be dropped, his detractor argued, the party could not fix upon "a stronger, nor a better man for its candidate than General Cass." Jackson was not convinced, and he shifted his support to James Polk, but other Democrats climbed aboard the Cass bandwagon.[36]

Encouraged by the political turn of events, Cass moved swiftly to capitalize on the expansion issue. He reassured a Boston supporter that the rumor he was no longer a candidate was "wholly without foundation" and hopefully added that "great doubt prevails respecting the action of the Baltimore Democratic Convention." To alleviate any lingering misgivings among the national delegates and rejuvenate his recently moribund candidacy, Cass followed Lucius Lyon's advice. Lyon reported that Van Buren's opposition to immediate annexation cost him the entire South, and he urged Cass to exploit the opportunity. He even provided specific guidelines for the candidate: "Write a short, forcible, patriotic, anti-British letter (such as you know how to write), say not a word about slavery," and avoid a tone of sectionalism. Lyon was certain Cass could "take the wind all out of the sails of Van Buren" and leave the New Yorker "hard aground in the mud." Acknowledging that the "Texas question has advanced like an avalanche," Cass agreed to undermine Van Buren's support.[37]

On May 10, Cass drafted letters to Joseph Wright and Edward Hannegan that clearly expressed his feelings on the annexation of Texas. The epistle to Senator Hannegan was published in the *Globe* on the sixteenth and soon thereafter in leading Democratic organs throughout the country. There was no time to lose, since the Baltimore convention met on the twenty-seventh. The letter to Hannegan was distinctly Anglophobic and played upon the fears of southern slaveholders. Cass briefly mentioned the economic benefits expected from annexation, then turned to the main thrust of his argument. In language evocative of his fight against the Quintuple Treaty, Cass warned that the United States must keep Texas from falling under the sway of Great Britain, the leading abolitionist power in the world. He raised the specter of a "servile war" in the South, should hostilities erupt over Texas, and painted a frightening picture of racial warfare: "What more favorable position could be taken for the occupation of English black troops, and for letting them loose upon our southern states, than is afforded by Texas?" With due regard for Democratic sensibilities, Cass asserted the majority of Americans were in favor of annexation: "Were they not—the measure ought not to be effected. But as they are—the sooner it is effected the better." Within days, Cass reinforced his position with letters to Robert J. Walker, Aaron Hobart, and others who could be counted on to support his nomination at the national convention. Cass claimed, "The annexation of Texas is essential to our national security," and felt confident the majority of Democratic delegates agreed.[38]

One final task remained for the candidate. He sent Lucius Lyon a "brief synopsis" of his political philosophy and views on major issues to share with the Democratic delegates passing through Washington. Cass declared his opposition to a national bank, a high protective tariff, distribution, and the assumption of state debts, and he called for a frugal federal government and no change in the veto power. He also favored "the one term principle" and pledged that "no consideration would induce me to serve a second time." Cass remained uncommitted on the subject of potential running mates and saw no reason to repeat his well-known sentiments regarding Oregon and Texas. Finding himself once more in the thick of the race for the presidential nomination, Lewis Cass settled back to await the outcome of the Democratic national convention.[39]

In the interim, the opposition selected a candidate. At the Whig national convention, called to order at Baltimore on May 1, Henry Clay was unanimously nominated for the presidency. Following passage of resolutions lauding the national ticket and Whig principles, the convention adjourned after only a single day. The Democrats, meeting in the same city near the end of the month, enjoyed no such unanimity or harmony.

The Texas question galvanized opponents of Martin Van Buren within the Democratic party and gave them the political ammunition to shoot down his nomination. Even Andrew Jackson acknowledged it would be as difficult "to turn the current of the Miss[iss]ippi, as to turn the democracy from the annexation of Texas." The strategy embraced by expansionists, and other opponents of Van Buren, was simple. Since most of the delegates were pledged to vote for the New Yorker on the initial ballot, a two-thirds majority would be required for nomination. The two-thirds rule had been passed at the first Democratic national convention, to demonstrate solidarity with the Jackson-Van Buren ticket, and was implemented again during the campaign of 1836, when Van Buren was the overwhelming choice for president. But it was rejected in 1840, when delegates could not unite on a vice presidential candidate. The opponents of Van Buren now intended to employ the two-thirds gambit to circumvent what it previously accentuated: majority rule. In fact, Robert J. Walker, who presided over the Washington annexation rally that nominated Cass for the presidency, advocated an even less scrupulous approach by encouraging his Mississippi colleagues to abandon Van Buren on the first ballot. Thus, the stage was set at Baltimore for a confrontation between the supporters of Martin Van Buren and Lewis Cass.[40]

Delegates to the fourth national Democratic convention converged on the Egyptian Saloon of Odd Fellows Hall late Monday morning, May 27, into quarters so cramped that one reporter likened the gallery to the Black Hole of Calcutta. Benjamin Butler, Van Buren's floor manager, predicted victory on the first ballot, "if we are not handcuffed & gagged by the ⅔ rule." Butler consulted with other Van Buren men, as they frantically rushed about pleading with delegates to vote against the rule. Those who led the charge to block Van Buren's nomination included Cass delegates Edward Bradley, of Michigan; Joseph Wright; William Roane, who headed the Virginia contingent; and Howell Cobb, of Georgia. The most prominent proponent of the two-thirds ploy was Robert J. Walker, who disagreed with Cass on the bank issue but was even more concerned with territorial expansion. To add to the confusion, "Tyler and Texas" men mingled with the Democratic delegates and pushed for immediate annexation. Tempers understandably heated up preceding the opening gavel.[41]

About twenty minutes before noon, the scheduled hour to convene, the opponents of Van Buren swung into action. Romulus Saunders, a congressman from North Carolina whose booming voice commanded attention, nominated Hendrick Wright, of Pennsylvania, to chair the convention. Some Van Buren delegates protested this "trick," but Butler recognized he could ill afford to antagonize the Keystone delegation prior to voting on the two-thirds rule, and the proposal was ratified by acclamation. John L. O'Sullivan put the best gloss on it, characterizing Wright as "a precious rascal . . . as likely to betray one way, as the other."[42] Further proceedings were suspended during the opening prayer and scripture reading. Governor Henry Hubbard of New Hampshire, Butler's original choice as convention chairman, subsequently headed the credentials committee, which reported late in the afternoon that 325 delegates shared a total of 266 votes. South Carolina, true to favorite son Calhoun, was not represented. Attention then focused on the crucial procedural issue.

Robert J. Walker presented the case for adoption of the two-thirds rule. The diminutive "Mississippi roarer" warned against "a mere majority" of delegates from a few larger states thwarting the national majority in favor of Texas annexation. Walker's arguments hardened feelings in the overcrowded convention hall, which one delegate described as "hot as Belshazzar's furnace." Benjamin Butler obtained the floor and insisted the two-thirds rule would lead to the "dismemberment" of the Democratic party. On that divisive note, the convention adjourned until the following morning.[43]

The Democrats reassembled at nine o'clock on Tuesday and resumed the debate. When they proceeded to vote four hours later, it became clear with the defection of five Massachusetts delegates that the two-thirds rule would pass. A Van Buren stalwart recorded that the final tally, 148 to 116, was greeted with "Great Cheering from the World of Traitordom." Most of the yea votes came from western and southern delegations; the Northeast and Ohio generally remained loyal to the New Yorker. In the pungent words of one journalist, passage of the two-thirds rule "cooked Mr. Van Buren's goose."[44]

The balloting for the presidential nomination began at three o'clock that afternoon. As expected, Van Buren received a majority of the votes cast on the first ballot, but his total of 146 fell short of the 178 needed. Cass was second with 83 votes; Johnson picked up 24. During the succeeding ballots, Van Buren's support steadily eroded, until Cass overcame his lead on the fifth ballot. With the seventh vote, Cass led 123 to 99. Butler shouted for an adjournment, while the Cass forces demanded another ballot. The convention floor was "a scene of violent commotion" and confusion, and it was agreed to reconvene on Wednesday morning.[45]

The Cass delegates were jubilant. Victory appeared certain as news spread during the night that Johnson was formally withdrawing and throwing his support to the candidate from Michigan. Van Buren's managers, however, were obstinately opposed to the nomination of Cass—the major benefactor of the two-thirds rule—and Butler and Bancroft worked into the early morning hours seeking a compromise candidate. Butler suggested Silas Wright, but he remained loyal to Van Buren. Gideon J. Pillow, of Tennessee, meanwhile lobbied strenuously for the selection of

James Knox Polk. Polk's credentials were impeccable; a protégé of Old Hickory, he favored the immediate annexation of Texas and was not aligned with the Cass forces that blocked Van Buren's nomination. And so, a hasty bargain was struck between the unyielding New York faction and supporters of "Young Hickory."

The first vote on Wednesday demonstrated the persuasiveness of Polk's advocates, who were no longer content to settle for second place on the national ticket. Cass maintained a plurality over Van Buren, 114 to 104, but the Tennesseean received 44 votes, from a total of seven states. Pandemonium greeted the results, and some despaired of a nomination ever being made. "In God's name," one exasperated Democrat implored, "are we to be kept here to all eternity?" Butler received permission to caucus, and the New York delegation left the floor amid derisive cries "they might never come back again." As the ninth ballot proceeded, Polk picked up most of the Van Buren votes, cutting so deeply into Cass's support that he led 74 to 20 when the New York delegation returned and joined the stampede. This opened the floodgates, and after Cass delegates switched their votes, Polk was declared the unanimous choice of the convention. So complete and swift was Young Hickory's victory, Bradley did not get the opportunity to read the conciliatory letter from Cass he carried in his pocket. The Michigan contender had authorized the withdrawal of his name, should "a division of opinion" prevent "a hearty and united exertion" on his behalf. To assuage the feelings of New Yorkers following the selection of Polk, Silas Wright was slated as his running mate, but Wright immediately, and repeatedly, declined the nomination from Washington via the recently installed telegraph. George M. Dallas ultimately was named to complete the ticket, and the Democratic platform naturally emphasized the newly important issue of expansion.[46]

The choice of James Knox Polk as the Democratic nominee, in the words of Thomas Hart Benton, "was a surprise and a marvel to the country,"[47] but the Baltimore delegates returned home convinced they had selected a winning team. Martin Van Buren had outfoxed himself with the Hammett letter. The New Yorker's uncharacteristically forthright stance cost him dearly. Lewis Cass, in contrast, did not gain the nomination because his followers necessarily led the charge to pass the two-thirds rule, thereby alienating a significant proportion of the delegates. Van Buren viewed Cass as a spoiler and an unscrupulous truckler not qualified for the White House; under the circumstances, Polk was an acceptable choice. Young Hickory and Lewis Cass embraced the same basic Democratic principles, and both were expansionists. Although his selection may have surprised the country, the Democracy entered the national campaign solidly united under the Polk banner.

Lewis Cass and Martin Van Buren endorsed the Democratic ticket, but their attitudes toward each other differed considerably. Cass insisted that since his heart was not set on the nomination, he felt no bitterness toward Van Buren for denying it to him. Although not as indifferent as he claimed, Cass personally bore no ill will toward his New York rival. The same cannot be said for Van Buren and his supporters. A Michigan Democrat recalled that during the previous presidential campaign, Cass was "secretly engaged in opposition" to Van Buren's reelection, and the Baltimore proceedings seemingly confirmed these suspicions. James Wadsworth, who labored ceaselessly for the New Yorker at the national convention, vilified Cass as a "disorganizing, treacherous, Hybrid" political scoundrel for pushing the two-thirds rule. One particularly incensed Ohio delegate proclaimed that "the *damned rotten corrupt*" Cass men "should be *guillotined*," and took cold comfort in thinking the Van Buren delegations had "saved the Nation from *the curse* of the nomination of Cass." This discontent proved to be particularly significant four years later, when the Michigan Democrat captured his party's nomination. Neither Cass nor Van Buren, however, was engaged in looking that far ahead in the months following the Baltimore convention; there was a national campaign to be won.[48]

Lewis Cass flung himself tirelessly into the effort to elect Polk president. At a mass meeting of Detroit Democrats, he enthusiastically pledged to support the nomination. Cass referred to Polk as the next president and predicted he "will follow in the footsteps of Washington and Jefferson, of Madison and of Jackson!" If that proved to be the case, the *Charleston Courier* sardonically retorted, "he will have to walk all sorts of ways."[49]

Cass carried the campaign to partisan crowds throughout much of the Old Northwest and Polk's home state. A throng numbering close to fifteen thousand turned out at Ann Arbor, on the Fourth of July, to hear "one of the best democratic speeches" ever delivered in the state; and Cass then made plans to travel to Nashville for a massive Democratic rally scheduled for the middle of August. He intended, as well, to pay a "final tribute of respect at the Hermitage, before the tomb closes upon the illustrious man." For his part, Jackson announced, "I will rejoice to see him." The Nashville rally attracted an estimated fifty thousand, and rostrums were erected outdoors so several orators could speak simultaneously. The local Democratic organ praised Cass's "eloquent and powerful speech" as the "master effort of a great statesman; and the popular thunders of applause with which it was received by the FIFTY ACRES OF FREEMEN in attendance, rang through the valleys and reverberated from hill to hill." Lewis Cass met privately with Andrew Jackson at the Hermitage, before leaving Nashville.[50]

The journey home to Detroit was punctuated with frequent campaign speeches in Indiana and Ohio. Cass was indefatigable, and the *Free Press* crowed he was "on the stump . . . doing efficient service in the Democratic cause." While pausing at Cleveland to catch his breath, Cass outlined to Polk his schedule for the final weeks of the campaign. "I trust I shall reach home tomorrow, Saturday, for I must set out for Indiana on Monday, where the Central Committee of that State have assigned to me nine different places to address the people." Richard Rush chimed in from Philadelphia with words of praise for Cass's efforts on behalf of Polk: "I observe that you are active all over the country, and rejoice at it. It cannot fail to do . . . great good." Cass also contributed several thousand dollars to the Democratic coffers.[51]

James Knox Polk narrowly defeated Henry Clay for the White House. Following the election, there was speculation Lewis Cass might enter the cabinet. The president-elect, instead, heeded the advice of Andrew Jackson to keep from his administration "all aspirants for the presidency." Young Hickory, had he been so inclined, might also have questioned the efficacy of Cass's contributions. Ohio, a state in which Cass campaigned vigorously, was carried by Clay with nearly a six thousand vote plurality (although the Whig margin was reduced from what it had been in 1840). The rest of the Northwest went Democratic, however, and Polk was too chagrined over the close loss in Tennessee to point fingers elsewhere. Cass, nonetheless, recognized political realities. Polk was his own man; he owed the Michigan politician nothing but thanks for a job well done. The only cabinet appointee considered to be a Cass supporter was Secretary of the Treasury Robert J. Walker. The Van Buren faction of the party was totally unrepresented, and a New Yorker opposed to the former president, William Marcy, headed the War Department. This further exacerbated the friction between radical Van Burenites, led by Silas Wright, and conservative "Hunker" Democrats, who looked to Cass for national leadership in 1848.[52]

Long before Polk announced his cabinet appointments, Lewis Cass set his sights on a seat in the U.S. Senate. Although some advisers, including

Edward Hannegan and Joseph Wright, warned that Cass might hurt his chances for the presidency, most agreed the Senate provided a forum for relaunching his national aspirations. The Michigan Democrats were united behind Cass; at a caucus of state legislators, he was endorsed by forty-three of the forty-eight party members present. On February 4, 1845, the Michigan Senate voted 16 to 2 in favor of Cass over Epaphroditus Ransom, a radical Democrat from Kalamazoo. There were no Whig senators. Cass carried the Michigan House overwhelmingly as well, with only the eight Whigs supporting Hezekiah Wells. Lewis Cass was elected to the Senate to replace Augustus S. Porter, a Whig and an original investor in the Cass Company.[53]

Shortly before the senator-elect left Detroit to take up his duties in Washington, the Cass home was thrown open for a "very large & very agreeable" party. Four rooms were prepared for the festivities, and in two of them carpets were removed for dancing. The dark woodwork and papered walls were brilliantly lighted with chandeliers and candelabra, and the china brought from France elegantly adorned the table. The Parisian cook Cass employed observed a continental fashion, providing the partygoers only half the food usually served at such functions in America. One guest remarked, "They call it *French,* but the truth is 'tis *meanness.* But never mind—we had enough." Catherine Mason was less charitable, insisting "the Casses have no taste—& with all their advantages still dress badly." Such opinions, however, were not universally held; and Cass left Detroit with the political approbation of its citizens. The people of Michigan were confident he would well represent their interests. Even the Whigs expected him to prove helpful regarding issues of concern to the Northwest. Lewis Cass, who received his first appointment to public office from President Thomas Jefferson, was sixty-two years old when he took his seat as the junior senator from Michigan.[54]

This house stood on the Cass farm until it was moved to the north side of Larned Street, between First and Second, when Cass was minister to France. It was demolished in 1882. *(Courtesy of the Burton Historical Collection of the Detroit Public Library)*

This substantial dwelling, located at Cass and Fort Streets, was built in the early 1840s, upon Cass's return from France. *(Courtesy of the Burton Historical Collection of the Detroit Public Library)*

Major Jonathan Cass, a veteran of the Revolution and commander of Fort Hamilton, Ohio, instilled in his eldest son an abiding sense of nationalism. *(Courtesy of the Burton Historical Collection of the Detroit Public Library)*

Henry Ledyard accompanied Cass to France as his personal secretary and returned as his son-in-law. Later he was mayor of Detroit. *(Courtesy of the Michigan State Archives)*

Henry B. Ledyard was the recipient of affectionate letters from Grandfather Lewis. He spent the Civil War years as a cadet and instructor at West Point. *(Courtesy of the Michigan State Archives)*

This painting by Gilbert Stuart portrays an elderly General William Hull, Cass's predecessor as governor of Michigan Ter-

Father Gabriel Richard was instrumental in the religious, educational, and political history of Michigan Territory. The first Catholic priest to serve in Congress, he died during the

This drawing of Augustus B. Woodward is the only known likeness of the eccentric territorial judge, who conceived of the Catholepistemiad, or University of Michigania, in 1817. *(Courtesy of the Michigan State Archives)*

William Woodbridge met Cass in Marietta, Ohio, when they read law in the office of Matthew Backus. Woodbridge served as secretary of Michigan Territory during most of Cass's governorship, later joining the Whig party and being elected governor of the state and a United States senator. *(Courtesy of the Michigan State Archives)*

John R. Williams was a partner in several real estate investments with Cass, the first mayor of Detroit, and adjutant general in the territorial militia. *(Courtesy of the Michigan State Archives)*

Charles C. Trowbridge was a young man when he accompanied Cass on the expedition of 1820 as the assistant topographer. He rose to be president of the Bank of Michigan, which served as a federal depository when Cass was a member of Andrew Jackson's cabinet. *(Courtesy of the Michigan State Archives)*

James M. Doty was the official secretary of the Cass expedition. He was appointed a territorial judge for the western counties and was later elected governor of Wisconsin. *(Courtesy of the State Historical Society of Wisconsin, neg. no. x346657)*

Henry Rowe Schoolcraft, mineralogist of the Northwest expedition, accompanied Cass to the Chicago treaty negotiations in 1821. Appointed Indian agent at the Sault the following year, Schoolcraft later wrote a campaign biography of Cass. *(Courtesy of the Michigan State Archives)*

Edmund Brush faithfully oversaw Cass's extensive business interests during the mission to France. Despite Brush's best efforts, Cass

Lucius Lyon was an occasional business associate of Cass and a staunch political ally. While serving in Congress, Lyon was a driving force in Cass's unsuccessful campaign for the Democratic presidential nomination in 1844. *(Courtesy of the Michigan*

Alpheus Felch, Cass's senatorial colleague, joined in supporting the Compromise of 1850. Felch's letters to his wife reveal the respect and affection he felt toward the fatherly Cass. *(Courtesy of the Michigan State Archives)*

Robert McClelland, despite voting for the Wilmot Proviso as a congressman, served as Cass's chief campaign manager in Michigan during the 1848 canvass. He represented the Cass wing of the Democratic party as President Pierce's secretary of the interior. *(Courtesy of the Michigan State Archives)*

Zachariah Chandler, a founder of the Michigan Republican party, replaced Cass in the Senate in 1857. He served three terms before being appointed secretary of the interior by President Grant. *(Courtesy of the Michigan State Archives)*

General Lewis Cass, shortly after being appointed governor of Michigan Territory, sat in Washington for this portrait by John Vanderlyn, who studied under Gilbert Stuart. *(Courtesy of the Burton Historical Collection of the Detroit Public Library)*

Chapter Six

United States Senator (1845–1848): "In These Great Questions of National Bearing, I Acknowledge No Geographical Claims"

WHIG SENATOR William Woodbridge presented the credentials of Lewis Cass, his erstwhile friend, to the United States Senate on March 1, 1845. Cass was sworn in three days later, at the convening of the Twenty-ninth Congress. Although his only legislative experience was acquired during a single term in the Ohio assembly, nearly forty years earlier, Cass was not treated as a typical congressional freshman. He was rightly regarded as a veteran Democratic statesman. After all, Cass had served in military, executive, and diplomatic stations, and as runner-up at the Baltimore convention the preceding year, he was the leading contender for the presidential nomination in 1848. His mission to France and protracted debate with Daniel Webster enhanced his reputation as a party spokesman, and he was appointed to the prestigious Committee on Foreign Relations, chaired by another western expansionist, William Allen of Ohio. Cass and Allen, in spite of a slight personal rivalry, emerged as the chief advocates of the "all of Oregon" movement. Indeed, Cass became the Senate's most consistent and enthusiastic promoter of American territorial expansion. Unquestionably, this furthered his presidential ambitions, but Cass also passionately believed it was the country's destiny to spread across the continent. His desire for more territority was motivated by nationalistic, economic, and ideological impulses. Cass wished to enhance trade opportunities in Asian markets by obtaining Pacific Coast ports, at the same time fostering Jefferson's ideal of an agrarian republic and expanding the areas of freedom and liberty under the aegis of American democratic institutions.[1]

After the inauguration of James Polk, Congress adjourned for the summer and Senator Cass returned home to face a family ordeal. Lewis, Jr., thirty years of age and somewhat adrift in terms of his life's work, was a source of deep concern to his parents. The elder Casses had attempted to provide for their only son by transferring some Detroit property to him, "in consideration of the natural love & affection" they bore, but their love was now sorely tested when a son fathered by Lewis was born out of wedlock to Cornelia Platt. She and her father, Zephaniah Platt, a former state attorney general, moved to New York City. The child, George Stephens, took his surname from the family that raised him in Des Moines, Iowa. Stephens eventually became a successful hardware merchant in Dubuque and an officer of the Norwegian Plow Company, but he was not recognized by the Cass family as an heir of Lewis, Jr., who died in 1878 without other issue. Lewis, "though he promised his Mother that he would do so," made no provision for his bastard son, despite bequeathing as much as thirty thousand dollars to various individuals. George Stephens received no satisfaction, either, from the several letters he wrote to Augustus Cass Canfield, Henry Ledyard, and Charles Trowbridge asking them to intervene with his aunts, "to secure some recognition of what I conceive to be my natural rights." Lewis, Jr., behaved in a shameful manner throughout this sordid affair.[2]

With a profound sense of relief, Senator Lewis Cass turned his attention to public matters during the congressional summer recess. The Michigan Democrat frequently wrote President Polk and members of the cabinet seeking federal posts for personal supporters and assorted dignitaries. Cass's recommendations carried a measure of weight, and sometimes yielded results, although on at least one occasion he came to regret it. Secretary of War William Marcy later complained that Sheldon McKnight, appointed assistant superintendent of mineral lands at the Sault upon Cass's endorsement, had abandoned his station to explore the copper region. Fortunately, most of the senator's attempts to influence the patronage process ended more happily. Jerome Napoleon Bonapart, for instance, asked Cass for help in getting his son admitted to West Point, while Francis Parkman, already "so much indebted" for past courtesies, sought letters of introduction to facilitate his studies of Indians on the Missouri and Upper Mississippi.[3]

In addition to flexing his limited patronage muscle, Cass spent part of the summer communicating with political supporters. He made plans to visit the homes of Aaron Hobart and Richard Rush on his return trip to Washington but took pains not to turn the stops into campaign rallies. That would be premature, and "repugnant" to Cass's sensibilities; he had "an almost invincible aversion" to such public displays of ambition. The politicking was left to the *Detroit Free Press,* while Cass quietly devoted these months to strengthening his following within the Democratic party. This meant deciding to vote against the Senate confirmation of nominees loyal to Van Buren and staking out positions on key issues—consistent with his principles—that appealed to the national electorate. Territorial expansion proved to be the hobbyhorse that Lewis Cass mounted on his quest for the White House.[4]

Cass and fellow expansionists were able to focus on the Oregon controversy when Congress reconvened in December, because the admission of Texas to the Union was virtually settled. Following the election of 1844, a joint resolution of annexation was signed by President Tyler on March 1. "One bone of contention is now out of the way," which "renders the prospects of the party . . . much better," Cass was pleased to report shortly before he took his Senate seat. A Texas convention agreed to annexation on the Fourth of July, and after Congress accepted its slave-state constitution in December, President Polk officially welcomed the Lone Star State into the Union. Polk crowed it was "a bloodless achievement," although the suspension of diplomatic relations between the United States and Mexico portended trouble. One plank of the Democratic platform was thus resolved. The "re-occupation of Oregon," however, temporarily proved to be a thornier problem than the "re-annexation of Texas."[5]

The Texas question was the first national political issue to polarize sentiment in Michigan along sectional lines. Most Whigs opposed the addition of slave territory, as evidenced by the negative votes of Senators Woodbridge and Porter on the joint annexation resolution. Democrats split over the issue, although most followed the lead of Cass and supported the incorporation of Texas into the Union. Lucius Lyon loyally voted in favor of the joint resolution, but the other Democratic members of the Michigan delegation, James B. Hunt and Robert McClelland, opposed it. The addition of Texas was generally favored by state politicians and the public at large; and the Michigan legislature, in January 1845, called for annexation "at the earliest practical period." Cass's stand on the

Texas issue was backed by a majority of Michiganites, while his position regarding Oregon was universally applauded.[6]

In his inaugural address, President Polk asserted that the American claim to the Oregon country was "clear and unquestionable" and urged Congress to extend the jurisdiction of federal law to the region. He repeated this call in his first annual message on December 2, 1845, after the British minister to Washington, Richard Pakenham, rejected the administration's offer to compromise the boundary at the forty-ninth parallel. In an effort to apply diplomatic pressure, the president requested Congress to give notice that after one year, in accordance with the conventions of 1818 and 1827, the United States would terminate the joint occupancy of Oregon. Polk declared the British offer to divide the country at the Columbia River to be unacceptable. That evening, Senator Cass called upon Polk and "expressed his entire concurrence" with his arguments. The president, in fact, simply echoed what Cass and other Democrat expansionists had been saying for years.[7]

With his election to the Senate, Cass took the lead in the expansionist movement, publicly supporting President Polk's call for abrogating joint occupancy. Cass believed the United States was entitled to all of the disputed Oregon territory: up to 54°40' north latitude. In his Fourth of July oration at Fort Wayne in 1843, Cass forcefully opposed British pretensions to the far Northwest: "Let us have no red lines upon the map of Oregon; let us hold on to the integrity of our just claim; and if war comes, be it so." He ominously concluded war could not long be avoided, since "the great tide" of American civilization "will not stop till it reaches the boundary of the continent." Such bellicose sentiments were well suited for public consumption, but Cass privately fretted the United States would be "humbugged" out of the Oregon country if it came "down to a mere party question."[8]

The Oregon controversy was tailor-made for a northwestern Democrat with presidential aspirations, and such was Lewis Cass. He was an aggressive advocate of increased foreign trade, a spread-eagle expansionist, and an Anglophobe—all of which combined to make Cass a staunch 54°40' man. On December 9, after consultations with Polk, Senator Cass submitted a series of resolutions designed to put some teeth in the president's notice proposal. The salient resolution called upon the Military Affairs Committee "to inquire into the condition of the national fortifications and . . . into the state of the means possessed by the Government for the defense of the country." Six days later, after the formal organization of the Senate, Lewis Cass took the floor to defend his preparedness resolutions. He acknowledged "war is a great calamity and ought to be avoided by all proper means; but there are calamities greater than war; among these is national dishonor." After urging the Senate to give the one year's notice, Cass unflinchingly declared that if the British government did not abandon "a large portion" of their claim, "we shall find ourselves involved in a war." This speech, unwavering in its opposition to British pretensions in Oregon, was not a shrill cry for "fifty-four forty or fight!" At this juncture Cass did not state what boundary line ought to be drawn, although he was on record as favoring American claims to all of Oregon. He merely recommended that the United States not settle for less than the forty-ninth parallel, since "we have a better and a juster title" than Great Britain.[9]

The implication, that war with Britain over the Oregon controversy was inevitable, overshadowed Cass's cautiously phrased position regarding settlement of the Oregon boundary dispute. With some justification, and not simply because of his personal animus, Cass was convinced the British might use military force to extend their Pacific holdings southward to California, thereby blocking American access to western ports. In a private communication, he warned that the country faced its "most imminent crisis . . . since 1812. I fear I do not see, how war is to be avoided." Cass did not shrink from the thought of war; in fact, he publicly upped the ante regarding expansion, contending the Polk administration "would secure imperishable honor" with "the peaceful annexation of California." Oregon and the possible acquisition of additional western territory motivated Cass to submit the military defense resolutions. If hostilities with Britain were imminent, the former secretary of war wished the nation to be better prepared than in 1812, when he commanded Ohio volunteers.[10]

The Cass resolutions met a partisan response in the Senate. Whigs blanched at the thought of going to war with the greatest naval power on the globe, solely to extend American territory to the boundary of Russian Alaska. Willie P. Mangum complained the resolutions were "unnecessarily pressed on the Senate" and sought to postpone their consideration. William Archer of Virginia warned that even the rumor of war was destructive to the American economy and denied that the federal government was responsible for the fate of citizens emigrating beyond national boundaries. "Strange doctrine this!" he exclaimed, "that the Government must control a vagrant population, escaping with no request or authority, . . . even to the extent of war." As the debate continued the following day, both John J. Crittenden and Daniel Webster questioned the necessity of the resolutions. Democratic senators naturally tended to play down the bellicose sentiments of Cass's speech. In the final analysis, no one wished to oppose resolutions calling for an examination of military preparedness, and they passed without a negative vote on December 16.[11]

The unanimous support ultimately accorded the Cass resolutions did not reflect American opinion regarding war with Britain over the Oregon boundary. In an editorial printed in the *New York Tribune,* Horace Greeley sarcastically thanked "Senator Gas" for his martial speech. Greeley claimed President Polk was "trying to determine how near he can graze a War and yet avoid it, but the demagogues who are taking the lead in Congress aim beyond this. They mean War. Gen. Cass means War. . . . And all who advocate and vote for the extension of our jurisdiction over all Oregon up to 54°40' either mean War, or they have not wit enough to be trusted to go out of doors." Other observers disparagingly viewed Cass's actions as the opening salvos of a campaign to secure the Democratic nomination in 1848.[12]

Despite the carping from Whigs, Cass took a position on the Oregon issue consistent with his principles. The United States was destined to extend its political and economic institutions over much of the Western Hemisphere, and to ensure American expansion, the acquisitive pretensions of Britain must be quashed. Cass claimed the nation was "surrounded by the territories and possessions, he would not say of an enemy, but of a great commercial rival," and warned the United States was "penetrable at every point, having scarcely a gun mounted, scarcely a soldier with a musket in his hand." He continually pleaded with the Senate to prepare for war. He also supported mandatory retirement for aged army officers, the construction of ten steamships-of-war, and a resolution instructing the secretary of the navy to investigate the need for armaments on Lake Superior. When President Polk recommended increased military forces in March, Cass took the floor to remark that "this matter had been allowed to sleep for many weeks" and he was "glad to find it was now pressed upon their attention by the Executive message, and not by British cannon." Clearly, he was growing impatient over the dilatory pace of the Senate regarding the notice proposal and American military preparedness.[13]

The resolute expansionism embraced by Lewis Cass was strongly supported by northwestern Americans. The Michigan legislature on February 20, 1845, resolved that Congress should extend federal jurisdiction over the Oregon country and abrogate the joint occupancy agreement with Britain. Mass meetings held in Detroit, and dominated by Cass Democrats, emphasized these demands and called for federal action. Even the leading Whig newspaper declared that "our title to the whole of Oregon" was "clear and unquestionable," although the editor of the *Detroit Advertiser* contended Cass's prediction of war was a political ploy. "Our Senator is probably gassing a little. A candidate for the Presidency naturally seeks to ride the popular war hobby. Still if war is desired, let us have it." Cass plainly had identified himself with the spirit of territorial expansion prevalent in the West.[14]

In February, the Senate took up a number of conterminous resolutions relating to the Oregon country, notably those submitted by William Allen, David Atchison, Edward Hannegan, and John C. Calhoun. The resolution introduced by Allen advised the president to give notice terminating the joint occupation. Atchison, one of the few slave-state senators whose enthusiasm for expansion knew no geographical bounds, recommended the organization of a government for the territory. Hannegan declared the entire region to 54°40' to be "the property, and part and parcel of the United States," while Calhoun advocated a policy of "masterly inactivity" regarding the controversy. His amendment, which placed the Oregon boundary at the forty-ninth parallel, reflected a more cautious approach favored by many southern Democrats, as well as Whigs in general. Webster contended arbitration was the best solution to the dispute. Cass responded to the call for compromise by declaring, "England must make a more liberal offer, or I am afraid that greater difficulty will ensue." Most western and northern Democrats lined up with Lewis Cass in favor of the notice resolution and the acquisition of all of Oregon. Sidney Breese of Illinois reminded his colleagues their national platform was unequivocal on this issue. Daniel Dickinson, a New Yorker who supported Cass's presidential aspirations, rhetorically inquired: "We have a right to Oregon; if our right embraces the whole, shall we not claim the whole? It will be time enough for us to say we will give Great Britain a part when she makes out a title to a part."[15]

While Whig senators enjoyed a unified stand on the Oregon question, southern Democrats held the balance of power. When the subject was first raised by Allen's resolution, Calhoun opposed giving the one year's notice. As the debate continued, he persistently pushed the forty-ninth parallel as a compromise boundary. The South Carolinian's call for a negotiated settlement was endorsed by numerous southern Democrats, including Thomas Hart Benton, who was nettled because Cass emerged as the administration spokesman in the Senate. Benton grew more conservative at the same time Cass and other western expansionists became more extreme in their demands for all of Oregon. It was, therefore, with no little anticipation that the Missourian listened, on the last day of March, to Cass's major speech on the Oregon controversy. Benton was already preparing his rebuttal.[16]

Lewis Cass addressed the Senate for three hours, in his typically humorless and impassive manner, supporting the notice resolution and 54°40' as the boundary of Oregon. Cass read this speech, as he did all his major discourses, speaking rapidly and occasionally placing one hand behind his back. As usual, his delivery lacked dramatic flair, flamboyant gestures, and rhetorical flourishes; he was not, in brief, an inspiring orator in the mold of Webster or Clay. A Senate page recalled that Cass "had a habit of ordering a glass of lemonade to be placed before him while making a speech, and would take a sip of it after each dry remark." And yet, the Michigan senator was generally accorded marked attention. His well-reasoned arguments influenced many of his listeners, and when declaiming on national mission and honor, he spoke with a fundamental passion that lent eloquence to his efforts. One observer called the speech of March 31, 1845, the greatest of his career.[17]

Drawing upon the research of a State Department translator, Cass argued that Robert Greenhow's *History of Oregon and California* supported the validity of the American title to 54°40'. If the forty-ninth parallel was the boundary between British and French possessions under the Treaty of Utrecht, as Benton and other advocates of compromise insisted, Britain had no just claim to any territory south of that line. And since the American government frequently had proposed the forty-ninth parallel as the border but the British each time refused, he reasoned, the United States was no longer bound to accept that compromise. Warming to his argument, Cass speciously professed, "Our claim to the country west of the Rocky mountains is as undeniable as our right to Bunker's Hill and New Orleans; and who will call in question our title to these blood-stained fields?" The question was "not whether peace is a blessing and war a curse, but whether peace can be preserved, and war avoided," consistent with national honor. "The eagle and the lion will not always lie down in peace together," Cass reminded the senators on the other side of the chamber, and he denounced those Americans who claimed "we are powerless to defend ourselves." The results of two wars with Britain impress "the stamp of error upon these sad forebodings." The far-flung British Empire and its discontented subjects forecast "an abundant harvest of ruin and disaster" should the United States forcefully defend its claims to the Oregon country. Certainly, American naval vessels and armed privateers possessed the "capacity to annoy a maritime adversary, and to sweep the British flag from this part of the continent," while "we can neither be overrun nor conquered. England might as well attempt to blow up Gibraltar with a squib, as to attempt to subdue us." Cass then turned to Calhoun's prediction that a protracted war with Britain would destroy American democratic institutions. It pained the Michigan senator to hear such allusions to the disruption of the Union, "not because they inspire me with any fear, but because we ought to have one unpronounceable word, as the Jews of old, and that word is *dissolution.*" To Cass's eye, the United States remained "the city upon a hill," with "the strongest government on the face of the earth for good, and the weakest for evil." The world need not fear American expansion; and since the United States possessed a just claim to all of Oregon, Cass concluded, national honor must be vigorously defended against British avarice. "I am among those who mean to march, if we can, to the Russian boundary."[18]

Benton rose the following day to answer Cass. The Missourian again claimed that the Utrecht treaty of 1713 recognized the forty-ninth parallel as the boundary and, since Cass promised to abandon his call for 54°40' if such proved to be the case, the senator from Michigan was "a prisoner . . . in the hands of the Forty-Nines. He is now their prisoner, doomed to dwell at 49. He is not killed, but taken." Benton described Cass's position as "a sad termination—almost ridiculous—of his warlike commencement."[19]

Cass was not in the Senate chamber during Benton's speech, but the pointed reference to being taken prisoner definitely stung, and he responded on April 2. After thanking his faithful Hoosier supporter, Edward Hannegan, for rising to his defense the previous day, Cass stated: "I have come here this morning to free myself. Twice in my life I have been captured by enemies—once fighting against British pretensions in war, and again fighting against British pretensions in peace. My country redeemed me in the former case—I come to redeem myself in the latter." Cass stood by Greenhow's assessment of the Utrecht agreement, and bluntly asked Benton whether he believed the treaty commissioners drew the boundary along the forty-ninth parallel west of the Rocky Mountains. The Missourian sat silently, and Cass then renewed his pledge to battle for America's just claims to 54°40'. Cass was correct regarding Greenhow's research, but he failed to sway Benton, who drifted further toward a compromise settlement. One congressman who was present during this "most exciting and animating debate" concluded that the Michigan senator was "the victor in the fight, and the effort of Benton to paralyze the effort of Cass's speech will be foiled."[20]

Two weeks after the spirited sparring between Cass and Benton, the Senate finally voted on the notice resolution. The original version, passed by the House in early February, was supported by expansionists since it called upon the president to terminate the joint occupancy. Senators seeking compromise backed a moderately worded amendment submitted by Reverdy Johnson, which gave the president discretionary authority regarding a notice. Thus amended, the resolution passed the Senate by a vote of 30 to 24. Fourteen intractable expansionists voted against engrossing the amended resolution, but this parliamentary maneuver was easily blocked. Lewis Cass, in both cases, supported the all-of-Oregon position. The final version passed by Congress, on April 23, authorized the president, "at his discretion," to give notice of the abrogation of joint occupation. Cass again voted with the minority (the tally was 42 to 10) that favored taking a stronger stand.

Passage of the notice resolution gave President Polk added leverage in negotiations with Great Britain. Young Hickory's sights were set on acquiring California from Mexico, and he had never ruled out compromise over the Oregon boundary. Furthermore, he was increasingly concerned that Democratic presidential contenders were playing politics with the controversy. He included Senators Allen and Calhoun in this category and acknowledged, "Gen'l Cass has aspirations but is more prudent than some." The Michigan senator had successfully impressed upon the president his desire "to keep peace and harmony in the party." When the British minister, on June 6, proposed a compromise boundary along the forty-ninth parallel, the president acted decisively before the dispute further eroded party discipline. Polk polled the cabinet and found only Secretary of State Buchanan hesitant about transmitting Pakenham's proposal to the Senate. The president attributed Buchanan's attitude to envy, alluding to the enhancement of Cass's political reputation that resulted from the Oregon debates. Polk also consulted privately with nine leading Democratic senators. Only Allen advised against sending the British offer to the Senate, and only Cass told Polk he would vote against the compromise boundary.[21]

On the afternoon of June 10, President Polk transmitted the British proposal to the Senate and asked for its advice. The following morning, Cass and Dickinson visited the White House and assured Polk that despite opposing the compromise boundary, they believed it was his duty to submit the offer to the Senate. During the ensuing debate, Cass urged his colleagues to seek further concessions, but the proposal was overwhelmingly accepted. In the next few days, Buchanan and Pakenham drafted a formal treaty, which was ratified by a Senate vote of 41 to 14 on June 18, despite pleas by Cass to proceed slowly. All twenty-four Whigs and seventeen Democrats favored the treaty, and fourteen Democrats—only two from slave states—opposed it. Cass, of course, voted with the minority expansionists, although as a good party man, he pledged to acquiesce in the result.

The Michigan senator made certain his views on the Oregon controversy were broadcast to the American electorate. He took the liberty of sending a key Massachusetts supporter one hundred printed copies of his speech, in franked envelopes, for distribution to prominent Democrats and party newspapers. Alfred O. P. Nicholson and Samuel Treat, a Missourian, received similar instructions, and Robert McClelland wrote on Cass's behalf to influential party members in a number of states. A devout expansionist, Cass had not trimmed his sails during the debate to catch the prevailing political breeze, as Buchanan was rightly accused of doing. And unlike William Allen, he gracefully accepted the compromise settlement. Following ratification of the treaty, the Ohio senator angrily quit as chairman of the Foreign Relations Committee and pressed other Democratic members to resign as well. To a man, they refused, and Cass continued to sit on the committee after George McDuffie was selected chairman. The Oregon boundary was thus adjusted peaceably with Great Britain—to the relief of President Polk, and the chagrin of ardent expansionists such as Lewis Cass.[22]

Polk and Cass did agree on another issue tackled by Congress in the spring of 1846. Tariff reduction was a plank in the Democratic platform. The agrarian-based party of Jefferson and Jackson traditionally favored low import taxes on manufactures. In his first annual message, President Polk advocated a revenue tariff (providing only incidental protection to American industry) to replacc the higher Whig duties of 1842. Senator Cass called at the White House that evening and gushed to the president: "You have struck out the true doctrine, you have cut the Gordian Knot." Perhaps, but the administration's tariff bill faced a difficult time in the

Senate. The House version came to a vote in the upper chamber on July 28, and the outcome was in doubt until the roll call was completed. Gideon Welles, observing from the gallery, reported that "Cass and his little troop are as timid as mice on this great question. He knows not what to say, or do, or how to vote, . . . but wishes the whole thing was in purgatory and not out troubling candidates for the Presidency." Welles was writing to Martin Van Buren, so his interpretation of the proceedings was hardly impartial. Cass simply was apprehensive about the close vote; he fully supported the tariff measure, since it was faithful to party ideology and the principles he had espoused during the campaign for the Democratic nomination. The bill passed with a majority of one, as both the recently seated Texas senators voted in favor. Two days later, President Polk signed into law the Walker Tariff. A Democratic campaign pledge was thereby fulfilled in a more satisfactory manner than the "reoccupation of Oregon."[23]

The compromise agreement ending the Oregon dispute disrupted Democratic unity at a critical juncture—the United States and Mexico were at war. Lewis Cass publicly stifled his opposition to the boundary settlement, as promised, but there was no need for the sake of party harmony to repress his feelings regarding the Mexican conflict. Cass became the administration's most martial spokesman in the Senate, advocating an aggressive military policy and the acquisition of Mexican territory.

Relations between the United States and Mexico, prior to the outbreak of hostilities, deteriorated precipitously for a number of reasons. The chief points of contention included the annexation of Texas, with the Rio Grande as its southwestern border; millions of dollars in unpaid, inflated claims by American citizens against the Mexican government; and President Polk's driving desire to obtain California. Since Tyler had begun the formal process of admitting the Lone Star Republic to the Union, Polk turned his attention to the claims impasse. During the Jackson administration, arbitration reduced the claims from over ten million dollars to slightly more than two million, and the Mexicans made several installments on the debt before an empty treasury led to default. The controversy was subsequently complicated by the suspension of diplomatic relations between the two republics after the United States moved to annex Texas. Nonetheless, Polk heavy-handedly attempted to settle the outstanding issues through negotiation. Acting on the advice of William S. Parrott, an erstwhile dentist pressing highly exaggerated claims of

$450,000 on the Mexican government, Polk appointed John Slidell of Louisiana to represent the United States at Mexico City. Slidell was given full diplomatic credentials, although the Mexicans could not accept a minister plenipotentiary without tacitly acquiescing in the annexation of Texas. A succession of Mexican governments refused to receive Slidell, and he prepared to return to Washington in the spring of 1846. President Polk, meanwhile, in separate interviews with Cass, Benton, Allen, and Calhoun, received the concurrence of each senator regarding a secret appropriation to facilitate treaty negotiations.[24]

While pursuing a diplomatic solution to the Mexican problem, Polk took military measures to defend Texas and obtain California. In the spring of 1845, General Zachary Taylor was ordered to proceed from Fort Jesup, Louisiana, with a contingent of regular army troops and occupy a point "on or near the east bank" of the Rio Grande. Texas claimed the Rio Grande as its southwestern border although, as a department of the Mexican Republic, its boundary had been the Nueces River, 150 miles to the north. The Lone Star Republic failed to extend military control over the disputed territory, and Mexico continued to govern the region as part of Tamaulipas. General Taylor subsequently camped on the south bank of the Nueces near Corpus Christi, the westernmost American settlement in Texas. In the months that followed, Taylor was instructed by Secretary of War Marcy to advance as near to the Rio Grande "as prudence will dictate," and to call upon neighboring states for volunteers should Mexican troops cross the river. When word reached Washington of Slidell's first diplomatic rebuff at Mexico City, General Taylor was explicitly ordered to the Rio Grande. By late March, American troops had begun constructing fortifications on the north bank of the river across from the Mexican town of Matamoras. An uneasy truce followed, as Taylor refused to comply with General Pedro de Ampudia's demand that he withdraw beyond the Nueces. Taylor instead ordered a blockade of the Rio Grande, thus cutting Ampudia's supply line. This was an act of war.[25]

Senator Cass closely followed the latest intelligence from Texas. He observed on May 1 that tensions were near the breaking point between the United States and Mexico. "If not actually at war, we are every moment upon the eve of it, & the slightest accident may bring it on." It was Cass's mistaken impression that if an amicable settlement to the Oregon controversy were reached with Britain, war would be averted with Mexico. Elizabeth Cass spent part of that May Day at the White House in an unsuccessful effort to persuade the president to appoint Lewis, Jr., to a diplomatic post. Polk was surprised that "Mrs. C. should have called in person," but he ultimately acceded to her request.[26]

As negotiations proceeded apace with Britain regarding the Oregon controversy, President Polk decided on sterner measures to resolve the Texas stalemate. On May 9, at a regular Saturday meeting of the cabinet, Polk announced the United States "had ample cause of war." Only Secretary of the Navy George Bancroft opposed seeking an immediate declaration of war based upon the claims dispute and the rejection of Slidell. That evening, dispatches arrived from General Taylor notifying the president of a skirmish on April 25 with Mexican cavalry—on the north bank of the Rio Grande—that left eleven Americans dead. Polk reassembled the cabinet, and it was unanimously agreed that a message be sent to Congress on Monday, urging a prompt and vigorous prosecution of the conflict then existing between the United States and Mexico.[27]

President Polk spent much of Sunday drafting a war message to Congress. That evening, he summoned to the White House Senator Allen, of the Foreign Relations Committee, and James McKay, chairman of the House Ways and Means Committee, both of whom approved the president's message. The next morning, Polk sent for Cass and Benton. The Michigan senator called first, and after the message was read he "highly approved it." Cass, too, believed "the cup of forbearance was exhausted" and was fully prepared to lead the fight in the Senate to support the administration's military policy. Benton, who arrived before Cass left the White House, argued against an offensive strategy since he was not persuaded the disputed territory was American. Following these discussions, Polk sent his message to the Congress.[28]

The president succinctly stated: "Mexico has passed the boundary of the United States, has invaded our territory, and shed American blood upon American soil." Whigs readily accepted only the fact that American blood had been shed, but Polk immediately called for "a large and overpowering" military force to bring hostilities "to a speedy and successful termination." After only a few hours of debate, the House passed a bill authorizing the enrollment of fifty thousand volunteers. The president's message received closer scrutiny in the Senate. Allen asserted the nation was at war and called for swift action. Calhoun disagreed, claiming, "There may be invasion without war." Lewis Cass was in no mood to debate a seemingly meaningless distinction between hostilities and war. "One nation can create a state of war," he sensibly noted. Cass ridiculed

Calhoun's suggestion that the president concentrate merely on repelling the invasion. "Can it be said that our troops may chase the Mexicans over the boundary, and then take off their hats and say, 'Good bye, gentlemen, until you come back, when we shall be ready for you again'?" The Michigan senator, who had supported the American military presence in Texas and unquestioningly accepted the Rio Grande boundary, called for an offensive into Mexico, "not to hold the country; but compel her to make such a peace as we have a right to demand." Calhoun then repeated that a state of war did not formally exist until Congress declared it to be so. Cass replied, "Any one nation may go to war, and of necessity, put its antagonist in a state of war." Following this exchange, Crittenden presented the fundamental Whig position. He implied President Polk was solely responsible for the commencement of hostilities, and he pledged support for the defense of the country, while calling for peace at the first opportunity. Soon thereafter, the Senate turned to other matters.[29]

Cass advocated a vigorous prosecution of the war, as the debate over the president's message continued the next day. He rejected the suggestion of Delaware Whig John Clayton (whose son Cass had befriended in Paris) that the Senate deal strictly with the defense of the country and postpone action on a declaration of war. Appalled at such pusillanimity, the Michiganite exhorted his colleagues to carry the fight into the enemy country—meaning beyond the Rio Grande. The country faced a singular opportunity to shape the American character and "destiny for a long series of years." Cass reminded his listeners the United States had "no admirers among the monarchical and aristocratical Governments of the Old World," but if the Mexican attack was met with resolve, the lesson would reverberate around the globe. "We have but one safe course before us," Cass thundered, to "conquer a peace at the point of the bayonet." He advocated marching into the enemy capital: "Let us take possession of the city of Montezuma, and dictate our own conditions." Such a feat of arms certainly would impress the British government, even as negotiations commenced over the Oregon controversy. Cass joined the Senate majority in passing the declaration of war with only two dissenting votes. The House concurred on minor amendments the same day, and President Polk signed the act of war on May 13. Two weeks later, the administration organ, the *Washington Union,* mirrored Cass's aggressive sentiments. "We shall invade her territory; we shall seize her strongholds; we shall even TAKE HER CAPITAL, if there be no other means of bringing her to a sense of justice."[30]

The American military forces were uniformly successful during the brief conflict with Mexico. As news of the outbreak of hostilities was relayed around the country, General Taylor invaded northern Mexico and won decisive victories against numerically superior forces at Palo Alto and Resaca de la Palma. Old Rough and Ready, his ranks swelled with inexperienced and ill-trained volunteers, pushed on to Monterrey in late September and, after fierce house-to-house fighting, forced General Ampudia to seek a negotiated surrender. Taylor's men were exhausted and he agreed to an eight-week truce, allowing the enemy troops to retreat with their arms. President Polk opposed the Monterrey armistice and ordered Taylor to take up a defensive position in northern Mexico. The president also detached some nine thousand veteran troops to bolster the expedition against Mexico City, leaving Taylor with fewer than five thousand men. Polk was influenced by the political enthusiasm for Taylor that greeted these early victories. Although his party affiliation was unclear at this juncture, "Old Zach" was being mentioned as presidential timber—more by Whigs than Democrats—and that was enough to turn Polk against him.

Political partisanship led Polk to seek a congressional bill creating a lieutenant generalship, the highest rank in the army. He planned to appoint Senator Benton to the post and send him to draft a peace treaty with Mexico. If successful, the president would steal some of the Whig's martial thunder as the national election campaign commenced. The vainglorious Missouri senator encouraged the scheme, although the president discerned only lukewarm support within the cabinet. Polk then asked Secretary of War Marcy to explore the subject with Lewis Cass, but was again disappointed. The Michigan senator advised against the bill because Whig opposition would work to the detriment of vital war legislation, and naturally he was not enthusiastic about another western Democrat covering himself in military glory. Cass "would not withhold his assent" if Polk made it a party measure, but he predicted the bill would fail. And so it did: the Senate tabled the proposal in early 1847. Meanwhile, Whig generals continued to win battles.[31]

Relegated to occupation duty and chafing under Polk's criticism of the Monterrey armistice, Zachary Taylor's pride was sorely wounded. But there turned out to be one more triumph for him. General Santa Anna led an army across two hundred miles of desert, in late February, to attack Taylor's force of untested volunteers at Buena Vista. Outnumbered three to one, the Americans were nearly overrun before the tide of battle turned, owing in large measure to the valiant stand of the First Mississippi Rifles, under the command of Colonel Jefferson Davis. Taylor and his chief subordinate, General John Wool, inspired the green troops by exhibiting personal courage under withering fire, and the American forces held the field at day's end. Buena Vista was Taylor's greatest victory. He was granted leave to return home in November, where he received a jubilant welcome. Old Zach's next fight would be for the White House.

General Wool was placed in command of the American occupation forces in northern Mexico, following Taylor's departure. His staff included Major Lewis Cass, Jr., of the Third Michigan Dragoons, commanded by Colonel Andrew T. McReynolds. Lewis was following a family tradition in responding to the call to arms, although (unlike several of his forefathers) Major Cass saw no military action. Rather, he faced tedious garrison duty and was soon at odds with his commanding officer, a courageous soldier but a strict disciplinarian detested by his subordinates. Wool was particularly vituperative toward Captain Irvin McDowell, and Major Cass pleaded with his father to intercede, "in a quiet way," with Adjutant General Roger Jones.[32] Senator Cass received this letter in the late spring of 1848, as the volunteers were being mustered out of service, so no action was necessary.

American military and naval forces in other regions of Mexico proved equally as effective as Taylor's troops. General Stephen Watts Kearny, with the support of Commodores Sloat and Stockton and the ineffectual Captain John Charles Frémont, pacified California. The decisive victories of the war were fought during the drive to Mexico City, commanded by General Winfield Scott—"Old Fuss and Feathers." The capture of the Mexican capital, in September 1847, ended the military phase of the conflict, just as Senator Cass had predicted. President Polk and his fellow Democrats, already apprehensive because the chief military commanders during the war were Whigs, found themselves in a partisan political struggle that threatened the fruits of victory. At issue was the question of slavery extension.[33]

It was apparent from the commencement of hostilities that any indemnity secured from the impoverished Mexican government would take the form of territory. This prospect pleased President Polk, who coveted New Mexico and Upper California, and he found a ready ally in Lewis Cass. On the last day of July 1846, they discussed a two million dollar congressional appropriation designed to induce a Mexican cession. The Michigan expansionist "fully concurred" with the proposal and helped guide the Two

Million bill swiftly through the Senate.[34] The House took up the measure on Saturday, August 8, before the scheduled adjournment of the first session of the Twenty-ninth Congress. Reasoned and deliberate debate was impossible, especially in light of the partisan feelings rubbed raw by the Mexican conflict; many northern Whigs viewed "Mr. Polk's War" as a conspiracy to conquer additional slave territory. It was a sweltering, humid day in Washington, and an already heated debate on the House floor was stoked with the introduction of an amendment by David Wilmot. Employing the language of the Northwest Ordinance, the Pennsylvania Democrat proposed that slavery be prohibited in any territory acquired from Mexico. This "Wilmot Proviso" was adopted by a vote of 83 to 64 and the amended bill sent back to the Senate.

The Senate assembled early Monday morning to clear its calendar and did not consider the Two Million bill until about thirty minutes before the scheduled noon adjournment. Dixon Lewis of Alabama moved to delete the Wilmot amendment and sought an immediate vote, but John Davis, an antislavery Whig from Massachusetts who opposed war, cautioned against the "high degree of steam-pressure" being exerted to push through the appropriation. As Davis continued to hold the floor, the impatient Lewis frequently asked his leave to introduce a resolution postponing adjournment. Davis refused to yield but assured the Alabama Democrat he would conclude in time for a vote on the bill. The Senate clock was not synchronized with that of the lower chamber, however, and Lewis laconically interrupted a final time to declare the House had adjourned. The Senate soon did the same, without voting on the Wilmot Proviso.[35]

As a result of Davis's possibly inadvertent filibuster, it was not necessary for Lewis Cass to take a public stand on the proviso. Nonetheless, eventually it became clear he would have voted in favor of the Two Million bill with the Wilmot amendment. George Rathbun, a Democratic congressman from New York, shared a railroad car with Cass between Washington and Baltimore shortly after Congress adjourned and later recalled they "spoke freely and with a good deal of energy on the subject of the 'Proviso.'" Cass revealed that every Democratic senator from the free states was prepared to support the amended bill, and "he regretted very much" not receiving the opportunity to vote on it. During the ensuing presidential campaign, Cass acknowledged he opposed the Wilmot Proviso from its inception but would have voted for the Two Million bill with it attached rather than have the appropriation fail. He noted the amendment "provoked almost no discussion and the excited feelings of the South since developed had not then been made known." In a Senate speech delivered in 1850, Cass publicly confirmed that when the proviso was introduced, "had it been pushed to a vote, I should have voted for it." He simply did not yet appreciate the groundswell of opposition to slavery restriction emerging in the South.[36]

The Wilmot Proviso brought out the political opportunist in Lewis Cass. By the time Congress reassembled in December, he was adamantly—and publicly—opposed to the "mischievous & foolish" amendment. Cass clearly bowed to growing southern opposition, but he also was aware the proviso jeopardized the acquisition of any Mexican territory. With two other members of the Foreign Relations Committee, the Michigan senator met at the White House, on December 23, to plot legislative strategy. Ambrose Sevier of Arkansas and Charles Atherton of New Hampshire joined Cass in accepting the president's assessment that no Mexican government could negotiate a peace treaty unless adequate funds were available to placate the army. The senators pledged to support another appropriation bill, unencumbered by a Wilmot amendment. There were political risks involved for Cass and Atherton, who "would be in great peril with their constituents" if they voted against the proviso, but they agreed to consult with other northern Democrats in an effort "to stand together & vote against the restriction." That was the plan; following this conference, a three million dollar appropriation bill was introduced in Congress.[37]

The political battle line was formed in the Senate with the introduction, in early February, of amendments to the Three Million bill. John Berrien, a Georgia Whig, drew a warm response from Lewis Cass when he declared the American government should not prolong the Mexican War, "with any view to the dismemberment of that republic, or to the acquisition by conquest of any portion of her territory." The Michigan senator instead proposed that the United States "vigorously" prosecute the war and seek "a reasonable indemnity . . . from Mexico for the wrongs she has committed." Cass blamed the Wilmot Proviso for southern opposition to the acquisition of Mexican territory. Privately, he referred to the explosive issue of slavery expansion as "a firebrand thrown among us which threatens the most disastrous results to the [Democratic] party." This was an astute characterization. Cass considered the proviso to be an inexpedient abstraction which "would conclude nothing," if passed, since the subject of slavery expansion would remain open to legislative wrangling. He pragmatically argued there would be time enough to face the issue after the war was brought to a successful termination and the territorial indemnity secured. Until then, discussion of the subject served no other purpose than to increase divisions among Democrats. Cass predicted the proviso could not pass the Senate, because its sectional nature spelled "death to the war—death to all hopes of getting an acre of territory, death to the administration, and death to the Democratic party."[38]

Lewis Cass took the Senate floor on February 10 and delivered a major oration on the Mexican conflict. He had become disheartened by the incessant political attacks against the administration's war effort. Whigs continued to blame the president for instigating hostilities, and opposition to the acquisition of Mexican territory was solidifying among antislavery northerners and southerners leery of the Wilmot Proviso or the annexation of a racially mixed foreign population. The previous day, Calhoun proposed establishing a fortified defense line until a peace treaty was concluded, again arguing that a prolonged war could not be waged "without great sacrifice and injurious effects to our institutions." In his far-ranging speech, Cass addressed such concerns.

The Michigan senator began by tracing the causes of the war to Mexican "injustice." The United States therefore was entitled to "a reasonable indemnity, either pecuniary or territorial, or both, for the injuries we have sustained," and to guarantee Mexican compliance, American military forces must remain on the offensive and Congress pass the Three Million bill. Cass dismissed Calhoun's defensive strategy as impractical, because of the lack of natural barriers along the frontier; furthermore, it would not compel the Mexicans to reach a peace settlement or cede territory. Cass also deplored the South Carolinian's contention that a costly conflict threatened the stability of the republic. On the contrary, the democratic government instituted by the Founding Fathers "has survived many a shock, and it will survive many more." He likened the Constitution to a "cliff of eternal granite, which overlooks the ocean, and drives back the ceaseless waves that assail its base." The simple answer to complex sectional problems, such as the expansion of slavery, was to "cling to this Constitution, as the mariner clings to the last plank, when night and the tempest close around him." Calhoun, clearly, had struck a chord. Cass's love for the constitutional Union was palpable. "In these great questions of national bearing, I acknowledge no geographical claims. What is best for the United States is best for me." And that plainly included territorial expansion.

Cass was a moderate politician, but his vision of America's mission and his defense of national honor knew no bounds. The United States, by extending across the North American continent, would avoid the governmental and social evils that plagued densely populated European nations. "We want almost unlimited power of expansion," Cass cried. "That is our safety valve." He conceded Calhoun had made some particularly "sound observations respecting the diversity of character, of races, and of institutions" between the United States and Mexico, and he smugly rejected any "amalgamation" with the Mexican people. "All we want is a portion of territory, which they nominally hold, generally uninhabited, or . . . sparsely so, and with a population which would soon recede, or identify itself with ours." The benefits from the conflict were not limited to land acquisition. The military victories and noble sacrifices of the American soldier "redeemed" the country's reputation in the eyes of the world. Cass mourned "the loss of life—of much precious life," but "wherever our banner is borne, by land or by sea, it will be pointed to, as the national emblem of a people, who have done those deeds, which give character now, and security henceafter."[39]

The bellicose expansionism embodied by Lewis Cass was denounced both within and without the Senate chamber. Ohio Whig senator Thomas Corwin, in a speech that strengthened his standing in the antislavery movement, chided Cass for ignoring the danger to the Union presented by the war. "To his serene, and as I fear too apathetic mind, all is calm. . . . The ship of State seems to him to expand her sails under a clear sky, and move on, with prosperous gales, upon a smooth sea." In words that outraged many of his listeners, Corwin scathingly denounced Cass's claim that the United States must expand to provide for its citizens. "The Senator from Michigan says we will be two hundred million in a few years, and we want room. If I were a Mexican I would tell you, 'Have you not room in your own country to bury your dead men? If you come into mine, we will greet you with bloody hands, and welcome you to hospitable graves.'" While refraining from such sanguinary prose, the *New York Tribune* reported that Cass's speech "demonstrated his intention . . . of marching to the Presidency, with flags flying, amid the clangor of trumpets, the rolls of drums, and all the pomp and circumstance of *glorious* war." Clearly, Cass failed to sway the opinions of those opposed to an aggressive war policy and the annexation of Mexican territory.[40]

The debate in the Senate on the Three Million bill culminated on March 1. After ascertaining a lack of support, Cass withdrew his amendment and voted with the 29 to 24 majority against Berrien's resolution rejecting a territorial indemnity. The Senate then turned to consideration of a Wilmot amendment proposed by William Upham, a Vermont Whig. Cass again spoke against such premature restrictions: "It will be quite in season to provide for the government of territory, not yet acquired from foreign countries, after we shall have obtained it." The introduction of the proviso restriction served solely to exacerbate sectional feeling, and "of all the questions, that can agitate us, those which are merely sectional in their character, are the most dangerous, and the most to be deprecated." He joined in defeating the Upham amendment by a vote of 31 to 21. As the evening session continued into the early morning hours, the Three Million bill was passed and the Senate ended its long day.[41]

Passage of the bill temporarily quieted the slavery expansion debate, much to Cass's relief. In the months following the introduction of the proviso, he had demonstrated an unstatesmanlike approach to the question. He was prepared to support the Wilmot amendment in August 1846, but his paramount concern was the acquisition of Mexican territory. When it became clear the proviso threatened the war effort and Democratic harmony, Cass opposed it for those practical reasons. Political principle was not an overriding motivation. He likewise supported passage of an unencumbered Three Million bill. There was, by the spring of 1847, no ideological underpinning to his position regarding slavery expansion; that would come in his famous letter to Alfred O. P. Nicholson, dated December 24.

The Wilmot Proviso marked an important milestone in Cass's political career. He had faithfully represented the political sentiments of the Old Northwest for more than forty years, but for the remainder of his public life, an ever-widening gulf separated him from his constituents on the subject of slavery. As expected, Senator Woodbridge and his fellow Whigs supported the Wilmot amendment. More significantly, the Michigan congressional delegation—all Democrats—twice during this session split two to one in favor of the proviso. And on the same day the Senate defeated the Upham amendment, Cass dutifully presented resolutions from the Michigan legislature "in favor of extending the provisions of the ordinance of 1787 over any territory which may be acquired by the United States." Within a few months, the *Charleston Mercury* complained that ten states had passed Wilmot resolutions.[42]

Northern Democratic senators who voted against the proviso came under heavy political assault. Detroit's Whig newspaper zeroed in on its favorite target: "There stands GEN. CASS, as we predicted, allied with every slave holder in the Senate save one, in favor of an unlimited extension of slave territory!" The *Advertiser* identified Cass and the four other northern opponents of the Wilmot restriction as "the doughfaces,—worthy compeers on the black list." (Senators Breese, Bright, Dickinson, and Hannegan stood with Cass against the Upham amendment; Atherton did not.) The *New York Tribune* singled out Cass for his speech of March 1. "He denounced the Wilmot Proviso as an abstraction," noted the reporter before pointedly adding, "Calhoun says the Constitution is an abstraction." The article wittily assailed Cass's logic that the proviso debate was premature since senators "should not legislate for the Future." The reporter agreed, "They certainly cannot legislate for the Past, and while they legislate the Present escapes them. If the Future is also to be excluded, for what time will the senator prescribe? The rhetorical Senator confounds more than time in some of his apothegms." Convoluted reasoning aside, the *Tribune* correspondent predicted political disaster: "I never knew a man to destroy his *future* more easily or rapidly than Gen. Cass in this speech. He will be abandoned by the North, whom he deserts, and despised by the South, to whom he succumbs."[43]

Attacked by northerners opposed to the annexation of additional slave territory, Cass never wavered. He was as staunchly in favor of extending the southern and western boundaries of the United States as he had been in acquiring Oregon. Anglophobia again played a role. Cass believed that unless the United States annexed the entire Southwest, it would come under the sway of Great Britain. It did not matter to Cass whether the territory would be slave or free; he was concerned only that the American flag—not the British—fly over the region.

Cass was not only a zealous expansionist, he was also an astute politician. He realized he had underestimated the emotional impact the slavery controversy generated in the North, among Democrats and Whigs alike. The issue additionally presented Cass, as a presidential contender, with an immediate political problem. It was no longer feasible to dismiss the Wilmot amendment as a mere abstraction impeding the acquisition of Mexican territory. By the autumn of 1847, Cass accepted the southern view that the proviso principle was unconstitutional—although he was less than candid as to when he reached that conclusion. Jefferson Davis was pleased to report: "Cass is heartily with us, and says he always was but saw the necessity last spring of caution, lest the fire which would go out if let alone should be kindled by attempting to extinguish it too suddenly."[44] Several weeks later, with the publication of his Nicholson letter in the *Washington Daily Union,* Cass broadcast to the American electorate his opposition to the proviso.

Lewis Cass took a public position on slavery extension only after long conversations with influential Democratic politicians, including Stephen Douglas and Jefferson Davis. As late as December 12, he tried to dodge the issue with the explanation that his name was before the people as a candidate for the presidential nomination. He was, however, "entirely opposed to the Wilmot proviso, in whatever form it may present itself," and believed "the question of slavery should be left to the people" of the territories, not Congress. These principles were not original to Cass. Both supporters and opponents of the Wilmot Proviso had argued that only territorial residents could properly decide the slavery question. Congressmen Caleb Blood Smith of Indiana and Shelton Leake, a Virginian, disagreed over the efficacy of the proviso, but each spoke during the early months of 1847 in favor of allowing westerners to decide the issue. Vice President Dallas expressed the same opinion at Pittsburgh on September 18, and three months later, Senator Dickinson presented resolutions supporting territorial self-determination regarding slavery. While Lewis Cass certainly did not formulate the concept of "popular sovereignty," he provided its ideological framework that December when he wrote to Nicholson, his ardent Tennessee supporter.[45]

The Nicholson letter was a clever piece of work. It secured for Cass the Democratic presidential nomination, as well as the sobriquet "Father of Popular Sovereignty." The Michigan senator began by reiterating his call for a territorial indemnity from Mexico, then turned to the question of whether slavery should be permitted in the region. In an effort to explain his turnabout on the Wilmot Proviso, Cass claimed that "a great change has been going on in the public mind upon this subject—in my own as well as others." After emphasizing his opposition to congressional restrictions, Cass asserted that federal authority over the territories "should be limited to the creation of proper governments," leaving to residents the right "to regulate their internal concerns in their own way." Thus, the doctrine of popular sovereignty was predicated upon the principle of self-government and Cass's interpretation of the Constitution. He chose to ignore the legislative precedents of 1787 and 1820, in this regard. After all, it was the Confederation Congress that passed the Northwest Ordinance, and the

Missouri Compromise line was not based upon a literal construction of the Constitution. Simply put, Cass believed the federal government did not possess the authority to interfere with slavery in either states or territories. True, the Constitution granted Congress the power "to dispose of and make all needful rules and regulations, respecting the territory and other property belonging to the United States," but the phrase referred to "territory" solely in the sense of "property"—not as a governmental entity. Cass embraced this narrow constitutional interpretation, which echoed the arguments of southern spokesmen, in an earnest effort to quiet disunionist sentiment. He was not vexed that the price paid to secure sectional harmony was black bondage. Cass viewed Negroes as inferior to whites and portrayed the southern slave system as a benevolent institution. The concept of popular sovereignty recognized whites as having the right to seek self-government; blacks—slave or free—were politically beyond the pale.

Cass favored treating slavery as a local matter, thereby removing the divisive issue from the halls of Congress. In this sense, the doctrine of popular sovereignty was a call for nonaction by the federal government. Cass reasoned that since the people of a territory were as capable as those of a state, it was the height of irresponsibility to raise the slavery question during the relatively brief territorial period. Popular sovereignty was not designed as a smoke screen behind which slavery would be insinuated into any Mexican cession. Cass was an early advocate of the theory that slavery had reached its "natural limits." California and New Mexico were "agricultural regions, similar in their products to our middle States, and generally unfit for the production of the great staples, which can alone render slave labor valuable." He also pointed out that Mexico had abolished the institution of slavery, so the region would remain free, in accordance with "the feelings of the inhabitants and the laws of nature." Cass buttressed his arguments with corroborating statements from James Buchanan and Robert J. Walker. (Ironically, these three Democrats would become involved in a bitter political struggle over the slavery issue in Kansas.) The concluding sentence of the Nicholson letter summarized his position: "Leave to the people, who will be affected by this question, to adjust it upon their own responsibility, and in their own manner, and we shall render another tribute to the original principles of our Government, and furnish another guarantee for its permanence and prosperity." Cass characteristically attempted to steer a middle course regarding slavery in the western territories—an issue destined to play a prominent part in the presidential campaign of 1848.[46]

The position Cass took on the subject of slavery expansion was construed by his political opponents as a cynical attempt to broaden his support among the American electorate. Although the political expediency of the Nicholson letter cannot be ignored, the popular sovereignty doctrine was perfectly consistent with Cass's principles. He was, above all else, a true democrat who firmly believed in local self-government. Cass reasoned that since the federal government was not specifically empowered to deal with this explosive issue, it was best left to the people. The Michigan senator was willing to compromise on slavery expansion because he refused to view it as a moral question; to Cass, it was strictly a constitutional problem. While he paid lip service to the idea that bondage was evil, he considered sectional agitation of the controversy to be a greater danger to the Union than the continued existence of slavery. Popular sovereignty, in summary, was a blending of the ideals of self-government, democracy, federalism, and the national Union—principles to which Lewis Cass was utterly devoted. He presented the doctrine to quiet the debate over the Wilmot Proviso and, of course, to further his presidential ambitions. He had no inkling its eventual implementation in Kansas would exacerbate sectional tensions.

As the new year dawned, Senator Cass refocused his attention on the Mexican War. Although political opponents attacked the Nicholson letter as politically self-serving, no such interpretation could be placed on his continued support of an aggressive war policy and territorial indemnity from Mexico. In fact, Cass alienated important segments of the electorate with his bellicose stance. When the Thirtieth Congress convened in December 1847, the Michigan senator gave up his seat on the Foreign Relations Committee to accept the chairmanship of the Committee on Military Affairs. Even though American troops occupied the enemy capital, no peace treaty had been signed, despite the efforts of Nicholas P. Trist, the chief clerk of the State Department sent by Polk to negotiate with Mexican officials. The president grew so impatient with the lack of progress, he ordered Trist recalled and decided to replace General Scott with William O. Butler, one of the few high-ranking Democrats in the regular army. Under these circumstances, Cass reported separate bills to enlist ten thousand regulars and twice that number of volunteers. He contended the thirty additional regiments were needed to garrison conquered territory and to convince the Mexican people, "by the exhibition of our overwhelming force, that resistance was out of the question." He also announced that preventing "the American people from taking possession of

Mexico, if they demand it, would be as futile in effect as to undertake to stop the rushing of the cataract of Niagara."[47]

As the Mexican War dragged on, Cass escalated his demands for territorial cessions. In the spring of 1847, another aspirant for the Democratic presidential nomination, Secretary of State Buchanan, reported that Cass was reluctant to acquire any territory south of the Missouri Compromise line because of the difficulty in governing the indigenous "mongrel race." Nevertheless, a year later, Cass indicated "the rich mineral region of Zacatecas and San Luis [Potosi] must be taken and held," in addition to the conquered regions of California and New Mexico. Once again, he refrained from explicitly calling for the annexation of all of Mexico, but these remarks led many to conclude that such were his intentions. On January 10, 1848, the *Congressional Globe* recorded a revealing exchange in the Senate chamber:

> Mr. Cass. I hope that the Executive will say, in so many words, that its object is, in any circumstance, to conquer Mexico.
> Mr. Mangum (in his seat). To conquer Mexico?
> Mr. Cass. I repeat, to conquer Mexico.
> Several Senators. The whole?
> Mr. Cass. The whole, but not to hold it all.[48]

Cass's statement naturally caused quite a stir. John Niles, a Van Buren Democrat from Connecticut shifting toward the free soil position, wrote: "The real or ultimate shame of the administration & the partisans of Cass, are daily becoming more apparent. . . . Their object is the conquest of Mexico & its annexation to the United States." While conceding that the Michigan senator added he was not for annexing "*all* of Mexico," Niles pointed out that several of his supporters had already gone that far. Edward Hannegan, for example, introduced a resolution declaring it was "within the constitutional capacity of this Government . . . to hold Mexico as a territorial appendage." Alexander Stephens was convinced "the War party, [with] Cass at their head in the Senate, was ready to swallow all Mexico, and really intended to do it."[49]

The arrival in Washington of a peace treaty temporarily ended the debate. Trist had ignored the president's recall order and signed an agreement with Mexican representatives at Guadalupe Hidalgo on February 2, 1848. The pact recognized the Rio Grande as the boundary of Texas and ceded Upper California and New Mexico to the United States, in return for fifteen million dollars and the assumption by the federal government of the claims owed Americans. President Polk was uncertain whether to submit the treaty for Senate ratification; it contained only the minimal territorial indemnity he authorized Trist to accept before the fall of Mexico City. Polk, in fact, portentously had sought the opinions of Senators Sevier and Cass regarding Trist's "most reprehensible conduct" in defying his recall, and they agreed that if he returned with a treaty "it would present a question of great responsibility and embarrassment." Sevier leaned toward submitting any peace agreement for Senate ratification, while Cass, perhaps wary of having been abandoned by the president on the Oregon boundary, stated, "it would be time enough to decide that question, if such a Treaty was made." Polk's cabinet split on the issue as well. Despite personal misgivings and divided counsel, once the Treaty of Guadalupe Hidalgo arrived at the White House, Polk sent it to the Senate. The president preferred a larger cession, but he was convinced the Whigs and a few disaffected Democrats would block additional men and money to continue the war. Lewis Cass voted with the 38 to 14 majority in favor of the treaty on March 10, and President Polk proclaimed the peace to the American people on the Fourth of July.[50]

The war was formally ended, but expansionists such as Cass already were urging American involvement in yet another region of Mexico. Yucatan had declared its independence from the central government in 1842. The region remained neutral at the outbreak of hostilities between the United States and Mexico, but the peace was shattered when local Indians rose against the whites. In November 1847, Yucatan leaders appealed to the United States for aid in quelling the natives. Their emissary, Justo Sierra, was received in Washington, but further action was postponed for several months. By late April, Sierra agreed to transfer the "dominion and sovereignty" of the peninsula to the United States if military assistance was granted, and Polk sent a message to Congress supporting a favorable response. Expansionists responded with a bill authorizing the president "to take temporary military occupation of Yucatan."[51]

Lewis Cass, on May 4, called for quick action on the Yucatan resolution, labeling it "a case of crying necessity." In his eyes, the conflict was "a war of races," in which the United States was "called on by humanity . . . to prevent the entire extermination of the white race" from the peninsula. Cass additionally based his plea on another familiar motivation: Anglophobia. The Yucatan government had also appealed for assistance to Britain and Spain, and Cass reported British artillery units were already in the southern portion of the country. When Britain "lays the lion's paw on Yucatan, it will be difficult to displace it," he ominously warned. Echoing sentiments expressed by southern senators seeking control over the Gulf of Mexico, Cass argued: "While Cuba and Yucatan are held by feeble Powers, having no ambition to interfere with our commercial interests, there is no danger. But let these places fall into the hands of a Power like England, and the danger will be evident." The Michigan senator proclaimed that the gulf "should be American," and he broadened the scope of the debate by recommending Spain be warned that "the United States would not see Cuba transferred to any other Power." Before congressional action was taken on the Yucatan bill, however, the Mexican government managed to settle its difficulties with the rebellious province.[52]

Cass seized upon the situation in Yucatan to insist the United States extend its boundaries whenever circumstances permitted. He once more demonstrated it made no difference to him whether the expansion take place to the south, north, or west, or whether the acquisitions be free or slave. It mattered only that they become part of the United States and thus be saved from European—especially British—interference. Cass rejoiced at the vast Mexican cession to the United States, and he was disappointed the Yucatan controversy was settled before annexation of the peninsula. Nonetheless, he had no time to brood over the lost opportunity. Following official notification from the Democratic national convention that he had been nominated for the presidency, Cass resigned from the Senate on May 29. His long years of service to the party were rewarded, and the political prize which he vainly sought in 1844 was now within his grasp.

Chapter Seven

Democratic Presidential Candidate (1848): "A Statesman Renowned for His Patience, Wisdom, and Energy"

James K. Polk pledged himself to a single term of office during the election campaign of 1844, and soon after his inauguration political maneuvering began among his potential successors. Lewis Cass shrewdly attempted to discourage the use of his name as a candidate for the presidential nomination during the early years of Polk's administration. The Michigan senator was keenly aware the Democrats were "broken into two fractions, and under the names of 'barn burners' and 'old hunkers,' . . . a great deal of ill feeling has been generated." The Barnburners, with a nucleus of antibank Van Burenites, increasingly advocated a more "radical," free-soil position regarding slavery extension, while the Hunkers, continuing to stake out the middle ground, were content to compromise with Southern defenders of the peculiar institution. The party division was especially acute in the pivotal states of New York and Ohio, and under such circumstances it was "better to give time for the councils of moderation to be heard." His political instincts and personality equally dictated "a prudent course," and Cass proposed "to sit still and wait the developments of public opinion, rather than seek to guide them," because if he advocated a position taken by one wing of the party, the other was "sure to oppose him." In truth, complained a dismayed President Polk more than a year before the national convention met at Baltimore, "faction rules the hour, while principle & patriotism is forgotten." Cass did acknowledge that "if the Democratic Party select me as their candidate I shall submit to their decision." Such was his public stance; privately, he labored mightily to attain the nomination.[1]

Cass's political appeal was widespread, but certainly not on the basis of his personal appearance or campaign style. By the time of the national election, he was sixty-six years old, and his formerly husky body had long since become obese. An uncomplimentary newspaper report described "the rotundity and extent of the parts surrounded by the General's waistband," and continued, "It is hard to tell whether he swallowed his meals or his meals him." Another Whig organ reprinted a disparaging article declaring that his face "denotes neither intellect, nor any other high quality; it is a stolid unmeaning countenance." The correspondent concluded by observing that "his frame is neither graceful, nor well formed; he is stoutly made, and has a very undue amount of those physical endowments which are considered prerequisite in an Alderman." A reddish wig that tended to meander over his pate, and prominent facial warts and moles, added to Cass's less-than-distinguished appearance. Furthermore, he was a teetotaler (something of a rarity among western politicians) not noted for his wit or sparkling conversation. Cass was neither a convivial dinner companion nor a stirring stump orator; he simply did not command political allegiance because of compelling personal qualities.[2]

Cass's shortcomings as a political campaigner were amply counterbalanced by his extensive record of public service and administrative experience. He had ably governed Michigan Territory for eighteen years and enjoyed the support of many younger politicians from the Old Northwest. His vocal opposition to British territorial pretensions—climaxed by his role in the Oregon debates—and his unfaltering support of the Mexican War strengthened his political base. One Whig newspaper conceded, in early 1848, that his "action against the Oregon Treaty now tells in his favor. . . . The West pours in for him." Cass was, in brief, the elder statesman among Northwest Democrats, and his appeal transcended sectional boundaries. The leadership he demonstrated in the Senate as an administration spokesman impressed party regulars. The president acknowledged, "Gen'l C[ass] has given to my administration an honest and hearty support, and if he is the nominee I will support him with great pleasure." Polk's attitude was echoed by the administration organ, the *Washington Union.* Cass's generally moderate stance on national issues also served to make him an acceptable candidate.[3]

To secure the presidential nomination, Lewis Cass needed to conciliate the differences among Democrats on the explosive issue of slavery extension. The extreme northern position was embodied in the Wilmot Proviso, which proscribed slavery in any territory ceded by Mexico. The uncompromising southern view, presented by Senator Calhoun in February 1847, was that all citizens must be allowed to emigrate "with their property," slaves included, into any American territory. It soon became apparent Democrats would alienate many of the rank and file should either of these radical positions be accepted as party doctrine.[4]

The leading candidates for the Democratic presidential nomination scrambled to present a suitable compromise to the problem. In a letter published in August 1847, Secretary of State Buchanan advocated extending the Missouri Compromise line over any territory ceded by Mexico, a position subsequently embraced by President Polk and Stephen Douglas. Vice President George M. Dallas, Buchanan's chief political rival in Pennsylvania, naturally took a different tack. Speaking at Pittsburgh in September, Dallas proposed allowing territorial residents to settle the slavery question for themselves. Before the year ended, however, publication of the Nicholson letter appropriated for Lewis Cass the popular sovereignty doctrine.[5]

As formulated by Cass, popular sovereignty adroitly offered both extreme factions of the Democratic party the opportunity to unite on the convulsive issue of slavery in the territories. Advocates and opponents of slavery expansion could pursue their separate goals and still agree that Congress had no authority regarding the matter. In fact, Supreme Court Justice John McLean argued in the *National Intelligencer* that the Constitution granted no specific powers to Congress regarding the establishment of territorial governments, with the sole exception of the District of Columbia.[6] Cass, accepting this reasoning, endeavored to broaden the appeal of popular sovereignty with the Nicholson letter, dated two days after the appearance of McLean's article. The Michigan senator did not specify *when* the people of a territory could decide the question of slavery, or whether such a decision would be binding throughout the territorial stage of government. Southerners were free to conclude residents could not prohibit slavery until they drafted a state constitution and entered the Union. Northerners, in contrast, were left with the hope that climatic conditions and a rapid influx of free soil residents would combine to prevent the spread of slavery into the western territories. Again, it may be emphasized, Cass was willing to compromise on the subject of slavery extension because he viewed it as a constitutional—not a moral—problem. Popular sovereignty was a formula for party harmony, and with the Nicholson letter, Lewis Cass staked out a moderate position on the major political issue of 1848.

The doctrine of popular sovereignty deftly was left ambiguous by Lewis Cass. One confused Florida delegate to the Democratic national convention inquired whether territorial residents, "*before* they form a State Government, have a right to establish or prohibit slavery." Cass chose to ignore this specific question and referred the Floridian to the Nicholson letter—the very document he had been asked to clarify. Popular sovereignty was a flexible policy, its creator hoped, behind which the Democrats could rally in an effort to encourage party unity and territorial expansion. Undeniably, it was designed to further purely partisan aims and win for Cass the presidential nomination. It was a politically astute position to adopt as the campaign of 1848 commenced. What Cass did not foresee was that its implementation ultimately exacerbated sectional tensions—and thus undermined party harmony—by focusing attention on the issue of slavery during the volatile period of territorial government.[7]

The popular sovereignty precept espoused by Lewis Cass completely satisfied neither extreme faction of the Democratic party, thereby demonstrating it was a true compromise. Southern criticism was led by the *Charleston Mercury*, which warned that while Cass had rejected the Wilmot Proviso, he nonetheless indicated the western territories would remain free unless the inhabitants specifically endorsed slavery. Hence, Cass's doctrine was "infinitely worse" than Wilmot's: "It is calculated to mislead, to betray. If not understood and exposed, it will be a trap into which the South will fall."[8] Some southerners who favored the unrestricted extension of slavery obviously viewed popular sovereignty as a threat to their institutions.

Most opposition to the Cass doctrine was centered in the free states. Northerners who resisted the spread of slavery considered the Nicholson letter to be little more than a blatant attempt to placate the South in order to capture the presidential nomination. The *St. Lawrence Republican*, a New York newspaper loyal to Van Buren, labeled Cass "the most truckling, subservient and unprincipled of all the dough-faces." The *Buffalo Republican* similarly blasted the Michigan senator as a man seduced by blind ambition to "abandon the cause of freedom." An editorial by Walt Whitman in the *Brooklyn Eagle* avoided such abusive language, but Whitman disagreed with Cass's contention that Congress lacked the authority to prohibit slavery in the territories. This was the thrust of the debate among Michigan Democrats as well; they feared an impotent federal government in the face of southern demands that slavery be protected in the West. One Wayne County politician acknowledged the Nicholson letter "caused some fluttering," and "were the Genl. not a resident here, an attempt would be made to organize a head against him." A Michigan Whig recorded that Cass's views were "novel and not universally concurred in here," but the Democrats quickly rallied. James B. Hunt, who voted for the Wilmot amendment in the House of Representatives, predicted the state convention would "nominate Genl. Cass & slip round the proviso some way." The Michigan treasurer captured the feelings of most Democrats when he philosophically asserted that the "present disturbances" over popular sovereignty represented "the necessary fermentation" in the political process that "will result in harmony." This proved to be the case, although James Buchanan crowed that the "foolish & uncalled for" Nicholson letter further alienated Cass from "his deadly foes, northern antislavery men."[9]

Those who vigorously opposed popular sovereignty constituted a national minority among Democrats. It was indicative of the general support given the Cass doctrine that two days after Whitman's editorial appeared, the *Eagle* approvingly printed long extracts from the Nicholson letter. The *Albany Argus* insisted Cass's reasoning was "impregnable," and a New Haven editor declared "at least nine-tenths of the Democracy of New England" accepted his position. The *Detroit Free Press* neatly concluded that "all the old, sound democratic papers of the Union, most cordially approve of the Patriotic letter." Southerners joined in the chorus of praise, and a member of the Georgia legislature confessed, "Much if not all of the doubt and suspicion that before rested upon my mind relative to his soundness on the 'Wilmot Proviso' has been removed." The *Tallahassee Floridian* echoed most southern Democratic newspapers with its hearty endorsement: "He takes the ground, which is the true one, that the power to regulate the internal and domestic institutions of Territories and States belongs to the people thereof, and not to the Congress." The *Richmond Enquirer* referred to the Nicholson letter as a "noble and patriot paper," and the *Washington Union* commended "the just views and the unanswerable reasoning of Gen. Cass upon this point." The political appeal of the Cass doctrine knew no geographical bounds.[10]

The Nicholson letter admirably fulfilled its purpose. Popular sovereignty was politically acceptable to most Democrats not affiliated with the Van Buren or Calhoun factions, and both northerners and southerners could interpret the doctrine to suit their separate purposes. Coupled with Cass's refusal to view the issue of slavery as a moral question, this ambiguity added to his attractiveness as a national candidate. Popular sovereignty demonstrated the Michigan senator's "availability," to all factions of the Democratic party, and helped him capture the presidential nomination.

The Cass political machine was put into operation shortly before publication of the Nicholson letter. The Michigan Democrat inspired loyalty, and his followers threw themselves zealously into the campaign for the presidential nomination. Correspondents were pressed into action to broadcast the Cass message at the local and state levels of the party, where the battle for delegates would be lost or won. The most effective of these regional lieutenants included Aaron Hobart and Daniel Dickinson in the Northeast, Michigan congressman Robert McClelland and Senator Alpheus Felch in Washington, Andrew Stevenson of Virginia, David Disney at Cincinnati, and Alfred Nicholson of Tennessee. Henry Rowe Schoolcraft set to work on a campaign biography. These diligent efforts were rewarded. Democratic newspapers began hoisting Cass's name, and state and local party gatherings in Missouri and Tennessee nominated the Michigan senator for the White House. Cass was elated that Democrats from President Polk's congressional district supported him, and just before the end of 1847, he wrote from Washington there was not "a man here, who dreams of the election of Mr. Van Buren." In short, "Things could not look better . . . especially in the South."[11]

As the time approached to select delegates for the Baltimore convention, Cass's political stock was rising. Several other potential contenders no longer appeared to be in the hunt for the nomination. Calhoun, who had claimed in July 1847 that his position was "the most eligible of all the publick men of our country," weakened his national appeal by opposing the Mexican War, and his break with the Polk administration and fierce proslavery image diluted his support among party regulars. The sudden death of Silas Wright, in August, brought a shockingly final halt to the candidacy of another leading Democrat. A New Yorker, Wright had been groomed by Van Buren as his political heir, and party members who advocated the Wilmot Proviso thus lost their chief national spokesman. The aspirations of Vice President Dallas received a severe setback when Cass emerged as the Father of Popular Sovereignty.[12]

By early 1848, the leading contenders for the Democratic nomination were Lewis Cass, James Buchanan, and Levi Woodbury. Buchanan's proposal to extend the Missouri Compromise line to the Pacific gained him support in several upper slave states and Louisiana but hurt him among Pennsylvania Democrats. The secretary of state ultimately carried his home-state delegation to the national convention, although resolutions were passed supporting popular sovereignty and complimenting "Gen. Lewis Cass as a great and glorious man." According to one observer, "the declaration of Gen. Cass as the *second choice* of Pennsylvania, is virtually looked upon as the nomination of Gen. Cass by that State. What lady in giving her hand to a gentleman, ever made a declaration as to whom she would marry if she were left a widow?" Dallas conceded defeat, henceforth serving as a stalking-horse for the Cass forces in the Keystone State. Buchanan stewed over his Michigan rival's growing strength but remained hopeful he would triumph at Baltimore on the second or third ballot.[13]

Levi Woodbury, recently appointed by Polk to the Supreme Court, was perceived as a "northern man with southern principles." One North Carolina newspaper flatly declared he was "the choice of the SOUTH," notably the Deep South. As part of a concerted political strategy, Justice Woodbury remained silent on the issue of slavery extension, and his supporters scrambled to further his cause prior to the Baltimore convention.[14]

With Buchanan and Woodbury demonstrating political strength in the Northeast and Southeast, Cass sought to maintain a following among conservatives in those regions, while consolidating control of his power base in the West. The expansionism of Lewis Cass was embraced by disappointed 54°40' men, and the doctrine of popular sovereignty, although rankling to "provisoists," was generally endorsed by westerners as a viable compromise to the slavery extension controversy. Ohio was the key state in the Northwest. In the previous campaign for the nomination, Ohioans had staunchly backed Martin Van Buren; but as Samuel Medary complained to him in late 1847, "Since the death of Silas Wright every thing seems to be at loose ends. At many of our meetings some one gets up & proposes a resolution" supporting Cass, which "passes without a word." An editorial in the *Clark County Democrat,* which raised the Cass banner in October 1846, proclaimed: "If the west is true to itself, General Cass will not only be the next democratic candidate, but the next democratic President." Most Ohio Democrats agreed with those sentiments. The state gathering at Columbus in early January resolved that Congress had no authority over the question of slavery in the territories, and nominated Lewis Cass for the presidency by a vote of 227 to 22.[15]

The triumph in Ohio was echoed throughout most of the West. During his years in Washington, Cass maintained control of the Michigan Democratic organization through the judicious dispersal of federal patronage. This domination was revealed when his home-state convention, ignoring the objections of free soilers, chose to take no official position on the question of slavery extension. Fortunately for the Cass forces, "Nothing in connection with the subject of slavery was agitated & every thing went off well." Michigan Democrats, unable to slow the Van Buren juggernaut four years before, proudly united behind their favorite son. "There was but one opinion—one wish—one feeling, and that an enthusiastic one for Gen. Cass," who was unanimously nominated for the presidency by the Lansing delegates. Although the other western state delegations were officially unpledged, in each case Cass was the acknowledged front-runner. The Illinois Democrats were typical. They met at Springfield and expressed a preference for Cass, whose "life of arduous service in various responsible posts has evinced the highest endowments of the soldier and statesman, the diplomatist and patriot." Kentuckian Richard M. Johnson wrote Cass: "You must be the candidate . . . you will get this state & the whole west, I think, in convention." Only Texas (which remained true to Sam Houston) and Louisiana (which favored Buchanan) kept the Michigan senator from a clean sweep of the western and southwestern states.[16]

In the weeks preceding the Baltimore convention, Cass men became convinced they had blunted the challenges of James Buchanan and Levi Woodbury. The *Jackson Mississippian* reported the "great western statesman" was "looked upon with more favor by the people of the whole Union." Alpheus Felch asserted it was "scarcely possible that he should fail of a nomination." Supporters of Buchanan and Woodbury, however, were not about to concede. Divisions within the national party organization, and the particularly unsettled condition of the New York Democracy, with its large bloc of thirty-six delegate votes, left the nomination in doubt.[17]

Democrats during the 1840s faced a series of political controversies that strained party unity. Northeasterners were upset with the Walker Tariff, and westerners felt equally betrayed by Polk's passive acceptance of the Oregon boundary settlement and his veto of an internal improvements bill—which Senator Cass supported. None of these issues, however, threatened the very existence of the national party organization as did the argument over slavery extension. The focus was on New York, where

Democrats had split into rival factions years earlier. The "radical" or "Barnburner" element, under the leadership of Silas Wright, Azariah Flagg, John Dix, Benjamin Butler, Churchill Cambreleng, Preston King, and John Van Buren, favored restrictive economic practices. The "conservative" or "Hunker" faction, led by William Marcy and Daniel Dickinson, more closely represented the political principles of Lewis Cass. New York Democrats had rallied behind Polk during the election campaign of 1844, and the state slate—headed by gubernatorial candidate Silas Wright—carried the party to victory.

By 1848, Democratic party unity in the Empire State was shattered. Patronage struggles widened the breach between radicals and conservatives, and when Barnburners embraced the Wilmot Proviso, the rupture became irreparable. Ideological differences were exacerbated by the death of Silas Wright in August 1847. Early the following month, Hunkers dominated the state convention at Syracuse, defeating the renominations of Flagg and John Van Buren and rejecting a Wilmot resolution. The furious radicals invoked Wright's name and demanded the conservatives do justice to his memory, but a Hunker callously retorted it was too late for that—"He is dead." Cass supporters bemoaned such "childish" behavior but were powerless to heal the breach. The result was a sweeping Whig victory in the state elections. The Barnburners had embarked on an emotional crusade that spelled trouble for the political fortunes of moderates, including Lewis Cass. Rather than view the results of the state election as a mandate to unite before the national convention, both groups became even more intransigent. The Hunkers stubbornly refused to work with the Barnburners at Utica and met at Albany to select a competing slate of national delegates. The response of the Baltimore convention to this split in the New York Democracy influenced not only the presidential nomination but the outcome of the election.[18]

On Sunday, May 21, when Lewis Cass attended church services in Washington, the full focus of his attention plainly was not on spiritual matters. For the past several days, delegates to the Democratic national convention had traveled through the capital on their way to Baltimore. A Whig complained, "The city is inundated with Loco-Focoism," and Cass took the opportunity to confer with some of his trusted supporters: Lucius Lyon, David Disney, Wright and Hannegan of Indiana, and Daniel Dickinson, head of the Hunker delegation from New York. The Cass forces continued hammering away at Buchanan's southern support, in the hope such efforts would soon bear fruit. Final plans were put into operation, and by that Sunday Cass was one of the few influential Democrats still in Washington. Congress, announced the *New York Tribune,* "has adjourned to Baltimore."[19]

The throng of delegates, correspondents, and curious bystanders that descended upon Baltimore taxed the city's capacity. Every hotel room, one disgruntled Whig reported, "was occupied with two, three, and even in some cases, with six or eight beds." The saloons and taverns did a brisk business, as "mint juleps, sherry-cobblers, brandy, and soda, were poured in large quantities." Strangely enough, the chief topic of conversation was not the fortunes of the leading contenders for the presidential nomination; rather, "in every corner was seen a clique of politicians talking over the stereotyped phrases of *Barnburner* and *Hunker*." Martin Van Buren had suggested the provisoists participate in the convention and accept the decision of the delegates, provided James Polk was not renominated. It remained to be seen if the more zealous free soilers—and Van Buren himself—were inclined to follow this advice.[20]

Shortly after noon on Monday, May 22, the Democratic national convention was called to order. Three thousand spectators and delegates were squeezed into the Universalist Church, which four years before had housed the Whigs. The first order of important business was balancing the conflicting claims presented by the New York delegations. To tackle the problem, a committee of credentials was appointed, consisting of one delegate from every state except New York. During the evening session it presented an interim report. The committee noted that 446 delegates were in attendance (including the two factions from the Empire State), dividing among them a total of 290 votes. South Carolina was represented by a single delegate, James M. Commander, who was authorized to cast all nine of his state's votes. Calhoun had urged South Carolinians to boycott the national convention, but a meeting of fifty-four men at Georgetown selected Commander (sarcastically styled "the Palmetto cat o' nine tails") as a delegate. After accepting the credential committee's findings, the convention selected Andrew Stevenson as permanent chairman and adjourned the first day's session.[21]

The delegates reconvened at nine o'clock the following morning. They swiftly adopted the two-thirds rule, without the rancor marking their debate in 1844, and then turned to the vexatious New York question. Benjamin Howard, of Maryland, reported that the credentials committee had decided not to proceed with its investigations until both factions agreed to support the nominations of the convention. Since the Barnburners refused to accept this condition, Howard recommended the Hunkers be seated. Further action was postponed until Wednesday.

When the delegates met for their third session, it became increasingly evident a compromise solution needed to be found to maintain even a semblance of party unity. Cass supporters believed that with the two-thirds rule in effect, it was imperative the Hunkers be seated. New England followers of Levi Woodbury were more inclined to favor admitting the Barnburners, while southern delegates naturally opposed the provisoists. The situation was most delicate. In a futile attempt to placate the feuding New York factions, the delegates decided on Thursday morning to allow both groups to share the state's thirty-six votes. For once, the Hunkers and Barnburners were in agreement: each side rejected this compromise, rightly contending it nullified the influence of New York by evenly dividing its vote. Nonetheless, both delegations stubbornly refused to withdraw from the convention. The schism between Hunkers and Barnburners effectively disfranchised the most populous state at the Democratic national convention.

Unable to resolve the division within the New York Democracy, the delegates of the remaining twenty-nine states selected a presidential candidate. After John Ramsey of Tennessee read a letter from Polk unequivocally stating he was not a candidate for renomination, three names were placed in contention: Buchanan, Cass, and Woodbury. On the first ballot, Cass received 125 votes, one short of a majority of those cast; Buchanan polled 55, and Woodbury 53. Eighteen other votes were scattered among Calhoun, Dallas, and William J. Worth of Georgia. This ballot revealed surprisingly strong support for Cass. He virtually swept the western delegations, cracked Woodbury's stranglehold on New England, and easily carried Louisiana, Delaware, Maryland, and Virginia, which were supposed to be solidly in Buchanan's camp. The Pennsylvanian sourly complained the Virginia delegates defected in order to secure the vice presidential nomination for Secretary of the Navy John Y. Mason. Cass continued to increase his strength on the second and third ballots, primarily at the expense of Buchanan. The Michigan senator finally received more than two-thirds of the votes on the fourth tally, and Andrew Stevenson declared him duly nominated, amid "enthusiastic and long-continued applause, the members of the various delegations almost universally springing to their feet, and uniting in one spirit-stirring shout of approbation." After the prolonged wranglings over New York, it was with joyous relief the Democrats so quickly chose a presidential candidate. Two events, however, forecast problems for Cass's candidacy: the Barnburners walked out of the convention to protest the nomination, and southern extremist William L. Yancey refused to switch Alabama's vote to Cass until a suitable platform was adopted. The Hunkers, at least, announced their "cordial and enthusiastic support." The following day, delegates turned to the selection of a running mate, and General William O. Butler was chosen on the second ballot over Mississippian John A. Quitman and several other candidates. Butler, a former congressman from Kentucky who served under Jackson at New Orleans, was a Mexican War hero. As a slaveholder, he "balanced" the national ticket.[22]

On Friday morning, Benjamin Hallett of Massachusetts submitted the platform committee report to the convention. The resolutions praised the achievements of President Polk and emphasized familiar Democratic doctrine: the federal government possessed limited powers and should not institute a general system of internal improvements, establish a protective tariff, or charter a national bank. The chief plank dealing with slavery was taken from the platform of 1840. It left to the individual states the regulation of their domestic institutions and excoriated abolitionists for endangering "the stability and permanency of the Union." No specific mention was made of popular sovereignty. A minority report, submitted by Yancey and two other southerners, called for adoption of a resolution guaranteeing "the doctrine of non-interference with the rights of property . . . be it in the States or in the Territories." This proposal was resoundingly defeated by a vote of 216 to 36. Amidst assorted jeers and catcalls, Yancey angrily led a small contingent of proslavery men off the convention floor. Most delegates obviously did not intend to place the Democratic party on record regarding the issue of slavery in the territories; the equivocal Nicholson letter would serve nicely during the campaign. After the rejection of Yancey's resolution, the platform was unanimously adopted. A national committee was subsequently appointed, consisting of one member from each state. This was the first central committee of a major political party formed to wage a presidential campaign. The fifth Democratic convention then adjourned *sine die.* At a rally in Monument Square, stump speakers praised the nominations, guns and rockets were fired, and "mighty rejoicing took place."[23]

It had been an acrimonious five days for the Baltimore delegates. The relative ease with which the national ticket was selected belied the sectional tensions simmering over the question of slavery extension. The Democratic organ of Milwaukee astutely observed it was "all important" that the convention nominate "a statesman who would be regarded as a *national* candidate." Lewis Cass was such a candidate, and "throughout the West and the North-West" his selection "will be regarded as the strongest that could have been made."[24] Cass succeeded in his quest for the nomination because, as a western nationalist, he bridged the expanding gap between northern and southern Democrats.

Cass's nomination, of course, did not meet with universal Democratic approval. Yancey represented the extreme proslavery position. He stalked home and refused to support the national ticket, although attempts to form a third-party organization in the South failed dismally. The influential *Charleston Mercury* echoed Yancey's fears that popular sovereignty was a device to prohibit slavery from the western territories, denouncing it as "too monstrous to be tolerated, . . . too degrading to be endured." The *Mercury* added that of all the candidates before the convention, Cass "was the least acceptable to the Democracy of South Carolina." Southern Whig newspapers correspondingly portrayed the nominee as a vacillating politician, "a mere nose of wax in the hands of stronger men."[25]

Northern Democratic newspapers that had endorsed the Wilmot Proviso were chilled by the selection of Cass. The *Chicago Democrat* hesitated to place his name on its masthead. Instead, chided its Whig rival, the *Democrat* came out for "'the nominee of the Baltimore Convention' without the name of Mr. Cass. It is perhaps as well—for next to his name, a blank is the most expressive way of announcing who is the nominee of the Baltimore Convention." The most strident northern opposition came from New York, where the Barnburners were determined to defeat Cass. The *Rochester Advertiser* insisted the Baltimore ticket was chosen "by a 'section' of the Democracy of the Union," and those excluded were "at perfect liberty to . . . withhold their support." A Wisconsin antislavery newspaper blasted as "cowardly" the decision to split the New York vote between both delegations, asserting it "vitiated the whole proceedings of the convention." The *Racine Advocate* called for a separate nomination by northern Democrats: "Defeat, we should look upon, as something of a misfortune, but not as so great a one as success under such circumstances." The national platform and the nomination of Cass plainly alienated northern and southern zealots.[26]

Despite opposition to his nomination within the party, most Democrats cheerfully hailed Cass's candidacy. Alpheus Felch wrote from

Washington that the nomination "has created great enthusiasm here—all are pleased with the result and all predict . . . success at the election." Cass's hotel suite was "literally hung with wreaths and festoons of flowers, . . . the gifts of the ladies, who have presented them to him with their own hands." President Polk, who found the nominee in "a fine humour," extended his personal congratulations. Democratic newspapers joined in the celebration. The *North Carolina Standard* referred to Cass as "a statesman renowned for his prudence, wisdom, and energy" and added that the Baltimore ticket was "worthy, in every sense, of the cordial and undivided support of the Democracy of the whole country." The *Cleveland Plain Dealer* was still less restrained in its praise. "Let every WESTERN MAN, every inhabitant of the original 'North-West Territory,' give his loudest shout for the CITIZEN NOMINEE!!" In general, even those Democratic organs that backed a different contender for the nomination rallied to the Cass-Butler banner once it was unfurled.[27]

While accepting the plaudits of political admirers in Washington, Cass received from Andrew Stevenson official notification of his nomination. Cass had been working on an acceptance letter for several days, seeking the advice of President Polk and editor Thomas Ritchie. He swiftly acknowledged the "distinguished honour" and pledged adherence to the Democratic platform. He also assured Polk that plans to purchase Cuba from Spain would not hinder his chances in November. Ever the expansionist, Cass asserted the island was "immensely valuable, & that he would be willing to pay a large sum for it." He then resigned his senate seat and made arrangements to return home. Felch, the junior senator from Michigan, professed an emotional loss at the impending parting. "He has been kind as a father to me," he informed his wife. "I regard him as one of the best and kindest-hearted men I have ever known." Cass and Benjamin Hallett, chairman of the newly formed Democratic central committee, dined at the White House on Saturday evening, June 3, and discussed campaign strategy with the president. Hallett then joined Senators Allen, Benton, Foote, and Houston, in accompanying Cass on his trip to Detroit.[28]

It proved to be a leisurely homeward journey. Leaving Washington on Monday, Cass stopped to pay his respects to those delegates still lingering at Baltimore, while members of his entourage participated in an enthusiastic campaign rally. After pausing at Wilmington, Delaware, where Cass entertained a friendly crowd with reminiscences of his youthful sojourn there, the company arrived at Philadelphia and took lodgings at the Jones Hotel, the principal headquarters for many of the Whigs attending their national convention. It was during this layover that Senator Allen earned the nickname "Fog Horn," for extolling the political virtues of Cass in spite of a deafening cacophony of steamboat whistles. The peace of the city was also shattered by several partisan altercations, "in some of which knives were drawn." By the time the Cass party departed for New York, Philadelphia Democrats "had worked themselves into a considerable fever of excitement."[29]

Not to be outdone, the regular Democracy of the Empire State turned out in large numbers to welcome Lewis Cass. His arrival at New York City was greeted with lusty cheering, flag waving, and the firing of ceremonial cannon. The presidential candidate was described by a Brooklyn reporter as "very winning" in "his personal bearing . . . wherever he goes he cannot fail to make friends." Following an immense ratification rally at Tammany Hall, Cass boarded the steamer *Hendrik Hudson.* The customary program was repeated at Albany, where the nominee was met by a reception committee and various members of his entourage addressed the assembled crowd. Lewis Cass was heartened by the response he received on the Barnburners' home ground. Even Gideon Welles softened his opinion, claiming he "would as soon see Cass president as either of his two competitors" for the nomination. "I think he has more heart" than Buchanan or Woodbury, the radical Democrat concluded, and if elected "would get along as well as some others." After traveling through Schenectady, Utica, Rome, Syracuse, and Rochester, Cass arrived in Buffalo, where the Democratic newspaper announced that between five and eight thousand citizens turned out to salute the candidate. Cass and his escort then proceeded by steamer to Cleveland and, finally, home.[30]

Cass arrived at Detroit on the morning of June 16, and when the boat "touched the wharf, cheer after cheer; and shout on shout arose to welcome the illustrious statesman." One proud Democrat called it "the *largest* reception meeting . . . *ever held in Detroit.* The whigs admit this themselves." But, sneered the local Whig organ, the crowd "did not exceed 500 or 600, at the most. . . . The whole thing more resembled a funeral procession than anything else." The homeward journey from Washington was the only occasion when Cass personally took to the stump. Upon reaching Detroit, the Democratic nominee settled into an outwardly tranquil routine. Cass confined his campaign efforts to writing letters of encouragement and advice to intimate supporters, and he awaited the outcome of the November election with apparent equanimity. Meanwhile, the Whig national convention completed its work.[31]

There were several contenders for the Whig nomination. Henry Clay, Daniel Webster, and John McLean claimed widespread respect and attention, and others mentioned as potential candidates included General Winfield Scott and Senator Thomas Corwin. The strongest challenger, however, was a political neophyte—General Zachary Taylor. Cass's nomination by the Democrats, in fact, greatly aided Taylor's candidacy and blighted the hopes of Clay and other Whig opponents of the Mexican War. Since Cass had been the leading Senate spokesman for President Polk's aggressive military policy, it was considered prudent to nominate a war hero. Old Rough and Ready's complete lack of political experience and expressed principles tended to appeal to all sections of the nation, and following his early victories in Mexico, it was evident a Taylor boom was underway.[32]

When his name first was mentioned as a presidential candidate, General Taylor modestly wrote to a son-in-law he desired "to have nothing to do with that high office." After all, he was an army veteran of forty years who had never even voted in a national contest. As private citizens and politicians began imploring the general to run, however, his aspirations increased proportionately. After accepting the endorsements of various public conventions, Old Zach acknowledged he would accept either the Whig or Democratic nomination, if unencumbered by a partisan platform. This disconcerted many Whig politicians, and Taylor responded with a letter to Captain John Allison, a brother-in-law, declaring he was "a Whig but not an ultra Whig." The Allison letter rallied to his standard many wavering Whigs bent on victory.[33]

Delegates, politicians, newspaper correspondents, and other observers poured into Philadelphia during the first days of June. Adding to the tumult was the presence of Lewis Cass and his traveling party, although the most vociferous political struggle took place between the supporters of Taylor and Clay. The Taylorites pounded away relentlessly at a single theme. It was senseless "to think of running Mr. Clay again . . . *simply because he cannot be elected.*"[34] This feeling permeated the convention, and Taylor was nominated on the fourth ballot. Millard Fillmore, a New York supporter of Clay, was selected as his running mate. The Whigs then passed a series of resolutions praising Old Zach's military record and personal virtues. No mention was made in the party "platform" of specific political issues.

While most delegates joined in the celebration following Taylor's nomination, the antislavery "Conscience" Whigs of Massachusetts denounced his selection. The Philadelphia convention thus adjourned under similar circumstances to the Democratic gathering at Baltimore—with a vocal antislavery faction from a northeastern state vehemently opposed to the party's presidential candidate. "The only consolation" from the nominations of Cass and Taylor, observed a northwestern antislavery Democratic organ, "is that they are so ridiculous that another must be made that will command the votes of those who do not choose to be disgraced by the dictation of the South."[35]

Conscience Whigs and other antislavery men wasted no time in organizing against Taylor. Led by Henry Wilson, fifteen Philadelphia delegates issued a call for a national free soil convention to meet at Buffalo in early August. Some four hundred erstwhile Whigs and Democrats and sundry abolitionists assembled at Columbus, Ohio, on June 21, under the leadership of Salmon P. Chase. This "People's Convention," scheduled to coincide with a Liberty party conference in the same city, repudiated the nominations of Taylor and Cass and repeated the call for a national free soil meeting. The Liberty party delegates, in turn, also endorsed the Buffalo convention, after nominating John P. Hale to head their national ticket. More than five thousand Conscience Whigs gathered at Worcester, Massachusetts, a week later to hear Charles Sumner castigate the Taylor nomination as the manifestation of "an unhallowed union . . . between the lords of the lash and the lords of the loom." Sumner was equally opposed to Cass, on the grounds that popular sovereignty would encourage the introduction of slavery into western territories. Before adjourning, the Worcester convention chose six delegates for Buffalo.[36]

Following the nomination of Lewis Cass, antislavery men throughout the North viewed the actions of dissident New York Democrats with considerable curiosity. A mass meeting of some ten thousand Barnburners, held at City Hall Park on the evening of June 6, served notice the internecine feud would not be easily settled. The few Cass supporters present broke into a smattering of groans and hisses, as resolutions were passed claiming the regular nomination had "no validity or force whatever."[37] Democrats opposed to Cass were urged to assemble at Utica, on June 22, to select an antislavery slate.

Lewis Cass and his advisers certainly understood that the split among Democrats represented serious campaign problems. Thomas Hart Benton and Francis P. Blair were among those recruited to placate the Barnburners. Benton, no unabashed admirer of Cass, was assigned the delicate task of persuading Martin Van Buren to rebuff "any separate organization on the presidential question." Van Buren responded in a conciliatory manner, and in late June Benton informed Cass the New Yorker would "advise against" a free soil slate at the Utica convention. Butler and Flagg also urged Van Buren not to repudiate the party affiliation he had spent decades fostering. At the same time, younger and generally more radical Barnburners, including Preston King, Samuel Tilden, and John Van Buren, argued that a fusion party would focus national attention on the antislavery crusade.[38]

The Utica convention demonstrated the implacability of the more extreme Barnburners. Under the direction of Preston King, the first day's session was largely spent in reading a lengthy, uncharacteristically candid letter from Martin Van Buren. The former president derided popular sovereignty and cannily remarked, "If no other candidates than those now before the country are presented, I shall not vote for President." The following morning, Van Buren and Henry Dodge of Wisconsin were nominated by acclamation. Dodge, who had expressed confidence Cass would prevail in November, "unless New York is the cause of our defeat," remained true to the regular party ticket and rejected the Utica nomination. After some soul searching, Van Buren accepted the Barnburner candidacy shortly before the free soil delegates gathered at Buffalo.[39]

Van Buren's reasons for accepting the Utica nomination were varied and complex. His initial hesitancy was the natural reaction of a born politician who had devoted his adult life to the Democratic party; and yet, a combination of personal and political motives drove him inexorably into the radical Barnburner camp. He felt no personal allegiance to Cass. The two politicians had been acquainted for more than three decades, but there was no intimate bond between them. Additionally, Van Buren viewed Cass as the prime mover in the drive to deny him the nomination in 1844. The former president was spurred by more than a visceral sense of revenge, however. He hoped to retain control of the New York Democracy by assuming the leadership of the powerful free soilers. Furthermore, he fervently disagreed with Cass's interpretation of the Constitution. The idea that Congress had no power to legislate on the issue of slavery expansion was alien to Van Buren, who viewed the doctrine of popular sovereignty as nothing more than submission to the proslavery position. So in accepting the Barnburner nomination for president, Van Buren expected to frustrate the ambitions of Lewis Cass while focusing attention on the dangers faced by the Union if radical southerners were not kept in check.

Van Buren's candidacy unleashed a torrent of bitter criticism from the Democratic faithful. President Polk led the chorus of party regulars who excoriated his "selfish, unpatriotic, and wholly inexcusable" betrayal. The *Cincinnati Enquirer* charged that "as an act of ingratitude," there was "no justification, nor even palliation," for Van Buren's acceptance of the Utica nomination. Lewis Cass characteristically kept his emotions under control in the midst of all the name-calling. He expressed astonishment at Van Buren's course but chose to put the best gloss possible on the situation: "The New York defection does little injury out of that State. It seems to band the party more firmly together, and probably carries more Whigs than Democrats with it." Nonetheless, the growing free soil movement was a decided threat to Cass's candidacy.[40]

On August 9, twenty thousand Barnburners, Conscience Whigs, and assorted abolitionists met at Buffalo to found the Free Soil party. The atmosphere was similar to a revival meeting, as eloquent and determined orators whipped up the enthusiasm of the fervent throng. Speaking under a huge "Oberlin tent" erected to ward off the fierce summer sun, Charles Francis Adams urged the Free Soilers to pull together toward "the model of a Christian commonwealth." The nominations of Cass and Taylor were vigorously denounced as the machinations of unholy forces. Joshua Giddings belittled the aspirations of Lewis Cass, declaring, "No one thinks of supporting *him* now." As the crowd expressed its agreement with chants of "No . . . No . . . No . . . ," Giddings concluded: "I will speak of him as of the others, one who *has been.*" New York delegate Erastus Culver indelicately disposed of the Whig candidate. "I greased Gen. Taylor and tried for a long time to swallow him," announced the former Whig, but "he got right across my throat and there he sticks. . . . I can not get him down."[41]

While the mass gathering was being entertained, Free Soil "conferees" met at the Universalist Church to draft resolutions and nominate a national ticket. Salmon Chase presided, and Benjamin Butler was chosen chairman of the resolutions committee. Although the platform made reference to cheap postage, government retrenchment, river and harbor improvements, free homesteads, and eradication of the national debt, most of the planks naturally focused on slavery. Conceding state governments had final juprisdiction over their internal institutions, the Free Soilers nonetheless resolved: "No more Slave States and no more Slave Territory." The platform was unanimously adopted and sent to the general convention, where it was ratified by acclamation amid shouts of "FREE

SOIL, FREE SPEECH, FREE LABOR, AND FREE MEN." The conferees then turned to the task that threatened to dissolve the harmony of the Buffalo meeting—selection of a presidential nominee.[42]

Each of the three major dissident groups that gathered at Buffalo had a favorite candidate for the nomination. The former Whigs preferred Supreme Court Justice John McLean; the Liberty party endorsed Hale; the Barnburners, Martin Van Buren. After Salmon Chase spread the word that McLean wished to withdraw, an informal poll revealed Van Buren as the clear choice for president. Joshua Leavitt thereupon urged that the recommendation be made unanimous, emotionally proclaiming, "The Liberty party is not dead, but translated." Novelist Richard Henry Dana, a Massachusetts delegate, observed that "many were moved to tears" by Leavitt's words, and the former Whigs and Liberty men quickly fell into line. The more radical conferees thus overlooked the racist undercurrents of the Barnburner creed (which sought to exclude free blacks, as well as slaves, from the western territories). They accepted Van Buren's candidacy because the Free Soil platform embraced their principles, and he was expected to rally a large following in November. Charles Francis Adams was selected to complete the Free Soil ticket.[43]

The nominations were received by the mass convention with unbridled enthusiasm. Hats were tossed into the air, banners and handkerchiefs were waved, and the cheering crowd marched through the streets chanting support for "VAN BUREN AND FREE SOIL, ADAMS AND LIBERTY." Charles Francis Adams, wearing a crepe band on his white hat in memory of his father, must have been momentarily struck with the irony of a Van Buren–Adams political alliance; the prototypical Jacksonian and the scion of Federalists made strange bedfellows indeed. President Polk spoke for loyal Democrats when he declared, "Mr. Van Buren is the most fallen man I have ever known." Although Lewis Cass maintained his public silence on the proceedings at Buffalo, his chances to gain the White House were seriously jeopardized.[44]

Chapter Eight

The Presidential Election of 1848: "The Election of Gen. Cass Is *Certain*— but That of Gen. Taylor a *Leetle More So*"

EIGHTEEN FORTY-EIGHT was an exciting year in the history of Western civilization. Americans viewed the revolutionary events in Europe with wonderment as the post-Napoleonic order established by the Congress of Vienna began to unravel. From Tipperary to Wallachia, from the Baltic to the Balkans, popular insurrections and nationalistic rebellions rolled across the continent, promising a more liberal Europe, before being brutally suppressed by autocratic governments. American society as well underwent significant, albeit less violent, changes. In January, gold was discovered in California, and the stampede of fortune seekers to the West Coast forever altered the political and economic structure of the country. John Jacob Astor, the wealthiest man in America, died in New York City on March 29, and the public was titillated by reports he bequeathed little of an estimated twenty million dollar fortune to charity or civic improvements. Women's rights advocates under the leadership of Elizabeth Cady Stanton and Lucretia Mott gathered at Seneca Falls, New York, to agitate for equality. And on the national political scene, the country was engaged in another quadrennial exercise to choose a chief executive.

The presidential race was well underway by the time the Free Soilers adjourned their convention at Buffalo. The political sniping commenced with the Baltimore nomination of Lewis Cass and developed into total warfare after the selection of Zachary Taylor by the Whigs. Until the Free

Soil nominations in August, the major parties largely ignored the anti-slavery movement and concentrated on their traditional rivalry. It was an exciting contest. One participant recalled, more than forty years later, "There has been no canvass since conducted with more zeal and fervor." The Taylor men marched with banners depicting Mexican battlefields in "flaming pictures of blood and carnage." The Cass standards "were full of civic honors and the victories of peace; but these triumphs showed dim and pale, contrasted with the lurid glories of the battle-flags of Taylor." Partisan orators took to the stump denouncing their opponents, and the party faithful held parades and barbecues to rally support. Most of the Democratic operations originated with an executive committee consisting of Mississippi senator Henry S. Foote, Edmund Burke of New Hampshire, and Indianan William J. Brown. The candidates themselves followed the contemporary practice of remaining aloof from the campaign and retired to their respective homes. Cass kept in touch with his chief lieutenants by writing letters, but decided to issue no public communications. A key Virginia supporter claimed, "The wisdom of your determination not to write letters for the public, is apparent—And I trust, you will under no circumstances depart from it." He did not; but Taylor did. From his plantation north of Baton Rouge, Old Rough and Ready wrote several letters for publication, in part because his political principles and policies were not as well known as those of Cass. Taylor's electioneering yielded mixed results.[1]

The Whigs put more imagination and verve into their campaign songs and literature. "The Ladies" boasted:

> Most of the ladies go for Zack,
> There's many a Taylor lass,
> Will give her loco beau the sack,
> Because he goes for Cass.

The reason the fairer sex backed Taylor became clear in the concluding stanza:

> Then come young ladies, lend your aid,
> Be constant, true, and steady;
> She never can be an old maid
> Who goes for Rough and Ready.

Whig women served the cause by persuading their husbands to vote for Taylor. One campaign anecdote humorously informed the reader *"How to make a Taylorite."* While traveling by steamboat, "One fair creature grew wroth with her Cass husband because he swore he wouldn't vote for Taylor. She just went to bed and locked the door, vowing that her lord should not 'come in' until he swore that he *would* vote for Taylor. Before morning he *did*." With such wholehearted support from the ladies, the Whigs predicted victory. The *Chicago Daily Journal* facetiously reported that "a man in the State of New York persists in expressing the belief that Gen. Cass will be the next President. . . . his friends have concluded to send him to the Lunatic Asylum at Utica. Proper diet and November weather may be beneficial."[2]

Democratic songs and anecdotes were more pedantic and labored than those of the Whigs. Cass was portrayed as a distinguished candidate for the presidency, who sought "to outdo" his neighbors only "in acts of charity and mercy." The Democrats marched and sang, to the tune of "Auld Lang Syne":

> With Cass and Butler at our head,
> Though traitors all combine,
> We'll win the day as we have won
> In the days of auld lang syne.
> *Chorus.*
> For auld lang syne, my boys,
> For auld lang syne,
> We'll vote for CASS and BUTLER now
> For auld lang syne.

The Hickory Sprout, a campaign paper published at Freehold, New Jersey, offered a song to the sprightly air of "O Susanna":

> I'm all the way from Michigan,
> The old White House to see;
> I'm going on to Washington,
> "My country calls for me."
> The sun shone bright the morn I left,
> The weather it was dry—
> I heard the Whigs along the road
> Say "Zachy, don't you cry."[3]

Some songs inspired rejoinders. The Whigs imagined Cass inquiring:

> Pray, tell me, Rough and Ready,
> How did it come to pass
> That you were made a President
> And I was made an ass?

The Democrats swiftly (and inaccurately) responded:

> Our candidate's an "Ass" you say,
> If but a "C," you take away;
> But from your own an *a* remove,
> And *Taylor* would a *Tyler* prove.[4]

The parades and rallies conducted to keep enthusiasm high among the rank and file were marred occasionally by drunkenness and violence. An intoxicated female partisan in Philadelphia informed the police she was "Rough and Ready," and they incarcerated her under that pseudonym. In New Orleans, a Democratic parade was tramping past a Rough and Ready Club when a Whig supporter began jeering the marchers with shouts of "Hurrah for Taylor and Fillmore!" After the heckler was threatened with torches and pistols, to no avail, the clubhouse was set afire by the Democrats and reduced to ashes.[5]

The presidential contest was fought as well with the pen. Documents extolling the personal and political attributes of the candidates were broadcast throughout the nation. The Democratic national committee, under Benjamin Hallett, labored mightily to publish biographical sketches of Cass and Butler. Pamphlets praised the long and honorable political career of the Michiganite, and stressed his qualifications for the presidency. The widely distributed *Sketch of the Life and Public Services of Gen. Lewis Cass* asserted he was "the man for the times, . . . he is, in every sense of the word, a Democrat." Henry Rowe Schoolcraft lauded the nominee's nationalistic fervor, characterizing him as "a man of broad, comprehensive principles and firm integrity—not sectional, but viewing the whole Union, north and south, and every part of the Union as a brotherhood of equal interests and rights." Schoolcraft was sincere in his praise, but he expected to advance in the Indian Office once his mentor reached the White House.[6]

Democrats emphasized traditional differences between the two major parties. Claiming the central government possessed limited powers, their platform eschewed a national bank, protective tariff, federally funded internal improvements, and distribution to the states of the proceeds from the sale of public lands. Having thus dealt with specific issues, Democrats proudly announced their reliance on "the popular will" of the American people and branded their opponents "the wily enemies of popular government." According to the *Detroit Free Press,* the Democratic party was governed by a strict adherence to principle, whereas the Whigs were swayed by the political charms of unprincipled individuals. In his letter accepting the presidential nomination, Cass maintained, "The very first article of the democratic creed teaches that the people are competent to govern themselves." Whigs contrastingly questioned "the capacity of man for self government."[7]

The Whig campaign organization, under the able leadership of Connecticut congressman Truman Smith, was equal to the Democratic challenges. Hobbled with a platform that totally ignored specific issues and party ideology, Whigs pledged fealty "to the principles of the Constitution as administered by its founders." They also compared General Taylor with an earlier warrior: "In the great essential qualities of wisdom, justice, integrity, humanity, and moral as well as physical courage," Senator John M. Clayton asserted, "Taylor approaches nearer to the character of Washington than any man who has occupied the Presidential chair since his day."[8]

Although party principles and the personal virtues of the candidates were primary topics of partisan propagandists, less erudite issues surfaced during the campaign. Democrats delighted in portraying the nomination of Taylor as being motivated by an abject desire to capture the White House. Jacob Thompson, a congressman from Mississippi, informed his colleagues that Taylor "is a soldier, a lucky and fearless soldier, I admit; but still no less the mere soldier." One exasperated Democrat was hard pressed to understand how "the American people could under any circumstances be guilty of the palpable insanity . . . of elevating to the Presidency a man who has acknowledged that he never took interest enough in the Government to cast a vote in his life!!" Taylor's political image was satirized by the antislavery poet James Russell Lowell:

> Ez to my principles, I glory
>   In hevin' nothin' o' the sort;

I aint a Wig, I aint a Tory,
  I'm jest a candidate, in short;
Thet's fair an' square an' parpendicler,
  But, ef the Public cares a fig
To hev me an'thin' in particler,
  Why, I'm a kind o' peri-wig.

The *Ohio Watchman* offered a fifty dollar reward to anyone who could "produce one *principle,* now contended for by the universal whig party that is not contained in the following four lines":

Sound the kewgag, strike the tonjon
  Beat the Fuzguzzy, wake the gonquong;
Let the loud hozanna ring,
  Bum tum fuzzlegum dingo bim.

A journal aptly named the *Campaign,* published by the proprietors of the *Washington Union,* caustically claimed the Whig convention "adjourned with the assertion of but *one principle,* that we have heard of—and that was the one *so honorable* to the whigs of Ohio, that *they would vote for a HORSE for Vice President!*"[9]

Stung by Whig accusations that Cass was too much a politician, Democrats ridiculed Taylor's indifference to national affairs. A widely reprinted anecdote described an acquaintance who called upon the general and asked, "What is your opinion of the ordinance of '87?" Taylor replied, "I don't know that I have ever seen any as old as that, but no doubt they were of poor metal—the *ordnance* of this day is certainly the best in the world." Taylor himself unwittingly provided the opposition with campaign fodder. In an effort to stem the flood of unsolicited political advice pouring in from around the country, he asked the Baton Rouge postmaster to stop delivering letters with insufficient postage. Unfortunately, the official notification of his nomination was subsequently sent to the dead-letter office. The Democrats seized upon this example of political insensibility and parsimony to deride "economical, comical Old Zack." Taylor's lack of experience did not hinder the Whig cause, however, because he placed himself in the hands of seasoned politicians. The general convolutedly assured one adviser, in late September: "I lost no time as you suggested in replying at length to the enclosed letter referred to, immediately destroying it, as requested."[10]

In a decidedly more serious vein than twitting his frugality, the northern Democratic press censured Taylor because he was a slaveholder. In addition to his Louisiana plantation, the general owned Cypress Grove (on the Mississippi River north of Natchez) and more than one hundred slaves. The *Detroit Free Press* reprinted articles from a New England Whig newspaper that portrayed Taylor as a rapacious slave monger who "FURNISHES CREOLE VIRGINS FOR THE HELLS OF NEW ORLEANS, AND RIOTS ON THE RUIN OF SOULS." Such verbal assaults were especially effective since "the Whigs pretend to be horror-stricken at slavery . . . and have declared that they would never vote for a slaveholder." Taylor's supporters feebly responded he did only "what every man at the South must do, if he would have servants, . . . either own or hire slaves." And in another comparison of the Whig nominee with the first president, it was noted that "Washington had no love for slavery, and Taylor has as little." Lowell mockingly referred to "Ole Zach" in the glossary of *Biglow Papers* as "a second Washington, an antislavery slaveholder, a humane buyer and seller of men and women, a Christian hero generally."[11]

Taylor was denounced as a slaveholder in the North, while Millard Fillmore was labeled an abolitionist by southern Democrats. One campaign song crudely linked the general to his running mate:

> Old Zack they say, has won great fame
> By pulling of the trigger,
> And Fillmore he is coming South,
> To liberate the Nigger.

Whigs countered with the charge that Cass was unreliable on the slavery issue since he was a northerner. Three topics were emphasized by Whig orators in the South, noted one observer: "miscellaneous abuse of Cass and the Democrats, comments on the danger to slavery and the impossibility of trusting any Northern man, . . . and lastly a glorification of Old Taylor's battles."[12]

In addition to impugning Zachary Taylor's qualifications and lack of principles, Democrats assailed the Whig party in general for opposing the Mexican War. Senator Cass was the Polk administration's staunchest advocate of an aggressive military strategy, in sharp contrast to the actions of congressional Whigs. This was the theme of a campaign poem, "The Soldier's Reply to the Whig Appeal for his Vote," in which a Mexican War veteran makes perfectly clear his political allegiance:

> Give you my vote! No! not to save
> This shattered body from the grave.
> Your perjured party I disclaim—
> Treason in nature, whig in name.
> To those who would my reason know—
> 'Tis this—I've fought in Mexico.

Even General Taylor was besmirched by the patriotism issue. An Indiana newspaper carried a fabricated testimonial from Whig senator Thomas Corwin for "Dr. Z. Taylor's Sugar-Coated Pills," which "worked out of my blood all my former attachment for the Mexicans, and my hatred of the American army." The Democrats were especially emphatic in their charge of "moral treason" against the Whig party because of Taylor's stature as a military hero.[13]

The Whigs likewise attacked the personal and political frailties of the Democratic candidate. The *Detroit Advertiser* dutifully reprinted an article that characterized Cass as "the most plethoric man in the Senate, and decidedly a heavy speaker. His eye is dull, his voice wheezey, his actions awkward, and his style is forever running after a climax that it does not reach." The writer concluded, "He reminds one of Shakespeare's fat knight, minus the fun; a Falstaff without wit." Cass was portrayed as "a radical, reckless Democrat," not to be trusted with the presidency. He was "a sly, artful, intriguing" politician who took a stand only after weighing whether it would further his personal aspirations. As one Whig poet expressed it:

> I charge thee Lewis fling away
> Oh, fling away, ambition;
> Oh, Lewis cease to be, I pray,
> *A scheming politician.*

Lewis Cass was most certainly a politician—a cautious, middle-of-the-road politician who took a measured stance on every substantive issue except those involving national honor or territorial expansion. He was dispassionate and restrained, always willing to negotiate and compromise. This left him open to charges he was a mere truckler. In truth, Cass was simply a partisan Democrat who placed the Constitution above personal morality; but this, coupled with his generally moderate political opinions, provided his opponents with ammunition during the campaign. To the

Whigs, he was unfit for the White House. "'I intend,' said a good, stiff Loco-foco, 'to give General Cass my unqualified support.'—'And if he succeeds,' replied his Whig interlocutor, 'you will have an *unqualified* President.'"[14]

Virtually every aspect of Cass's extensive public career was scrutinized during the canvass, and determined Whigs found much to criticize. The old charge that he had been a Federalist in his youth was resurrected, bolstered with the imputation that his diplomatic service in France revealed a streak of antirepublicanism. Henry Clay hit upon this theme shortly before the Baltimore convention. Senator Alpheus Felch, then forty-two years of age, joined his Michigan colleague in calling upon Clay, and the Kentuckian attempted to put the younger man at ease with some remarks "about age not being always necessary to wisdom." Senator Cass cheerfully responded that Clay's early career plainly demonstrated that fact. "'See now,' said Mr. Clay, 'what a residence at a foreign court does for a man—He cannot forget the courtier.'"

The genial tone of Clay's sally was lost by the Whig press once the campaign commenced. The *Battery*, a campaign organ published at Washington, imaginatively depicted the former minister as a sybarite, "basking in the sunshine of royalty, and revelling in all the splendors and luxuries of that voluptuous metropolis, rosying his gills with 'bewitching Burgundy,' swelling his portly dimensions with frogs, filets, and Perigord pies." Whig newspapers reprinted Cass's laudatory portrait (written while minister to France) of the recently dethroned Louis Philippe. The *Boston Post* explained Cass was merely comparing the energetic and relatively liberal administration of the Citizen King with those of his "weak and besotted" predecessors. Lewis Cass personally took pains to defuse this issue at a public gathering held in Washington before his nomination. The aspiring candidate acknowledged that the government installed by Louis Philippe ultimately began "to forget its promises," and he expressed wholehearted approval of the recent popular uprising. Cass proclaimed, "The shouts of liberty reach us from the Old World: let us send back their echoes from the New." This speech was printed as a pamphlet and circulated during the campaign.[15]

Coupled with Cass's purported leanings as an aristocratic monarchist was the issue of a Michigan territorial bill he signed while governor. This act provided that vagrants, and those incapable of supporting their families, could be sentenced to a whipping "not exceeding ten stripes" or to three months labor. According to Cass, the *Battery* admonished,

"POVERTY IS A CRIME, and he who is a vagrant, though from sickness and mere destitution, deserved to be whipped and sold into bondage." A Whig campaign song grimly warned:

> The wife, the widow, and the lass,
> Though their votes are not polled,
> Yet if their smiles elected CASS;
> They might be whip't and sold.

Democrats had to content themselves with the explanation that the Michigan law was taken verbatim from a Vermont statute and that William Henry Harrison (the Whig candidate in 1840) signed a similar bill while territorial governor of Indiana.[16]

Not satisfied with denouncing Cass as a clandestine aristocrat, the Whigs depicted him as a dangerous man who would engulf the nation in perpetual wars of conquest. One campaign pamphlet vividly noted: "He seems to look upon the United States as if the country were some monster reptile, that must subsist and swell its huge, unsightly bulk, by gorging itself with every living thing, small and great, that comes in its way." The *Boston Atlas* cautioned that the election of Cass "will be followed by wars of aggression on weak neighboring republics, bringing as their inevitable result, acquisition of territory, amalgamation with a barbarous, hostile population, further extension of slavery, . . . and a Public Debt." This was the theme of a campaign poem, "My Voice Is Still for War":

> He's chaw'd up half of Mexico,
> The balance he will swallow,
> Of Cuba he will make a foe,
> Then War again, must follow.

After documenting Cass's bellicose nature and unbridled expansionism, the Whig press argued their candidate was a soldier who deprecated war and opposed the annexation of additional Mexican territory.[17]

The Whigs plainly hit the mark with their portrayal of Cass as a zealous expansionist. His positions on the annexation of Texas and the Oregon and Mexican treaties were well known. And during the summer of 1848, he declared the United States must soon acquire not only "Mexico, but Cuba and all the islands in the Atlantic and Pacific which naturally belong to this continent. It is our destiny to spread over the whole of North America." Cass's ardent expansionism and vocal opposition to the territorial pretensions of Great Britain were attacked by the Whigs, but Democrats used these issues for their own purposes. When a London *Times* editorial praised Taylor as "the fittest and best man" then nominated for the presidency, Democratic organs eagerly printed the story under the headline: "General Taylor the Candidate of the London *Times.*" The *Detroit Free Press* chided eastern editors for forgetting the impressment issue and warned, "The West will never forget nor forgive the murder and massacre of her citizens." Cass, who unreservedly placed the honor and interests of his country over those of foreign powers, was to be commended and supported, because "we are not yet so reduced as to ask England who we shall elevate to the Presidency."[18]

In addition to critizing Cass's voracious appetite for territorial conquest, the Whigs ridiculed his war record. This was in direct response to Democratic representations of Cass as "The Brave Old Volunteer," betrayed by General William Hull's ignominious capitulation of Detroit in 1812:

> When Hull surrendered to the foe,
> And quailed his heart with fear,
> Bold Cass refused his sword to yield—
> The brave old volunteer!

The *Battery,* referring to the claim that Cass was the first American ashore during the invasion of Canada, facetiously remarked: "One would suppose that, since the landing of Columbus, there were really no landings on record to be compared with the landing of Cass in Canada." A Whig journal gleefully informed its readers that Congressman Andrew Stewart had "taken out a search-warrant to find the battle-field on which Gen. Cass distinguished himself." The story continued a week later. The Pennsylvania Whig, "failing to find Gen. Cass' glorious battle-field by means of a search warrant, has concluded to resort to the use of a Microscope of immense magnifying powers. We hope he may be more successful this time." The Democratic newspaper of Indianapolis rose to the challenge, alleging Stewart's search would "no doubt be more successful than if he was on the hunt after 'whig principles.'" A great deal of silly bickering also ensued over the question of whether Cass actually broke his sword rather than surrender it to a British officer.[19]

On July 27, a devastating campaign speech was presented by Abraham Lincoln to the House of Representatives. The Illinois Whig belittled Cass's contributions as an aide to General Harrison at the Battle of the Thames, recalling that during the canvass of 1840, the Democrats charged that "Harrison was picking whortleberries two miles off, while the battle was fought." Lincoln likewise disposed of the sword controversy. "Some authors say he broke it; some say he threw it away; and some others, who ought to know, say nothing about it. Perhaps it would be a fair historical compromise to say, if he did not break it, he did not do anything else with it." Lincoln concluded with a pledge that if he ever were taken up as a candidate for the presidency, his supporters "shall not make fun of me, as they have of General Cass, by attempting to write me into a military hero." The Illinois congressman subsequently entertained rapt audiences during a campaign swing through New England, a region that generally supported the Whig ticket.[20]

Not all the attacks on Lewis Cass's war record were good-natured. Congressman Thomas Butler King, of Georgia, argued that since Colonel Cass surrendered the forces under his command following the fall of Detroit, "if Hull committed treason, is not General Cass a traitor?" King denounced the Democratic candidate as *"an ass and a villain,"* and added, "*He should have been tried and shot,* at that very time."[21]

Several other issues of a military nature were discussed in partisan newspapers and campaign documents. Cass was accused of callousness toward the Mexican War volunteers because he introduced a Senate bill reducing their monthly clothing allowance from $3.50 to $2.50. Democrats retorted the decrease was more than counterbalanced by another aspect of the law, which enabled the soldiers to buy directly from government stores at wholesale prices. In an attempt to demonstrate concern for the plight of Mexican War volunteers, a lachrymose anecdote was circulated in which Cass visited a Detroit barracks housing some of the returned veterans.

> The Old General seemed as much at home as in the Senate of the United States, and as the wearied and wornout soldiers would relate to him the sufferings they had undergone, the tears started in his eyes as he replied "I have been through the same scenes, my boys; I know full well how to appreciate your story." . . .
>
> As the gallant old General left the room, he called the warden to him, and placing in his hands a roll of money, says he, "See that

> their wants are all supplied; and when this is gone, recollect that my purse is ever open to the call of those who have so nobly sustained our country's flag in the hour of danger." Many a heart beat with joy at this announcement, and breathed a long life and happiness to the soldier's friend.

The Democrats further argued that while secretary of war, Cass instituted several reforms to benefit the regular army troops. Drunkenness, for instance, declined after the War Department prohibited the sale of liquor by sutlers and the daily allowance of whiskey was replaced with a ration of coffee and sugar. This appealed especially to the large temperance segment of the American electorate; the soldiers themselves were reminded Cass gave them a day of rest by canceling Sunday inspections and parades.[22]

The Whigs capitalized on Old Rough and Ready's military victories and the esteem in which he was held by his troops, while Democrats made the most of stories that the general denigrated volunteers in Mexico. According to his opponents, Taylor questioned the courage and martial spirit of some regiments from Indiana. The *Evansville Democrat* reprinted the official report of Brigadier General Joseph Lane of the Second Indiana, which refuted Taylor's charge that Hoosier volunteers broke, *"could not be rallied and took no further part in the action, except a handful of men under its gallent Col. Bowles."* Lew Wallace was driven into the Free Soil ranks by this single issue: he "cared nothing" for Cass or Van Buren, his "only thought" was to defeat Taylor. "Let every *Indianan* remember," the *State Sentinel* thundered, that in voting "for the vile old SLANDERER of our brave volunteers, . . . he votes *his own disgrace for all time."* The Whigs countered by publishing a letter from Zachary Taylor to editor John Defrees of the *State Journal* in which the general claimed he had not lost confidence in the Indiana regiments. Democrats, however, refused to accept such an explanation, "written by *solicitation.*" After all, "Taylor's *report* is in the archives of the nation, where it will be regarded as historical data, for all time to come. His private letter . . . is in Defrees's breeches pocket, perhaps, where historical facts are not very likely to be sought for." Hoosier Democrats pointedly held barbecues in honor of their volunteers.[23]

General Taylor's troubles with the Mexican War volunteers extended beyond the borders of Indiana. Democrats claimed that when "an almost famished soldier" from Ohio was discovered to have plundered a chicken, Taylor abusively declared, *"all the volunteers were a God damned set of thieves and cowards.*" It also was reported the general ordered that several hundred Bibles, sent for distribution to the soldiers, be shredded for cartridges and wadding. When some of the troops expressed compunctions regarding this treatment of the holy book, Old Zach bellowed: "Now then, you cowardly fools, let me see how you can spread the gospel in Mexico!" Democrats piously concluded this blasphemous oath "was the last speech heard upon earth by many a gallant soul."[24]

As the campaign intensified, supporters of Cass and Taylor devoted a great deal of energy to impugning the character of their opponents. Whigs charged that during his tenure as governor of Michigan Territory, Cass received some sixty thousand dollars in compensation, additional to his regular salary. Andrew Stewart amused his House colleagues by stating the Democratic candidate "takes especial care of the people's money—especially when he gets it in his own pocket." Focusing on the fact Cass was entitled to ten rations per day as territorial superintendent of Indian affairs, Abraham Lincoln illustrated his gustatory capabilities: "We have all heard of the animal standing in doubt between two stacks of hay, and starving to death; the like of that would never happen to General Cass. Place the stacks a thousand miles apart, he would stand stock still midway between them, and eat them both at once."[25]

Democrats retaliated against the "gross, malicious, and wilful misrepresentations" made by Whig orators. Claiming the figures presented by Stewart were greatly inflated, Cass supporters countered that General Taylor had received over $70,000 in extra allowances. Moreover, while Cass immediately resigned his Senate seat upon accepting the presidential nomination, General Taylor still was receiving $691.33 per month in salary and expenses. "With the whigs," one partisan Democratic editor emphasized, "the motto, *'few die and none resign,'* has a significant application."[26]

Specific political questions also were debated during the campaign. The single most troublesome issue to Lewis Cass in the Northwest was the internal improvements controversy. Whigs traditionally espoused federally funded projects, but Democrats were not united on the question. Their platform of 1844 stated, "The Constitution does not confer upon the General Government the power to commence or carry on a general system of internal improvements," and President Polk declared his opposition to any "attempt to make improvements in the interior at points unconnected with foreign commerce." Political pressure to support such appropriations mounted on Democratic politicians, despite party doctrine, as the annual value of commerce conducted on the Great Lakes rose to an estimated hundred million dollars. A Milwaukee resident complained to his congressional delegate, after a particularly brutal gale, it was "a pity" the wrecked ships "were not all loaded with Senators and members of Congress." Northwestern Democrats responded positively in the summer of 1846 to a bill that provided federal funds for improvements on Lake Michigan and the Mississippi and Ohio Rivers. Lewis Cass and eleven other congressional Democrats joined every northern Whig in voting for passage, but President Polk vetoed the appropriation.[27]

Advocates of river and harbor improvements lost little time in attacking the president's veto. In the summer of 1847, ten thousand delegates to the Northwestern River and Harbor Convention descended upon Chicago. Adding to the press of visitors were newspaper correspondents from as far away as Boston and Richmond and the usual assortment of "gambling sharks, . . . pickpockets, hotel robbers, general thieves, and counterfeiters." Most of the actual delegates were from northern or Mississippi Valley states, although South Carolina, Georgia, and Florida were represented. Whigs predominated, but Democrats such as "Long John" Wentworth also attended. The city fathers delayed the Independence Day celebration until July 5 so the convention could open on a truly festive note. The vast assemblage listened for three days as a parade of speakers beseeched the federal government to improve navigable rivers and lake harbors.[28]

On the second day of the proceedings, messages were read from distinguished political figures who did not attend the Chicago gathering. Most of the communications, including those from Democrats, praised the aims of the convention and lauded the delegates for their contributions to the improvement of rivers and harbors. Martin Van Buren, Silas Wright, and Alpheus Felch were among those who called for federal support to improve navigation on the Great Lakes, and the crowd cheered their sentiments. The letter which stirred the greatest interest, however, was a terse note from Lewis Cass. Addressed to William Whiting, one of the convention organizers, the entire text was read aloud to the delegates: "I am much obliged to you for your kind attention to transmitting me an invitation to attend the Convention on Internal Improvements, which will meet in Chicago in July. Circumstances, however, will put it out of my power to be present at that time." This missive "was received at first with incredulous surprise," declared the *American Whig Review,* "and then (when assured by a second reading, clamorously called for, that the note, and the whole note, was before them) with such a shout of derision as no public man can survive, or should provoke." The *New York Herald* reported Cass's message was greeted by the audience with "a perfect shout of real western laughter." Horace Greeley joined in the chorus, informing the *Tribune*'s readers the cursory note "was listened to with hardly less astonishment than indignation." In fact, the brevity of the Cass communication, and its noncommittal attitude toward river and harbor improvements, proved a serious political blunder. Thurlow Weed, editor of the *Albany Evening Journal,* cheerfully concluded that the "cold, formal, and almost disrespectful Letter to this Convention has forever blasted his [Cass's] hopes." The Whig press swiftly denounced the Michigan Democrat as a truckler to public opinion and a slave to party doctrine. The *American Review* proved more prescient than most partisan journals when it predicted Cass had made "a mistake . . . irrevocable, potent, . . . which will be remembered to his damage by the whole lake and river country."[29]

Most of the political rhetoric on the internal improvements issue was directed at the Democrats, since the Free Soilers advocated federally funded programs "of national concern," and Zachary Taylor promised to abide by "the will of the people." If the voters were "willing that millions and hundreds of millions shall be expended in foreign wars," wrote one Whig editor with a jibe at the Democrats' handling of the Mexican conflict, "and nothing shall be granted to improve the Rivers and Harbors of the West, let Lewis Cass be President." The attacks continued throughout the campaign, as Whigs and Free Soilers repeatedly reminded the voters of Cass's perfunctory letter to the Chicago convention. Many northwestern newspapers, such as the *Indiana State Journal,* simply reprinted the entire note without comment. With grim mockery, a Philadelphia journalist reported that "all masters of vessels and seamen upon the lakes and western rivers propose to carry the insulting letter of Candidate CASS to the Chicago Convention at half-mast during the political campaign; it will be printed upon a very little flag, and thrown to the breeze." One campaign song admonished the Democratic candidate:

> Yes truth is mighty and it must
> Prevail with honest minds, sir,
> The people cannot put their trust
> In letters of five lines, sir.

Hoosier congressman Caleb B. Smith was equally disparaging, waving on the floor of the House a ludicrously tiny book, "about two inches square," which contained the brief communication.[30]

The negative impact of the Chicago letter was reinforced by Lewis Cass's own actions soon after he received the Democratic nomination. On his homeward journey to await the outcome of the election, Cass paused at Cleveland. The opportunity to undo some of the damage on the improvements issue arose when a local Democratic politician, Judge Reuben Wood, presented the candidate to a hastily assembled crowd. In a short introduction, Wood asked for his opinion on the extension of slavery and "the improvement of our Western Rivers and Harbors." Cass dissembled, claiming that "the noise and confusion which pervade this vast assembly will, I apprehend, prevent me from being distinctly heard by all present." Following these abrupt remarks, Cass demonstrated in a brief address that it was not the boisterous crowd which prevented him from commenting on such controversial subjects.[31]

Cass's refusal to discuss important political issues, and his unfortunate use at Cleveland of the phrase "noise and confusion," provided his opponents with a considerable amount of campaign material. The Detroit Whig newspaper rhetorically inquired if there was "ever one who better deserved the cognomen of 'Artful Dodger,' than Gen. Cass?" In a heavy-handed attempt at wordplay, the *Scioto Gazette* pugnaciously predicted, "At the election in November the 'river and harbor' boys will knock the 'C' off" Cass's name. Whig marchers sang:

> Poor Cass they did interrogate,
> His silence has revenged us,
> "Confusion" seized the candidate
> The "noise," it was tremendous.

According to a *Battery* reporter, Cass found himself "unexpectedly in hot water" at Cleveland; his expression was likened to that of a lobster "at the very first moment of his being boiled." The national Whig campaign organ placed above the title of each issue an illustration of General Taylor on horseback, commanding his artillery officer to fire "A Little More Grape." The cannon was aimed at an obese figure saying, "Sir, the noise and confusion which pervade this assembly will prevent my being heard on the important topics to which you have called my attention." Lest the reader miss the allusion, the target of Captain Bragg's shot was labeled *"Cass at Cleveland."* Partisan orators exuberantly picked up this theme, and sarcastic references to "noise and confusion" rarely failed to draw derisive laughter. When Senator Reverdy Johnson proposed that ten thousand copies of the "Memorial of the Chicago Convention" be printed and distributed, Democratic votes tabled the resolution.[32]

In the face of incessant attacks, Democrats defended their candidate's position regarding river and harbor improvements. The *Campaign* dismissed the "noise and confusion" incident by insisting the remarks made by Cass were "most shamefully misrepresented by the whig press." On the broader issue of federal funding for rivers and harbors, one Cass journal hedged by stating he was "in favor of internal improvements within the limits prescribed by the constitution." John Wentworth, a zealous advocate of river and harbor improvements, remarked that since entering Congress, he and Cass "voted invariably alike on this question. . . . I wish there was as good proof that General Taylor would sign our harbor and river bills." Richard W. Thompson, a Whig congressman from Indiana, grudgingly conceded that Cass "stood up manfully at all times, for the Harbor and River improvements" bills.[33]

Democrats took the offensive, questioning their opponents' stand on rivers and harbors. In yet another sarcastic reference to Zachary Taylor's lack of expressed principles and ignorance of the issues, a Democratic journal inquired of the candidate: "'How are you on internal improvements?' 'Thank you, my internals are well enough, for I never employed a doctor in all my life, I never balk the course of nature.'" The *Detroit Free Press* similarly concocted a letter from the Whig nominee. "I don't know how big your lakes are," Taylor supposedly wrote, "but if boats can run on them, the harbors ought to be made good." The general added he was "in favor of improving the harbor at Baton Rouge, and the clearing out of *snags* (that I suppose means Allegators) but I have somewhere read that there were no snags or allegators in the north." In brief, while the Whigs attempted to exploit the internal improvements controversy, Democrats confidently relied upon their candidate's voting record to help carry the Northwest.[34]

Lewis Cass was a firm and consistent supporter of internal improvements. Soon after taking his Senate seat in December 1845, he presented resolutions concerning deepening the channel at the mouth of the St. Clair River and constructing a canal around the falls at the Sault. Cass did not confine his support of such legislation to his home state. He voted in favor of bills providing land grants to Mississippi for a railroad, and appropriations for the improvement of the Ohio, Mississippi, and Arkansas Rivers. He persuaded his colleagues to reinstate a twelve thousand dollar appropriation for Little Fort Harbor, Illinois, reminding them "the God of nature had imposed the most formidable difficulties" on the Great Lakes. Cass based the constitutionality of such measures on the "landowner argument." The federal government, which held more than half the nation's territory, was "empowered by the Constitution *to dispose of and make all needful rules and regulations respecting the territory or other property belonging to the United States.*" Cass reasoned that any property owner, "seeking to dispose of his large landed interest, would ask himself what improvements he could make to give it greater value and a readier sale. This is a dictate of common sense, as well of every day's experience. Roads, every one knows, facilitate settlements," as do canals and railroads. While Cass was silent on the subject of internal improvements during the presidential campaign, he had unwaveringly supported such projects in the Senate with his voice and vote. The issue undoubtedly cost the Democratic ticket some popular support in the Northwest, but Cass remained serenely confident of the region's electoral votes.[35]

Although the internal improvements controversy did Lewis Cass no irreparable political harm, he was not so fortunate with the tariff question. The highly protective Whig tariff of 1842 was superseded four years later by the Walker Act. Whigs argued the lower Democratic schedules took "the daily bread from the orphan" and cast millions out of work. Senator Cass's vote for the Walker Tariff and the Democratic policy of favoring only incidental protection were attacked during the presidential race in the Northeast and Louisiana. Senator John Davis lyrically praised the Whig policy, or "the black tariff, as the enemies of American industry are pleased to call it," under which "our finances became prosperous, . . . the hammer and the shuttle were again heard in unison with the cheerful songs of the laborer—and light hearts with strong arms gave unexampled prosperity to our industrial pursuits." The Massachusetts Whig criticized Cass and other supporters of the Walker Act for encouraging "foreign labor while they bankrupted our own." This theme was especially effective in Pennsylvania, where the iron industry was mired in a slump.[36]

The Democrats did not waver under the Whig attack. They consistently opposed high tariff schedules, aware that this aided their cause in the South. The *Detroit Free Press* typically contended, "There can be no other object in creating a protective tariff than to benefit the rich at the expense of the poor, and to build up a set of manufacturing aristocrats, to draw the life's blood from the hard working portion of [the] community." The *Washington Union* characterized the Whigs as "a pampered and avaricious combination of manufacturing capitalists." According to the article, Taylor personally favored a high tariff because he was "a large Sugar maker in Louisiana—or rather his human chattels make it for him." His business interests placed the Whig candidate in the position of seeking a protective tariff, "by which he can control the market and make people buy their sweetening of him at such price as he may see fit to fix." Additionally, Taylor was linked to the northeastern Whig cotton manufacturers, who would conspire with him "to get the tariff raised."[37]

Democrats, though opposed to protective tariffs as a matter of policy, sought to play down the negative effects of the Walker Act on the American economy. The *Philadelphia Pennsylvanian* noted the iron industry expanded its domestic market and increased exports under the lower schedules, and Robert Rantoul informed his fellow Massachusetts Democrats the textile industry had enjoyed similar benefits. Party orators and newspapers warned the laboring masses not to be swayed by Whig claims that the Walker Tariff was responsible for throwing so many of them out of work. The *Boston Post* printed a conversation "between a broken down whig proprietor and an honest-hearted Irish operative." Since the local foundry was closed owing to an economic slump blamed on the Democratic tariff, the Whig owner inquired of his unemployed laborer:

> "You surely won't vote *again* for men who throw you out of employment?"
>
> "It's the *dimocrathic* ticket, you say?"
>
> "Yes, Murphey—yes."
>
> "I think I will, sir."
>
> "You're a *fool,* Murphey. Will you submit to treatment like *this,* from your friends?" . . .
>
> "I'm jes thinkin', sir, *if it's our friends, as you say, that trate us so badly, wat the divil our innemies 'ill do, ef they could get a chance!*"
>
> "You're a fool, I say."
>
> "May be so, masther, But I'll vote for Cass and Butler—so I will!"

Supporters of Cass and Butler hoped the laboring classes would remain as firmly committed to their cause as the fictitious Patrick Murphey. They would, however, be disappointed. The tariff issue hindered the Democratic ticket in several key northeastern states.[38]

The internal improvements and tariff controversies were emphasized in various regions of the country to the detriment of Lewis Cass, but the major issue that transcended sectional boundaries was slavery extension. The Democratic platform made no mention of the Wilmot Proviso or popular sovereignty; it was generally believed the Nicholson letter better served the party and ticket. Cass agreed. His position on the question of slavery in the western territories was widely known, and he consistently chose to ignore requests for clarification. Cass avowed he would write no more political letters: "I have said I would not, and I have been cautioned against doing it, time and again, by some of our best friends." Democratic organs throughout the nation adopted popular sovereignty as orthodox party doctrine following the Baltimore convention, and they carried the Cass message to the electorate. The *Democratic Review* dismissed supporters of the Wilmot amendment as "broken down politicians and disappointed office-seekers, banded together for an unholy purpose." Southern Democrats argued that Cass was a "firm and avowed opponent" of the "distracting and pestiferous" proviso and could be counted on to veto any bill prohibiting slavery in the territories. Northern Cass supporters, on the other hand, focused on his New England origins and claimed popular sovereignty would keep the West free. Obviously, the disparate factions still loyal to the regular party ticket were able to unite under the multihued banner of the Father of Popular Sovereignty.[39]

The Wilmot Proviso was the only significant issue during his long public career upon which Cass completely reversed his stand, and his political opponents made the most of it. The Whigs contended he took ambiguous positions in a characteristic attempt to garner political support from both the North and South. Southerners recalled Cass's claim, while minister to France, that he had never been a slaveholder and prayed for the total abolition of slavery. Antislavery Whigs emphasized he opposed the proviso, in early 1847, because its passage would interfere with the annexation of Mexican territory. Abraham Lincoln joined in the attack by citing Cass's change of position, trenchantly characterizing the candidate as a doltish beast blindly responding to his master, the Democratic party:

> When the question was raised in 1846, he was in a blustering hurry to take ground for it. He sought to be in advance, and to avoid the uninteresting position of a mere follower; but soon he began to see

> glimpses of the great Democratic ox-gad waving in his face, and to hear, indistinctly, a voice saying, "Back," "back, sir," "Back a little." He shakes his head; and bats his eyes, and blunders back to his position of March, 1847; but still the gad waves, and the voice grows more distinct, and sharper still—"Back, sir!" "Back, I say!" "Further back!" and back he goes to the position of December, 1847; at which the gad is still, and the voice soothingly says—"So!" "Stand at that."

Northern Whigs insisted that although Taylor was a slaveholder, he would not veto the proviso; whereas Cass, "the Boss Dough-face of the country," would preside over the extension of slavery into the territories.[40]

The accusation that Cass was "two faced" on slavery extension was reinforced by divergent editions of a Democratic campaign pamphlet. The *Sketch of the Life and Public Services of Gen. Lewis Cass* intended for the North contained a section praising the recent European revolutions. The version distributed in the South, however, deleted that section, and inserted an extract from the Nicholson letter repudiating the Wilmot Proviso. A Whig congressman from Virginia read aloud from the two pamphlets and fulminated: "Talk about tricks; about sneaking into power unworthily! Where was so palpable an attempt to do so as here, in this defeated instance?" Cass, he concluded, plainly could not be trusted. Democrats explained that the northern edition was prepared, after Cass left Washington, solely to take into account recent events in Europe. Moreover, as Howell Cobb contended, if Cass shifted on the proviso issue, "the reason was to be found in the course pursued by every honest man, who, when the conviction was made on his mind that he was wrong, changed the position which he had erroneously taken." The Democrats further stressed there were fourteen different campaign biographies of Taylor in circulation.[41]

The Whigs, too, ignored the subject of slavery extension when drafting a platform, and questions were raised concerning Zachary Taylor's "two faces" on the issue. Northern supporters pointed to his pledge never to use the veto power, "except in cases of clear violation of the Constitution," claiming this precluded blocking the proviso. The candidate himself appeared to sanction this interpretation in a loosely worded letter to free soil Democrat James W. Taylor, a Cincinnati newspaper editor. A clipping from the *Morning Signal,* declaring, "The extension over the continent beyond the Rio Grande of the ordinance of 1787 is an object too high and permanent to be baffled by presidential vetoes," was submitted to the general, who responded evasively, concluding, "I trust you will pardon me for thus briefly replying to you, which I do with a high opinion and approval of the sentiments and views embraced in your editorial." Southern Democrats seized upon this as evidence that Zachary Taylor was unreliable on the proviso issue. His northern opponents contrastingly noted that Taylor later repudiated the *Signal* editorial. Moreover, the Whig candidate was "a southern man and a slaveholder, and therefore identified with southern interests." An extract from an Alabama newspaper, circulated throughout the North, warned, "*We must elect a man for the President of the United States who lives in our own sunny South;* who is willing to peril all for the Constitution; who loves the South and HER CHERISHED INSTITUTIONS." Regarding the potentially most explosive political issue of the national election, both Whigs and Democrats attempted to obfuscate the stance of their candidate. At the same time, each side accused the other of deliberately deceiving the electorate by taking an equivocal position on the question of slavery extension.[42]

In the weeks after the Baltimore and Philadelphia conventions, the majority of Democrats and Whigs united behind their respective tickets, but important factions of both parties remained implacably opposed to Cass and Taylor. The outcome of the presidential race would depend in large measure on the success of the candidates in mollifying those disaffected by their nominations. Many northern Whigs were upset with the selection of a slaveholder, and those who opposed the Mexican War were further alienated by the choice of a military man as their candidate. One Michigan Democrat smugly assessed the predicament of the antiwar Whigs: "These gentlemen see their inconsistency. They denounced the war, . . . charged Genl. Taylor with being a woman & child killer & praying to God that the Genl. & his army might find graves in Mexico & now to have this same Genl. forced upon them as their standardbearer makes the blood run cold in their vains."[43]

Massachusetts Whigs, in particular, were divided over the question of supporting Taylor. While Rufus Choate, Senator John Davis, and Speaker of the House Robert Winthrop rallied to the regular party nomination, many others turned to Daniel Webster for guidance. "Black Dan," who was disappointed and offended by Taylor's candidacy, flirted briefly with the notion of joining the Free Soil organization. After correctly assessing the political strength of the antislavery movement in the Northeast, however, he decided the presidential race was between Taylor and Cass. Since Webster viewed Cass as "the most dangerous man in whom the powers of the executive Chief Magistracy could well be placed," he tepidly endorsed Taylor in an address delivered near his home at Marshfield on September 1. The acrimonious public debate over the Treaty of Washington and the right-of-search issue had brought Cass national attention and helped secure the presidential nomination, but it just as certainly ensured that Daniel Webster ultimately supported the Whig ticket in 1848.[44]

The response to Webster's Marshfield speech was predictable. The *Detroit Free Press* rejoiced at his unenthusiastic endorsement of Taylor and crowed, "He has killed him with faint praise." Robert Winthrop, however, shrewdly ascertained that "a sulky support is better than opposition"; and indeed, most Massachusetts Whigs remained loyal to the regular ticket. Somewhat halfheartedly, Webster blunted the appeal of the Free Soil party among northeastern Whigs—damaging the political prospects of Lewis Cass in the process.[45]

Henry Clay was another Whig leader disappointed with the Taylor candidacy. Embittered by the lack of support he received at Philadelphia, the Kentuckian could not forgive Taylor for threatening to remain in the presidential race if he failed to receive the nomination. The prideful Clay resolved to remain aloof from the hurly-burly of the canvass, but the actions of northeastern Whigs forced his hand.[46]

In early September, New York Whigs, enraged that Taylor publicly accepted the support of a group of Charleston Democrats, defiantly nominated a ticket of Henry Clay and Millard Fillmore. Clay declined the draft. Although he entertained partisan "apprehensions from the election of General Cass," he did "not see enough of hope and confidence in that of General Taylor to stimulate my exertions and animate my zeal." The Kentuckian therefore adopted a policy of "silence and reserve" during the campaign, but his rejection of the independent New York Whig nomination, and his public opposition to Cass, aided the Taylor cause.[47]

The influential publisher of the *New York Tribune* was similarly shocked by the nomination of Taylor and the refusal of the Whig national convention to adopt a specific party platform. Following his return home from "the late National Slaughter-House at Philadelphia," Horace Greeley refused to endorse the ticket and counseled his readers to take "time for reflection." He wistfully wrote Clay of his desire to "spend this season on some quiet farm, and see the play acted out by those interested in its results." Greeley nevertheless adamantly opposed the election of that "pot-bellied, mutton-headed cucumber, Lewis Cass," and after it became clear Clay would not enter the race, he reluctantly endorsed Taylor on September 29. Since Van

Buren could not be elected, the *Tribune* editorial argued, Taylor must be supported to guarantee the defeat of Cass, "the least worthy and most dangerous among the candidates." Greeley thus joined Webster and many other northeastern Whigs in reluctantly backing Taylor.[48]

Many Whigs came to support the Philadelphia nomination with some trepidation, fearing Zachary Taylor would not be a steadfast defender of party principles. The candidate himself contributed to this image. After accepting the Whig nomination, Taylor proclaimed in a widely circulated letter to George Lippard, "I AM NOT A PARTY CANDIDATE, and if elected shall not be the President of a party." To compound the confusion, Taylor accepted the nomination of a group of Charleston Democrats who refused to support Lewis Cass because he did not specifically endorse the right to hold slaves in the western territories. Taylor's acceptance of this nomination, with Democratic vice presidential candidate William Butler as his running mate, infuriated New York Whigs, who logically interpreted it as a public insult to Millard Fillmore. Henry Clay smugly observed that a few more communications, such as those sent to Lippard and the independent Charleston Democrats, would give Taylor "the *coup de grace*." A Cass campaign journal delightedly agreed with this appraisal: "The letters of Gen. Taylor are like the stones thrown at frogs. They may be sport to him, but they are death to his friends!"[49]

In light of the reception accorded his Lippard and Charleston letters, Zachary Taylor made a final effort to assuage the feelings of his Whig followers. In a second communication to Captain Allison, dated September 4, he wrote that from the first mention of his name for the presidency, he declared himself "to be a Whig on all proper occasions." Turning to the Charleston controversy, Taylor reasoned he could no more "repel nominations from political opponents" than "refuse the vote of a democrat at the polls." His avowal of party principles, and a complimentary allusion to Fillmore, had the desired effect of quieting northern dissatisfaction with his nomination. Philip Hone represented many New York Whigs when he maintained party discipline in November and voted against Lewis Cass, the "embodiment of political humbug and demogogism." A smaller contingent of Whigs either joined the Free Soilers or refused to participate in the election. As Thurlow Weed phrased it, the second Allison letter "inspired the confidence and awakened the zeal of the now united Whig party."[50]

The Democrats suffered from similar schisms during the course of the campaign. With the exception of Van Buren loyalists, those opposed to

Cass generally were either fervid proslavery southerners or northerners devoted to prohibiting the expansion of the peculiar institution. A North Carolina newspaper astutely observed that the Baltimore delegates "found it impossible to please the two extremes of South Carolina and New York." The Barnburners refused to support Gen. Cass "because he goes *too far* for Southern rights," while slave state Democrats denounced him "because he does not go *far enough!*"[51] At this juncture of the slavery debate, Lewis Cass and his popular sovereignty doctrine represented a distinctly moderate position, untenable only to Van Burenites and the more radical sectionalists. As a national candidate, Cass had no acceptable alternative beyond holding tightly to the political allegiance of the vast majority of the Democrats while reluctantly yielding the support of the uncompromising segments of the party. It turned out, however, that the number of Democrats who broke ranks and failed to rally to the Cass banner was electorally significant.

William Yancey, who bolted the Baltimore convention over the question of federal protection for slavery in the territories, led the extremist southerners opposed to the national ticket. Yancey warned that Cass could not be trusted on the Wilmot Proviso but admitted that among his fellow Democrats, "nine-tenths, and I fear even a greater proportion, are determined to vote for the regular ticket." The recipient of this disheartened political forecast, John C. Calhoun, shared Yancey's objections to the nomination of Lewis Cass. In a public letter dated September 1, the South Carolinian urged his friends to "regard me as taking no part between the two candidates, and as standing on independent ground." As a result, many Democrats actively opposed Cass, including the dissidents who met at Charleston and nominated Zachary Taylor for president. The Taylor boom among Democrats in South Carolina, however, was dampened by the second Allison letter. The previously wavering *Charleston Mercury,* and politicians such as Robert Barnwell Rhett and Andrew Pickens, led the Cass resurgence. When South Carolina voters went to the polls in early October to select the legislature that would choose the presidential electors, a decisive victory for the regular Democratic ticket was predicted.[52]

Most northern Democrats opposed to Cass were equally against the extension of slavery, but many refused to support the party ticket because of personal allegiance to Martin Van Buren. This was especially the case in New England and New York. Additionally, antislavery Democrats blamed the defeat of Governor Silas Wright's bid for reelection, in 1846, on lackadaisical campaigning by the regular party organization. After Wright's sudden death, Whig newspapers stoked the internecine flames by reminding Barnburners that "Lewis Cass and the Polk administration originated and countenanced the political assassination of that great and good man." Supporters of Cass, in turn, railed at the "treachery" displayed by Van Buren in running as a Free Soiler. It was charged the New Yorker vindictively entered the race because Cass supported the two-thirds rule at the national convention of 1844, which "tricked & cheated" Van Buren out of the nomination. Daniel Dickinson informed Cass the Free Soil candidate's "vengeful appetite had eaten up his good sense. . . . he is left like an old lecher with all his hurts, but destitute of power." The *Detroit Free Press* branded Van Buren "a traitor," the *Washington Union* referred to him as "the Arch Apostate," and an Illinois journal flippantly dismissed the former president as "the 'Great Sore-Head' of Kinderhook." A Michigan newspaper summarized the animosity felt toward Van Buren by regular Democrats: "There has never been a man in existence who has fallen from so high to so low a station in the hearts of his countrymen . . . save and except perhaps, the traitor, Aaron Burr." Although he generally kept silent during the campaign, Cass denounced the opposition of Van Buren as "equally unexpected and lamentable," and supported President Polk's purge of Free Soilers.[53]

When Barnburners raised "the guerrilla standard" of Martin Van Buren at Utica in June, Democrats loyal to the Baltimore ticket called upon President Polk to dismiss the defectors from federal posts. Senator Dickinson led the call, and among his chief targets was New York district attorney Benjamin F. Butler. Polk, however, was urged to be cautious during private consultations with vice presidential candidate William Butler, Senator Alpheus Felch, and Congressman Robert C. McClelland. Cass personally favored an immediate purge, but he accepted the president's decision to move deliberately so as not to drive wavering Democrats into the Barnburner ranks. After the Free Soil convention at Buffalo, however, Cass and Polk agreed on the necessity of removal, lest the administration appear to countenance the third-party nominations. Ironically, the politically motivated removals of Butler and other Van Burenites, which were characterized as vindictive and petty, strengthened the resolve of some northeastern Democrats to oppose the Cass nomination.[54]

Whigs and Democrats could not agree among themselves whether Van Buren's candidacy aided or damaged their respective campaigns. Some Whigs hopefully predicted:

Cass used Van up in '44,
His plotting did defeat him,
But Van is healing up the sore
By helping Zach to beat HIM.

The *Illinois Journal* concluded the Free Soil ticket "strikes a death blow to all lingering hopes of the friends of Gen. Cass." Other Taylor organs, however, warned the third party would attract antislavery Whigs. Democrats were likewise divided in their assessments. Benton optimistically reasoned the defection "may do us no harm—that it may cut as much one way as the other." Wentworth echoed these sentiments, convinced "Van Buren's coming out saves New York from Taylor," while another Cass supporter boasted the new states admitted since 1844 would more than "make good the loss" of New York. The Democratic candidate himself correctly assumed that the nomination of Van Buren hurt the ticket in New York, "but elsewhere our prospects look encouraging." Less sanguine Democratic observers shared with Cass, and many of his Whig opponents, distinct misgivings about the entry of the Free Soilers into the campaign.[55]

In part because the Free Soilers were feared by both Whigs and Democrats, "almost the whole of the virulence and animosity" generated during the election was directed against them. Democratic campaign literature castigated the third party as little more than a fractious group of "barn burners, bolters, sore-heads, cock-eyes, sick Whigs, and darkies," threatening the stability of the Union. The Free Soil convention was ridiculed as "the mongrel assembly of Buffalo"; Martin Van Buren was portrayed as a "desperate man," driven "by disappointed ambition and rankling revenge," who willingly renounced past principles in a reckless venture to defeat Cass. A Whig pamphlet, informatively entitled *Inconsistency and Hypocrisy of Martin Van Buren on the Question of Slavery,* outlined the Free Soil candidate's prosouthern leanings since the time of the Missouri Compromise. James Russell Lowell captured the mood of many antislavery men when he declared:

I used to vote fer Martin, but, I swan, I'm
clean disgusted,—
He aint the man thet I can say is fittin'
to be trusted.

To underscore Van Buren's flexible principles, a pamphlet written by Charles Francis Adams during the previous presidential election was reprinted. The Free Soil vice presidential candidate had characterized his running mate as a politician who "*bargained away* much that the free States deem valuable" to gratify his personal ambition. Although Adams now claimed Van Buren was a staunch antislavery man, doubts lingered regarding the sincerity of his political conversion. Some abolitionists joined the assault against the Free Soil organization. "Its name rightly describes it," explained William Lloyd Garrison, "it is a party for keeping *Soil* free, and not for setting *Men* free."[56]

Despite the vituperation heaped upon Van Buren, Free Soil organizations were formed throughout the northern states, with an exuberance unmatched by the Democrats or Whigs. Antislavery forces faithfully attended rallies and barbecues and sang:

> Come, ye hardy sons of toil,
> And cast your ballots for Free soil;
> He who'd vote for Zacky Taylor
> Needs a keeper or a jailor.
> And he who still for Cass can be,
> He is a Cass without the C;
> The man on whom we love to look,
> Is Martin Van Buren from Kinderhook.

One campaign document succinctly stated, "There is absolutely no difference between Cass and Taylor. You must vote for enslaving 1,800,000 square miles—or vote for Van Buren and Adams." The *North Star* declared the traditional parties "are chained to the bloody car of Slavery, and . . . every man in them is but a pitiful pack-horse, with bit in mouth, to be guided by the rein, and urged on by the whip of his Southern masters." Cass, "too much of a politician," and an avowed opponent of the Wilmot Proviso, was portrayed by Free Soil orators as a traitor to the North. "Why does Lewis Cass live in this glorious North West? Why has he been educated on this free soil? Tell me why, on the richest meadows grow the largest toadstools, and I will answer you." The antislavery men presented an anecdotal response to Democrats who claimed the election of Cass would guarantee the freedom of the western territories:

> FREE SOILER—Well, neighbor, what do you think of this matter of extending slavery?

CASS MAN—What do I think of it? Why, I am opposed to its extension, of course! I go for Free Soil.
FREE SOILER—O, I'm glad to hear it. Then you will vote for Van Buren of course.
CASS MAN—Not as you know of! I go for Cass and Free Soil!
FREE SOILER—O, ah, yes! You remind me of a man I knew once who married a colored lady, but resolved to have none but white children!

Zachary Taylor similarly was dismissed by the Free Soilers as a soldier "wholly destitute of political experience." Moreover, he was "born and bred a slaveholder." If either Taylor or Cass won the White House, slavery would be extended, along with "lust, rapine, and the lowest grade of licentiousness."[57]

In the face of criticism from both Democrats and Whigs, who questioned his devotion to the antislavery cause, Van Buren was defended by the Free Soilers with a zealousness characteristic of recent converts. The *National Era* argued that even if the New Yorker had been "subservient to the slave power" in the past, "he is not, like Gen. Cass, a vassal of it, or, like Gen. Taylor, its embodiment, in 1848." One campaign journal ebulliently predicted that with Van Buren and Adams as candidates, "we can not doubt success." As the November election approached, however, the political prospects of the Free Soilers were greatly diminished.[58]

The result of the presidential campaign was foreshadowed in the state elections held during the summer and autumn months. Michigan, Indiana, Illinois, Wisconsin, and Iowa were considered to be solidly Democratic. Those five northwestern states totaled 34 of the 290 electoral votes. Michigan, Indiana, and Illinois voted for Polk in 1844 (Wisconsin and Iowa not then being states), and favorite son Lewis Cass was expected to achieve even greater majorities. The candidate assured Nicholson early in the campaign that "north of the Ohio, our friends are in the best spirits," but the Free Soil nomination of Martin Van Buren upset his optimistic calculations. Austin Blair, Isaac P. Christiancy, and Flavius Littlejohn led the Free Soilers in Michigan, and George Washington Julian emerged as the foremost antislavery crusader in Indiana, although only small pockets of Free Soil strength developed in those two states and Iowa. Northern Illinois and portions of Wisconsin, however, demonstrated vigorous support for Van Buren. Jesse Bright spearheaded the Democratic assault against the Free Soilers, and when opponents to slavery extension (such as John Wentworth) remained loyal to the national ticket, it became apparent the Northwest would be carried by Cass. Despite the yeoman service of Abraham Lincoln to rally local Whigs, voters in Illinois, Indiana, and Iowa went to the polls in August and elected the Democratic slates. Cass was buoyed by these encouraging election returns in his home region and reported that "in the North west generally all looks well."[59]

The prospects of the Democrats were equally favorable in the southwestern states, with several notable exceptions. Alabama, Mississippi, Louisiana, Arkansas, and Missouri cast their electoral votes for Polk in the previous canvass. Although Yancey opposed Cass in Alabama, that traditionally Democratic state was expected to support the national ticket, and so was Mississippi, under the leadership of Henry Foote, Jefferson Davis, and John A. Quitman. Arkansas, Missouri, and Texas were also conceded by the Whigs. Local elections during the summer months confirmed that the twenty-nine electoral votes of those five states were securely in the Cass column. Louisiana, in contrast, could not be counted on by the Democrats. The Walker Tariff was unpopular among sugar planters, and party unity was damaged by feuding between John Slidell and Pierre Soulé. Louisiana was expected to cast her six electoral votes for the local hero, Zachary Taylor. The Whigs were confident they likewise would carry Kentucky's twelve electoral votes, but Tennessee was not so readily conceded by Cass. Embarrassed by the failure to carry his home state in 1844, President Polk joined with Nicholson and Andrew Johnson in predicting a Democratic victory. Objective observers nonetheless placed the thirteen electoral votes of Tennessee in the Whig column.[60]

The southeastern states were split in their support. Delaware, Maryland, and North Carolina—with a total of twenty-two electoral votes—consistently backed the Whig national ticket during the 1840s. Zachary Taylor was a native of traditionally Democratic Virginia, and a valiant attempt to carry the Old Dominion was led by William C. Rives, a former Democrat who had pushed for Cass's nomination in 1844. Virginia Whigs assailed Cass as "one of the greatest political prostitutes of the age," while Democrats adhered to their southern strategy, and concentrated on the "Abolition candidate for Vice President," Millard Fillmore. Virginia's seventeen electoral votes appeared to be destined for the Democratic column. So did the nine votes of South Carolina. Initially, Cass's nomination inspired slight enthusiasm in the Palmetto State. Calhoun remained publicly aloof from the campaign, but Robert B. Rhett eventually rallied most Democrats to the Cass banner. The *Charleston*

Mercury admitted that a neutral stand "would be a position of imbecility" and threw its support behind the Baltimore ticket. South Carolina was the only state that still chose its presidential electors by vote of the legislature, and the Democrats overwhelmingly carried the local races in early October. The state election in neighboring Georgia, with ten electoral votes, did not indicate a clear victory for either political party. Howell Cobb stumped the state for Cass, and his Whig congressional colleagues, Alexander Stephens and Robert Toombs, were equally active in urging Georgians to support Taylor. Florida joined Wisconsin, Iowa, and Texas in voting for the first time in a presidential election, and received little national attention. Democratic newspapers informed their readers that "Gen. Cass is perfectly sound on all questions of slavery," and typically pointed to the abolitionist stance of Fillmore. But Floridians had more confidence in slaveholder Zachary Taylor, a popular figure from his role in the Seminole conflict of the 1830s. When the Whig slate carried the state election, it was evident Florida would cast her three electoral votes for Old Rough and Ready.[61]

The Northeast proved to be a pivotal section. Most New England states were expected to follow accustomed political patterns. Maine tended to be Democratic, and after the state races in September, the *Campaign* boasted her nine electoral votes may "be set down *as already counted for Cass and Butler.*" Cass's native New Hampshire, under the leadership of Levi Woodbury and Franklin Pierce, was also considered to be firmly behind the regular ticket. Vermont and Connecticut were expected to back the Whig candidate, especially since the Free Soil party drew support from former Democrats such as John M. Niles. New Hampshire, Vermont, and Connecticut each held six electoral votes. Rhode Island, a Providence correspondent reminded Cass, had been "under whig control for many years," and her four votes were conceded to Taylor. Massachusetts, traditionally a Whig stronghold, was the scene of the most vocal and enthusiastic Free Soil campaign in New England. Many Whigs followed Sumner, Wilson, and Samuel Hoar into the Free Soil ranks; but the regular party organization soon roused itself, and it became apparent the Bay State would contribute her twelve electoral votes to the Taylor column. The Whigs were assured, as well, of New Jersey's seven votes.[62]

The most populous state in the Union was the scene of a bitter three-way presidential race. New York Democrats were sharply divided between Cass and Van Buren, and the Free Soilers presented a distinguished slate headed by John Dix. A few regular Democrats continued to predict Van Buren would siphon off more votes from Taylor, but by October, Cass privately confessed he did not harbor "the most distant hope" of victory. John Van Buren gloated: "Lewis Cass stood as much chance of carrying the great state of New York as Louis Philippe." Whig partisans agreed, and confidently counted on the Empire State's thirty-six electoral votes.[63]

Notwithstanding the apparent Whig ascendancy in the Northeast, Democrats retained "full confidence and belief in the election of our President." Prior to the Baltimore convention the *Detroit Free Press* optimistically declared, "We *can* and *shall* elect the nominee" without the vote of New York. Although Whig newspapers objected to this "insulting boast," it was understood that success in both Ohio and Pennsylvania would place Cass in the White House. The arithmetic was elementary, based on the 146 electoral votes necessary for election. With the race in Georgia too evenly contested to ascribe its votes to either candidate, Taylor could reasonably count on a total of 127 and Cass 104. The Democrats therefore needed to sweep Ohio and Pennsylvania, with a combined 49 electoral votes. The Whig national campaign manager calculated in early October that if the party carried either Ohio or Pennsylvania, "we are safe."[64]

The Whigs carried Ohio in the two previous presidential campaigns but were by no means assured of success in 1848. Cass was closely identified with the Buckeye State because he served in the state legislature before the War of 1812 and spent eighteen years governing neighboring Michigan. Most Ohio Democrats accepted popular sovereignty as a fair solution to the slavery extension question, and "Fog Horn" Allen stumped the state on behalf of the national ticket. The Democratic cause was aided by widespread opposition among Whigs to the Philadelphia nomination. Governor William Bebb, Benjamin Wade, and Thomas Corwin threw themselves into the campaign, but Taylor received rather listless support from Ohioans. He was further damaged by the Free Soilers, who were especially active in the Western Reserve. Joshua Giddings led the antislavery exodus from the Whig ranks, and he teamed with Salmon Chase to give the Free Soil organization a moral fervor unmatched in any other state. Cass supporters confidently calculated that "Van Buren will take off five to ten Whigs to one democrat," and the election returns in October bolstered their hopes. The Democrats increased their representation in state and federal offices, and missed capturing the governorship by only a few hundred votes. Ohio seemed destined for the Democratic column in November.[65]

The probability of a Cass victory in Ohio made the contest in Pennsylvania crucial. Although Harrison narrowly carried the state in 1840, Pennsylvanians usually voted Democratic. In 1848, however, the Whig organization was united behind Taylor, and several key issues aided their cause. The voters of Pittsburgh and other iron and coal regions blamed a recent economic slump on the Walker Tariff, and wool growers in western Pennsylvania were also sensitive to this issue. The Whig ticket was further strengthened by fusion with the local Native American party, headed by Philadelphia congressman Lewis C. Levin. As one Cass supporter bitterly phrased it, the Whigs "went to work dividing the spoil[s] of office with the Natives." Although Democrats derided this "crazy cabal," Taylor's prospects in Philadelphia brightened.[66]

In contrast to the Whigs and their Nativist allies, Pennsylvania Democrats were divided and dispirited. Vice President Dallas and Secretary of State Buchanan, both disappointed aspirants for the presidential nomination, unenthusiastically attempted to hold the party together in support of Cass. Gideon Welles branded Buchanan and his cohorts "the very worst managers of a good cause that ever afflicted a state." The fragmented Democrats received another setback with the resignation in June of Governor Francis Shunk, who was terminally ill. Cass's chances were hurt as well by the antislavery movement. David Wilmot, of the Towanda district, announced he planned to "support Van Buren with the whole strength of my patriotism," despite Robert McClelland's efforts to gain his endorsement of the regular ticket. The October returns indicated that Pennsylvania, until recently a bellwether Democratic state, was carried by the Whigs in a remarkably close vote. The national Democratic campaign organ acknowledged its disappointment at the shocking results but claimed the state "is now safe, because she is roused. . . . Our friends will redeem themselves." Still, the twenty-six electoral votes of the aptly nicknamed Keystone State remained doubtful on the eve of the national election.[67]

On November 7, 1848, the presidential election for the first time was held on the same day throughout the United States. Partisan journals and politicians urged vigilance at the polls and predicted victory before the final returns were tabulated. The *Battery* admonished its readers to arrive at the polling stations, "rain or shine, hail or snow, at least an hour or two before they are opened," since "the Cassites no doubt will attempt some of their usual frauds, and must therefore be watched." It was a closely contested race and, as expected, Pennsylvania proved to be decisive. At about midnight, Henry Ledyard handed Lewis Cass a telegraphic message from Allegheny County, which showed the Democrats carrying Pittsburgh. The festive crowd gathered about the Cass home cheered the news, but the candidate himself understood that the relatively small majority portended defeat statewide. "I am beaten," Cass calmly remarked, and retired to his bed. By Friday, it was apparent his analysis was correct. The Democratic *Cleveland Plain Dealer* conceded, on November 10, "We deliberately record our opinion that the election of Gen. Cass is *certain*—but that of Gen. Taylor a *leetle more so.*" Lewis Cass was defeated for the presidency by an electoral tally of 163 to 127. Van Buren and the Free Soilers did not carry a solitary state or attain a single electoral vote. More than three-quarters of the electorate participated. In round figures, the popular vote totals were 1,360,000 for Taylor, 1,220,000 for Cass, and 290,000 for Van Buren. Table 1 provides a comparison of the presidential returns for the elections of 1844 and 1848.[68]

In a losing effort, Lewis Cass garnered significant support throughout the nation. He carried a majority of the counties and fifteen of the thirty states (eight free and seven slave), receiving seventy-two northern electoral votes and fifty-five from the South. Taylor, however, outpolled Cass in both sections: ninety-seven in the North and sixty-six in the slave states. The Whig candidate carried every state, except Ohio, which had backed Clay in 1844, and he gained the electoral votes of New York, Pennsylvania, Georgia, and Louisiana. Additionally, Cass lagged almost five percentage points behind Taylor's share of the popular vote.

Van Buren was the choice of slightly more than one-tenth of the national electorate. The Free Soiler received almost five times as many popular votes as James G. Birney, the Liberty candidate in 1844, and outpolled Cass in three northeastern states. Furthermore, the Free Soilers elected nine congressmen and (after the state legislatures met) two senators, Hale and Chase. For a party organized only three months before the election, the Free Soilers had "high cause for satisfaction." Van Buren concluded, "Every thing was accomplished by the Free Soil movement that the most sanguine friend could hope for & much more than there was good reason to expect." An antislavery advocate from Brooklyn declared the people were "no longer willing to be Governed by Northern men with Southern principles—Cass men are very scarce now in New York & they are as quiet as mice." A Michigan Free Soil weekly exulted

TABLE I
Presidential Election Returns

	1848			1844		
	Taylor	*Cass*	*Van Buren*	*Clay*	*Polk*	*Birney*
Northeast	615,594	468,252	210,120	618,225	621,061	44,806
Connecticut	30,318	27,051	5,005	32,832	29,841	1,943
Maine	35,273	40,195	12,157	34,378	45,719	4,836
Massachusetts	61,072	35,281	38,333	67,062	53,039	10,830
New Hampshire	14,781	27,763	7,560	17,866	27,160	4,161
New Jersey	40,015	36,901	829	38,318	37,495	131
New York	218,583	114,319	120,497	232,482	237,588	15,812
Pennsylvania	185,730	172,186	11,176	161,195	167,311	3,139
Rhode Island	6,705	3,613	726	7,322	4,867	
Vermont	23,117	10,943	13,837	26,770	18,041	3,954
Northwest	308,801	342,410	81,170	292,996	305,842	17,297
Illinois	52,853	55,952	15,702	45,854	58,795	3,469
Indiana	69,668	74,695	8,031	67,866	70,183	2,108
Iowa	9,930	11,238	1,103		(not a state)	
Michigan	23,947	30,742	10,393	24,185	27,737	3,638
Ohio	138,656	154,782	35,523	155,091	149,127	8,082
Wisconsin	13,747	15,001	10,418		(not a state)	
Southwest	251,885	241,981		216,336	239,802	
Alabama	30,482	31,173		26,002	37,401	
Arkansas	7,587	9,301		5,604	9,546	
Kentucky	67,145	49,720		61,249	51,988	
Louisiana	18,487	15,379		13,083	13,782	
Mississippi	25,911	26,545		19,158	25,846	
Missouri	32,671	40,077		31,200	41,322	
Tennessee	64,321	58,142		60,040	59,917	
Texas	5,281	11,644			(not a state)	
Southeast	185,113	170,817	211	172,447	172,789	
Delaware	6,440	5,910	82	6,271	5,970	
Florida	4,120	3,083			(not a state)	
Georgia	47,532	44,785		42,100	44,147	
Maryland	37,702	34,528	129	35,984	32,706	
North Carolina	44,054	35,772		43,232	39,287	
Virginia	45,265	46,739		44,860	50,679	
Total North	924,395	810,662	291,290	911,221	926,903	62,103
Total South	436,998	412,798	211	388,783	412,591	
Total Nation	1,361,393	1,223,460	291,501	1,300,004	1,339,494	62,103
Total Vote	2,876,354			2,701,601		

over the results: Lewis Cass, "the eyesore of Freemen, and a burdensome stone to his own friends, has met the retribution he has so richly deserved. The election being over, his friends will drop him as they would a dead dog in July."[69]

Democrats could find little to cheer in the election returns. Although the *Kalamazoo Gazette* graciously noted Cass tallied "a larger number of electoral votes than any defeated candidate," he attained a smaller percentage of the popular votes cast in each northwestern state than Polk had in 1844. Wisconsin was carried by Cass with less than 39 percent of the popular vote; only Iowa gave him a clear majority in the region. Van Buren took away more Democrats than Whigs in Illinois and Wisconsin; conversely, the Free Soilers hurt Taylor in Indiana and ensured a Democratic victory in Ohio. Voters in the commercial cities of Cleveland, Detroit, and Chicago were susceptible to the internal improvements issue. In Cuyahoga County (Cleveland), the Free Soil vote increased dramatically over the Liberty party totals in 1844, while Cass polled slightly fewer votes than had Polk. Cass's home county demonstrated even more clearly the impact of this issue: Polk carried Wayne County with 52 percent of the vote, Cass received 45 percent, and Van Buren more than doubled the number of votes previously attained by Birney. The two Illinois counties that border Lake Michigan gave the Democratic candidate 28 percent of their vote in 1848. While the improvements issue added to the excitement of the presidential campaign and cost the Democratic ticket northwestern votes, it did not determine the outcome of the election. Lewis Cass was vindicated for remaining silent on the subject and relying solely on his Senate voting record.[70]

In the South, Taylor's military reputation and the fact he was a slaveholder greatly aided the Whig cause. Cass opposed the Wilmot Proviso, but many southerners feared popular sovereignty would prevent the establishment of slavery in the western territories. The Cass-Butler ticket nevertheless succeeded in traditionally strong Democratic states, although Alabama, Arkansas, Mississippi, Missouri, and Virginia were carried with

---

Note to Table 1: The vote totals listed above include figures from the three major parties only. Gerrit Smith, the Liberty League candidate in 1848, received some 2,500 votes in New York. There were also several hundred "scattered" ballots cast throughout the nation. The "scattered" vote in 1844 totaled more than 2,000. Other sources additionally credit Van Buren in 1848 with 85 votes in North Carolina, 9 in Virginia, 3 or 4 in Texas, and 1 in Louisiana.

reduced majorities. Georgia and Louisiana shifted to the Whig column; Florida cast its first electoral votes for Taylor; and the Whig margin of victory was substantially increased in Kentucky, Tennessee, and North Carolina.

The Democratic ticket was particularly damaged by the Free Soil party in the Northeast. Van Buren ran second to Taylor in Massachusetts, New York, and Vermont and, by splitting the Democratic vote in New York, allowed Taylor to carry the Empire State. The Free Soil ticket was also an important factor in Pennsylvania, which joined New York in switching allegiance. One Cass supporter lamented that "the delusive cry of *'Free Soil,'* got up by the friends of Van Buren" seeking revenge, led to the defeat.[71] Nonetheless, the impact of the Free Soil party on the outcome of the presidential race was minimal. Although Van Buren's candidacy lost New York for the Democrats, the antislavery vote shifted Ohio from the Whig to the Democratic column. In short, had there been no viable third party in 1848, Zachary Taylor still would have been elected president of the United States. The Free Soilers did, however, serve notice that a growing segment of northerners was adamantly opposed to the extension of slavery.

The outcome of the presidential election was not a true indication of the relative strength of the major parties. Democrats generally embraced the doctrine of popular sovereignty as a politically acceptable compromise to the slavery extension controversy. Although leaders from the different sections interpreted it to suit themselves, the Cass precept was ambiguous enough to satisfy most party members in 1848. The Whigs, on the other hand, did not maintain even a semblance of unity on the issue of slavery and the western territories. Taylor's election represented, in the North, a victory of personality and party loyalty over principle. Southern Whigs (and Democrats) who voted for General Taylor did so because he was a planter and war hero. Taylor's victory in the slaveholding states was a triumph of sectionalism. Lewis Cass, the stolid public servant, proved incapable of instilling in Democrats the unrestrained political fervor necessary to prevent defections to the Whig or Free Soil tickets. Cass thus lost the election because of the same characteristics that had gained him the nomination. He was a venerable, moderate politician who served his party faithfully but without flair, thereby making few political enemies, and attracting even fewer passionate supporters.

Cass accepted his defeat with equanimity. He harbored no personal regrets for the loss, yet bemoaned "the results for the sake of our great party, and for the sake of my true friends." Although Cass was not a man to denounce political opponents, he did "not envy Mr. Van Buren his feelings or his position." Other Democrats were less charitable to the former president, who was blamed for the loss of New York and, hence, the election. One Democratic newspaper stated that "the defeat of the democracy may properly be attributed to the course pursued by Mr. Van Buren and his friends." Van Buren himself insisted, "The result of the election of 1848 was altogether occasioned by divisions in the Democratic party."[72]

The election of a Whig military hero, "without a single civil qualification," was particularly galling to the Democrats. Taylor, claimed the disappointed losers, was elected because his supporters deliberately concealed his "opinions on the political questions of the day." President Polk contended the "poor old man! can have no mind of his own, for he has no fixed principles,—and is totally ignorant of public affairs." After extending his personal condolences to Cass, Polk predicted Taylor would have little impact on the federal government, since his actions would be directed by the Whig leadership. "It is the first instance in our history, in which the Government will be committed to a *Ministry.*" The *New York Tribune* portentously observed: "The Whigs of course rejoice, but in general very moderately; for they do not feel that Gen. Taylor is entirely 'bone of their bone and flesh of their flesh,' and they cannot forget the great disappointment and disaster which followed swiftly on the sweeping triumph of 1840."[73]

Lewis Cass and the Democrats were defeated, but the election of 1848 held deeper significance. Both major parties were affected by sectionalism. Cass received over one hundred thousand fewer votes in the North than had Polk, in spite of an additional four hundred thousand ballots cast. The Democratic totals in the South were virtually identical with those of 1844, even though the electorate increased by almost fifty thousand. The Whigs faced similar problems. Taylor polled more than ten thousand fewer votes than the unsuccessful Clay in northern states participating in both elections. The Whigs demonstrated increased strength in the South, but this was attributable to the nomination of a military hero and planter. It was inevitable that when forced to take a firm position on slavery expansion, the Whig leadership would alienate important factions of the party. Lewis Cass rightly believed "the Whig party can not hold together. It contains the seeds of dissolution: of speedy dissolution." So, too, did the Democratic party. The great increase in the Free Soil vote, over that of the Liberty party, demonstrated that a growing number of northerners sought a political solution to the slavery extension issue. And yet, abolitionists were also disturbed by the election results. Garrison castigated the president-elect as a "MAN-STEALER" who "richly deserves to be hung." The *North Star* dismissed both Taylor and Cass as being better fitted for "the state prison or a lunatic asylum" than the White House.[74]

The traditional parties were losing their hold on the electorate. National politics was in a state of flux and transition, as the differences between Whigs and Democrats on substantive issues appeared to be diminishing. This was unacceptable to the growing segment of antislavery voters. "It is evident," insisted a Wisconsin Free Soil newspaper, "the day has arrived when the question must be between the North and the South, and the sooner settled the better. Those who stick to the old organizations, stick to the South, for if they were so weak before that the south could dictate to both parties, will they not be infinitely weaker now?" Not, party regulars hoped, if a moderate political solution could be found to the emerging sectional controversy. The question of slavery extension was on the agenda of the Thirty-first Congress, and Lewis Cass played an important role in framing the ensuing compromise.[75]

Chapter Nine

United States Senator (1849–1857): "Life Is a Compromise . . . From the Cradle to the Grave"

Lewis Cass encountered strong opposition in his bid to return to the United States Senate following the election of 1848. At stake was the seat he resigned after being nominated for the presidency. Although Michigan staunchly backed Cass in the campaign, a growing number of Democrats embraced the free soil philosophy. Michigan antislavery men had begun to organize during the 1830s, in an attempt to aid fugitive slaves and further the cause of abolition, but the real impetus for concerted political action came in the late 1840s. The notorious Crosswhite case served as a catalyst.

By 1846, an estimated one hundred escaped slaves were settled in central Michigan. Six of the fugitives—Adam Crosswhite, his wife, and four children—lived outside of Marshall. The Crosswhites were the property of Frank Giltner of Carroll County, Kentucky, who authorized his grandson, Francis Troutman, to apprehend them. In January 1847, Troutman and three other Kentuckians solicited the services of Deputy Sheriff Harvey Dickson and proceeded to the Crosswhite residence, where they kicked in a door and seized the fugitives. Meanwhile, the alarm was sounded throughout the community that slave catchers were afoot, and hundreds of residents responded to prevent the return of the family to slavery. With the situation becoming uncontrollable, Dickson arrested Troutman on charges of assault and trespass. Troutman was subsequently fined one hundred dollars and court costs.

The Crosswhites resumed their flight to Canada and safety, while the Kentuckians returned home. A mass meeting held in Carroll County passed a series of resolutions urging the legislature to denounce the Marshall abolitionists and petition Congress for a more stringent fugitive slave act. Furthermore, Giltner brought suit against several Marshall residents to recover the value of the Crosswhites. The first trial held at Detroit ended with a hung jury, but at a second trial, which began as the presidential election took place, the defendants were found guilty and more than nineteen hundred dollars awarded the plaintiff. The verdict infuriated free soilers, and Zachariah Chandler led the subscription drive to pay the fines and court costs. Chandler accepted the commonly held belief the Crosswhite case was prosecuted to enhance Cass's candidacy in the South.

The Crosswhite verdict energized the free soil movement in the Northwest, but antislavery sentiment remained tinctured with racism. Most white Michiganites opposed the settlement of free blacks, and the first state constitution prohibited Negroes from voting because they "belonged to a degraded caste of mankind." In 1850, more than 70 percent of the electorate refused to extend the franchise to black residents. Thus, Cass represented the feelings of the majority of his constituents regarding slavery and civil rights during this period, but an increasingly vocal and politically potent antislavery faction was steadily gaining strength. And after the presidential contest of 1848, antiextension Democrats from southwestern Michigan united with Free Soilers and Whigs in a determined effort to prevent the election of Lewis Cass to the Senate.[1]

Democratic governor Epaphroditus Ransom of Kalamazoo captured the antislavery passions aroused by the Crosswhite case in a message to the state legislature. Directly contradicting Cass's popular sovereignty doctrine, Ransom argued Congress possessed the authority to regulate slavery in the federal territories, and the West should remain free. One Democrat conceded that the governor "rather out-witted Cass" in seizing the high moral ground on the slavery issue. A bloc of western Democrats, demanding that their region be represented in the U.S. Senate, joined antislavery legislators in supporting Ransom's bid for the seat. The minority Whigs backed Edwin Lawrence of Washtenaw County but appeared willing to vote for Ransom to block Cass. The antislavery men demonstrated their strength with the passage of resolutions instructing Michigan's federal senators to support the Wilmot Proviso. "The opposers of Cass are waxing bold," one observer noted, adding with some exaggeration that "nine-tenths of the people are with them." On January 9, the lower house nominated Cass, but the state senate wrangled for almost two weeks before finally choosing Ransom. It was apparent the antiextensionists held the balance of power between conservative Democrats and the Whig–Free Soil coalition. An opponent of Cass was hopeful the legislature would "doom him to a retired life, for a season at any rate," and the *New York Tribune* trumpeted that the schism within the Michigan Democratic party guaranteed "no election will be held this Winter."[2]

Lewis Cass broke the legislative impasse by bringing the full weight of his personal prestige to bear on recalcitrant Democrats. After all, Cass men argued, he had led the party since its formation and was the only Michigan politician of national stature. The conservatives therefore refused to settle on a compromise candidate. Cass himself was hard at work behind the scenes, and when he promised to obey any instructions from the legislature, enough antiextensionists were swayed to break the deadlock. In a joint legislative session, Cass received a majority of the votes cast for federal senator, and a resolution certifying his election was passed by a vote of 14 to 7 in the Michigan Senate, and 39 to 21 in the House. "Genl. Cass is a good man and will do well," noted a pleased supporter, and a Kalamazoo Democrat concluded the choice was "highly satisfactory to the people of the whole state, excepting the local desire for a Western man." Cass was the clear victor in this legislative infighting—he still dominated the Michigan Democratic party structure—but antislavery legislators placed him on a short tether with their free soil instructions. Although scarcely accorded the overwhelming vote of confidence he wished following his defeat at the hands of Zachary Taylor, Lewis Cass was grateful for the opportunity to return to Washington.[3]

A Michigan antislavery Whig gloated that, in light of the legislative instructions, Cass "cannot possibly take one single step that shall not bring disaster." If he supported the Wilmot Proviso, southerners would surely "denounce him as a driveller and an apostate. If he disobeys instructions, he is deemed a juggling traitor by the people of Michigan and the North. And if he fails to vote . . . his reputation will be that of a cowardly dodger." In a decidedly more sympathetic vein, President Polk informed Cass he had "reflected much on the subject" and concluded "that you should consent to return to the Senate.—I should hope that *instructions* by your Legislature might be prevented by your friends; but if not and instructions should follow you—you could only resign—and in doing so—make a patriotic appeal to the people of all sections, in favour of the preservation of the Union." Lewis Cass agreed with this advice and made arrangements to rejoin the Senate, determined to resign his seat rather than support the Wilmot Proviso.[4]

It was a consolation to Lewis Cass that President Polk appointed Lewis, Jr., to a diplomatic post before Taylor's inauguration. In late September 1848, word arrived in Washington of the death of the American chargé d'affaires to Rome, and the younger Cass called at the White House seeking the position. Polk frankly informed Lewis such an appointment would injure his father's chances in November, and the son then "insisted" the president "promise him the office as soon as the election was over." This Polk refused to do, so Lewis returned three days after the presidential election. Again, Polk put him off, although he confided in his diary that out of "great respect for his father," he would probably gratify the request. A month later, following a private discussion with the elder Cass, Polk submitted the nomination of Lewis, Jr., as chargé to the Papal States. The Senate confirmed the appointment, and Lewis served in Rome for the duration of the ensuing Whig administration, rising to the position of minister to Italy in 1854. A political opponent remarked that "the Casses have had a small victory to comfort them for a great defeat—General Cass has been re-elected Senator and his illustrious son is now on his way to Rome." Especially grateful was Elizabeth Cass, who two years before fruitlessly sought a diplomatic post for Lewis. Mrs. Cass, suffering from failing health and virtually an invalid in the family home at Detroit, rested easier knowing her only son held a responsible foreign mission.[5]

Lewis Cass arrived at Washington in late February 1849, politically bruised by his reelection struggle and burdened with free soil instructions from the Michigan legislature. Such concerns were momentarily forgotten, however, as he took up bachelor's lodgings at the United States Hotel and then called upon Zachary Taylor to offer the most cordial congratulations he could muster. On Thursday evening, March 1, Cass and Taylor were guests at a White House dinner party. Sarah Childress Polk, seated between the two recent presidential antagonists, handled the delicate task with aplomb. Her husband recorded, "Not the slightest allusion was made to any political subject . . . the whole company seemed to enjoy themselves." Two days later, Lewis Cass was sworn in as senator. Congress remained in session until seven o'clock Sunday morning, establishing the Department of the Interior and passing important civil and diplomatic appropriations. President Polk signed these measures, although he was disappointed Congress failed to provide a territorial government for California. The next day, Zachary Taylor took the oath as president of the United States. Lewis Cass attended the inauguration and then returned to Detroit, deeply aware a daunting task faced the Thirty-first Congress. The slavery extension issue threatened to "ruin" Democratic party accord—and even the Union itself—if a political compromise was not fashioned to maintain sectional peace. Cass informed a group of New York Democrats, during the legislative recess, that "we have but one danger to fear": sectionalism. "If we are not struck by judicial blindness, we shall hold on to the Constitution with a tenacity defying time and accident." In words that sounded the tocsin for congressional action, Cass cautioned that "a spirit of compromise was necessary to create this confederation, and it is equally necessary to preserve it in its integrity and efficiency." The summer months at home provided time for reflection and allowed the Michigan senator to recoup his physical strength before the fateful session that convened in December. Lewis Cass, molded in the image of the nationalistic—and accommodating—Founding Fathers, was prepared to face the challenge that endangered the republic.[6]

The Thirtieth Congress bequeathed to its successor the controversial issue of slavery and the western territories. President Polk, following the establishment of a free territorial government for Oregon, urged Congress in December 1848 to provide governments for California and New Mexico. The federal legislators quarreled over Wilmot amendments, and no action was taken at that time; but with the continued exodus of Americans to the California gold fields, it became imperative Congress act promptly. President Polk expressed his fears to Lewis Cass. Referring to the "state of anarchy" on the West Coast, Polk warned that Californians might "organize an Independent Government" and "induce *Oregon* to join them." The president was concerned that the Whigs, "in order to relieve *Genl. Taylor* from the embarrassment in which he is placed on the *Wilmot Proviso,* may be willing . . . to give up the country."[7] Although Polk remained chary of Taylor's intentions following a brief chat between the two men on inauguration day, the new president was strongly in favor of admitting California to the Union. So, too, was Senator Cass. The Thirty-first Congress, however, was not united on the issue.

Lewis Cass was in a jovial mood as he returned to Washington, after the summer recess, in the company of his home-state colleague Alpheus Felch. Mary Bingham, the wife of a Michigan antislavery Democratic congressman, joined the two senators at Syracuse and was impressed with Cass's unassuming and pleasant nature. "He talks so familiarly with one, just as if you were an old acquaintance." Mrs. Bingham, fortified at dinner with champagne that "seemed to go to the right spot," recounted Cass remarked "he was very glad I was going to Washington to take care of my husband, for indeed, said he, 'I must tell you that Mr. Bingham is no better than the rest of us.'—We all laughed."[8] But Cass's high spirits were soon dispelled.

It was a distinguished and contentious group that met in the Senate chamber on December 3, 1849. Henry Clay, showing signs of his seventy-two years, was united for the final time with Webster and Calhoun. Jefferson Davis, Stephen Douglas, Salmon Chase, and William Seward represented a new generation of national politicians. Senator Cass, mindful of his reputation as a prestigious elder statesman of the Democratic party, declined to serve on any standing committee. He avoided such tedious routine in part because of advancing age, husbanding his energies to moderate the spirit of sectionalism that pervaded the Senate. Once again, Lewis Cass was determined to lend his voice to the cause of political compromise, and it quickly became clear he faced a difficult task.

The intensity of sectional feeling was demonstrated as the Thirty-first Congress organized. The selection of Speaker of the House was prevented for weeks, largely because Democrats held only seven more seats than the Whigs, and the thirteen Free Soilers denied them an absolute majority. Representatives also quarreled along sectional lines, with some antislavery Democrats refusing to support Howell Cobb, and certain southern Whigs withholding their ballots from Robert Winthrop. House members eventually decided to elect the Speaker by a plurality vote, and Cobb was chosen on the sixty-third ballot.[9]

While the House was wrangling, the Senate argued over a resolution honoring a distinguished clerical visitor from Ireland. Father Theobald Mathew—the "Apostle of Temperance"—was accused by Jefferson Davis of inciting naturalized Irish-Americans "to unite as a body with Abolitionists in their nefarious designs." Seward immediately leaped to Mathew's defense and pointedly remarked, "If slavery be an error, if it be a crime, if it be a sin, we deplore its existence among us." After the sponsor of the resolution, Isaac Walker of Wisconsin, explained that he viewed the Irish friar simply as "a philanthropist connected with temperance reform," Lewis Cass obtained the floor. The Michigan senator confessed his ignorance of the reverend visitor's antislavery tendencies and added that he opposed any discussion of the subject. Recalling his leadership of the temperance movement in Washington during the 1830s, Cass urged the Senate to grant a seat to Father Mathew, solely in recognition of his crusade against drink. This suggestion fell on deaf ears. The slavery question could not be ignored; rather, it proved to be the paramount national issue for the remainder of Cass's public career. Following a rancorous debate, Father Mathew was granted the privilege of sitting within the bar of the Senate by a vote of 33 to 18. All of the dissenting ballots were cast by slave state members. Despite Cass's plea, notice was served the Thirty-first Congress would not easily compromise sectional questions.[10]

After the delayed organization of the House, President Taylor sent his first annual message to Congress on December 24. Anticipating that California and New Mexico would apply for statehood, Taylor recommended Congress respond favorably. On the same day, Henry Foote notified the Senate he intended to introduce a bill organizing territorial governments for California, Deseret (Utah), and New Mexico. The Mississippian formally presented the resolution several days later, and John Hale of New Hampshire offered an amendment excluding slavery from the western territories. Defenders of slavery, in turn, no longer relied on Calhoun's precept of congressional nonintervention. They began to insist that since the western region was the common possession of the states, the property of all emigrating citizens must be protected by the federal government. Cass's doctrine of popular sovereignty took a middle position. By denying congressional authority and leaving the question entirely to the territorial residents, Cass characteristically sought to avoid a collision on the explosive issue of slavery extension.

Firmly convinced political catastrophe would result from resuming the Wilmot Proviso debate, Cass deplored the sectionalism demonstrated in Congress by January 1850. In a confidential communication, he bluntly warned that "this Union is in the most imminent danger. There is a fixed determination with many Southern members to dissolve it." Faced with political extremism, he concluded the only solution lay in "a spirit of moderation from the North and West."[11] Although vainly wishing to avoid the entire controversy, instructed as he was to support the principle of the proviso, Senator Cass forthrightly presented his position in a two-day speech that commenced on January 21. Reading rapidly from a carefully prepared text, he forcefully reaffirmed the thesis of the Nicholson letter: "There is no clause in the Constitution which gives to Congress express power to pass any law respecting slavery in the Territories." He repeated that the clause authorizing Congress "to make all needful rules and regulations respecting, the territory or other property belonging to the United States" referred to "territory" in the sense of "land."

Cass again refuted the basic arguments that Congress possessed the authority to decide the issue of slavery in the territories. There were a dozen in all, including sovereignty, nationality, the right of ownership and settlement, and treaty-making powers. In each case, Cass found no constitutional basis for the claim Congress had control over local institutions, because "the term 'territory,' as here used, is merely descriptive of one kind of property" and did not refer to a political community. By utilizing this narrow interpretation of the Constitution (which Calhoun and Chief Justice Taney ultimately embraced), Cass maintained Congress had no jurisdiction over the territories beyond the creation of proper governments. Hence, the Wilmot Proviso was unconstitutional; and, by implication, so was the southern call for federal protection of slavery in the territories. After devoting most of his allotted time to an explicit refutation of the constitutionality of the proviso, Cass acknowledged Congress was forced to institute territorial governments out of "necessity," although the authority to do so came "from the people of the United States," not the Constitution. Only territorial legislatures were empowered to regulate slavery, because the western settlers received the right of self-government from "Almighty God; from the same omnipotent and beneficent Being who gave us our rights." Interestingly, Cass later attacked Seward's "higher law" precept for being extraconstitutional. "Almighty God" apparently granted self-government to white Americans, while maintaining the bonds of black slavery.

Lewis Cass was frightened by the prospects facing the nation. "Sad will be the day when the first drop of blood is shed in the preservation of the Union." There could be no peaceable dismemberment of the federal republic, but he held out the hope civil war need not occur, "if the same spirit of compromise . . . which animated our fathers continues to animate us and our children." Because he was a free state senator advocating sectional accommodation, Cass emphasized he was "no panegyrist of the South. . . . I am a northern man by birth, a western man by the habits and associations of half a century; but I am an American above all." He concluded by acknowledging the obligation he felt toward the instructions from the largely Democratic Michigan legislature. Cass announced that when called upon to cast a vote regarding the Wilmot Proviso, he would reconcile his "duty to the Legislature with my duty to myself, by surrendering a trust I can no longer fulfill." Senator Cass remained true to the principles enunciated in the Nicholson letter. At the same time, popular sovereignty was being repudiated by northern provisoists, and by southerners who demanded federal protection for slavery in the territories.[12]

Reaction to Cass's speech naturally split along ideological lines. The *Savannah Georgian* praised his moderate stand on the slavery issue and encouraged other senators to seek a compromise settlement. A visitor to the capital, in contrast, insisted Cass "has not convinced a single man." The *New York Tribune* similarly declared that after giving the discourse "a careful reading, we decided . . . our columns could be far better employed than in printing it, and omit it accordingly." Popular sovereignty was a "humbug, it is knavery to talk of awaiting the action of the people of the Territories on this subject." The following day, the *Tribune* erroneously reported the Michigan senator was preparing to resign and return home in anticipation of the presidential contest. Instead, Cass remained in Washington and brooded over the rising sectionalism.[13]

Henry Clay shared a deep concern for the stability of the Union, and he, too, sought a compromise solution to the slavery controversy. A week after Cass's speech, the Kentucky senator introduced eight resolutions designed to calm the sectional storm. Clay implicitly supported the popular sovereignty principle in his proposals relating to the Mexican Cession. California would be admitted to the Union under the free-state constitution proposed by its inhabitants. And since Mexico had proscribed slavery in the region, Clay reasoned it was "inexpedient for Congress to provide by law, either for its introduction into or exclusion from any part of said territory." Therefore, governments would be established for Utah and New Mexico "without the adoption of any restriction or condition on the subject of slavery."[14]

His health deteriorating under the harsh winter weather, Henry Clay, in early February, addressed the Senate a final time in favor of sectional compromise. There was, remarked Senator Felch, "a greater throng about the Senate Chamber than I have ever seen before." Urging his colleagues to adjust the slavery controversy through mutual compromise, Clay implored them "solemnly to pause—at the edge of the precipice, before the fearful and disastrous leap is taken in the yawning abyss below, which will inevitably lead to certain and irretrievable destruction." The Kentucky senator, visibly fatigued by his oratorical labors, concluded on the following day and was immediately besieged by admirers who believed "the Great Pacificator" had again saved the Union.[15]

Clay's compromise proposals sought a popular sovereignty solution to the question of slavery expansion. Various senators, however, attacked his specific resolutions, and even questioned the validity of maintaining the republic in light of the slavery controversy. Hale, for example, presented a petition from Quakers "praying for the immediate and peaceful dissolution of the Union." Lewis Cass rose on February 11, to speak against this "wicked and foolish proposition." After declaring his respect for the moral qualities of the Society of Friends, Cass bluntly added that "he who expects such a result is either already in an insane hospital or ought to be placed there." Strong words, certainly, which demonstrated the Michigan senator's rage; but even within Cass's home state, disunionist sentiments were taking root. A professor at the University of Michigan affirmed that "of the two evils, the extension & perpetuation of slavery; & the dissolution" of the Union, he preferred the latter. Cass rejected such reasoning; he was incapable of accepting the dismantling of the Union to remove the taint of slavery from the consciences of northerners. Talk of secession was a call for civil war. The Michigan senator, instead, pleaded with his colleagues to seek a compromise solution.[16]

Despite the leadership of Clay and Cass, the festering specter of disunion was not easily quashed. Many proslavery southerners were as opposed to compromise as their northern counterparts. Jefferson Davis fanned the flames of sectionalism on the Senate floor, arguing neither Congress nor territorial legislatures could ban slavery. Davis repudiated popular sovereignty, as well as the proviso. Other slave state senators, including Andrew P. Butler of South Carolina, went on record opposing the admission of California without political concessions to the South.

Lewis Cass and his fellow moderates began to despair of a peaceful settlement. If popular sovereignty were discarded, no legislative accord was possible; the extension of the Missouri Compromise line to the Pacific could not garner sufficient support for passage. Moreover, Senator Cass demonstrated his ideological consistency by rejecting such a solution. Although not making his objection public at this time, because it was not part of the debate, Cass staked out a position he maintained for the remainder of his public career. Since Congress was not explicitly granted the power to legislate for the territories on the slavery question, the 36° 30' restriction was patently unconstitutional. With no compromise in sight, the outlook was bleak. By the end of February, Cass believed the country faced its most "perilous crisis" since the adoption of the Constitution. He was equally appalled that northern and southern "fanaticism" openly advocated "a dissolution of the Union." A dejected Cass sadly wrote that the Taylor administration was "an utter failure" in dealing with the controversy. "There is *no* day light yet."[17]

John C. Calhoun was not the man to dispel the darkness of sectionalism and disunion. Too ill to speak, his final thoughts on slavery were read to the Senate by James M. Mason of Virginia. The South Carolinian placed the entire blame for the controversy on the North, which had chipped away at the political equality of slaveholders since the Ordinance of 1787. The Clay proposals were simply unacceptable; the South had "no compromise to offer." Instead, the North must concede to the South the right to carry slaves into the western territories, return fugitive slaves, and completely "cease the agitation of the slave question." Calhoun died before the month ended (Cass, Clay, and Webster served as pallbearers during the Senate funeral ceremonies), but the spirit of unyielding opposition to compromise was not laid to rest with his body.

Senator Daniel Webster did his best to mollify southern intransigence when he spoke on March 7. The Massachusetts Whig rejected the sectionalism of his South Carolina colleague and backed the compromise proposals. Webster echoed Cass in labeling the proviso a mere abstraction and warning that unless a legislative solution could be found, civil war would result, since peaceful secession was impossible. This appeal for political compromise and mutual forbearance was decried by New England abolitionists.[18]

Webster disappointed those who turned to him for a defense of the proviso position, but a younger contingent of northeastern politicians personified the radical antislavery argument. William Seward, elected to the Senate the previous year, spoke four days after Webster. The forty-eight-year-old New York Whig was an implacable foe of legislative compromises, which he denounced as "radically wrong and essentially vicious." He demanded the immediate admission of California as a free state, without any concessions to the South. While conceding the Constitution "regulates our stewardship" of the territories, Seward argued that "there is a higher law than the Constitution, which regulates our authority over the domain." He thus agreed with Calhoun—not Cass—that Congress had the power to determine the issue of slavery in the territories. The New York senator's sentiments were ably seconded by Hale and Chase.

Three days after Seward spoke, Cass obtained the Senate floor and declared it was "essential to calm this agitation." Although sectional feelings could not be eradicated through legislation, Cass urged his colleagues to take all possible steps to promote a tranquil settlement of the controversy. This included admitting California as a free state without further delay, enacting a stronger fugitive slave law, and allowing "the people of the territories to govern themselves, without any Wilmot proviso." If Congress heeded the calls for compromise, and accepted the principle of popular sovereignty, Cass was hopeful the Union could be saved. In fact, the advocates of accommodation were optimistic that all was not lost.[19]

Despite the railings of inflexible southerners and northerners, Senator Cass noted in late April that "matters here have assumed a little more promising aspect. Feelings have become a little more allayed, and . . . we have opened the way for action." Congress plainly reflected the distinct lessening of tensions throughout the nation on the issue of slavery. The actions of the Michigan legislature were representative of this changing mood. Starting in 1847, the state's federal senators were repeatedly instructed to support the Wilmot Proviso principle. Lewis Cass naturally chafed under the free soil resolutions and gave notice he would resign rather than adhere to them. This spurred moderate legislators to seek their rescission. A Michigan Whig newspaper complained that the senator wished to take the responsibility "off his shoulders, and leave him free to vote for the Wilmot Proviso, or dodge the question, as party or popularity may dictate." Democrats, however, could ill afford to lose their most influential spokesman in Congress, and party newspapers and county organizations called upon the legislature to rescind the "unwise" and "pernicious" instructions. The esteem in which Cass was held by Michiganites—and the gravity of the sectional controversy—contributed to their success, as the legislators narrowly voted to repeal. It was with a great deal of pride, tinged with no little relief, that Cass presented to the Senate this "peace-offering upon the altar of our common country," and again called upon his colleagues to forge a compromise solution to the slavery question. Cass did not gloat over the withdrawal of the free soil instructions; it was enough that a spirit of cooperation was in the air.[20]

On April 18, the Senate passed a resolution establishing a select thirteen-man committee to draft compromise legislation. The following day, Henry Clay was chosen to chair the Committee of Thirteen; the other members represented equally the North and South, and the Democratic and Whig parties. Lewis Cass, recognized by his colleagues as a Senate leader and a vocal supporter of compromise, was selected as a member, and the other northern Democrats (Daniel S. Dickinson and Jesse D. Bright) were his supporters.[21]

During deliberations of the Committee of Thirteen, chairman Clay was flanked by Senators Cass and Webster. They formed a determined troika, pulling in unison to save the republic. Cass related to a political confidant, after the committee's first meeting, "Tho' nothing definitive has been done, yet opinions have been drawn, from which some thing may be augured." The eventual proposals made by the committee had been agreed to in principle, and "the reasonable men are all in favour, but whether they will be able to carry the others is doubtful." Cass predicted the major difficulty would be with "the extreme Southern men." His hopes for a compromise settlement alternately rising and falling, Cass believed by early May that substantial progress toward an agreement had been made. At the committee's third session, it was decided to admit California as a free state and establish the western territorial governments without reference to slavery. Plans also were drawn to settle the Texas boundary, abolish the slave trade in Washington, and amend the Fugitive Slave Law "to give general satisfaction, North and South." Several days later, Cass worried the committee proposals "will meet with strong opposition from the extreme Southern men, on account of California, and I am not sure, but they will defeat it." He prophetically confessed his "hopes of success are not sanguine." By the end of the month, he had good reason to "despair as to the present state of things."[22]

The Committee of Thirteen reported three bills to the Senate. The first, consisting of thirty-nine sections, was dubbed the "Omnibus" bill. It called for the admission of a free California, settled the Texas–New Mexico boundary dispute, and established territorial governments for Utah and New Mexico. The other bills provided for the more effective return of fugitive slaves and abolished the slave trade in the District of Columbia. It soon became apparent that the Omnibus bill solidified both northern and southern opposition to compromise. Free Soilers insisted upon the immediate admission of California and the incorporation of the proviso principle into any bill establishing territorial governments for Utah and New Mexico. Southern senators opposed the admission of a free California and demanded federal protection for slavery in the territories. Some senators, led by Thomas Hart Benton, rejected various aspects of the compromise relating to Texas. President Taylor favored the admission of California but rejected the immediate establishment of territorial governments for Utah and New Mexico. Henry Clay rightfully warned that unless compromise measures were passed embracing all the controversial issues, "instead of healing and closing the wounds of the country, instead of stopping the effusion of blood, it will flow in still greater quantities, with still greater danger to the Republic."[23]

Cass threw his single-hearted support behind the compromise proposals, which tacitly adhered to the popular sovereignty principle. The debates in the Senate so frequently revolved around the Cass doctrine, he felt obliged to defend the "somewhat historical" Nicholson letter. In so doing, he once more sidestepped the question of when territorial residents might decide the question of slavery, and recommended the Supreme Court be the final "umpire" on that point. In words that foreshadowed Stephen Douglas's Freeport Doctrine, Cass declared that if westerners opposed slavery, "you cannot make them legislate in favor of it." On the other hand, he stated Congress had no right to prohibit slavery if territorial residents supported it. The solution to the controversy remained quite simple: popular sovereignty must be accepted by Congress. "That done," Cass concluded, "we should enter again upon a glorious career, *with none to trouble us or to make us afraid.*"

Lewis Cass attempted to steer the Senate on a moderate course regarding the slavery issue because it was constitutionally sound—not because he found it the path of least resistance. Quite the contrary. Cass became exasperated during the compromise debates and lashed out at extremists from both sections who supported disunion rather than negotiation. Proslavery southerners, for instance, faced "an easy task" in presenting their arguments, being "supported and applauded by a constituency which feels as they do." The Michigan senator similarly had no patience with abolitionists, who were prepared "to cover the country with blood and conflagration to abolish slavery." He rhetorically inquired which took greater moral courage, "to minister to the popular feeling where we live, or to endeavor to moderate it, to hold back, to survey the whole subject coolly and impartially, and to restore harmony to a distracted country?" Unfortunately, Cass bemoaned, conservative northerners were placed in difficult circumstances. "They are throwing themselves into the breach; and yet their condition is not at all appreciated here." Beleaguered moderates, who accepted the constitutional right of southerners to decide the issue of slavery for themselves, were derided by their fellow citizens as "dough-faces." Cass scorned that opprobrious term. The true doughfaces, he reasoned, were those who swam with the political current, not against it. "I am an American, with the most kindly feelings to every portion of our beloved country. Its strength is in its union; its prosperity in its union; its hopes in its union." Throughout these debates, he urged his colleagues to hold to the Constitution, "as the mariner clings to the last plank, when night and the tempest close around him." Cass vowed to continue supporting sectional compromises to guarantee the permanency of the Union, but he faced a formidable challenge.[24]

Throughout the oppressive summer months, Cass labored diligently for the compromise bills. His junior colleague indelicately observed that the fleshy Cass "sweats like a butcher these hot days," but he did not slacken. On June 11, he urged the Senate to seek common ground. In words that may be taken as his political credo, Cass declared, "Life is a . . . compromise, from the cradle to the grave." He dismissed the president's plan, which called only for the admission of California, as totally inadequate. Cass argued that "the admission of California is demanded by a strong public feeling," and so was the establishment of territorial governments for Utah and New Mexico. He correctly observed that opposition to the compromise bills was headed by intractable ideologues from the North and South. This proved the adage, "Politics, like misery, make strange bedfellows," but he reserved his harshest criticisms for antislavery men. Cass singled out Horace Mann, the author of a recent article against compromise published in the *Liberator*. He bitingly derided such abolitionist sentiment as the type of "philanthropy [that] costs nothing personally but studied phrases," since Mann was "safely removed from the difficulties and dangers of the question." Cass's attitude toward abolitionists and other northerners who rejected popular sovereignty was hardening. While he continued to rebuke proslavery politicians in his private correspondence, in public Cass increasingly blamed antiextentionists. He focused on abolitionists, because to attack southerners would exacerbate sectional tensions, and the growing antislavery movement in the Northwest was a political threat to Cass and the Democratic party.[25]

Cass's oratorical attack on abolitionists was indicative of the strained relations between politicians who advocated a negotiated solution to the slavery controversy and those opposed to compromise. The pent up emotionalism reached a climax with a confrontation in the Senate chamber between Benton and Henry Foote. The diminutive Mississippian drew a pistol after Benton advanced toward him during debate. As Vice President Fillmore attempted to restore order and senators leaped to disarm Foote, Benton tore open his coat and bellowed: "I have no pistols! Let him fire! . . . Stand out of the way, and let the assassin fire!" When it became clear Benton presented no physical threat to Foote, tempers subsided and the debate over the compromise proposals continued.[26]

In a less dramatic vein, Lewis Cass and John Hale traded gibes on June 17. Cass took the Free Soiler to task for "lecturing" moderate northerners on the slavery issue and remarked, "If the Senator will attend to his own conscience, he will have quite enough to do." Hale evoked "roars of laughter" from his listeners when he retorted: "I never once assumed that the Senator from Michigan had a conscience, or anything of that sort." As to lecturing senators, "It is the last thing that I could be thinking of, for I have more than I can do to digest one half of the lectures that are given to me." Cass elicited the final chuckle when he said if Hale "did not deliver a lecture, I am sure I anticipated it, for we have one from him so often that every time he gets up I expect one."[27]

Amid the strident sectionalism, and notwithstanding the valiant efforts of Cass, Clay, and other congressional moderates, passage of the compromise measures drafted by the Committee of Thirteen appeared doubtful. Cass privately blamed different types of southerners for the continuing stalemate: those who opposed any settlement that hindered the secession movement, and those who favored extending the Missouri Compromise line to the Pacific. He flatly predicted the Omnibus bill would fail. However, two events took place during the summer that aided the cause of accommodation. In June, the Nashville convention met pursuant to the call of radical southerners. Nine slave states sent representatives but moderates controlled the proceedings. Although proslavery delegates denounced the compromise measures, no overt steps toward disunion were taken. Another serious obstacle facing the Omnibus bill was removed with the sudden death of Zachary Taylor on July 9. Lewis Cass served with Clay and Webster as pallbearers, and the Michigan Democrat eulogized the fallen president before the Senate. "The statesman, occupying as proud a position as this world offers to human hopes, has been struck down in a crisis which demanded all his firmness and wisdom." Cass personally believed Taylor had not been sufficiently conciliatory, and he took solace from the hope that "this afflicting dispensation of Providence may not be without its salutary influence upon the American people and upon their representatives." His death "will not be in vain, if it tends to subdue the feelings that have been excited, and to prepare the various sections of our country for a mutual spirit of forbearance." Indeed, Millard Fillmore was pledged to support a legislative compromise.[28]

As the summer wore on, despite the change of occupants in the White House, both Cass and Clay realized they faced a stiff fight. A majority of the Senate still opposed at least part of the proposed settlement, and on July 31, southerners and antislavery men banded together and emasculated the Omnibus bill. All that remained was the provision establishing a territorial government for Utah, which was agreed to the next day. Bitterly disappointed, Henry Clay gave up the struggle and left Washington for the more healthful climate of the Rhode Island seashore. Lewis Cass also despaired of the Senate's actions and viewed the defeat of the Omnibus bill as "a national misfortune. What we are to do, I am sure I do not know."[29]

The prospects were gloomy, but the victory of those opposed to a comprehensive compromise was short-lived. During Clay's absence, Stephen Douglas assumed the task of steering individual bills through the Senate. The Texas boundary dispute was soon settled, and Cass proclaimed, "We have at length advanced a step, which gives us hope of a final adjustment." It came quickly, with the admission of California as a free state, the establishment of New Mexico Territory, a more stringent fugitive slave law, and the prohibition of the slave trade in Washington. Cass supported all of these measures during the debates, but abstained from voting on the Fugitive Slave bill. By late September, the legislation collectively known as the Compromise of 1850 was signed into law, and Cass pithily concluded that the slavery question "is settled in the public mind." Californians had determined their own fate regarding slavery, and the residents of the western territories would have the opportunity to do the same. Popular sovereignty triumphed. Moderate politicians—Democrats and Whigs—who desperately sought a solution to the issue of slavery expansion, embraced the Cass precept embodied in the Compromise of 1850. The accord endorsed a strict construction of the Constitution and a federal government of limited powers. Lewis Cass was extremely pleased with the settlement.[30]

The American people generally supported the Compromise of 1850, although the Fugitive Slave Act was galling to the sensibilities of many northerners. During the months of debate, Lewis Cass invariably supported more stringent regulations for the rendition of escaped slaves. Several days before the Senate finally acted on the bill, he pledged to vote for legislation that contained:

1. The right of the master to arrest his fugitive slave wherever he may find him.
2. His duty to carry him before a magistrate in the State where he is arrested, that the claim may be adjudged by him.

3. The duty of the magistrate to examine the claim, and to decide it, like other examining magistrates, *without a jury,* and then to commit him to the custody of the master.
4. The right of the master then to remove the slave to his residence.

However, Cass abstained from engrossing the bill for its third reading, contradictorily claiming he opposed the final version because it did not guarantee accused slaves jury trials in the states from which they fled (a provision of the original Omnibus bill).[31]

Democratic newspapers in Michigan tended to regard the Fugitive Slave Act as an essential concession to the South and accepted Cass's explanation for withholding his vote. The *Hillsdale Gazette* argued that "the panicites" were attempting to make political capital out of the Fugitive Slave Act by perverting its provisions, but the "essential features" of the new law were constitutional. The Whig press naturally lambasted Senator Cass. One editor surmised that unlike Congressman Alexander Buel, who courageously supported the Fugitive Slave bill, Cass "did not dare to vote for it, because it would kill him at the North, (as it had Mr. Buel) and he did not dare to vote against it, because it would kill him at the South. What could he do? He did *nothing.*" The Detroit Whig newspaper conceded the Fugitive Slave Act was constitutional but opposed its implementation "because we believe it inequitable and over-stringent." This theme was echoed throughout the North. The accused fugitive was not permitted to testify during the hearing to determine his fate; federal marshals were responsible "for the full value" of any slave who escaped their custody; and "all good citizens" were "commanded to aid and assist in the prompt and efficient execution of this law," under penalty of fine and imprisonment. These harsh provisions, soon put to the test, served to exacerbate sectional tensions.[32]

One of the first arrests under the Fugitive Slave Act occurred in October at Detroit. Giles Rose, employed as a farm laborer by former governor William Woodbridge, was accused of escaping from slavery in Tennessee and was placed in the custody of the federal marshal. Armed blacks, including some three hundred who crossed over from Canada, surrounded the jail and threatened to free Rose. Before blood was shed or a rescue effected, a public meeting was called and presided over by the city's mayor. Following a rousing exhortation from Congressman Bingham, the assembly contributed to a subscription for the purchase of Rose, and five hundred dollars was subsequently paid for his freedom.

Although other arrests in various states led to outbursts of indignation directed at the Fugitive Slave Act, most northerners were satisfied the Compromise of 1850 had permanently resolved the sectional conflict. There was a corresponding lessening of partisan tensions among supporters of the settlement. Daniel Webster wrote it was "impossible" for him to "entertain hostile feelings or political acrimony" toward Cass and other moderate Democrats. One Whig teased Cass he "should not be much surprised to find you, ere long, as good a Union *whig* as I am!" Similarly, the Michigan senator introduced a Detroit acquaintance as a Whig, but added, "What redeems [him] some in my view, is that [he] is a Union Whig. . . . and as I do not expect to make him a Democrat, I am willing to leave him there." This sentiment was reflected at numerous mass gatherings, frequently designated "Union Meetings." Those who assembled at New Haven, Connecticut, were typically entreated to enforce the Fugitive Slave Act, "so long as it continues to be the law of the land."[33]

Senator Cass personally benefited from the spirit of conciliation that accompanied the Compromise of 1850. Once again, the vast majority of Michiganites accepted him as their political leader. Although he was opposed by Whigs and Free Soilers, his own party closed ranks behind him; westerners no longer demanded representation in the Senate. When the legislature convened in early 1851, he was easily reelected during the first day's session. Lewis Cass, the Father of Popular Sovereignty, had not changed his political stance one jot; his constituents, rather, discarded for the moment the Wilmot Proviso and accepted the compromise as the conclusive adjustment of sectional issues that threatened to dissolve the Union. The prevailing mood favored Cass and compromise. Congressman Buel, however, was not so fortunate. He was defeated for reelection in the fall of 1850, despite Cass's campaigning on his behalf, while indignation over the Fugitive Slave Law was at its height. Whigs, in fact, carried two of Michigan's three congressional seats, but Democrats maintained control of the legislature.[34]

Senator Cass's contributions to the Compromise of 1850 were recognized beyond the borders of his home state. He was tendered a public reception in New York, in November, and took the opportunity to extol the settlement as "reasonable and equitable." With a jab at Senator Seward, the Michigan Democrat lined up with those who believed "the constitution is a law high enough for American citizens." Cass warned that any tampering with the accord—such as repealing the Fugitive Slave Act—"would dissolve this confederation," and he implored his listeners to cease all further debate over slavery. Privately, Cass was "sick of those wretched attempts to continue the agitation; which puts the Union in danger." He repeated this theme in a public letter to a group of Baltimore Democrats, beseeching "every true American" to "rescue the ark of the constitution, from the perils that surround it." His message was emphatic: the principle of popular sovereignty, if given a fair test in Utah and New Mexico, would put to rest the wrangling over slavery in the western territories. This doctrine and the other compromise provisions must be supported to secure the Union.[35]

Notwithstanding the efforts of Cass and other moderates, it became clear when Congress reconvened in December that sectional agitation was not completely quieted. Several times during the session, antislavery members unsuccessfully urged the Senate to rescind the Fugitive Slave Act. Cass groused, "There seems to be a moral epidemic spreading over the land," and he took no part in the debates. He remained firmly convinced repeal was "out of the question," since it would contribute to disunion. When Bostonians aided the escape of fugitive slaves, the Michigan Democrat deplored their actions. As the debate continued, he intensified his oratorical assault on abolitionists. When a town meeting in Weymouth, Massachusetts, urged all slaves to escape from slavery "by running away, or by such other means as in their opinion are right and best," Cass denounced the resolution as nothing less than "a direct invitation to murder." He insisted, "It may be necessary to recapture some fugitive slaves, at almost any cost, to assert the power of the law, and to prevent escapes by showing that fugitives will be retaken." Two years after passage of the compromise measures, Cass acknowledged he "would have voted for twenty fugitive slave laws, if I had believed the safety of the Union depended upon my doing so." The Michigan Democrat was hopeful "the peace of the country has been assured" by the Compromise of 1850. The fact that both northern and southern extremists assailed the accord proved it to be "a wise and patriotic" solution to the slavery question. This sentiment was shared by Stephen Douglas, who agreed that "the whole country is acquiescing in the compromise measures . . . as a final settlement of an unprofitable controversy."[36]

Cass's personal aversion to political extremism, and his unstinting defense of the compromise, earned him a measure of political support from various "Union" groups prior to the presidential election of 1852. The New York Union Committee, for example, urged a national ticket of either Fillmore and Cobb or Clay and Cass. In November 1851, Senator Foote was persuaded by influential northeasterners to explore the possibility of presenting Clay and Cass under the Union banner. Although in feeble health and destined to die within a year, Clay apparently consented on the condition that Cass also agreed. After consulting with influential Democrats, including Daniel Dickinson and Stephen Douglas, Cass refused the invitation. The Michigan senator had been a Democrat for half a century; he would not abandon the party organization to run on a compromise fusion ticket. Instead, Lewis Cass hoped again to be the Democratic presidential candidate.[37]

Following his defeat in 1848, Cass resignedly confessed, "My publick career is over, and I trust I have sense enough to know it. I would not run another such race, for any honour." But as the next election approached, it became evident a large number of conservative Democrats still looked to the Michigan senator as a presidential candidate. Cass attempted to maintain his equanimity in the face of an increasing number of appeals to seek the nomination, acknowledging, in the fall of 1851, he was "too old to set my heart upon farther elevation." His loyal supporters naturally ignored such disclaimers and continued campaigning on his behalf. Michigan Democrats nominated their favorite son for the presidency following passage of the Compromise of 1850 and repeated their endorsement a year later. Although opponents within the party claimed his loss to Taylor eliminated Cass as a suitable candidate, other Democrats blamed the defeat on the Barnburners. They believed Cass deserved another chance because of his distinguished career of service, capped by his ardent support of the compromise measures. The venerable Democrat remained true to his political principles, urging fellow party members to "go on with a steady step, turning neither to the right hand nor the left, and all will yet be right." Even some former Free Soilers were anxious to return to the Democratic fold and support the candidate they opposed in 1848. Although he remained unpopular with sectional spokesmen, of course, Cass's moderate positions on controversial issues had widespread national appeal. Henry Clay, in fact, privately endorsed Cass for the Democratic nomination: "He is, I think, more to be relied on than any of his competitors."[38]

Cass's chances to gain the nomination were hindered by severe personal and political handicaps. The Democratic senator would be seventy years old at the time of the election, and age combined with obesity to make him a sluggish campaigner. One visitor to the Michigan state fair unflatteringly characterized Cass as "a regular old fidgety-granny" whose speech consisted of "his usual song—old times—British & Indians and this big country—interspersed with quotations from Scripture and Shakespear[e] thrown in indiscriminately like jewels in a hog trough." A more subtle, female observer declared that "the Michigan statesman would well fill the Presidential chair, for what he lacks in height, he makes up in breadth." Cass recognized that his shortcomings as a campaigner, and an aversion to seeking the nomination aggressively, made him "a bad candidate." Nonetheless, he retained substantial political support among conservative Democrats, especially in the West.[39]

As the campaign for the nomination intensified, Cass became caught up in the enthusiasm generated for his candidacy. He continued to inform correspondents he did "not care two cents for the Presidency," but by August 1851, he acknowledged that "if the future brings me political advancement so be it. I shall perform my part, as well as I can." This theme was repeated several months later, when he confided, "If the Democratic party think that my name will be useful in the approaching contest, I shall submit and do the best I can." The Michigan senator took pains to send Andrew Jackson Donelson, Old Hickory's nephew, reports of conventions that named him for the presidency. Donelson, who became editor of the *Washington Union* in early 1851, after Thomas Ritchie ran into financial difficulties, pledged to remain neutral in the contest for the nomination, but his sympathies were with Cass. One of the senator's opponents complained the *Union* "was clearly for Cass from the start, and all the time." One month prior to the national convention, Cass confidently disclosed that since he owed a political debt to the Democratic party, "I can best fulfill my obligations by discharging faithfully my duty . . . if nominated and elected." Alpheus Felch believed his colleague's prospects for the nomination were "very good" but cautioned there were "many other candidates and some of them are very active. We cannot tell what will transpire."[40]

By late spring 1852, it was evident that Cass faced vigorous challenges for the presidential nomination. Following the death of Levi Woodbury the previous November, many New England Democrats shifted their political allegiance to Cass's former running mate, William Butler. The Kentucky slaveholder was an appealing national candidate because he personally opposed the extension of slavery and favored gradual emancipation. Butler's political positions were suitably vague on other controversial issues, and he appeared to be gaining support. In January, the Kentucky party convention endorsed him for the presidency and passed a series of resolutions declaring that Congress had no authority to prevent a slaveholder from emigrating with his property to any western territory. Butler's subsequent endorsement of this platform effectively destroyed his candidacy in the North. Other Democrats, such as Joseph Lane, Sam Houston, and William Marcy, likewise enjoyed brief booms of political support. Lane was the choice of Indiana, Houston was touted by various New Englanders, and the aging Marcy received the backing of New York (although Daniel Dickinson and other Cass men captured eleven seats on the state's national delegation). Marcy boldly predicted the political star of General Cass "has passed quite beyond the zenith," but it was the New Yorker who had dropped from serious contention by the time the Democratic convention assembled. The choice apparently was between experienced party spokesmen Lewis Cass and James Buchanan and the youthful Stephen Douglas.[41]

Sixty-year-old James Buchanan ostensibly retired from politics after his stint as Polk's secretary of state, but like Cass, the Pennsylvanian was a Democratic warhorse who believed his years of public service earned him the presidential nomination. Following the admission of California as a free state, Buchanan enjoyed increasing support from southerners who agreed the Missouri Compromise line should be extended to the Pacific. Although disappointed when the Louisiana delegation (still split between John Slidell and Pierre Soulé) pledged its allegiance to Cass, Buchanan was consoled by the endorsement of the most populous cotton states and Virginia. Proslavery spokesmen distrusted the popular sovereignty doctrine, and after the Compromise of 1850, one political observer noted that "the Southern Rights Party is dead against" Cass. As early as December 1851, it was reported "the South would not touch . . . any one who was in Congress & voted for the compromise measures—but they were willing to go for Buchanan." The Pennsylvanian, hopeful he would receive the nomination, concluded that "one thing is certain,—General Cass is out of the question." Buchanan was premature, although Cass's support outside the Northwest was soft.[42]

The political fortunes of Lewis Cass in the South were further damaged by his ardent support of European nationalism. The controversy revolved around Louis Kossuth, a leader in the Hungarian rebellion for independence from Austria. In December 1849, Cass introduced a resolution instructing the Committee on Foreign Relations "to inquire into the expediency of suspending diplomatic relations with Austria," but no formal action was taken on the motion after it was opposed by Henry Clay.

Following suppression of the Hungarian revolt by the combined military forces of Austria and Russia, Kossuth fled to safety. Congress, in early 1851, authorized dispatching a naval vessel to escort the Hungarian nationalist to the United States, and he arrived from Turkey aboard the USS *Mississippi* in December. The Senate, meanwhile, debated a resolution welcoming Kossuth, and Hale proposed an amendment reflecting the "earnest desire" of Americans "that the time may speedily arrive when the rights of man shall be universally recognized and respected by every people and Government of the world." Although Cass denounced the amendment as a veiled attack against the institution of slavery, he praised Kossuth as "the Washington of Hungary" and attended several public dinners given in his honor. Cass therefore was viewed with suspicion by slaveholders, who repudiated the liberal doctrines espoused by European revolutionaries. The Michigan senator was "too mixed up with all this Kossuth movement" to satisfy many southern delegates to the Democratic national convention. A Virginia politician emphasized, "We are dead against Genl. Cass," and expressed a preference for Buchanan, Marcy, or Douglas.[43]

Buchanan, a strong contender in the South for the Democratic nomination, faced an obstinate challenge from the Cass forces in his home state. Shortly after adoption of the compromise measures, one newspaper reported that twenty-six county organizations in Pennsylvania endorsed the Michigan senator for president. Buchanan soon rallied his supporters, however, and a "terrible quarrel" ensued, with Cass men "criticising Buchanan's refusal to come out for the *whole* Compromise as well as the *Fugitive Law.*" Simon Cameron privately informed Cass that "Buchanan acts like a desperate gambler with the last stake in his hand, and so hostile have his feelings become towards you that on all occasions he speaks . . . in disrespectful terms." Buchanan, in fact, accused Cass of being "deficient in moral firmness" and repeatedly warned the party would meet defeat if Cass were again selected the Democratic standard-bearer.[44]

The rivalry between Buchanan and Cass supporters reached comic heights at a Philadelphia County Democratic meeting. A resolution was offered instructing delegates to the state convention to support Cass, but the "Buchaneers" smoothly substituted their own candidate's name and abruptly adjourned. The indignant Cass men attempted to restrain the chairman from fleeing the hall through a rear window but succeeded only in tearing his coat. The Buchananites, ably led by Jeremiah Black, David Porter, J. Glancy Jones, and John Forney, acted more decorously at the state gathering in Harrisburg. After all, they were in firm control of the proceedings. The majority supported Buchanan by a vote of 94 to 31, and imposed the unit rule for the Baltimore national convention. While Buchanan was cheered by these actions and remained confident his prospects "never were so bright," beyond Pennsylvania and much of the South he enjoyed only marginal support.[45]

Lewis Cass was not a man easily angered by political attacks, but he chafed under Buchanan's continual belittling of his chances in 1852. "As to Mr. Buchanan," Cass wrote an influential Democratic editor, "I never refer to him, but with respect. But I am told he is resorting to strange means such as little become the high prize he has in view." Cass's pique did not linger; he was not a man to bear grudges. Two months before the Baltimore convention, a political confidant of Buchanan reported after meeting with the Michigan senator: *"General Cass prefers you for the Presidency to any other person named, in case he cannot himself succeed."* If so, Cass was not making such sentiments known; instead, the Michigan Democrat praised the other leading contender for the nomination. "As to Douglas, he is a good fellow. I am confident he feels friendly to me, and I do not believe he ever did or will do the least improper thing, to attain the Presidency." By the time the national convention convened some months later, however, Cass's favorable attitude toward Douglas was sorely tested.[46]

Stephen Douglas was thirty-eight years old in the spring of 1851, when he began to be mentioned for the presidency. The Illinois senator originally supported the nomination of Lewis Cass, the Northwest's most prominent Democrat. But Douglas's youth, ambition, and belief in manifest destiny combined to make him the ideal candidate for "Young America," an aggressively nationalistic political movement that championed territorial and economic expansion. He reported from New York to Robert M. T. Hunter, a Virginia supporter frequently mentioned as a running mate, that "everything looks well—much better than either of us had a right to expect." As his candidacy gained strength in the Northwest and New England, the Illinois Democrat agreed with a political advisor that his "name should not be brought too prominently before the public at this time. More can be done by private correspondence with our friends in other states than by any other mode." Unfortunately, one of his most vociferous supporters embroiled Douglas in partisan controversy.[47]

George N. Sanders was a Kentuckian who personified the principles of Young America. He purchased the *Democratic Review* from John L. O'Sullivan, in December 1851, and commenced to bolster the candidacy of Douglas by systematically attacking all other contenders for the nomination. The January issue set the tone, declaring, "Age is to be honored, but senility is pitiable." Without mentioning Douglas by name, Sanders urged the party to choose "a statesman who can bring young blood, young ideas, and young hearts to the councils of the Republic." The editor later focused on William Butler as "a good sample of the no-policy statesman" and a "beaten horse." Lewis Cass was dismissed as "the patriarch of old fogyism," "the most self-aggrandizing old fogy." The term "old fogy" had been in use for years, but it might have been coined with Cass in mind. Sanders hammered away at the contrast between "fogyism" and Young America. Additionally, the *Review* scathingly characterized the Michigan senator as "this variable weather-vane, this human contradiction, this American Janus, with one face of yesterday, and another of to-day, whose whole cranial formation from the neck up is pivotal." Douglas pleaded in vain with Sanders to curtail these brutal attacks, since they focused the ire of his rivals on the Illinois senator. Nonetheless, when the Democrats convened at Baltimore, Douglas, Buchanan, and Cass were considered the front-runners for the presidential nomination.[48]

At noon on Tuesday, June 1, the Democratic national convention was called to order at the Maryland Institute. Nearly seven hundred delegates were present, including a large Cass contingent headed by Daniel Dickinson, Robert McClelland, Simon Cameron, and Jesse Bright. Two days were spent organizing the convention, choosing committees, and settling credential disputes; the two-thirds rule was instituted, making 197 of the 296 accredited votes necessary for nomination. When the first ballot to select the presidential candidate was taken on Thursday morning, Cass garnered a plurality of 116 votes, demonstrating strength in New England, New York, New Jersey, Delaware, Maryland, Louisiana, and the western states. Seventeen ballots were cast during the day, and Cass remained in the lead, although his total slipped under 100. Buchanan consistently received about 90 votes, and Douglas increased his tally from 20 to 50, passing a fading Marcy in the process.

At nine o'clock Friday morning, the delegates reconvened and cast another sixteen fruitless ballots. After falling to 27 votes, while first Buchanan and then Douglas gained pluralities, Cass recovered on the thirty-third roll call to total 123. The nomination seemed within reach once again, as his political opponents hastily pushed through an adjournment. "The Cass men are in ecstacies," reported a New York correspondent that evening, "and think that they will elect their favorite to-morrow," but the reporter cautioned, "The Buchananites are caucussing to-night and forming combinations to thwart him."[49]

The Buchaneers, led by Jeremiah Black and David Porter, repaired to Carroll Hall and devised their strategy. It was decided that on Saturday each potential candidate would be briefly supported, in turn, to demonstrate none could gain two-thirds of the votes. It would then be possible, the plotters hoped, to settle upon Buchanan as the Democratic nominee. The following morning, Virginia put the plan into operation by casting 15 votes for Daniel Dickinson of New York. Dickinson, however, remained loyal to Lewis Cass and withdrew his name from consideration. A similar attempt to rally support for Marcy revealed his inability to secure the nomination. A third possible compromise candidate, Franklin Pierce, then received Virginia's votes. After thirteen more inconclusive ballots, the frustrated delegates plodded through the forty-ninth roll call with little change in the voting pattern, until North Carolina was called. James Dobbin, a Buchanan supporter, rose and eloquently urged the selection of Pierce in the spirit of "harmony and conciliation." The exhausted delegates responded with alacrity, and chairman John W. Davis announced the results of the final ballot: "Cass 2, Douglas 2, Butler 1, Houston 1, FRANKLIN PIERCE of New Hampshire, (God bless him!) 282 votes." After nominating William King, of Alabama, for vice president, and hurriedly passing a platform that supported the Compromise of 1850, the Democratic national convention adjourned.[50]

Lewis Cass was denied the presidential nomination, due to the opposition of Buchanan and proslavery southerners who distrusted the doctrine of popular sovereignty. His supporters, "exceedingly chagrined & disappointed," bravely predicted that once Pierce was elected, the Michigan senator "will be the power behind the throne—greater than the throne itself." Cass himself accepted the defeat with characteristic good grace. "I am as cool as any man in the nation. I never had my heart upon the nomination, nor did I ever believe I should receive it. I knew too well the influences, that were at work against me." He thanked Daniel Dickinson for his unwavering support at Baltimore and exhorted Democrats to "all team in and support" the candidate. Cass personally congratulated Pierce, referring to the nomination as "a most fortunate event for our party and the Country."[51]

The other major political parties soon made their nominations. Meeting at Baltimore, the Whigs selected General Winfield Scott to head the ticket. Their platform "acquiesced" in the compromise measures "as a settlement in principle and substance, of the dangerous and exciting question which they embrace." The Free Soilers—now calling themselves Free Democrats—assembled at Pittsburgh, where they nominated John P. Hale on a platform strongly opposed to the Compromise of 1850.[52]

Once again, Lewis Cass hurled himself enthusiastically into a presidential election campaign. At a ratification meeting in June, at Detroit City Hall, he was greeted with "tremendous cheering." The stalwart Democrat lauded Pierce as a candidate who "will go for the Union, for the whole Union, and for nothing but the Union and the constitution." After fulfilling the melancholy task of accompanying the mortal remains of Henry Clay from Washington to Lexington, Kentucky, the following month, Cass returned to the campaign trail, speaking on behalf of the national ticket at Washington, Baltimore, and New York. Upon returning to Detroit, he campaigned extensively in the Northwest. A Democratic weekly expansively reported that "Gen. Cass' abilities as a stump speaker have not been over-rated by even his warmest friends.—He is courteous, dignified and argumentative, and at the same time has a fund of pleasantry and good humor." Douglas joined Cass at Cleveland on September 10, and soon thereafter at the Michigan state fair. They also campaigned together at Chicago, where Cass's speech was received "amid deafening and protracted cheers." Despite his advanced age, Cass continued to stump for Pierce until election day, when Michigan was firmly in the Democratic column. Pierce won all but four states, and trounced Scott by a 259 to 42 electoral margin; Hale attained slightly more than half the Free Soil popular vote in 1848. Cass was pleased, too, with the reelection of his political protégé, Governor Robert McClelland, for whom he campaigned vigorously. Zachariah Chandler, the defeated Whig candidate, portentously remarked: "I am afraid it will take General Cass's Senatorial seat to balance the account between us."[53]

Franklin Pierce was determined to put his personal stamp on cabinet selections. The president-elect showed no inclination to invite any of his chief rivals for the nomination to join the administration, and Lewis Cass ruled himself out for "any office whatever," immediately following the election. "I can foresee no possible state of things, which would induce me to go into the cabinet," he informed David Disney, his loyal Ohio lieutenant. "It can not be." Pierce kept his own counsel, and took the Michigan senator at his word, not consulting him regarding departmental appointments. Nonetheless, Pierce understood that certain geographical and ideological divisions within the Democratic party needed to be represented in his official family. He therefore discussed the situation with Alfred O. P. Nicholson (his former colleague in the Senate) to ascertain Cass's wishes, and also wrote to James Buchanan for suggestions. The Cass faction of the party joined southerners in effectively vetoing the selection of former Barnburner John Dix—although the New York cabinet seat subsequently went to William Marcy, despite Cass's endorsement of Daniel Dickinson. Robert McClelland was appointed secretary of the interior, and he found posts for other Cass men, such as George Manypenny, who headed the Indian Office. Treasury nominee James Guthrie, of Louisville, was recommended by Nicholson; he, too, received Cass's imprimatur. Jefferson Davis and James Dobbin were the notable southern cabinet members, and James Campbell was the choice of Buchanan. Only the Douglas faction was largely ignored. There were not enough patronage positions available to satisfy everyone, and it nettled Cass to notify his many supplicants that he enjoyed little personal influence on the distribution of federal offices.[54]

Senator Cass did not attend the inaugural festivities or the opening session of Congress in the spring of 1853, because Elizabeth's health had deteriorated to the point where he rarely left her bedside. She died on March 31, and Cass wrote the president he had suffered "a stroke from which I can never recover . . . life has no future for me." He continued in a morbid tone: "I am an old man.—My race is almost run.—I ask nothing of mortal man." His helpmate of forty-seven years was gone, but Lewis Cass took solace from the rest of his family. His only son was proving to be an able diplomat in revolution-torn Italy, and his daughters were raising families of their own. Grandfather Cass was a doting and indulgent patriarch, ever ready with a few dollars or equally unsolicited advice, as Henry B. Ledyard discovered when he went off to school. "You have it in your power to make yourself a dependable, useful man," Cass reminded the young boy, adding to accomplish that "you must study well and behave well. . . . I feel a deep interest in you, and you must think of that & study the harder." His grandchildren were a great source of joy to the grieving widower, who was also comforted by the Democratic presidential victory, and the firm belief that the Compromise of 1850 had permanently settled the sectional conflict.[55]

Lewis Cass returned to Washington in the fall of 1853 and took a suite at Willard's Hotel. Robert McClelland, acting increasingly more like a surrogate son than a political protégé, arranged for the purchase of a splendid span of horses to transport the senator in style between his lodgings and the Capitol. Still mourning Elizabeth's death, Cass rarely entertained or dined out. He became something of a recluse, choosing to concentrate his energies on public affairs. The natural diminution of his physical capabilities forced Cass to take a less active role among the Democratic leadership. He confided to a longtime political acquaintance, "I shall never hold another office than the one I now fill, never," and regretfully saw himself as a "spectator of passing events, rather than an actor in them." For the remainder of his Senate term, Cass chose to serve on only one standing committee: the Committee on the Library. This appointment indicates the esteem in which he was held as a scholar, and reveals an important personal characteristic. His many publications regarding Indian culture, world travel, and history were recognized as significant contributions to American learning, while his positions on controversial political questions demonstrated an intellectual, studious approach to government. Cass grounded his principles upon a strictly constitutional, legalistic foundation. He was not swayed by emotional or moralistic appeals, and he remained committed to seeking compromise solutions to explosive sectional issues. His spirit of political moderation found a forum, as the doctrine of popular sovereignty again became the focus of Senate debate during the ensuing months. Once more, the question of slavery expansion threatened the stability of the Union and roused Lewis Cass from lethargy.[56]

Ironically, the impetus for reopening the sectional controversy came from an avowed proponent of popular sovereignty. Shortly after the Thirty-third Congress convened in December, Senator Augustus Caesar Dodge of Iowa introduced a bill organizing that portion of the Louisiana Purchase north of 36°30' as the territory of Nebraska. The bill was referred to the Committee on Territories, chaired by Stephen Douglas. The Illinois Democrat, who introduced similar legislation in both the House and Senate during the preceding decade, wasted little time in reporting the Nebraska bill on January 4. A second version, published six days later, added a section previously omitted because of a "clerical error." The revised measure incorporated the Cass doctrine; the slavery question was "left to the decision of the people residing therein." Douglas, morally obtuse regarding the institution of slavery, futilely hoped to secure southern support for his proposal without explicitly repealing the Missouri Compromise line. Senator Archibald Dixon, a Kentucky Whig, attempted to remove the ambiguity from Douglas's bill by offering an amendment allowing citizens "to take and hold their slaves within any of the Territories of the United

States." When Charles Sumner responded the following day that the Nebraska bill in no way contravened the Missouri Compromise, the sectional battle lines were clearly drawn. Douglas subsequently endorsed the southern demand for abrogating the Missouri Compromise line, doubtless aware of the political firestorm this would ignite. On January 23, he submitted a third bill creating two territories—Nebraska and Kansas. The issue of slavery, again, was to be decided by territorial residents; the Missouri Compromise, "superseded" by the Compromise of 1850, was declared "inoperative." Douglas, "profoundly impressed with the point of view outlined by Lewis Cass" in the Nicholson letter, by this time was a devout disciple of the popular sovereignty creed.[57]

Antislavery men opposed any attempt to subvert the Missouri Compromise proscription. Even before Douglas reported the third Kansas-Nebraska bill, abolitionist and antiextension congressmen organized against any territorial measure that did not maintain the 36°30' line. On Tuesday, January 24, the *National Era* published an "Appeal of the Independent Democrats in Congress to the People of the United States." Primarily the work of Senator Salmon Chase and Congressman Joshua Giddings, this manifesto condemned the Douglas bill as a "falsification of the truth of history"; the Compromise of 1850 was not intended to repeal the "sacred pledge" of the Missouri accord, it argued. Five northern state legislatures passed resolutions condemning the latest proposal to open the western territories to slavery.[58]

After an initial hesitation, President Pierce made the Kansas-Nebraska bill a test of party orthodoxy. He was won over by Douglas's argument that repealing the Missouri Compromise line was necessary to secure essential southern support. The administration organ in Washington called upon "every true democrat" to support the bill as a reaffirmation of the settlement of 1850. Lewis Cass answered his party's call with a heavy heart. Only months before, the Michigan senator confided, "I have been a Democrat all my days, and I mean to die one," but he was appalled that Douglas's machinations resurrected sectional antagonisms and completely dissipated the spirit of political conciliation fostered by the compromise measures. The two prominent Northwest Democrats also had conflicting personalities. Douglas reveled in the rough-and-tumble of the congressional arena, while Cass dispassionately sought accommodation. The Michiganite privately described Douglas as "just about the most overrated man in the country, and so he will come out. . . . It is all humbug." Cass, moreover, complained he was not consulted during the drafting of the various Nebraska bills; the Illinois senator did not think it necessary to include the Father of Popular Sovereignty in his legislative plans. When urged by supporters to regain some control over events by moving for repeal of the Missouri Compromise line, Cass replied that he "could not make such an atrocious proposition, whatever others might do." The Kansas-Nebraska bill, he asserted, "was fraught with infinite evil," and Cass denied a *New York Herald* report he would vote to rescind the 36°30' line. He personally "begged" the president to avoid a direct confrontation on the issue. Pierce ultimately disregarded this advice, and Cass then refocused his wrath. A New York congressman astutely observed that Cass "looks upon the whole movement and the manner in which it has been made as a despicable piece of demagogism on the part of Douglas." Lewis Cass was not a rigid ideologue. He was shocked and dismayed by Douglas's attempt to substitute popular sovereignty for the Missouri Compromise proscription. The threat to the Union embodied in the Kansas-Nebraska bill was palpable. And yet, after it was embraced by President Pierce as a party measure, Salmon Chase surmised that Cass "was decidedly against renewal of the agitation—but he will *vote* with the proslavery side."[59]

Senator Cass did not immediately announce his support of the Kansas-Nebraska bill. He did, however, make good on his vow to take part in its adjustment "frankly and fearlessly." It was in response to his argument that the term "superseded," as used in the bill, was "an entire logical fallacy," that Douglas proposed an amendment declaring the Missouri Compromise line to be "inconsistent" with the principle of congressional nonintervention with slavery in the territories. Cass voted with the Senate majority in approving this amendment on February 15 and thereafter was a vocal advocate of the Kansas-Nebraska bill. After all, while he regretted its introduction and quibbled over the wording, Cass had no quarrel with its popular sovereignty core. As one congressman observed, Cass supported the bill "as a matter of course, it being simply an embodiment of the principle upon which he fought the battle of 1848." During the debates, the Michigan senator cautioned his colleagues they lacked any constitutional authority to regulate the domestic concerns of territorial residents, because self-government was "an inalienable right of the people, consecrated by the blood of our fathers, and hallowed by the affection of their sons." He once again opposed both the northern demand that Congress exclude slavery from the territories and the southern insistence that slavery in the western regions be protected by federal legislation. Cass believed the popular sovereignty principle, which he referred to simply as "the right of men to govern themselves," was acceptable to most Democrats, and would ensure the pacific organization of Kansas and Nebraska.[60]

Senator Cass proved to be wrong. Truman Smith, of Connecticut, presented resolutions opposed to the introduction of slavery into the western territories, and suggested to Cass they represented "the sentiments of an overwhelming majority of the people of Michigan." Cass responded to the goad and defiantly declared that his constituents supported self-government, not restrictions on the rights of territorial inhabitants.[61] But instead of rallying to the popular sovereignty standard, Michigan antislavery men joined other northerners in castigating the Kansas-Nebraska bill. The Cass doctrine could not be employed in this case as intended, due to sectional intransigence. Lewis Cass simply could not fathom why southerners and northerners adamantly refused to compromise. This was his blind spot: refusing to link morality to the slavery controversy, he continued to approach the question from a strictly legalistic perspective. He was, in brief, losing touch with political realities by remaining bent on seeking a moderate solution to the problem. Popular sovereignty was no longer an ambiguous device aiding the cause of union. It was now the instrument that reopened in Congress the divisive subject of slavery and the territories.

Cass helped to strip his doctrine of its carefully contrived ambiguity. In response to critics of "squatter sovereignty," who demanded to know when the population of a territory was sufficient for its organization, Cass replied "the smallest number of persons" were entitled to regulate their local affairs. He finally repudiated the southern claim that territorial residents could not prohibit slavery prior to statehood. Instead, the underlying principles of the American republic—liberty and equality—were to be implemented in the West. Lewis Cass, like Douglas, never believed that repealing the Missouri Compromise line would actually open the region to slavery. From the introduction of the Cass doctrine, in the Nicholson letter, through the debates over the Kansas-Nebraska bill, popular sovereignty was not meant as a confirmation of the right of southerners to carry their slaves into any territory. Cass steadfastly maintained that regardless of any congressional action, slavery would fail to take root in the western prairies and plains, and he buttressed this belief with his vote. Cass promoted an unsuccessful Homestead bill that would have retarded the spread of slavery in the western territories, and favored an amendment restricting the grants to "free white[s]." Convinced the territories would remain free, owing to soil and climate conditions, he supported the popular sovereignty concept embodied in the Kansas-Nebraska bill simply as a matter of principle and, once the question was unavoidable, political expediency.[62]

Passage of the Kansas-Nebraska bill was well managed by Stephen Douglas. In early March, Cass voted with the Senate majority in favor of the bill, and he likewise supported the final version worked out with the House. On May 30, President Pierce signed the Kansas-Nebraska Act. Several days later, Senator Cass stated it was "a wise measure" that would forever withdraw the slavery controversy from Congress. He conceded that repeal of the Missouri Compromise line "excited a good deal of opposition" in Michigan and aroused a groundswell of antisouthern sentiment, but he confidently concluded that "the more it is examined and becomes known, the more favor it will meet from reasonable men of both parties." This optimistic analysis proved to be lamentably mistaken. The Father of Popular Sovereignty was blinded to the political havoc his doctrine had unleashed.[63]

Lewis Cass and Stephen Douglas, committed to popular sovereignty and political accommodation, underestimated the moral indignation that swept through the North with the Kansas-Nebraska Act. Following the adjournment of Congress, the Illinois senator discovered he "could travel from Boston to Chicago by the light of my own effigy." Anti-Nebraska sentiment was particularly strong in the Northwest, with the notable exceptions of Indiana and southern Illinois. A free soil Michigan newspaper denounced the measure as "the most impudent insult to legislative integrity ever conceived in the corrupt Congress of this slavery-ridden nation." Lewis Cass was derided as "one of the insects" who hastened to do the South's bidding; the *Battle Creek Journal* reported local citizens hanged him in effigy. Antislavery northwesterners were in no mood to accept Cass's contention that popular sovereignty would keep Kansas and Nebraska free. They wanted explicit restrictions on the spread of slavery, and wasted little time in exploiting the issue. In Ohio, anti-Nebraska conventions were organized in early 1854, and abolitionists, Whigs, Know Nothings, and free soil Democrats united to form a state Republican party. This scene was repeated in Wisconsin and Iowa, as antislavery Whigs and Democrats abandoned their former allegiance and adopted the Republican name. Michiganites also responded with alacrity, and mass rallies were held in Detroit, and several other cities, to protest the

Kansas-Nebraska Act. An estimated three to five thousand former Free Soilers, Whigs, and Free Democrats gathered at Jackson, in July, and organized the Michigan Republican party. They passed resolutions that condemned slavery as "a great moral, social and political evil"; called for its abolition in the District of Columbia; and urged repeal of the Fugitive Slave Law and the Kansas-Nebraska Act. In direct contrast to Lewis Cass, Republicans argued Congress had the authority to prohibit slavery in the territories, and they pledged to oppose its extension by all constitutional means. Free soil western emigrants were urged to "remember the Republican motto, 'THE NORTH WILL DEFEND YOU.'" Following selection of a state ticket headed by former Democratic congressman Kingsley Bingham, the first Michigan Republican convention adjourned.[64]

Democrats met at Detroit City Hall, in September, and Lewis Cass sounded the keynote of the campaign. He declared that although the Kansas-Nebraska Act was widely denounced, "the principle it contained was *right*." Taking note of the Republican platform, Cass acknowledged slavery was a social and political evil but asserted Congress had no authority "to abolish or establish it in the territories." Repeal of the Missouri Compromise line, quite simply, was constitutional. Cass concluded with an earnest plea to support popular sovereignty in the settlement of Kansas and Nebraska, because slavery could not exist there unless the residents desired it. His fellow Democrats responded by adopting resolutions affirming the Cass doctrine. John Barry, who had served three terms as governor, was selected to head the ticket. The election campaign was off to a fast start in Michigan.[65]

Cass anguished over the disarrangement of the American political system triggered by the Kansas-Nebraska Act and the founding of the Republican organization. He firmly believed a powerful, sectional party threatened the Union. Cass therefore threw himself into the canvass with a vigor belying his seventy-two years, and carried his message to Chicago before stumping the more populous areas of Michigan. His theme did not vary in the almost daily speeches he delivered to attentive audiences. To bolster his argument, Cass warned the voters that the power to prohibit slavery entailed the power to establish it. He rhetorically inquired at Kalamazoo: "Congress cannot say to the people of Michigan, 'you shan't have this or that institution.' Why, then, shall it say to the people of Nebraska, 'you shan't have this or that institution'? Are not American citizens equal?" He chose to ignore any constitutional distinction between states and territories on the slavery issue.[66]

On Saturday evening, November 4, Lewis Cass delivered his final address of the campaign at Detroit City Hall. One of those present, a local attorney opposed to the extension of slavery, observed he "had a very large & attentive audience; but . . . I thoroughly suspect that a majority of the crowd were not Nebraska Democrats." The senator devoted much of his two-hour speech to addressing a *Richmond Enquirer* editorial that took him to task for terming slavery a social and political evil. Cass previously complained, on the floor of the Senate, southerners were no longer satisfied that northern politicians accepted, "firmly and unflinchingly, the rights of the slaveholding portion of the Union"; instead they demanded an acknowledgment "that *slavery is the best condition of human society.*" Speaking to his neighbors, the senator reaffirmed that "there is a natural feeling in the human breast against the existence of slavery." Nevertheless, the question for every patriotic citizen "is not whether he regrets the existence of slavery, but what right he has to touch it." Cass supported the Kansas-Nebraska Act because it sanctioned "the true doctrine of congressional non-intervention" and repealed the unconstitutional Missouri Compromise line, which restricted "the rights of self-government." Cass pledged to maintain the constitutional rights of southerners and castigated the Republicans and their Know Nothing allies. He closed with an admonition to fellow Democrats not to "abolitionize" their party. Apparently, the senator failed to sway the opinions of many in his audience. One listener recalled that when Cass alluded to the Know Nothings, nativists opposed to the political aspirations of immigrants and Roman Catholics, "there were double the number of cheers that greeted any other portion of his speech, and when he went on to denounce them, it was very evident that he met with very little sympathy from any except Irishmen."[67]

Lewis Cass did not have an appreciable impact on the election of 1854. The Democratic *Free Press* loyally reported in October that "his masterly vindication of the Nebraska bill, made a deep and lasting impression" on the electorate, but the antislavery press more closely mirrored the mood of Michigan's voters. The free soil *Detroit Democrat* noted the senator labeled slavery an evil only after returning to the North, and concluded Cass was "the subservient mouthpiece and apologist and advocate of slavery and slave-holders." Indeed, Michigan election returns vindicated the Republican party. Kingsley Bingham was elected governor, and Republicans captured three of the state's four congressional seats. The

Democrats also lost the legislative majority they had held for thirteen years. Lewis Cass was bitterly disappointed. He grossly underestimated the antislavery sentiment in his home region, and the result was a devastating defeat that forever tarnished the luster of the popular sovereignty doctrine.[68]

When the Michigan legislature convened in January 1855, Republicans immediately served notice they rejected any compromise on the slavery issue. A Personal Liberty bill was passed, which provided legal protection (including the benefit of habeas corpus and trial by jury) for all accused fugitive slaves. The legislators formally condemned slavery "as a great moral, social, and political evil" and called upon Congress to abolish the institution in the District of Columbia. The legislature instructed Senators Lewis Cass and Charles Stuart to vote for repeal of the Fugitive Slave Law and to support any bill prohibiting slavery in the territories—"especially in Kansas and Nebraska."[69]

Stuart dutifully presented the Michigan resolutions to the U.S. Senate on February 5. Following their reading, Cass obtained the floor and acknowledged that five years earlier he pledged to resign if similar instructions regarding the Wilmot Proviso were not rescinded. Since the Republican party now controlled the Michigan legislature, however, Cass declared he was not bound to honor the current resolutions. Furthermore, Cass believed repeal of the Fugitive Slave Act, or the prohibition of slavery in Kansas and Nebraska, would trigger "the dissolution of this Confederacy." The Union was imperiled by political extremism and sectionalism, and Senator Cass attacked the coalition of free soilers and Know Nothings that shaped the Republican party. "We want no new parties, no new platforms, no new organizations, and the sooner these dangerous efforts are abandoned, the better will it be for us, and those who are to follow us in this heritage of freedom." He singled out for criticism advocates of religious and political intolerance who, while "humbly affecting to know nothing," are "resolutely determined to direct everything." It was imperative, in the face of this threat, that Democrats maintain a national organization firmly committed to moderation on divisive issues. Popular sovereignty, Cass hoped, might yet be the ideological bridge within the party between North and South.[70]

Lewis Cass was understandably concerned about the impact of Republicans, although the American party, as the Know Nothings were formally known, did not achieve the political influence in Michigan it did in other states. Repeal of the Missouri Compromise line was a significant catalyst in the formation of the Republican party. Other factors and issues affecting the realignment of political allegiance during the 1850s included nativism, temperance, and religious antagonisms—particularly between Catholics and evangelical Protestants. The Know Nothings effectively exploited nativist and anti-Catholic sentiment, and vied with Republicans to challenge the established Democratic party. In a number of northern states, in fact, nativists and anti-Nebraska men formed fusion tickets. Such was not the case in Michigan. In 1854, the state elections clearly presented a choice between the nascent Republicans and the Democrats, although the Americans generally supported Republican candidates. The following year, Know Nothings won some local races, but the Democrats carried Detroit, and Henry Ledyard, Cass's son-in-law, was elected mayor. By 1856, the contest was again between Democrats and Republicans. The Know Nothing influence was on the wane, in Michigan as well as nationwide. Internal and sectional dissension, especially over slavery, led to the decline of the American party, which correspondingly added to Republican strength in the North. Lewis Cass's devotion to the constitutional Union caused him to view the growing antislavery sentiment with alarm, and he increasingly came to rely on southern Democrats to maintain the party's supremacy over the Republicans.[71]

Slavery extension was the chief domestic problem during the Pierce administration, but Lewis Cass was concerned, as well, with foreign affairs and personal family matters. A recurring diplomatic issue was the future of Cuba. Cass feared the island was coming under the influence of the British; as long as Spain retained Cuba, he acknowledged, the United States had no right to interfere. Cass deplored filibustering expeditions to seize the island, several years before the Ostend Manifesto sought to make that official policy, but he was willing to purchase Cuba, "even at an extravagant price," to safeguard national interests in the Caribbean. "The Gulf of Mexico," he told his colleagues, "must be practically an American lake, for the great purpose of security."[72] His Anglophobia and sense of national honor, in this instance, were neatly coupled with one of Cass's lifelong public pursuits: territorial expansion. The fact that Cuba was coveted by slaveholders added to its allure. The Michigan senator wished to demonstrate to southern Democrats that northern conservatives were steadfast allies.

It was with equal fervor that Cass engaged in a public debate with the archbishop of New York over religious rights abroad. The senator called upon the administration to secure religious freedom for Americans in foreign lands, while Archbishop Hughes pointedly noted Catholics were persecuted by Protestant mobs in the United States. There was plenty of blame to share, but the Senate passed a brace of harmless resolutions, submitted by Cass, urging that future treaties, "if practicable," guarantee to Americans residing abroad both freedom of worship and consecrated "burial places." The deaths of close family members, and his own advancing age, no doubt added to Cass's concern about such matters. This was underscored when Cass's son-in-law Augustus Canfield died a year after Elizabeth, leaving his widow, Mary, to her father's care. The senator wrote to H. A. Willard in the fall of 1855 expressing his needs for the approaching congressional session: "I want a parlor, and two bed rooms, one for myself, and one for my daughter," and an additional room for the footman; the coachman could board near the stables. If possible, Cass wished "to avoid mounting more than one pair of stairs." With the settlement of such sacred and mundane matters, Senator Cass turned his attention once more to the volatile slavery controversy.[73]

Republicans and southern defenders of slavery expansion had rejected popular sovereignty, but Cass clung to the doctrine with increasing zeal as the election of 1856 approached. Senator Cass faced a difficult reelection campaign, and the Republicans were serious challengers for the White House, but national attention first focused on events in Kansas. Following passage of the Kansas-Nebraska Act, it generally was acknowledged Nebraska would enter the Union as a free state, and the southern territory became the scene of a desperate struggle between free soilers and proslavery men. The *New York Tribune* fiercely declared Kansas was "the battle-ground of freedom and must never be surrendered." Organizations such as the New England Emigrant Aid Company were formed to assist northerners in migrating westward. Nevertheless, by the end of 1854, fewer than five hundred such emigrants were settled in Kansas, and the proslavery men gained the upper hand in the contest for political control of the territory. Free soilers were frustrated in their attempts to secure a legislative majority because neighboring Missourians, encouraged by Senator David Atchison, flocked across the border to support the proslavery candidates. Governor Andrew Reeder, a Pierce appointee from Pennsylvania who was deeply involved in shady land speculations, had conducted a rough census which counted fewer than three thousand eligible territorial voters. After election returns gave the proslavery ticket a 5,427 to 791 margin of victory, a congressional investigation revealed that nearly five thousand fraudulent ballots had been cast. The illegal votes of "border ruffians," as Horace Greeley dubbed the Missourians, enabled proslavery men to organize a territorial assembly at Shawnee Mission. This legislature promptly expelled the free soil members before adopting, over Reeder's veto, a stringent territorial slave code. The governor was subsequently removed by President Pierce, who cited speculative irregularities but was largely influenced by southern opposition to Reeder's popular sovereignty stance.[74]

Antislavery Kansans countered by forming a provisional territorial government at Topeka. Led by James Lane (a former Hoosier Democrat and Mexican War veteran), Dr. Charles Robinson (a product of abolitionist Massachusetts), and former governor Andrew Reeder, the free staters drafted a constitution prohibiting slavery and sent a copy to Washington, where Lewis Cass presented it to the Senate on March 24, 1856. Cass made it clear he did so to honor a previous pledge, and because every American citizen had the right to petition Congress. Shortly after this less than enthusiastic introduction, Cass withdrew the document from the "self-styled Legislature," since it represented the sentiments of only free soil Kansans. In spite of the formal retraction of the Topeka constitution, Congress was confronted with competing territorial governments as the national political wrangling escalated.[75]

Cass was dispirited by the situation in Kansas Territory. He addressed the Senate during two days in May in an attempt "to redeem from obloquy a cherished American principle, which lies at the foundation of free institutions"—popular sovereignty. Cass devoted most of his allotted time on May 12 to yet another tedious refutation of the claim that Congress had the authority to regulate slavery in the territories. He concluded: "You can find in the Constitution no recognition of sovereignty in Congress"; sovereignty resides in "the people of the United States." Summarizing the principles originally presented in the Nicholson letter, the Michigan senator said territorial residents "are fully competent to administer their own domestic affairs." The next day, Cass turned specifically to the Kansas problem. That the principle of self-government embodied in the Kansas-Nebraska Act had not led to a peaceful adjustment of the dispute was attributable, in his view, to "external interference." Antislavery northerners were the most culpable, including clergymen (such as Henry Ward Beecher) who aided free soil emigrants. Cass protested, "The house of prayer is now made an armory for the collection of weapons to arm Americans against their countrymen." The entire slavery controversy was exacerbated by a spirit of fanaticism emanating from the northern press. "The world had been inundated with log-cabin books," Cass continued with a thrust at Harriet Beecher Stowe, "about as worthy of credit as the travels of the renowned Gulliver, too often drawing their conclusions from the dictates of a wild or false heart, or of a disordered head." Although he castigated Missourians who entered Kansas solely to cast proslavery ballots, he found their actions unsurprising in light of the influx of armed adventurers from the North. He chose to ignore the fact that northern farmers moved west to settle Kansas, not merely to influence territorial elections. He stated the proslavery legislature was legally constituted, while the free staters who met at Topeka "resorted to a revolution." In short, Lewis Cass held northerners morally responsible for the deplorable conditions in Kansas. The answer to the unrest remained political compromise. Since "the South intermeddles not with the social institutions of the North," Cass urged northerners "to exhibit the same spirit of toleration" by adhering to "the great doctrine of the right of man to govern himself." This required no sacrifice of principle from either side, and "there is no other ground on which we can stand together."[76]

Reactions to Cass's speech, as usual, divided along partisan lines. The Democratic *Washington Union* praised the Michigan senator's "able and argumentative manner" and concluded he "handled abolitionism without gloves." Greeley's *Tribune* disparagingly dismissed the address as "a post-mortem examination of Squatter Sovereignty"; Cass "was its father, and will be its undertaker." Popular sovereignty was spurned as "a stepping-stone pitched into the water to enable the Northern Democracy to pass over on dry land from the doctrines of Freedom to those of Slavery." The New York editor disdainfully rejected Cass's call for a compromise settlement of the Kansas controversy. "Slavery or Freedom must rule in the territories, and not Squatter Sovereignty."[77]

Lewis Cass was no more successful in allaying the spirit of sectionalism within the halls of Congress. One week after he pleaded for moderation, Charles Sumner rose to speak. In a vituperative address laced with sexual imagery, the Massachusetts senator called for the immediate admission of Kansas as a free state, and scathingly attacked Andrew Butler and Stephen Douglas. He portrayed the South Carolinian as a self-deceiving Don Quixote whose mistress, "though polluted in the sight of the world, is chaste in his sight—I mean the harlot, Slavery." Douglas played Sancho Panza, "the squire of Slavery" who performed "all its humiliating offices." As soon as Sumner finished, Cass pushed himself up from his desk to condemn "the most un-American and unpatriotic [speech] that ever grated on the ears of the members of this high body." He had listened "with equal regret and surprise" to the sectional rantings and fervently wished "never to hear again here or elsewhere" such disunionist sentiments. Cass later denounced Sumner's "reprehensible language" and "prurient imagination." To Lewis Cass, agitation of the slavery controversy was nothing more than disloyalty to the American republic, and he was disgusted with the growing inflexibility demonstrated by both sections.[78]

After a temporary respite, the violence in Kansas escalated. In late 1855, Wilson Shannon, a former governor of Ohio who succeeded Reeder, had defused the almost bloodless "Wakarusa War" by personally dissuading twelve hundred Missourians and their Kansas allies from attacking the free soil settlement at Lawrence. The day after Sumner's infamous speech, however, proslavery men descended upon the town. In a rampage that resulted in the death of one of the invaders, they destroyed two newspapers, attacked and burned the fortified Free State Hotel, and ransacked several homes. The northern press made the most of this "Sack of Lawrence." Several days later, the fanatical John Brown led a small band of free soilers in retaliation; during a midnight raid along Pottawatomie Creek, they murdered five proslavery settlers. As further depredations convulsed "Bleeding Kansas," emotions throughout the country reached fever pitch.

The Senate chamber was likewise the scene of physical conflict. Congressman Preston Brooks of South Carolina, incensed at the slanderous attack on his elder kinsman, Andrew Butler, stalked onto the floor where Sumner was sitting defenseless at his desk and repeatedly struck him about the head with a stout walking stick. The Massachusetts senator, bleeding profusely, collapsed under this outrageous assault and did not return to his seat for more than two years. Lewis Cass, despite objecting the task would be too demanding for a man of his age, was selected to serve on the Senate committee that investigated the incident. Precedents were examined, and the select committee reported that any action against Brooks would have to come from the House of Representatives. These findings were accepted and the matter was closed, insofar as the Senate was concerned. While he promptly denounced Sumner's inflammatory address, Cass never commented publicly on the brutal assault administered by Preston Brooks. Senator Cass thereby contributed to his growing political differences with northern antislavery men. In a futile effort to assuage southern sensibilities, Cass again ignored the moral and emotional implications of the sectional quarrel.

In the midst of these frenzied events, a compromise settlement to the Kansas controversy was presented to the Senate. Robert Toombs of Georgia sponsored a bill calling for the election of delegates to a state constitutional convention. Voting was to be supervised by federal commissioners and take place in November, when nonresidents were preoccupied with the presidential contest. Toombs sought nothing less than to eliminate Bleeding Kansas as a national campaign issue. This bill plainly was based on the popular sovereignty principle, and Cass eagerly supported it in order to "secure a fair expression of the public will." After all, Congress would simply be guaranteeing honest territorial elections, not dictating the future of slavery in Kansas. The Toombs bill was sanctioned by the Pierce administration, as well, and passed the Senate in July. Because of Republican opposition, however, the House took no action before Congress adjourned the following month. Lewis Cass lost heart. "I am tired of it all. I am tired of this everlasting harping upon slavery and this hazarding the best and happiest government on the face of the Globe, running the risk of sacrificing it to sectional divisions." He was "too old to witness this state of things much longer" but still held a "deep attachment to our glorious Union. God help us." Cass was resigned to seeking divine intervention because Republicans apparently wanted the Kansas conflict to remain an explosive issue throughout the presidential campaign. The gulf between the moderate Michigan senator and antislavery men was widening, and popular sovereignty no longer bridged the gap. Henceforth, the question was whether enough Democrats would rally around the Cass doctrine to maintain a semblance of party harmony on the slavery issue. This was essential, in light of the formation of the Republican party, if the Union was to be preserved. Such were Cass's beliefs, and the election of 1856 bore him out.[79]

Several major contenders emerged for the Democratic nomination, but Lewis Cass was not among them. Although in April 1855 he wrote to a political confidant that if selected, "I shall meet the results, as best I may," by the end of the year, it had become clear his deteriorating health and advanced age would not permit Cass to pursue the presidency. In response to a request urging him to seek the nomination, the Michigan Democrat replied he did not wish his name to be placed in contention at the national convention. At a Senate caucus in December, Cass publicly declared he was not a candidate. Although the *Washington Union* reported he exhibited "in his enjoyment of uncommon strength and health, the benefits of a life of strict temperance and regularity," the senator confided that physical infirmities forced him to abandon all social functions—he no longer even dined out. Any lingering presidential ambitions were dispelled by an accident that occurred in February. While descending the icy steps of the Interior Department building, Cass slipped and struck his head, losing consciousness. He suffered a severe gash above the left eye, and it was first feared his skull was fractured. Such was not the case, fortunately, although it was many weeks before he fully recovered. Cass wrote in April that he had been incapacitated for over two months and insisted, "No earthly consideration could induce me to be a Candidate for the Presidency." To Alpheus Felch he confessed: "I know my time had come, and that I am too old to enter the Presidential race again." During his recuperation, Cass endorsed the candidacy of James Buchanan.[80]

The Democratic national convention met at Cincinnati on June 2. After drafting a platform that basically echoed traditional party tenets, delegates turned to the selection of a presidential candidate. Samuel Inge of California, "to the astonishment of many," nominated Lewis Cass, "who was honored with a rattle of surprise rather than approving animation." Most delegates obviously had accepted Cass's declarations he was "unwilling to have his name used as a Presidential candidate for all he means by it." The Californian originally intended to back Buchanan but balked when the Pennsylvania delegation joined in tabling a platform resolution calling upon the federal government "to provide a safe and speedy communication" between the coasts. With Buchanan no longer acceptable, Inge turned to Cass, in appreciation of his support for California during the compromise debates in 1850. Although Cass attracted a few additional votes from Ohio, he never was a serious contender for the nomination. Instead, the choice narrowed to Buchanan and Douglas when President Pierce's strength dissipated after fourteen ballots. During the months prior to the convention, the Illinois senator vainly hoped to receive united support from the northwestern delegations. Lewis Cass, however, blamed the younger man for diluting his own support in 1852, and for the turmoil in Kansas. Jesse Bright, engaged in a continuing struggle with Douglas over party patronage, joined Cass in the Buchanan camp. With Michigan and Indiana giving the Pennsylvanian their complete support and—except for Illinois—the other northwestern states splitting their votes, Buchanan was selected on the seventeenth ballot. John Breckinridge of Kentucky was nominated as his running mate.[81]

Stephen Douglas was frustrated by Cass (among others) in his quest for the presidential nomination, but he heartily united with the elder Democrat in support of the national ticket and platform. The Cincinnati delegates vindicated Douglas for his role in the Kansas controversy and supported Cass on two important points. The principles of popular sovereignty and congressional nonintervention, regarding slavery in the territories, were endorsed in the platform. "The only sound and safe solution of the 'slavery question'" was "NON-INTERFERENCE BY CONGRESS WITH SLAVERY IN STATE AND TERRITORY, OR IN THE DISTRICT OF COLUMBIA." The term "non-interference" replaced "non-intervention" in the Democratic lexicon, but the ambiguity of the Cass doctrine remained, since the delegates made no attempt to resolve the question of when a territory could legislate on slavery. Cass and most northern Democrats contended the settlers could determine their domestic institutions through territorial legislation; the common southern interpretation was that slavery could not be prohibited prior to statehood. Popular sovereignty thus continued to serve as a sectional bridge between Democrats on the divisive issue of slavery expansion, in keeping with Cass's original purpose.[82]

The first Republican national convention was called to order in Philadelphia soon after the Democrats adjourned. Mexican War veteran John C. Frémont was selected as the presidential candidate and William Drayton, a former senator from New Jersey, completed the ticket. The platform supported a Pacific railroad and federal appropriations for internal improvements, but most of the planks dealt with slavery and Kansas. After all, the Republicans organized in response to the repeal of the Missouri Compromise line and slavery expansion. The Philadelphia delegates denounced slavery as a relic of barbarism and claimed "it is both the right and the imperative duty of Congress" to exclude it from the western territories. The Republicans charged that Kansas had been "invaded by an armed force" of proslavery men, and they demanded its immediate admission as a free state. The temporary chairman of the convention, Robert Emmet of New York, laid the blame for the strife on "squatter sovereignty," a doctrinal "fallacy" that enabled "the quasi-squatters from Missouri, who came in there with their bowie-knives and revolvers, to control the elections." Cass's worst political nightmare was taking shape: a formidable sectional party opposed to popular sovereignty and dedicated to the nonextension of slavery was emerging as a national force.[83]

While Cass focused his concern on the Republicans, other political organizations entered the presidential fray. The Know Nothings faced a sectional split when they met at Philadelphia, prior to the Democratic and Republican conventions. Southerners, aided by New York votes, controlled the proceedings, and a large contingent of delegates from northern states withdrew in protest. The mainly southern Know Nothings adopted resolutions recognizing the right of territorial residents "to regulate their domestic and social affairs in their own mode" and nominated a ticket of Millard Fillmore and Andrew Jackson Donelson. The northern Know Nothings (or "Know Somethings") subsequently endorsed Frémont for the presidency. This schism signaled the end of the American party as a viable national organization. The electoral field was completed, in September, when a generally elderly remnant of Whigs, aptly termed the "Silver Grays," met and seconded the nomination of Fillmore. Henceforth during the campaign, three candidates nominated by five political conventions vied for the White House.[84]

Senator Cass, although discomfited by the unsolicited Know Nothing endorsement of popular sovereignty, was delighted with the work of the Democratic national convention. He acknowledged the platform embodied "the true faith of our party" and praised the nominations of Buchanan and Breckinridge as being in "every way worthy of our confidence." At a Washington ratification meeting, Cass joined President Pierce and Senator Douglas in endorsing the national ticket. He was "repeatedly interrupted with loud and enthusiastic cheers" as he called upon every true Democrat to "buckle on his armor" and "go forth to the combat." An opposition newspaper asserted that "poor old Cass, stupid Pierce, and bitter Douglas were hauled forth to amuse the crowd by a hollow pretence of happiness at the auspicious result" of the Cincinnati convention. "How mankind revenges itself upon the demagogues." The nation's leading Democrats, however, willingly closed ranks behind the banner of "Buck and Breck." "Poor old Cass" was painfully aware, too, that he faced an uphill fight for reelection to the Senate.[85]

Lewis Cass campaigned vigorously for the Democratic cause after the adjournment of Congress. He wasted no time in addressing various mass rallies during his westward journey to Detroit, first stumping on Buchanan's behalf at Frederick, Maryland, where "the reception of the old war-worn veteran was of the most enthusiastic character." A Democratic correspondent praised his "eloquence and solemnity, which produced a visible effect upon all within the reach of his voice." The Michigan senator also spoke in Illinois and Ohio, and joined vice presidential nominee Breckinridge, Stephen Douglas, Jesse Bright, John Van Buren, and other distinguished orators at the site of the Tippecanoe battlefield. A throng estimated to number more than one hundred thousand, "the largest political assemblage ever convened at the West," applauded as the speakers lambasted the Republican party. Senator Cass understood the Democrats faced "a hard contest north of the Ohio, and to be successful will require the most strenuous exertions." No effort, certainly, was spared in Michigan, as prominent Democrats from throughout the country campaigned for Buchanan and Cass. The presence on the same platform of Daniel Dickinson and John Van Buren, leaders of the rival factions of New Yorkers in 1848, demonstrated the Barnburner rift was healed. The national Democracy was united on a popular sovereignty platform, and in support of Lewis Cass.[86]

During campaign swings through his home state, Senator Cass continually attacked sectionalism and emphasized the importance of political compromise in preserving the Union. His speech at Kalamazoo was typical, although Democratic newspapers reported it with accustomed hyperbole. After his introduction to an audience of some thirty thousand, Cass "came forward with trembling lips, eyes dewy with tears," and when the cheering that greeted his appearance finally subsided, "the vast assemblage hung with breathless attention on every word he uttered." Cass warned that the country was in danger because a sectional Republican party, aided by the clash in Kansas, threatened to gain the White House. The Kansas-Nebraska Act must be supported, because it "allows the people of Kansas to govern themselves." He again singled out for condemnation antislavery clergymen, and applause greeted his declaration that it was "their business to distribute the Gospel, and not Sharp's [*sic*] rifles." Such meddling could only serve to benefit Republicans and stoke the fires of sectionalism. At a Democratic mass meeting at Centreville, Senator Cass spoke for an hour and a half in a similar attempt to beat back "the uprising of this new and formidable republican party." It was an eloquent effort. "There were parts of his speech in which he alluded to the past history of the democratic party, and which was but the history of his own experience, which held that vast gathering spell-bound during its narration." Each one of his "ten thousand listeners, whether democrats or republicans, (as many of the latter were in the crowd) looked up to him as a venerable and wise statesman." A few days before the election, the *Washington Union* boasted that "the Veteran Cass still [is] in the Field," driven by concerns for his own reelection and abhorrence of the Republican creed. The Michigan senator viewed the Democracy as the true "American party" and believed "the fate of this great republic" depended upon its success. He did not exaggerate the importance of keeping the Democratic party united and dominant in the face of Republican and proslavery sectionalism: it was the sole nationwide political institution.[87]

Republican orators were also on the hustings in Michigan. William Seward journeyed from New York to inform voters the Democratic party was controlled by southern interests, a theme exploited by senatorial candidate Zachariah Chandler. Another local Republican shadowed Cass on the campaign trail, attacking his principles and stance on slavery. Wirt Dexter's "wit and power of ridicule" were put to good use, a Republican in his audience cheerfully recorded, as he cut and slashed through Cass's speech, until "there seemed to be nothing left of it."[88]

Despite Cass's unstinting efforts, the Republicans triumphed in Michigan. They elected all four congressmen (a gain of one seat) and maintained control of the legislature. It was especially galling to Cass that Frémont received 57 percent of the vote—his greatest margin of victory in the Northwest. The Republicans also carried Illinois and Indiana. Nonetheless, Buchanan was elected president with the support of five northern states and every slave state except Maryland, which went to Fillmore.

Lewis Cass obviously would not be returned to the Senate. "The election of a black-republican legislature in Michigan," a national Democratic newspaper bemoaned, "is one of the most unpleasant incidents of the canvass." While his party regretted the loss "of the venerable sage and patriot," Cass's political opponents rejoiced. John Judson Bagley, a young Republican who later served as governor, crowed: "Thank God, Gen. Cass is a defunct institution." The *New York Tribune* gloated that "the old man has been stuck so full of pins by his ungrateful constituents . . . he is more than commonly awake." Cass claimed, "As to *myself*, the result of the late election is nothing," but conceded it was "mortifying that we lost our State." The Republican cause in Michigan was aided by platform resolutions calling for federal funding of internal improvements; however, the overriding national issue of the campaign was the emotionally charged Kansas controversy. Recognizing this, Cass blamed the Democratic defeat on "the spirit of fanaticism, which has spread its roots broader and deeper than I expected." The Michigan senator had attempted to quiet the passions engendered by "Bleeding Kansas" and "Bleeding Sumner," but his repeated calls for toleration and political accommodation went unheeded. Republicans cynically exploited the civil unrest in Kansas and appealed to antisouthern sentiments among the northern electorate, although they offered no lasting solution to the country as a whole. The result was a repudiation of Democratic doctrine by the voters of Cass's own state.[89]

James Buchanan was elected on a platform that endorsed popular sovereignty, but Lewis Cass realized the Democratic presidential victory did not settle the question of slavery expansion. "You may end a Bank question, and a tariff question, and all other political questions, but there is no end to a fanatical question. The Union is nothing to those, who are under the influence of this feeling." He ominously added that "Mr. Buchanan will have a difficult time" resolving the Kansas conflict. By a strictly partisan vote, in January 1857, Zachariah Chandler was selected by the Michigan legislature to succeed Cass in the U.S. Senate. Chandler made good his pledge to unseat the Democratic senator, but the election of 1856 did not signal the end of Lewis Cass's public life.[90]

Chapter Ten

Secretary of State and Union Advocate (1857–1866): "I Am Sometimes Filled with Apprehension . . . I May Yet Outlive the Union and Constitution of My Country"

THE ELECTION of 1856 marked a milestone for Lewis Cass. With Republicans in control of the Michigan legislature his senatorial tenure was drawing to a close, but one more important public office beckoned before his extensive career ended. Following the November election, president-elect James Buchanan, with the aid of a few political advisers including Howell Cobb, John Slidell, and Jesse Bright, began the process of picking a cabinet. The sixty-five-year-old Pennsylvanian was determined to preside over a harmonious administration, free from political extremism and sectionalism. He therefore sought as department heads politically conservative nationalists from all regions of the country. The most delicate decision Buchanan faced was selecting a secretary of state. He originally favored his close personal friend, Howell Cobb, a forty-one-year-old Georgia congressman who would reside at the White House during his wife's frequent trips back home. Cobb campaigned vigorously for the Democratic cause in the Northeast, and made it clear he would accept only the State Department. His appointment, however, was opposed by vocal southern spokesmen, such as Jefferson Davis, as well as by northern expansionists who preferred Robert J. Walker. One of Walker's prominent backers was Stephen Douglas, still engaged in a struggle with Jesse Bright for control of the Democratic organization in the Old Northwest. Buchanan disliked Douglas, his rival for the presidential nomination, but the influential Illinois senator could be neither unceremoniously ignored nor deliberately antagonized during the cabinet selection process. Senator Bright, a longtime Hoosier supporter of Lewis Cass, suggested a simple solution to the dilemma: appoint Cass to the State Department, and give Cobb the powerful position of treasury secretary. Neither Douglas nor Walker would oppose the selection of the Father of Popular Sovereignty, and Cobb would acquiesce in the choice of his "venerable old friend." Fittingly, as an elder statesman acceptable to all factions of the party, Cass would serve as a symbol of Democratic unity during a period of increased sectional strain. Thus the impasse was broken.[1]

Buchanan informed both Cass and Cobb of his intentions on February 21. He tendered Cass the appointment as secretary of state, disingenuously adding it was his "desire to do [so] from the beginning, & I have only doubted in consideration of your age." The president-elect assured Cobb he was originally slated for either the Treasury or State Department, and the choice of "our venerable and patriotic friend General Cass," for the senior post, "cannot fail to be agreeable to you." The other cabinet appointments presented fewer difficulties to Buchanan, although the selections were not completed until shortly after his inauguration. In all, the cabinet consisted of four slaveholders and three northerners, none of whom was unsympathetic to southern rights and interests. The Buchanan administration demonstrated the locus of Democratic strength was unmistakably in the South.[2]

James Buchanan named Cass to the chief cabinet post for both political and personal reasons. The two experienced Democratic politicians had never developed a close friendship; in fact, they did not completely trust or respect each other. Buchanan believed that Cass, nine years his senior, was indolent and indecisive, an opinion bolstered by an adviser who warned that Cass was "burdened with a great weight of useless flesh" and, "according to the course of nature, he must soon begin to decline, if indeed he already has not." Such dire predictions proved to be unwarranted, but Cass's corpulence and advanced age made even a light workload at the State Department burdensome. "The truth is," he complained to his son, "the labour and responsibility of this office are enough to break me down." The *New York Tribune* sarcastically reported that it was "an imposition to saddle him with the foreign service at a time of life when prayers and not protocols should be his daily occupation. Still the old General has a hankering for place." His home-state opponents were even more brutal in their assessment of the appointment. The Detroit Republican organ, before Cass was formally nominated, declared: "Michigan cares not upon whom Gen. Cass becomes a stipendiary, so that she is free from that burden and reproach. . . . Let him go to Washington in any capacity which Buchanan may dole out to him, he will not carry Michigan thither, 'in his breeches pocket.'"[3]

Buchanan never expected Cass's duties at the State Department to become cumbersome. Rather, the Michigan Democrat was expected to serve primarily as a figurehead, while the president directed American diplomacy. Buchanan, a former minister to Russia and Britain and secretary of state under Polk, had more foreign policy experience than any president since John Quincy Adams. Before choosing Cass, Buchanan sent John Slidell to sound him out regarding the appointment of an assistant secretary to handle the daily affairs of the department. Slidell indicated the secretary-designate obligingly preferred "leaving that matter in your hands." Actually, Cass favored his son-in-law Henry Ledyard for the post but agreed to let Buchanan name his assistant, because he lacked both the patience for routine paperwork and the desire to retire to Michigan. Slidell predicted that with Cass at the helm in the State Department, Buchanan might "be compelled to take the laboring oar out of the ordinary course of duty," yet he was firmly convinced the president could "get along with the General better than with any other person." Buchanan maintained a private office in the Department of State, but he soon discovered Cass was capable of pulling his own oar.[4]

Lewis Cass was aware his tenure at the State Department represented the swan song of his public life, and he made the most of it. He enjoyed the celebrity that came with being a member of the cabinet, and joined the Washington social swirl with unfeigned relish. Cass moved into a large "double" house with his widowed daughter, Mary Canfield, and entertained lavishly, when his health permitted. Henry Ledyard, a former mayor of Detroit who served briefly as a state senator during these years, brought his family to reside for a time with the secretary of state, and Lewis, Jr., was told by his father to sell his house in Rome and ship the furnishings to the family compound. There was room for all. The secretary's every physical need was attended to by family members; Mrs. Canfield wrapped her father in flannels during the winter months, and sent him off to bed at nine o'clock. It was an untroubled and pleasant final chapter to his public life, and Cass took advantage of the comfortable circumstances to devote his energies to professional duties.[5]

Shortly after formally taking office on March 6, Cass inexplicably assured the incumbent assistant secretary of state, John Thomas, that his position was secure. The next day, the president asked Cass to appoint as his assistant John Appleton, a former congressman from Maine who caught Buchanan's attention while serving under him as secretary of the legation in London. The *New York Tribune* reported the removal of Thomas "was expected, but . . . the dismissal was ordered from the White House without consultation with Mr. Cass." William Marcy surmised that if Cass continued as secretary of state, "he will be called on to submit to what a high spirited man would regard as an indignity." Indeed, the secretary was forced to recall Lewis Cass, Jr., from his station in Rome. This was consistent with the removal policy of the Buchanan administration, however, and not a personal slight to the senior Cass. Nonetheless, his lack of influence regarding patronage rankled the secretary of state, who complained "it is most amazing, and even distressing. I have not made a single appointment in my department, except to put into the lowest clerkship, a young man, who has been in my employment some years."[6]

Despite some irritation relating to patronage, Lewis Cass and James Buchanan worked in basic harmony until the secession crisis following the election of 1860. During the course of the administration, Secretary of State Cass was much more than the figurehead the president intended. He was instrumental in implementing foreign policy, and presided over cabinet meetings when Buchanan was absent from Washington. On such occasions, Cass sought a consensus among those present and passed their findings on to Buchanan for a final decision. The personal relationship between the president and the secretary of state warmed considerably, although in rare situations Buchanan bypassed Cass in matters of diplomacy. The most notable example, in early 1860, regarded the possible purchase of Alaska. Baron de Stoeckl, Russian minister to the United States, was informed by California senator William Gwin that Appleton would conduct the discussions, not Cass. Buchanan wanted the assistant secretary to deal with Russian diplomats before being sent to St. Petersburg, as the American minister, but he also wished to keep firm personal control over foreign policy. This was not a hinderance to a smoothly functioning State Department, as it turned out, because Buchanan and Cass agreed on virtually every major policy issue until the secession crisis. One observer claimed, with exaggeration, that "nearly all of the important [diplomatic] correspondence" was dictated by the president; yet, rather than signaling a conflict within the administration, this reflected the unanimity of opinion, and spirit of cooperation, between Buchanan and Cass. The secretary of state proved his worth to the administration, and the president himself came to place increasing trust in his judgment. When Nicaragua's new minister visited Bedford Springs, Pennsylvania, in the summer of 1858, the vacationing president wrote Cass he would hear what the envoy had "to say & speak plainly to him; but enter into no engagement of any kind. Of course I shall refer him to you."[7]

Freed from the responsibility of the routine functions of the State Department, and despite Buchanan's initial reluctance, Lewis Cass played an active role in several longstanding diplomatic and domestic controversies. The chief foreign policy goals of the administration included territorial and commercial expansion throughout the Americas, and a corresponding lessening of European—especially British—geopolitical influence in the hemisphere. The time appeared propitious for accomplishing such objectives, although the specter of slavery cast a pall over the efforts. In Latin America the British were increasingly focusing on economic interests, rather than on expanding their colonial empire, and if the United States brought political stability to the region, this would open up markets and commercial opportunities for all. Cass, of course, was a champion of American aggrandizement. His reputation as a spread-eagle expansionist outstripped that of the president, and he embraced the administration policy with enthusiasm. "It is idle to tell me," the secretary of state wrote in 1858, "we have land enough." The "constant torrent" of immigration "requires more land, more territory upon which to settle, and just as fast as our interests and our destiny require additional territory in the North, or in the South, or on the Islands of the Ocean, I am for it." Cass and Buchanan were northern conservatives who desired to placate slaveholders, and both had long advocated the acquisition of Cuba. Prior to the election of 1848, Cass remarked it was the destiny of the United States to possess the Caribbean island, "and the sooner it is done, the better it will be for us, . . . and for the world." Four years later, he divulged a willingness to "swallow Cuba." As secretary of state, Cass consistently supported the inquiries made by the administration regarding a possible purchase of the island from Spain. Shortly after Senator Slidell introduced a bill, in January 1859, allocating thirty million dollars to facilitate negotiations, Cass claimed acquiring Cuba was of "paramount importance" to all regions of the country. Zachariah Chandler, however, successfully mobilized congressional opposition to the addition of more slave territory. This set the tone for foreign affairs during the Buchanan administration. Sectionalism transcended domestic politics, and with only one major exception, Republicans uniformly acted to thwart the policies of the president and secretary of state.[8]

Cass likewise joined Buchanan in casting avaricious eyes toward Mexico. During the 1850s, a series of revolutions south of the Rio Grande resulted in the deaths of several American citizens and claims of ten million dollars against the Mexican government. Shortly after taking office, Secretary of State Cass received a confidential letter from a prominent Louisiana politician, Senator Judah P. Benjamin, urging the administration to purchase Lower California and Sonora and to obtain the right of transit across the Isthmus of Tehuantepec. Benjamin warned, "You must strike *now*—Six months hence, the golden opportunity will be gone." Cass and Buchanan were already committed to such a policy. In July 1857, the secretary of state authorized the American minister at Mexico City, John Forsyth, to offer between twelve and fifteen million dollars for Lower California and substantial portions of Sonora and Chihuahua. Forsyth was further instructed to seek a separate treaty granting the right of transit across Tehuantepec. The minister approached a succession of Mexican leaders and, after consistent rebuffs, vented his frustration by severing diplomatic relations. Forsyth was ordered home. His replacement, Robert McLane of Maryland, was instructed by Cass to concentrate on commercial matters rather than territorial cessions. In December 1859, McLane reached an agreement with the Benito Juarez government that guaranteed a perpetual right of transit across the isthmus, but Senate ratification was soundly defeated by the Republicans. President Buchanan and Secretary of State Cass were thwarted from achieving their foreign policy goals, regarding Cuba and Mexico, by an obdurate Congress split along sectional lines. Cass was philosophical about the setbacks. The Mexican Cession temporarily provided enough room for America's surging population; the nation could afford to wait until Cuba and Mexico were obtained peaceably. In the meantime, attention focused further south.[9]

The Buchanan administration was ultimately quite successful in its dealings with Latin America and Great Britain. The appointment of Lewis Cass as secretary of state, of course, did not meet with unbridled enthusiasm within the British government. "All the world except the English," one of his apologists contended, "know that General Cass is a great and Good Man and one of the ablest statesmen of the day." James Buchanan felt an explanation was in order and privately informed the

British foreign secretary that "no Englishman need feel the least uneasiness on this account. His Anglophobia, as you used facetiously to term it, if it ever existed, no longer exists." Lord Clarendon diplomatically phrased his response. "I am glad to learn from you that the Anglophobia of General Cass no longer exists & I am not disposed to believe the report of the *Times* Correspondent that I am the object of this special aversion. . . . I dare say we shall get on well together." Cass, recalling his own diplomatic experiences, pledged to evince "overflowing love & kindness for John Bull if deemed necessary." Such proved to be the case, as the United States and Britain faced several vexatious problems during the 1850s. In his first annual message, President Buchanan lamented that "it has been our misfortune almost always to have had some irritating, if not dangerous, outstanding question with Great Britain." During Cass's tenure as secretary of state, the most troublesome issue proved to be the Clayton-Bulwer Treaty.[10]

In April 1850, Secretary of State John Clayton and British minister Sir Henry Bulwer pledged that their respective governments would not exert exclusive control over any isthmian canal; nor would they colonize or seek "dominion over Nicaragua, Costa Rica, the Mosquito coast, or any part of Central America." Senator Lewis Cass supported ratification of the Clayton-Bulwer Treaty, but events in Latin America soon caused him misgivings. Following an altercation off the coast of Nicaragua in 1851, between an American steamship and a British man-of-war, Cass lashed out at his perennial nemesis. He termed the seizure of the American vessel "indefensible" and reminded Britain "she had stipulated with us that she will *not assume or exercise dominion over . . . any part of Central America.*" The British government, however, placed a very different gloss on the Clayton-Bulwer accord. Her Majesty's ministers maintained the agreement was prospective, rather than retrospective—that it sanctioned those colonies already held. Bulwer, in fact, handed Clayton a note before the formal exchange of ratifications that explicitly exempted from the treaty the British settlement at Honduras, "and its dependencies." Acting upon this construction of the pact, in 1852 Britain proclaimed the diminutive archipelago near Honduras to be the Colony of the Bay Islands.[11]

Lewis Cass consistently opposed British arrogation in Latin America. In a series of Senate speeches, he repeatedly claimed that he voted for the Clayton-Bulwer Treaty because Britain thereby abjured all dominion and jurisdiction over Central America. But, he complained, the British government never considered Belize (British Honduras) or the Bay Islands to be a part of that pact, and had so notified the State Department. Senator Cass also attacked the British protectorate over the Mosquito Indians as another violation of the treaty, characteristically contending it was a ruse to gain dominion along the Nicaraguan coast. He looked "with a feeling of loathing upon this interference of one civilized nation with savage tribes living . . . within the dominions of another Power. And the feeling reaches indignation, when the measure is cloaked by hollow professions of philanthropy, while, in fact, it is dictated by the purposes of power." Cass piously prayed that America's "aboriginal inhabitants be everywhere delivered from the protection of such a protector!" Such British intrigues served to nullify the treaty, and Cass called for a reaffirmation of the principles of the Monroe Doctrine. His unchanging theme was that Britain should abide by the American interpretation of the Clayton-Bulwer Treaty; otherwise, the administration should "act accordingly, be the consequences what they may." Senator Cass ominously concluded it was time "to assert the honor and interests of the United States."[12]

President Buchanan's message to Congress in December 1857 concurred with Secretary of State Cass's sentiments concerning Central America. In an attempt to prod the British government into settling the controversy, Buchanan argued that since the two nations interpreted the Clayton-Bulwer Treaty "in senses directly opposite, the wisest course" would be to begin negotiations anew. The Buchanan administration similarly sought peaceful settlements with individual Latin American states. Secretary Cass signed a general treaty of amity and commerce, in November, with Antonio José de Yrissari, newly appointed Nicaraguan envoy to Washington. The right of transit through Nicaragua was granted the United States. In return, Cass pledged the international neutrality of any railroad or canal. Cass hastened to advise diplomats in London and Central America that this pact did not violate the Clayton-Bulwer Treaty, because the United States guaranteed to keep the isthmus open to all nations. Such questionable assurances proved to be unnecessary, however, since the Nicaraguan government, distrustful of American intentions, rejected the Cass-Yrisarri Treaty.[13]

Nicaragua and the other Central American states were particularly alarmed with filibustering expeditions launched from the United States. On the same day Cass and Yrissari concluded their negotiations, the most notorious filibuster, William Walker, embarked from a southern port on his second bid to conquer Nicaragua. The irrepressible Tennessee adventurer previously had seized power, only to be driven out by the combined military strength of neighboring nations. Upon landing at Punta Arenas, near Greytown, Walker and his band were taken into custody by American naval forces under Commodore Hiram Paulding. Following his return to the United States and release from federal custody, an unchastened Walker began planning a third expedition.

The Buchanan administration attempted to suppress filibustering ventures through the halfhearted enforcement of neutrality laws. Cass telegraphed customs officials and federal attorneys at Mobile and New Orleans, urging them to prevent "any illegal expeditions," but the impact of these instructions was lessened by public knowledge of an earlier Cass letter praising Walker's exploits. Senator Cass had confessed that "the heroic effort of our countrymen in Nicaragua excites my admiration, . . . he who does not sympathize with such an enterprize has little in common with me." Southerners who supported the acquisition of potential slave territory also argued Cass conceded the right of emigrating Americans, "at all times, to take their arms with them." Although President Buchanan denounced the filibustering campaigns as "robbery and murder," Latin American leaders believed the administration opposed them only because they made it difficult for the United States to gain hegemony across the isthmus through diplomacy. So, in response to armed threats by marauding adventurers and the presumed acquiescence of the American government, the presidents of Nicaragua and Costa Rica issued the Rivas Manifesto, placing their countries under the protection of France, England, and Sardinia.[14]

Tensions increased between the United States and Central American nations, but a solution to the controversy was in the making. The first step was to improve diplomatic relations with Great Britain through settlement of the right-of-search issue. The Webster-Ashburton Treaty pledged the United States and Britain to maintain separate naval squadrons to suppress the African slave trade. Although these warships were not authorized to detain or seize vessels of any foreign nation, zealous British sailors frequently boarded American ships suspected of being slavers. Such actions naturally led to vociferous complaints, and when the British expanded their searches to the Caribbean, the Buchanan administration formally protested.

Secretary Cass enthusiastically supported the president's position on the search issue. After all, while governor of Michigan Territory, he argued British boardings of American ships on the Great Lakes were a gross violation of national honor, and he became further embroiled in the controversy during his mission to France. Cass therefore instructed the minister at London, former vice president George Dallas, to inform the British Foreign Office that American ships were being "interfered with" at Havana. The secretary of state asserted that the administration viewed "with horror the prostitution of the American flag" by slavers; and to combat the nefarious practice, the United States increased its naval presence off the African coast and declared the illegal traffic to be a capital offense. But while remaining committed to suppressing the slave trade, Cass informed Dallas the administration would never "legalize the entrance of a British armed force into our vessels." To emphasize that point, President Buchanan ordered the navy to cruise the Gulf of Mexico and protect American ships "from search or detention by the vessels-of-war of any other nation." Secretary of State Cass, meanwhile, kept up the pressure on the diplomatic front.[15]

On April 10, Cass addressed a long communication to the British minister at Washington, Lord Napier. While conceding that searches might be employed in an honest effort to combat the slave trade, Cass argued they threatened legitimate maritime rights and would not be countenanced by the United States. Again he rejected the distinction made by the British regarding "visitation" to determine a vessel's nationality. "Search, or visit, it is equally an assault upon the independence of nations." He pointed out that a British admiralty judge had denied the validity of any right to visit and search foreign ships in peacetime. The secretary of state supported this decision, because visitation "cannot be submitted to by any independent nation without injury and dishonor." The United States, Cass succinctly summarized to Napier, denied any foreign power the right to board an American ship "for any purpose whatever."[16]

The firm stand taken by Buchanan and Cass received broad nonpartisan support in the United States, which, in turn, influenced British opinion. The Senate unanimously adopted a resolution denouncing visitation as a "derogation" of national sovereignty. Republican William Seward, who continued to clash with Cass over slavery, expressed his party's concurrence with the administration by claiming that "the United States have never recognized this right [of search], and never will." The London *Times,* meanwhile, noted most Britons sought a peaceful adjustment of the maritime controversy, because Americans had "a just cause of complaint against us." Were the cases reversed, "the spirit of every Englishman" would be roused. The British foreign secretary prudently bowed to public and diplomatic pressure. Dallas jubilantly informed the secretary of state that Lord Malmesbury recognized "the principles of international law as laid down by General Cass in his note of the 10th of April" and conceded that nothing in the Webster-Ashburton Treaty "supersedes that law."[17]

Cass took a great deal of personal pride in Buchanan's subsequent announcement that "the question of visitation and search has been amicably adjusted." American national honor was satisfied, and the accord embodied principles Cass espoused sixteen years before, in his public debate with Daniel Webster. Unfortunately, British abandonment of visitation inevitably led to an increase in the slave trade under the United States flag. The British government invited the Buchanan administration to enter into joint measures to suppress the illegal traffic, but it was not until after the secession of southern states that such a treaty was signed.[18]

Following settlement of the search controversy, attention once more turned to Central America. Secretary Cass urged Lord Napier to resolve the differences arising from the Clayton-Bulwer Treaty. He emphasized that substantial agreement had been achieved on the questions of isthmian transit-route neutrality and the Mosquito protectorate. Two other weighty matters remained: British control of the Bay Islands, and the boundary of Belize. "Is it possible," Cass cordially inquired that, "if approached in a spirit of conciliation and good feeling, these two points of difference" might be reconciled?[19]

The British government responded in kind. Lord Malmesbury applauded Cass's "friendly tone," and recalled from Central America Sir William Gore Ousley, who had helped scuttle ratification of the Cass-Yrisarri Treaty, and years before tangled with Cass in a pamphleteering war of words over the Quintuple Treaty. Ousley's arguments carried the field in that verbal encounter, but his recall completed Cass's vindication. Ousley's replacement quickly negotiated a treaty with Guatemala, delineating the boundaries of Belize. In November 1859, the Bay Islands were restored to Honduras, and three months later, Britain formally relinquished her protectorate of the Mosquito coast. In the meantime, the presidents of Nicaragua and Costa Rica disavowed the sentiments of the Rivas Manifesto, claiming it was drafted precipitously under the threat of filibustering expeditions. The American minister subsequently concluded a treaty with Nicaragua that essentially recapitulated the Cass-Yrissari pact. The Central American controversies were settled peacefully to the satisfaction of all concerned parties. Aside from an inability to attain territorial cessions, President Buchanan and Secretary of State Cass fulfilled their foreign policy goals.[20]

The Buchanan administration was not nearly as successful in dealing with domestic matters, however, and this shortcoming eventually led to Lewis Cass's resignation. The chief problem remained sectionalism, aggravated by the strife in Kansas. Until he took up the reins of the State Department (which was responsible for the general management of territorial affairs), Lewis Cass consistently maintained Congress had no authority over slavery in the territories. He presented this position to the public with the Nicholson letter, and frequently repeated it during the debates on the Compromise of 1850 and the Kansas-Nebraska bill. Cass held firm to the idea that only the people of a territory possessed the power to regulate their domestic institutions. Popular sovereignty was manifested in the Kansas-Nebraska Act and endorsed by the delegates to the Democratic convention in 1856. Despite personal reservations concerning the act and the principle it embodied, Buchanan accepted both as party doctrine during the presidential campaign. And in his inaugural address, Buchanan again endorsed the Cass doctrine, hoping to lessen sectional tensions. On that sunny day in March, the president exclaimed: "What a happy conception, then, was it for Congress to apply this simple rule, that the will of the majority shall govern, to the settlement of the question of domestic slavery in the Territories!" He acknowledged that opinions differed as to when a territorial legislature might decide the issue, and to Cass's chagrin, he added his personal observation that slavery could not be prohibited until statehood. Buchanan concluded by disingenuously pledging to submit "cheerfully" to the *Dred Scott* decision then being prepared by the Supreme Court.[21]

Lewis Cass emphatically disagreed with the contention that western residents could not legislate on slavery before drafting a state constitution. Cass, and most northern Democrats, believed the question could be decided after the formation of a territorial government. In fact, it was because of Cass's opposition that President Buchanan presented merely his individual opinion on the issue. On the other important point, however, Buchanan and Cass strongly concurred: the Supreme Court should be the final arbiter regarding slavery extension. By shifting the question from the political realm to the judiciary, Cass hoped this nettlesome controversy would be transformed into a strictly legalistic, constitutional problem. He therefore joined in supporting the basic principles presented by Chief Justice Roger Brooke Taney in the *Dred Scott* case. Dred Scott was a Missouri slave who sued for his freedom on the ground that his former owner had taken him to live in Illinois and then to Wisconsin Territory, where slavery was forbidden by the Missouri Compromise.

Two days after the inauguration, with each of the nine justices issuing either a concurring or dissenting opinion, the Supreme Court ruled that Dred Scott remained a slave. Chief Justice Taney, writing for the majority, argued two main points: no Negro could be an American citizen and Congress could not prohibit the introduction of slavery into the territories. The aged Marylander echoed Cass's narrow constitutional interpretation that the powers granted Congress over "the territory or other property belonging to the United States" referred simply to land and not a governmental entity. Nevertheless, unlike Buchanan, Cass disapproved of the chief justice's claim that a territorial legislature could not decide the slavery question. The secretary of state did accept Taney's ruling that Negroes were not American citizens, and continued the general policy of denying passports to northern blacks who wished to travel abroad. When Senator Henry Wilson requested a passport for a Boston physician, Cass replied that since such a document was tantamount to "a certificate of citizenship," it was never "granted to persons of color. No change in this respect has taken place in consequence of the decision of the Dred Scott case." Despite Cass's disclaimer, in certain instances papers that served as passports had been issued to free blacks. The *Boston Bee* swiftly cited half a dozen examples for the edification of the new secretary of state, but no passports were granted to African Americans during Cass's tenure at the State Department.[22]

The Buchanan administration moved quickly to settle the Kansas controversy, and Cass applauded the plans. Robert J. Walker, the prominent expansionist and popular-sovereignty advocate who served as Polk's treasury secretary, was appointed territorial governor and instructed by Cass to supervise the drafting of a state constitution. Frederick P. Stanton, a Virginian and former congressman from Tennessee, was named secretary of the territory, which made him acting governor in Walker's absence. Both men were sympathetic to slavery as an institution (each had held slaves), but they were committed to bringing Kansas into the Union as a Democratic state through fair elections. Since the overwhelming majority of territorial residents were antislavery, Kansas—even if Democratic—would be a free state. In his letter of acceptance, Governor Walker indicated Kansans "must decide for themselves what shall be their social institutions."

Lewis Cass expressed his full support of this policy, affirming the institutions of the territory "should be established by the votes of the people of Kansas, unawed and uninterrupted by force or fraud." This meant "foreign voters must be excluded, come whence they may." In a private letter, the secretary of state confidently predicted that if not stymied "by causes beyond his control," Walker would restore political order in the territory. Governor Walker, who agreed with Cass that Kansas was geographically unsuited for slavery, was determined to carry out the popular sovereignty principle of the Kansas-Nebraska Act and shepherd a free, Democratic state into the Union. He believed compromise was possible, because the conflict was not a moralistic crusade; it was a political struggle for control of the territory. Ironically, by not insisting on fair elections or submitting the proposed state constitution for voter ratification, the Democratic administration prevented Walker from accomplishing his goals.[23]

Shortly after Governor Walker arrived in Kansas, delegates were elected to the constitutional convention. Proslavery candidates were chosen, as free staters and those who feared increased taxes refused to participate. Only two thousand votes were cast. The antislavery men did take part in the legislative election held in October, and a Republican was selected as congressional delegate. The legislative races were closely contested, but Walker threw out the obviously fraudulent returns from two districts, and antislavery men gained a majority. The governor thereby violated Cass's explicit instructions that "in no case of a contested election" was he "authorized to act as a judge in any stage of the proceedings." Walker explained to the secretary of state if the "pretended votes had been counted," the administration would be "accomplices in a most disgraceful fraud." Acceptance of the "spurious" returns represented nothing less than "a gross outrage upon the elective franchise and the sacred rights of the people of this territory." In short, Walker chose not to violate the spirit of popular sovereignty.[24]

The constitutional convention met at Lecompton soon after the legislative election, and drafted a proslavery document. Proclaiming the rights of slaveholders to be "inviolable," the Lecompton constitution stated: "The legislature shall have no power to pass laws for the emancipation of slaves without the consent of the owners." The Fugitive Slave Law was to be rigidly enforced and free blacks excluded from the state. The institution of slavery was thereby secured, with constitutional amendments prohibited until after 1864. The convention delegates, aware free staters were a territorial majority, decided the entire document would not be submitted to the voters. Instead, a referendum in December would choose between the "constitution with slavery" or the "constitution with no slavery." In either case, slaves already in Kansas would remain in bondage.[25]

Governor Walker, upset with the Lecompton convention, hastened to Washington to register his protest with the president. Prior to this time, the governor held the free staters mostly responsible for the turmoil racking the territory, but he rightly perceived the constitution to be a blatant attempt to shackle Kansas with slavery. Robert J. Walker, as partisan a Democrat as Lewis Cass, reasoned that the political struggle was against a Republican-abolitionist coalition, and party members who favored a free Kansas needed to ally themselves with the proslavery faction to achieve a Democratic majority. Walker realized the brewing Lecompton controversy irreparably damaged party unity, in Kansas and the nation as a whole. Unfortunately, he was unable to sway Buchanan. "It is greatly to be regretted," the *New York Times* editorialized, the president did not understand "that fidelity to the great principle of Popular Sovereignty" required the Lecompton constitution be "sanctioned by the People themselves."[26]

During Walker's absence, Frederick Stanton called the newly elected Kansas legislature into extraordinary session. The acting governor informed Cass it was "only just and proper" that territorial residents be allowed to vote on the Lecompton constitution.[27] The free state legislators naturally agreed, and scheduled a referendum for early January on the entire constitution, not merely the slavery provision. The plebiscite held in December, under the auspices of the Lecompton delegates, recorded fewer than seven thousand votes in support of the constitution. The following month, more than ten thousand Kansans rejected the Lecompton constitution outright; fewer than two hundred favored ratification. Nevertheless, President Buchanan decided to throw the full weight of the administration behind the proslavery document.

Lewis Cass sided with the president, despite the demonstrated free state majority in Kansas. Henry Foote recalled that the secretary of state "confessed, frankly, his entire condemnation of Mr. Buchanan's conduct in the Lecompton matter," but Cass publicly sustained administration policy, just as he had with the Kansas-Nebraska bill. Once again, Cass was overly concerned with demonstrating to southerners that popular sovereignty was not a trick to keep the territories free. Stanton was removed from office, following his unauthorized call for a special legislative session, and Governor Walker resigned in protest. In a prolix letter to

Secretary Cass, Walker complained that the president reneged on a pledge to submit any proposed state constitution to the voters. This was nothing less than a repudiation of "the true doctrine of popular sovereignty" and a "violation of the right of self-government." Walker warned that an overwhelming majority of Kansans opposed the Lecompton constitution, and forcing it upon them "will, I fear be attended by civil war, extending, perhaps, throughout the union.[28]

Cass accepted Walker's resignation, without the slightest public sign his criticisms struck a chord of understanding. It was important to Cass the administration present a united front on the question of slavery in Kansas, thereby demonstrating to southerners that their constitutional rights were respected by northern Democrats. In defending Buchanan's support of the Lecompton convention, Cass dutifully reminded Walker that the president was committed to submitting only the slavery issue to the people. The Lecompton constitution, therefore, represented the sentiments of those who exercised their franchise in the December referendum. This was tortuous reasoning, and it represented a significant deviation in the conduct of Lewis Cass. He was again taking a strictly legalistic approach to a controversy fraught with moralistic considerations, but in so doing, he ignored the fundamental concept of popular sovereignty: that the majority should rule. The Father of Popular Sovereignty spurned his ideological progeny.

Despite the concerted efforts of the Buchanan administration, the unrepresentative Lecompton constitution was not accepted by Congress. The opposition was led by Stephen Douglas, who embraced the doctrine of popular sovereignty prior to introducing the Kansas-Nebraska bill and (unlike Cass) saw no reason to abandon it. The Illinois senator contended the referendum of January demonstrated the will of the people. Although the Senate passed a bill to admit Kansas under the proslavery constitution, the House of Representatives decided to submit the entire document to the voters of the territory. A joint conference committee then worked out a plan to admit Kansas as a state, under the proslavery constitution, if the residents accepted a reduction in their federal land-grant request. In August, the territorial voters overwhelmingly turned down this proposal, thus rejecting the Lecompton constitution. Kansas had spurned slavery, but it remained a territory until southern congressmen resigned during the secession crisis. The Buchanan administration failed in its efforts to bring Kansas into the Union as a Democratic slave state; in the process, sectional tensions worsened, shattering party solidarity.

Lewis Cass supported President Buchanan during the Lecompton controversy not simply out of a sense of party loyalty. He truly believed the Union was at stake. The Father of Popular Sovereignty realized the proslavery constitution made a sham of his cherished doctrine, but failure to support it would dangerously polarize political feeling. As applied to Kansas, the ambiguity of the Cass precept had outlived its usefulness. It actually jeopardized the republic, by exacerbating the explosive issue of sectional honor during the difficult period of territorial settlement. Jefferson Davis, for instance, while acknowledging that "squatter" sovereignty "was ushered in by a great and good man," repudiated it as "a fallacy—a fallacy fraught with mischief." Yet to Cass, reaching an accord on slavery extension was a higher aim than adherence to ideological principle. Popular sovereignty, after all, was introduced to prevent a Democratic schism and alleviate sectional antagonisms, not aggravate them. Cass believed the security of the nation depended upon a concordant, dominant Democratic party. The real peril lay in the Republicans' exploiting Bleeding Kansas to capture the White House or gain a majority in the House of Representatives. According to Cass, the Republican creed called for abolishing slavery in the District of Columbia, repealing the Fugitive Slave Law, prohibiting slavery in the territories, and preventing the admission of any more slave states. If these sectional goals were met, a dissolution of the republic would follow—a measureless catastrophe, he somberly warned. As the rhetoric of Republicans became more impassioned, Cass toughened his stand. The issue of slavery was "a constitutional and practical question"; the Negro belonged to an "inferior" race, and slavery could not be abolished "without exciting the apprehensions of every right-minded man. I would not emancipate the slaves in the southern States to-morrow, were it in my power." He closed this tirade by echoing the sentiments of Fisher Adams. "I am sometimes filled with apprehension, that, old as I am, I may yet outlive the Union and Constitution of my country. God grant that no such misfortune may be in store for me."[29]

Lewis Cass believed Republicans endangered the Union by fanning the sectional flames consuming Kansas. He therefore joined Buchanan in backing the Lecompton constitution, to demonstrate to anxious southerners their interests would be protected. Cass argued that the proslavery document was certainly legal, even if it did not represent the sensibilities of most Kansans. Such a perspective enabled Cass to accept it without explicitly repudiating popular sovereignty. The Cass creed, in the hands of its creator, was transformed from an instrument of compromise into one of conciliation; southern Democrats must be appeased. After statehood was granted, Kansans could amend their constitution to prohibit slavery, and Republicans would be deprived of a menacing political issue.

Cass's effort to safeguard the republic from the scourge of sectionalism demonstrated a myopic view of the slavery extension controversy. His ineffectual attempts to placate southerners and maintain Democratic solidarity, through a strictly legalistic approach to the Kansas question, served to alienate him from mainstream northern opinion. The administration's stubborn adherence to the proslavery position, coupled with political fallout from the Panic of 1857, led to Republican gains in the ensuing elections. Throughout the North, Democrats lost a total of twenty-two congressional seats. The most significant exception to the trend was Illinois, where Douglas was reelected to the Senate, and Democrats carried five of nine congressional districts.

In response to the Republican triumphs, northern Democratic moderates frantically attempted to patch together the national party organization. The old guard, symbolized by Buchanan and Cass, continued to sustain Taney's ruling that slavery could not be prohibited from the territories, and vainly railed against the increasingly perilous sectional strife. Following John Brown's raid on Harper's Ferry, Lewis Cass lamented: "We have fallen upon evil times, and they seem to me to grow worse and worse. The northern abolition feeling and the invasion of southern rights, which it has produced, has led to its natural consequence, and the South is in a high state of excitement which threatens the most serious results. . . . I have almost lost my hope in men." Cass remained convinced that the survival of the republic depended upon a united Democratic party, presenting viable compromises to divisive issues. To ensure this, northerners must be willing to accommodate slaveholders.[30]

The rift within Democratic ranks was not healed before the presidential campaign of 1860 commenced. Consequently, Senator Douglas was nominated by a convention dominated by northern Democrats while Vice President Breckinridge was selected by the southerners. Michigan Democrats met at Detroit, in late June, and swiftly ratified the nomination of Douglas and his popular sovereignty platform. A resolution commending the policies of the Buchanan administration was defeated by a vote of 140 to 6. A more personal humiliation was in store for Secretary of State Cass, who spent the summer in his hometown; the delegates tabled a resolution encouraging him to attend their proceedings. A Washington newspaper caustically inquired: "Whither is the democratic party drifting when Lewis Cass is deemed unworthy to be invited to a seat in a democratic convention?"[31] To the old political warhorse the answer was plain. His cherished party was disintegrating.

In a fruitless attempt to present an image of national harmony, Cass, Buchanan, and Pierce joined a forlorn remnant of northern Democrats in supporting the Breckinridge nomination. These longtime party leaders viewed the candidacy of Douglas as an abandonment of southern interests. His popular sovereignty platform was essentially an abolitionist program, since it effectively banned slavery from the western territories. For the final time, Lewis Cass publicly repudiated the popular sovereignty principle, in a futile effort to uphold a still more precious ideal—the federal union. He was willing to bend and twist and ultimately forsake his doctrine, in a desperate attempt to restore Democratic unity—a unity that he linked inexorably with the survival of the republic. Following the Michigan party meeting, a "State Convention of the National Democracy" convened to ratify the nomination of Breckinridge. This small group of conservative Democrats, which included Henry Ledyard, adjourned to the Cass home after the completion of business.

The result of the national election was foretold in the Democratic schism. The Republican party swept the North, and Abraham Lincoln was elected president. Every northwestern state was solidly in the Republican column. Michigan gave Lincoln a twenty-three thousand vote majority over Douglas; Breckinridge polled a mere eight hundred votes. The event Lewis Cass so dreaded had occurred. A sectional party was in control of the White House, and the disunion that he predicted would follow a Republican victory was swift in coming. Led by South Carolina, southern states began to implement plans for secession. When the dispirited Buchanan cabinet met a few days after the election, sectional differences were clearly delineated. Howell Cobb and Secretary of the Interior Jacob Thompson defended the legitimacy of secession and prepared to follow Georgia and Mississippi out of the Union. Secretary of War John Floyd, a Virginian, did not consider Lincoln's election to be valid grounds for the dissolution of the national government but acknowledged the right of a state to secede. Isaac Toucey, of the Navy Department, opposed secession, as did most New Englanders, but this amiable son of Connecticut recoiled at the thought of using armed force to maintain the federal republic. Kentuckian Joseph Holt, who headed the Post Office

Department; Attorney General Jeremiah Black, of Pennsylvania; and seventy-eight-year-old Lewis Cass led the nationalist faction within the cabinet. Four years previously, Cass proclaimed he did "not believe in the right of secession under the Constitution," and his devotion to the Union remained steadfast. William H. Trescott, Appleton's successor as assistant secretary of state and an unyielding secessionist from South Carolina, recorded a characteristic Cass conversation. "I speak to Cobb, . . . and he tells me he is a Georgian; to Floyd, and he tells me he is a Virginian. . . . I am not a Michigander; I am a citizen of the United States." Cass simply did not accept secession as a constitutional prerogative; he still placed the welfare of the country over that of any state or section.[32]

James Buchanan and Lewis Cass, two inveterate advocates of political compromise, came to a parting of the ways following the election of 1860. In early December, the president formally responded to the secession crisis in his final annual address to Congress. Buchanan condemned northerners who threatened the very existence of slavery; in the face of personal liberty laws and abolitionist legislation intended to keep the territories free, the southern states had a constitutional right to seek a judicial redress of grievances. While dismissing the concept of secession as nothing less than "revolution," the president declared neither he nor Congress could "coerce" a state into remaining in the Union. Buchanan called for passage of a constitutional amendment to strengthen the Fugitive Slave Act and protect slavery throughout the territories and states where it existed. In the meantime, the commander in chief pledged to execute the federal laws, but he weakened this warning by announcing the troops at Charleston, South Carolina, were under orders "to act strictly on the defensive." It was Buchanan's fervent wish that secession (or, at least, any armed clash between the federal government and southern states) could be prevented until Lincoln assumed the presidency.[33]

Cass concurred with most of Buchanan's notions on the secession crisis. Both men blamed radical antislavery men for the widening breach between North and South, believed secession to be unconstitutional, and denied that the federal government possessed the authority to coerce a state to remain in the Union. In fact, following a reading of the original draft to the cabinet, Secretary Cass suggested Buchanan disclaim any such power in more forceful terms. (As Lincoln subsequently discovered, effective resistance to secession inevitably entailed military coercion.) On one significant point, however, Cass vehemently disagreed with the president's message. He urged that federal forts located in the South be

This satirical cartoon, published in 1836, fancifully depicts the White House reception of a popular French dancer. Lewis Cass (who was soon appointed minister to France) is seated with other members of Old Hickory's administration: Secretary of the Navy Mahlon Dickerson, Attorney General Benjamin F. Butler, Postmaster General Amos Kendall, Treasury Secretary Levi Woodbury, and Vice President Van Buren. *(Courtesy of the Library of Congress)*

These portraits of Lewis and Elizabeth Cass were painted in

François Guizot to pose for Healy, as well. *(Courtesy of Henry Led-*

This Alvah Bradish painting of Cass hangs in the Michigan capitol. It dates to after his tenure as governor; observe his "Protest" against the Quintuple Treaty under the inkstand. *(Courtesy of the Michigan State Archives)*

This engraving of a romanticized drawing of Cass by J. B. Longacre appeared in *The National Portrait Gallery of Distinguished Americans* in 1834, when Cass was secretary of war. *(Courtesy of the State Historical Society of Wisconsin, neg. no. x318069)*

Nathaniel Currier printed this lithograph of the Democratic ticket in 1848, with a stern-looking Lewis Cass and General William O. Butler. *(Courtesy of the Library of Congress)*

This Whig campaign lithograph from the election of 1848 portrays a bellicose "President Gas" engaging in wars of conquest. Cass made no secret of his desire to acquire Cuba and additional Mexican territory (including Yucatan), but targeting Peru was certainly an exaggeration. *(Courtesy of the Library of Congress)*

"The Buffalo Hunt" envisions Free-Soiler Martin Van Buren (who was nominated at Buffalo) stampeding Cass and Taylor in 1848. Cass's hat, already in the proverbial "Salt River," contains a copy of the Wilmot Proviso; Taylor's cap has some of the "dead letters" that became a minor campaign issue. *(Courtesy of the William L. Clements Library, University of Michigan, Ann Arbor)*

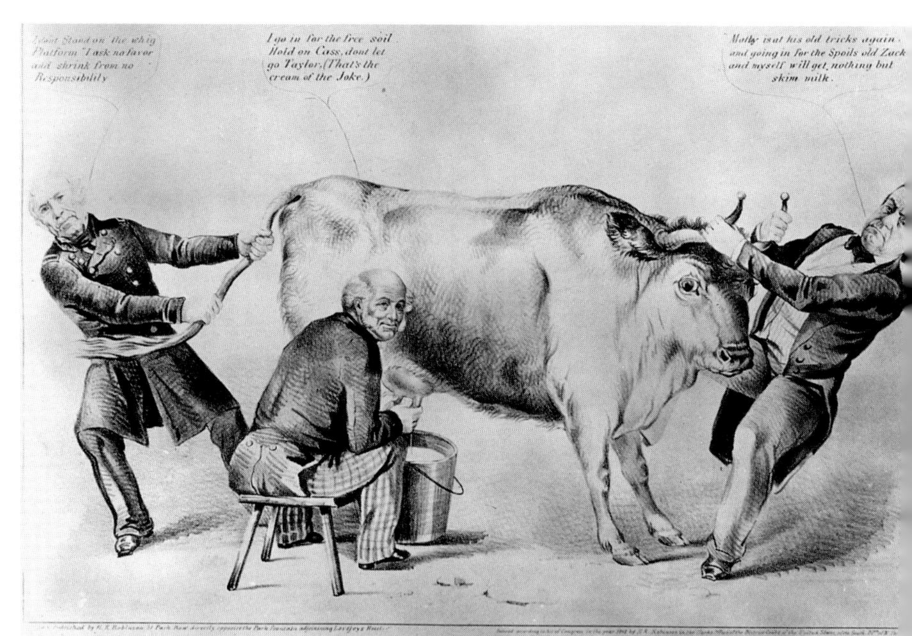

The two chief protagonists for the White House in 1848, Zachary Taylor and Lewis Cass, try to pull the electoral cow in opposite directions while Martin Van Buren calmly continues his milking. The cartoonist was correct in predicting that Cass would "get nothing but skim milk." *(Courtesy of the Michigan State Archives)*

Zachary Taylor, standing firmly on the rock of the Constitution, leads "The Presidential Fishing Party of 1848." Van Buren, who stole the bait of former Liberty party candidate John P. Hale, breaks his line after hooking the fish labeled "New York." Cass bemoans his lack of foresight in not supporting river and harbor improvements. *(Courtesy of the Michigan State Archives)*

This engraving of a daguerreotype taken at Matthew Brady's studio depicts Senator Cass at the apogee of his political career, when the doctrine of popular sovereignty was sustained by the Compromise of 1850. *(Courtesy of the Library of Congress)*

A drunken President Pierce leads his "border ruffians" into Bleeding Kansas. James Buchanan and William Marcy plunder the body of a free soiler, Stephen Douglas lifts a scalp, and a rotund Cass licks his lips over the carnage. *(Courtesy of the William L. Clements Library, University of Michigan, Ann Arbor)*

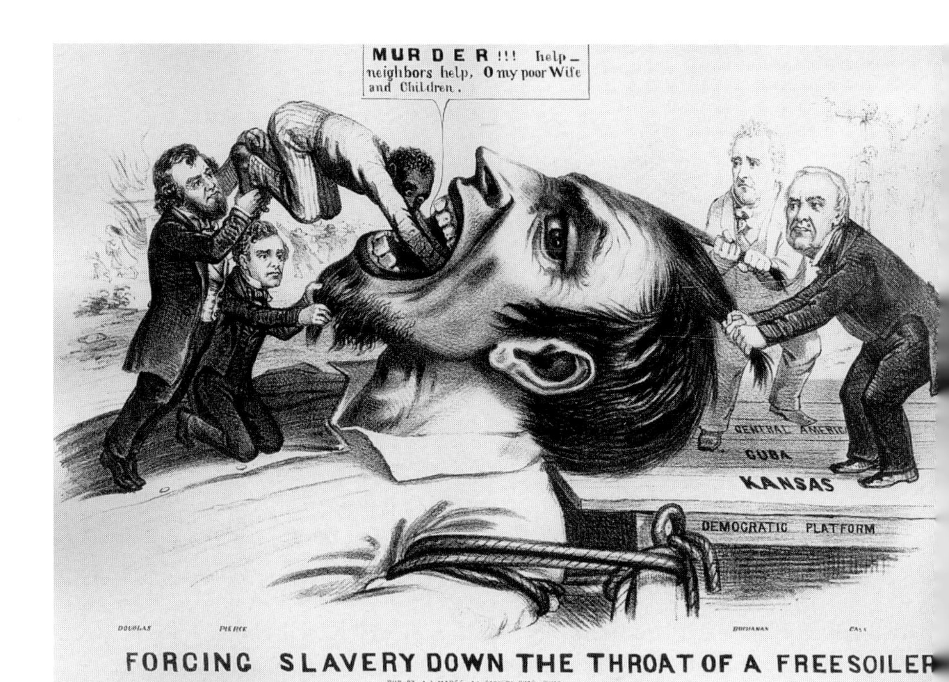

This lithograph castigates leading Democrats for the violence unleashed by the Kansas-Nebraska Act. Following the election of 1856, Buchanan appointed Cass (who joins him on the Democratic platform) to head the State Department. *(Courtesy of the Library of Congress)*

This formal photograph of the Buchanan cabinet shows Secretary of State Cass standing to the right, while Howell Cobb, who settled for the Treasury post, is on Buchanan's immediate left. The others (from left to right) are: Jacob Thompson, John B. Floyd, Isaac Toucey, Joseph Holt, and Jeremiah S. Black. *(Courtesy of the Library of Congress)*

This daguerreotype shows Cass in the twilight of his public life, shortly before he resigned from Buchanan's cabinet and retired to Detroit, dispirited over the sundering of the Union. *(Courtesy of the Chicago Historical Society, ICHi—09742)*

This previously unpublished photograph was taken by C. C. Randall a few months before Cass's death. It reveals an unadorned old Democrat, without pretense or wig. Cass, who personified antebellum nationalism and political moderation, lived to see the republic restored. *(Courtesy of the Burton Historical Collection of the Detroit Public Library)*

This stalwart figure of Lewis Cass stands in the United States Capitol, signifying his importance to the history of Michigan. The sculptor was Daniel Chester French, a fellow native of Exeter, New Hampshire, renowned for his Minute Man monument and the magnificent Lincoln Memorial. *(Courtesy of the Library of Congress)*

strengthened immediately, and warned the Charleston garrison was particularly vulnerable. This recommendation was seconded by the commanding officer, Major Robert Anderson, who requested additional troops. Cass and Attorney General Black entreated Buchanan to send reinforcements to Anderson, but Secretary of War Floyd persuaded the president to wait until after conferring with Commanding General Winfield Scott. In the interim, Cass received a communication from General John Wool, of the Eastern Department, pleading that relief forces be sent at once. Wool declared such a show of force would "prevent a civil war."[34] This advice braced Cass's resolve, and he again called for reinforcements when the cabinet met on December 13. Buchanan still refused to act.

Buchanan's decision not to reinforce federal posts in the South triggered Cass's resignation. Nearly thirty years before, as secretary of war under Andrew Jackson, Cass assumed responsibility for the defense of Charleston during the nullification crisis. The old nationalist could not now remain in the cabinet of a president who shrank from acting forcefully under similar circumstances. In a letter of resignation delivered to Buchanan by Jeremiah Black, Cass emphasized his differences with the president's course. The garrison at Charleston should be reinforced, and armed revenue cutters sent to assist in the collection of customs duties. Cass expressed his "warmest regard" for Buchanan personally but retired from the cabinet in protest over his handling of the crisis. Buchanan publicly expressed his "surprise and regret" and reminded Cass that the secretaries of war and the navy "did not concur in your views." Privately, the president complained that Cass was a most ineffectual secretary of state, because of his age and indecisiveness. James Buchanan, who had anguished over Cobb's resignation a week before, did not regard Cass's departure "as a calamity, but rather as a good riddance." The president also derided his stated reason for leaving the cabinet, since the secretary of state had declared the annual message *"was not sufficiently strong against the power of Congress to make war upon a State for the purpose of compelling her to remain in the Union."* But on this point, Buchanan missed the mark. What Cass insisted upon was the defense of federal property at Charleston, not the coercion of a state. He was hopeful a civil war might be averted; after all, secession was not yet an accomplished fact.[35]

Buchanan responded gracelessly to Cass's resignation. The old bachelor belittled the important contributions made by the departing secretary of state, because of personal pique and the fact that his withdrawal damaged the president's standing among northern moderates. Nonetheless,

Buchanan correctly surmised that advanced age and deteriorating health had diminished the secretary's decisiveness. Cass actually postponed official notification of his resignation, following Thursday's cabinet meeting; his letter to Buchanan was dated Wednesday, December 12, but not submitted until several days later. Although there is some doubt as to precisely when Cass resigned, the correspondence of those directly involved indicates it probably took place on December 15. The *New York World,* under a dateline of the fourteenth, reported that "there is no doubt whatever that Gen. Cass has resigned as Secretary of State." The *Herald* announced, "Early this afternoon the national capital was startled by a rumor" Cass had retired. "In due time the report was fully confirmed." Assistant Secretary of State Trescot, however, sent Cass a private note on the same day the articles appeared, explaining he had received "no official information whatever as to any change in the Head of this Dep[artment]." The president recorded Cass's letter was delivered on Saturday evening, December 15.[36]

In addition to confusion surrounding the date of his resignation, there is reason to believe Cass attempted to retract his letter after it was submitted to the president. In a private memorandum, Buchanan disclosed that on Monday, December 17, both Thompson and Black informed him they had conversed with Cass regarding "his resignation & that he had expressed a desire to withdraw it & return to the Cabinet. I gave this no encouragement." Isaac Toucey, at Buchanan's prodding several years later, recalled a cabinet meeting in which the president deemed a retraction of the letter to be "inadmissible." Attorney General Black confirmed that after the resignation was accepted, Cass "repented himself, admitted that it was all wrong, and would have been glad to take it back." Trescot similarly remembered the secretary of state saying he had acted in haste, "that he had yielded to a pressure brought upon him by those about him." It is quite probable Lewis Cass inquired into the possibility of withdrawing his letter of resignation, after a weekend's reflection; but it is highly unlikely he would have rejoined the cabinet without a reversal of the president's policy, and this Buchanan was not yet prepared to do. The beleaguered president made no efforts to strengthen federal posts in the South prior to the secession of South Carolina. Lewis Cass received cold comfort from quitting public life while the Union was still intact.[37]

Whatever second thoughts Cass had, they were quickly dispelled by the reception he received. Admirers thronged his rooms, and words of lavish praise poured in from throughout the free states. "Your recent course in regard to Major Anderson has but added a new laurel to your already lustrous brow," one Pennsylvanian effusively wrote. Another correspondent from Buchanan's home state assured Cass, "An extensive reading of the press re-echoes a general verdict of satisfaction and admiration for your conduct, although regretting your loss." A Detroit neighbor predicted, "If you were now to come home, dear General, the whole city . . . would welcome you with open hearts and hands." Northern approval of Cass's resignation was confirmed by the Republican *Detroit Advertiser;* while the editors "had occasion to differ from Gen. Cass on questions of public policy," they cordially approved of his "manly act." The *New York Evening Post* stated that "even General Cass has at last found himself at the frontier of concession. He has been obliged to leave the cabinet, that he might not remain in it a perjured traitor." In a similar vein, a political opponent contended, "Cass has shown total depravity impossible by demonstrating that there is a point at which even such a wretched old sneak as he finds enough inextinguishable residu[u]m of conscience to be forced to stop." The Democratic newspaper of Detroit was surprisingly restrained in its commendation. "We are glad he has retired *finally,* for thereby he will separate his fame from that which shall distinguish the last days of Mr. Buchanan's administration." Robert McClelland, too, congratulated Cass, adding his "only regret" was that you "remained so long in the Cabinet." Francis Blair, whose political attachments reached back to Old Hickory, took the unkindest thrust: "Old Cass, like the lame Captain ran first, being too heavy to run fast." In direct contrast to Blair and Buchanan, one northerner viewed Cass's resignation as "the crowning act and glory" of an illustrious life. "Lewis Cass could not possibly end his long public career with a nobler act," the *New York World* agreed. "Nothing has occurred to produce so decided a sensation for a long time."[38]

The resignation created an especially profound impact on the northern consciousness because Cass, a consistent advocate of sectional compromise, submitted it following the president's decision not to strengthen federal fortifications in the South. Throughout his long public career, Lewis Cass labored mightily to expand and defend the boundaries of the United States. When he failed to convince President Buchanan to send reinforcements to Charleston, he felt honor bound to retire from his cabinet. Cass's resignation, as evidenced by the tepid efforts he made to retract it, was not a defiant gesture directed at Buchanan personally.

Instead, it was the act of a despondent old man who had outlived his time and feared he was witnessing the crumbling of the Union.

Lewis Cass savored the northern acclaim that greeted his withdrawal from the Buchanan administration, but privately he fretted over "the state of our Country, and the evils which threaten us." South Carolina seceded a week later. When Cass received this "startling" news, "tears started from his eyes." The venerable politician, in an overly dramatic retelling of the event, exclaimed: "Can it be! Can it be! . . . I had hoped to retire from the public service, and go home to die with the happy thought, that I should leave to my children, as an inheritance from patriotic men, a united and prosperous republic. But it is all over!" Cass was urged to stay in Washington as a symbol of national unity, but he had "lost faith in man" and desired to retreat to Detroit. "While the pillars of the Temple are shaking, there is no place [here] for me. . . . I am utterly powerless." His departure, however, was delayed by the illness of his daughter, Mary Canfield. Cass remained quietly in the capital, slipping deeper into depression, as six other states followed South Carolina out of the Union. He received little consolation from the fact Buchanan finally agreed to send reinforcements to Fort Sumter. The *Star of the West* expedition vindicated the former secretary of state, but it was driven back by shore batteries without accomplishing its purpose. George Boutwell, who visited Cass during this period, observed he "appeared like a man for whom life had nothing of interest." Cass remarked he was "going home to Michigan to die," and morosely added, "If I wanted the office of constable, there isn't a town in the State that would elect me."[39]

Despite his gloomy prophecy, Lewis Cass was warmly welcomed home in late February. Accompanied by his son and Mary and her children, Cass was met at Toledo by a deputation sent from Detroit to escort their distinguished neighbor on the final leg of his journey. The tired old Democrat was cheered when he reached his hometown, and he soon settled into secluded retirement at the residence of his daughter. He put his private affairs in order, and donated several lots to provide the city with a public market, parks, and a school. St. John's Episcopal Church benefited from his largess in the form of a final tribute to Elizabeth. An acquaintance who called upon Cass found him looking "quite well" but convinced "disunion [is] a fixed fact." And then Confederate guns opened fire on Fort Sumter, and the United States flag was lowered in surrender. Lewis Cass, who prior to Lincoln's election was an open ally of southern expansionists and proslavery ideologues, experienced a personal epiphany. He placed the blame for civil war squarely on Southern shoulders. "You know how much I thought they had a right to complain of," he wrote, "but nothing ever justified . . . secession." Cass summarized his feelings in a letter to his grandson: "The course of the South is without excuse and deserves universal reprobation."[40]

The attack on Fort Sumter galvanized the old warrior, and Cass enthusiastically addressed several recruitment rallies. On April 17, he and Zachariah Chandler appeared arm in arm at the Board of Trade in Detroit. They were "greeted by cheer after cheer," demonstrating republican sentiment in Michigan transcended political partisanship. Cass fervently proclaimed: "I come to do honor to that beautiful flag just flung to the breeze. . . . My only hope is that I may die under it, with its stars and stripes still unsullied." A week later, he presided over a mass meeting of ten thousand excited Unionists. Declaring "he who is not *for* his country is *against* her," Cass warned, "There is no neutral position to be occupied." It was "the duty of all zealously to support the government in its efforts to bring this unhappy civil war to a speedy and satisfactory conclusion." The venerable Democrat subscribed several thousand dollars to help equip volunteer regiments, and when Michigan soldiers returned to Detroit after the First Battle at Bull Run, he delivered a welcoming address. The former secretary of war also contributed military advice. Chandler informed the War Department, soon after the first skirmishes, that Cass admonished: "Don't defend Washington. Don't establish batteries on Georgetown Heights. March your troops into Virginia. . . . By this bold policy you will save the border States."[41]

Lewis Cass additionally aided the Union cause in the field of foreign affairs. In November 1861, a federal cruiser overhauled the British steamer *Trent* in West Indian waters and took into custody two Confederate agents, James M. Mason and John Slidell. The Southerners were bound for Europe aboard a neutral vessel, and Britain justifiably demanded their immediate release and an official apology from the American government. War fever ran high in both countries as, ironically, traditional national policy on the right-of-search issue was reversed. Cass cautioned the Lincoln administration to act prudently. He promptly cabled Secretary of State Seward, recommending he take the opportunity to commit Great Britain more firmly to the American position by "discharging" Mason and Slidell. Cass supported this argument in a letter the following day, warning that war with Britain would prevent the restoration of the Union. Mason and Slidell could do little actual harm, he wrote

Seward, because the question of European recognition of the Confederacy would be decided by national interests, not diplomatic negotiations. President Lincoln received similar advice from Senator Charles Sumner, of the Foreign Affairs Committee, and defused the crisis by ordering the release of Mason and Slidell. Secretary Seward subsequently penned a personal note to Cass, expressing appreciation for his "considerate, kind and patriotic counsel in the *Trent* case."[42]

As the Civil War dragged on, Lewis Cass experienced "the most melancholy forebodings." His health and disposition seemed to ebb and flow with the fortunes of the Northern armies. In January 1862, he confessed to being "more and more dispirited every day"; in all of recorded history, no "nation has fallen from the height of prospects to the depths of adversity, in as little time, as we have done." Although Cass steadfastly expected the republic to be restored, he lamented the "fatal error" made by the North in raising "that abominable Negro question," which encouraged secession. Still, Southerners bore the "major responsibility for their insane attempt to break up the government." His heart remained "set upon the integrity of the Union, and . . . the restoration of the Seceding States to the Supremacy of the Constitution." Cass spoke at a military rally in Detroit on July 22, a week after an anti-Union mob disrupted a similar meeting, and he made his last public appearance on August 13, at Hillsdale. He acknowledged "evil days are upon us," but held out hope that "if we are prepared for the exertions and sacrifices which the crisis calls for, the issue will be equally glorious for us, and encouraging for the cause of free governments throughout the world."[43]

Following the Hillside address, Cass's health further deteriorated. The *Free Press* reported that "his case is considered very critical," and the aged Democrat admitted to "suffering a good deal." He did not respond publicly to the Emancipation Proclamation or the military triumphs at Gettysburg and Vicksburg. In the spring of 1864, he complained he had been confined indoors "since last fall." Cass naturally played no active role in the presidential campaign, although he remained faithful to the Democracy and favored McClellan over Lincoln. Nonetheless, he successfully appealed to President Lincoln for the release of two Confederate prisoners of war related to the Canfield branch of the family. (A grandson, Henry B. Ledyard, spent the war as a cadet and, then, instructor at West Point.)[44]

Although Cass "sometimes appeared sad, discouraged and despondent" during his final years, as one personal friend observed, "he never faltered in the support of the Union cause and never ceased to hope for its final triumph." Lewis Cass lived to see his beloved country reunited. By the spring of 1866, he was bedridden and failing fast. On Saturday evening, June 16, a doctor was summoned, and family members gathered to keep the final vigil. Lewis Cass died quietly, shortly after four o'clock on Sunday morning, and several days later was buried beside his wife Elizabeth.[45]

EPILOGUE

Lewis Cass was interred in Detroit's Elmwood Cemetery on June 20, 1866. A Presbyterian burial service was read, and "the sublime ceremonies of the Masonic order" were performed over the body of the former grand master. Following these rites, the grave was covered with sod, and his mortal remains returned to the earth. Thus ended the saga of Michigan's most famous son. President Andrew Johnson proclaimed a period of national mourning, and Cass's personal character was praised by eulogists throughout the United States. A Detroit newspaper testified he was without peer "in honesty of purpose, in purity of character—both public and private." Lewis Cass embodied the virtues of probity, faithfulness, temperance, and constancy; he was a decent, cultured (albeit ethnocentric), and guileless man.[1]

Cass led a remarkable life. Born in the same year as Benton, Calhoun, Van Buren, and Webster, he remained in the public arena long after those prominent politicians departed the scene. For well over half a century, he held a succession of local, state, and federal posts. Although his duties carried him far afield, he remained closely connected to the Northwest; more than any other individual, Governor Cass was responsible for the growth and settlement of Michigan. His political principles were molded during this period, and remained steadfast.

Lewis Cass personified the vigorous Americanism prevalent in the Old Northwest during the first half of the nineteenth century. Above all, he was a true democrat, believing in the ability and right of the people to govern themselves. Additionally, he was an unabashed promoter of territorial expansion. Convinced of the superiority of American political institutions, he felt it was the nation's destiny to spread the blessings of democracy throughout the Western Hemisphere. Appropriately, Cass's extensive career spanned the decades when the United States emerged as a continental republic. He was shaped, too, by an intense Anglophobia. As his father before him, Lewis Cass took up arms to defend his country against British encroachments, and remained an aggressive champion of American honor. Unswerving nationalism was the keystone to his political principles. He was a constitutional unionist, a member of the second generation of United States citizens who clung passionately to the document drafted by their Revolutionary fathers. And Cass was a republican. He believed the federal government possessed explicitly limited powers and defended the rights guaranteed to the states. The ideology of popular sovereignty flowed intuitively from the mind of Lewis Cass.

To ensure the preservation of the republic in the face of increasing sectional tensions, Cass worked unceasingly for political compromise. He was an opponent of slavery, in the abstract, yet blithely accepted its existence as a condition of federal union. Cass heatedly denied he was a doughface, but in truth, he was an accommodating constitutionalist, who evolved into a northern apologist for the peculiar institution. Slavery was a political question to him, not a moral one; disunion was a greater evil than the continuation of black bondage. Shortly before becoming secretary of state, Cass characteristically decried the sentiment pervasive among sectional extremists. "Men talk about the dissolution of the Union as they talk about the division of a township. But a few years since we had one unpronounceable word, and we ought to have it now, like the interdicted name among the Jews, and that word is 'Dissolution.'"[2] This overriding concern for the Union left Cass blinded to the greatest injustice of his era.

Lewis Cass was a thoroughly partisan politician. He harbored personal reservations about Democratic policy concerning Indian removal, the national bank, federal funding for internal improvements, the Oregon boundary, and the Kansas-Nebraska bill; yet, at least publicly, Cass dutifully supported the official party position. By the time of Polk's presidency, in fact, he was looked upon as the leading Democratic spokesman in the Senate. Cass served his party faithfully, and was rewarded with the nomination for president in 1848. By the mid-1850s, he was convinced the future security of the country depended upon a dominant and united Democracy.

Lewis Cass relied on his intellect and judgment; he abhorred demagoguery. He was unable to comprehend the emotionally charged moral fervor, inexorably linked with the struggle for political power, that motivated northerners to spurn the Kansas-Nebraska Act and form the Republican party. Favoring political conciliation, he lost his Senate seat because Michiganites rejected further compromise on slavery extension. The Cass doctrine, likewise, ultimately failed, but only after a decade of providing an expedient solution to the sectional dilemma. Popular sovereignty passed its first major test when Americans were willing to accept its ambiguity. The Compromise of 1850 implicitly endorsed congressional nonintervention regarding slavery and the territories, and few politicians pressed the question of when westerners might decide the issue for themselves. Within half a dozen years, however, the Cass precept outlived its effectiveness. The inflamed political atmosphere, brought about by Bleeding Kansas and the *Dred Scott* case, destroyed the artfully contrived popular sovereignty principle; and when Stephen Douglas broke with the Buchanan administration, the Cass creed no longer functioned as a viable ideological bridge between Democrats. It tragically failed its final test, and the Father of Popular Sovereignty abandoned his doctrinal brainchild. Ironically, jettisoning popular sovereignty as Democratic dogma led to increased sectional tensions; the inability of moderate politicians to compromise on slavery expansion pushed the nation closer to disunion. But to be fair, of course, no individual or political party was able to provide a permanent, pacific solution to the explosive slavery problem.

It is appropriate that Cass survived the Civil War he labored so mightily to prevent. A discarded symbol of antebellum nationalism and political moderation, he adjusted to political realities, and spent his final years as a forthright advocate of the federal cause. Cass ended a lifetime of public service as he commenced it: defending the United States against foreign and domestic assault. He rejoiced to see the country again united. A veteran Washington reporter recalled that he was "the most pronounced American that ever sat in Congress."[3] This is a fitting epitaph for Lewis Cass.

ABBREVIATIONS

AHR	*American Historical Review*
ASP	*American State Papers*
AWR	*American Review: A Whig Journal of Politics, Literature, Art and Science* (title varies)
Burton	Burton Historical Collection, Detroit Public Library
CG	*Congressional Globe*
Clements	William L. Clements Library, University of Michigan, Ann Arbor
DR	*United States Magazine and Democratic Review* (title varies)
HSP	Historical Society of Pennsylvania
Huntington	Huntington Library, San Marino, California
LC	Library of Congress
MH	*Michigan History Magazine* (title varies)
MHC	Michigan Historical Collections, Bentley Historical Library, University of Michigan, Ann Arbor
MHR	*Michigan Historical Review*
MHS	Massachusetts Historical Society
MPHC	*Michigan Pioneer and Historical Collections* (title varies)
MVHR	*Mississippi Valley Historical Review*
NA	National Archives
NAM	National Archives Microfilm
NAR	*North American Review*
NYHS	New-York Historical Society
NYPL	New York Public Library
OAHQ	*Ohio Archaeological and Historical Quarterly* (title varies)

OSAHSL	Ohio State Archaeological and Historical Society Library
RDS	Records of the Department of State, National Archives
RG 75	Records of the Bureau of Indian Affairs, Record Group 75, National Archives
RG 107	Records of the Office of the Secretary of War, Record Group 107, National Archives

NOTES

Unless otherwise noted, all references to manuscript collections refer to Lewis Cass Papers.

PREFACE

1. William T. Young, *Sketch of the Life and Public Services of General Lewis Cass* (Detroit, 1852), 2; W[illiam] L. G. Smith, *The Life and Times of Lewis Cass* (New York, 1856); Andrew C. McLaughlin, *Lewis Cass,* rev. ed. (Boston, 1899), vii.

2. Lewis Cass to Henry Ledyard, Jan. 1, 1853, Clements; Cass to Andrew McReynolds, Dec. 26, 1846, Clements; Andrew Stevenson to Cass, Mar. 6, 1840, Stevenson letterbook, Jan. 1, 1840–Oct. 8, 1841, LC.

3. Frank B. Woodford, *Lewis Cass: The Last Jeffersonian* (New Brunswick, N.J., 1950); Willis Frederick Dunbar, *Lewis Cass* (Grand Rapids, Mich., 1970).

INTRODUCTION

1. Lewis Cass to Henry B. Ledyard, June 19, 1858, Clements.

2. Lewis Cass to Alfred O. P. Nicholson, in the *Daily Washington Union,* Dec. 24, 1847.

CHAPTER ONE
Youth & Soldier (1782–1813)

1. James Abram Garfield, *The Works of James Abram Garfield,* ed. Burke A. Hinsdale, 2 vols. (Boston, 1883), 2:774.

2. Warren Brown, *History of the Town of Hampton Falls, New Hampshire,* 2 vols. (Manchester, N.H., 1900), 1:230–32; Charles H. Bell, *History of the Town of Exeter, New Hampshire* (Exeter, N.H., 1888), 394; Francis B. Heitman, *Historical Register of the Officers of the Continental Army* (Washington, D.C., 1914), 147; Arthur Gilman to Andrew McLaughlin, Nov. 28, 1890, McLaughlin Papers, MHC; Cass K. Shelby, "The Paternal Ancestry of Lewis Cass," Sept. 1947, typewritten manuscript, Burton. It is possible that Jonathan's marriage to Mary Gilman was his second; it is probable that he fathered several children in addition to his offspring with Mary. Regarding Cass genealogy, I am grateful to Dorothy J. Cody and Donald J. Berry for sharing with me the fruits of their individual research.

3. Jonathan Cass to Nicholas Gilman, May 7, 1790, Clements; *Niles Weekly Register* 47 (Sept. 13, 1834): 18.

4. Jonathan Cass to William Woodbridge, Aug. 30, 1803, Woodbridge Papers, Burton.

5. Leverett Saltonstall to Cass, Feb. 24, 1823, Clements; Webster quoted in McLaughlin, *Cass,* 38.

6. Debby Cass to Lewis Cass, Dec. 2, 1794, George W. Cass to Lewis Cass, May 7, 1795, and Charles Lee Cass to Lewis Cass, May 8, 1795, Clements; Jonathan and Mary Cass to Lewis Cass, Apr. 19, 1796, Burton.

7. Copy of Lewis Cass's Exeter Academy certificate, Oct. 2, 1799, Burton.

8. Debby Cass to Betsy Gilman, Jan. 2 and 25, 1800, Burton; Smith, *Cass,* 18–22.

9. Jonathan Cass to Simeon Ladd, Mar. 20, 1802, Burton.

10. D. W. Silliman to Elizabeth Gilman, Oct. 14, 1804, and Jonathan Cass to Simeon Ladd, July 30, 1804, Burton; Dudley Woodbridge to William Woodbridge, May 30, 1803, and Lewis Cass to William Woodbridge, Feb. 28, 1803, Dec. 6, 1806, Woodbridge Papers, Burton; [Lewis Cass], *France, Its King, Court, and Government; and Three Hours at Saint Cloud,* 2d ed. (New York, 1841), 109–21.

11. Lewis Cass's application for membership, American Union Lodge No. 1, Nov. 7, 1803, photostatic copy from Roscoe Bonistal, Clements; Charles Fey Papers, MHC.

12. The Ohio constitution of 1802 vested virtually all political power in the legislative branch of government. Most officials were appointed by the assembly, as were all judges; the patronage available to the governor was strictly limited, and there was no provision for an executive veto. William T. Utter, "Judicial Review in Early Ohio," *MVHR* 14 (1927): 3–4.

13. Dudley Woodbridge to William Woodbridge, June 19, 1802, and June 7, 1806, Woodbridge Papers, Burton (emphasis deleted); "Some of the Ancestry of Mrs. Governor Cass," undated manuscript, Reuben Hyde Walworth Papers, Clements.

14. Lewis Cass to his wife, Dec. 6, 1806, quoted in Cass Canfield, ed., *General Lewis Cass: 1782–1866* (Norwood, Mass., 1916), 9–11.

15. Draft of Lewis Cass to Thomas Jefferson, Dec. 26, 1806, Clements; Cass to Thomas Worthington, Dec. 16, 1806, Burton.

16. *Chillicothe (Ohio) Supporter,* Jan. 26, 1809. Although Tod and another Federalist judge were acquitted, it was a short-lived victory. The next year the assembly vacated all state judgeships and filled the posts with more pliant individuals.

17. Jonathan Cass to his sister, Aug. 14, 1812, Burton.

18. Allen Trimble, "The Autobiography of Allen Trimble," *"Old Northwest" Genealogical Quarterly* 10 (1907): 38; Paris M. Davis, *An Authentic History of the Late War between the United States and Great Britain* (New York, 1836), 28; Cass address quoted from the *Trump of Fame,* June 1812, in "Ohio in the War of 1812," *OAHQ* 28 (1919): 292–93, and enclosed in Lewis Cass to William Hull, July 17, 1812, Clements.

19. Lewis Cass to Thomas Worthington, May 19, 1812, in Richard C. Knopf, transcriber, *Document Transcriptions of the War of 1812 in the Northwest,* 10 vols. (Columbus, Ohio, 1957–62), 3:89; Trimble, "Autobiography," 37.

20. Estimates vary; see Fred C. Hamil, "Michigan in the War of 1812," *MH* 44 (1960): 265; Emilius O. Randall and Daniel J. Ryan, *History of Ohio,* 6 vols. (New York, 1912–15), 3:263; John G. Van Deusen, "Detroit Campaign of Gen. William Hull," *MH* 12 (1928): 572; Woodford, *Cass,* 58.

21. [Robert Breckinridge McAfee], *History of the Late War in the Western Country . . .* (1816; reprint, Ann Arbor, Mich., 1966), 93–94; [Henry R. Schoolcraft], *Outlines of the Life and Character of Gen. Lewis Cass* (Albany, N.Y., 1848), 9; *Sketch of the Life and Public Services of Gen. Lewis Cass* (Washington, D.C., 1848), 2.

22. Proclamation of General Hull, in "Ohio in the War of 1812," 310–11; D. B. Read, *Life and Times of Major-General Sir Isaac Brock* (Toronto, 1894), 125; Cass to Benson J. Lossing, May 17, 1862, Lossing Papers, Burton; Mrs. Maria Campbell and James Freeman Clarke, *Revolutionary Services and Civil Life of General William Hull*... (New York, 1848), 338. Cass indirectly stated that he wrote the proclamation in a letter to Worthington, Jan. 15, 1813, Burton.

23. Cass to Worthington, July 13, 1812, Burton; Cass to Hull, July 17, 1812, Hull Papers, Burton; Robert Lucas, *The Robert Lucas Journal of the War of 1812 during the Campaign under General William Hull,* ed. John C. Parish (Iowa City, 1906), 35.

24. *Life of General Lewis Cass: Comprising an Account of His Military Services in the North-West during the War with Great Britain, His Diplomatic Career and Civil History*... (Philadelphia, 1848), 31; Van Deusen, "Detroit Campaign," 576.

25. Alex R. Gilpin, *The War of 1812 in the Old Northwest* (East Lansing, Mich., 1958), 106; Cass to Worthington, Aug. 12, 1812, John Stiles Gano Papers, Cincinnati Historical Society.

26. Talcott E. Wing, ed., *History of Monroe County, Michigan* (New York, 1890), 91. There is some dispute as to when Cass and McArthur left camp, but Smith (*Cass,* 43) and Woodford (*Cass,* 65) date it August 14. See also Francis F. Beirne, *The War of 1812* (New York, 1949), 105; Samuel Perkins, *A History of the Political and Military Events of the Late War between the United States and Great Britain* (New Haven, Conn., 1825), 86.

27. William Hull quoted in Van Deusen, "Detroit Campaign," 582; *Daily National Intelligencer,* Sept. 8, 1812 (dateline: Aug. 26; Chillicothe, Ohio); *Lucas Journal,* 61–67; Daniel Dobbin's account of Sept. 11, 1812, enclosed in Joseph Gales to Cass, Aug. 16, 1833, Clements.

28. [Schoolcraft], *Life of Cass,* 12; *Life of General Lewis Cass,* 37.

29. Cass to William Eustis, Sept. 10, 1812, in "Documents Relating to Detroit and Vicinity, 1805–1813," *MPHC* 40 (1929): 477–85; *Lucas Journal,* vii–viii.

30. Richard Rush to William Eustis, Sept. 12, 1812, photostatic copy, Burton; *National Intelligencer,* Sept. 15, 1812.

31. Cass to Worthington, Jan. 31, 1813, Worthington Papers, Ohio State Library; Cass to Worthington, Jan. 15, 1813, Burton; Harrison to Armstrong, Oct. 9, 1813, in John Brannon, ed., *Official Letters of the Military and Naval Officers of the United States, during the War with Great Britain*... (Washington, D.C., 1823), 238; *Life of General Lewis Cass,* 55; William Hull, *Memoirs of the Campaign of the North Western Army of the United States, A.D. 1812* (Boston, 1824), 156; E. Alexander Cruikshank, ed., *The Documentary History of the Campaign on the Niagara Frontier,* 9 vols. (Welland, Ontario, [1896]–1908), 5:60–62; Exchange of Prisoners, Sept. 17, 1813, "Copies of Papers on File in the Dominion Archives at Ottawa, Canada, Pertaining to the Relations of the British Government with the United States During the Period of the War of 1812," *MPHC* 15 (1889): 388–89; James Monroe to Harrison, Dec. 26, 1812, in *Messages and Letters of William Henry Harrison,* ed. Logan Esarey, 2 vols. (New York, 1975), 2:268; General Orders issued by Adjutant-General E. P. Gaines, Oct. 17, 1813, Madison Papers, LC; General Orders Respecting the Exchange of Prisoners of War, Feb. 8, 1813, "Copies of Papers on File in the Dominion Archives at Ottawa, Canada, Pertaining to Michigan, As Found in the Colonial Office Records," *MPHC* 25 (1896): 424–26. Cass was reappointed governor of Michigan Territory in 1817, 1820, 1822, 1825, and 1828.

32. John Mathews to Solomon Sibley, June 22, 1816, Sibley Papers, Burton; Cass to Worthington, Jan. 15, 1813, Burton. Cass was not alone in receiving military promotion prior to testifying for the prosecution at General Hull's court-martial; McArthur became a brigadier general, Van Horne a lieutenant colonel, Snelling a major, and McCormick and Daliby captains.

CHAPTER TWO
Governor of Michigan Territory (1813–1831)

1. Cass to Charles Larned, Dec. 29, 1813, Clements; Cass to Worthington, Dec. 11, 1813, Burton.

2. Cass to General Gano, Oct. 26, 1813, Cass to Robert Brent [Nov. 1813], and Cass to Samuel Huntington, Nov. 19, 1813, Clements.

3. Cass to John Armstrong, Oct. 28, 1813, in "Documents Relating to Detroit," 541; William Woodbridge to I. W. Taylor, Feb. 5, 1825, Woodbridge Papers, Burton; Cass to William Crawford, May 31, 1816, RG 107; Cass to Alexander Dallas, July 22, 1815, RG 107; Crawford to Cass, July 2, 1816, in Clarence Edwin Carter, ed., *The Territorial Papers of the United States,* vol. 10, *The Territory of Michigan: 1805–1820;* vol. 11, *The Territory of Michigan: 1820–1829;* vol. 12, *The Territory of Michigan: 1829–1837* (Washington, D.C., 1942–45), 10:657.

4. Cass to [Sec. of War?], Dec. 4, 1813, in "Documents Relating to Detroit," 544–46; Cass to John Armstrong, July 25, Sept. 3, 1814, RG 107; *CG,* 33d Cong., 2d sess., 511.

5. Cass to Sec. of War, Aug. 13, 1814, RG 107; Acting Sec. of War to Cass, Aug. 30, 1814, in Carter, *Territorial Papers,* 10:474.

6. Cass to Acting Sec. of War James Monroe, Sept. 1814, Acting Sec. of War to Cass, Aug. 30, 1814, and enclosure, Cass to Sec. of War, Sept. 3, 1814, RG 107; Carter, *Territorial Papers,* 10:474–80; Cass to [Sec. of War Armstrong?], Dec. 4, 1813, in "Documents Relating to Detroit," 545.

7. Mrs. Dudley Woodbridge to Dudley Woodbridge, July 6, 1817, Woodbridge Papers, Burton; Cass to Sec. of War A. J. Dallas, July 2, 1815, RG 107; Friend Palmer, "Detroit in 1827 and Later On," *MPHC* 35 (1907): 280; Bela Hubbard, "The Early Colonization of Detroit," *MPHC* 1 (1877): 357–58; "The Old Cass House," *Detroit Evening News,* Aug. 30, 1882, reprinted in *MPHC* 4 (1883): 95–96; "Detroit Half a Century Ago . . . ," ibid., 91–92; various real estate contracts and deeds, Burton; document dated Aug. 11, 1836, Townbridge Papers, Burton. The patent holders for the Cass farm were John, William, and David Macomb.

8. Cass to Calhoun, Oct. 17, 1821, in *The Papers of John C. Calhoun,* ed. Robert L. Meriwether et al. (Columbia, S.C., 1959–), 6:440–43; Cass to William Woodbridge, Jan. 16, 1828, Woodbridge Papers, Burton.

9. William Gerald Shade, *Banks or No Banks: The Money Issue in Western Politics, 1832–1865* (Detroit, 1972), 34–35; R. Carlyle Buley, *The Old Northwest: Pioneer Period, 1815–1840,* 2 vols. (Indianapolis, Ind., 1950), 1:126–30, 574–75, 630–31.

10. Levi Bishop, "Biographical Sketch of John Roberts," *MPHC* 22 (1894): 429; George B. Catlin manuscript, Burton; Mrs. E. M. S. Stewart, "Childhood's Recollections of Detroit," *MPHC* 18 (1892): 465; Charles C. Trowbridge to Henry Schoolcraft, Mar. 9, 1826, in Carter, *Territorial Papers,* 11:957; Cass to Joseph Vance, Dec. 2, 1824, ibid., 618–19; *MPHC* 36 (1908): 511–12; *MPHC* 1 (1877): 333.

11. Cass to Elkanah Watson, Nov. 3, 1815, Burton.

12. *Annals of the Congress of the United States,* 15th Cong., 2d sess., 2479; Carter, *Territorial Papers,* 11:278–91, 320–22; *Detroit Gazette,* Feb. 28, 1823.

13. Cass to Worthington, Nov. 28, 1813, Burton; Cass to James Madison, May 26, 1814, in Carter, *Territorial Papers,* 10:461; William Woodbridge to Charles Lanman, Mar. 13, 1823, Woodbridge Papers, Burton; Cass to Joel Poinsett, Sept. 9, 1840, Poinsett Papers, HSP; Cass to Thomas McKenney, Mar. 11, 1826, RG 75; Cass to William Woodbridge, Jan. 16, 1828, Woodbridge Papers, Burton.

14. Cass to James Madison, Nov. 15, 1814, Burton; Edward Tiffin to Josiah Meigs, Nov. 30, 1815, in George H. Cannon, "The Early Surveys of Michigan," *MPHC* 10 (1888): 61–62; William Crawford to Cass, May 22, 1816, in Carter, *Territorial Papers,*

10:637. Edward Tiffin served as governor of Ohio during the time of the Burr conspiracy; Josiah Meigs was the uncle of Return Jonathan Meigs, Ohio's governor when the War of 1812 began.

15. Cass to Sec. of War William Crawford, May 31, 1816, in Carter, *Territorial Papers,* 10:642–45; Cass to Josiah Meigs, May 11, 1816, ibid., 633–36.

16. Tiffin quoted in Madison Kuhn, "Tiffin, Morse, and the Reluctant Pioneer," *MH* 50 (1966): 118; Cass to Edward Tiffin, Nov. 1, 1817, Mar. 24, 1822, in Carter, *Territorial Papers,* 10:709–10, 11:232; J. R. Williams, "Internal Commerce of Michigan, Present and Prospective," *The Merchants' Magazine and Commercial Review* 19 (1848): 21; James H. Lanman, *History of Michigan* (New York, 1839), 221.

17. Cass to John Johnston, June 12, 1817, Johnston Papers, Cincinnati Historical Society; Cass to Solomon Sibley, [Aug. 1817], Sibley Papers, Burton.

18. Cass and Duncan McArthur to George Graham, Sept. 29, 1817, Michigan Papers, Clements; Cass to Elkanah Watson, Nov. 3, 1815, Burton; Cass to Josiah Meigs, May 11, 1816, in Carter, *Territorial Papers,* 10:633–35, 709–23.

19. Letter dated Oct. 1, 1823, in *Detroit Gazette,* Feb. 6, 1824, quoted in Morris C. Taber, "New England Influence in South Central Michigan," *MH* 45 (1961): 306; Cass to Solomon Sibley, Jan. 29, 1823, Lanman Papers, Clarke Library, Central Michigan University.

20. Cass to Calhoun, Apr. 17, 1818, Aug. 3, 1819, RG 107; Cass to James Monroe, Feb. 17, 1815, RG 107; Cass to Calhoun, Oct. 8, Nov. 21, 1819, Dec. 16, 1820, Oct. 24, 1821, RG 107; Calhoun to Cass, Feb. 11, 1822, in *Papers of Calhoun,* 6:685.

21. Cass to Calhoun, Aug. 3, May 27, 1819, Apr. 17, 1818, Apr. 25, July 9, 1822, RG 107; Cass to Calhoun, June 11, 1823, Chicago Historical Society; Cass to Solomon Sibley, Oct. 21, 1821, Sibley Papers, Burton; Cass to President of the United States, Apr. 10, 1827, in "Territorial Records: Schoolcraft Papers," *MPHC* 36 (1908): 541–42.

22. Cass to Calhoun, Aug. 15, 1823, in Carter, *Territorial Papers,* 11:401–2; Cass to Calhoun, Dec. 4, 1823, in *Papers of Calhoun,* 8:393; Cass to Calhoun, May 4, 1821, June 5, 11, 1823, in RG 107; Calhoun to Cass, June 27, 1823, in Carter, *Territorial Papers,* 11:374–75.

23. Lt. Col. William James to Cass, July 8, 1815, and Cass to James, July 9, 1815, RG 107.

24. Cass to Commodore Sir Edward W. C. R. Owen, Sept. 5, 7, 1815, and Owen to Cass, Sept. 5, 6, 7, 1815, in "Copies of Papers on File in the Dominion Archives at Ottawa, Canada, Pertaining to the Relations of the British Government with the United States During and Subsequent to the Period of the War of 1812," *MPHC* 16 (1890): 238–42, 247–50.

25. William James to Cass, Oct. 5, 1815, and Cass to James, Oct. 5, 7, 1815, ibid., 313–14; Cass proclamation, Oct. 27, 1815, in Carter, *Territorial Papers,* 10:718–19; *Niles Weekly Register* 9 (Dec. 2, 1815): 243.

26. Cass to Elkanah Watson, Nov. 3, 1815, Burton; Cass to Sec. of State John Quincy Adams, Oct. 31, 1823, in Carter, *Territorial Papers,* 11:416–17 and Sec. of War Peter B. Porter to Alexander Macomb, Oct. 25, 1828, ibid., 1207.

27. Cass to the Commanding Officer of the *Tecumseh,* June 6, 1816, in Smith, *Cass,* 104–5; John R. Williams to Cass, July 24, 1816, in Charles Moore, comp., "The Beginnings of Territorial Government in Michigan—Manuscripts in the Department of State, Washington," *MPHC* 31 (1902): 521–22; Cass to Acting Sec. of War James Monroe, in Woodford, *Cass,* 102; Charles Bagot to James Monroe, Nov. 18, 1816, in "Copies of Papers . . . War of 1812," 16:546–48.

28. Cass proclamation, Aug. 1814, Woodbridge Papers, Burton; Cass to William Puthuff, July 4, 1818, in Carter, *Territorial Papers,* 10:778; *Laws of the Territory of Michigan,* 2 vols. (Lansing, Mich., 1871–74), 1:180–81; Cass, "Regulations for the Indian Department," broadside in Clements; Cass to Henry R. Schoolcraft, June 10, 1823, in Reuben Gold Thwaites, ed., "The Fur-Trade in Wisconsin: 1812–1825," *Collections of the State Historical Society of Wisconsin* 20 (1911): 306–7.

29. Cass to Sec. of War John Armstrong, Sept. 3, 1814, in Carter, *Territorial Papers,* 10:476; Cass to Sec. of War John Calhoun, Sept. 14, Oct. 1, 1818, RG 75; Cass to Calhoun, May 23, July 18, 1822, RG 107; Cass to Charles Lanman, Jan. 19, 1820, Burton; Laurence F. Schmeckebier, *The Office of Indian Affairs: Its History, Activities and Organization* (Baltimore, 1927), 23–24.

30. Cass to Calhoun, Oct. 26, 1821, RG 75; Cass to William Puthuff, June 8, 1817, in Reuben Gold Thwaites, ed., "The Fur-Trade in Wisconsin: 1815–1817," *Collections of the State Historical Society of Wisconsin* 19 (1910): 461; Major Matthew Irwin, Jr., to Col. Thomas McKenney, [1819?], in [Lyman C. Draper, ed.], "The Fur Trade and Factory System at Green Bay: 1816–21," ibid., 7 (1876): 278; Puthuff to Cass, Oct. 29, 1816, in Carter, *Territorial Papers,* 10:668–69; Ramsay Crooks to Cass, May 29, 1818, ibid., 760–62; Cass to Calhoun, Oct. 20, 1818, RG 107. Congress, in 1816, forbade the issuance of trading licenses to non-Americans. The president, however, granted Governor Cass and several Indian agents the authority to grant such licenses at their discretion.

31. *New York Press,* Nov. 2, 1892, quoted in Kenneth Wiggins Porter, *John Jacob Astor: Businessman,* 2 vols. (Cambridge, Mass., 1931), 2:723–25n; Cass to John Tipton, Apr. 21, 1825, Tipton Papers, Indiana State Library; *MPHC* 14 (1890): 37–38; American Fur Co. Letterbook, D3:1817, Montreal, and 1817–19, Mackinac, Burton.

32. Cass to Calhoun, Nov. 18, 1819, RG 107; *ASP: Indian Affairs,* 2:318–19.

33. *Detroit Gazette,* May 26, 1820; Calhoun to Cass, Jan. 14, 1820, RG 75; Henry Rowe Schoolcraft, *Travels through the Northwestern Regions of the United States,* reprint of *Narrative Journal of Travels from Detroit Northwest through the Great Chain of American Lakes to the sources of the Mississippi River in the year 1820* (1820; reprint, Ann Arbor, 1966), 67–70; Charles C. Trowbridge, "Detroit, Past and Present," *MPHC* 1 (1877): 383–84.

34. Schoolcraft, *Travels,* 107; Cass to Calhoun, Mar. 10, 1820, RG 107.

35. Sassaba quoted in George Johnston, "Reminiscences of Sault Ste. Marys," *MPHC* 12 (1888): 608–11.

36. "General Cass and the British Flag: From the *Detroit Democratic Free Press,* August 17, 1843," *MPHC* 6 (1884): 502; Cass to Calhoun, June 17, 1820, in Carter, *Territorial Papers,* 11:36–37; "Gen. Cass at Ste. Marie in 1820," *Report and Collections of the State Historical Society of Wisconsin* 5 (1868): 410–13; Henry R. Schoolcraft, *Summary Narrative of an Exploratory Expedition to the Sources of the Mississippi River in 1820* (Philadelphia, 1855), 78–81. John Johnston, the Indian agent at the Sault, was temporarily absent from his post during Cass's visit.

37. Schoolcraft, *Travels,* 253–54.

38. Cass to Calhoun, Sept. 14, 1820, RG 107; *The Journal of David Bates Douglass,* ed. Sydney W. Jackman and John F. Freeman (Marquette, Mich., 1969); Schoolcraft, *Summary Narrative* and *Travels.*

39. Cass to Calhoun, Sept. 14, 27, 1820, RG 107; Cass to Calhoun, Oct. 12, 21, 1820, RG 75; Cass to Robert Stewart, Aug. 30, 1820, Clements.

40. Schoolcraft to Calhoun, Apr. 3, 1822, in *Papers of Calhoun,* 7:8–10; Schoolcraft to wife, quoted in Richard G. Bremer, *Indian Agent and Wilderness Scholar: The Life of Henry Rowe Schoolcraft* (Mount Pleasant, Mich., 1987), 233; Cass to Calhoun, Sept. 14, Oct. 3, 1820, RG 107 and RG 75; Cass to Sec. of State John Quincy Adams, Dec. 5, 1821, in Carter, *Territorial Papers,* 11:207. Cass later recommended Douglass for a lieutenant colonelcy in the corps of topographical engineers: Cass to John W. Taylor, Mar. 23, 1826, Taylor Papers, NYHS. Secretary of War Calhoun placed the total cost of the expedition at $6,318.02: Calhoun to Philip Barbour, Feb. 9, 1822, in *Papers of Calhoun,* 6:683.

41. Cass and Solomon Sibley to Calhoun, Feb. 1, 1822, in *Papers of Calhoun,* 6:667–72; Schoolcraft to Calhoun, Sept. 18, 1821, ibid., 374–75; Cass to Charles Noble, Oct. 9, 1823,

Noble Papers, Burton; Bremer, *Indian Agent,* 46–49; Sue I. Silliman, "The Chicago Indian Treaty of 1821," *MH* 6 (1922): 194–97. For a censorious view of Cass's use of alcohol in treaty negotiations, see Bernard C. Peters, "Hypocrisy on the Great Lakes Frontier: The Use of Whiskey by the Michigan Department of Indian Affairs," *MHR* 18 (1992): 1–13. Peters, a geography professor, is unconvincing in arguing that a governmental cover-up existed regarding alcohol and Indian land cessions.

42. Cass message to the Legislative Council, Nov. 6, 1826, in George N. Fuller, *Messages of the Governors of Michigan,* 4 vols. (Lansing, Mich., 1925–27), 1:32; Cass to William Crawford, May 31, 1816, in Carter, *Territorial Papers,* 10:644; *Detroit Gazette,* Nov. 28, Dec. 12, 1817, Feb. 28, 1823; Cass proclamation, in Carter, 10:769–71; Memorial to Congress by Inhabitants of the Territory, Memorial to Congress by Inhabitants of Wayne County, and Cass to Alexander Macomb, ibid., 11:278–91, 320–22, 419.

43. Cass message to Legislative Council, June 7, 1824, in Fuller, *Messages,* 1:13; Cass to William Woodbridge, Oct. 26, 1822, Woodbridge Papers, Burton; Cass to Benjamin I. Woodruff, Jan. 2, 1827, in "Territorial Records," 533. The Antimasonic party in Michigan was formed in 1829, and the two major parties organized shortly thereafter. William Preston Vaughn, *The Antimasonic Party in the United States* (Lexington, Ky., 1983), 167.

44. William Woodbridge to Cass, Apr. 6, 1826, A. E. Wing to Woodbridge, Apr. 29, 1826, and Woodbridge to James Lanman, Mar. 13, 1823, Woodbridge Papers, Burton.

45. Woodbridge to Lanman, Mar. 13, 1823, Woodbridge Papers, Burton; Cass proclamation, July 21, 1818, in Carter, *Territorial Papers,* 10:796–98; Cass to Charles Trowbridge, Nov. 7, 1831, Trowbridge Papers, Burton.

46. Northwest Ordinance, art. 3; Lewis Cass, *Address Delivered Before the New England Society of Michigan, December 22, 1848* (Detroit, 1849), 37–39, and *Address of Lewis Cass, of Michigan, LL.D.: Delivered, by Appointment, before the Association of the Alumni of Hamilton College, at their Anniversary Meeting, August 25, 1830* (Utica, N.Y., 1830), 28.

47. Cass to Lemuel Shattuck, Nov. 17, 1820, Shattuck Papers, Burton; Carter, *Territorial Papers,* 10:731–32; *Laws of the Territory of Michigan,* 1:879–81.

48. Cass address to Legislative Council, Nov. 6, 1826, in Fuller, *Messages,* 1:28; D. Bethune Duffield to Cass, Jan. 19, 1860, Clements; George B. Catlin, "Neighborhood House, Detroit Industrial School," *MH* 18 (1934): 255.

49. Lewis Cass, *A Discourse Delivered at the First Meeting of the Historical Society of Michigan: September 18, 1829* (Detroit, 1830); John T. Mason to Emily Mason, Aug. 22, 1830, Mason Papers, Burton; C. C. Gilbert to Cass, Jan. 25, 1845, Clements.

50. Cass, *Address . . . Hamilton College;* Cass to Schoolcraft, July 7, 1822, in Carter, *Territorial Papers,* 11:252; William Woodbridge to A. E. Wing, Mar. 29, 1826, and Wing to Woodbridge, Apr. 29, 1826, Woodbridge Papers, Burton; Tom S. Applegate, comp., "A History of the Press in Michigan," *MPHC* 6 (1884): 62–98.

51. Cass to Dr. Richard S. Satterlee, Dec. 31, 1831, Burton; Elizabeth Cass (daughter) to Charles C. Trowbridge, Apr. 9, 1832, Trowbridge Papers, Burton.

52. Cass to Col. [Ralph?] Earle, undated, Burton; Cass to William Woodbridge, July 28, 1831, Woodbridge Papers, Burton; Isaac McCoy, *History of the Baptist Indian Missions . . .* (New York, 1840); notes signed by Elizabeth Cass, July 9, 1821, Woodbridge Papers, Burton.

53. *History of St. Clair County, Michigan . . .* (Chicago, 1883), 104; Alexander Macomb to Cass, Oct. 20, 1818, Clements; John T. Blois, *Gazetteer of Michigan . . .* (Detroit, 1838), 151; William Darby and Theodore Dwight, Jr., *A New Gazetteer of the United States . . .* (Hartford, Conn., 1833), 300; [Lewis Cass], *An Examination of the Question, Now in Discussion, Between the American and British Governments, Concerning the Right of Search* (Baltimore, 1842), 47.

54. Cass to Edward Everett, Apr. 29, 1826, Everett Papers, NYHS; Cass to Jefferson Scott, June 16, 1828, in "Territorial Records," 559–60; Cass to George Dallas, Sept. 11, 1860, RDS microfilm, Diplomatic Instructions, Great Britain, 17:341.

55. *Administration of Gen. Cass in the Northwest* [1848], 4; Cass to Charles J. Lanman, Jan. 19, 1820, Burton; Cass to John Johnston, July 30, 1818, *Papers of Calhoun,* 2:443; Christopher Vandeventer to Cass, June 6, 1818, RG 75; Calhoun to Cass, Oct. 16, 1820, Feb. 13, May 28, 1821, RG 75; Cass to A. J. Dallas, July 10, 20, 1815, in Carter, *Territorial Papers,* 10:566–67, 573–82; Cass to William H. Crawford, Oct. 27, 1815, ibid., 606–8; George Graham to Cass, Dec. 29, 1815, ibid., 613; Charles Lee Cass appointment, Feb. 6, 1826, Burton; Cass to Rev. James Finley, Feb. 6, Mar. 22, 1826, photostatic copies of originals from Hayes Memorial Library, Fremont, Ohio, in Burton. Indian agents were paid between $1,200 and $1,800; subagents received $500, even though in some cases they essentially were doing the work of an agent.

56. Calhoun to Cass, May 29, 1822, in *Papers of Calhoun,* 7:129–31; Cass to Sec. of War John Armstrong, Sept. 3, 1814, in Carter, *Territorial Papers,* 10:475–80; George Boyd to Calhoun, Jan. 20, 25, 1820, and Calhoun to Boyd, Feb. 17, 1820, in *Papers of Calhoun,* 4:586–87, 597–602, 669–70; Calhoun to Cass, Apr. 2, 1821, RG 75, and Dec. 9, 1818, Feb. 19, 22, 1820, Nov. 19, 1821, in *Papers of Calhoun,* 3:365, 4:676, 6:502; Cass to Calhoun, Oct. 21, 1821, in *Papers of Calhoun,* 6:480–83, and Dec. 27, 1821, RG 75.

57. Calhoun to Cass, Dec. 9, 1821, Clements; Calhoun to Samuel D. Ingham, June 1, 1823, in *Papers of Calhoun,* 8:82; Calhoun to Cass, Oct. 24, 1823, Apr. 24, 1824, Clements.

58. Drafts of letters from De Witt Clinton to Cass, Nov. 26, 1822, Dec. 5, 1827, Clinton Papers, Columbia University; Cass to Henry Clay, Apr. 14, 1825, in *The Papers of Henry Clay,* ed. James F. Hopkins et al., 11 vols. (Lexington, Ky., 1959–92), 4:257.

59. Cass to Calhoun, Oct. 27, 1821, RG 107; Cass to John Johnston, Johnston Papers, Cincinnati Historical Society; Cass to Thomas Hart Benton, Jan. 19, 1823, Records of the Michigan Superintendency of Indian Affairs, NA; [Lewis Cass], "Policy and Practice of the United States and Great Britain in Their Treatment of Indians," *NAR* (April 1827), 365–442; Cass to Calhoun, Jan. 9, 1823, in *Papers of Calhoun,* 7:412–13, and Apr. 6, 1821, in Carter, *Territorial Papers,* 11:116–17.

60. Cass to Charles J. Lanman, Jan. 19, 1820, Burton; Cass to William H. Crawford, June 6, 1816, in Carter, *Territorial Papers,* 10:648–49; Cass to Gen. John Tipton, Jan. 28, 1818, Tipton Papers, Indiana State Library; Cass to Rev. James Finley, Mar. 25, 1825, photostatic copy of original from Hayes Memorial Library, Burton; Cass to Calhoun, Mar. 22, 1823, in Carter, *Territorial Papers,* 11:353; Crawford to Cass, July 2, 1816, ibid., 10:657–59; Cass to Isaac McCoy, July 16, 1822, in McCoy, *Indian Missions,* 143–51; Calhoun to John Hays, May 29, 1821, in *Papers of Calhoun,* 6:153; Cass to Calhoun, Jan. 6, Aug. 31, 1822, ibid., 6:610, 7:261–62.

61. [Lewis Cass], "Indians of North America," *NAR* (Jan. 1826), 119; Cass and Duncan McArthur to Calhoun, Sept. 18, 1818, RG 75; St. Mary's Treaty, Clements.

62. Cass to Calhoun, Mar. 2, 1821, RG 75; Calhoun to John Lewis, Mar. 2, 1825, in *Papers of Calhoun,* 9:612; Cass to Calhoun, Sept. 30, 1819, in Carter, *Territorial Papers,* 10:863–65.

63. [Lewis Cass], "Removal of the Indians," *NAR* (Jan. 1830), 64–76; [Cass], "Indians of North America," 112–13.

64. Cass to John Johnston, May, 3, 1824, RG 75; typewritten transcript of original from Elizabeth Cass Goddard, Daughters of the War of 1812, Michigan Papers, Burton; Leslie Thorn [or, Thom], "Dr. John L. Whiting . . ." *MPHC* 4 (1883): 119.

65. O-ge-maw-keke-too, quoted in Ephraim S. Williams, "The Treaty of Saginaw in the Year 1819," *MPHC* 7 (1886): 264; Cass to Calhoun, Sept. 30, 1819, in Carter, *Territorial Papers,* 10:863–65, and Jan. 23, 1822, RG 107.

66. Cass to Ramsay Crooks, June 30, 1821, Clements; [Lewis Cass], *Inquiries Respecting the History, Traditions, Languages, Manners, Customs, Religion, &c. of the Indians Living Within the United States* (Detroit, 1823; originally published as two pamphlets); Cass to Calhoun, Dec. 15, 1824, in *Papers of Calhoun,* 9:444; Cass to Benjamin Drake, Dec. 24, 1821, State Historical Society of Wisconsin; Daniel Webster to George Tichnor, Mar. 1, 1826, in George T. Curtis, *Life of Daniel Webster,* 2 vols. (New York, 1870–72), 1:260; Phillip P. Mason, ed., *Schoolcraft: The Literary Voyager or Muzzeniegun* (East Lansing, Mich., 1962), xx.

67. Peter B. Porter to Cass, July 28, 1828, in Carter, *Territorial Papers,* 11:1194–96; Cass to Henetman, Jan. 8, 1849, Clements; Herman J. Viola, *Thomas L. McKenney, Architect of America's Early Indian Policy: 1816–1830* (Chicago, 1974), 114–15, 173.

68. Bremer, *Indian Agent,* 66–70, 74; Viola, *McKenney,* 136–51. The United States Senate rejected the land-grant section of the treaty.

69. Smith, *Cass,* 173–78; Young, *Cass,* 91–92.

70. Cass to James Barbour, July 4, 1827, in Carter, *Territorial Papers,* 11:1093–95; *Detroit Gazette,* Aug. 28, 1827; Cass to Capt. McNair, July 4, 1827, and to James Barbour, July 10, 1827, in Carter, *Territorial Papers,* 11:547–48, 1101–4; Gen. Atkinson to Gen. Gaines, Sept. 27, 28, 1827, in House Ex. Doc. No. 2, 20th Cong., 1st sess., 149–50, 155–58. Red Bird died while in custody; the other tribesmen were sentenced to be hanged but pardoned by President John Quincy Adams.

71. In Carter, *Territorial Papers:* Alexander Macomb to Cass, Aug. 19, 1828, 11:1198–99; Cass to James Barbour, Sept. 4, 1827, 1116–17; Thomas McKenney to Sec. of War, Jan. 24, 1828, 1157–58; Cass to William B. Lewis, Nov. 30, 1830, 12:215–16; McKenney to Cass, July 2, 1829, 52–53. Also Cass to Calhoun, May 4, 1821, *Papers of Calhoun,* 6:91–92.

72. Martin Van Buren to Andrew Jackson, July 16, 1831, and Jackson to Van Buren, July 11, 1831, Van Buren Papers, LC; Austin E. Wing to William Woodbridge, Feb. 27, 1817, Mar. 22, 1824, Jan. 28, 1826, and Woodbridge to Wing, Feb. 16, 1826, Woodbridge Papers, Burton; Charles Trowbridge to Henry Schoolcraft, Jan. 23, 1826, Jan. 10, 1829, in Carter, *Territorial Papers,* 11:935–37, 12:4–6; Jackson's appointment of Cass as secretary of war, Aug. 1, 1831, Clements; *Niles Weekly Register,* 40 (July 16, 1831): 337; Schoolcraft to Cass, June 28, 1831, in Carter, *Territorial Papers,* 12:304–5; Edward Livingston to Cass, July 8, 1831, and Cass to Livingston, July 20, 21, 1831, ibid., 307, 310–11; Robert V. Remini, *Andrew Jackson,* 3 vols. (New York, 1977–84), 2:316–19; Donald B. Cole, *The Presidency of Andrew Jackson* (Lawrence, Kans., 1993), 86.

73. John Biddle quoted in Young, *Cass,* 118; Lanman, *Michigan,* 236.

74. Lewis Cass quoted in Smith, *Cass,* 237.

75. William Woodbridge to James Lanman, Mar. 13, 1823, Woodbridge Papers, Burton; Julius P. Bolivar McCabe, *Directory of the City of Detroit, with its Environs, and Register of Michigan, for the Year 1837* (Detroit, 1837), 8.

CHAPTER THREE
Secretary of War (1831–1836)

1. Louis McLane to Cass, July 25, Oct. 24, 1833, Nov. 20, 1834, Clements.

2. Richard Johnson to Cass, Aug. 24, 1831; Thomas Hart Benton to Cass, Aug. 11, 1831; Nicholas Biddle to Cass, Aug. 10, 1831; Benjamin Abbot to Cass, Aug. 5, 1831; Winfield Scott to Cass, Aug. 1, 1831; William Henry Harrison to Cass, Aug. 29, 1831, all in Clements.

3. Emily Mason to Elizabeth Mason, July 6, 1835, Mason Papers, Burton.

4. Sec. of War Cass report, Nov. 25, 1832, House Doc. No. 2, 22d Cong., 2d sess., 1:20; Andrew Jackson's First Inaugural Address, Mar. 4, 1829, in James D. Richardson, comp., *A*

Compilation of the Messages and Papers of the Presidents: 1789–1897, 10 vols. (Washington, D.C., 1897), 2:438.

5. Mrs. Stephen Decatur to Cass, Dec. 31, 1831; Wool to Cass, June 27, 1834; Ritchie to Cass, Sept. 28, 1836; Massie to Cass, June 5, 1832; Buchanan to Cass, Mar. 2, 1832; McLane to Cass, May 7, 1832; Johnson to Cass, Apr. 8, 1834; Taney to Cass, Dec. 31, 1835; Bryant to Cass, Mar. 19, 1834; and Irving to Cass, Mar. 20, 1834, all in Clements. Also Cass to Dix, Nov. 20, 1834, Dix Papers, Columbia University; Philip R. Fendall to Henry Clay, Oct. 24, 1832, *Papers of Clay,* 8:588–89.

6. Cass to William Woodbridge, Sept. 8, Oct. 10, 1831, Jan. 25, May 2, 1832, Jan. 2, 1833, Jan. 6, 1835, and Woodbridge to Cass, July 30, Dec. 15, 1831, Feb. 9, 1832, Jan. 13, 1834, Woodbridge Papers, Burton.

7. Cass to Col. Zachariah [*sic*] Taylor, Maj. W. G. McNeil, and Maj. T. F. Smith, July 16, 1836, House Doc. No. 278, 25th Cong., 2d sess., 9–12; *ASP: Military Affairs,* 4:815–16, 5:512–13, 6:149–55, 7:777–86; Cass to Jackson, Apr. 7, 1836, in Sen. Doc. No. 293, 24th Cong., 1st sess., 4; Zachary Taylor to Maj. Gen. Thomas Jesup, July 5, 1834, Clements.

8. Sec. of War Cass report, Nov. 30, 1835, *CG,* 24th Cong., 1st sess., app., 1; Benton to Cass, Aug. 11, 1831, Clements; William Gordon to Cass, Oct. 3, 1831, photostatic copy of original from Missouri Historical Society, in Burton; Sec. of War Cass report, 1832, 18–19; Sec. of War Cass report, Nov. 29, 1833, *CG,* 23d Cong., 1st sess., 14–15; Sec. of War Cass report, Nov. 27, 1834, in House Doc. No. 2, 23d Cong., 2d sess., 33–34.

9. Sec. of War Cass report, Nov. 21, 1831; *ASP: Military Affairs,* 4:709.

10. *ASP: Military Affairs,* 4:709, 712; Sec. of War Cass report, 1832, 1:21; Sec. of War Cass report, 1833, 15; Cass to Gen. Dearborn, Feb. 19, 1833, LC. Abolition of the daily liquor ration did not, of course, eliminate the problem of alcohol abuse in the army. The "fatigue ration" of alcohol, for example, continued to be issued, and veteran soldiers managed to obtain illegal whiskey: "The Middle West in 1837 . . . ," ed. Lynne M. Case, *MVHR* 20 (1933): 381–99. I thank William Unrau, my colleague at Wichita State University, for sharing his current research regarding the use (and abuse) of alcohol in the West during this period.

11. Newspaper clipping, "Letter from the Hon. Lewis Cass, Secretary of War, to the Reverend Dr. Edwards, Secretary of the American Temperance Society: Washington City, February 27, 1836," Clements; *Proceedings and Speeches at a Meeting for the Promotion of the Cause of Temperance, . . . February 24, 1833* (Washington, D.C., 1833), 6–14.

12. John Fairfield to his wife, Feb. 8, 1836, in *The Letters of John Fairfield,* ed. Arthur G. Staples (Lewiston, Maine, 1922), 96; Cass to William Woodbridge, July 28, 1831, Woodbridge Papers, Burton; Theodore Frelinghuysen to Cass, Feb. 6, 12, 1834, Clements; *Proceedings and Speeches at a Meeting Held in the Capitol, at Washington, January 13, 1832 . . .* (Washington, D.C., 1832), 3–14.

13. John E. Wool to Cass, Nov. 7, 1831, Clements; Sec. of War Cass report, 1832, 20–21; Sec. of War Cass report, 1834, 34–35; Cass to Callender Irvine, June 23, 1832, Michigan Papers, Clements.

14. Sec. of War Cass report, 1831, 708–16; Cass-Clark proposals, Feb. 9, 1829, in House Doc. No. 117, 20th Cong., 2d sess., 52–77; Sec. of War Cass report, 1834, 33–40; Report on Regulating the Indian Department, May 20, 1834, House Report No. 474, 23d Cong., 1st sess.

15. John Wesley Hunt to Col. Leslie Combs, December 1831, Clements; Buchanan quotes Jackson in George T. Curtis, *Life of James Buchanan,* 2 vols. (New York, 1883), 2:399; Andrew Jackson to Martin Van Buren, Dec. 17, 1831, Van Buren Papers, LC. My characterization of Andrew Jackson is drawn largely from Robert V. Remini's published biographies.

16. Cass to John Reynolds, May 5, 1832, NAM, Sec. of War, Letters Sent, 13:188–89.

17. Cass to Gen. Henry Atkinson, May 31, 1832, and Cass to Gen. Winfield Scott, June 15, July 24, Sept. 4, 1832, ibid., 209–12, 265–67, 274–75.

18. Jackson to Cass, Aug. 20, 1832, Clements; Sec. of War Cass report, 1832, 17–18, 30. Father Gabriel Richard was among those at Detroit who died of the cholera.

19. Sec. of War Cass report, 1833, 16.

20. Taylor to Thomas S. Jesup, July 15, 1834, Clements.

21. Sec. of War Cass reports, 1832, 29–37; 1833, 15–16; 1834, 38–39.

22. Joseph Blunt [*A Statement of Indian Relations: with a Reply to the Article in the Sixty-Sixth Number of the North American Review, on the Removal of the Indians* (New York, 1830)], Samuel M. Worcester article [*Spirit of the Pilgrims* 3 (March 1830): 141–61], and Evarts to Eleazer Lord, cited in Francis Paul Prucha's introduction to Jeremiah Evarts, *Cherokee Removal: The "William Penn" Essays and Other Writings* (Knoxville, Tenn., 1981), 19–23; [Evarts], *The Removal of the Indians* . . . (Boston, 1830).

23. Sec. of War Cass report, 1831, 713–16.

24. Sec. of War Cass reports, 1832, 26–27; 1833, 15–16; Sen. Doc. No. 1, 21st Cong., 2d sess., 1:19–20.

25. Arthur H. DeRosier, Jr., *The Removal of the Choctaw Indians* (Knoxville, Tenn., 1970), 148–49, 158. Total expenditures for Choctaw removal exceeded five million dollars, a sum greater than the administration's estimate for removal of all the eastern tribes.

26. Cass to Montford Stokes and Robert Vaux, July 14, 1832, in Sec. of War Cass report, 1832, 32–37; Stokes commission to Cass, Feb. 10, 1834, in House Report No. 474, 23d Cong., 1st sess., 78–131. The Stokes commission was authorized by an act of Congress; Cass made the appointments.

27. Cass to Creek Nation of Indians, Nov. 1, 1831, in Office of Indian Affairs, Letters Sent, Aug. 3, 1830–Dec. 31, 1831, 7:446–47, NA; Cass to Creeks, Jan. 16, 1832, Indian Office Letterbook No. 8 (Jan. 1–July 4, 1832): 17, NA.

28. Cass to Thomas Jesup, May 19, 1836, in *ASP: Military Affairs*, 6:622–23; Cass to Crawford, Apr. 5, Oct. 10, 1832, and Crawford to Cass, Apr. 27, July 5, 1832, RG 75; Cass to John B. Hogan, Sept. 19, 1835, in House Ex. Doc. No. 276, 24th Cong., 1st sess., 41; Jesup to Cass, July 2, 1836, Clements.

29. [Cass], "Removal," 71–72; Francis Paul Prucha and Donald F. Carmony, eds., "A Memorandum of Lewis Cass: Concerning a System for the Regulation of Indian Affairs," *Wisconsin Magazine of History* 52 (1968): 39; Sec. of War Cass report, 1831, 715; Cass to Benjamin F. Curr[e]y, Sept. 1, 1831, Return J. Meigs Papers, LC; Cass to Cherokee delegation, Jan. 10, 1832, Indian Office Letterbook, 8:6, NA; Jackson to Cass, Aug. 29, 1831, Clements. In a letter dated April 17, 1832, Cass urged the Cherokees to remove to the West. The Indians responded on August 6: they refused to relocate, and called upon the president to protect their national rights. House Doc. No. 2, 22d Cong., 2d sess., 1:37–40.

30. *Worcester* v. *Georgia*, 6 Peters, 515–96; *Cherokee Nation* v. *Georgia*, 5 Peters, 1–80.

31. *Washington Globe*, Mar. 31, 1832; U.S. Constitution, art. 4, sec. 3; Smith, *Cass*, 249–62.

32. Cass to Cherokees, Jan. 10, 1832, RG 75; Cass to Cherokees, Apr. 17, 1832, and Cherokee General Council to Cass, Aug. 6, 1832, in Sec. of War Cass report, 1832, 37–40.

33. Cass to Lumpkin, Dec. 24, 1832, RG 107; Lumpkin to Cass, Jan. 2, 19, 1833, in Wilson Lumpkin, *The Removal of the Cherokee Indians from Georgia*, 2 vols. in 1 (New York, 1907), 1:196–200, 207 (emphasis deleted). The Georgia legislature issued a formal apology for the treatment of the missionaries in 1992.

34. A commonly accepted figure for the death toll during the Cherokee Trail of Tears is roughly four thousand of the sixteen thousand emigrants. A demographic study by Donald R. Englund, however, places the total at about two thousand, or one-eighth of those removed by the military. "A Demographic Study of the Cherokee Nation" (Ph.D. diss., University of Oklahoma, 1973), cited in Francis Paul Prucha, *The Great Father: The United States Government and the American Indians*, 2 vols. (Lincoln, Nebr., 1962), 1:241n.

35. Jackson to Cass, Oct. 29, 1832, Jackson Papers, LC; General Macomb to Brevet Major J. F. Heilman, Oct. 29, 1832, in Sen. Doc. No. 71, 22d Cong., 2d sess., 1:4; Cass to Scott, Nov. 18, Dec. 3, 1832, Clements.

36. Jackson's proclamation, in Richardson, *Messages of the President,* 2:654. The proclamation was probably written by Secretary of State Edward Livingston, but Cass, among others, was thought by some to have had a hand in its final draft. See *The Diary of Philip Hone: 1828–1852,* ed. Allan Nevins (New York, 1936), 84; Richard P. Longacre, "Was Jackson's Kitchen Cabinet a Cabinet?" *MVHR* 44 (1957): 105.

37. *Richmond Enquirer,* Dec. 13, 1832. Much of the correspondence cited relating to the nullification crisis was published in Sen. Doc. No. 71, 22d Cong., 2d sess. and *ASP: Military Affairs,* 5:156–61. I have followed the punctuation of the copies written in Cass's hand, Clements.

38. Cass to Scott, Jan. 26, 1833, Clements; Jackson to Cass, Dec. 17, 1832, *Correspondence of Andrew Jackson,* ed. John Spencer Bassett, 7 vols. (Washington, D.C., 1926–35), 4:502–3.

39. "Major Jack Downing" quoted in James Parton, *Life of Andrew Jackson,* 3 vols. (New York, 1860), 3:489–90.

40. Barrington Anthony to Alpheus Felch, Apr. 13, 1848, Felch Papers, MHC; *National Intelligencer,* June 11, 18, 20, 22, 1833; *Washington Globe,* June 12, 14, 17, 18, 29, 1833; *New York Journal of Commerce,* June 13, 1833.

41. Cass quoted in [William J. Duane], *Narrative and Correspondence Concerning the Removal of the Deposites, and Occurences Connected Therewith* (Philadelphia, 1838), 99–100; Lewis memorandum in Parton, *Jackson,* 3:501–8.

42. Paper read to the cabinet, Sept. 18, 1833, in *Correspondence of Jackson,* 5:192–203, Richardson, *Messages of the Presidents,* 3:15–19, and *The Statesmanship of Andrew Jackson as Told in His Writings and Speeches,* ed. Francis Newton Thorpe (New York, 1909), 261–81; *Washington Globe,* Sept. 26, 1833; Cass quoted by Francis P. Blair to Martin Van Buren, Nov. 13, 1859, in "The Autobiography of Martin Van Buren," ed. John C. Fitzpatrick, *Annual Report of the American Historical Association for the Year 1918,* 2:608.

43. Taney quoted in "Roger B. Taney's 'Bank War Manuscript,'" ed. Carl Brent Swisher, *Maryland Historical Magazine* 53 (1958): 126; William Henry Harrison to Cass, Oct. 5, 1833, Clements; Jackson to Van Buren, Sept. 24, 25, 1833, in "Autobiography of Van Buren," 603–4; Daniel Webster to Samuel Jaudon, Sept. 26, 1833, *The Papers of Daniel Webster: Correspondence,* ser. 1, ed. Charles M. Wiltse (Hanover, N.H., 1974–86), 3:276.

44. Van Buren to Cass, Sept. 10, 1835, Clements; W. L. Newberry to Lucius Lyon, Jan. 22, 1836, Newberry Library, Chicago; E. A. Brush to Cass, Oct. 25, 1836, Clements; Lewis Cass, Jr., to Charles C. Trowbridge, Oct. 8, 1836, and document signed by Cass, Oct. 7, 1831, Trowbridge Papers, Burton; indenture dated Nov. 1, 1832, Burton; Arthur Bronson to Cass, June 2, 1834, Clements; deeds dated Oct. 6, Nov. 18, 1834, Aug. 12, 1836, Burton; Lyon to John P. Sheldon, July 5, 1836, Sheldon Papers, Burton; sale agreement for Cass farm, June 11, 1835, and bond dated June 18, 1835, Burton; undated document regarding Cass Company, Trowbridge Papers, Burton; undated document regarding real estate partnership, Austin E. Wing Papers, Burton; Brush to Cass, Jan. 29, Sept. 15, 29, 1836, Clements; document signed by Lewis and Elizabeth Cass, Oct. 10, 1836, Trowbridge Papers, Burton.

45. Fuller, *Messages,* 1:28–29.

46. Cass to Stevens T. Mason, May 1, 1835, Mason Papers, MHC; Mason to Cass, May 10, 1835, Clements.

47. Cass to Mason, May 1, 9, July 16, Aug. 16, 1835, Mason Papers, MHC, and July 16, Dec. 26, 1835, Clements; Mason to Cass, Apr. 18, 1835, Clements; Cass to John A. Bryan, May 10, 1835, Cincinnati Historical Society; Cass to John Forsyth, Nov. 19, 1835, OSAHSL. Mason was appointed territorial secretary in July 1831, when Cass resigned the governorship

to accept the War Department post; Mason was then nineteen years of age. Upon the death of Governor George B. Porter three years later, Mason became acting governor, and he was later elected first governor of the state of Michigan.

48. John Eaton to Cass, Mar. 8, 1835, in [Woodburne Potter], *The War in Florida: Being an Exposition of its Causes, and an Accurate History of the Campaigns of Generals Clinch, Gaines and Scott* (1836; reprint, Ann Arbor, Mich., 1966), 35–37; Cass to Thompson, Nov. 24, 1834, in Report of Secretary of War, Communicated to the House of Representatives May 26, 1836, in *ASP: Military Affairs,* 6:436; Cass to John Eaton, [1835], in [Potter], *War in Florida,* 37–38.

49. Cass to General Clinch, Apr. 14, 1835, in John T. Sprague, *The Origin, Progress, and Conclusion of the Florida War . . .* (New York, 1848), 85.

50. Sec. of War Cass reports, 1836, 436; 1835, 1; Clinch to Adjutant General, Jan. 22, 1835, in "D. L. Clinch's Reply to Governor Cass," *Washington Globe,* reprinted in *Niles Weekly Register* 52 (July 15, 1837): 315–17.

51. Thompson to Cass, in Sec. of War Cass report, 1836, 437.

52. Sec. of War Cass report, 1835, 3.

53. Cass to General Scott, Jan. 21, 1836, in Sen. Doc. No. 224, 24th Cong., 2d sess., 3:199–201; John H. Eaton to Cass, Jan. 1836, Clements.

54. George Walton, *Fearless and Free: The Seminole Indian War, 1835–1842* (Indianapolis, Ind., 1977), 205–11; John K. Mahon, *History of the Second Seminole War: 1835–1842* (Gainesville, Fla., 1967), 96–111.

55. Eaton to Cass, Feb. 22, 1836, Clements; Cass, *To the Public* (Paris, 1837), 2–8.

56. "Clinch's Reply to Cass"; Amos Adams Lawrence to his father, Jan. 10, 1836, in "Letters from Washington, 1836," MHS *Proceedings* 53 (1919): 55.

57. *A Discourse Pronounced at the Capitol of the United States, In the Hall of Representatives, Before the American Historical Society, January 30, 1836, by the Hon. Lewis Cass, President of the Society* (Washington, D.C., 1836), 45.

58. Cass to John P. Sheldon, Sept. 19, 1833, Burton; Duff Green to Calhoun, July 8, 1833, *Papers of Calhoun,* 12:160–62; Sheldon to Cass, Sept. 5, 1833, Burton; Ambrose Spencer to Clay, Dec. 14, 1833, *Papers of Clay,* 8:677–78; John McLean to Samuel D. Ingham, Feb. 4, 1833, Van Buren Papers, LC.

59. Cass to Gaines, Jan. 23, Apr. 25, May 4, 12, 1836, and Gaines to Cass, Mar. 29, Apr. 8, 1836, in *ASP: Military History,* 6:416–24; Jackson to Cass, Aug. 31, 1836, Clements.

60. Cass to Lewis, June 13, 1836, in *Correspondence of Jackson,* 5:437n.

61. Jackson memorandum, [Nov. 15, 1836?], and Jackson memorandum respecting A. Pageot, Nov. 15, 1836, ibid., 436–38; Jackson to Lewis, Oct. 19, 1839, and Lewis to Jackson, Nov. 5, 1839, Jackson & Lewis Papers, NYPL. In his magisterial biography, Robert Remini contends that "Jackson came within an ace of recalling Cass" during this dispute, but I take exception with his claim Jackson was "justifiably furious" with Cass. As Major Lewis pointed out to the president, Jackson read Cass's letter before it was posted, and the king did not use it in a public fashion (as Jackson claimed). See Remini, *Andrew Jackson,* 3:291; Lewis to Jackson, Nov. 5, 1839, Jackson & Lewis Papers, NYPL. Pageot was promoted to the rank of envoy extraordinary and minister plenipotentiary to the United States during the Polk administration. James K. Polk, *The Diary of James K. Polk,* ed. Milo Milton Quaife, 4 vols. (Chicago, 1910), 3:308.

62. [Cass], *Discourse . . . American Historical Society,* 23–31; honorary degree from Harvard, 1836; Edgar Allan Poe to Cass, July 4, 1836; and Cass to Henetman, Jan. 8, 1849, all in Clements. Cass was granted honorary membership in numerous learned organizations, including the United States Navy Lyceum; New England Historic, Genealogical Society; Jefferson Literary and Historical Society of Philadelphia; Union Literary Society; Rhode

Island Historical Society; and the Buffalo Historical Society. Cass to James S. Whitney, Apr. 25, 1851, and Cass to J. W. Vermillion, Mar. 23, 1860, Clements; documents dated Dec. 18, 1835, Apr. 7, 1847, July 19, 1853, Clements; Walter W. Stevens, "The Scholarship of Lewis Cass," *MH* 44 (1960): 59–66.

63. Cass to Jackson and Jackson to Cass, Oct. 4, 1836, Jackson Papers, LC; and, all in Clements: John E. Wool to Cass, Sept. 11, 1836; Ordnance Office clerks to Cass, Oct. 4, 1836; Cass to clerks, Oct. 9, 1836; Buchanan to Cass, Oct. 3, 1836; George W. Cass, Jr., to Lewis Cass, July 22, 1836. George Washington Cass, Jr., later served as president of the Pittsburgh, Fort Wayne, and Chicago Railroad; the Northern Pacific; and the Adams Express Company.

CHAPTER FOUR
Minister to France (1836–1842)

1. [Cass], *France,* 64–67.

2. Ibid., 68–69, 86, 201; *Life of General Lewis Cass,* 98; "General Cass on European Monarchy," *DR* 30 (1852): 456–69; [George H. Hickman], *The Life of General Lewis Cass, with his Letters and Speeches on Various Subjects* (Baltimore, 1848), 28.

3. Cass to Andrew Jackson, Feb. 21, 1837, Van Buren Papers, LC; Ashbel Smith to Anson Jones, Apr. 11, 1843, in George P. Garrison, ed., "Diplomatic Correspondence of the Republic of Texas," *Annual Report of the American Historical Association for the Year 1908,* 2:1433; J. P. Henderson to B. E. Bee, Mar. 10, 1839, and to David G. Burnet, Mar. 5, June 13, 1839, ibid., 1243–44, 1265–66; Cass to Van Buren, Aug. 5, 1839, Van Buren Papers, LC.

4. Elliot to Cass, Feb. 16, 1836, Feb. 5, 1837, Clements.

5. Edgar Allan Poe to Cass, July 4, 1837, Clements; [Cass], "A Recent Visit to Lady Hester Stanhope," *Southern Literary Messenger* 4 (1838): 496–99; [Cass], "The Island of Cyprus," ibid., 7 (1841): 93; [Cass], "Island of Candia," ibid., 5 (1839): 709–20; Cass diary of tour, Clements; Smith, *Cass,* 337–73.

6. [Cass], *France,* 49, 54–59, 74, 78, 86, 125–26, 134, 201.

7. John Carroll Brent to George D. Ramsay, Dec. 22, 1838, Clements; Edward L. Pierce, ed., *Memoir and Letters of Charles Sumner,* 4 vols. (London, 1878–93), 1:253; Edward Everett to Cass, Nov. 3, 1837, Clements; Leverett Harris to Edward C. Burd, Jan. 25, [18??], HSP. Among those who wrote introductions to the American minister in 1841 (his last full year at Paris), were Richard Rush, Mar. 31; Benjamin F. Butler, Apr. 23 and July 23; James A. Hamilton, May 5; Leverett Saltonstall, May 12; George Bancroft, June 19; Rufus Choate, June 23; Cave Johnson, July 7; Daniel Webster, July 16 and Nov. 8; Theodore Frelinghusen, Aug. 19; Andrew Stevenson, Aug. 20; Enos T. Throop, Aug. 29; John E. Wool, Sept. 12; George M. Dallas, Oct. 2; Albert Gallatin, Oct. 5; John C. Spencer, Nov. 15; and John Gorham Palfrey, Dec. 15, all in Clements.

8. Clayton to Cass, Oct. 12, Dec. 25, 1841, Clements.

9. [Caroline Webster], *"Mr. W. & I": Being the Authentic Diary of Caroline Le Roy Webster during a Famous Journey with the Honle. Daniel Webster to Great Britain and the Continent in the Year 1839* (Binghamton, N.Y., 1942), 171–84, 190–204; Cass to Webster, June 23, 1839, in *Papers of Webster,* ser. 1, 4:373–74.

10. Cass to Andrew Stevenson, Dec. 29, 1836, Stevenson Papers, LC; Cass to Col. Webb, Mar. 31, 1837, Burton.

11. Emily Mason to John T. Mason, June 26, 1842, Mason Papers, Burton.

12. Cass to Van Buren, Feb. 4, 1832, Van Buren Papers, LC; Mary Stocking Knaggs, "Memoir of James Knaggs, of Monroe," *MPHC* 17 (1892): 223; Cass to Col. Webb, Mar. 31, 1837, Burton; Harrison to Cass, Oct. 5, 1833, Clements.

13. Power of attorney in Trowbridge Papers, Burton; Cass to Austin Wing, Apr. 15, 1837, Burton; memorandums dated June 18, 1835, Dec. 5, 1836, May 6, 1829, Nov. 25, 1840,

Burton; Cass Co. sales agreement, June 11, 1835, Burton; George Watterston, *A New Guide of Washington* (Washington, D.C., 1842), 218n.

14. Brush to Cass, Apr. 20, May 20, June 23, Aug. 4, Sept. 13, 1837, and Trowbridge to Cass, May 27, Aug. 14, Oct. 12, 1837, Clements; Nathaniel Ray Thomas to Webster, July 27, 1838, in *Papers of Webster,* ser. 1, 4:316–18; Henry Hubbard to Webster, Aug. 1, 1838, ibid., 318–19; Webster to Samuel Jaudon, Jan. 12, 1839, ibid., 338–40; Charles Butler to Henry Whiting, Dec. 10, 1840, Butler Papers, Burton.

15. Trowbridge to Cass, Aug. 24, 1838, Clements; Cass to Andrew Stevenson, Apr. 19, 1838, Stevenson Papers, LC; Brush to Cass, Aug. 4, 1837, Feb. 9, June 13, 1838, Jan. 22, Nov. 6, 22, 1839, Mar. 21, Oct. 31, 1840, Jan. 18, Aug. 17, 1841, Apr. 21, July 22, 1842, Clements; Lewis Cass, Jr., to Lucius Lyon, May 17, 1843, Clements; Lewis Cass to Lyon, June 8, 1843, Clements; Henry T. Backus to William Woodbridge, June 2, 1841, Woodbridge Papers, Burton; Schoolcraft to Woodbridge, Sept. 4, Nov. 3, 1841, Clements; tax statement, Wayne County treasurer's office, Oct. 5, 1844, Clements.

16. J. M. Howard to H. Hall, Apr. 27, 1843, in Floyd Benjamin Streeter, *Political Parties in Michigan, 1837–1860* (Lansing, Mich., 1918), 148n; *Life of General Lewis Cass,* 98; Henry D. Brown, "Pioneer Riverfront Development," *Bulletin: Detroit Historical Society* 13 (1957): 8–13.

17. Cass to Webster, Mar. 5, 15, 1841, in *The Papers of Daniel Webster: Diplomatic Papers,* ser. 3, ed. Kenneth E. Shewmaker and Kenneth R. Stevens (Hanover, N.H., 1983–87), 1:37–38, 44–45.

18. Andrew Stevenson to Lord Palmerston, Feb. 17, 1840, in Sen. Doc. No. 377, 29th Cong., 1st sess., 15–16 (hereafter, Sen. Doc. 377); James Bandinel, *Some Account of the Trade in Slaves from Africa . . .* (London, 1842), 254–55; Hugh G. Soulsby, "The Right of Search and the Slave Trade in Anglo-American Relations," *Johns Hopkins University Studies in Historical and Political Sciences* 51 (1933): 192; Lord Aberdeen to Edward Everett, Dec. 20, 1841, in House Rep. Doc. No. 192, 27th Cong., 3d sess., 5:9 (hereafter, House Doc. 192).

19. Edward Everett to Cass, Feb. 15, 1842, Burton; *Niles Weekly Register* 62 (Mar. 26, 1842): 54–60.

20. [Cass], *Examination,* 3, 6, 7, 13, 25, 27, 38, 53, 46, 48, 49, 47, 55.

21. The *Times* and *Examiner* quoted in *Sketch of the Life and Services of General Lewis Cass, of Ohio* (Harrisburg, Pa., 1843), 23; [Sir William Gore Ouseley], *Reply to An "American's Examination" of the "Right of Search"* . . . (London, 1842), iii, 6, 59, 25, 111.

22. Charles Sumner to George Sumner, Mar. 29, 1842, in Pierce, *Sumner,* 2:204–5; [Cass], *Examination,* 38; Lord Aberdeen to Edward Everett, Dec. 20, 1841, in House Doc. 192, 8; Lord Brougham speech in the House of Lords, Feb. 21, 1842, in *Hansard's Parliamentary Debates,* ser. 3, 60:718; Robert Peel speech to the House of Commons, Feb. 2, 1843, ibid., 66:88.

23. Cass to François Guizot, in *Niles Weekly Register* 62 (June 11, 1842): 229–30 and Duff Green Papers, LC.

24. John Tyler's First Annual Message to Congress, Dec. 7, 1841, in Richardson, *Messages of the Presidents,* 4:77; Tyler to Webster, undated, in Lyon G. Tyler, *Letters and Times of the Tylers,* 3 vols. (Richmond, Va., 1884–96), 2:233 and Curtis, *Webster,* 2:183; Webster to George Ticknor, Feb. 18, 1842, and Webster to Edward Everett, Apr. 26, 1842, in *Papers of Webster,* ser. 3, 1:26, 543–44; diary entries, Aug. 24, 1842, Mar. 15, 1843, in *Memoirs of John Quincy Adams, Comprising Portions of His Diary from 1795–1848,* ed. Charles Francis Adams, 12 vols. (Philadelphia, 1874–77), 11:243, 338. Cass's opposition to ratification of the Quintuple Treaty was seconded by the American chargé at Berlin, Henry Wheaton, and Duff Green, an intimate of President Tyler visiting Paris at the time.

25. Cass to Rives, Apr. 27, May 31, 1842, Rives Papers, LC; Cass to Duff Green, May 11, 24, 1842, Green Papers, LC; Rives to Cass, June 12, 1842, Clements; Calhoun to Cass, [ca.

February 1842], *Papers of Calhoun,* 16:155; Everett to Webster, May 20, 1842, *Papers of Webster,* ser. 1, 5:210.

26. Cass to Rives, May 31, 1842, Rives Papers, LC; Cass to Webster, May 26, 1842, in Sen. Doc. 377, 199; Cass to Henry Ledyard, May 16, 1842, LC.

27. Legaré to Cass, Apr. 5, 1842, and Rives to Cass, June 12, 1842, Clements. Jesse S. Reeves notes that an antisearch amendment to the official reply to the king's speech was unanimously adopted by the Chambers before Cass's pamphlet was published or his protest to Guizot delivered. *American Diplomacy Under Tyler and Polk* (Baltimore, 1907), 36.

28. Cass to Webster, Jan. 24, 1842, Clements; Cass to ——, May 17, 1842, Lee Kohns Papers, NYPL; Everett to Cass, Feb. 15, 1842, Burton.

29. Emily Mason to John Mason, June 26, [1842], and Emily Mason to Laura Mason, [1842], Mason Papers, Burton; Lewis Cass, Jr., to Emily Mason, May 1842, and Rebecca Marsh Herrick to Freeman Parker, Dec. 11, 1844, Burton; Lewis Cass, Jr., to Ledyard, Nov. 29, [1842], Clements; Emily Mason to Elizabeth Chew, Feb. 27, 1842, Mason Papers, Burton.

30. Cass to J. Watson Webb [?], Feb. 13, 1842, NYPL; Cass to Webster, Feb. 15, 1842, in Sen. Doc. 377, 187–92, and *Papers of Webster,* ser. 3, 1:502–9; Everett to Webster, Dec. 31, 1841, and Webster to Everett, Jan. 29, 1842, in House Doc. 192, 6–7, 11–12, and *Papers of Webster,* ser. 3, 1:173–85, 496–97.

31. Tyler to Cass, June 29, 1842, Clements; Webster to Everett, Apr. 26, 1842, in Curtis, *Webster*, 2:118n; Webster to Cass, Apr. 5, 1842, in John Bassett Moore, *A Digest of International Law,* 8 vols. (Washington, D.C., 1906), 2:929; Webster to Cass, Apr. 25, 1842, in Curtis, *Webster*, 2:186.

32. Webster to Everett, Mar. 28, 1843, in Sen. Doc. 377, 132–40, and *Papers of Webster,* ser. 3, 1:807–17; President Tyler's message to the House of Representatives, Feb. 28, 1842, in House Doc. 192, 3.

33. Cass to Webster, Sept. 17, Oct. 3, 1842, in Sen. Doc. 377, 203–6, and *Papers of Webster,* Ser. 3, 1:716–21. Cass was informed the president granted his request to return home in a communication from Acting Secretary of State Fletcher Webster, dated October 11, 1842. Sen. Doc. 377, 207.

34. Cass to Webster, Oct. 3, 1842, in Sen. Doc. 377, 203–6, and *Papers of Webster,* ser. 3, 1:717–21.

35. *Boston Post,* Dec. 7, 8, 1842; *Daily National Intelligencer,* Dec. 9, 10, 1842; *Washington Globe,* Dec. 9, 1842; Enos T. Throop et al., to Cass, Oct. 20, 1842, and Cass to Webster, Dec. 6, 1842, Clements. Henry Ledyard remained the chargé at Paris until 1844, when President Tyler appointed Senator William King of Alabama minister to France. Tyler to Cass, Apr. 11, 1844, Clements.

36. Webster to Cass, Nov. 14, 1842, in Sen. Doc. 377, 208–16, and *Papers of Webster,* ser. 3, 1:724–34.

37. Cass to Webster, Dec. 11, 1842, and Webster to Cass, Dec. 20, 1842, in Sen. Doc. 377, 216–28, and *Papers of Webster,* ser. 3, 1:734–49.

38. Tyler to Webster, [Dec. 1843 and Feb. 1843], *Papers of Webster,* ser. 3, 1:261, 750.

39. Cass to Webster, Mar. 7, 1843, in Sen. Doc. 377, 229–48, and *Papers of Webster,* ser. 3, 1:750–75.

40. Cass speech, Mar. 30, 1846, *CG,* 29th Cong., 1st sess., app., 423; Kenneth E. Shewmaker, "The 'War of Words': The Cass-Webster Debate of 1842–43," *Diplomatic History* 5 (1981): 151–63. John Quincy Adams characterized Cass's correspondence to Webster as "insolent, inconsistent, sophistical, and prevaricating": diary entry, Mar. 15, 1843, in *Memoirs of J. Q. Adams,* 11:338. More temperate observers who favor Webster's arguments include Richard N. Current, "Webster's Propaganda and the Ashburton Treaty," *MVHR* 34 (1947): 198;

Curtis, *Webster*, 2:187–204; Claude M. Fuess, *Daniel Webster,* 2 vols. (Boston, 1930), 2:123–24; Gerald W. Johnson, *America's Silver Age: The Statecraft of Clay, Webster, and Calhoun* (New York, 1939), 248; Henry Cabot Lodge, *Daniel Webster* (Boston, 1899), 253; and Soulsby, "Right of Search," 226–29. Cass is not without his defenders. See *Detroit Democratic Free Press*, Mar. 11, 1843, and Americanus (pseud.), *Comments on Lord Brougham's Attack Upon General Lewis Cass* (Harrisburg, Pa., 1843). Young claims that "the reasoning and argument of Gov. Cass stand without even an attempt at refutation" (208). Smith (*Cass,* 479) and Woodford (*Cass,* 214) take similar positions in support of Cass.

41. Edward Everett to Webster, Mar. 3, 1842, *Papers of Webster,* ser. 3, 1:713–14; Lord Ashburton to Lord Aberdeen, Apr. 25, 26, 1842, ibid., 544–47; Brougham's speech, Apr. 7, 1843, *Hansard's Parliamentary Debates,* 3d ser., 68:605–6; Henry D. Gilpin to Martin Van Buren, May 29, 1842, Van Buren Papers, LC.

42. Horace Greeley, *The American Conflict . . . ,* 2 vols. (Hartford, Conn., 1864–66), 1:177.

CHAPTER FIVE
Candidate for the Presidential Nomination (1842–1844)

1. By the time party lines and ideologies were more clearly delineated in the 1840s, Rives and Tallmadge joined the Whig party.

2. James C. N. Paul, *Rift in the Democracy* (Philadelphia, 1951), 10, 17–23, 53–61.

3. Cass to Levi Reynolds, May 16, 1842, Burton; Cass to John P. Sheldon, Mar. 21, 1842, Sheldon Papers, Burton; Cass to Duff Green, July 1, 1842, Green Papers, LC; Charles E. Anderson to Stevens T. Mason, July 30, 1838, Mason Papers, Burton; Cass to A. C. Pepper, Dec. 20, [1841], and Cass to Harrisburg committee, May 16, Sept. 14, 1842, Clements.

4. William C. Rives to Cass, Aug. 13, 1842, Clements; Enos Throop to Van Buren, Sept. 27, 1842, Van Buren Papers, LC; Nathaniel Niles to Nathaniel P. Tallmadge, May 18, 1841, Tallmadge Papers, State Historical Society of Wisconsin; Cass to Thomas Worthington, Mar. 4, 1844, Huntington; James H. Hammond to Calhoun, Sept. 10, 1842, *Papers of Calhoun,* 16:453–56; Duff Green to Calhoun, Nov. 10, 1842, ibid., 540–41; Francis P. Blair to Calhoun, Nov. 11, 1842, ibid., 541–43; Henry D. Gilpin to Van Buren, Nov. 23, 1842, Van Buren Papers, LC; George Bancroft to Van Buren Nov. 23, 1842, in "Van Buren-Bancroft Correspondence, 1830–1845," [ed. Worthington Chauncey Ford], MHS *Proceedings* 42 (June 1909): 394.

5. Cass to Rives, Sept. 14, 19, 1842, Rives Papers, LC; Lewis to Cass, July 1844, Clements.

6. Levi Reynolds to Cass, misdated Dec. 28, 1842 [postmarked Nov. 29, 1842], Clements; *Niles Weekly Register* 63 (Nov. 19, 26, 1842): 182, 202; *Harrisburg Keystone,* Nov. 23, 1842; *New York Herald,* Nov. 28, 1842.

7. Enos Throop to Van Buren, Sept. 27, Oct. 28, 1842, Van Buren Papers, LC; Calhoun to James H. Hammond, Sept. 24, [1842], *Papers of Calhoun,* 16:469–71; *New York Herald,* Dec. 20, 1842; Cass to Duff Green, Oct. 1, 1842, Green Papers, LC; Everett to Webster, Oct. 17, Dec. 3, 1842, *Papers of Webster,* ser. 3, 1:700–3 and ser. 1, 5:254.

8. William Marcy to Van Buren, Dec. 20, 1842, Van Buren Papers, LC; George Bancroft to Van Buren, Nov. 23, 1842, in [Ford], "Van Buren–Bancroft," 394.

9. Cass to Boston citizens, Dec. 8, 1842, Clements; George Bancroft to Van Buren, Dec. 9, 1842, in [Ford], "Van Buren–Bancroft," 396; New England citizens to Cass, Dec. 7, 1842, Clements; *Boston Post,* Dec. 12, 1842. Neither Bancroft nor Governor Marcus Morton signed the Faneuil Hall invitation.

10. Henry Gilpin to Van Buren, Nov. 23, 1842, and Conrad Ten Eyck to Van Buren, Sept. 16, 1840, Van Buren Papers, LC; *New York Herald,* Nov. 15, 1842; George Bancroft to

Van Buren, Nov. 23, 1842, in [Ford], "Van Buren–Bancroft," 394; Charles Sumner to Lord Morpeth, Dec. 16, 1842, in Pierce, *Sumner,* 3:228.

11. Mahlon Dickerson to Cass, Dec. 10, 1842, and Cass to Dickerson, Dec. 10, 1842, in *New York Standard,* Dec. 12, 1842, *Boston Post,* Dec. 14, 1842, and [Hickman], *Cass,* 39–40 (punctuation varies).

12. Philip Hone diary entry, Dec. 13, 1842, in *Diary of Hone,* 638–39; *New York Herald,* Nov. 28, Dec. 10, 1842; John T. Mason to Emily V. Mason, Dec. 13, 1842, Mason Papers, Burton; *Boston Post,* Dec. 14, 1842; Robert H. Morris to Cass, Dec. 10, 1842, Clements.

13. *New York Herald,* Dec. 20, 1842; Henry Gilpin to Van Buren, Nov. 23, Dec. 14, 1842, Van Buren Papers, LC; Democratic citizens of Philadelphia to Cass, Dec. 15, 1842, Clements.

14. Cass to William Rives, Jan. 10, 1843, Rives Papers, LC; *New York Daily Tribune,* Jan. 16, 1843; Cass to Andrew Jackson, May 26, 1843, Jackson Papers, LC; Thomas Hart Benton to Van Buren, Jan. 1, 1843, Van Buren Papers, LC; *CG,* 27th Cong., 3d sess., 54, 94, 99; Sen. Doc. No. 223, 27th Cong., 3d sess., vol. 4; John Davis to Van Buren, Nov. 16, 1842, Van Buren Papers, LC.

15. Reynolds to Cass, [Nov.] 28, 1842, Clements; Cass to David Disney, Feb. 9, 1843, Burton; Cass to Democratic state convention of Indiana, in Young, *Cass,* 214–17; Cass to Mahlon Dickerson, Dec. 10, 1842, in [Hickman], *Cass,* 40; *Detroit Daily Advertiser,* Jan. 31, 1843; *New York Daily Tribune,* Mar. 22, 1842; Cass to Duff Green, Oct. 1, 1842, Green Papers, LC; *Niles Weekly Register* 64 (May 13, 1843): 167–69.

16. *Cincinnati Enquirer,* Feb. 3, 1843.

17. Cass to David Disney, Feb. 9, 1843, Burton; Moses Dawson to Van Buren, Feb. 4, 1843, Van Buren Papers, LC.

18. Moses Dawson to Van Buren, Feb. 4, 1843, Van Buren Papers, LC.

19. Jackson to Van Buren, Sept. 22, 1843, Van Buren Papers, LC; Cass application to join the American Union Lodge of Marietta, Ohio, dated Nov. 7, 1804, Clements; A. Harper to Cass, Mar. 11, 1815, Clements; promissory note, Apr. 3, 1827, signed by "Lewis Cass, Grand Master," Clarke Library, Central Michigan University; Moses Dawson to Jackson, Aug. 2, 1843, Jackson Papers, LC.

20. Cass to Duff Green, Feb. 21, 1843, Green Papers, LC; *Detroit Democratic Free Press,* Feb. 15, 16, 1843.

21. Henry R. Schoolcraft to John S. McKeon, Oct. 4, 1843, Schoolcraft Papers, LC.

22. Cass to Duff Green, Feb. 21, 1843, Green Papers, LC; *Painesville (Ohio) Telegraph,* Dec. 7, 1842.

23. Schoolcraft to McKeon, Oct. 4, 1843, Schoolcraft Papers, LC; Cass to Niles, Aug. 31, 1843, Burton; Cass to C. O. [or, G. O.] Wittemore, Feb. 27, 28, 1843, newspaper clipping, John B. Yates Scrapbook, 1856–70, MHC; Cass to John H. Dean, Oct. 10, 1843, and Cass to George Savage, Dec. 26, 1843, Clements; A. O. P. Nicholson to William Allen, Nov. 5, 1843, Allen Papers, LC; Edward Brooks to J. C. Spencer, Oct. 14, 1843, Burton.

24. William B. Lewis to Cass, July 2, 1843, Clements; Cass to Jackson, May 26, 1843, Jackson Papers, LC.

25. Jackson to Cass, July 8, 1843, Clements; Cass to Jackson, Aug. 11, 1843, Jackson Papers, LC; John Norvell to editors of the *Washington Globe,* Aug. 18, 1843, enclosed in Norvell to William B. Lewis, Aug. 18, 1843, Clements; Jackson to Lewis, Sept. 12, 1843, Jackson & Lewis Papers, NYPL.

26. [Richard Rush], *Biography of General Lewis Cass: Including a Voice from a Friend* (New York, 1843), 17, 20–24; Cave Johnson to James Polk, Dec. 9, 1843, Polk Papers, LC; Richard Rush to Cass, Aug. 28, 1844, Clements.

27. McLaughlin, *Cass,* 203–4; *New York Daily Tribune,* July 18, 1843.

28. *Oration Delivered at the Celebration of the Completion of the Wabash and Erie Canal, by Gen. Lewis Cass, at Fort Wayne, I[ndian]a, on the Fourth of July, 1843* (Fort Wayne, Ind., 1843), 15; *Niles Weekly Register* 64 (Aug. 12, 1843): 378–81; John Law to Van Buren, Sept. 22, 1843, Van Buren Papers, LC.

29. G. Mott Williams to Thomas Williams, July 1, 1843, John R. Williams Papers, Burton.

30. George Bancroft to Van Buren, Sept. 14, 1843, and Gideon Welles to Van Buren, Oct. 26, 1843, Van Buren Papers, LC.

31. Jackson to Van Buren, Nov. 29, 1843, and John Bragg to Van Buren, Oct. 28, 1843, Van Buren Papers, LC; Polk to Van Buren, Nov. 30, 1843, *Correspondence of James K. Polk,* ed. Herbert Weaver et al. (Nashville, Tenn., 1969–), 6:364–65.

32. *Cincinnati Enquirer,* June 30, 1843; *New York Daily Tribune,* Nov. 7, Dec. 26, 1843; George R. Davis to Van Buren, Aug. 4, 1843, and Samuel Medary to Van Buren, Nov. 19, 1843, Van Buren Papers, LC; William Medill to William Allen, Jan. 11, 1844, Allen Papers, LC.

33. John Norvell to Van Buren, Sept. 10, 1843, Van Buren Papers, LC; Lucius Lyon to David Skerrett, Oct. 18, 1843, in "Letters of Lucius Lyon," ed. L. G. Stuart *MPHC* 27 (1897): 563; *New York Daily Tribune,* July 6, 1843; R. P. Eldridge and C. G. Hammond to Van Buren, July 2, 1843, Van Buren Papers, LC; *Detroit Democratic Free Press,* Jan. 11, 1844; *Detroit Daily Advertiser,* Jan. 12, 1844.

34. Cass to Duff Green, Jan. 29, 1844, Green Papers, LC; Lyon to John McLean, Jan. 25, 1844, Lyon to Cass, Apr. 6, 1844, and Lyon to Gen. J. Burdick, Mar. 31, 1844, in "Letters of Lyon," 568, 574, 573; Cass to Lyon, Apr. 13, 1844, Lyon Papers, Clements; *Detroit Daily Advertiser,* Mar. 19, 1844; Henry Whiting to H. R. Schoolcraft, Mar. 2, 1844, Schoolcraft Papers, LC.

35. Henry Clay to the editors of the *Daily National Intelligencer,* Apr. 17, 1844, and Martin Van Buren to William H. Hammett, Apr. 20, 1844, in *Niles Weekly Register* 66 (May 4, 1844): 152–57; John C. Calhoun to Richard Pakenham, Apr. 18, 1844, Sen. Doc. No. 341, 28th Cong., 1st sess., 50–51.

36. William B. Lewis to Jackson, Apr. 26, 1844, Jackson Papers, LC; *New York Daily Tribune,* July 18, 1843.

37. Cass to Aaron Hobart, May 6, 1844, Clements; Lucius Lyon to Cass, Apr. 29, May 2, 1844, in "Letters of Lyon," 577–78; Cass to Lyon, May 10, 1844, typewritten transcript, LC.

38. Cass to Edward Hannegan, May 10, 1844, in *Niles Weekly Register* 66 (May 25, 1844): 197; Cass to Robert J. Walker, May 12, 1844, NYHS; Cass to George N. Sanders, May 6, 1844, Sanders Papers, LC. The *Washington Globe* printed Cass's annexation letter on May 16, and the *New York Daily Tribune* carried it two days later; it thereafter appeared in leading western Democratic journals, including the *Detroit Democratic Free Press* (May 20) and the *Cincinnati Enquirer* (May 22).

39. Cass to Lyon, May 11, 12, 1844, LC.

40. Andrew Jackson to Benjamin F. Butler, May 14, 1844, in "Letters of Gideon J. Pillow to James K. Polk, 1844," ed. Jesse S. Reeves, *AHR* 11 (July 1906): 833; Silas Wright to Van Buren, May 20, 1844, Conrad Ten Eyck to Van Buren, May 20, 1844, John C. Rives to Van Buren, May 21, 1844, Henry Gilpin to Van Buren, May 23, 1844, and A. C. Flagg to Van Buren, May 23, 1844, Van Buren Papers, LC; *Washington Globe,* May 4, 1844; Richard C. Bain, *Convention Decisions and Voting Records* (Washington, D.C., 1960), 30–31.

41. Benjamin Butler to Van Buren, May 27, 1844, Van Buren Papers, LC; *Niles Weekly Register* 66 (June 1, 1844): 218–28.

42. John L. O'Sullivan to Van Buren, May 27, 1844, Van Buren Papers, LC.

43. *Niles Weekly Register* 66 (June 1, 1844): 211–15; Daniel Dickinson to his wife, May 27, 1844, in *Speeches, Correspondence, Etc., of the late Daniel S. Dickinson, of New York,* ed. John R. Dickinson, 2 vols. (New York, 1867), 2:369; *New York Daily Tribune,* May 27, 29, 1844.

44. John L. O'Sullivan to Van Buren, May 28, 1844, Van Buren Papers, LC; Beman Brockway, *Fifty Years in Journalism* (Watertown, N.Y., 1891), 64; *Niles Weekly Register* 66 (June 1, 1844): 215–16; *Daily National Intelligencer,* May 29, 1844; James L. English to Cass, Mar. 21, 1844, Clements.

45. *New York Herald,* May 30, 1844; Gideon J. Pillow to Polk, May 28, 1844, *Correspondence of Polk,* 7:158.

46. *Niles Weekly Register* 66 (June 1, 1844): 211, 216–18; Cass to Michigan delegates, May 19, 1844, in Young, *Cass,* 223–24; Lucius Lyon to Cass, May 31, 1844, in "Letters of Lyon," 582; Benjamin Butler to Van Buren, May 31, 1844, Van Buren Papers, LC; Gideon Pillow to Polk, May 29, 1844, in Reeves, "Pillow to Polk," 841–42.

47. [Benton], *Thirty Years' View,* 2:594.

48. Conrad Ten Eyck to Van Buren, Sept. 16, 1840, and James I. Wadsworth to Van Buren, June 1, 1844, Van Buren Papers, LC; Henry C. Whitman to William Allen, May 29, 1844, Allen Papers, LC; Benjamin Butler to Van Buren, May 31, 1844, Van Buren Papers, LC; Lucius Lyon to Cass, May 31, 1844, in "Letters of Lyon," 582–83; Frederick J. Blue, *The Free Soilers: Third Party Politics, 1848–1854* (Urbana, Ill., 1973), 18–19.

49. Anthony Ten Eyck to Van Buren, June 4, 1844, Van Buren Papers, LC; *Charleston Courier* quoted in the *Daily National Intelligencer,* June 24, 1844; Cass to Robert McClelland, June 8, 1844, McClelland Papers, Burton; *Detroit Democratic Free Press,* June 4, 1844.

50. *Detroit Democratic Free Press,* July 1, 5, 1844; Cass to Andrew Jackson Donelson, July 29, 1844, Donelson Papers, LC; Jackson to William B. Lewis, Aug. 15, 1844, in *Correspondence of Jackson,* 6:315; *Nashville Union,* Aug. 17, 1844.

51. *Detroit Democratic Free Press,* Sept. 24, 1844; Cass to Polk, Oct. 4, 1844, Polk Papers, LC; Richard Rush to Cass, Aug. 28, 1844, Clements; Lucius Lyon to P. H. Brown, Dec. 24, 1844, in "Letters of Lyon," 594.

52. Jackson to Polk, Dec. 13, 1844, Polk Papers, LC; Cass to Nathaniel Niles, Nov. 26, 1844, LC; George Sanders to Polk, July 12, 1844, and Austin Wing to Polk, Aug. 2, 1844, Polk Papers, LC.

53. Lucius Lyon to Cass, Dec. 4, 1844, Jan. 28, 1845, in "Letters of Lyon," 593; *Brighton (Michigan) Livingston Courier,* Jan. 29, Feb. 12, 1845; *Detroit Democratic Free Press,* Feb. 4, 5, 1845; *Detroit Daily Advertiser,* Feb. 5, 1845; *Journal of the (Michigan State) Senate* (Detroit, 1845), 90–91; John Tyler to Senators of the United States, Jan. 8, 1845, Clements.

54. Emily Mason to John T. Mason, Jan. 26, 1845, and Catherine Mason to Laura [Mason], Feb. 9, 1845, Mason Papers, Burton; Thomas Rowland to William Woodbridge, Feb. 20, 1845, Woodbridge Papers, Burton; Pierre Margry to Cass, Mar. 14, 1844, Clements.

CHAPTER SIX
United States Senator (1845–1848)

1. *CG,* 28th Cong., 2d sess., 383, 397; *CG,* 29th Cong., 1st sess., 66.

2. Deed from Lewis and Elizabeth Cass to Lewis, Jr., Apr. 8, 1844, Burton; James F. Joy to Charles C. Trowbridge, Oct. 3, 1878, and George Stephens to Trowbridge, Sept. 29, Nov. 6, 1879, Trowbridge Papers, Burton; J. S. Desnoyers to Emily Mason, May 22, 1845, Mason Papers, Burton; last will and testament of Lewis Cass, Jr., Feb. 8, 1878, Burton; *Dubuque Daily Times,* Oct. 1, 1879. Augustus Cass Canfield, a nephew, was co-executor with Emily Mason of the estate of Lewis Cass, Jr. Two children of Major George Browne each received $30,000; other specific bequests ranged up to $10,000. Emily Mason received

Cass's private papers, and his surviving sisters received the remainder of the estate. No mention was made of George Stephens in the will.

3. Francis Parkman, Jr., to Cass, Mar. 19, 1846; Cass to Polk, July 21, 30, 1845; Cass to Marcy, July 21, 1845; Marcy to Cass, July 24, 1845, June 4, 1846, Jan. 27, 1848; Jerome Napoleon Bonaparte to Cass, Jan. 18, 1846; Cass to Cave Johnson, Aug. 15, 1845; Cass to Robert J. Walker, Sept. 24, 1845, May 25, 1847; Simon Cameron to Cass, Jan. 6, 1846; and George Bancroft to Cass, May 29, 1846, all in Clements.

4. Cass to Hobart, Mar. 10, Oct. 10, Nov. 21, 1845, Jan. 28, Feb. 3, 28, 1846, and Cass to Rush, Oct. 27, 1845, Clements; Alexander Hamilton Buel to John Sherman Bagg, Feb. 17, 1845, Bagg Papers, Huntington. Cass voted against the confirmation of Marcus Morton and Silas Wright.

5. Cass to Hobart, Mar. 1, 1845, Clements; Polk's annual message, Dec. 2, 1845, in Richardson, *Messages of the Presidents,* 4:387; Kirk H. Porter and Donald Bruce Johnson, comps., *National Party Platforms: 1840–1960,* 2d ed. (Urbana, Ill., 1961), 4.

6. Streeter, *Political Parties,* 69–71, 76; *CG,* 28th Cong., 2d sess., 194, 362.

7. Polk's inaugural address, Mar. 4, 1845, and Polk's message, Dec. 2, 1845, in Richardson, *Messages of the Presidents,* 4:38, 395–98; *Diary of Polk,* 1:109–10.

8. [Cass], *Oration at Fort Wayne,* 3–4; Cass to T. Worthington, Mar. 4, 1844, Huntington.

9. *CG,* 29th Cong., 1st sess., 30, 45–47; *Niles Weekly Register* 69 (Dec. 27, 1845): 258.

10. Cass to Dutee Jerould Pearce, Dec. 23, 1845, Clements; *CG,* 29th Cong., 1st sess., 47.

11. *CG,* 29th Cong., 1st sess., 48–60.

12. *New York Daily Tribune,* Dec. 22, 1845; Daniel Mallory to Willie P. Mangum, Dec. 22, 1845, in *The Papers of Willie Person Mangum,* ed. Henry Thomas Shanks, 5 vols. (Raleigh, N.C., 1950–56), 4:341.

13. *CG,* 29th Cong., 1st sess., 101, 113, 267, 337, 339, 541.

14. Resolution of the Michigan Legislature, Feb. 20, 1845, Woodbridge Papers, Burton; *Detroit Daily Advertiser,* Dec. 23, 1845; petition from Charles Fletcher to Cass, undated, Clements; Cass to Alpheus Felch, Feb. 6, 1846, Felch Papers, Burton.

15. *CG,* 29th Cong., 1st sess., 75–76, 351–57, 370–74, 415–19, 432, 436–37, 443–48.

16. *Diary of Polk,* 1:154, 265; *CG,* 29th Cong., 1st sess., 378–82, 456, 502–6, 577–78, 604–7, 667–68 (in printing the full text of Cass's speech, the *Congressional Globe* incorrectly dated it as March 30: app., 422–30).

17. Christian F. Eckloff, *Memoirs of a Senate Page (1855–1859),* ed. Percival G. Melbourne (New York, 1909), 31; *Niles Weekly Register* 70 (Apr. 4, 1846): 65.

18. *CG,* 29th Cong., 1st sess., 577–78, and app., 422–30; Currente Calamo to editor of the *Detroit Daily Advertiser,* Mar. 12, 1853; Smith, *Cass,* 518–68; Young, *Cass,* 235–92.

19. *CG,* 29th Cong., 1st sess., 583–84.

20. Ibid., 587–91; Howell Cobb to his wife, Apr. 3, 1846, in "The Correspondence of Robert Toombs, Alexander H. Stephens, and Howell Cobb," ed. Ulrich B. Phillips, *Annual Report of the American Historical Association for the Year 1911,* 2:75.

21. *CG,* 29th Cong., 1st sess., 680–83, 691, 716, 721; *Diary of Polk,* 1:345, 280, 268, 139, 147, 151–55, 462–63.

22. Cass to Hobart, Apr. 27, June 20, Sept. 2, Oct. 5, 1846, Clements; Cass to Franklin Pearce [*sic*], Sept. 2, 1846, Pierce Papers, LC; Cass to Robert McClelland, Sept. 4, 21, 1846, McClelland Papers, Burton; Cass to A. O. P. Nicholson, Sept. 22, 1846, NYHS; Cass to Seth P. Beers, Sept. 21, 1846, LC; Cass to Samuel Treat, Nov. 7, 1846, photostatic copy of original from Missouri Historical Society, in Burton; *Diary of Polk,* 1:462–63, 465–66, 470–72; *Substance of a Speech Delivered by Hon. Lewis Cass, of Michigan, in Secret Session of the Senate of the United States, on the Ratification of the Oregon Treaty, with Additions* (Detroit, 1846);

George Bancroft to Louis McLane, June 23, 1846, in M. A. DeWolfe Howe, *The Life and Letters of George Bancroft,* 2 vols. (New York, 1908), 1:285. David Atchison (Missouri) and James Wescott (Florida) voted against ratification of the Oregon treaty.

23. *Diary of Polk,* 1:110; Gideon Welles to Van Buren, July 28, 1846, Van Buren Papers, LC.

24. Parrott quoted in Eugene Irving McCormac, *James K. Polk: A Political Biography* (1922; reprint, Berkeley, Calif., 1965), 352–72, 383–407; Joel Poinsett to Van Buren, May 26, 1846, Van Buren Papers, LC; *Diary of Polk,* 1:33–35.

25. Marcy to Taylor, July 30, Aug. 23, 30, 1845, in House Exec. Doc. No. 60, 30th Cong., 1st sess., 82–89.

26. Cass to Joel Poinsett, May 1, 1846, Poinsett Papers, HSP; *Diary of Polk,* 1:305–13, 372.

27. *Diary of Polk,* 354, 382, 384–85.

28. Ibid., 387–91.

29. *CG,* 29th Cong., 1st sess., 783–88.

30. Ibid., 795–803; *Washington Union,* May 29, 1846 (punctuation altered). Senators Thomas Clayton of Delaware (a cousin of John Clayton) and John Davis of Massachusetts voted nay. Two other Whigs, John Berrien of Georgia and George Evans of Maine, were present but abstained from voting, as did Calhoun. The House of Representatives passed the original declaration of war bill by a vote of 174 to 14. The House vote on the final bill was 117 to 50. All three Michigan congressmen voted in favor of both bills. *CG,* 29th Cong., 1st sess., 795, 810.

31. *Diary of Polk,* 2:271–76.

32. Lewis Cass, Jr., to Lewis Cass, Apr. 13, 1848, Clements.

33. *Diary of Polk,* 2:180–86.

34. Ibid., 56–57.

35. *CG,* 29th Cong., 1st sess., 1211, 1217–18, 1220–21. Michigan Democrat John Chipman voted against the proviso, but his two Democratic colleagues, Robert McClelland and James Hunt, supported it.

36. George Rathbun speech to the delegates of the Utica, New York, Democratic convention of February 1848, in O. C. Gardiner, *The Great Issue: Or, the Three Presidential Candidates; Being a Brief Historical Sketch of the Free Soil Question in the United States, from the Congresses of 1774, and '87 to the Present Time* (1848; reprint ed., Westport, Conn., 1970), 94; Cass to W. J. Brown, Sept. 16, 1848, Franklin Elmore Papers, LC; *CG,* 31st Cong., 1st sess., 398.

37. *Diary of Polk,* 2:75, 291–92.

38. *CG,* 29th Cong., 2d sess., 325–26; Cass to Alpheus Felch, Feb. 4, 1847, Felch Papers, Burton; Cass to Robert S. Wilson, Feb. 19, 1847, in *Chicago Daily Journal,* Aug. 31, 1848.

39. *CG,* 29th Cong., 2d sess., 356–57, 367–75, and app., 189–96, 323–27, 367–68; Young, *Cass,* 303–18; Smith, *Cass,* 585–99.

40. *CG,* 29th Cong., 2d sess., 211, 216–18; *New York Daily Tribune,* Feb. 12, 1847.

41. *CG,* 29th Cong., 2d sess., 541–56. The twenty-one senators favoring the Upham amendment, with the exception of John Clayton of Delaware, were from northern states; seven were Democrats. Thirty-one opposed the amendment, with Cass joining four other northerners. The House also passed the Three Million bill unencumbered by a Wilmot amendment.

42. Ibid., 540, 555–56; *CG,* 29th Cong., 1st sess., 1217–18; *Charleston Mercury,* June 26, 1847.

43. *Detroit Daily Advertiser,* Mar. 11, 12, 1847; *New York Daily Tribune,* Mar. 3, 1847.

44. Jefferson Davis to Stephen Cocke, Nov. 30, 1847, in *Jefferson Davis, Constitutionalist: His Letters, Papers and Speeches,* ed. Dunbar Rowland, 10 vols. (Jackson, Miss., 1923), 1:180–81.

45. *Washington Daily Union* Dec. 30, 1847; *[Nicholson] Letter from Hon. Lewis Cass, of Michigan, on the War and the Wilmot Proviso* (Washington, D.C., 1847); *CG,* 29th Cong., 2d sess., 124, 354, 444, and app., 242; *CG,* 30th Cong., 1st sess., 27. The original Nicholson letter is not known to exist; it was reprinted in Democratic newspapers and published in pamphlet form. The term "popular sovereignty" did not come into general use until the debate over the Kansas-Nebraska bill in 1854.

46. *[Nicholson] Letter,* 2–5; *Washington Daily Union,* Dec. 30, 1847; Young, *Cass,* 320–27; Smith, *Cass,* 607–16; *U.S. Constitution,* art. 4, sec. 3.

47. *CG,* 30th Cong., 1st sess., 21, 63, 74–90, 111–14, 150, 183–84, 214–16, 485–95, 503, 593, 648. The Ten Regiment bill passed the Senate shortly after the peace treaty with Mexico was ratified; more than a month later, Cass was still advocating passage of the volunteer bill.

48. James Buchanan to General Shields, Apr. 23, 1847, in *The Works of James Buchanan: Comprising his Speeches, State Papers, and Private Correspondence,* ed. John Bassett Moore, 12 vols. (Philadelphia, 1908–11), 7:287 ("mongrel race" was Buchanan's phrase); *CG,* 30th Cong., 1st sess., 79, 114, 215, 220.

49. John M. Niles to Van Buren, Jan. 20, 1848, Van Buren Papers, LC; *CG,* 30th Cong., 1st sess., 136; Stephens quoted in *Recollections of Alexander Hamilton Stephens,* ed. Myrta Lockett Avary (New York, 1910), 19.

50. *Diary of Polk,* 3:309–11, 344–50.

51. Ibid., 430, 436; *CG,* 30th Cong., 1st sess., 709, 727.

52. *CG,* 30th Cong., 1st sess., 754, 591–610, and app., 591; Sen. Doc. No. 52, 30th Cong., 1st sess., 7:36. Mississippi senators Henry Foote and Jefferson Davis called for the United States to control the gulf.

CHAPTER SEVEN
Democratic Presidential Candidate (1848)

1. Cass to Andrew T. McReynolds, Dec. 26, 1846, Clements; *Diary of Polk,* 2:368, 3:319–21.

2. *New York Daily Tribune,* Feb. 5, 1848; *Boston Atlas* quoted in *Detroit Daily Advertiser,* Jan. 17, 1848.

3. *New York Daily Tribune,* May 24, 1848; *Diary of Polk,* 3:335.

4. *CG,* 29th Cong., 2d sess., 455.

5. Buchanan to Charles Kessler et al., Aug. 25, 1847, in *Works of Buchanan,* 17:385–87; Dallas speech in *Washington Daily Union* Sept. 24, 1847.

6. Although McLean later changed his views, Cass remained convinced the Constitution did not confer upon Congress the power to regulate slavery in the territories. Don E. Fehrenbacher, *The Dred Scott Case: Its Significance in American Law and Politics* (New York, 1978), 142–43; *Daily National Intelligencer,* Dec. 22, 1847.

7. R. J. Moses to Cass, May 19, 1848, in *Savannah Republican,* reprinted by *Chicago Daily Democrat,* Oct. 2, 1848 (emphasis added). It was not until a Senate debate on June 3, 1850, that Cass plainly stated the inhabitants had the authority to decide the question of slavery while forming a territorial government. *CG,* 31st Cong., 1st sess., 1120.

8. *Charleston Mercury,* Jan. 6, 17, 1848.

9. *St. Lawrence Republican and Advertiser* and *Buffalo Republican,* Jan. 7, 1848, in *New York Weekly Tribune,* May 6, 1848; *Brooklyn Daily Eagle and Kings County Democrat,* Jan. 3, 1848, in *The Gathering of the Forces: Editorials, Essays, Literary and Dramatic Reviews and Other Materials Written by Walt Whitman as Editor of the Brooklyn Daily Eagle in 1846 and 1847,* ed. Cleveland Rodgers and John Black, 2 vols. (New York, 1920), 1:227–28; George Griswold to Alpheus Felch, Jan. 16, Feb. 27, Mar. 26, 1848, Jacob Howard to Felch, Jan. 17,

1848, Hunt to Felch, Jan. 24, 1848, and Cooper to Felch, Jan. 28, 1848, Felch Papers, MHC; Buchanan to John M. Reed, Jan. 18, 1848, Buchanan Papers, HSP.

10. *Daily Albany Argus,* Jan. 4, 1848; *New Haven Columbian Register,* reprinted by *Illinois State Register,* Feb. 11, 1848, in Joseph G. Rayback, *Free Soil: The Election of 1848* (Lexington, Ky., 1970), 120; *Detroit Free Press,* Jan. 21, 1848; Luther J. Glenn to Howell Cobb, Feb. 12, 1848, in Phillips, "Toombs, Stephens, Cobb," 96; *Tallahassee Floridian,* Jan. 15, 1848; *Richmond Enquirer,* in *Detroit Free Press,* Jan. 21, 1848; *Washington Daily Union* Dec. 30, 1847; Rodgers and Black, *Gathering of the Forces,* xxx–xxxi; *Athens (Ga.) Southern Banner,* Apr. 20, 1848; *Montgomery Tri-Weekly Flag and Advertiser,* Jan. 15, 1848.

11. Cass to J. H. Harmon, Dec. 29, 1847, Bagg Papers, Huntington.

12. Calhoun to Thomas G. Clemson, July 24, 1847, in "Correspondence of John C. Calhoun," ed. J. Franklin Jameson, *Annual Report of the American Historical Association for the Year 1899,* 2:735; Cass to Disney, Sept. 20, 1847, Burton; Cass to Hobart, Dec. 3, 1847, Clements.

13. *Detroit Free Press,* Mar. 16, 1848; *Philadelphia Ledger,* in *Detroit Free Press,* Mar. 20, 1848; *Baltimore Sun,* Jan. 12, 1848; *Philadelphia Pennsylvanian,* Mar. 6, May 22, 1848.

14. *Lincoln (County, N.C.) Courier,* in *St. Louis Union,* Mar. 24, 1848; A. H. H. Clapp to Levi Woodbury, May 10, 17, 18, 1848, John D. Kellogg to Woodbury, May 11, 1848, Nehemiah Moses to Woodbury, Mar. 23, 1848, Richard Jenness to Woodbury, May 15, 1848, J. E. Dow to Woodbury, May 17, 1848, J. M. Brodhead to Woodbury, May 13, 1848, Asa Whitney to Woodbury, May 13, 1848, and William Yancey to Woodbury, Mar. 10, 1848, Woodbury Papers, LC; *New Hampshire Patriot & State Gazette,* Apr. 6, 1848; *Montgomery Tri-Weekly Advertiser,* Feb. 17, 1848. In addition to the states mentioned in the text, Buchanan was particularly strong in New Jersey, Delaware, Maryland, North Carolina, and Virginia; Woodbury in Alabama, Georgia, Florida, and South Carolina.

15. Samuel Medary to Van Buren, Dec. 27, 1847, Van Buren Papers, LC; *Clark County Democrat,* in *Detroit Free Press,* Jan. 24, 1848; J. A. Potter to Felch, Dec. 30, 1847, Felch Papers, MHC; *New York Evening Post,* Jan. 28, 1848; *Detroit Daily Advertiser,* Jan. 19, 1848; *Ohio State Journal,* Jan. 10, 1848.

16. George R. Griswold to Felch, Jan. 16, Feb. 13, 27, Mar. 26, 1848, and H. Stone to Felch, Feb. 14, 1848, Felch Papers, MHC; *Chicago Daily Democrat,* May 4, 1848; Richard M. Johnson to Cass, Apr. 21, 1848, Clements.

17. *Jackson Mississippian,* Mar. 24, 1848; Alpheus Felch to his wife, May 22, 1848, Felch Papers, MHC.

18. *Albany Atlas,* Oct. 4, 1847; Stone to Alpheus Felch, Feb. 14, 1848, Felch Papers, MHC.

19. *New York Daily Tribune,* May 23, 24, 1848; Alpheus Felch to his wife, May 22, 1848, Felch Papers, MHC.

20. *New York Daily Tribune,* May 24, 1848.

21. Frederick W. Seward, *[William Henry] Seward at Washington, as Senator and Secretary of State: A Memoir of his Life, with Selections from his Letters, 1846–1861* (New York, 1891), 68.

22. *The Proceedings of the Democratic National Convention, Held at Baltimore, May 22, 1848* (Washington, D.C., [1848]), 1–18; *Baltimore Sun,* May 22, 25, 26, 1848.

23. *New York Daily Tribune,* May 27, 1848; *Proceedings of the Democratic Convention, 1848,* 18–28.

24. *Weekly Wisconsin,* May 31, 1848.

25. *Charleston Mercury,* June 2, May 30, 1848; *Milledgeville Southern Recorder,* May 30, 1848; *Nashville Republican Banner,* May 31, 1848.

26. *Chicago Daily Journal,* May 27, 1848; *Rochester Daily Advertiser,* May 30, 1848; *Racine Advocate,* May 31, June 28, 1848.

27. Alpheus Felch to his wife, May 25, 1848, Felch Papers, Burton; *Diary of Polk,* 3:463; *North Carolina Standard,* May 31, 1848; *Cleveland Daily Plain Dealer,* May 26, 1848; *Buffalo Daily Courier,* May 26, 27, 1848; *Brooklyn Daily Eagle and Kings County Democrat,* May 26, 1848; *Cincinnati Daily Enquirer,* May 27, 1848; *Detroit Free Press,* May 27, 1848; *Savannah Georgian,* June 8, 1848; *Richmond Enquirer,* May 26, 27, June 2, 1848.

28. *Life of General Lewis Cass,* 143–49; Alpheus Felch to his wife, June 3, 1848, Felch Papers, MHC; *Diary of Polk,* 3:470–81.

29. *New York Daily Tribune,* June 8, 1848; *Baltimore Sun,* June 9, 1848; *CG,* 30th Cong., 1st sess., 792; *Campaign* 1 (May 31, 1848): 1; *Philadelphia Pennsylvanian,* June 7, 1848, in *Daily Albany Argus,* June 10, 1848; *Washington Daily Union* June 10, 1848.

30. *Brooklyn Daily Eagle and Kings County Democrat,* June 10, 1848; Welles to ——, May 26, 1848, Welles Papers, LC; *New York Daily Tribune,* June 9, 13, 1848; *Daily Albany Argus,* June 12, 1848; *Washington Daily Union* June 20, 1848; *Buffalo Daily Courier,* June 14, 1848; *Cleveland Daily Plain Dealer,* June 15, 1848; *Cincinnati Weekly Herald,* June 28, 1848.

31. *Detroit Free Press,* June 17, 1848; C. C. Jackson to Alpheus Felch, June 17, 1848, Felch Papers, MHC; *Detroit Daily Advertiser,* June 17, 1848.

32. *Chicago Daily Journal,* June 6, 1848; *Chicago Gem of the Prairie,* June 3, 1848; A. T. Burnley to John Crittenden, Dec. 12, 1847, Crittenden Papers, LC; *A Sketch of the Life and Character of Gen. Taylor, The American Hero and People's Man; Together with a Concise History of the Mexican War, . . . By the One-Legged Sergeant* (New York, 1847), 12; *Niles Weekly Register* 72 (Apr. 17, 1848): 112.

33. Zachary Taylor to Robert Crooke Wood, Aug. 4, Dec. 10, 1846, Sept. 27, 1847, Feb. 18, 1848, in *Letters of Zachary Taylor from the Battlefields of the Mexican War: Reprinted from the Originals in the Collection of Mr. William K. Bixby, of St. Louis, Mo.,* ed. William H. Samson (Rochester, N.Y., 1908), 35, 76, 134, 154; Taylor to John S. Allison, Apr. 22, 1848, in Holman Hamilton, *Zachary Taylor, Soldier in the White House,* 2 vols. (Indianapolis, Ind., 1951), 2:79–81. In a letter dated September 27, 1847, Taylor stated: "I would have voted for Mr. Clay at the last election, had I voted at all, which I have never done for any one of our chief magistrates since I entered the army or before, which is near forty years." *Letters of Taylor,* 134.

34. A. T. Burnley to John J. Crittenden, Dec. 12, 1847, Crittenden Papers, LC.

35. *Racine Advocate,* June 14, 1848.

36. *Charles Sumner: His Complete Works,* ed. George Frisbie Hoar, 20 vols. (1900; rept.; New York, 1969), 2:233; *Niles Weekly Register* 74 (July 5, 1848): 8–9. The estimated figure of four hundred delegates to the People's Convention is taken from the *Niles* issue cited. The *Chillicothe (Ohio) Scioto Gazette* of June 28, a Taylor organ, estimated "about 150" attended; while Frederick J. Blue puts the figure at "over one thousand" (*Free Soilers,* 55). Although few Liberty party members (and fewer Democrats) attended the Worcester convention, the delegation to Buffalo was evenly proportioned in an effort to appeal to free soilers of all parties.

37. *New York Herald,* June 1, 7, 1848.

38. Thomas Hart Benton to Cass, [June 1848], Clements; Benton to Van Buren, May 29, 1848, and Benjamin Butler to Van Buren, May 29, 1848, Van Buren Papers, LC.

39. Martin Van Buren letter to the Utica convention, in *New York Herald,* June 25, 1848; Dodge to Alpheus Felch, June 15, 1848, Felch Papers, MHC.

40. *Diary of Polk,* 3:502; *Cincinnati Daily Enquirer,* July 4, 1848; Cass to Henry Hubbard, July 29, 1848, NYHS; *New York Herald,* May 26, 1848.

41. *Oliver Dyer's Phonographic Report of the Proceedings of the National Free Soil Convention at Buffalo, N.Y.: August 9th and 10th, 1848* (Buffalo, [1848]), 7–12, 27–32. Some estimates placed the number present at the Buffalo convention at forty thousand.

42. Porter and Johnson, *Party Platforms,* 13–14; Richard Henry Dana, Jr., *Speeches in Stirring Times and Letters to a Son,* ed. Richard Henry Dana III (Boston, 1910), 149–63.

43. Leavitt quoted in Blue, *Free Soilers,* 76–78; Richard Henry Dana, Jr., *The Journal of Richard Henry Dana, Jr.,* ed. Robert F. Lucid, 3 vols. (Cambridge, Mass., 1968), 1:347–55; journal of Richard Henry Dana, Jr., Aug. 10, 1848, MHS; Benjamin Stanton to Samuel Lewis and Salmon Chase, [July 3], 1848, and Charles Sumner to Chase, July 7, 1848, Chase Papers, LC; Chase to John McLean, Aug. 2, 1848, McLean Papers, LC. *Dyer's Report* (32) records the informal poll of the 466 conferees as follows: Van Buren, 244; Hale, 183; Giddings, 23; Charles F. Adams, 13; and William Ellsworth, 3. Dana states that Van Buren received 244 votes and Hale 181, with 41 scattering (Dana journal, MHS).

44. *Dyer's Report,* 27, 32; *Diary of Polk,* 4:67; Dana, *Speeches in Stirring Times,* 159–63.

CHAPTER EIGHT
The Presidential Election of 1848

1. Reuben Davis, *Recollections of Mississippi and Mississippians* (Boston, 1890), 293–94; John Y. Mason to Cass, Sept. 25, 1848, Clements; Cass to W. J. Brown, Sept. 16, 1848, Franklin H. Elmore Papers, LC.

2. E. M. P. Rose, *The Poetry of Locofocism; or Modern Democracy and Cassism Unmasked, A Political and Personal Poem Containing 275 Stanzas* (Wellsburgh, Va., 1848), 20, 40; *St. Louis Reveille,* in *Milledgeville Southern Recorder,* Nov. 7, 1848; *Chicago Daily Journal,* Sept. 15, 1848.

3. *Campaign,* July 19, Aug. 30, Sept. 6, Oct. 11, 1848; *Hickory Sprout,* Nov. 4, 1848, Clements.

4. Hamilton, *Taylor,* 2:129–30.

5. Holman Hamilton, "Election of 1848," *History of American Presidential Elections to 1968,* ed. Arthur M. Schlessinger, Jr., and Fred L. Israel, 4 vols. (New York, 1971), 886–91.

6. *Sketch of Gen. Lewis Cass* (Globe Office), 8; [Schoolcraft], *Life of Cass,* 63.

7. Porter and Johnson, *Party Platforms,* 10–11; *Detroit Free Press,* July 22, 1848; Cass to the Democratic Convention of 1848, in Young, *Cass,* 360–62.

8. Porter and Johnson, *Party Platforms,* 14–15; *Gen. Taylor's Moral, Intellectual, & Professional Character*... [1848], 2; *Reasons Good and True for Supporting the Nomination of General Zachary Taylor* [1848]; *A Sketch of the Life and Public Services of Gen. Zachary Taylor, the People's Candidate for the Presidency, with Considerations in Favor of His Election* (Washington, D.C., 1848), 29; Truman Smith to Alexander H. Stephens, Oct. 2, 1848, Stephens Papers, LC; [Daniel D. Barnard], "The Whigs and Their Candidate," *AWR* 8 (Sept. 1848): 222.

9. *CG,* 30th Cong., 1st sess., 975; William S. Brown to Alpheus Felch, July 22, 1848, Felch Papers, MHC; [James Russell Lowell], *The Biglow Papers, Edited, with an Introduction, Notes, Glossary, and Copious Index by Homer Wilbur, A.M.* . . . (Cambridge, Mass., 1848), 91; *Ohio Watchman,* in *Tallahassee Floridian,* July 29, 1848; *Campaign,* July 12, 19, 26, Aug. 2, 9, 1848.

10. *Tallahassee Floridian,* July 29, 1848; Hamilton, *Taylor,* 2:117–18; Zachary Taylor to John Crittenden, Sept. 23, 1848, Taylor Papers, NYHS; *Washington Daily Union* July 23, 1848; *Campaign,* Aug. 2, Oct. 27, 1848.

11. *Detroit Free Press,* reprinted in *Campaign,* Aug. 23, 1848; *Taylor Whig[g]ery Exposed,* [1848], 3; *Reasons Good and True,* 8; [Lowell], *Biglow Papers,* 147; *General Taylor: A Buyer of Men & Women!* [1848].

12. *Jackson Mississippian,*, Oct. 6, 20, 1848; Arthur Charles Cole, *The Whig Party in the South* (Washington, D.C., 1914), 132 (punctuation altered); Millard Fillmore to W. Mills, Oct. 17, 1838, in *Address of the National Democratic Republican Committee. Millard Fillmore, Proved to be an Abolitionist! General Taylor, Probably Pledged to the Whigs of the North, in*

Favor of the Wilmot Proviso [Washington, D.C., 1848], 3–4; *Jefferson City (Mo.) Inquirer,* Oct. 7, 1848; *Campaign,* Sept. 6, 13, 20, 1848.

13. F. A. Durivage, "The Soldier's Reply to the Whig Appeal for his Vote," in *Boston Daily Times,* reprinted in *Campaign,* July 12, 1848; *Vincennes Western Sun and General Advertiser,* Aug. 12, Sept. 30, 1848; *The Executive Committee of the 7th Ward, Cass and Butler Club, in Washington City, Submit the following Extracts to the consideration of the people, and respectfully ask the candid of all parties to give them a careful perusal* [1848], 1; untitled circular published under the authority of the National and Jackson Democratic Association Committee [1848], 4.

14. *New York Mirror,* in *Detroit Daily Advertiser,* Jan. 19, 1848; *Address Adopted by the Whig State Convention, at Worcester, September 13, 1848* [Worcester, Mass., 1848], 7; Rose, *Poetry,* 35; *Diary of Hone,* 854; *The Cass Platform* [Washington, D.C., 1848], 4–7.

15. Alpheus Felch to his wife, Jan. 16, 1848, Felch Papers, MHC; *Battery,* July 6, Aug. 3, 1848; *Boston Post,* July 12, 1848; *Remarks of General Lewis Cass, on the Late French Revolution, Delivered at a Public Meeting held in Odd-Fellows Hall, in the City of Washington, March 28, 1848* [Washington, D.C., 1848].

16. *Cass Platform,* 6; *Battery,* July 6, Sept. 28, 1848; Rose, *Poetry,* 26; *Campaign,* Aug. 2, 9, 1848; *Address of the Democratic Republican Young Men's General Committee, of the City of New-York, to the Republican Young Men of the State* (1840); *The Grape-Shot,* July 27, 1848.

17. [Barnard], "The Whigs," 225; *Boston Atlas,* July 31, 1848, in Rayback, *Free Soil,* 235; Rose, *Poetry,* 19; Taylor to John Crittenden, Sept. 23, 1848, Taylor Papers, NYHS; *Address of the Young Men's Committee.* In a letter to a political adviser, dated September 4, 1848, Taylor reiterated his opposition "to the further annexation of Mexican territory . . . beyond the lower Rio Grande and the Compromise line of 36°30'." Taylor to John M. Clayton, Clayton Papers, LC.

18. John Lewis Peyton, *Over the Alleghanies and Across the Prairies. Personal Recollections of the Far West One and Twenty Years Ago* (London, 1870), 159; *Washington Daily Union* Aug. 1, 1848; *Campaign,* Aug. 2, 9, 1848; *Detroit Free Press,* July 13, 1848; *CG,* 30th Cong., 1st sess., 754.

19. "The Brave Old Volunteer," in *Campaign,* June 21, 1848; *Battery,* July 6, 1848; *Indiana State Journal,* July 31, Aug. 7, 1848.

20. *CG,* 30th Cong., 1st sess., app., 1042; *Grape-Shot,* July 13, Sept. 16, 1848.

21. Thomas B. King address at Paterson, N.J., quoted by Robert Smith to Thomas S. Jesup, in *Campaign,* Oct. 4, 1848.

22. *Rochester Courier,* quoted in Untitled Circular, 4; *Detroit Daily Advertiser,* July 24, 1848; C. B. Flood to Alpheus Felch, June 19, 1848, Felch Papers, MHC.

23. *Evansville Democrat,* July 12, Aug. 15, 19, Sept. 1, 1848; Lew Wallace, *An Autobiography,* 2 vols. (New York, 1906), 1:201–5; *(Indiana) State Sentinel,* Jan. 11, June 21, Sept. 14, 27, Oct. 11, 1848; Taylor to Defrees, Mar. 3, 1848, in *Perrysville Eagle,* Apr. 8, 1848.

24. *Campaign,* July 26, 1848; [Thomas Prentice Kettell], "The Election," *DR* 23 (1848): 287n.

25. *CG,* 30th Cong., 1st sess., app., 779–83, 1041–43; Hamilton, "Election of 1848," 886. The figures presented by the opposition as extra allowances to Cass varied greatly. Stewart fixed upon $60,412; one campaign document placed the amount at $96,412; while the Detroit Whig organ claimed Cass received precisely $234,231.49 in salary and allowances during his thirty-six years of public service. *CG,* 30th Cong., 1st sess., app., 1043; *Cass Platform,* 1; *Detroit Daily Advertiser,* Oct. 4, 1848.

26. *Campaign,* June 14, July 12, 13, 20, Sept. 27, Oct. 25, 27, 1848; *Allowances and Extra Pay. A Plain Statement of Facts from the Record, Showing Gen. Taylor to Have Received $74,864 of "Allowances," Besides His Regular Pay, and General Cass to Have Received Not One Cent,*

Except for Actual Services Rendered the Government [Washington, D.C., 1848]; Untitled Circular, 7–8; *A Refutation of Andrew Stewart's Fabrication Against General Lewis Cass* [1848].

27. Porter and Johnson, *Party Platforms*, 3; Richardson, *Messages of the Presidents*, 4:460–66; E. Starr to J. D. Doty, May 9, 1840, in House Exec. Doc. No. 236, 26th Cong., 1st sess., 6:6. Colonel John J. Abert presented the hundred million dollar estimate of the lake trade in the "Annual Report of the Chief of the Corps of Topographical Engineers," House Exec. Doc. No. 2, 29th Cong., 1st sess., 1:297. Seven northwestern Democrats abstained from voting on the improvements bill in 1846, and only three (two from Illinois and one from Indiana) opposed it.

28. *Chicago River and Harbor Convention: An Account of Its Origins and Proceedings by William Mosley Hull, John Wentworth, Samuel Lisle Smith, Horace Greeley, Thurlow Weed; together with Statistics Concerning Chicago; By Jesse B. Thomas, and James L. Barton,* comp. Robert Fergus, (Chicago, 1882), 15–17; *New York Daily Tribune,* July 14, 1847; *New York Herald,* July 8, 12, 1847; *Weekly Chicago Democrat,* July 6, 13, 1847; *Chicago Daily Democrat,* July 9, 1847; "The Chicago Convention," *AWR* 6 (1847): 111–14. Delegations to the Chicago convention represented Connecticut, Florida, Georgia, Indiana, Illinois, Iowa, Kentucky, Maine, Massachusetts, Michigan, Missouri, New Hampshire, New Jersey, New York, Ohio, Pennsylvania, Rhode Island, South Carolina, and Wisconsin. Fergus, *Chicago Convention,* 52–68.

29. Cass to W. L. Whiting, May 17, 1847, in Smith, *Cass,* 622; "Chicago Convention," 118; *New York Herald,* July 14, 1847; *New York Tribune,* July 14, 15, 1847; *Albany Evening Journal,* July 13, 1847; Fergus, *Chicago Convention.*

30. Porter and Johnson, *Party Platforms*, 14–15; Taylor to John S. Allison, Apr. 22, 1848, in Hamilton, *Taylor,* 2:80; *Perrysville (Ind.) Eagle,* June 3, 1848; *Indiana State Journal,* July 3, 1848; *Philadelphia North American and United States Gazette,* June 20, 1848; Rose, *Poetry*, 25; *CG,* 30th Cong., 1st sess., 883, 966.

31. *Cleveland Herald,* June 15, 1848, in *Cincinnati Weekly Herald,* June 28, 1848; *Campaign,* June 28, 1848.

32. *Detroit Daily Advertiser,* June 24, 1848; *Chillicothe (Ohio) Scioto Gazette,* July 5, 1848; Rose, *Poetry*, 32; *Battery*, Aug. 3, 10, 1848; *Indiana State Journal,* June 26, 1848; *CG,* 30th Cong., 1st sess., 883, 893, 899, 966–67, and app., 780, 1041. Caleb B. Smith of Indiana and Robert C. Schenck of Ohio were two Whig speakers who sardonically referred to "noise and confusion" within the House chambers. *CG,* 30th Cong., 1st sess., 966.

33. *Campaign,* Aug. 2, 1848; *Boston Post,* Oct. 31, 1848; *CG,* 30th Cong., 1st sess., 899, 966; *Indiana State Sentinel,* Sept. 20, 1848.

34. *Indiana State Sentinel,* Sept. 20, 1848; *Detroit Free Press,* June 28, 1848.

35. *CG,* 29th Cong., 1st sess., 93, 101, 113, 743–44, 752, 1013, 1084, 1116–17, 1123, 1136.

36. James Simmons address to the Senate, July 28, 1846, in *CG,* 29th Cong., 1st sess., 1158; John Davis to A. H. Bullock et al., June 23, 1848, in *Reasons Good and True,* 1; William H. Seward, Oct. 15, 1848, address to Boston Whigs, and address to New York Whig meeting, Oct. 5, 1848, in *The Works of William H. Seward,* ed. George E. Baker, 3 vols. (New York, 1853), 3:288, 303; Gideon Welles to Martin Van Buren, July 28, 1846, Van Buren Papers, LC. Spencer Jarnagin of Tennessee, following state legislative instructions, was the only Whig to support the Walker Tarriff. Three Democrats—Simon Cameron and Daniel Sturgeon of Pennsylvania and John M. Niles of Connecticut—voted against the Walker bill.

37. *Detroit Free Press,* July 27, 1848; *Washington Daily Union* Oct. 18, 1848; *Weekly Chicago Democrat,* Sept. 5, 1848.

38. *Philadelphia Pennsylvanian,* Oct. 26, 1848, in Rayback, *Free Soil,* 262; *Boston Post,* June 15, 1848; Robert Rantoul quoted by *New Haven Daily Register,* Oct. 20, 1848, reprinted in *Washington Daily Union* Oct. 28, 1848.

39. Cass to Henry Foote, Sept. 18, 1848, Clements; "The Wilmot Proviso," *DR* 23 (1848): 219–26; *Richmond Enquirer*, June 6, 1848, and *Louisville Democrat,* Sept. 28, 1848, in Rayback, *Free Soil,* 242–43; Cass to W. J. Brown, Sept. 16, 1848, Franklin H. Elmore Papers, LC.

40. *CG,* 30th Cong., 1st sess., app., 1042; *Indiana State Journal,* July 3, 1848; [Cass], *Examination,* 47.

41. *CG,* 30th Cong., 1st sess., 889, 974; Taylor to Allison, Apr. 22, 1848, in Hamilton, *Taylor,* 2:80.

42. *Cincinnati Morning Signal,* Apr. 13, 1847; Zachary Taylor to James W. Taylor, May 18, 1847, in *Niles Weekly Register* 72 (July 3, 10, 1847): 288, 295; *General Taylor's Two Faces* (Washington, D.C., 1848), 1–7; *Aberdeen Whig,* in [John Calvin Adams], *General Taylor and the Wilmot Proviso* [Boston, 1848]; *Facts for those who will understand them. Gen Cass's Position on the Slavery Question Defined by Himself and His Friends . . .* [1848], 1–5; *Cass Platform,* 8; *Campaign,* June 21, Sept. 20, 27, Nov. 1, 1848. (The two Taylors were not related.) Although his position on the proviso was never clearly stated during the campaign, Zachary Taylor favored extending the Missouri Compromise line to the Pacific. Balie Peyton to John J. Crittenden, Jan. 25, 1848, Crittenden Papers, LC.

43. William Andersen to Alpheus Felch, June 20, 1848, Felch Papers, MHC.

44. *Mr. Webster's Speech at Marshfield, Mass. Delivered September 1, 1848, and his Speech on the Oregon Bill, Delivered in the United States Senate, August 12, 1848* (Boston, 1848), 4–6, 8, 13, and *Papers of Webster,* ser. 4, 2:489–512; Webster to his son Fletcher, June 19, 1848, and Webster to Everett, May 29, 1848, *Papers of Webster,* ser. 1, 6:299, 290.

45. *Detroit Free Press,* Sept. 9, 1848; Robert Winthrop to John P. Kennedy, Sept. 19, 1848, in Allan Nevins, *Ordeal of the Union,* 2 vols. (New York, 1947), 1:211. Webster stated, in a letter to R. M. Blatchford, his Marshfield speech was meant to serve several purposes: "First, to make out a clear case for all true Whigs to vote for [Taylor]. . . . Second, to place myself in a condition of entire independence . . . from his failure or his success. . . . Thirdly, and most especially, to show the preposterous conduct of those Whigs who make a secession from their party and take service under Mr. Van Buren." Sept. 18, 1848, in *Private Correspondence of Daniel Webster,* ed. Fletcher Webster, 2 vols. (Boston, 1857), 2:286.

46. Henry Clay to James Harlan, Aug. 5, 1848, in *The Private Correspondence of Henry Clay,* ed. Calvin Colton (New York, 1855), 571.

47. Clay to James Lynch et al., Sept. 20, 1848, in Mrs. Coleman Chapman, ed., *The Life of John J. Crittenden, with Selections from his Correspondence and Speeches,* 2 vols. in 1 (Philadelphia, 1873), 1:324–26; Clay to Thomas B. Stevenson, Sept. 4, 1848, in *Works of Henry Clay: Comprising His Life, Correspondence and Speeches,* ed. Calvin Colton, 7 vols. (New York, 1897), 3:483; *New York Weekly Tribune,* Sept. 16, 1848.

48. *New York Daily Tribune,* June 12, 14, Sept. 29, 1848; Greeley to Clay, June 21, 1848, Clay Papers, LC; Henry Luther Stoddard, *Horace Greeley* (New York, 1946), 123; Greeley to Joshua Giddings, June 20, 1848, Greeley Papers, NYHS.

49. Taylor to George Lippard, July 24, 1848, in *Taylor Whig[g]ery,* 13; Clay to Thomas B. Stevenson, Sept. 4, 1848, in *Works of Clay,* 3:484; *Campaign,* Sept. 6, 1848.

50. Taylor to Allison, Sept. 4, 1848, in Hamilton, *Taylor,* 2:121–24; *Diary of Hone,* 850–51; *Autobiography of Thurlow Weed,* ed. Harriet A. Weed (Boston, 1883), 579; William Bull Pringle to Taylor, July 26, 1848, and Taylor to Pringle, Aug. 9, 1848, in *Charleston Courier,* Aug. 22, 1848; Fillmore to Solomon G. Haven, Aug. 19, 1848, Fillmore Papers, LC.

51. *North Carolina Standard,* June 7, 1848.

52. William Yancey to Calhoun, June 14, 1848, in "Correspondence Addressed to John C. Calhoun, 1837–1849," ed. Chauncey S. Boucher and Robert P. Brooks, *Annual Report of the American Historical Association for the Year 1929,* 2:441; Calhoun letter to the

editor, *Charleston Mercury,* Sept. 5, 1848; *Campaign,* Aug. 30, 1848. Although Yancey took no active role in support of the regular Democratic ticket, he did publish *Address to the People of Alabama.* This pamphlet was an account of the adoption of the Alabama Platform, and an explication of the author's conduct at the Baltimore convention.

53. *Detroit Daily Advertiser,* Nov. 1, 1848; Simon Cameron to Cass, July 12, 1848, Clements; Pierpont Potter to John Van Buren, June 15, 1848, Van Buren Papers, LC; Daniel Dickinson to Cass, July 10, 1848, Clements; *Detroit Free Press,* July 2, 1848; *Washington Daily Union,* Sept. 20, 1848; *Illinois State Register,* Sept. 15, 1848; *Niles (Mich.) Republican,* July 22, 1848; Cass to Samuel Treat, July 3, 1848, Treat Papers, Missouri Historical Society, photostatic copy in Burton.

54. Phineas Homan to Alpheus Felch, July 20, 1848, Felch Papers, MHC; *Diary of Polk,* 4:9–12, 36–37, 57–58, 114; John Y. Mason to Cass, Sept. 25, 1848, Clements; Dickinson to Cass, July 10, 1848, Clements; Cass to Felch, July 17, 25, 1848, Felch Papers, Burton.

55. Rose, *Poetry,* 20; *Illinois Journal,* Aug. 16, 1848; Benton to Cass, July 10, 1848, Clements; Wentworth to E. S. Kimberly, June 27, 1848, Kimberley Papers, Chicago Historical Society; Allen Haines to Alpheus Felch, June 30, 1848, Felch Papers, MHC; Cass to Samuel Beardsley, Oct. 6, 1848, Clements.

56. Gideon Welles to Martin Van Buren, Sept. 30, 1848, Henry B. Learned transcript, Welles Papers, LC; *Cleveland Plain Dealer,* in *Indiana State Sentinel,* Aug. 23, 1848; *Campaign,* Aug. 16, 23, 30, Sept. 6, Oct. 4, 1848; *Inconsistency and Hypocracy of Martin Van Buren on the Question of Slavery* [1848]; [Lowell], *Biglow Papers,* 131; *Liberator,* Aug. 18, 1848.

57. Blue, *Free Soilers,* 132; *American Free Soil Almanac for 1849: Astronomically and Politically Calculated for the States and Territories of the Union* (Boston, [1848]), 19; *North Star,* June 16, 1848; *Address by the Whig State Convention,* 7; *Chicago Gem of the Prairie,* July 8, 1848; *Milford (N.H.) Standard,* in *New York Daily Tribune,* Oct. 25, 1848; Charles Stearns, *Facts in the Life of Gen. Taylor; the Cuba Blood-Hound Importer, the Extensive Slave-Holder, and the Hero of the Mexican War!!* (Boston, 1848), 28; *The Free Soil Question . . .* (New York, [1848]), 15; *Milwaukee American Freeman,* Aug. 30, 1848.

58. *National Era,* in *Chicago Gem of the Prairie,* Sept. 9, 1848; *Racine Advocate,* Aug. 16, Oct. 11, 1848.

59. Cass to Nicholson, Aug. 5, 1848, Burton; Cass to Samuel Beardsley, Oct. 6, 1848, Clements; *Campaign,* Aug. 2, 16, Sept. 6, 13, 20, 1848. The Democratic popular vote majorities in the state elections of August totaled approximately ten thousand in Illinois, seven thousand in Indiana, and thirteen hundred in Iowa. *Albany Argus,* in *Campaign,* Sept. 20, 1848.

60. George S. Houston to Howell Cobb, Oct. 23, 1848, and Richard French to Cobb, Sept. 10, 1848, in Phillips, "Toombs, Stephens, and Cobb," 132, 126; Polk to Cass, Aug. 24, 1848, Joseph B. Gilman to Cass, Oct. 18, 1848, and Simon Cameron to Cass, July 12, 1848, Clements.

61. *Wheeling Times,* in *Richmond Enquirer,* June 8, 1848; *Richmond Enquirer,* Sept. 2, 1848; *Charleston Mercury,* Aug. 27, 1848; *Tallahassee Floridian,* Aug. 5, 1848; *Campaign,* Aug. 30, Sept. 20, Oct. 11, Nov. 1, 1848.

62. *Campaign,* Sept. 20, 27, 1848; Walter S. Burges to Cass, June 15, 1848, Clements; *New Hampshire Patriot & State Gazette,* Aug. 10, 1848.

63. Cass to Samuel Beardsley, Oct. 6, 1848, Clements; Van Buren quoted in *New Orleans Daily Picayune,* Sept. 24, 1848; John A. Dix to Azariah C. Flagg, June 5, 1848, Flagg Papers, Columbia University.

64. N. Baylor to Alpheus Felch, Oct. 20, 1848, Felch Papers, MHC; *Detroit Free Press,* Apr. 29, 1848; *Grand Rapids Grand River Eagle,* June 20, 1848; Truman Smith to Alexander Stephens, Oct. 2, 1848, Stephens Papers, LC.

65. George Fries to Howell Cobb, Sept. 14, 1848, in Phillips, "Toombs, Stephens, and Cobb," 124; *Campaign,* Oct. 18, 20, Nov. 1, 1848. The returns, published October 27, gave the

Whig candidate for governor 148,666 votes, to 148,321 for his Democratic opponent. Erwin H. Price, "The Election of 1848, in Ohio," *OAHQ* 36 (1927): 288–89.

66. J. G. Schott to Alpheus Felch, Sept. 21, 1848, Felch Papers, MHC; *Campaign*, Oct. 27, Nov. 1, 1848.

67. Gideon Welles to ——, Oct. 21, 1848, Henry B. Learned notes, Welles Papers, LC; David Wilmot letter, June 29, 1848, in Henry R. Mueller, "The Whig Party in Pennsylvania," Columbia University *Studies in History, Economics, and Public Law* 101 (1922): 151–56; *Campaign*, July 19, Oct. 4, 18, 20, 25, Nov. 1, 1848. Although Cameron characterized Shunk's resignation as "ill-advised," it was unavoidable; the former governor died eleven days later. In the race for governor, the Whig candidate received 168,523 votes to his opponent's 168,221. The Whigs carried fourteen of the twenty-four congressional seats; Nativist Lewis Levin and Free Soiler David Wilmot were reelected. Cameron to Cass, July 12, 1848, Clements; *Campaign*, Nov. 1, 1848; Mueller, "Whig Party," 156.

68. *Battery*, Oct. 12, 1848; Charles Moore, *History of Michigan*, 4 vols. (Chicago, 1915), 1:400; *Detroit Free Press*, Nov. 6, 1848; *Cleveland Plain Dealer*, Nov. 10, 1848. The popular vote figures for the election vary somewhat in different sources; I have generally relied on the statistics in *Guide to U.S. Elections* (Washington, D.C., 1975), 268.

69. Charles Sumner to Salmon Chase, Nov. 16, 1848, Chase Papers, LC; Martin Van Buren to Francis P. Blair, Sr., Dec. 11, 1848, Blair Family Papers, LC; John R. Hinchman to Theodore Hinchman, Nov. 19, 1848, Hinchman Papers, Burton; *Ann Arbor (Mich.) True Democrat*, Nov. 16, 1848.

70. *Kalamazoo (Mich.) Gazette*, Nov. 17, 1848; *Racine (Wisc.) Advocate*, Nov. 15, 1848; *Campaign*, Apr. 11, 1849.

71. Charles D. Tuell to Alpheus Felch, Dec. 9, 1848, Felch Papers, MHC.

72. Cass to Aaron Hobart, Mar. 9, 1849, and Cass to Samuel Beardsley, Dec. 12, 1848, Clements; *Jefferson City Inquirer*, Nov. 18, 1848; Martin Van Buren, *Inquiry into the Origin and Course of Political Parties in the United States*, ed. by his sons (1867; reprint, New York, 1967), 349. The *Chicago Gem of the Prairie*, a Free Soil weekly, boasted on November 11, "If it had not been for the Free Democracy, Cass would have been elected, beyond all question." The Free Soilers are also credited with Cass's defeat by (among others) DeAlva Stanwood Alexander, *A Political History of the State of New York*, 4 vols. (New York, 1906–23), 2:144; John Hubbell, "The National Free Soil Convention of '48. Held in Buffalo," *Publications of the Buffalo Historical Society* 4 (1878): 162; and Roy F. Nichols, *The Stakes of Power, 1845–1877* (New York, 1961), 21. W. L. G. Smith summarized, "The Wilmot Proviso had done its work. It alone had caused the defeat" of Cass (658). McLaughlin (*Cass*, 260) and Woodford (*Cass*, 269) concluded that Cass lost because the South did not trust him on the slavery issue.

73. *Cleveland Daily Plain Dealer*, Nov. 10, 1848; *Richmond Enquirer*, Nov. 11, 1848; Polk to Cass, Nov. 14, 1848, Clements; *New York Weekly Tribune*, Nov. 25, 1848, 547–60.

74. Cass to Samuel Treat, Dec. 8, 1848, Treat Papers, Missouri Historical Society, photostatic copy in Burton; *Liberator*, Nov. 11, 1848; *North Star*, Nov. 10, 1848.

75. *Racine (Wisc.) Advocate*, Nov. 15, 1848; *Milwaukee Weekly Wisconsin*, Nov. 15, 1848; *Kenosha (Wisc.) Southport Telegraph*, Nov. 10, 1848.

CHAPTER NINE
United States Senator (1849–1857)

1. Eugene H. Berwanger, *The Frontier Against Slavery: Western Anti-Negro Prejudice and the Slavery Extension Controversy*, 2d ed. (Urbana, Ill., 1971), 32, 40; John C. Patterson, "Marshall Men and Measures in State and National History," *MPHC* 38 (1912): 244–79. A fifth child was born to the Crosswhites while they lived in Michigan. The verdict in the Crosswhite case was returned after the election of 1848.

2. Jonathan Lamb to Alpheus Felch, Jan. 6, 1849 [misdated 1848], Felch Papers, MHC; John R. Hinchman to Theodore Hinchman, Nov. 19, 1848, Hinchman Papers, Burton; *New York Daily Tribune,* Jan. 20, 1849.

3. H. V. Man to Felch, Jan. 29, 1849, and Edmund Rice to Felch, Jan. 31, 1849, Felch Papers, MHC; *Detroit Free Press,* Jan. 15, 20, 22, 1849; *Detroit Daily Advertiser,* Jan. 12, 15, 23, 1849. Thomas Fitzgerald, who was appointed to fill the seat vacated by Cass until an election could be held, presented to the Senate on February 2, 1849, the Michigan resolutions "against the introduction of slavery into the new Territories." They were read, ordered to be printed, and laid on the table. *CG,* 30th Cong., 2d sess., 432.

4. Charles A. Loomis to his father, Feb. 11, 1849, in William L. Jenks, "Senator Charles A. Loomis," *MH* 10 (1926): 220; Polk to Cass, Dec. 15, 1848, Jan. 9, 1849, Clements.

5. *Diary of Polk,* 4:134–35, 188, 239–40, 333; Louisa Hinchman to aunt of the same name, Jan. 22, 1849, Hinchman Papers, Burton; Polk to Cass, Nov. 14, 1848, Clements.

6. *Diary of Polk,* 4:358–59; Cass to Robert McClelland, June 12, 1849, Burton; Cass to Campbell P. White et al., Nov. 26, 1849, in Smith, *Cass,* 663–65; *Washington Daily Union* Feb. 28, 1849; *CG,* 30th Cong., 2d sess., 692.

7. Polk to Cass, Dec. 15, 1848, Clements.

8. Mary Bingham to her sister, Dec. 11, 1849, Bingham Papers, MHC (punctuation added).

9. *CG,* 31st Cong., 1st sess., 1–66, passim. The Senate Democrats held an eight-vote majority over the twenty-four Whigs and two Free Soilers.

10. Ibid., 51–59, 75, 87, 99–100.

11. Cass to Samuel Medary, Jan. 26, 1850, photostatic copy of original in Samuel Medary Collection, OSAHSL, Burton; Cass to Robert McClelland, June 12, 1849, Burton.

12. *CG,* 31st Cong., 1st sess., app., 58–74.

13. *Savannah Georgian,* in *Detroit Free Press,* May 14, 1850; Francis Lieber note, [January 1850], Huntington; *New York Daily Tribune,* Jan. 23, 24, 1850.

14. *CG,* 31st Cong., 1st sess., 244–47. Clay's second resolution stated: "That as slavery does not exist by law, and is not likely to be introduced into any of the territory acquired by the United States from the Republic of Mexico, it is inexpedient for Congress to provide by law, either for its introduction into or exclusion from any part of the said territory; and that appropriate Territorial governments ought to be established by Congress in all of the said territory, not assigned as the boundaries of the proposed State of California, without the adoption of any restriction or condition on the subject of slavery" (245).

15. Alpheus Felch to his wife, Feb. 5, 1850, Felch Papers, MHC; *CG,* 31st Cong., 1st sess., app., 115–27.

16. *CG,* 31st Cong., 1st sess., 319, 331; J. Holmes Agnew to Alpheus Felch, Feb. 10, 1849, Felch Papers, MHC.

17. Cass to N. Niles, Feb. 25, 1850, LC; Cass letter, Feb. 24, 1850, in *Hillsdale (Mich.) Gazette,* Mar. 19, 1850.

18. *CG,* 31st Cong., 1st sess., 371, 397, 451–55, 476–83, and app., 148–57; *New York Daily Tribune,* Mar. 6, 1850.

19. *CG,* 31st Cong., 1st sess., app., 260–69, 468–80, 527, 1054–65.

20. Cass to Robert McClelland, Apr. 23, 1850, McClelland Papers, Burton; *Michigan Expositor,* Feb. 19, 1850; Roger L. Rosentreter, "Michigan and the Compromise of 1850," *Old Northwest* 6 (1980): 157–58; *CG,* 31st Cong., 1st sess., 493, 702–3; *Detroit Free Press,* Mar. 22, 1850.

21. The remaining committee members were northern Whigs Daniel Webster, Samuel Phelps, and James Cooper; southern Democrats William R. King, James Mason, and Solomon Downs; and southern Whigs Willie P. Mangum, John Bell, and John Berrien. Stephen Douglas, who previously submitted bills to the Senate dealing with the

admission of California and the establishment of territorial governments for New Mexico and Utah, believed the select committee was unnecessary and therefore did not allow his name to be submitted as a potential member. Three of those chosen—Berrien, Dickinson, and Mason—left Washington on April 22 to accompany the body of John Calhoun to South Carolina and thus did not attend committee deliberations after that date.

22. Cass to Robert McClelland, Apr. 23, May 5, 30, 1850, McClelland Papers, Burton; Cass to Daniel Dickinson, May 1, 1850, in *Speeches of Dickinson,* 2:430–31; Cass to John Sherman Bagg, May 2, 1850, Bagg Papers, Huntington.

23. *CG,* 31st Cong., 1st sess., app., 612–16; *CG,* 31st Cong., 1st sess., 944–48. That portion of the Omnibus bill regarding California, Utah, and New Mexico was taken from two earlier bills submitted to the Senate by Douglas. The committee, in the words of the Illinois senator, "took my two printed Bills & put a wafer between & Reported them back without changing or writing a single word, except one line. The one line inserted prohibited the territorial Legislatures from Legislating upon the subject of slavery." Neither Cass nor Clay supported the proscription on territorial legislation; the bills that were ultimately passed by Congress contained no such clause. Douglas to Charles H. Lanphier and George Walker, Aug. 3, 1850, in *The Letters of Stephen A. Douglas,* ed. Robert W. Johannsen (Urbana, Ill., 1961), 192; *CG,* 31st Cong., 1st sess., 780; Johannsen, *Stephen A. Douglas* (New York, 1973), 285–86.

24. *CG,* 31st Cong., 1st sess., 1120–22; Smith, *Cass,* 694–703.

25. Alpheus Felch to his wife, June 28, 1850, Felch Papers, MHC; *CG,* 31st Cong., 1st sess., app., 803–10; Cass to McClelland, June 25, Aug. 10, 1850, McClelland Papers, Burton.

26. *CG,* 31st Cong., 1st sess., 762–64.

27. Ibid., app., 908–9.

28. *CG,* 31st Cong., 1st sess., 1364, 1490–91, and app., 1405–14; Cass to Henry Ledyard, June 13, 1850, Clements; Cass to Robert McClelland, June 25, 1850, McClelland Papers, Burton.

29. Cass to Samuel Beardsley, Aug. 8, 1850, Clements.

30. Cass to Robert McClelland, Aug. 10, 1850, McClelland Papers, Burton; *CG,* 31st Cong., 1st sess., 399, 1504, 1573, 1589, 1659–60, 1858–59.

31. *CG,* 31st Cong., 1st sess., app., 1583 (emphasis added); *Washington Daily Union* Sept. 5, 1852. All the southern senators voted in favor of engrossing the Fugitive Slave bill for a third reading, and twelve northerners made up the 27 to 12 minority in opposition. Cass joined fifteen northern senators who abstained from voting.

32. *Hillsdale (Mich.) Gazette,* Oct. 10, 1850; *Michigan Expositor,* Oct. 29, 1850; *Detroit Daily Advertiser,* Oct. 8, 28, 1850; Henry Steele Commager, ed., *Documents of American History,* 5th ed., s.v. "The Compromise of 1850"; *CG,* 31st Cong., 2d sess., app., 1124–25.

33. Webster to Peter Harvey, Oct. 2, 1850, *Papers of Webster,* ser. 1, 7:155–56; George Edmund Badger to Cass, Nov. 6, 1850, Clements; Cass to A. H. Stewart, Apr. 25, 1851, Burton; *The Proceedings of the Union Meeting, Held at Brewster's Hall, October 24, 1850* (New Haven, Conn., 1851), 16.

34. Robert McClelland to Alpheus Felch, Nov. 21, Dec. 23, 1850, Felch Papers, MHC; Cass to McClelland, Dec. 8, 31, 1850, McClelland Papers, Burton; *Washington Daily Union* Feb. 7, 1851; *Journal of the [Michigan] House of Representatives* (Lansing, 1851), 4; *Detroit Daily Advertiser,* Oct. 23, Nov. 2, 1850. Cass received a 14 to 6 majority in the Michigan Senate, and a 39 to 23 victory in the House.

35. Cass New York address and letter to the Baltimore committee of the Union Festival, in Young, *Cass,* 402–7; Cass to Robert McClelland, Oct. 15, 1850, McClelland Papers, Burton.

36. Cass to Samuel Beardsley, Dec. 19, 1850, Clements; Cass to Robert McClelland, Nov. 21, 1850, McClelland Papers, Burton; *CG,* 31st Cong., 2d sess., 249, 580, 673, and app., 296, 313; *CG,* 32d Cong., 1st sess., 145–46, and app., 48–61, 68, 1124.

37. Henry S. Foote, *Casket of Reminiscences* (Washington, D.C., 1874), 83–86.

38. Cass to Buchanan, Jan. 16, 1849, and Cass to Lewis Coryell, Oct. 14, 1851, Buchanan Papers, HSP; Cass to Capt. David Robinson, Dec. 27, 1848, Burton; Henry Clay to Daniel Ullmann, June 14, 1851, in *Correspondence of Clay,* 619.

39. D. H. Pease to S. A. Keeney, Sept. 28, 1851, MHC; [Sarah Jane Clarke Lippincott], *Greenwood Leaves: A Collection of Sketches and Letters,* 2d ser. (Boston, 1854), 345; Cass to Andrew J. Donelson, Oct. 31, 1851, Donelson Papers, LC.

40. Cass to Robert McClelland, Oct. 13, 1851, McClelland Papers, Burton; Cass to Aaron Hobart, Aug. 25, 1851, Clements; Cass to David Robinson, October 1851, Burton; Edmund W. Hubard to Hunter, May 8, 1852, in "Correspondence of Robert M. T. Hunter: 1826–1879," ed. Charles Henry Ambler, *Annual Report of the American Historical Association for the Year 1916,* 2:142; Cass to Lyman Norris, Apr. 30, 1852, Norris Family Papers, MHC; Alpheus Felch to his wife, Feb. 22, 1852, Felch Papers, MHC. One of the more curious letters of support Cass received prior to the Baltimore convention was from the wife of a cousin. Sarah Gilman wrote on October 25, 1851, "So far as I know the Democratic Party of Tennessee is for you for the Presidency in 1852," and asked to borrow one thousand dollars because for the previous two years her husband had been seeking his fortune in California; Clements.

41. Marcy to Buchanan, Mar. 10, 1850, HSP.

42. Salmon Chase to E. S. Hamlin, Dec. 21, 1850, in "Sixth Report of the Historical Manuscripts Commission: With Diary and Correspondence of Salmon P. Chase," *Annual Report of the American Historical Association for the Year 1902,* 2:227; Marcy to James Berret, Dec. 14, 1851, Marcy Papers, LC; Buchanan to J. S. Yost, June 16, 1851, Buchanan Papers, NYHS; Thomas H. Benton to Montgomery Blair, Aug. 29, 1851, Blair Family Papers, LC.

43. *CG,* 31st Cong., 1st sess., 75, 113–17; *CG,* 32d Cong., 1st sess., 21–25, 66, 69, 90, 157, and app., 159–65, 309–11; Hubard to Hunter, May 8, 1852, in "Correspondence of Hunter," 140–41; *Proceedings, Speeches, &c., at the Dinner Given to Louis Kossuth, at the National Hotel, Washington, January 7, 1852* (Washington, D.C., [1852]).

44. C. Eames to William Marcy, Sept. 14, 1851, Marcy Papers, LC; Simon Cameron to Cass, Apr. 10, 1851, Clements; Buchanan to Andrew J. Donelson, Mar. 20, 1851, in "Selected Letters, 1846–1856, from the Donelson Papers," ed. St. George L. Sioussat, *Tennessee Historical Magazine* 3 (December 1917): 269; *Baltimore Sun,* Sept. 13, 1850.

45. James Buchanan to Cave Johnson, Dec. 22, 1851, Mar. 30, 1852, in *Works of Buchanan,* 8:429–30, 447–49.

46. Cass to Andrew J. Donelson, Oct. 31, 1851, Donelson Papers, LC; George Plitt to Buchanan, Apr. 4, 1851, Buchanan Papers, LC.

47. Stephen Douglas to Robert M. T. Hunter, May 6, 1851, Douglas to William J. Brown, June 21, 1851, and Douglas to George N. Sanders, Feb. 10, Apr. 15, 1852, in *Letters of Douglas,* 218, 226–27, 239–40, 246–47.

48. "Eighteen Fifty-Two and the Presidency," "The Presidency and the Review," "General Cass on European Monarchy," "The Roman Republic—'Rome to America,'" "The Nomination—the 'Old Fogies' and Fogy Conspiracies," and "Congress, the Presidency and the Review," *DR* 30 (1852): 9–12, 183–85, 466, 344, 371, 202–24. A political broadside dated April 14, 1852, and presumably penned by "A Middle-Aged Fogy," was circulated during the campaign. It was subtitled: "Proving by facts and figures that Gen. CASS cannot be elected President, even if nominated by the National Convention"; Burton.

49. *New York Daily Tribune,* June 5, 1852.

50. *Proceedings of the Democratic National Convention, Held at Baltimore, June, 1852,* reported by William Hincks and F. H. Smith (Washington, D.C., 1852), 36–37; *Convention Decisions,* 44–47. The organizing committee for the Baltimore convention futilely specified

that the number of delegates be limited to the number of electoral votes, a total of 296. The *Proceedings* of the convention states that, "the whole number of votes being 296," 197 were necessary to gain the nomination (21). Nichols, in *The Democratic Machine* (131), and Johannsen (*Douglas*, 367) accept these figures; however, Nichols claims in his biography *Franklin Pierce* (203) that there were only 288 total votes, and Nevins agrees (*Ordeal*, 2:19). According to statistics listed in the *Proceedings* (21–44), on three different ballots more than 288 votes were cast; the 296 total-votes figure is correct. The Democratic platform avoided labeling the Compromise of 1850 the "final solution" to the slavery controversy, but it urged a "faithful execution of the acts known as the compromise measures settled by the last Congress." On this issue, the delegates followed the position of all the leading candidates for the presidential nomination. Porter and Johnson, *Party Platforms*, 17; *New York Herald*, May 25, 1852.

51. O. D. Richardson to Alpheus Felch, June 7, 1852, and William S. Brown to Felch, June 17, 1851, Felch Papers, MHC; Cass to Aaron Hobart, June 10, 1852, Clements; Cass to Dickinson, June 10, 1852, in *Speeches of Dickinson*, 2:470; Cass to Franklin Pierce, June 6, 1852, Pierce Papers, LC.

52. Porter and Johnson, *Party Platforms*, 18–21.

53. *Washington Daily Union* June 11, 1852; *Adrian (Mich.) Watchtower*, Oct. 12, 1852; *Weekly Chicago Democrat*, Oct. 4, 1852; Zachariah Chandler quoted in Woodford, *Cass*, 294; Cass to Robert McClelland, June 23, July 5, 1852, McClelland Papers, Burton; *New York Herald*, Sept. 3, 1852; *Detroit Daily Free Press*, July 14, Sept. 11, 13, 15, 21, 24, 29, Oct. 19, 1852.

54. Cass to David Disney, Nov. 9, 1852, NYHS; Cass to John Sherman Bagg, Jan. 30, 1853, Bagg Papers, Huntington; Cass to Samuel Beardsley, Dec. 8, 1852, and Cass to Aaron Hobart, Jan. 18, 23, 1853, Clements; Cass to Robert McClelland, Feb. 14, 1853, McClelland Papers, Burton.

55. Cass to Pierce, Aug. 30, 1853, Cass to Henry B. Ledyard, Jan. 1, 1853, and Cass to W. L. Helfurstein, Mar. 17, 1853, Michigan Papers, Clements.

56. Cass to Samuel Beardsley, Dec. 13, 1853, and Robert McClelland to Cass, Sept. 17, 1853, Clements; *CG*, 33d Cong., 1st sess. 1605; *CG*, 34th Cong., 1st sess., 22–23, and 3d sess., 43.

57. Senate Doc. No. 15, 33d Cong., 1st sess., 4; *CG*, 32d Cong., 2d sess., 1117; *CG*, 33d Cong., 1st sess., 1, 44, 221–22; Robert W. Johannsen, "Stephen A. Douglas, Popular Sovereignty and the Territories," *Historian* 22 (August 1960): 384–85.

58. "Appeal of the Independent Democrats in Congress to the People of the United States," *CG*, 33d Cong., 1st sess., 281–82. Giddings wrote the first draft and Chase revised the "Appeal"; Senator Charles Sumner and Congressmen Edward Wade (Ohio), Gerrit Smith (New York), and Alexander De Witt (Massachusetts) also affixed their signatures.

59. *Washington Daily Union* Jan. 22, 1854; Cass to William A. Seaver, Sept. 30, 1853, Clements; Cass to McClelland, May 19, 1853, NYHS; Gideon Welles diary, June 29, 1855, Welles Papers, LC; *New York Herald*, Jan. 18, 1854; Congressman Michael Walsh letter, Feb. 11, 1854, in *New York Herald*, Feb. 13, 1854; Salmon Chase to E. L. Hamlin, Jan. 23, 1853, Chase Papers, LC.

60. *CG*, 33d Cong., 1st sess., 343–44, 421, 450–8, 532, 1321, and app., 270–79; Walsh letter, *New York Herald*, Feb. 13, 1854.

61. *CG*, 33d Cong., 1st sess., 1256.

62. Ibid., app., 278; *CG*, 33d Cong., 1st sess., 553, 1662, 1740, 1744. Cass claimed Calhoun coined the phrase "squatter sovereignty." The Michigan senator refrained from using that "reproachful term," favoring "self-government" or "popular sovereignty." Ibid., 688.

63. Cass to J. H. Cleveland, June 4, 1854, in McLaughlin, *Cass*, 299–300.

64. Douglas quoted in George F. Milton, *The Eve of Conflict: Stephen Douglas and the Needless War* (Boston, 1934), 175; *Detroit Democrat*, in *New York Herald*, Feb. 4, 1854; *Detroit Daily Democrat*, Feb. 15, Oct. 10, 1854; *Battle Creek Journal*, June 23, 1854; Frank A. Flower,

History of the Republican Party, Embracing its Origin, Growth and Mission, Together with Appendices of Statistics and Information Required by Enlightened Politicians and Patriotic Citizens (Springfield, Ill., 1884), 171–81.

65. *Detroit Daily Advertiser,* Sept. 16, 1854; *Detroit Daily Free Press,* Sept. 15, 1854; Cass to Nicholson, Sept. 30, 1854, NYHS; Cass to A. Harris, Oct. 1, 1854, Douglas Papers, University of Chicago. Barry served as governor from 1841 to 1845 and 1850 to 1851; the Michigan state constitution limited the incumbent to two consecutive two-year terms.

66. *Detroit Daily Free Press,* Sept. 8, 11, 12, 14, Oct. 17, 1854; *Chicago Daily Democratic Press,* Oct. 21, 1854; *Hillsdale (Mich.) Standard,* Oct. 31, 1854; *Detroit Daily Advertiser,* Oct. 30, 1854.

67. Frederick Bissell Porter journals, Nov. 4, 6, [1854], MHC; *Daily Richmond Enquirer,* Sept. 22, 1854; *CG,* 33d Cong., 1st sess., app., 277; *Address of General Cass to the Democracy of Detroit, Delivered at the City Hall, November 4, 1854* ([Detroit, 1854]); *Washington Daily Union,* Nov. 14, 1854.

68. *Detroit Daily Free Press,* Oct. 8, Nov. 19, 1854; *Detroit Daily Democrat,* Oct. 10, 1854; *Marshall (Mich.) Statesman,* Dec. 27, 1854; *Kalamazoo (Mich.) Gazette,* Dec. 29, 1854. The Michigan Democrats were not alone in their defeat; throughout the North, the party lost sixty-six congressional seats, while surrendering only four in the slave states. Michigan Republicans captured twenty-five of the thirty-two senate seats, and forty-eight of seventy-two seats in the house.

69. *CG,* 33d Cong., 2d sess., 555.

70. Ibid., 555–56. Stuart joined Cass in disregarding the instructions.

71. William E. Gienapp, *The Origins of the Republican Party, 1852–1856* (New York, 1987), 103–6; Ronald P. Formisano, *The Birth of Mass Political Parties, Michigan, 1827–1861* (Princeton, N.J., 1971), 249–53, 258–65; *Detroit Free Press,* Nov. 8, 1854; *Detroit Daily Advertiser,* Nov. 8, 1854. Wisconsin was the other northwestern state that presented a united Republican party to voters in 1854, rather than a fusion with Know Nothings.

72. *CG,* 32d Cong., 2d sess., 140–42; Smith, *Cass,* 720–26.

73. *CG,* 32d Cong., 2d sess., 183; *CG,* 33d Cong., 1st sess., 463, 482, 506, 551, 580, 630, 703, 773, 834, 929, 1133, 1854, and app., 681–91; *CG,* 33d Cong., 2d sess., 228, 1032; Cass to H. A. Willard, Sept. 20, 1855, Clements; *Letter of the Most Rev. Archbishop Hughes on the Madiai. Speech of Hon. Lewis Cass, on Religious Freedom Abroad. Letter of the Most Rev. Archbishop Hughes, in Reply to Hon. Lewis Cass, on Religious Toleration* (Baltimore, [1854]).

74. *New York Daily Tribune,* Apr. 10, 12, 1857.

75. *CG,* 34th Cong., 1st sess., 864, 698, 826–27, 839, 853.

76. Ibid., app., 512–26.

77. *Washington Daily Union,* May 13, 14, 1856; *New York Daily Tribune,* May 14, 1856.

78. *CG,* 34th Cong., 1st sess., 1279–80.

79. Ibid., 1317, 1439, 1574, and app., 529–44; *CG,* 34th Cong., 3d sess., 90; Cass to John P. Cook, June 29 and July 4, 1856, Cook Papers, MHC.

80. Cass to Aaron Hobart, Apr. 15, 1855, Clements; Cass to Andrew J. Webster et al., Nov. 23, 1855, in Smith, *Cass,* 777; *Washington Daily Union* Dec. 14, 1855; Cass to James Jesse Strang, Apr. 8, 1856, Clements; Cass to McClelland, Apr. 9, 1856, MHS; Cass to Alpheus Felch, Feb. 23, 1856, Felch Papers, Burton; *Detroit Daily Free Press,* Feb. 14, 1856.

81. William B. Hesseltine and Rex G. Fisher, ed., *Trimmers, Trucklers & Temporizers, Notes of Murat Halstead from the Political Conventions of 1856* (Madison, Wis., 1961), 47; William Marcy to Buchanan, Dec. 23, 1855, in Ivor Debenham Spencer, *The Victor and the Spoils: A Life of William L. Marcy* (Providence, R.I., 1959), 367; *Official Proceedings of the National Democratic Convention, Held in Cincinnati, June 2–6, 1856* (Cincinnati, Ohio, 1856), 56–58, 61–68; McKee, *Conventions,* 87.

82. Porter and Johnson, *Party Platforms*, 23–27.

83. Ibid., 22–23; *Proceedings of the [Republican] National Convention Held at Philadelphia, on the 17th, 18th, and 19th June, 1856* . . . [1856], 6.

84. Porter and Johnson, *Party Platforms*, 27–28.

85. Cass to Daniel Dougherty et al., June 24, 1856, Clements; *Washington Daily Union*, June 7, 1856; *Cincinnati (Ohio) Commercial*, June 11, 1856, in Hesseltine and Fisher, *Trimmers*, 64–65.

86. *Washington Daily Union*, Aug. 9, 1856; *Cleveland Plain Dealer*, in ibid., Sept. 13, 1856; Cass to Howell Cobb Sept. 9, 1856, photostatic copy, Illinois Historical Survey, University of Illinois; *Detroit Daily Free Press*, Aug. 16, Sept. 4, 9, 11, 1856.

87. A. D. P. Van Buren, "Michigan in Her Pioneer Politics; Michigan in Our National Politics, and Michigan in the Presidential Campaign of 1856," *MPHC* 17 (1892): 277–86; *Detroit Daily Free Press*, Sept. 7, 1856; *Washington Daily Union* Sept. 13, Nov. 1, 1856; Cass to the editor of the *Detroit Free Press*, Aug. 22, 1855, in Smith, *Cass*, 771–76.

88. Van Buren, "Michigan," 283–84; A. D. P. Van Buren, "The Log Schoolhouse Era in Michigan," *MPHC* 14 (1890): 388–89.

89. *Washington Daily Union*, Nov. 12, 1856; Robert McClelland to Cass, Nov. 10, 1856, McClelland letterbook, LC; John J. Bagley to ——, May 1, 1857, in George H. Hopkins, "John Judson Bagley," *MPHC* 5 (1884): 199; *New York Daily Tribune*, Dec. 15, 1856; Cass to McClelland, Nov. 29 [or 24], 1856, McClelland Papers, Burton.

90. Cass to McClelland, Nov. 29 (or 24), 1856; *Detroit Daily Advertiser*, Jan. 12, 13, 1857; *Detroit Daily Free Press*, Jan. 11, 13, 1857. Zachariah Chandler was not a unanimous choice for the Senate seat. Most of Michigan's Republican officeholders and the *Detroit Advertiser* favored Jacob M. Howard, a Detroit lawyer who served as chairman of the platform committee at the state convention in July 1854. Isaac P. Christiancy, who issued the call for that first meeting of Michigan Republicans, also enjoyed substantial support. Republican members of the assembly, however, met in caucus and ultimately decided on Chandler; he was then swiftly selected to replace Lewis Cass.

CHAPTER TEN
Secretary of State & Union Advocate (1857–1866)

1. Howell Cobb to his wife, Jan. 6, 1857, and Robert McLane to Cobb, Feb. 14, 1857, in Phillips, "Toombs, Stephens, and Cobb," 389; 395–96.

2. Buchanan to Cass, Feb. 21, 1857, in *General Lewis Cass*, 29; Buchanan to Cobb, Feb. 21, 1857, in Phillips, "Toombs, Stephens, and Cobb," 397. In addition to Cass and Cobb, the original Buchanan cabinet included John Floyd of Virginia (War Department), Aaron Brown of Tennessee (Post Office), Jacob Thompson of Mississippi (Interior Department), Isaac Toucey of Connecticut (Navy Department), and fellow Pennsylvanian Jeremiah Black as attorney general.

3. George Butler to Buchanan, Dec. 6, 1856, Buchanan Papers, HSP; Cass to his son, Dec. 7, 1858, Clements; *New York Daily Tribune*, Jan. 1, 1857; *Detroit Daily Advertiser*, Nov. 11, 1856.

4. John Slidell to Buchanan, Feb. 19, 1857, J. Glancy Jones to Buchanan, Feb. 14, 1857, and Cass to Buchanan, Feb. 23, 1857, Buchanan Papers, HSP.

5. Cass to his son, Apr. 27, 1857, Clements; Mrs. Roger A Pryor, *Reminiscences of Peace and War* (New York, 1904), 100. Lewis Cass, Jr., apparently married one Mary Ludlum in May 1854; she died, childless, a year later. *New York Observer*, in *Detroit Daily Free Press*, April 17, 1855.

6. *New York Daily Tribune*, Apr. 3, 1857; "Diary and Memoranda of William L. Marcy, 1857," contrib. Thomas M. Marshall, *AHR* 24 (1919): 647–48; Cass to McClelland, May 12, 1857, McClelland Papers, Burton; Cass to his son, Apr. 27, 1857, Clements; *Harper's Weekly*, Mar. 7, 1857, 150.

7. Ben Perley Poore, *Perley's Reminiscences of Sixty Years in the National Metropolis,* 2 vols. (Philadelphia, 1886), 1:519; Buchanan to Cass, Aug. 9, 1858, July 28, 1859, Clements; Cass to Buchanan, Aug. 21, 1860, Buchanan Papers, HSP.

8. Cass to ——, Aug. 27, 1858, LC; Peyton, *Alleghanies,* 159; *Detroit Daily Advertiser,* Sept. 24, 1852; Cass to George Washington Hopkins, Jan. 20, 1859, Clements.

9. Judah P. Benjamin to Cass, Mar. 19, 1857, and John Forsyth to Cass, Aug. 31, 1858, Clements; Cass to Forsyth, July 17, 1857, in Sen. Ex. Doc. No. 72, 35th Cong., 1st sess., 39–48; Robert McLane to Cass, Apr. 20, 1860, and Buchanan to Cass, Jan. 27, 1859, Clements. Article 8 of the Gadsden Treaty stated, "The United States may extend its protection" along the Tehuantepec route "as it shall judge wise," when "sanctioned and warranted by the public or international law." Buchanan sought a more precise understanding from Mexico. *Treaties, Conventions, International Acts, Protocols, and Agreements Between the United States of America and Other Powers: 1776–1909,* comp. William M. Malloy, 2 vols. (Washington, D.C., 1910), 1:1124.

10. Robert M. Harrison to Alvah Bradish, Oct. 25, 1848, Bradish Papers, Burton; Buchanan to Lord Clarendon, Feb. 23, 1857, in *Works of Buchanan,* 10:103; J. Glancy Jones to Buchanan, Feb. 14, 1857, Buchanan Papers, HSP; Clarendon to Buchanan, Mar. 13, 1857, in *Works of Buchanan,* 10:115 (punctuation added); Buchanan's First Annual Message to Congress, Dec. 8, 1857, in Richardson, *Messages of the Presidents,* 5:441–42.

11. Malloy, *Treaties,* 1:659–63; *CG,* 32d Cong., 1st sess., 81; Sir Henry Bulwer declaration, June 29, 1850, in Moore, *International Law,* 3:137. Bulwer's declaration of June 29, 1850, and Clayton's reply, dated July 4, in which he acknowledged that he "understood British Honduras was not embraced in the treaty," were not at first made public. They came to light in response to a Cass resolution of December 1852, calling upon the president to communicate to the Senate any information regarding the establishment of the Bay Island Colony. Clayton stated to the Senate in March 1853 that since Belize comprised a portion of the Yucatan peninsula, it was not part of Central America. Clayton quoted in Moore, *International Law,* 3:137; *CG,* 32d Cong., 2d sess., 158, 174; *CG,* 32d Cong., 3d sess., app., 247–51.

12. *CG,* 32d Cong., 2d sess., 199, 269, 391, and app., 90–95; *CG,* 33d Cong., 1st sess., 28, 107, and app., 61–72; *CG,* 34th Cong., 1st sess., 109, 794–96, and app., 68–74.

13. Richardson, *Messages of the Presidents,* 5:442–44; Cass to Mirabeau B. Lamar, June 3, 1858, in Lewis Einstein, "Lewis Cass," *The American Secretaries of State and Their Diplomacy,* vol. 6 (New York, 1928), 351; Cass-Yrissari Treaty, in Senate Ex. Doc. No. 112, 46th Cong., 2d sess., 102–7; Cass to George Dallas, Nov. 23, 1857, RDS, Diplomatic Instructions, Great Britain, 17:92, NAM.

14. Cass to Collector of the Customs at New Orleans, Jan. 2, 1858, in House Ex. Doc. No. 24, 35th Cong., 1st sess., 38 (the same communication was sent to the collector of customs at Mobile and to the federal attorneys at Mobile and New Orleans); Cass letter quoted in William O. Scroggs, *Filibusters and Financiers: The Story of William Walker and His Associates* (New York, 1916), 173; Lt. John J. Almy to Isaac Toucey, Oct. 29, 1857, in Sen. Ex. Doc. No. 13, 35th Cong., 1st sess., 13; Richardson, *Messages of the Presidents,* 5:448. The Rivas Manifesto, named for the town in which it was signed by Thomas Martinez and Juan Rafael Mora, was dated May 1, 1858. France, England, and Sardinia were named as "the three powers who have caused the independence and nationality of the Ottoman empire to be respected." Sen. Ex. Doc. No. 1, 35th Cong., 2d sess., 62–64.

15. Cass to George Dallas, May 12, 1858, Feb. 23, 1859, Oct. 27, 1860, RDS, Diplomatic Instructions, Great Britain, 17:103, 150–67, NAM; Cass to Dallas, Mar. 18, 1859, Dallas Papers, Huntington; *CG,* 35th Cong., 1st sess., 3061.

16. Cass to Napier, Apr. 10, 1858, in Sen. Ex. Doc. No. 49, 35th Cong., 1st sess., 42–55.

17. *CG,* 35th Cong., 1st sess., 3061; London *Times,* June 15, 1858; Dallas to Cass, June 8, 1858, General Records of the Department of State, Diplomatic Dispatches, Great Britain,

vol. 72, NA; minute of conversation between Dallas and Malmesbury, June 8, 1858, in Sen. Ex. Doc. No. 1, 35th Cong., 2d sess., 35.

18. Buchanan's second annual message to Congress, Dec. 6, 1858, in Richardson, *Messages of the Presidents,* 5:507; Soulsby, "Right of Search," 167–68.

19. Cass to Napier, Nov. 8, 1858, in Moore, *International Law,* 3:164–75.

20. Malmesbury to Napier, Dec. 8, 1858, ibid., 175–76; Buchanan to Clarendon, Apr. 8, 1859, in *Works of Buchanan,* 10:316; Juan R. Mora to Mirabeau B. Lamar, Sept. 16, 1858, in Sen. Ex. Doc. No. 1, 35th Cong., 2d sess., 64–67; Buchanan's fourth annual message to Congress, Dec. 3, 1860, in Richardson, *Messages of the Presidents,* 5:639.

21. Buchanan's inaugural address, in Richardson, *Messages of the Presidents,* 431; *CG,* 31st Cong., 1st sess., 1121; *CG,* 34th Cong., 1st sess., 85, 96; *CG,* 34th Cong., 3d sess., 86. Buchanan had been privately assured the *Dred Scott* ruling would conform to his views regarding slavery in the territories.

22. Cass to Henry Wilson, in *New York Times,* Apr. 12, 1858; *Charleston Daily Courier,* Mar. 9, 1857; J. Glancy Jones to Buchanan, Feb. 14, 1857, Buchanan Papers, HSP; *Boston Daily Bee,* in *Liberator,* Apr. 16, 1858;

23. Walker to Buchanan, Mar. 26, 1857, Cass to Walker, Mar. 30, 1857, and Walker's inaugural address, in "Governor Walker's Administration," *Transactions of the Kansas State Historical Society* 5 (1889–96): 290, 322–23, 328–41; Cass to Robert McClelland, Apr. 6, 1857, Clements.

24. Cass to Walker, Sept. 2, 1857, Walker to Cass, Nov. 3, 1857, and Walker's proclamations to the people of Kansas, Oct. 19, 22, 1857, in "Walker's Administration," 382–84, 402–8. Walker rejected the returns from Oxford precinct in Johnson County, situated across the border from Kansas City, Missouri. The governor toured the area and found only "six houses, including stores," although Oxford submitted returns totaling 1,628 votes. Walker also threw out the returns from three precincts in the extreme southeastern portion of the territory bordering Missouri. Fourteen ballots had been cast there in the previous election; and while Walker estimated one hundred qualified voters lived in the area, 1,266 votes were reported.

25. Lecompton constitution, in House Report No. 377, 35th Cong., 1st sess., 73–92.

26. *New York Times,* Dec. 4, 1857.

27. Stanton to Cass, Dec. 9, 1857, and message of Stanton, Dec. 8, 1857, in "Walker's Administration," 414–19.

28. Foote, *Reminiscences,* 117; Walker to Cass, Dec. 15, 1857, and Cass to Walker, Dec. 18, 1857, in "Walker's Administration," 421–31.

29. *CG,* 36th Cong., 1st sess., 1940; *CG,* 34th Cong., 3d sess., 85–91; *CG,* 35th Cong., 1st sess., app., 196. The new governor of Kansas reported the Lecompton/land-grant proposal was rejected by a vote of 11,300 to 1,788. James W. Denver to Cass, Aug. 24, 1858, in "Walker's Administration," 540.

30. Cass to F. W. Pieham [?], Dec. 12, 1859, photostatic copy, Burton; Cass to John S. Bagg, Nov. 10, 1858, Bagg Papers, Huntington.

31. *Washington Constitution,* June 30, 1860.

32. *CG,* 34th Cong., 3d sess., 91; William H. Trescot quoted in Samuel Wylie Crawford, *The Genesis of the Civil War: The Story of Sumter, 1860–1861* (New York, 1887), 23.

33. Richardson, *Messages of the Presidents,* 5:626–39.

34. Gen. Wool to Cass, Dec. 6, 1860, Clements.

35. Cass to Buchanan, Dec. 12, 1860, and Buchanan memorandum, Dec. 15, 1860, Buchanan Papers, HSP; Buchanan memorandums, Dec. 11, [17], 1860, in *Works of Buchanan,* 11:57, 67.

36. *New York World,* Dec. 15, 1860; *New York Herald,* Dec. 15, 1860; Trescot to Cass, Dec. 14, 1860, Clements; Buchanan memorandum, [Dec. 17, 1860], in *Works of Buchanan,* 11:67.

37. Buchanan memorandum, [Dec. 17, 1860], Isaac Toucey to Buchanan, May 25, 1864, and Jeremiah Black to George T. Curtis, Sept. 26, 1881, *Works of Buchanan,* 11:364, 64; Trescot quoted in Crawford, *Genesis,* 44. Cass's biographers tend to dismiss the claim he attempted to withdraw his resignation, citing a complete lack of corroborative testimony from his family. But if Cass was persuaded to resign "by those about him," he would have been loath to inform them of a change of mind. Black, in fact, was convinced that son-in-law Henry Ledyard "simply got scared" of the political consequences of the secession crisis "and communicated his fright to the General." Black to Curtis, Sept. 26, 1881, *Works of Buchanan,* 11:64; McLaughlin, *Cass,* 348–49; Woodford, *Cass,* 328.

38. J. D. Mendenhall to Cass, Jan. 3, 1861, T. J. Lewis to Cass, Dec. 17, 1860, and George Frost to Cass, Dec. 19, 1860, Clements; *Detroit Daily Advertiser,* Dec. 17, 1860 (emphasis added); *New York Evening Post,* Dec. 15, 1860; E. Peshure Smith to Henry C. Carey, Dec. 16, 1860, E. C. Gardiner Papers, HSP; *Detroit Free Press,* Dec. 16, 1860; McClelland to Cass, Jan. 4, 1861, Clements; Francis P. Blair to Martin Van Buren, Mar. 7, 1861, Van Buren Papers, LC; *New York World,* Dec. 15, 1860; *New York Daily Tribune,* Dec. 15, 1860; *Cincinnati Daily Enquirer,* Dec. 16, 1860; *New York Herald,* Dec. 15, 1860.

39. Cass to Ephraim G. Squirer, Dec. 21, 1861, Clements; Benson J. Lossing, *Pictorial History of the Civil War in the United States of America,* 3 vols. (Philadelphia, 1866–74), 1:141; Cass to William Woodbridge, Jan. 10, 1861, Woodbridge Papers, Burton; George S. Boutwell, *Reminiscences of Sixty Years in Public Affairs,* 2 vols. (1902; reprint, New York, 1968), 1:275–76; McClelland to Cass, Jan. 4, 1861, Clements.

40. John S. Bagg to his wife, Mar. 3, 1861, Bagg Papers, Burton; Cass to Dr. Ira Davis, May 13, 1861, Cass to Henry B. Ledyard, Oct. 4, 1861, and D. Bethune Duffield to Cass, Jan. 19, 1860, Clements; deeds and documents dated Sept. 26, 1859, Jan. 23, July 1860, Feb. 15, 1862, in Burton and the Clarke Library, Central Michigan University.

41. *Detroit Daily Advertiser,* Apr. 18, 25, 1861; McLaughlin, *Cass,* 350–51; Zachariah Chandler to Simon Cameron, Apr. 17, 1861, in *The War of the Rebellion: A Compilation of the Official Records of the Union and Confederate Armies,* ser. 3, 1:78.

42. Cass to Seward, Dec. 18, 19, 1861, in *War of the Rebellion,* ser. 2, 2:1130–32; Seward to Cass, Jan. 2, 1862, Clements (italics added). A Detroit newspaper editor gave a highly dramatic (and inaccurate) account of the *Trent* crisis in William E. Quinby, "Reminiscences of Michigan Journalism," *MPHC* 30 (1904): 515–16.

43. Cass to Lewis Coryell, July 3, 1862, Coryell Papers, HSP; Cass to Henry Ledyard, Jan. 13, 1862, Clements; manuscript of Cass speech, Aug. 13, 1862, in J. P. Cook Papers, MHC.

44. *Detroit Free Press,* Sept. 15, 1863; Cass to Charles C. Trowbridge, May 16, 1863, Burton; Cass to Henry Ledyard, Mar. 14, 1864, and Montgomery Blair to Cass, June 30, 1864, Clements.

45. Alpheus Felch to Edwin C. Lyons, June 20, 1893, Felch Papers, Burton; *Detroit Free Press,* June 17, 1866.

EPILOGUE

1. *Detroit Free Press,* June 17, 20, 21, 1866.
2. *CG,* 34th Cong., 3d sess., 91.
3. John McElhone quoted in *Detroit Tribune,* Feb. 17, 1889.

BIBLIOGRAPHY

The eight sections of this bibliography reflect the different types of sources consulted for this book: principal published works of Lewis Cass; manuscript collections; newspapers; public documents; printed collections of documents, letters, and private diaries; doctoral dissertations; general works, monographs, and pamphlets; and journal and magazine articles.

MANUSCRIPT COLLECTIONS

Boston Public Library.
Webster, Daniel. Papers.
Buffalo and Erie County Historical Society. Buffalo, New York.
Fillmore, Millard. Papers.
Burton Historical Collection. Detroit Public Library. Detroit.
Bagg, John S. Papers.
Bishop, Levi. Papers.
Bradish, Alvah. Papers.
Butler, Charles. Papers.
Cass, Lewis. Papers.
Catlin, George B. Papers.
Douglass, Samuel T. Papers.
Felch, Alpheus. Papers.
Hinchman, Theodore H. Papers.
Hull, William. Papers.
Lossing, Benson J. Papers.
Lyon, Lucius. Papers.
Macomb, Alexander. Papers.
Mason, John Thomas. Papers.
Mason, Stevens T. Papers.

McClelland, Robert. Papers.
Michigan, State of. Papers.
Noble, Charles. Papers.
Satterlee, Richard S. Papers.
Shattuck, Lemuel. Papers.
Shelby, Cass K. Papers.
Shelby, George Cass. Papers.
Sheldon, John P. Papers.
Sibley, Solomon. Papers.
Trowbridge, Charles C. Papers.
Voorhees, Henry P. Papers.
Wilkins, William D. Papers.
Wilkinson, James. Papers.
Williams, John R. Papers.
Wing, Austin E. Papers.
Witherell, Benjamin Franklin H. Papers.
Woodbridge, William. Papers.

Chicago Historical Society.
Cass, Lewis. Papers.
Kimberly, Edmund Stoughton. Papers.

University of Chicago Library.
Douglas, Stephen A. Papers.

Cincinnati Historical Society.
Cass, Lewis. Papers.
Gano, John Stites. Papers.
Hatch, William Stanley. Papers.
Johnston, John. Papers.
Torrence, Aaron. Papers.

Clarke Library. Central Michigan University. Mount Pleasant.
Cass, Lewis. Papers.
Lanman, Charles. Papers.

William L. Clements Library. University of Michigan. Ann Arbor.
Cass, Lewis. Papers.
Lyon, Lucius. Papers.
Michigan. Papers
Van Deventer, Christopher. Papers.
Walworth, Reuben Hyde. Papers.

Columbia University Library. New York City.
Clinton, De Witt. Papers.
Dix, John A. Papers.
Flagg, Azariah C. Papers.

Henry A. Huntington Library. San Marino, California.
Bagg, John Sherman. Papers.
Cass, Lewis. Papers.
Dallas, George M. Papers.

Titus, Charles Henry. Papers.
Indiana State Library. Indianapolis.
Tipton, John. Papers.
Library of Congress. Manuscripts Division. Washington, D.C.
Allen, William. Papers.
Biddle,Nicholas.Papers.
Black, Jeremiah. Papers.
Blair, Francis P. Family Papers.
Blair, Francis P., and William C. Rives. Papers.
Buchanan, James. Papers.
Calhoun, John C. Papers.
Cass, Lewis. Papers.
Chase, Salmon P. Papers.
Clay, Henry. Papers.
Clayton, John M. Papers.
Crittenden, John J. Papers.
Donelson, Andrew J. Papers.
Elmore, Franklin H. Papers.
Fillmore, Millard. Papers.
Force, Peter. Papers.
Garrett, I. W. Family. Papers.
Green, Duff. Papers.
Hammond, James H. Papers.
Jackson, Andrew. Papers.
Jesup, Thomas S. Papers.
Madison, James. Papers.
Mangum, Willie P. Papers.
Manypenny, George W. Papers.
Marcy, William L. Papers.
McClelland, Robert C. Letterbook.
McLean, John. Papers.
Meigs, Return J. Papers.
Niles, Nathaniel. Papers.
Pierce, Franklin. Papers.
Polk, James K. Papers.
Rives, William C. Papers.
Sanders, George N. Papers.
Schoolcraft, Henry R. Papers.
Stephens, Alexander H. Papers.
Stevenson, Andrew. Papers.
Taylor, Zachary. Papers.
Van Buren, Martin. Papers.
Welles, Gideon. Papers.
Woodbury, Levi. Papers.
Massachusetts Historical Society. Boston, Massachusetts.

Cass, Lewis. Papers.
Webster, Daniel. Papers.
Michigan Historical Collections. Bentley Historical Library. University of Michigan. Ann Arbor.
Alpha Nu Society. Papers.
Bingham, Kingsley S. Papers.
Cook, John Potter. Papers.
Crapo, Henry Howland. Papers.
Felch, Alpheus. Papers.
Fey, Charles. Papers.
Goodrich, Enos. Papers.
Lyon, Lucius. Family Papers.
Mason, Stevens Thomson. Papers.
McLaughlin, Andrew C. Papers.
Norris, Mark. Family Papers.
Porter, Frederick Bissell. Journals.
Rickey, Joseph. Papers.
Thomas, Nathan Macy. Papers.
Yates, John B. Scrapbook.
National Archives. Washington, D.C.
Indian Office. Letterbooks.
Office of Indian Affairs/Letters Sent.
Secretary of War/Letters Sent/Indian Affairs.
Newberry Library. Chicago, Illinois.
Cass, Lewis. Papers.
New Hampshire Historical Society. Concord, New Hampshire.
Pierce, Franklin. Papers.
New-York Historical Society. New York City.
Astor, John Jacob, and Ramsey Crooks. Papers.
Buchanan, James. Papers.
Cass, Lewis. Papers.
Everett, Edward. Papers.
Greeley, Horace. Papers.
Taylor, John W. Papers.
Taylor, Zachary. Papers.
New York Public Library. New York City.
Jackson, Andrew, and William B. Lewis. Papers.
Kohns, Lee. Papers.
Tilden, Samuel J. Papers.
Ohio State Library. Columbus, Ohio.
Worthington, Thomas. Papers.
Pennsylvania, Historical Society of. Philadelphia, Pennsylvania.
Buchanan, James. Papers.
Coryell, Lewis. Papers.
Gardiner, Edward Corey. Papers.
Poinsett, Joel R. Papers.
State Historical Society of Wisconsin.

Doty, James D. Papers.
Tallmadge, Nathaniel P. Papers.

NEWSPAPERS
(Listed alphabetically by city)

(Adrian) Michigan Expositor
Adrian Watchtower
Daily Albany Argus
Albany Evening Journal
Ann Arbor True Democrat
Athens (Ga.) Southern Banner
(Baltimore) Niles Weekly Register
Baltimore Sun
(Battle Creek) Michigan Liberty Press
Boston Daily Advertiser
Boston Emancipator
Boston Liberator
Boston Post
Boston Semi-Weekly Advertiser
Bradford (County, Mich.) Reporter
(Brighton and Howell, Mich.) Livingston Courier
Brooklyn Daily Eagle and Kings County Democrat
Buffalo Daily Courier
Charleston Courier
Charleston Mercury
Chicago Daily Democrat
Chicago Daily Democratic Press
Chicago Daily Journal
Chicago Gem of the Prairie
Weekly Chicago Democrat
Chicago Western Citizen
Chillicothe (Ohio) Scioto Gazette
Chillicothe Supporter
Cincinnati Enquirer
Liberty Hall and Cincinnati Mercury
Cincinnati Weekly Herald
Cleveland Daily Plain Dealer
Cleveland Herald
Coldwater (Mich.) Sentinel
(Columbus) Ohio State Journal
(Concord) New Hampshire Patriot & State Gazette
Detroit Advertiser & Tribune
Detroit Daily Advertiser
Detroit Daily Democrat

Detroit Daily Post
Detroit Free Press
Detroit Gazette
Detroit Tribune
(Grand Rapids, Mich.) Grand River Eagle
Harrisburg (Pa.) Keystone
Hillsdale (Mich.) Gazette
Hillsdale Standard
(Indianapolis) Indiana State Journal
(Indianapolis) Indiana State Sentinel
Jackson Mississippian
Jackson (Mich.) Patriot
Jacksonville Floridian
Jefferson (City, Mo.) Inquirer
Kalamazoo (Mich.) Gazette
(Kenosha, Wisc.) Southport Telegraph
London Times
Marshall (Mich.) Democratic Expounder
Marshall Statesman
Milledgeville (Ga.) Federal Union
Milledgeville Southern Recorder
Milwaukee American Freeman
Milwaukee Weekly Wisconsin
Mobile Register and Journal
Montgomery Tri-Weekly Flag & Advertiser
Nashville Republican Banner
Nashville Union
New Orleans Daily Crescent
New Orleans Daily Picayune
New-York Daily Tribune
New York Evening Post
New-York Herald
New York National Anti-Slavery Standard
New-York Standard
New-York Times
New-York Weekly Tribune
New York World
Niles (Mich.) Republican
Painesville (Ohio) Telegraph
Perrysville (Ind.) Eagle
Philadelphia North American and United States Gazette
Philadelphia Pennsylvanian
Pontiac (Mich.) Gazette [variously, *Oakland Gazette*]
Racine (Wisc.) Advocate
(Raleigh) North Carolina Standard
Richmond Enquirer

Rochester (N.Y.) Daily Advertiser
Rochester North Star
Salem (Mass.) Free World
Savannah Georgian
(Springfield) Illinois Journal
(Springfield) Illinois State Journal
(Springfield) Illinois State Register
(St. Clair, Mich.) Port Huron Observer
St. Louis Union
Tallahassee Floridian
(Tallahassee, Fla.) Southern Journal
(Vincennes, Ind.) Western Sun and General Advertiser
(Washington, D.C.) Battery
(Washington, D.C.) Campaign
(Washington, D.C.) Constitution
(Washington, D.C.) Daily National Intelligencer
(Washington, D.C.) Daily Union
(Washington, D.C.) Globe
(Washington, D.C.) National Era

PUBLIC DOCUMENTS

American State Papers, Indian Affairs
American State Papers, Military Affairs
Annals of Congress
Congressional Globe
Congressional Record
Hansard's Parliamentary Debates
House Documents
House Executive Documents
House Reports
Senate Documents
Senate Executive Documents

PRINCIPAL PUBLISHED WORKS OF LEWIS CASS

"Aboriginal Structures." *North American Review* (October 1840): 396–433.

Address Delivered Before the New England Society of Michigan, Dec. 22, 1848. Detroit: F. P. Markham & Brother, 1849.

Address of Gen. Lewis Cass, Delivered Before the Kalamazoo County Agricultural Society, on Friday, October 11, 1850. Washington, D.C.: Towers, n.d.

Address of General Cass to the Democracy of Detroit, Delivered at the City Hall, November 4, 1854. [Detroit, 1854.]

Address of Lewis Cass, of Michigan, LL.D.: Delivered, by Appointment, before the Association of the Alumni of Hamilton College, at their Anniversary Meeting, August 25, 1830. Utica, N.Y.: William Williams, 1830.

Address of the Hon. Lewis Cass, Delivered before the Michigan State Agricultural Society, at its Third Annual Fair, Held at Detroit, September 24, 25 & 26, 1851. Detroit: Barns, Brodhead, 1851.

A Discourse Delivered at the First Meeting of the Historical Society of Michigan: September 18, 1829. Detroit: Geo. L. Whitney, 1830.

"Discourse Delivered Before the Historical Society of Michigan." In *Historical and Scientific Sketches of Michigan. Comprising a Series of Discourses Delivered Before the Historical Society of Michigan, and Other Interesting Papers Relative to the Territory,* 5–50. Detroit: Stephen Wells & George L. Whitney, 1834.

A Discourse Pronounced at the Capitol of the United States, In the Hall of Representatives, Before the American Historical Society, January 30, 1836, by the Hon. Lewis Cass, President of the Society. Washington, D.C.: P. Thompson, 1836.

An Examination of the Question, Now in Discussion, Between the American and British Governments, Concerning the Right of Search. Baltimore: N. Hickman, 1842.

France, Its King, Court, and Government; and Three Hours at Saint Cloud. 2d ed. New York: Wiley & Putnam, 1841.

"Indians of North America." *North American Review* (January 1826): 53–119.

Inquiries Respecting the History, Traditions, Languages, Manners, Customs, Religion, &c. of the Indians Living Within the United States. Detroit: Sheldon & Reed, 1823.

"Island of Candia." *Southern Literary Messenger* 5 (1839): 709–20.

"The Island of Cyprus." *Southern Literary Messenger* 7 (1841): 81–105.

Letter from Hon. Lewis Cass, of Michigan, on the War and the Wilmot Proviso. [The Nicholson Letter.] Washington, D.C.: Blair & Rives, 1847.

Letter from Lewis Cass, Late American Minister at Paris, to Daniel Webster, Secretary of State, on the Right of Search, Dated March 7, 1843. Washington, D.C.: Ritchie & Heiss, 1846.

Letter of the Most Rev. Archbishop Hughes on the Madiai. Speech of Hon. Lewis Cass, on Religious Freedom Abroad. Letter of the Most Rev. Archbishop Hughes, in Reply to Hon. Lewis Cass, on Religious Toleration. Baltimore: Murphy, [1854].

Oration Delivered at the Celebration of the Completion of the Wabash and Erie Canal, by Gen. Lewis Cass, at Fort Wayne, I[ndian]a on the Fourth of July, 1843. Fort Wayne, Ind.: T. Tigar, 1843.

"Policy and Practice of the United States and Great Britain in Their Treatment of Indians." *North American Review* (April 1827): 365–442.

"A Recent Visit to Lady Hester Stanhope." *Southern Literary Messenger* 4 (1838): 496–99.

Remarks of General Lewis Cass, on the Late French Revolution, Delivered at a Public Meeting held in Odd-Fellows Hall, in the City of Washington, March 28, 1848. [Washington, D.C.]: Congressional Globe Office, [1848].

"Removal of the Indians." *North American Review* (January 1830): 62–121.

"Stephens' Travels in the East." *North American Review* (January 1839): 181–256.

"Structure of the Indian Languages." *North American Review* (April 1828): 357–403.

Substance of a Speech Delivered by Hon. Lewis Cass, of Michigan, in Secret Session of the Senate of the United States, on the Ratification of the Oregon Treaty, with Additions. Detroit: Bagg & Harmon, 1846.

"Three Hours at Saint Cloud. By an American." *Knickerbocker* 17 (1841): 1–15.
To the Public. Paris, Mar. 6, 1837.

PRINTED COLLECTIONS OF DOCUMENTS, LETTERS, AND PRIVATE DIARIES

Adams, John Quincy. *Memoirs of John Quincy Adams, Comprising Portions of His Diary from 1795–1848.* Edited by Charles Frances Adams. 12 vols. Philadelphia: J. B. Lippincott, 1874–77.

Black, Jeremiah S. *Essays and Speeches of Jeremiah S. Black. With a Biographical Sketch.* Compiled by Chauncey F. Black. New York: D. Appleton, 1886.

Boucher, Chauncey S., and Robert P. Brooks, eds., "Correspondence Addressed to John C. Calhoun, 1837–1849." *Annual Report of the American Historical Association for the Year 1929.* Washington, D.C., 1930.

Brannon, John, ed. *Official Letters of the Military and Naval Officers of the United States, during the War with Great Britain in the Years 1812, 13, 14, & 15.* Washington, D.C.: Way & Gideon, 1823.

Brown, Aaron V. *Speeches, Congressional and Political, and Other Writings of Ex-Governor Aaron V. Brown, of Tennessee.* Nashville: John L. Marling, 1854.

Buchanan, James. *The Works of James Buchanan: Comprising his Speeches, State Papers, and Private Correspondence.* Edited by John Bassett Moore. 12 vols. Philadelphia: J. B. Lippincott, 1908–11.

Calhoun, John C. "Correspondence of John C. Calhoun." *Annual Report of the American Historical Association for the Year 1899.* Vol. 2. Edited by J. Franklin Jameson. Washington, D.C., 1900.

———. *The Papers of John C. Calhoun.* Edited by Robert L. Meriwether, W. Edwin Hemphill, and Clyde N. Wilson. Columbia, S.C.: University of South Carolina Press, 1959– .

Carter, Clarence Edwin, comp. and ed. *The Territorial Papers of the United States.* Vols. 10–12. Washington, D.C.: Government Printing Office, 1942–45.

Cass, Lewis. *General Lewis Cass: 1782–1866.* Edited by Cass Canfield. Norwood, Mass.: Plimpton, 1916.

Chase, Salmon P. "Sixth Report of Historical Manuscripts Commission: With Diary and Correspondence of Salmon P. Chase." *Annual Report of the American Historical Association for the Year 1902.* Vol. 2. Washington, D.C., 1903.

Clay, Henry. *The Papers of Henry Clay.* Edited by James F. Hopkins et al. 11 vols. Lexington: University Press of Kentucky, 1959–1992.

———. *The Private Correspondence of Henry Clay.* Edited by Calvin Colton. New York: A. S. Barnes, 1855.

———. *Works of Henry Clay: Comprising His Life, Correspondence and Speeches.* Edited by Calvin Colton. 7 vols. New York: Henry Clay, 1897.

Commager, Henry Steele, ed. *Documents of American History.* 5th ed. New York: Appleton-Century-Crofts, 1949.

"Copies of Papers on File in the Dominion Archives at Ottawa, Canada, Pertaining to Michigan, As Found in the Colonial Office Records." *Historical*

Collections: Collections and Researches Made by the Michigan Pioneer and Historical Society 25 (1896).
"Copies of Papers on File in the Dominion Archives at Ottawa, Canada, Pertaining to the Relations of the British Government with the United States During the Period of the War of 1812." *Historical Collections: Collections and Researches Made by the Michigan Pioneer and Historical Society* 15 (1889).
"Copies of Papers on File in the Dominion Archives at Ottawa, Canada, Pertaining to the Relations of the British Government with the United States During and Subsequent to the Period of the War of 1812." *Historical Collections: Collections and Researches Made by the Pioneer and Historical Society* 16 (1890).
Cruikshank, Ernest Alexander, ed. *The Documentary History of the Campaign on the Niagara Frontier.* 9 vols. Welland, Ont.: Lundy's Lane Historical Society, 1896–1908.
Dana, Richard Henry, Jr. *The Journal of Richard Henry Dana, Jr.* Edited by Robert F. Lucid. 3 vols. Cambridge: Harvard University Press, Belknap Press, 1968.
———. *Speeches in Stirring Times and Letters to a Son.* Edited by Richard H. Dana III. Boston: Houghton Mifflin, 1910.
Davis, Jefferson. *Jefferson Davis, Constitutionalist: His Letters, Papers and Speeches.* Edited by Dunbar Rowland. 10 vols. Jackson: Printed for the Mississippi Department of Archives and History, 1923.
Dickinson, Daniel S. *Speeches, Correspondence, Etc., of the Late Daniel S. Dickinson, of New York.* Edited by John R. Dickinson. 2 vols. New York: G. P. Putnam, 1867.
"Documents Relating to Detroit and Vicinity, 1805–1813." *Michigan Historical Collections* 40 (1929).
Douglas, Stephen A. *The Letters of Stephen A. Douglas.* Edited by Robert W. Johannsen. Urbana: University of Illinois Press, 1961.
Fairfield, John. *The Letters of John Fairfield.* Edited by Arthur G. Staples. Lewiston, Maine: Lewiston Journal, 1922.
Fox, J. Sharpless, ed. "Territorial Papers, 1831–1836, including Schoolcraft Papers." *Historical Collections and Researches Made by the Michigan Pioneer and Historical Society* 37 (1909–10): 207–419.
Fuller, George N., ed. *Messages of the Governors of Michigan.* 4 vols. Lansing: Michigan Historical Commission, 1925–27.
Garfield, James Abram. *The Works of James Abram Garfield.* Edited by Burke A. Hinsdale. 2 vols. Boston: James R. Osgood, 1883.
Garrison, George P., ed. "Diplomatic Correspondence of the Republic of Texas." *Annual Report of the American Historical Association for the Year 1908.* Vol. 2. Washington, D.C., 1911.
Garrison, William Lloyd. *The Letters of William Lloyd Garrison.* Edited by Walter M. Merrill. 5 vols. Cambridge: Harvard University Press, Belknap Press, 1971–79.
Harrison, William Henry. *Messages and Letters of William Henry Harrison.* Edited by Logan Esarey. 2 vols. New York: Arno, 1975.
Hone, Philip. *The Diary of Philip Hone: 1828–1851.* Edited by Allan Nevins. New York: Dodd, Mead, 1936.

Hunter, Robert M. T. "Correspondence of Robert M. T. Hunter: 1826–1876." *Annual Report of the American Historical Association for the Year 1916.* Edited by Charles Henry Ambler. Vol. 2. Washington, D.C., 1918.

Israel, Fred L., ed. *The State of the Union Messages of the Presidents.* 3 vols. New York: Chelsea House–Robert Hector, 1966.

Jackson, Andrew. *Correspondence of Andrew Jackson.* Edited by John Spencer Bassett. 7 vols. Washington, D.C.: Carnegie Institution, 1926–35.

———. *The Statesmanship of Andrew Jackson as Told in his Writings and Speeches.* Edited by Francis Newton Thorpe. Principles of American Statesmanship Series. New York: Tandy-Thomas, 1909.

Knopf, Richard C., trans. *Document Transcriptions of the War of 1812 in the Northwest.* 10 vols. Columbus: Ohio Historical Society, 1957–62.

Lincoln, Abraham. *The Collected Works of Abraham Lincoln.* Edited by Roy P. Basler. 8 vols. New Brunswick, N.J.: Rutgers University Press, 1953.

Lippincott, Sarah Jane Clarke. *Greenwood Leaves: A Collection of Sketches and Letters.* 2d ser. Boston: Ticknor, Reed, and Fields, 1854.

Lyon, Lucius. "Letters of Lucius Lyon." Edited by L. G. Stuart. *Historical Collections: Collections and Researches Made by the Michigan Pioneer and Historical Society* 27 (1897): 412–604.

Malloy, William M., comp. *Treaties, Conventions, International Acts, Protocols and Agreements Between the United States of America and Other Powers: 1776–1909.* 2 vols. Washington, D.C.: Government Printing Office, 1910.

Mangum, Willie Person. *The Papers of Willie Person Mangum.* Edited by Henry Thomas Shanks. 5 vols. Raleigh, N.C.: State Department of Archives and History, 1950–56.

Michigan Legislature. *Journal of the House of Representatives.* Lansing: Bagg & Harmon, 1848; R. W. Ingels, 1851.

———. *Journal of the Senate.* Detroit: Bagg & Harmon, 1845; Lansing: Munger & Pattison, 1849; R. W. Ingels, 1851.

———. *Laws of the Territory of Michigan.* 2 vols. Lansing: W. S. George, 1871–74.

———. *Some of the Acts of the Territory of Michigan, With the Titles and a Digest of all the Acts of the Said Territory: Now in Force.* Detroit: Theophilus Mettez, 1816.

Moore, Charles, comp. "The Beginnings of Territorial Government in Michigan—Manuscripts in the Department of State, Washington." *Historical Collections: Collections and Researches Made by the Michigan Pioneer and Historical Society* 31 (1902): 510–612.

Moore, John Bassett. *A Digest of International Law.* 8 vols. Washington, D.C.: Government Printing Office, 1906.

Permanent Temperance Documents of the American Temperance Society. Religion in America Series. Edited by Edwin S. Gaustad. 1835. Reprint. New York: Arno, 1972.

Phillips, Ulrich B., ed. "The Correspondence of Robert Toombs, Alexander H. Stephens, and Howell Cobb." *Annual Report of the American Historical Association for the Year 1911.* Vol. 2. Washington, D.C., 1913.

Polk, James K. *Correspondence of James K. Polk.* Edited by Herbert Weaver et al. Nashville: Vanderbilt University Press, 1969– .

———. *The Diary of James K. Polk: During His Presidency, 1845 to 1849*. Edited by Milo Milton Quaife. 4 vols. Chicago: A. C. McClurg, 1910.

Quaife, Milo Milton, ed. "The Movement for Statehood: 1845–1846." Publications of the State Historical Society of Wisconsin. *Collections* 26 (1918).

Richardson, James D., comp. *A Compilation of the Messages and Papers of the Presidents: 1789–1897*. 10 vols. Washington, D.C.: Government Printing Office, 1897.

Ross, John. *The Papers of Chief John Ross*. Edited by Gary E. Moulton. 2 vols. Norman: University of Oklahoma Press, 1985.

Russell, John, comp. *The History of the War, between the United States and Great-Britain, which Commenced in June, 1812, and Closed in Feb[ruary] 1815; . . . .* Hartford, Conn.: William S. Marsh, 1815.

Schoolcraft, Henry Rowe. "Territorial Records: Schoolcraft Papers." *Historical Collections: Collections and Researches Made by the Michigan Pioneer and Historical Society* 36 (1908): 383–620.

Seward, William H. *The Works of William H. Seward*. Edited by George E. Baker. 3 vols. New York: Redfield, 1853.

Sumner, Charles. *Charles Sumner: His Complete Works*. Edited by George Frisbie Hoar. 20 vols. 1900. Reprint. New York: Negro Universities Press, 1969.

Taylor, Zachary. *Letters of Zachary Taylor from the Battlefields of the Mexican War: Reprinted from the Originals in the Collection of Mr. William K. Bixby, of St. Louis, Mo.* Edited by William H. Samson. Rochester, N.Y.: Genesee, 1908.

Thwaites, Reuben Gold, ed. "The Fur-Trade in Wisconsin: 1815–1817." *Collections of the State Historical Society of Wisconsin* 19 (1910): 375–488.

———, ed. "The Fur-Trade in Wisconsin: 1812–1825." *Collections of the State Historical Society of Wisconsin* 20 (1911): 1–395.

Tilden, Samuel J. *The Writings and Speeches of Samuel J. Tilden*. Edited by John Bigelow. 2 vols. New York: Harper & Brothers, 1885.

Walker, William. "Governor Walker's Administration." *Transactions of the Kansas State Historical Society* 5 (1889–96): 290–464.

The War of the Rebellion: A Compilation of the Official Records of the Union and Confederate Armies. Washington, D.C.: Government Printing Office, 1897.

Webster, Daniel. *The Letters of Daniel Webster*. Edited by C. H. Van Tyne. New York: McClure, Phillips, 1902.

———. *The Papers of Daniel Webster: Correspondence*. Series 1. Edited by Charles M. Wiltse. 7 vols. Hanover, N.H.: University Press of New England, 1974–1986.

———. *The Papers of Daniel Webster: Diplomatic Papers*. Series 3. Edited by Kenneth E. Shewmaker and Kenneth R. Stevens. 2 vols. Hanover, N.H.: University Press of New England, 1983–87.

———. *The Papers of Daniel Webster: Legal Papers*. Series 2. Edited by Alfred S. Konefsky and Andrew J. King. 3 vols. Hanover, N.H.: University Press of New England, 1982–89.

———. *The Papers of Daniel Webster: Speeches and Formal Writings*. Series 4. Edited by Charles M. Wiltse. 2 vols. Hanover, N.H.: University Press of New England, 1986–1988.

———. *Private Correspondence of Daniel Webster*. Edited by Fletcher Webster. 2 vols. Boston: Little, Brown, 1857.

———. *The Works of Daniel Webster.* 17th ed. Boston: Little, Brown, 1877.
———. *The Writings and Speeches of Daniel Webster in Eighteen Volumes.* Boston: Little, Brown, 1903.

DOCTORAL DISSERTATIONS

Armold, Jack David. "The Compromise of 1850: A Burkeian Analysis." University of Illinois, 1959.
Beers, Henry Putney. "The Western Military Frontier: 1815–1846." University of Pennsylvania, 1935.
Hewlett, Richard G. "Lewis Cass in National Politics, 1842–1861." University of Chicago, 1952.
Hubbell, John Thomas. "The Northern Democracy and the Crisis of Disunion, 1860–1861." University of Illinois, 1969.
Mirani, Ronald Gregory. "Lewis Cass and Indian Administration in the Old Northwest, 1815–1836." University of Michigan, 1974.
Ndukwu, Maurice Dickson. "Antislavery in Michigan: A Study of its Origin, Development, and Expression from Territorial Period to 1860." Michigan State University, 1979.
Sherer, Timothy Frederick. "The Rule of the Governor and Judges in Michigan Territory, 1805–1823." Michigan State University, 1976.
Smith, Carlton Bruce. "The United States War Department, 1815–1842." University of Virginia, 1967.
Stevens, Walter William. "A Study of Lewis Cass and His United States Senate Speeches on Popular Sovereignty." University of Michigan, 1959.
Unger, Robert William. "Lewis Cass: Indian Superintendent of the Michigan Territory, 1813–1831." Ball State University, 1967.
Van Deventer, Carroll Francis. "The Free Soil Party in the Northwest in the Elections of 1848." University of Illinois, 1968.
Whitehurst, Alto Lee. "Martin Van Buren and the Free Soil Movement." University of Chicago, 1932.

GENERAL WORKS, MONOGRAPHS, AND PAMPHLETS

Adams, Charles Francis, [Jr.]. *Charles Francis Adams.* American Statesmen Series. Boston: Houghton Mifflin, 1900.
[Adams, John Calvin.] *General Taylor and the Wilmot Proviso.* [Boston: Wilson & Damrell, 1848.]
———. *A Northern No! Addressed to the Delegates from the Free States to the Whig National Convention. At Philadelphia, 1848.* [1848.]
Address Adopted by the Whig State Convention, at Worcester, September 13, 1848. [Worcester, Mass., 1848.]
Address of the Democratic Republican Young Men's General Committee, of the City of New-York, to the Republican Young Men of the State. [New York?]: Jared W. Bell, 1840.

Address of the National Democratic Republican Committee. Millard Fillmore, Proved to be an Abolitionist! General Taylor, Probably Pledged to the Whigs of the North, in Favor of the Wilmot Proviso. [Washington, D.C.]: Central National Democratic Republican Committee, [1848].

Administration of Gen. Cass in the Northwest. Published Under the Authority of the Committee, [1848].

Ahl, Frances Norene. *Andrew Jackson and the Constitution.* Boston: Christopher, 1939.

Alexander, DeAlva Stanwood. *A Political History of the State of New York.* 4 vols. New York: Henry Holt, 1906–23.

Allowances and Extra Pay. A Plain Statement of Facts from the Record, Showing Gen. Taylor to Have Received $74,864 of "Allowances," . . . and General Cass to Have Received Not One Cent . . . . [Washington, D.C.]: Published Under Authority of the National and Jackson Democratic Association, [1848].

American Free Soil Almanac for 1849: Astronomically and Politically Calculated for the States and Territories of the Union. Boston: White, Potter, & Wright, [1848].

Americanus [pseud.]. *Comments on Lord Brougham's Attack Upon General Lewis Cass.* Harrisburg, Pa.: Argus Office, 1843.

Ammon, Harry. *James Monroe: The Quest for National Identity.* New York: McGraw-Hill, 1971.

Anbinder, Tyler. *Nativism and Slavery: The Northern Know Nothings and the Politics of the 1850s.* New York: Oxford University Press, 1992.

Andrew, John A., III. *From Revivals to Removal: Jeremiah Evarts, the Cherokee Nation, and the Search for the Soul of America.* Athens: University of Georgia Press, 1992.

Armstrong, John. *Notices of the War of 1812.* 2 vols. in 1. New York: George Dearborn, 1836; New York: Wiley & Putnam, 1840.

Auchampaugh, Philip G. *James Buchanan and His Cabinet on the Eve of Secession.* Lancaster, Pa.: Privately printed, 1926.

Avary, Myrta Lockett, ed. *Recollections of Alexander H. Stephens.* New York: Doubleday, Page, 1910.

Bain, Richard C. *Convention Decisions and Voting Records.* Washington, D.C.: Brookings Institute, 1960.

Baker, Jean H. *Affairs of Party: The Political Culture of Northern Democrats in the Mid-19th Century.* Ithaca, N.Y.: Cornell University Press, 1983.

Bald, F. Clever. *Michigan in Four Centuries.* New York: Harper & Row, 1961.

Bancroft, Frederic. *The Life of William H. Seward.* 2 vols. New York: Harper & Brothers, 1900.

Bandinel, James. *Some Account of the Trade in Slaves from Africa as Connected with Europe and America; from the Introduction of the Trade into Modern Europe, Down to the Present Time; Especially with Reference to the Efforts Made by the British Government for its Extinction.* London: Longman, Brown, 1842.

Bartlett, Ruhl Jacob. *John C. Fremont and the Republican Party.* Ohio State University Studies, no. 13. Columbus: Ohio State University, 1930.

Bassett, John Spencer. *The Life of Andrew Jackson.* 2 vols. Garden City, N.Y.: Doubleday, Page, 1911.

Bauer, K. Jack. *The Mexican War: 1846–1848.* The Wars of the United States Series. General editor Louis Morton. New York: Macmillan, 1974.

———. *Zachary Taylor: Soldier, Planter, Statesman of the Old Southwest.* Southern Biography Series. Baton Rouge: Louisiana State University Press, 1985.

Baxter, Maurice G. *One and Inseparable: Daniel Webster and the Union.* Cambridge: Harvard University Press, Belknap Press, 1984.

Beardsley, Levi. *Reminiscences; Personal and Other Incidents; Early Settlement of Otsego County, Notices and Anecdotes of Public Men; Judicial, Legal and Legislative Matters; Field Sports; Dissertations and Discussions.* New York: Charles Vinten, 1852.

Beirne, Francis F. *The War of 1812.* New York: E. P. Dutton, 1949.

Bell, Charles H. *History of the Town of Exeter, New Hampshire.* Exeter: J. E. Farwell, 1888.

———. *The Phillips Exeter Academy.* Exeter: W. B. Morrill, 1883.

Belohlavek, John M. *George Mifflin Dallas: Jacksonian Patrician.* University Park: Pennsylvania State University Press, 1977.

———. *"Let the Eagle Soar!": The Foreign Policy of Andrew Jackson.* Lincoln: University of Nebraska Press, 1985.

Bemis, Samuel Flagg. *A Diplomatic History of the United States.* 5th ed. New York: Holt, Rinehart, & Winston, 1965.

[Benton, Thomas Hart.] *Thirty Years' View; or, A History of the Working of the American Government for Thirty Years, From 1820 to 1850.* 2 vols. New York: D. Appleton, 1854–56.

Bergeron, Paul H. *The Presidency of James K. Polk.* American Presidency Series. Lawrence: University Press of Kansas, 1987.

Berwanger, Eugene H. *The Frontier Against Slavery: Western Anti-Negro Prejudice and the Slavery Extension Controversy.* 2d ed. Urbana: University of Illinois Press, 1971.

Beveridge, Albert J. *Abraham Lincoln: 1809–1858.* 2 vols. Boston: Houghton Mifflin, 1928.

Bidlack, Russell E. *The Yankee Meets the Frenchman: River Raisin, 1817–1830.* Ann Arbor: Historical Society of Michigan, 1965.

Bigelow, John. *Retrospections of an Active Life.* 5 vols. New York: Baker & Taylor, 1909.

Billington, Ray Allen. *Westward Expansion: A History of the American Frontier.* New York: Macmillan, 1949.

Bird, Harrison. *War for the West: 1790–1813.* New York: Oxford University Press, 1971.

Bishop, Joseph Bucklin. *Presidential Nominations and Elections: A History of American Conventions, National Campaigns, Inaugurations, and Campaign Caricature.* New York: Charles Scribner's Sons, 1916.

Blois, John T. *Gazetteer of the State of Michigan, in Three Parts, . . . With an Appendix, Containing the Usual Statistical Tables, And a Directory for Emigrants, &c.* Detroit: Sydney L. Rood, 1838; New York: Robinson, Pratt, 1838.

Blue, Frederick J. *The Free Soilers: Third Party Politics, 1848–1854.* Urbana: University of Illinois Press, 1973.

———. *Salmon P. Chase: A Life in Politics.* Kent, Ohio: Kent State University Press, 1987.

Blumenthal, Henry. *France and the United States: Their Diplomatic Relations, 1789–1914.* Chapel Hill: University of North Carolina Press, 1970.

Bottorff, William K. *Thomas Jefferson.* Edited by Sylvia E. Bowman. Twayne's United States Authors Series. Boston: Twayne, 1979.

Boutwell, George S. *Reminiscences of Sixty Years in Public Affairs.* 2 vols. 1902. Reprint. New York: Greenwood, 1968.

[Bowditch, William Ingersoll.] *Cass and Taylor on the Slavery Question.* Boston: Damrell & Moore, 1848.

Bowers, Claude G. *The Party Battles of the Jackson Period.* Boston: Houghton Mifflin, 1928.

Brant, Irving. *James Madison.* 6 vols. Indianapolis: Bobbs-Merrill, 1941–61.

Brauer, Kinley J. *Cotton versus Conscience: Massachusetts Whig Politics and Southwestern Expansion, 1843–1848.* Lexington: University of Kentucky Press, 1967.

Bremer, Richard G. *Indian Agent and Wilderness Scholar: The Life of Henry Rowe Schoolcraft.* Mount Pleasant: Clarke Historical Library, Central Michigan University, 1987.

[Bridge, Horatio.] *The Journal of an American Cruiser; Comprising Sketches of the Canaries, the Cape De Verds, Liberia, Madeira, Sierra Leone, and Other Places of Interest on the West Coast of Africa.* Edited by Nathaniel Hawthorne. Aberdeen: George Clark & Son, 1848.

Brigance, William Norwood. *Jeremiah Sullivan Black.* Philadelphia: University of Pennsylvania Press, 1934.

Brinton, Crane. *The Americans and the French.* Cambridge: Harvard University Press, 1968.

Brock, William R. *Conflict and Transformation: The United States, 1844–1877.* Harmondsworth, Eng.: Penguin, 1973.

Brockway, Beman. *Fifty Years in Journalism.* Watertown, N.Y.: Daily Times, 1891.

Brown, Charles, H. *Agents of Manifest Destiny: The Lives and Times of the Filibusters.* Chapel Hill: University of North Carolina Press, 1980.

Brown, Warren. *History of the Town of Hampton Falls, New Hampshire from the Time of the First Settlement Within its Borders, 1640 until 1900.* 2 vols. Manchester, N.H.: John B. Clarke, 1900.

Bruce, David K. E. *Revolution to Reconstruction.* New York: Doran, 1939.

[Buchanan, James.] *Mr. Buchanan's Administration on the Eve of the Rebellion.* New York: D. Appleton, 1866.

Buley, R. Carlyle. *The Old Northwest: Pioneer Period, 1815–1840.* 2 vols. Indianapolis: Indiana Historical Society, 1950.

Burgess, John W. *The Middle Period: 1817–1858.* New York: Charles Scribner's Sons, 1900.

Burnham, W. Dean. *Presidential Ballots: 1836–1892.* Baltimore: Johns Hopkins Press, 1955.

Burton, Clarence Monroe. *The Building of Detroit.* N.p., 1912.

Campbell, James V. *Outlines of the Political History of Michigan.* Detroit: Schober, 1876.

Campbell, Maria, and James Freeman Clarke. *Revolutionary Services and Civil Life of General William Hull; Prepared from His Manuscripts, by His Daughter, Mrs. Maria Campbell. . . .* New York: D. Appleton, 1848.

Campbell, Stanley W. *The Slave Catchers: Enforcement of the Fugitive Slave Law, 1850–1860.* Chapel Hill: University of North Carolina Press, 1970.

Capers, Gerald M. *John C. Calhoun—Opportunist: A Reappraisal.* Gainesville: University of Florida Press, 1960.

Carpenter, Jesse Thomas. *The South as a Conscious Minority, 1789–1861; A Study in Political Thought.* New York: New York University Press, 1930.

Carr, Clark E. *My Day and Generation.* Chicago: A. C. McClurg, 1908.

Carter, Samuel, III. *Cherokee Sunset: A Nation Betrayed.* Garden City, N.Y.: Doubleday, 1976.

The Cass Platform. [Washington, D.C.: Towers, 1848.]

Casselman, Alexander Clark. *[Major John] Richardson's War of 1812.* Toronto: Historical Publishing, 1902.

[Catlin, George.] *Catlin's Notes of Eight Years' Travels and Residence in Europe, with his North American Indian Collection.* 2 vols. London, 1848.

Catlin, George B. *A Brief History of Detroit in the Golden Days of '49.* N.p., 1921.

———. *The Story of Detroit.* Detroit: Detroit News, 1923.

Chambers, William Nisbet. *Old Bullion Benton.* Boston: Little, Brown, 1956.

Chapman, Mrs. Coleman, ed. *The Life of John J. Crittenden, with Selections from his Correspondence and Speeches.* 2 vols. in 1. Philadelphia: J. B. Lippincott, 1873.

The Charles F. Adams Platform, or A Looking Glass for the Worthies of the Buffalo Convention. J. & G. S. Gideon, [1848].

[Cheever, George.] *The Removal of the Indians.* Boston: Peirce & Williams, 1830.

Chidsey, Donald Barr. *The War With Mexico.* New York: Crown, 1968.

Chittenden, L. E. *Personal Reminiscences Including Lincoln and Others: 1840–1890.* New York: Richmond, Croscup, 1893.

Cleaves, Freeman. *Old Tippecanoe: William Henry Harrison and His Time.* New York: Charles Scribner's Sons, 1939.

Cole, Arthur Charles. *The Era of the Civil War: 1848–1870.* Centennial History of Illinois Series. Springfield: Illinois Centennial Commission, 1919.

———. *The Whig Party in the South.* Washington, D.C.: American Historical Association, 1914.

Cole, Donald B. *Martin Van Buren and the American Political System.* Princeton, N.J.: Princeton University Press, 1984.

———. *The Presidency of Andrew Jackson.* Lawrence: University Press of Kansas, 1993.

Coles, Harry L. *The War of 1812.* Chicago: University of Chicago Press, 1965.

Colton, Calvin. *The Last Seven Years of the Life of Henry Clay.* New York: A. S. Barnes, 1856.

Comfort, Benjamin F. *Lewis Cass and the Indian Treaties.* Detroit: Charles F. May, 1923.

[Conneau, Theophile (Theodore Canot).] *Captain Canot; or, Twenty Years of an African Slaver: Being an Account of his Career and Adventures on the Coast, in the*

Interior, on Shipboard, and in the West Indies. Edited by Brantz Mayer. New York: D. Appleton, 1854.

Connor, Seymour V., and Odie B. Faulk. *North America Divided: The Mexican War, 1846–1848.* New York: Oxford University Press, 1971.

Cooley, Thomas McIntyre. *Michigan: A History of Governments.* Boston: Houghton Mifflin, 1899.

Cotter, Cornelius P., and Bernard C. Hennessy. *Politics Without Power: The National Party Committees.* New York: Atherton, 1964.

Covington, James W. *The Seminoles of Florida.* Gainesville: University Press of Florida, 1993.

Craven, Avery. *The Coming of the Civil War.* New York: Charles Scribner's Sons, 1942.

Crawford, Samuel Wylie. *The Genesis of the Civil War: The Story of Sumter, 1860–1861.* New York: Charles L. Webster, 1887.

Crippen, Lee F. *Simon Cameron: Ante-Bellum Years.* Oxford, Ohio: Mississippi Valley, 1942.

Crosbie, Laurence M. *The Phillips Exeter Academy: A History.* Norwood, Mass.: Plimpton, 1924.

Cunningham, Frank H. *Familiar Sketches of the Phillips Exeter Academy and Surroundings.* Boston: James R. Osgood, 1883.

Current, Richard N. *Daniel Webster and the Rise of National Conservatism.* Boston: Little, Brown, 1955.

Curtis, George Ticknor. *The Just Supremacy of Congress over the Territories.* Boston: A. Williams, 1859.

———. *Life of Daniel Webster.* 2 vols. New York: D. Appleton, 1870–72.

———. *Life of James Buchanan.* 2 vols. New York: Harper & Brothers, 1883.

Dain, Floyd R. *Detroit and the Westward Movement.* Detroit: Wayne State University Press, 1951.

Dalzell, Robert F., Jr. *Daniel Webster and the Trial of American Nationalism, 1843–1852.* Boston: Houghton Mifflin, 1973.

Darby, William. *A Tour from the City of New-York, to Detroit, in the Michigan Territory, Made Between the 2d of May and the 22d of September, 1818.* New York: Kirk & Mercein, 1819.

Darby, William, and Theodore Dwight, Jr. *A New Gazetteer of the United States of America; . . . Including Other Interesting and Valuable Geographical, Historical, Political, and Statistical Information; With the Population of 1830.* Hartford, Conn.: Edward Hopkins, 1833.

Darling, Arthur B. *Political Changes in Massachusetts: 1824–1848.* New Haven, Conn.: Yale University Press, 1925.

Davis, Burke. *Old Hickory: A Life of Andrew Jackson.* New York: Dial, 1977.

Davis, Paris M. *An Authentic History of the Late War [of 1812] Between the United States and Great Britain.* New York: Ebenezer F. Baker, 1836.

Davis, Reuben. *Recollections of Mississippi and Mississippians.* Boston: Houghton Mifflin, 1890.

Debo, Angie. *The Road to Disappearance.* Norman: University of Oklahoma Press, 1941.

Denman, Clarence Phillips. *The Secession Movement in Alabama.* Montgomery: Alabama State Department of Archives and History, 1933.
DeRosier, Arthur H., Jr. *The Removal of the Choctaw Indians.* Knoxville: University of Tennessee Press, 1970.
DeVoto, Bernard. *The Year of Decision, 1846.* Boston: Little, Brown, 1943.
Dix, Morgan, comp. *Memoirs of John Adams Dix.* 2 vols. New York: Harper & Brothers, 1883.
Dodd, William E. *The West and the War with Mexico.* Annual Address Before the Illinois State Historical Society, May 23, 1912. Reprinted from the Journal of the Society, July 1912.
Donald, David. *Charles Sumner and the Coming of the Civil War.* New York: Alfred A. Knopf, 1961.
Donovan, Herbert D. A. *The Barnburners. A Study of the Internal Movements in the Political History of New York State and of the Resulting Changes in Political Affiliation: 1830–1852.* New York: New York University Press, 1925.
Douglass, David B. *The Journal of David Bates Douglass.* Edited by Sydney W. Jackman and John F. Freeman. Marquette: Northern Michigan University Press, 1969.
Duane, William J. *Narrative and Correspondence Concerning the Removal of the Deposites, and Occurrences Connected Therewith.* Philadelphia, 1838.
Duberman, Martin. *Charles Francis Adams, 1807–1886.* Palo Alto, Calif.: Stanford University Press, 1968.
DuBois, W. E. Burghardt. *The Suppression of the African Slave-Trade to the United States of America: 1638–1870.* New York: Longmans, Green, 1896.
Dumond, Dwight L. *A History of the United States.* New York: Henry Holt, 1942.
Dunbar, Willis Frederick. *Lewis Cass.* A Great Men of Michigan Book. Edited by C. Warren Vander Hill. Grand Rapids, Mich.: William B. Eerdmans, 1970.
———. *Michigan: A History of the Wolverine State.* Grand Rapids, Mich.: William B. Eerdmans, 1965.
Dyer, Brainerd. *Zachary Taylor.* Baton Rouge: Louisiana State University Press, 1946.
Dyer, Oliver. *Great Senators of the United States Forty Years Ago, (1848 and 1849). With Personal Recollections and Delineations of Calhoun, Benton, Clay, Webster, General Houston, Jefferson Davis, and Other Distinguished Statesmen of that Period.* New York: Robert Bonner's Sons, 1889.
———. *Oliver Dyer's Phonographic Report of the Proceedings of the National Free Soil Convention at Buffalo, N. Y.: August 9th and 10th, 1848.* Buffalo: G. H. Derby, [1848]; New York: Andrews & Boyle, [1848]; Philadelphia:Dyer & Webster, [1848].
Eaton, Clement. *The Mind of the Old South.* [Baton Rouge]: Louisiana State University Press, 1967.
Eblen, Jack Ericson. *The First and Second United States Empires: Governors and Territorial Government, 1784–1912.* Pittsburgh, Pa.: University of Pittsburgh Press, 1968.
Eby, Cecil. *"That Disgraceful Affair," the Black Hawk War.* New York: W. W. Norton, 1973.

Eckloff, Christian F. *Memoirs of a Senate Page (1855–1859).* Edited by Percival G. Melbourne. New York: Broadway, 1909.

Ehle, John. *Trail of Tears: The Rise and Fall of the Cherokee Nation.* New York: Doubleday, 1988.

Einstein, Lewis. "Lewis Cass." *The American Secretaries of State and Their Diplomacy.* General editor Samuel Flagg Bemis. Vol. 6. New York: Alfred A. Knopf, 1928.

Ellis, Richard E. *The Union at Risk: Jacksonian Democracy, States' Rights, and the Nullification Crisis.* New York: Oxford University Press, 1987.

Evans, Estwick. *A Pedestrious Tour, of Four Thousand Miles, through the Western States and Territories, during the Winter and Spring of 1818.* 1819. Reprint. *Early Western Travels: 1748–1846.* Edited by Reuben Gold Thwaites. Vol. 8. New York: AMS, 1966.

Evarts, Jeremiah. *Cherokee Removal: The William Penn Essays and Other Writings.* Edited by Francis Paul Prucha. Knoxville: University of Tennessee Press, 1981.

———. *The Removal of the Indians. An Article from the American Monthly Magazine: An Examination of an Article in the North American Review; and an Exhibition of the Advancement of the Southern Tribes, in Civilization and Christianity.* Boston: Peirce and Williams, 1830.

Everest, Allan S. *The War of 1812 in the Champlain Valley.* Syracuse, N.Y.: Syracuse University Press, 1981.

The Executive Committee of the 7th Ward, Cass and Butler Club, in Washington City, Submit the following Extracts to the consideration of the people, and respectfully ask the candid of all parties to give them a careful perusal. [1848.]

Facts and Arguments Against the Election of General Cass, Respectfully Addressed to the Whigs and Democrats of All the Free States. New York: R. Craighead, 1848.

Facts for those who will understand them. Gen. Cass's Position on the Slavery Question Defined by Himself and His Friends. Also, a Brief Notice of Southern Objections to Millard Fillmore, the Whig Vice Presidential Candidate. G. S. Gideon [1848].

Farmer, Silas. *The History of Detroit and Michigan or the Metropolis Illustrated.* Detroit: Silas Farmer, 1884.

Fehrenbacher, Don E. *Chicago Giant: A Biography of "Long John" Wentworth.* Madison, Wisc.: American History Research Center, 1957.

———. *The* Dred Scott *Case: Its Significance in American Law and Politics.* New York: Oxford University Press, 1978.

———. *Prelude to Greatness: Lincoln in the 1850's.* Palo Alto, Calif.: Stanford University Press, 1962.

Fergus, Robert, comp. *Chicago River-and-Harbor Convention: An Account of Its Origin and Proceedings by William Mosley Hull, John Wentworth, Samuel Lisle Smith, Horace Greeley, Thurlow Weed. . . .* Fergus' Historical Series, no. 18. Chicago: Fergus, 1882.

Flower, Frank A. *History of the Republican Party, Embracing its Origin, Growth and Mission, Together with Appendices of Statistics and Information Required by Enlightened Politicians and Patriotic Citizens.* Springfield, Ill.: Union, 1884.

Foner, Eric. *Free Soil, Free Labor, Free Men: The Ideology of the Republican Party Before the Civil War.* New York: Oxford University Press, 1970.

Foner, Philip Sheldon. *Business & Slavery: The New York Merchants & the Irrepressible Conflict.* Chapel Hill: University of North Carolina Press, 1941.

Foote, Henry S. *Casket of Reminiscences.* Washington, D.C.: Chronicle, 1874.

Foreman, Grant. *Indian Removal: The Emigration of the Five Civilized Tribes of Indians.* Norman: University of Oklahoma Press, 1953.

———. *The Last Trek of the Indians.* Chicago: University of Chicago Press, 1946.

Formisano, Ronald P. *The Birth of Mass Political Parties, Michigan, 1827–1861.* Princeton, N.J.: Princeton University Press, 1971.

Forney, John W. *Anecdotes of Public Men.* New York: Harper & Brothers, 1874.

The Free Soil Question, and Its Importance to the Voters of the Free States, in an Address of the 18th Ward Jeffersonian League, New York. 3d ed. New York: William C. Bryant, [1848].

Frost, John. *A Pictorial Biography of Andrew Jackson.* New York: Henry Bill, 1863.

Fuess, Claude M. *Daniel Webster.* 2 vols. Boston: Little, Brown, 1930.

Fuller, George N., ed. *Michigan: A Centennial History of the State and Its People.* 5 vols. Chicago: Lewis, 1939.

Ganoe, William Addleman. *The History of the United States Army.* Rev. ed. New York: D. Appleton-Century, 1942.

Gara, Larry. *The Presidency of Franklin Pierce.* Lawrence: University Press of Kansas, 1991.

Gardiner, O. C. *The Great Issue: Or, the Three Presidential Candidates; Being a Brief Historical Sketch of the Free Soil Question in the United States, from the Congresses of 1774 and '87 to the Present Time,* 1848. Reprint. Westport, Conn.: Negro Universities Press, 1970.

Garraty, John Arthur. *Silas Wright.* New York: Columbia University Press, 1949.

General Cass on the Wilmot Proviso. Published Under the Authority of the [Democratic National] Committee, [1848].

General Taylor: A Buyer of Men & Women! [1848.]

General Taylor and His Staff: Comprising Memoirs of Generals Taylor, Worth, Wool, and Butler: Colonels May, Cross, Clay, Hardin, Yell, Hays, and Other Distinguished Officers Attached to General Taylor's Army: Interspersed with Numerous Anecdotes of the Mexican War, and Personal Adventures of the Officers. Philadelphia: Grigg, Elliot, 1848.

Gen. Taylor's Moral, Intellectual, & Professional Character, . . . together with his opinions on war, and anecdotes illustrative of his republican habits and simplicity of manners, his humanity, his indomitable courage, his fearlessness, . . . concluding with some remarkable specimens of brevity in composition . . . . J. & G. S. Gideon, 1848.

Gen. Taylor's Rough and Ready Almanac. 1848. Boston: James Fisher, 1848.

General Taylor's Two Faces. Washington, D.C.: National and Jackson Democratic Association Committee, 1848.

George, Mary Karl. *Zachariah Chandler.* East Lansing: Michigan University Press, 1969.

Giddings, Joshua R. *History of the Rebellion: Its Authors and Causes.* New York: Follet, Foster, 1864.

Gienapp, William E. *The Origins of the Republican Party, 1852–1856.* New York: Oxford University Press, 1987.
Gilpin, Alec R. *The Territory of Michigan [1805–1837].* East Lansing: Michigan State University Press, 1970.
———. *The War of 1812 in the Old Northwest.* East Lansing: Michigan State University Press, 1958.
Godwin, Parke. *A Biography of William Cullen Bryant, with Extracts from his Private Correspondence.* 2 vols. New York: D. Appleton, 1883.
Going, Charles B. *David Wilmot—Free Soiler.* New York: D. Appleton, 1924.
Goodell, William. *Address of the Macedon Convention, by William Goodell; and Letters of Gerrit Smith.* Albany, N.Y.: S. W. Green, 1847.
Graebner, Norman A. *Empire on the Pacific: A Study in American Continental Expansion.* New York: Ronald, 1955.
———. *An Uncertain Tradition: American Secretaries of State in the Twentieth Century.* New York: McGraw-Hill, 1961.
———, ed. *Ideas and Diplomacy.* New York: Oxford University Press, 1964.
Greeley, Horace. *The American Conflict: A History of the Great Rebellion in the United States of America, 1860–'65; Its Causes, Incidents, and Results: Intended to Exhibit Especially its Moral and Political Phases, with the Drift and Progress of American Opinion Respecting Human Slavery from 1776 to the Close of the War for the Union.* 2 vols. Hartford, Conn.: O. D. Case, 1864–66.
Green, Michael D. *The Politics of Indian Removal: Creek Government and Society in Crisis.* Lincoln: University of Nebraska Press, 1982.
Greene, Laurence. *The Filibuster: The Career of William Walker.* Indianapolis: Bobbs-Merrill, 1937.
Grinnell, Josiah Busnell. *Men and Events of Forty Years: Autobiographical Reminiscences of an active career from 1850 to 1890.* Boston: D. Lothrop, 1891.
Guide to U.S. Elections. Washington, D.C.: Congressional Quarterly, 1975.
Gusfield, Joseph R. *Symbolic Crusade: Status Politics and the American Temperance Movement.* 2d ed. Urbana: University of Illinois Press, 1986.
Hagan, William T. *The Sac and Fox Indians.* Norman: University of Oklahoma Press, 1958.
Hamilton, Holman. "Election of 1848." *History of American Presidential Elections to 1968.* Edited by Arthur M. Schlesinger, Jr., and Fred L. Israel. 4 vols. New York: Chelsea House, 1971.
———. *Prologue to Conflict: The Crisis and Compromise of 1850.* Lexington: University of Kentucky, 1964.
———. *Zachary Taylor, Soldier in the White House.* 2 vols. Indianapolis: Bobbs-Merrill, 1951.
Hamlin, Charles Eugene. *The Life and Times of Hannibal Hamlin.* Cambridge, Mass.: Riverside, 1899.
Hammond, Jabez D. *Life and Times of Silas Wright.* Syracuse, N.Y.: L. W. Hall, 1852.
Harlow, Ralph Volney. *Gerrit Smith: Philanthropist and Reformer.* New York: Henry Holt, 1939.
Harris, Alexander. *A Review of the Political Conflict in America, from the Commencement of the Anti-Slavery Agitation to the Close of Southern Reconstruction; Comprising also a Resume of the Career of Thaddeus Stevens: Being a Survey of the*

Struggle of Parties, which Destroyed the Republic and Virtually Monarchized its Government. 1919. Reprint. Westport, Conn.: Negro Universities Press, 1970.

Harrold, Stanley. *Gamaliel Bailey and Antislavery Union.* Kent, Ohio: Kent State University Press, 1986.

Hart, Albert Bushnell. *Salmon Portland Chase.* American Statesmen Series. Boston: Houghton Mifflin, 1899.

———. *Slavery and Abolition: 1831–1841.* American Nation Series. New York: Harper & Brothers, 1906.

Hatch, William Stanley. *A Chapter of the History of the War of 1812 in the Northwest.* Cincinnati, Ohio: Miami, 1872.

Hatcher, William B. *Edward Livingston.* Baton Rouge: Louisiana State University Press, 1940.

Headley, J. T. *The Second War with England.* 2 vols. New York: Charles Scribner, 1853.

Heale, M. J. *The Presidential Quest: Candidates and Images in American Political Culture, 1782–1852.* London: Longman, 1982.

Heitman, Francis B. *Historical Register of the Officers of the Continental Army during the War of the Revolution: April, 1775, to December 1783.* Washington: Rare Book Shop, 1914.

Hesseltine, William B., and Rex G. Fisher, eds. *Trimmers, Trucklers & Temporizers: Notes of Murat Halstead from the Political Conventions of 1856.* Madison: State Historical Society of Wisconsin, 1961.

Hickey, Donald R. *The War of 1812: A Forgotten Conflict.* Urbana: University of Illinois Press, 1989.

[Hickman, George H.] *The Democratic Text Book, Being a Compendium of the Principles of the Democratic Party.* New York: Burgess, Stringer, 1848; Philadelphia: G. B. Zieber, 1848.

———. *The Life of General Lewis Cass, with his Letters and Speeches on Various Subjects.* Baltimore: N. Hickman, 1848.

Hietala, Thomas R. *Manifest Design: Anxious Aggrandizement in Late Jacksonian America.* Ithaca, N.Y.: Cornell University Press, 1985.

History of St. Clair County, Michigan, . . . Preceded by a History of Michigan, and Statistics of the State. Chicago: A. T. Andreas, 1883.

History of the American War of 1812, from the Commencement, until the Final Termination Thereof, on the Memorable Eighth of January, 1815, at New Orleans. 3d ed. Philadelphia: William M'Carty, 1817.

Hoar, George F. *Autobiography of Seventy Years.* 2 vols. New York: Charles Scribner's Sons, 1903.

Holst, Hermann Eduard von. *The Constitutional and Political History of the United States.* Translated by John J. Lalor and Alfred B. Mason. 8 vols. Chicago: Callaghan, 1881–92.

———. *John C. Calhoun.* American Statesmen Series. Boston: Houghton Mifflin, 1882.

Holt, Michael F. *The Political Crisis of the 1850s.* New York: John Wiley & Sons, 1978.

———. *Political Parties and American Political Development from the Age of Jackson to the Age of Lincoln.* Baton Rouge: Louisiana State University Press, 1992.

Horsman, Reginald. *The War of 1812.* New York: Alfred A. Knopf, 1969.
Howe, M. A. DeWolfe. *The Life and Letters of George Bancroft.* 2 vols. New York: Charles Scribner's Sons, 1908.
Hull, William. *Memoirs of the Campaign of the North Western Army of the United States, A.D. 1812.* Boston: True & Greene, 1824.
Hunt, Gilbert J. *The Historical Reader; Containing "The Late War Between the United States and Great Britain, From June, 1812, to February, 1815. In the Scriptural Style."* 3d ed. New York: Daniel B. Smith, 1819.
Inconsistency and Hypocrisy of Martin Van Buren on the Question of Slavery. [1848.]
Isely, Jeter Allen. *Horace Greeley and the Republican Party, 1853–1861.* Princeton, N.J.: Princeton University Press, 1947.
Jackson, Helen Hunt. *A Century of Dishonor.* Edited by Andrew F. Rolle. 1881. Reprint. New York: Harper & Brothers, 1965.
Jahoda, Gloria. *The Trail of Tears.* New York: Holt, Rinehart & Winston, 1975.
James, Marquis. *Andrew Jackson: Portrait of a President.* Indianapolis: Bobbs-Merrill, 1937.
———. *The Life of Andrew Jackson.* Indianapolis: Bobbs-Merrill, 1938.
[Jarvis, Russell.] *Facts and Arguments Against the Election of General Cass, Respectfully addressed to the Whigs and Democrats of all the Free States.* New York: R. Craighead, 1848.
Jay, William. *A Review of the Causes and Consequences of the Mexican War.* 1849. Reprint. Freeport, N.Y.: Books for Libraries, 1970.
Jenkins, John S. *The Life of James Knox Polk.* Auburn, N.Y.: James M. Alden, 1850.
Johannsen, Robert W. *Frontier Politics and the Sectional Conflict. The Pacific Northwest on the Eve of the Civil War.* Seattle: University of Washington Press, 1955.
———. *Stephen A. Douglas.* New York: Oxford University Press, 1973.
———. *To the Halls of the Montezumas: The Mexican War in the American Imagination.* New York: Oxford University Press, 1985.
Johnson, Allen. *Stephen A. Douglas: A Study in American Politics.* 1908. Reprint. New York: Da Capo Press, 1970.
Johnson, Gerald W. *America's Silver Age: The Statecraft of Clay, Webster, and Calhoun.* New York: Harper & Brothers, 1939.
Johnson, Rossiter. *A History of the War of 1812–'15 between the United States and Great Britain.* New York: Dodd, Mead, 1882.
Jones, Wilbur Devereux. *The American Problem in British Diplomacy, 1841–1861.* Athens: University of Georgia Press, 1974.
Josephy, Alvin M. *American Heritage History of the Congress of the United States.* New York: American Heritage, 1975.
Julian, George W. *The Life of Joshua R. Giddings.* Chicago: A. C. McClurg, 1892.
———. *Political Recollections: 1840–1872.* Chicago: Jansen, McClurg, 1884.
Kent, Frank R. *The Democratic Party: A History.* New York: Century, 1928.
Kirwan, Albert D. *John J. Crittenden: The Struggle for the Union.* [Lexington]: University of Kentucky Press, [1962].
Klein, Philip Shriver. *President James Buchanan: A Biography.* University Park: Pennsylvania State University Press, 1962.

Lambert, Oscar Doane. *Presidential Politics in the United States: 1841–1844.* Durham, N.C.: Duke University Press, 1936.
Lanman, James H. *History of Michigan.* New York: E. French, 1839.
Lathrop, Thornton K. *William Henry Seward.* American Statesman Series. Boston: Houghton Mifflin, 1896.
Latner, Richard B. *The Presidency of Andrew Jackson.* Athens: University of Georgia Press, 1979.
Lavender, David. *The Fist in the Wilderness.* Garden City, N.Y.: Doubleday, 1964.
Lewis, Walker. *Without Fear or Favor: A Biography of Chief Justice Roger Brooke Taney.* Boston: Houghton Mifflin, 1965.
Life of General Lewis Cass: Comprising an Account of His Military Services in the North-West during the War with Great Britain. . . . To Which is Appended, a Sketch of the Public and Private History of Major-General W. O. Butler . . . . Philadelphia: G. B. Zieber, 1848.
Linn, William Alexander. *Horace Greeley.* New York: D. Appleton, 1903.
Litwack, Leon F. *North of Slavery: The Negro in the Free States, 1790–1860.* Chicago: University of Chicago Press, 1961.
Lloyd, Alan. *The Scorching of Washington: The War of 1812.* Devon, Eng.: David & Charles, n.d.
Lodge, Henry Cabot. *Daniel Webster.* American Statesmen Series. Boston: Houghton Mifflin, 1899.
Lomask, Milton. *Aaron Burr: The Conspiracy and Years of Exile, 1805–1836.* New York: Farrar, Straux, Giroux, 1982.
Lossing, Benson J. *Hull's Surrender of Detroit.* Philadelphia: John E. Potter, 1875.
———. *Pictorial History of the Civil War in the United States of America.* 3 vols. Philadelphia: George W. Childs, 1866–74.
Lothrop, Thornton K. *William Henry Seward.* American Statesmen Series. Boston: Houghton Mifflin, 1896.
[Lowell, James Russell]. *The Biglow Papers, Edited, with an Introduction, Notes, Glossary, and Copious Index by Homer Wilbur, A. M., Pastor of the First Church in Jaalam, and (Prospective) Member of Many Literary, Learned and Scientific Societies.* Cambridge, Mass.: George Nichols, 1848; New York: George P. Putnam, 1848.
Lucas, Robert. *The Robert Lucas Journal of the War of 1812 during the Campaign under General William Hull.* Edited by John C. Parish. Iowa City: State Historical Society of Iowa, 1906.
Lumpkin, Wilson. *The Removal of the Cherokees from Georgia.* 2 vols. in 1. New York: Dodd, Mead, 1907.
Lyell, Sir Charles. *A Second Visit to the United States of North America.* 2 vols. New York: Harper & Brothers, 1849.
Mabee, Carleton. *The American Leonardo—A Life of Samuel F. B. Morse.* New York: Alfred Knopf, 1943.
MacCabe, Julius P. Bolivar. *Directory of the City of Detroit, with its Environs, and Register of Michigan, for the Year 1837.* Detroit: William Harsha, 1837.
MacDonald, William. *Jacksonian Democracy: 1829–1837.* American Nation Series. New York: Harper & Brothers, 1906.

Macy, Jesse. *Political Parties in the United States: 1846–1861.* 1900. Reprint. New York: Arno Press, 1974.

Magoon, E. L. *Living Orators in America.* New York: Charles Scribner, 1860.

Mahon, John K. *History of the Second Seminole War: 1835–1842.* Gainesville: University of Florida Press, 1967.

———. *The War of 1812.* Gainesville: University of Florida Press, 1972.

Malone, Henry Thompson. *Cherokees of the Old South.* Athens: University of Georgia Press, 1956.

Mason, Phillip P., ed. [Henry Rowe] *Schoolcraft: The Literary Voyager or Muzzeniegun.* East Lansing: Michigan State University Press, 1962.

Mast, Sister M. Dolorita. *Always the Priest: The Life of Gabriel Richard.* Baltimore: Helicon, 1965.

Matloff, Maurice, ed. *American Military History.* Rev. ed. Army Historical Series. Washington: Office of the Chief of Military History, 1973.

Matson, Henry James. *Remarks on the Slave Trade and African Squadron.* 2d ed. London: James Ridgeway, 1848.

May, George S. *Pictorial History of Michigan: The Early Years.* Grand Rapids, Mich.: William B. Eerdmans, 1967.

[McAfee, Robert Breckinridge]. *History of the Late War in the Western Country, Comprising a Full Account of all the Transactions in that Quarter, from the Commencement of Hostilities at Tippecanoe, to the Termination of the Contest at New Orleans on the Return of Peace.* 1816. Reprint. Ann Arbor, Mich.: University Microfilms, 1966.

McCarty, Dwight G. *The Territorial Governors of the Northwest.* Iowa City: State Historical Society of Iowa, 1910.

McCormac, Eugene Irving. *James K. Polk: A Political Biography.* 1922. Reprint. Berkeley: University of California Press, 1965.

McCormick, Richard P. *The Second American Party System: Party Formation in the Jacksonian Era.* Chapel Hill: University of North Carolina Press, 1966.

McCoy, Isaac. *History of Baptist Indian Missions: Embracing Remarks on the Former and Present Condition of the Aboriginal Tribes, their Settlement within the Indian Territory and their Future Prospects.* Washington: William M. Morrison, 1840.

McGrane, Reginald C. *William Allen, A Study in Western Democracy.* Columbus: Ohio Archaeological and Historical Society, 1925.

McKee, Thomas Hudson. *The National Conventions and Platforms of All Political Parties: 1789–1900.* Baltimore: Friedenwald, 1900.

McKenney, Thomas L. *Sketches of a Tour to the Lakes, of the Character and Customs of the Chippeway Indians, and of Incidents Connected with the Treaty of Fond Du Lac.* 1827. Reprint. Barre, Mass.: Imprint Society, 1972.

McLaughlin, Andrew C. *History of Higher Education in Michigan.* Washington: Government Printing Office, 1891.

———. *Lewis Cass.* Rev. ed. American Statesmen Series. Edited by John T. Morse, Sr. Boston: Houghton, Mifflin, 1899.

McReynolds, Edwin C. *The Seminoles.* Norman: University of Oklahoma Press, 1957.

Melish, John. *A Geographical Description of the United States, with the Contiguous British and Spanish Possessions, Intended as an Accompaniment to Melish's Map of These Countries.* Philadelphia, 1816.

Merk, Frederick. *The Oregon Question: Essays in Anglo-American Diplomacy and Politics.* Cambridge: Harvard University Press, Belknap Press, 1967.

———. *Slavery and the Annexation of Texas.* New York: Alfred A. Knopf, 1972.

Merk, Frederick, with the collaboration of Lois Bannister Merk. *The Monroe Doctrine and American Expansionism: 1843–1849.* New York: Alfred A. Knopf, 1966.

Michigan Biographies. 2 vols. Lansing: Michigan Historical Commission, 1924.

Mills, James Cooke. *History of Saginaw County, Michigan.* 2 vols. Saginaw, Mich.: Seemann & Peters, 1918.

Mills, Robert. *Guide to the Capitol and to the National Executive Offices of the United States.* Washington, D.C.: J. C. Greer, 1854.

Milton, George F. *The Eve of Conflict, Stephen A. Douglas and the Needless War.* Boston: Houghton Mifflin, 1934.

Minnigerode, Meade. *Presidential Years: 1787–1860.* New York: G. P. Putnam's Sons, 1928.

Montgomery, H. *The Life of General Zachary Taylor, Twelfth President of the United States.* 20th ed. Auburn, N.Y.: Derby, Miller, 1850.

Moore, Charles. *History of Michigan.* 4 vols. Chicago: Lewis, 1915.

Morgan, Robert J. *A Whig Embattled: The Presidency under John Tyler.* Lincoln: University of Nebraska Press, 1954.

Morrison, Chaplain W. *Democratic Politics and Sectionalism: The Wilmot Proviso Controversy.* Chapel Hill: University of North Carolina Press, 1967.

Morse, Jedidiah, and Sidney Edward Morse. *Geography Made Easy, Being A New Abridgement of the American Universal Geography, on an Improved Plan; Containing General Views with Questions.* Boston: Richardson & Lord, 1820.

Murray, Paul. *The Whig Party in Georgia, 1825–1853.* James Sprunt Studies in History and Political Science. Vol. 29. Chapel Hill: University of North Carolina Press, 1948.

Myers, Gustavus. *History of the Great American Fortunes.* 3 vols. New York, 1907–10.

Nevins, Allan. *Ordeal of the Union.* 2 vols. New York: Charles Scribner's Sons, 1947.

Nichols, Roger L. *General Henry Atkinson: A Western Military Career.* Norman: University of Oklahoma Press, 1965.

Nichols, Roy Franklin. *The Democratic Machine: 1850–1854.* New York: Columbia University, 1923.

———. *The Disruption of American Democracy.* New York: Macmillan, 1948.

———. *Franklin Pierce.* Philadelphia: University of Pennsylvania Press, 1931.

———. *The Invention of the American Political Parties.* New York: Macmillan, 1967.

———. *The Stakes of Power, 1845–1877.* New York: Hill & Wang, 1961.

Niven, John. *John C. Calhoun and the Price of Union: A Biography.* Baton Rouge: Louisiana State University Press, 1988.

———. *Martin Van Buren: The Romantic Age of American Politics.* New York: Oxford University Press, 1983.

Nye, Russell B. *George Bancroft: Brahmin Rebel.* New York: Alfred A. Knopf, 1944.

O'Connor, Thomas H. *Lords of the Loom: The Cotton Whigs and the Coming of the Civil War.* New York: Charles Scribner's Sons, 1968.

Official Proceedings of the National Democratic Convention, Held in Cincinnati, June 2–6, 1856. Cincinnati: Enquirer Company Steam Printing Establishment, 1856.

Osborn, Charles S., and Stellanova Osborn. *Schoolcraft-Longfellow-Hiawatha.* Lancaster, Penn.: Jaques Cattell, 1942.

[Ouseley, Sir William Gore.] *Reply to An "American's Examination" of the "Right of Search": with Observations on some of the Questions at Issue Between Great Britain and the United States, and on Certain Positions Assumed by the North American Government. By an Englishman.* London: John Rodwell, 1842.

Paludan, Phillip Shaw. *The Presidency of Abraham Lincoln.* Lawrence: University Press of Kansas, 1994.

Parker, Joel. *The True Issue, and the Duty of the Whigs. An Address Delivered before the Citizens of Cambridge, October 1, 1856.* Cambridge, Mass.: James Munroe, 1856.

Parkins, Almon Ernest. *The Historical Geography of Detroit.* Lansing: Michigan Historical Commission, 1918.

Parks, Robert J. *Democracy's Railroads: Public Enterprise in Jacksonian Michigan.* Port Washington, N.Y.: National University Publications, 1972.

Parton, James. *Life of Andrew Jackson.* 3 vols. New York: Mason Brothers, 1860.

———. *The Life of Horace Greeley, Editor of the New York Tribune.* New York: Mason Brothers, 1855.

———. *The Presidency of Andrew Jackson.* Edited by Robert V. Remini. New York: Harper Torchbooks, 1967.

Paul, James C. N. *Rift in the Democracy.* Philadelphia: University of Pennsylvania Press, 1951.

Perkins, Samuel. *A History of the Political and Military Events of the Late War between the United States and Great Britain.* New Haven, Conn.: S. Converse, 1825.

Pessen, Edward. *Jacksonian America: Society, Personality, and Politics.* Rev. ed. The Dorsey Series in American History. Homewood, Ill.: Dorsey, 1978.

Peters, Virginia Bergman. *The Florida Wars.* Hamden, Conn.: Archon, 1979.

Petersen, Svend. *A Statistical History of the American Presidential Elections.* New York: Frederick Ungar, 1963.

Peterson, Charles J. *The Military Heroes of the War of 1812; with a Narrative of the War.* Philadelphia: James B. Smith, 1858.

Peterson, Merrill D. *The Great Triumvirate: Webster, Clay, and Calhoun.* New York: Oxford University Press, 1987.

Peterson, Norma Lois. *The Presidencies of William Henry Harrison & John Tyler.* Lawrence: University Press of Kansas, 1989.

Peyton, John Lewis. *Over the Alleghanies and Across the Prairies. Personal Recollections of the Far West One and Twenty Years Ago.* London: Simpkin, Marshall 1870.

Phillips, Ulrich Bonnell. "The Southern Whigs, 1834–1854." In *Essays in American History Dedicated to Frederick Jackson Turner.* New York: Henry Holt, 1910.

Pictorial Life of General Taylor, the Hero of Okee Chobee, Palo Alto, Resaca de La Palma, Monterey, and Buena Vista. Philadelphia: Lindsay & Blackiston, 1847.

Pierce, Edward L., ed. *Memoir and Letters of Charles Sumner.* 4 vols. London: Sampson Low, Marston, Searle, & Rivington, 1878–93.

Pletcher, David M. *The Diplomacy of Annexation: Texas, Oregon, and the Mexican War.* Columbia: University of Missouri Press, 1973.

Poage, George Rawlings. *Henry Clay and the Whig Party.* 1936. Reprint. Gloucester, Mass.: Peter Smith, 1965.

Poore, Ben Perley. *Perley's Reminiscences of Sixty Years in the National Metropolis.* 2 vols. Philadelphia: Hubbard Brothers, 1886.

"Popular Sovereignty." The Reviewer Reviewed: By a Southern Inquirer. Washington, D.C., 1859.

Popular Sovereignty in the Territories. The Democratic Record. Baltimore: Murphy, n.d.

Porter, Kenneth Wiggins. *John Jacob Astor: Business Man.* 2 vols. Cambridge: Harvard University Press, 1931.

Porter, Kirk H., and Donald Bruce Johnson, comps. *National Party Platforms; 1840–1960.* 2d ed. Urbana: University of Illinois Press, 1961.

Potter, David M. *The Impending Crisis, 1848–1861.* Completed and edited by Don E. Fehrenbacher. New York: Harper & Row, 1976.

[Potter, Woodburne.] *The War in Florida: Being an Exposition of its Causes, and an Accurate History of the Campaigns of Generals Clinch, Gaines and Scott.* 1836. Reprint. Ann Arbor, Mich.: University Microfilms, 1966.

Proceedings and Speeches at a Meeting for the Promotion of the Cause of Temperance, in the United States, Held at the Capitol, in Washington City, February 24, 1833. Washington, D.C.: Way & Gideon, 1833.

Proceedings and Speeches at a Meeting Held in the Capitol, at Washington, January 13, 1832, for the Purpose of Promoting the Cause of Temperance in the United States. Washington, D.C. 1832.

Proceedings at the Banquet of the Jackson Democratic Association, Washington, Eighth of January, 1852. [Washington]: Congressional Globe Office, [1852].

Proceedings of the Democratic National Convention, Held at Baltimore, May 22, 1848. Washington, D.C.: Blair & Rives, [1848].

Proceedings of the Democratic National Convention, Held at Baltimore, June, 1852. Reported by William Hincks and F. H. Smith. Washington, D.C.: Buell & Blanchard, 1852.

Proceedings of the National Convention Held at Philadelphia, on the 17th, 18th, and 19th June, 1856 . . . . [1856.]

Proceedings of the Union Meeting, Held at Brewster's Hall, October 24, 1850. New Haven, Conn.: William H. Stanley, 1851.

Proceedings, Speeches, &c., at the Dinner Given to Louis Kossuth, at the National Hotel, Washington, January 7, 1852. Washington: Globe Office, [1852].

Prucha, Francis Paul. *American Indian Policy in the Formative Years.* Lincoln: University of Nebraska Press, 1962.

———. *The Great Father: The United States Government and the American Indians.* 2 vols. Lincoln: University of Nebraska Press, 1984.
———. *Lewis Cass and American Indian Policy.* Detroit: Wayne State University Press, 1967.
———. *The Sword of the Republic: The United States Army on the Frontier, 1783–1846.* New York: Macmillan, 1969.
Pryor, Mrs. Roger A. *Reminiscences of Peace and War.* New York: Macmillan, 1904.
Quaife, Milo Milton. *The Doctrine of Non-Intervention with Slavery in the Territories.* Chicago: Mac. C. Chamberlin, 1910.
———, ed. "The Movement for Statehood: 1845–1846." Publications of the State Historical Society of Wisconsin: *Collections.* Vol. 26. Madison: State Historical Society of Wisconsin, 1918.
———, ed. *War on the Detroit: The Chronicles of Thomas Vercheres de Boucherville and the Capitulation by an Ohio Volunteer.* Chicago: Lakeside Press, 1940.
Quaife, Milo M., and Sidney Glazer. *Michigan: From Primitive Wilderness to Industrial Commonwealth.* New York: Prentice-Hall, 1948.
Randall, Emilius O., and Daniel J. Ryan. *History of Ohio: The Rise and Progress of an American State.* 6 vols. New York: Century History, 1912–15.
Rauch, Basil. *American Interest in Cuba: 1848–1855.* New York: Columbia University Press, 1948.
Rawley, James A. *Race & Politics: "Bleeding Kansas" and the Coming of the Civil War.* Lincoln: University of Nebraska Press, 1969.
Rayback, Joseph G. *Free Soil: The Election of 1848.* [Lexington]: University of Kentucky Press, [1970].
Rayback, Robert J. *Millard Fillmore: Biography of a President.* Buffalo: Henry Stewart, 1959.
Read, David Breakenridge. *Life and Times of Major-General Sir Isaac Brock, K. B.* Toronto: William Briggs, 1894.
Reasons Good and True for Supporting the Nomination of General Zachary Taylor. [1848].
Reeves, Jesse S. *American Diplomacy Under Tyler and Polk.* Albert Shaw Lectures on Diplomatic History, 1906. Baltimore: Johns Hopkins Press, 1907.
Refutation of Andrew Stewart's Fabrication Against General Lewis Cass. Published Under Authority of the National and Jackson Democratic Association Committee, [1848].
Remini, Robert V. *Andrew Jackson.* New York: Twayne, 1966.
———. *Andrew Jackson and the Bank War.* New York: W. W. Norton, 1967.
———. *Andrew Jackson.* 3 vols. New York: Harper & Row, 1977–84.
———. *Henry Clay: Statesman for the Union.* New York: W. W. Norton, 1991.
———. *The Legacy of Andrew Jackson: Essays on Democracy, Indian Removal, and Slavery.* Baton Rouge: Louisiana State University Press, 1988.
———. *The Life of Andrew Jackson.* New York: Harper & Row, 1988.
———. *Martin Van Buren and the Making of the Democratic Party.* New York: Columbia University Press, 1959.
Report of the Trial of Brig. General William Hull; Commanding the North-Western Army of the United States. By a Court Martial Held at Albany on Monday, 3[illegible] January, 1814, and Succeeding Days. Taken by Lieut. Col. Forbes, of the Forty-

Second Regt. U.S. Infantry, and a Supernumerary Member of the Court. New York: Eastburn, Kirk, 1814.

Review of the Life, Character and Political Opinions of Zachary Taylor. Boston: Eastburn's, 1848.

Riddle, Donald W. *Congressman Abraham Lincoln.* Urbana: University of Illinois Press, 1957.

Riddleberger, Patrick W. *George Washington Julian: Radical Republican.* Indiana Historical Bureau, 1966.

Rives, George Lockhart. *The United States and Mexico: 1821–1848.* 2 vols. New York: Charles Scribner's Sons, 1913.

Robison, Edgar E. *The Evolution of American Political Parties: A Sketch of Party Development.* New York: Harcourt, Brace, 1924.

Rodgers, Cleveland, and John Black, eds. *The Gathering of the Forces: Editorials, Essays, Literary and Dramatic Reviews and Other Materials Written by Walt Whitman as Editor of the Brooklyn Daily Eagle in 1846 and 1847.* 2 vols. New York: G. P. Putnam's Sons, 1920.

Rorabaugh, William J. *The Alcoholic Republic: An American Tradition.* New York: Oxford University Press, 1979.

Rose, E. M. P. *The Poetry of Locofocoism; or Modern Democracy and Cassism Unmasked, a Political and Personal Poem Containing 275 Stanzas.* Wellsburgh, Va.: J. A. Metcalf, 1848.

Ross, Robert B., and George B. Catlin. *Landmarks of Detroit: A History of the City.* Revised by Clarence Burton. Detroit: Evening News Association, 1898.

Roster of Ohio Soldiers in the War of 1812. Columbus, Ohio: Edward T. Miller, 1916.

Rough and Ready Annual; or Military Souvenir. New York: D. Appleton, 1848.

Rush, Richard. *Biography of General Lewis Cass. Including a Voice from a Friend.* New York: J. Winchester, 1843.

Russel, Robert R. *Critical Studies in Antebellum Sectionalism: Essays in American Political and Economic History.* Contributions in American History Series. Edited by Stanley I. Kutler. Westport, Conn.: Greenwood, 1972.

———. *Improvement of Communication with the Pacific Coast as an Issue in American Politics, 1783–1864.* Cedar Rapids, Iowa: Torch, 1948.

Sargent, Nathan. *Public Men and Events from the Commencement of Mr. Monroe's Administration, in 1817, to the Close of Mr. Fillmore's Administration, in 1853.* 2 vols. Philadelphia: J. B. Lippincott, 1875.

Satz, Ronald N. *American Indian Policy in the Jacksonian Era.* Lincoln: University of Nebraska Press, 1975.

Schlesinger, Arthur M., Jr. *The Age of Jackson.* Boston: Little, Brown, 1947.

Schmeckebier, Laurence F. *The Office of Indian Affairs: Its History, Activities and Organization.* Baltimore: Johns Hopkins Press, 1927.

Schoolcraft, Henry R. *Narrative Journals of Travels from Detroit Northwest through the Great Chain of American Lakes to the Sources of the Mississippi River in the Year 1820.* 1821. Reprint. New York: Arno Press, 1970.

———. *Outlines of the Life and Character of Gen. Lewis Cass.* Albany, N.Y.: Joel Munsell, 1848.

———. *Summary Narrative of an Exploratory Expedition to the Sources of the Mississippi River in 1820.* Philadelphia: Lippincott, Grambo, 1855.

———. *Travels through the Northwestern Regions of the United States.* March of America Facsimile Series, no. 66. Reprint of *Narrative Journal of Travels from Detroit Northwest through the Great Chain of American Lakes to the Sources of the Mississippi River in the Year 1820.* Albany, 1821. Ann Arbor, Mich.: University Microfilms, 1966.

Schroeder, John H. *Mr. Polk's War: American Opposition and Dissent, 1846–1848.* Madison: University of Wisconsin Press, 1973.

Schuckers, J. W. *The Life and Public Services of Salmon Portland Chase, United States Senator and Governor of Ohio, Secretary of the Treasury; and Chief-Justice of the United States.* 1874. Reprint. Miami, Fla.: Mnemosyne, 1969.

Schurz, Carl. *Henry Clay.* American Statesmen Series. 2 vols. Boston: Houghton Mifflin, 1899.

Schuyler, Eugene. *American Diplomacy.* New York: Charles Scribner's Sons, 1895.

Scroggs, William O. *Filibusters and Financiers: The Story of William Walker and His Associates.* New York: Macmillan, 1916.

Seager, Robert II. *And Tyler Too: A Biography of John & Julia Gardiner Tyler.* New York: McGraw-Hill, 1963.

Sears, Louis M. *John Slidell.* Durham, N.C.: Duke University Press, 1925.

Sellers, Charles G. "Election of 1844." *History of American Presidential Elections: 1789–1968.* Edited by Arthur M. Schlesinger, Jr., and Fred L. Israel. 4 vols. New York: Chelsea House, 1971.

———. *James K. Polk.* 2 vols. Princeton, N.J.: Princeton University Press, 1957–66.

Seward, Frederick W. *[William H.] Seward at Washington, as Senator and Secretary of State. A Memoir of his Life, with Selections from his Letters. 1846–1861.* New York: Derby & Miller, 1891.

———., ed. *Autobiography of William H. Seward, from 1801 to 1834. With a Memoir of his Life, and Selections from his Letters from 1831 to 1846.* New York: D. Appleton, 1877.

Sewell, Richard H. *Ballots for Freedom: Antislavery Politics in the United States, 1837–1860.* New York: Oxford University Press, 1976.

———. *A House Divided: Sectionalism and Civil War, 1848–1865.* Baltimore: Johns Hopkins University Press, 1988.

———. *John P. Hale and the Politics of Abolition.* Cambridge: Harvard University Press, 1965.

Shade, William Gerald. *Banks or No Banks: The Money Issue in Western Politics, 1832–1865.* Detroit: Wayne State University Press, 1972.

Shenton, James P. *Robert John Walker: A Politician from Jackson to Lincoln.* New York: Columbia University Press, 1961.

Shepard, Edward M. *Martin Van Buren.* American Statesmen Series. Boston: Houghton Mifflin, 1899.

Singletary, Otis A. *The Mexican War.* Chicago History of American Civilization Series. Edited by Daniel J. Boorstin. Chicago: University of Chicago Press, 1960.

Sketch of the Life and Character of Gen. Taylor, The American Hero and People's Man. Together with a Concise History of the Mexican War. . . . By the One-Legged Sergeant. New York: N. H. Blanchard, 1847.

Sketch of the Life and Public Services of Gen. Lewis Cass. Washington, D.C.: Boston Daily Times Extra, 1848.

Sketch of the Life and Public Services of Gen. Lewis Cass. Washington, D.C.: Congressional Globe Office, 1848.

Sketch of the Life and Public Services of Gen. Zachary Taylor, the People's Candidate for the Presidency, with Considerations in Favor of His Election. [Title varies.] Washington, D.C.: J. T. Towers, 1848.

Sketch of the Life and Services of General Lewis Cass, of Ohio. Harrisburg, Pa.,1843.

Sketches of the War, between the United States and the British Isles: Intended as a Faithful History of all the Material Events from the Time of the Declaration in 1812, to and Including the Treaty of Peace in 1815: Interspersed with Geographical Descriptions of Places, and Biographical Notices of Distinguished Military and Naval Commanders. Rutland, Vt.: Fay & Davison, 1815.

Smith, Alice E. *The History of Wisconsin.* Vol. 1: *From Exploration to Statehood.* General editor, William Fletcher Thompson. Madison: State Historical Society of Wisconsin, 1973.

Smith, Elbert B. *The Death of Slavery: The United States, 1837–65.* Chicago: University of Chicago Press, 1967.

———. *Francis Preston Blair.* New York: Free Press, 1980.

———. *Magnificent Missourian: The Life of Thomas Hart Benton.* Philadelphia: J. B. Lippincott, 1958.

———. *The Presidency of James Buchanan.* Lawrence: University Press of Kansas, 1975.

———. *The Presidencies of Zachary Taylor & Millard Fillmore.* American Presidency Series. Lawrence: University Press of Kansas, 1988.

Smith, Justin H. *The War With Mexico.* 2 vols. New York: Macmillan, 1919.

Smith, O. H. *Early Indiana Trials and Sketches.* Cincinnati, Ohio: Moore, Wilstach, Keys, 1858.

Smith, Theodore Clarke. *The Liberty and Free Soil Parties in the Northwest.* New York: Longmans, Green, 1897.

Smith, William Ernest. *The Frances Preston Blair Family in Politics.* 2 vols. New York: Macmillan, 1933.

Smith, William L. G. *The Life and Times of Lewis Cass.* New York: Derby & Jackson, 1856.

Snyder, Charles McCool. *The Jacksonian Heritage: Pennsylvania Politics, 1833–1848.* Harrisburg: Pennsylvania Historical and Museum Commission, 1958.

Spencer, Ivor Debenham. *The Victor and the Spoils; A Life of William L. Marcy.* Providence, R.I.: Brown University Press, 1959.

Sprague, John T. *The Origin, Progress, and Conclusion of the Florida War. . . .* New York: D. Appleton, 1848.

Stagg, J. C. A. *Mr. Madison's War: Politics, Diplomacy, and Warfare in the Early American Republic, 1783–1830.* Princeton, N.J.: Princeton University Press, 1983.

Stampp, Kenneth M. *And the War Came: The North and the Secession Crisis, 1860–1861.* [Baton Rouge]: Louisiana State University Press, 1950.

Stanton, Henry B. *Random Recollections.* New York: Harper & Brothers, 1887.

Stanwood, Edward. *A History of the Presidency.* Boston: Houghton Mifflin, 1898.

Stearns, Charles. *Facts in the Life of Gen. Taylor; the Cuba Blood-Hound Importer, the Extensive Slave-Holder, and the Hero of the Mexican War!!* Boston: Published by the Author, 1848.

Stewart, James Brewer. *Joshua R. Giddings and the Tactics of Radical Politics.* Cleveland: Press of Case Western Reserve University, 1970.

Stinnett, Ronald F. *Democrats, Dinners, & Dollars: A History of the Democratic Party, its Dinners, its Ritual.* Ames: Iowa State University Press, 1967.

Stocking, William, ed. *Under the Oaks: Commemorating the Fiftieth Anniversary of the Founding of the Republican Party, at Jackson, Michigan, July 6, 1854; Comprising a History of the Party in Michigan; the Proceedings of the Anniversary Celebration, and Portraits of Leading Michigan Republicans.* Detroit: Detroit Tribune, 1904.

Stoddard, Henry Luther. *Horace Greeley.* New York: G. P. Putnam's Sons, 1946.

Stone, Irving. *They Also Ran.* Garden City, N.Y.: Doubleday, Doran, 1943.

Streeter, Floyd Benjamin. *Political Parties in Michigan, 1837–1860.* Lansing: Michigan Historical Commission, 1918.

Summers, Mark W. *The Plundering Generation: Corruption and the Crisis of the Union, 1849–1861.* Lexington: University of Kentucky Press, 1987.

Sumner, William Graham. *Andrew Jackson.* American Statesmen Series. Boston: Houghton Mifflin, 1888.

Swisher, Carl Brent. *Roger B. Taney.* New York: Macmillan, 1935.

Taylor, William R. *Cavalier and Yankee: The Old South and American National Character.* New York: Harper Torchbooks, 1969.

[Zachary] *Taylor Whig*[g]*ery Exposed.* Published Under Authority of the National and Jackson Democratic Association Committee, [1848].

Terrell, John Upton. *Furs by Astor.* New York: William Morrow, 1963.

Thomas, Benjamin P. *Abraham Lincoln.* New York: Alfred A. Knopf, 1952.

Thompson, Richard W. *Recollections of Sixteen Presidents from Washington to Lincoln.* 2 vols. Indianapolis, Ind.: Bowen-Merrill, 1894.

Thomson, John Lewis. *Historical Sketches of the Late War Between the United States and Great Britain.* Philadelphia: Thomas Desilver, May 1818.

Trefousee, H. L. *Benjamin Franklin Wade: Radical Republican from Ohio.* New York: Twayne, 1963.

Tucker, Glenn. *Poltroons and Patriots: A Popular Account of the War of 1812.* 2 vols. Indianapolis, Ind.: Bobbs-Merrill, 1954.

———. *Tecumseh: Vision of Glory.* New York: Russell & Russell, 1956.

Tyler, Alice Felt. *Freedom's Ferment.* New York: Harper Torchbooks, 1944.

Tyler, Lyon G. *Letters and Times of the Tylers.* 3 vols. Richmond, Va.: Whittet & Shepperson, 1884–85; Williamsburg, Va., 1896.

Untitled Circular. Published Under Authority of the National and Jackson Democratic Association Committee, [1848].

Updyke, Frank A. *The Diplomacy of the War of 1812.* Albert Shaw Lectures on Diplomatic History, 1914. Baltimore: Johns Hopkins Press, 1915.

Utley, Henry M., and Byron M. Cutcheon. *Michigan As a Province, Territory, and State.* Edited by Clarence M. Burton. 4 vols. Publishing Society of Michigan, 1906.

Utter, William B. *The History of the State of Ohio: The Frontier State, 1803–1825.* Columbus: Ohio State Archaeological and Historical Society, 1942.

Van Buren, Martin. *Inquiry into the Origin and Course of Political Parties in the United States.* Edited by his sons. 1867. Reprint. New York: Augustus M. Kelley, 1967.

The Van Buren Platform, or Facts for the Present Supporters of Martin Van Buren. [Washington]: J. & G. S. Gideon, [1848].

Van Deusen, Glyndon G. *Horace Greeley: 19th Century Crusader.* Philadelphia: University of Pennsylvania Press, 1953.

———. *The Jacksonian Era: 1828–1848.* New York: Harper Torchbooks, 1959.

———. *The Life of Henry Clay.* Boston: Little, Brown, 1937.

———. *Thurlow Weed.* Boston: Little, Brown, 1947.

Van Every, Dale. *Disinherited: The Lost Birthright of the American Indian.* New York: Avon, 1967.

Varg, Paul A. *United States Foreign Relations: 1820–1860.* [East Lansing]: Michigan State University Press, 1979.

Vaughn, William Preston. *The Antimasonic Party in the United States, 1826–1843.* Lexington: University of Kentucky Press, 1983.

Viola, Herman J. *Thomas L. McKenney, Architect of America's Early Indian Policy: 1816–1830.* Chicago: Swallow, 1974.

Wakefield, John A. *History of the War Between the United States and the Sac and Fox Nations of Indians, and Parts of Other Disaffected Tribes of Indians, in the Years Eighteen Hundred and Twenty-seven, Thirty-one, and Thirty-two.* Jacksonville, Ill.: Calvin Goody, 1834.

Wallace, Anthony F. C. *The Long, Bitter Trail: Andrew Jackson and the Indians.* New York: Hill and Wang, 1993.

Wallace, Edward S. *Destiny and Glory.* New York: Coward-McCann, 1957.

Wallace, Lew. *An Autobiography.* 2 vols. New York: Harper Brothers, 1906.

Walton, George. *Fearless and Free: The Seminole Indian War, 1835–1842.* Indianapolis, Ind.: Bobbs-Merrill, 1977.

Ward, John William. *Andrew Jackson: Symbol for an Age.* London: Oxford University Press, 1962.

Warden, Robert B. *An Account of the Private Life and Public Services of Salmon Portland Chase.* Cincinnati, Ohio: Wilstach, Baldwin, 1874.

Watterston, George. *A New Guide to Washington.* Washington, D.C.: Robert Farnham, 1842.

[Webster, Caroline.] *"Mr. W. & I": Being the Authentic Diary of the Honle. Daniel Webster to Great Britain and the Continent in the Year 1839.* Binghamton, N.Y.: Ives Washburn, 1942.

Webster, Daniel. *Mr. Webster's Speech at Marshfield, Mass. Delivered September 1, 1848, and his Speech on the Oregon Bill, Delivered in the United States Senate, August 12, 1848.* Boston: T. R. Marvin, 1848.

Weed, Harriet A., ed. *Autobiography of Thurlow Weed.* Boston: Houghton Mifflin, 1883.

Weigley, Russell F. *The American Way of War: A History of United States Military Strategy and Policy.* New York: Macmillan, 1973.

———. *Towards an American Army: Military Thought from Washington to Marshall.* New York: Columbia University Press, 1962.

Weisenburger, Francis P. *The History of the State of Ohio: The Passing of the Frontier, 1825–1850.* Columbus: Ohio State Archaeological and Historical Society, 1941.

Weslager, C. A. *The Delaware Indian Westward Migration: With the Texts of Two Manuscripts (1821–22) Responding to General Lewis Cass' Inquiries About Lenape Culture and Language.* Wallingford, Pa.: Middle Atlantic Press, 1978.

West, Richard S., Jr. *Gideon Welles: Lincoln's Navy Department.* Indianapolis, Ind.: Bobbs-Merrill, 1943.

What's the Difference? What is the difference between the opinions of Gen. Cass and Gen. Taylor on the Wilmot Proviso? Boston: I. R. Butts & Son, [1848].

White, Laura A. *Robert Barnwell Rhett: Father of Secession.* New York: Century, 1931.

White, Leonard D. *The Jacksonians: A Study in Administrative History, 1829–1861.* New York: Macmillan, 1954.

Whittier, John Greenleaf. *The Complete Poetical Works of John Greenleaf Whittier.* Boston: Houghton, Osgood, 1878.

Wilkins, Thurman. *Cherokee Tragedy: The Story of the Ridge Family and of the Decimation of a People.* New York: Macmillan, 1970.

Williams, Mary Wilhelmine. *Anglo-American Isthmian Diplomacy: 1815–1915.* Washington, D.C.: American Historical Association, 1916.

Wilson, Henry. *History of the Rise and Fall of the Slave Power in America.* 3 vols. Boston: Houghton Mifflin, 1872–77.

Wiltse, Charles M. *John C. Calhoun.* 3 vols. Indianapolis, Ind.: Bobbs-Merrill, 1944–51.

Wing, Talcott E., ed. *History of Monroe County, Michigan.* New York: Munsell, 1890.

Winthrop, Robert C., Jr. *A Memoir of Robert C. Winthrop.* Boston: Little, Brown, 1897.

Withington, W. H. *Michigan in the Opening of the [Civil] War. A Paper Read Before Michigan Commandery of the Military Order of the Loyal Legion of the United States, March 2nd, 1887, by Companion W. H. Withington, Brevet Brigadier General U. S. Volunteers.* Detroit: Ostler, 1889.

Wittke, Carl. *Refugees of Revolution: The German Forty-Eighters in America.* Philadelphia: University of Pennsylvania Press, 1952.

Wolff, Gerald W. *The Kansas-Nebraska Bill: Party, Section, and the Coming of the Civil War.* New York: Revisionist, 1977.

Woodford, Frank B. *Lewis Cass: the Last Jeffersonian.* New Brunswick, N.J.: Rutgers University Press, 1950.

———. *Mr. Jefferson's Disciple: A Life of Justice Woodward.* East Lansing: Michigan State University Press, 1953.

Woodford, Frank B., and Arthur M. Woodford. *All Our Yesterdays: A Brief History of Detroit.* Detroit: Wayne State University Press, 1969.

Woodward, Grace Steele. *The Cherokees.* Norman: University of Oklahoma Press 1963.

Wyatt-Brown, Bertram. *Lewis Tappan and the Evangelical War Against Slavery* Cleveland: Press of Case Western Reserve University, 1969.

Young, William T. *Sketch of the Life and Public Services of General Lewis Cass with the Pamphlet on the Right of Search and Some of His Speeches on the Great Political Questions of the Day.* Detroit: Markham & Elwood, 1852.

Zachariah Chandler: An Outline Sketch of his Life and Public Services. Detroit: Post and Tribune, 1880.

Zwelling, Shomer S. *Expansion and Imperialism.* Chicago: Loyola University Press, 1970.

JOURNALS AND MAGAZINES

Applegate, Tom S., comp. "A History of the Press in Michigan." *Pioneer Collections: Report of the Pioneer Society of the State of Michigan. Together with Reports of County, Town, and District Pioneer Societies* 6 (1884): 62–98.

Aumann, F. R. "The Development of the Judicial System of Ohio." *Ohio Archaeological and Historical Quarterly* 41 (1932): 195–236.

"Baltimore Convention,—The Future." *Democratic Review* 30 (1852): 472–74.

"Bancroft Papers on the Mecklenburg Declaration, 1775, and on the Annexation of Texas, 1848, Communicated by Mr. Howe." Massachusetts Historical Society *Proceedings* 43 (1909): 101–21.

Barber, Edward W. "Michigan Men in Congress: The Chosen of the People." *Historical Collections: Collections and Researches Made by the Michigan Pioneer and Historical Society* 35 (1907): 444–517.

Barnard, Daniel D. "The Whigs and Their Candidate." *American Review: Devoted to Politics and Literature* 8 (1848): 221–34.

Barton, William E. "The Making of Abraham Lincoln and the Influence of Illinois in his Development." *Transactions of the Illinois State Historical Society for the Year 1921,* 32–53.

Bates, George C. "By-Gones of Detroit." *Historical Collections: Collections and Researches Made by the Michigan Pioneer and Historical Society* 22 (1894): 305–404.

Bemis, Edward W. "Local Government in Michigan and the Northwest." *Johns Hopkins University Studies in Historical and Political Science* 1 (1883), part 5.

Bestor, Arthur. "State Sovereignty and Slavery—A Reinterpretation of Proslavery Constitutional Doctrine, 1846–1860." *Journal of the Illinois State Historical Society* 54 (1961): 117–80.

Bigelow, Martha M. "The Political Services of William Alanson Howard." *Michigan History* 42 (1958): 1–22.

Bishop, Levi. "Biographical Sketch of John Roberts." *Historical Collections: Collections and Researches Made by the Michigan Pioneer and Historical Society* 22 (1894): 427–31.

Bittle, George C. "First Campaign of the Second Seminole War." *Florida Historical Quarterly* 46 (1967): 39–45.

Blackburn, George M. "George Johnston: Indian Agent and Copper Hunter." *Michigan History* 54 (1970): 108–21.

Boucher, Chauncey S. "In *Re* that Aggressive Slavocracy." *Mississippi Valley Historical Review* 8 (1921): 13–79.

Bradley, Cyrus P. "Journal of Cyrus P. Bradley." *Ohio Archaeological and Historical Publications* 15 (1906): 207–70.
Bright, Jesse D. "Documents: Some Letters of Jesse D. Bright to William H. English." *Indiana Magazine of History* 30 (1934): 370–96.
Brown, Elizabeth Gaspar. "Lewis Cass and the American Indian." *Michigan History* 37 (1953): 286–98.
Brown, Henry D. "Detroit Entertains a President, 1817." *Bulletin of the Detroit Historical Society* 2 (1946): 3–7.
———. "Pioneer Riverfront Development." *Bulletin:Detroit Historical Society* 13 (1957): 6–13.
Brown, Ralph H., ed. "With Cass in the Northwest in 1820: The Journal of Charles C. Trowbridge." *Minnesota History* 23 (1942): 126–48, 233–52, 328–48.
Buley, R. C. "Indiana in the Mexican War." *Indiana Magazine of History* 15 (1919): 260–326; 16 (1920): 46–68.
Butler, William Allen. "William Allen Butler Letter to George Bancroft." Massachusetts Historical Society *Proceedings* 60 (1927): 118–20.
Callahan, James Morton. "The Mexican Policy of Southern Leaders Under Buchanan's Administration." *Annual Report of the American Historical Association for the Year 1910*. 133–51.
Cannon, George H. "The Early Surveys of Michigan." *Historical Collections: Collections and Researches Made by the Pioneer and Historical Society of the State of Michigan* 10 (1888): 60–63.
Case, Lynn M., ed. "The Middle West in 1837: Translations from the Notes of an Italian Count, Francesco Arese." *Mississippi Valley Historical Review* 20 (1933): 381–99.
Catlin, George B. "Neighborhood House, Detroit Industrial School." *Michigan History Magazine* 18 (1934): 253–75.
———. "Oliver Newberry." *Michigan History Magazine* 18 (1934): 5–24.
———. "The Regime of the Governor and Judges of Michigan Territory." *Michigan History Magazine* 15 (1931): 19–41.
"Causes of the Success of the Whigs." *American Review: Devoted to Politics and Literature* 8 (1848): 547–60.
Chaddock, Robert E. "Ohio Before 1850: A Study of the Early Influence of Pennsylvania and Southern Populations in Ohio." *Studies in History, Economics, and Public Law* 31 (1908): 187–341.
"The Chicago Convention." *American Review: A Whig Journal of Politics, Literature, Art and Science* 6 (1847): 111–22.
Christiancy, I. P. "Recollections of the Early History of the City and County of Monroe." *Pioneer Collections: Report of the Pioneer Society of the State of Michigan, Together with Reports of County, Town, and District Pioneer Societies* 6 (1884): 361–73.
Clark, George P. "The Dunking of General Cass: A Hoosier Myth." *Traces of Indiana and Midwestern History* 5 (1993): 4–11.
Clark, Rachel. "Michigan 100 Years Ago." *Michigan History Magazine* 17 (1933): 163–74.
"Congress, the Presidency and the Review." *Democratic Review* 30 (1852): 202–24.

Current, Richard N. "Webster's Propaganda and the Ashburton Treaty." *Mississippi Valley Historical Review* 34 (1947): 187–200.
Curti, Merle Eugene. "Austria and the United States, 1848–1852." *Smith College Studies in History* 11 (1926): 139–206.
———. "Young America." *American Historical Review* 32 (1926): 34–55.
Curtis, James C. "Andrew Jackson and His Cabinet—Some New Evidence." *Tennessee Historical Quarterly* 27 (1968): 157–64.
Dain, Floyd R. "Public School Education in Detroit." *Michigan History* 45 (1961): 353–57.
Dancy, John C. "The Negro People in Michigan." *Michigan History Magazine* 24 (1940): 221–40.
Derosier, Arthur H., Jr. "Andrew Jackson and Negotiations for the Removal of the Choctaw Indians." *Historian* 29 (1967): 343–62.
"Detroit Half A Century Ago: Interesting Letters Written From and About Detroit—Some Predictions, and How They Have Been Fulfilled, From the *Detroit Post and Tribune,* Nov. 9th, 1879." *Pioneer Collections: Report of the Pioneer Society of the State of Michigan. Together with Reports of County, Town, and District Pioneer Societies* 4 (1883): 89–94.
Dillon, Merton L. "Elizabeth Chandler and the Spread of Antislavery Sentiment to Michigan." *Michigan History* 39 (1955): 481–94.
Doherty, Herbert J., Jr. "The Whigs of Florida: 1845–1854." *University of Florida Monographs: Social Sciences* 1 (1959): 1–73.
Douglas, Stephen A. "The Dividing Line Between Federal and Local Authority. Popular Sovereignty in the Territories." *Harper's New Monthly Magazine* 19 (September 1859): 519–37.
Draper, Lyman C., ed. "The Fur Trade and Factory System at Green Bay: 1816–21." *Report and Collections of the State Historical Society of Wisconsin* 7 (1876): 269–88.
Dunbar, Willis F. "A New Look at Lewis Cass." *Bulletin: Detroit Historical Society* 28 (1971): 4–9.
Dustin, Fred. "The Treaty of Saginaw, 1819." *Michigan History Magazine* 4 (1920): 243–78.
Dyer, Brainerd. "Zachary Taylor and the Election of 1848." *Pacific Historical Review* 9 (1940): 172–82.
"Eighteen-Fifty-Two, and the 'Coming Man.'" *Democratic Review* 30 (1852): 481–92.
"Eighteen-Fifty-Two and the Presidency." *Democratic Review* 30 (1852): 1–12.
Emery, B. Frank. "Fort Saginaw." *Michigan History Magazine* 30 (1946): 476–503.
Felch, Alpheus. "The Indians of Michigan and the Cession of their Lands to the United States by Treaties." *Historical Collections: Collections and Researches Made by the Michigan Pioneer and Historical Society* 26 (1896): 274–97.
Fennimore, Jean Joy L. "Austin Blair." *Michigan History* 48 (1964): 1–17, 130–66.
Fields, Harold B. "Free Negroes in Cass County Before the Civil War." *Michigan History* 44 (1960): 275–83.
Fitzgibbon, John. "King Alcohol: His Rise, Reign and Fall in Michigan." *Michigan History Magazine* 2 (1918): 737–80.

Fitzhugh, George. "The Administration and the Slave Trade." *DeBow's Review* 26 (1859): 144–48.
Fitzsimons, Matthew A. "Calhoun's Bid for the Presidency, 1841–1844." *Mississippi Valley Historical Review* 38 (1951): 39–60.
Foner, Eric. "Racial Attitudes of the New York Free Soilers." *New York History* 46 (1965): 311–29.
Ford, Worthington Chauncey, ed. "Van Buren–Bancroft Correspondence, 1830–1845, communicated by Mr. Ford." Massachusetts Historical Society *Proceedings* 42 (1909): 381–442.
"Free Soil Policy." *American Review: Devoted to Politics and Literature* 8 (1848): 193–99.
Fuller, George N. "Detroit: Michigan's Capital 100 Years Ago." *Michigan History Magazine* 20 (1936): 5–20.
———. "Settlement of Michigan Territory." *Mississippi Valley Historical Review* 2 (1915): 25–55.
Fuller, John D. P. "The Slavery Question and the Movement to Acquire Mexico, 1846–1848." *Mississippi Valley Historical Review* 21 (1934): 31–48.
Gardiner, T. C. "An Appeal to the Free Soil Party." *United States Magazine and Democratic Review* 23 (1848): 399–404.
"General Cass and the British Flag: From the *Democratic Free Press,* Detroit, August 17, 1843." *Pioneer Collections: Report of the Pioneer Society of the State of Michigan. Together with Reports of County, Town, and District Pioneer Societies* 6 (1884): 502.
"General Cass at St[e]. Marie, 1820." *Report and Collections of the State Historical Society of Wisconsin* 5 (1868): 410–16.
"General Cass Joins the Peace Society." *Harper's Weekly* 1 (March 7, 1857): 150.
"General Cass on European Monarchy." *Democratic Review* 30 (1852): 456–69.
"General Cass on the Winnebago Outbreak, 1827." *Report and Collections of the State Historical Society of Wisconsin* 5 (1868): 156–57.
"The General Issue." *United States Magazine and Democratic Review* 23 (1848): 381–90.
Glazer, Sidney. "In Old Detroit (1831–1836)." *Michigan History Magazine* 26 (1942): 202–14.
Golder, Frank A. "The Purchase of Alaska." *American Historical Review* 25 (1920): 411–25.
Gordon, John M. "The Michigan Land Rush in 1836," edited by Douglas H. Gordon and George S. May. *Michigan History* 43 (1959): 1–42, 129–49, 257–93, 433–78.
Graebner, Norman A. "1848: Southern Politics at the Crossroads." *Historian* 25 (1962): 14–35.
———. "Thomas Corwin and the Election of 1848: A Study in Conservative Politics." *Journal of Southern History* 17 (1951): 162–79.
Greer, James Kimmins. "Louisiana Politics, 1845–1861." *Louisiana Historical Quarterly* 12 (1929): 381–425, 555–610.
Hall, Kermit L. "Andrew Jackson and the Judiciary: The Michigan Territorial Judiciary as a Test Case, 1828–1832." *Michigan History* 59 (1975): 131–51.
Hamil, Fred C. "Michigan in the War of 1812." *Michigan History* 44 (1960): 257–91.

Hamilton, Holman. "Democratic Senate Leadership and the Compromise of 1850." *Mississippi Valley Historical Review* 41 (1954): 403–18.

Hamlin, L. Belle, ed. "Selections from the Follett Papers, II." *Quarterly Publication of the Historical and Philosophical Society of Ohio* 9 (1914): 69–100.

———., ed. "Selections from the William Greene Papers, I." *Quarterly Publication of the Historical and Philosophical Society of Ohio* 13 (1918): 1–38.

Harmon, George D. "Douglas and the Compromise of 1850." *Journal of the Illinois State Historical Society* 21 (1929): 453–99.

Hicks, John D. "The Third Party Tradition in American Politics." *Mississippi Valley Historical Review* 20 (1936): 525–36.

Hodder, F. H. "The Authorship of the Compromise of 1850." *Mississippi Valley Historical Review* 22 (1936): 525–36.

Holt, Edgar Allan. "Party Politics in Ohio, 1840–1850." *Ohio Archaeological and Historical Publications* 37 (1928): 439–591; 38 (1929): 47–182.

Hopkins, George H. "John Judson Bagley." *Pioneer Collections: Report of the Pioneer Society of the State of Michigan. Together with Reports of County, Town, and District Pioneer Societies* 5 (1884): 191–205.

Hubbard, Bela. "The Early Colonization of Detroit." *Pioneer Collections: Report of the Pioneer Society of the State of Michigan. Together with Reports of County, Town, and District Pioneer Societies* 1 (1887): 347–68.

Hubbart, Henry Clyde. "'Pro–Southern' Influences in the Free West: 1840–1865." *Mississippi Valley Historical Review* 20 (1933): 45–62.

Hubbell, John. "The National Free Soil Convention of '48. Held in Buffalo." *Publications of the Buffalo Historical Society* 4 (1878): 147–62.

Humphreys, Sexson E. "Lewis Cass, Jr. and Pope Pius IX, 1850–58." *Michigan History* 41 (1957): 129–61.

———. "Lewis Cass, Jr. and the Roman Republic of 1849." *Michigan History* 40 (1956): 24–50.

Isely, W. H. "The Sharps Rifle Episode in Kansas History." *American Historical Review* 12 (1907): 546–66.

Jamison, Knox. "The Survey of the Public Lands in Michigan." *Michigan History* 42 (1958): 197–214.

Jenks, William L. "Augustus Elias Brevoort Woodward." *Michigan History Magazine* 9 (1925): 515–46.

———. "Fort Gratiot Turnpike." *Michigan History Magazine* 9 (1925): 174–82.

———. "Henry Whiting." *Michigan History Magazine* 16 (1932): 174–82.

———. "Senator Charles A. Loomis." *Michigan History Magazine* 10 (1926): 212–20.

Johannsen, Robert W. "Stephen A. Douglas, 'Harper's Magazine,' and Popular Sovereignty." *Mississippi Valley Historical Review* 45 (1959): 606–31.

———. "Stephen A. Douglas, Popular Sovereignty and the Territories." *Historian* 22 (1960): 378–95.

Johnson, Allen. "The Genesis of Popular Sovereignty." *Iowa Journal of History and Politics* 3 (1905): 3–19.

Johnston, George. "Reminiscences of Sault Ste. Marys." *Historical Collections: Collections and Researches Made by the Pioneer and Historical Society of the State of Michigan* 12 (1888): 605–11.

Kern, John. "A Short History of Michigan." *Michigan History Magazine* 60 (1976): 3–69.

Kettell, Thomas Prentice. "The Election." *United States Magazine and Democratic Review* 23 (1848): 285–94.

King, Ameda Ruth. "The Last Years of the Whig Party in Illinois—1847 to 1856." *Transactions of the Illinois State Historical Society for the Year 1925*, 108–54.

Klunder, Willard Carl. "Lewis Cass and Slavery Expansion: 'The Father of Popular Sovereignty' and Ideological Infanticide." *Civil War History* 32 (1986): 293–317.

———. "Lewis Cass and the Surrender of Detroit." *Michigan History* 75 (1991): 12–21.

———. "The Seeds of Popular Sovereignty: Governor Lewis Cass and Michigan Territory." *Michigan Historical Review* 17 (1991): 64–81.

Knaggs, Mary Stocking. "Memoir of James Knaggs, of Monroe." *Historical Collections: Collections and Researches Made by the Michigan Pioneer and Historical Society* 17 (1892): 217–25.

Kuhn, Madison. "Tiffin, Morse, and the Reluctant Pioneer." *Michigan History* 50 (1966): 111–38.

Larzelere, Claude S. "The Boundaries of Michigan." *Historical Collections: Collections and Researches Made by the Michigan Pioneer and Historical Society* 30 (1906): 1–27.

Latner, Richard B. "The Eaton Affair Reconsidered." *Tennessee Historical Quarterly* 36 (1977): 330–51.

Lawrence, Amos Adams. "Letters from Washington, 1836." Massachusetts Historical Society *Proceedings* 53 (1919): 48–57.

Learned, Henry Barrett. "Cabinet Meetings Under President Polk." *Annual Report of the American Historical Association for the Year 1914*, 1:229–42.

Levi, Kate Everest. "The Wisconsin Press and Slavery." *Wisconsin Magazine of History* 9 (1926): 423–34.

"The Liberty Party." *United States Magazine and Democratic Review* 23 (1848): 97–108.

Lockwood, James H. "Early Times and Events in Wisconsin." *Second Annual Report and Collections of the State Historical Society, of Wisconsin, for the Year 1855* 2 (1856): 98–196.

Longaker, Richard P. "Was Jackson's Kitchen Cabinet a Cabinet?" *Mississippi Valley Historical Review* 44 (1957): 94–108.

Luthin, Reinhard H. "Abraham Lincoln and the Massachusetts Whigs in 1848." *New England Quarterly* 14 (1941): 619–32.

Lynch, William O. "Anti-Slavery Tendencies of the Democratic Party in the Northwest, 1848–50." *Mississippi Valley Historical Review* 11 (1924): 319–31.

Marsden, Michael T. "Henry Rowe Schoolcraft: A Reappraisal." *Old Northwest* 2 (1976): 153–82.

Marshall, Thomas M., contributor. "Diary and Memoranda of William L. Marcy, 1857." *American Historical Review* 24 (1919): 641–53.

Massie, Dennis. "Jacob Smith in the Saginaw Valley." *Michigan History* 51 (1967): 117–29.

McCain, Anne. "Charles Edward Stuart of Kalamazoo." *Michigan History* 44 (1960): 324–35.

McKenney, Thomas L. "The Winnebago War of 1827." *Report and Collections of the State Historical Society of Wisconsin* 5 (1868): 178–204.

McLaughlin, Andrew C. "The Influence of Governor Cass on the Development of the Northwest." *Papers of the American Historical Association* 3 (1889): 311–27.

McLemore, R. A. "The French Spoliation Claims, 1816–1836." *Tennessee Historical Magazine* 2 (1932): 234–54.

McMillan, Malcolm C., ed. "Joseph Glover Baldwin Reports on the Whig National Convention of 1848." *Journal of Southern History* 25 (1959): 366–82.

Merk, Frederick. "Presidential Fevers." *Mississippi Valley Historical Review* 47 (1960): 3–33.

Miller, Albert. "Detroit in 1814: Extracts from Articles Written in 1853 by Hon. B. F. H. Witherell." *Historical Collections: Collections and Researches Made by the Michigan Pioneer and Historical Society Including Reports of Officers and Papers Read at the Annual Meeting of 1888* 13 (1889): 503–7.

Moore, John Bassett. "Kossuth: A Sketch of a Revolutionist." *Political Science Quarterly* 10 (1895): 95–131, 251–91.

Moore, Powell. "James K. Polk: Tennessee Politician." *Journal of Southern History* 17 (1951): 493–516.

Mueller, Henry R. "The Whig Party in Pennsylvania." Columbia University *Studies in History, Economics and Public Law* 101 (1922): 247–517.

Naegely, Henry E. "Lewis Cass and the Saginaw Treaty of 1819." *Michigan History Magazine* 3 (1919): 610–16.

"The New Cabinet." *Harper's Weekly*, April 11, 1857, 229.

Nichols, Roy F. "The Kansas-Nebraska Act: A Century of Historiography." *Mississippi Valley Historical Review* 43 (1956): 187–212.

"The Nomination.—General Taylor." *American Review: Devoted to Politics and Literature* 8 (1848): 1–8.

"The Nomination.—The 'Old Fogies' and Fogy Conspiracies." *Democratic Review* 30 (1852): 366–84.

Odle, Thomas D. "The Commercial Interests of the Great Lakes and the Campaign Issues of 1860." *Michigan History* 40 (1956): 1–23.

"Ohio in the War of 1812." *Ohio Archaeological and Historical Publications* 28 (1919): 286–368.

"The Old Cass House: From the *Detroit Evening News,* August 30th, 1882." *Pioneer Collections: Report of the Pioneer Society of the State of Michigan, Together with Reports of County, Town, and District Pioneer Societies* 4 (1883): 95–96.

Oliver, John W. "Lewis Kossuth's Appeal to the Middle West—1852." *Mississippi Valley Historical Review* 14 (1928): 481–95.

O'Sullivan, John L. "Principles Not Men." *United States Magazine and Democratic Review* 23 (1848): 3–12.

Palmer, Friend. "Detroit in 1827 and Later On." *Historical Collections: Collections and Researches Made by the Michigan Pioneer and Historical Society* 35 (1907): 272–83.

Pargellis, Stanley. "Father Gabriel Richard." *Michigan History* 43 (1959): 165–72.

Patterson, John C. "Marshall Men and Measures in State and National History." *Historical Collections: Collections and Researches Made by the Michigan Pioneer and Historical Society* 38 (1912): 244–79.

Pelzer, Louis. "The History and Principles of the Democratic Party of Iowa, 1846–1857." *Iowa Journal of History and Politics* 6 (1908): 163–246.

Peters, Bernard C. "Hypocrisy on the Great Lakes Frontier: The Use of Whiskey by the Michigan Department of Indian Affairs." *Michigan Historical Review* 18 (1992): 1–13.

Pilcher, E. H. "Life and Times of Rev. Joseph Hickox." *Pioneer Collections: Report of the Pioneer Society of the State of Michigan. Together with Reports of County, Town, and District Pioneer Societies* 1 (1877): 472–81.

Poore, Ben Perley. "Reminiscences of Washington." *Atlantic Monthly* 46 (1880): 799–810.

Potter, William W. "The Michigan Judiciary Since 1805." *Michigan History Magazine* 27 (1943): 644–60.

"The Presidency and the Review." *Democratic Review* 30 (1852): 182–86.

Price, Erwin H. "The Election of 1848 in Ohio." *Ohio Archaeological and Historical Quarterly* 36 (1927): 188–311.

Prucha, Francis Paul. "Andrew Jackson's Indian Policy: A Reassessment." *Journal of American History* 56 (1969): 527–39.

Prucha, Francis Paul, and Donald F. Carmony, eds. "A Memorandum of Lewis Cass: Concerning a System for the Regulation of Indian Affairs." *Wisconsin Magazine of History* 52 (Autumn 1968): 35–50.

Quaife, Milo Milton. "General William Hull and His Critics." *Ohio State Archaeological and Historical Quarterly* 47 (1938): 168–82.

Quaife, Milo M., and Florence Emery, eds. "Lemuel Shattuck and the University of Michigania." *Michigan History Magazine* 18 (1934): 225–52.

Quinby, William E. "Reminiscences of Michigan Journalism." *Historical Collections: Collections and Researches Made by the Michigan Pioneer and Historical Society* 30 (1904): 507–17.

Ranck, James B. "Lewis Cass and Squatter Sovereignty." *Michigan History Magazine* 10 (1926): 157–74.

Rayback, Joseph G. "Martin Van Buren's Break with James K. Polk: The Record." *New York History* 36 (1955): 51–62.

———. "The Presidential Ambitions of John C. Calhoun, 1844–1848." *Journal of Southern History* 14 (1948): 331–56.

———, ed. "Martin Van Buren's Desire for Revenge in the Campaign of 1848." *Mississippi Valley Historical Review* 40 (1954): 707–16.

Reeves, Jesse S., ed. "Letters of Gideon J. Pillow to James K. Polk, 1844." *American Historical Review* 11 (1906): 832–43.

Riddle, A. G. "Rise of the Antislavery Sentiment on the Western Reserve." *Magazine of Western History* 6 (1887): 145–56.

"The Roman Republic—'Rome to America.'" *Democratic Review* 30 (1852): 336–46.

Rosentreter, Roger L. "Michigan and the Compromise of 1850." *Old Northwest* 6 (1980): 153–73.

Schouler, James. "Abraham Lincoln at Tremont Temple in 1848." Massachusetts Historical Society *Proceedings* 42 (1909): 70–83.
Schurtz, Shelby B. "Gabriel Richard and the University of Michigan." *Michigan History Magazine* 19 (1935): 5–18.
Sears, Louis Martin. "Slidell and Buchanan." *American Historical Review* 27 (1922): 709–30.
Sewell, Richard H. "John P. Hale and the Liberty Party, 1847–1848." *New England Quarterly* 37 (1964): 200–23.
Sherer, Timothy. "The Resistance to Representative Government in Early Michigan Territory." *Old Northwest* 5 (1979): 167–79.
Shewmaker, Kenneth E. "The 'War of the Words': The Cass-Webster Debate of 1842–43." *Diplomatic History* 5 (Spring 1981): 151–63.
Silliman, Sue I. "The Chicago Indian Treaty of 1821." *Michigan History Magazine* 6 (1922): 194–97.
Sioussat, St. George L. "Tennessee and National Political Parties, 1850–1860." *Annual Report of the American Historical Association* 1 (1914): 243–58.
———. "Tennessee, the Compromise of 1850, and the Nashville Convention." *Mississippi Valley Historical Review* 2 (1915): 313–47.
———, ed. "Selected Letters, 1846–1856, from the Donelson Papers." *Tennessee Historical Magazine* 3 (1917): 257–91.
Skelton, William B. "The Commanding General and the Problem of Command in the United States Army, 1821–1841." *Military Affairs* 34 (1970): 117–22.
Smith, Mrs. E. C., comp. "Extracts from old Letters." *Historical Collections: Collections and Researches Made by the Michigan Pioneer and Historical Society* 35 (1907): 672–79.
Snelling, William J. "Early Days at Prairie du Chien, and the Winnebago Outbreak of 1827." *Report and Collections of the State Historical Society of Wisconsin* 5 (1868): 123–53.
Soulsby, Hugh G. "The Right of Search and the Slave Trade in Anglo-American Relations, 1814–1862." *Johns Hopkins University Studies in Historical and Political Science* 51 (1933): 115–299.
Spencer, Donald S. "Lewis Cass and Symbolic Intervention: 1848–1852." *Michigan History* 53 (1969): 1–17.
Stebbins, C. B. "Report of the Memorial Committee: Ingham County." *Historical Collections: Collections and Researches Made by the Michigan Pioneer and Historical Society* 26 (1896): 408–17.
Stevens, Walter W. "Lewis Cass and the Presidency." *Michigan History* 49 (1965): 123–34.
———. "The Scholarship of Lewis Cass." *Michigan History* 44 (1960): 59–66.
Stewart, Mrs. E. M. S. "Childhood's Recollections of Detroit." *Historical Collections: Collections and Researches Made by the Michigan Pioneer and Historical Society* 18 (1892): 458–65.
Streeter, Floyd B. "The Factional Character of Early Michigan Politics." *Michigan History Magazine* 2 (1918): 165–91.
Sutherland, Daniel E. "Michigan Emigrant Agent: Edward H. Thomson." *Michigan History* 59 (1975): 3–37.

Swisher, Carl Brent, ed. "Roger B. Taney's 'Bank War Manuscript.'" *Maryland Historical Magazine* 53 (1958): 103–30, 215–37.

Taber, Morris C. "New England Influence in South Central Michigan." *Michigan History* 45 (1961): 305–36.

Thayer, George W. "Life of Senator Lucius Lyon." *Historical Collections: Collections and Researches Made by the Michigan Pioneer and Historical Society* 27 (1897): 404–12.

Thomas, Robert Charles. "Andrew Jackson Versus France: American Policy toward France, 1834–36." *Tennessee Historical Quarterly* 35 (1976): 51–64.

Thompson, Arthur W. "Political Nativism in Florida, 1848–1860: A Phase of Anti-Secessionism." *Journal of Southern History* 15 (1949): 39–65.

Thorn [or Thom], Leslie. "Dr. John L. Whiting." *Pioneer Collections: Report of the Pioneer Society of the State of Michigan, Together with Reports of County, Town, and District Pioneer Societies* 4 (1883): 116–21.

Tobias, Clifford I. "Henry D. Gilpin: 'Governor In and Over the Territory of Michigan.'" *Michigan History* 59 (1975): 152–70.

Trask, William Blake. "Lewis Cass." New England Historical-Genealogical Society *Memorial Biographies* 6 (1905): 163–65.

Travis, Ira Dudley. "The History of the Clayton-Bulwer Treaty." *Publications of the Michigan Political Science Association* 3 (1898–1900): 203–514.

Trimble, Allen. "The Autobiography of Allen Trimble." *"Old Northwest" Genealogical Quarterly* 9 (1906): 195–226, 275–87; 10 (1907): 1–54.

Trowbridge, Charles C. "Detroit Past and Present." *Pioneer Collections: Report of the Pioneer Society of the State of Michigan. Together with Reports of County, Town, and District Pioneer Societies* 1 (1877): 371–85.

Tuchalski, Yvonne. "Erastus Hussey, Battle Creek Antislavery Activist." *Michigan History* 56 (1972): 1–18.

Turner, Andrew Jackson. "The History of Fort Winnebago." *Collections of the State Historical Society of Wisconsin* 14 (1898): 65–102.

Utter, William T. "Judicial Review in Early Ohio." *Mississippi Valley Historical Review* 14 (1927): 3–24.

Valliere, Kenneth L. "The Creek War of 1836: A Military History." *Chronicles of Oklahoma* 57 (1979–80): 463–85.

Van Bolt, Roger H. "The Hoosiers and the 'Eternal Agitation,' 1848–1850." *Indiana Magazine of History* 48 (1952): 331–68.

———. "Sectional Aspects of Expansion, 1844–1848." *Indiana Magazine of History* 48 (1952): 119–40.

Van Buren, A. D. P. "The Log Schoolhouse Era in Michigan." *Historical Collections: Collections and Researches Made by the Michigan Pioneer and Historical Society Including Reports of Officers and Papers Read at the Annual Meeting of 1889* 14 (1890): 283–402.

———. "Michigan in Her Pioneer Politics; Michigan in Our National Politics, and Michigan in the Presidential Campaign of 1856." *Historical Collections: Collections and Researches Made by the Michigan Pioneer and Historical Society* 17 (1892): 238–95.

———. "Our Temperance Conflict." *Historical Collections: Collections and Researches Made by the Michigan Pioneer and Historical Society Including Reports of Officers and Papers Read at the Annual Meeting of 1888* 13 (1889): 388–407.

[Van Buren, Martin.] "The Autobiography of Martin Van Buren." Edited by John C. Fitzpatrick. *Annual Report of the American Historical Association for the Year 1918*, vol. 2.

Van Deusen, John G. "Court Martial of Gen. William Hull." *Michigan History Magazine* 27 (1943): 72–142.

———. "Detroit Campaign of Gen. William Hull." *Michigan History Magazine* 12 (1928): 568–86.

"War with America a Blessing to Mankind." *Fraser's Magazine for Town and Country* 23 (1841): 494–502.

"Washington Gossip—the Cabinet." *Harper's Weekly*, March 7, 1857, 150.

Watson, Richard L., Jr. "Congressional Attitudes Toward Military Preparedness, 1829–1835." *Mississippi Valley Historical Review* 34 (1948): 611–36.

Webber, William L. "Indian Cession of 1819, Made by the Treaty of Saginaw." *Historical Collections: Collections and Researches Made by the Michigan Pioneer and Historical Society* 26 (1896): 517–34.

Williams, Ephraim S. "The Treaty of Saginaw in the Year 1819." *Pioneer Collections: Report of the Pioneer Society of the State of Michigan. Together with Reports of County, Town, and District Pioneer Societies* 7 (1886): 262–70.

Williams, J. R. "Internal Commerce of the West: Its Conditions and Wants, As Illustrated by the Commerce of Michigan, Present and Prospective." *Merchants' Magazine and Commercial Review* 19 (1848): 19–40.

Williams, Mentor L. "The Background of the Chicago River and Harbor Convention, 1847." *Mid-America* 30 (1948): 219–32.

———. "The Chicago River and Harbor Convention, 1847." *Mississippi Valley Historical Review* 35 (1949): 607–26.

———. "'A Shout of Derision': A Sidelight on the Presidential Campaign of 1848." *Michigan History* 32 (1948): 66–77.

"The Wilmot Proviso." *United States Magazine and Democratic Review* 23 (1848): 219–26.

Wilson, Howard L. "President Buchanan's Proposed Intervention in Mexico." *American Historical Review* 5 (1900): 687–701.

Woodford, Frank B. "Lewis Cass—Frontier Diplomat." *Bulletin: Detroit Historical Society* 6 (1950): 4–8.

Young, Mary E. "The Creek Frauds: A Study in Conscience and Corruption." *Mississippi Valley Historical Review* 42 (1955): 411–37.

Young, Otis E. "The United States Mounted Ranger Battalion, 1832–1833." *Mississippi Valley Historical Review* 41 (1954): 453–70.

INDEX

Lewis Cass and the Politics of Moderation
was composed in
Adobe Caslon on a Macintosh Quadra 700 system
by Books International;
printed by sheet-fed offset
on 50-pound Glatfelter Supple Opaque Natural stock
(an acid-free recycled paper)
notch case bound over binder's boards in Arretox B cloth,
and wrapped with dustjackets printed in three colors
on 100-pound enamel stock finished with film lamination
by Thomson-Shore, Inc.;
designed by Will Underwood;
and published by
The Kent State University Press
KENT, OHIO 44242